Anachronic Renaissance

Anachronic Renaissance

Alexander Nagel

and

Christopher S. Wood

ZONE BOOKS · NEW YORK

2010

© 2010 Alexander Nagel and Christopher S. Wood
ZONE BOOKS
633 Vanderbilt Street
Brooklyn, NY 11218

First paperback edition 2020
ISBN 978-1-942130-34-5

Printed in the United States of America.

Distributed by The MIT Press,
Cambridge, Massachusetts, and London, England

.

Library of Congress Cataloging-in-Publication Data

Nagel, Alexander.
    Anachronic Renaissance / Alexander Nagel and
Christopher S. Wood.
            p. cm.
    Includes bibliographical references (p.   ) and index.
    ISBN 978-1-935408-02-4 (hardcover : alk. paper)
            1. Art, Medieval. 2. Architecture, Renaissance.
3. Building Materials—Recycling. I. Wood, Christopher S.
II. Title.

    N6370.N34 2—010
    709.02'4–DC22
                        2009026817

Contents

I   *Plural Temporality of the Work of Art* 7

II   *"The Image of the Image of Our Lady"* 21

III   *What Is Substitution?* 29

IV   *An Antique Statue of Christ* 35

V   *The Plebeian Pleasure of Anachronism* 45

VI   *Architectural Models* 51

VII   *Double Origins of the Christian Temple* 63

VIII   *Icon Maintenance* 71

IX   *Fashion in Painting* 85

X   *Ancient Painting* 97

XI   *Substitution Symbolized* 109

XII   *Author and Acheiropoieton* 123

XIII   *Antiquity of Buildings Overrated* 135

XIV   *Non-Actual Histories of Architecture* 147

XV   *Temples Painted, Printed, and Real* 159

XVI   *Citation and Spoliation* 175

XVII   *Neo-Cosmatesque* 185

XVIII   *Movable Buildings* 195

XIX   *The Titulus Crucis* 219

XX   *The Fabrication of Visual Evidence* 241

XXI   *Retroactivity*   251

XXII   *Forgery 1: Copy*   275

XXIII   *Forgery 2: Pastiche*   289

XXIV   *Anti-Architecture*   301

XXV   *The Primitive Hut Amidst the Ruins of St. Peter's*   313

XXVI   *Mosaic/Paint 1: Limits of Substitution*   321

XXVII   *Mosaic/Paint 2: Intermedial Comparison*   335

XXVIII   *Space for Fiction*   347

Acknowledgments   367

Notes   369

Index   447

Plural Temporality of the Work of Art

"The Imperial Palace does not have a restored look, nor has it an ancient one: this hesitation makes it appear not eternal but precarious and like an imitation of itself." This is Simone de Beauvoir describing the Forbidden City in Beijing in her travel memoir *The Long March* (1957). "There is nothing accidental about the impermanence of the materials; it is simultaneously the cause, the effect, the expression of a troubling fact; the traces left upon this palace by the past are so few that, paradoxically, I would hesitate to call it a historical monument."[1] These were buildings, Beauvoir recognized, that disguised their own histories of fabrication and subsequent restorations. The Forbidden City transcended the merely human circumstances of its life in time. In the European tradition of building and making to which Beauvoir was implicitly comparing the Chinese palace, an artifact's historicity is both the source of its authority and the basis for an eventual demystification of that authority. In the modern West, the very old building or painting is venerated for having survived and for testifying with its body to the corrosive effects of the passage of time, a passage that can sometimes be measured precisely, to the year. But by virtue of its anchorage in history, the European building is also a mere product of its time. It is all too obviously contrived by real agents—human beings, not giants, not gods. The Imperial Palace in Beijing seemed to evade all these conditions. Beauvoir did not feel invited either to contemplate the structure's great antiquity or to read it as the index of its times, and so she saw the palace as inauthentic, as an "imitation of itself." The palace's true self, for Beauvoir, was its historical self.

The premise of the present book is that the Forbidden City is no anomaly. Most cultures have created buildings and artifacts that "hesitate" in just the way Beauvoir describes. They resist anchoring in time. Societies tend to coalesce around artifacts that embody institutions, but often on the condition that the historicity of those artifacts—as much as that of the institutions—is masked. Like the buildings of the Forbidden City, such artifacts are not meant to look old, nor are they meant to look as if someone has tried to recover their original look. There is no premium placed on their historical moment of origin because they are supposed to deliver still older truths, or even timeless truths. For anyone can see that the possible gain in legitimacy conferred by the marks of time is easily offset by the risk of loss of aura through fixing in time. To fix an image or temple in time is to reduce it to human proportions.

Most societies also recognize, alongside the timeless object, a completely different kind of object whose historicity, its link to a point in time, is the entire basis of its value. Such an object is called a *relic*. The relic is irreplaceable. But even here societies have tended to provide for loopholes, for the consequences of loss or destruction of the relic are too great. The ancient Roman historian Suetonius, for example, reported that the emperor Nero in his megalomania and want of money "stripped many temples of their gifts and melted down the images of gold and silver, including those of the Penates," the household gods of the Romans. This outrage proved easy to correct, however. The next emperor, Galba, simply had the statues recast.[2]

The work that manages to retain its identity despite alteration, repair, renovation, and even outright replacement was a sustaining myth of art in premodern Europe. Ontological stability across time was figured by the Ship of Theseus, a relic of the Athenian state. In this ship the hero-king Theseus had returned from Crete together with the Athenian youths, destined for sacrifice, whom he had rescued from the Minotaur. According to Plutarch, the ship "was preserved by the Athenians down even to the time of Demetrius Phalereus [that is, late fourth century BCE], for they took away the old planks as they decayed, putting in new and stronger timber in their place, insomuch that this ship became a standing example among the philosophers, for the logical question of things that grow; one side holding that the ship remained the same, and the other contending that it was not the same."[3] The Ship of Theseus is a paradigm of the object defined by its structure rather than by its material make-up. The age of the planks is accidental; essential is the form. To grasp an object's structure is to abstract from the mere object as given to the senses. The identity of such an object is sustained across time by the stability of its name and by the tacit substitution of its parts. The "structural object," in the phrase of Rosalind Krauss, here following Roland Barthes, has "no other causes than its name, and no other identity than its form."[4] The Ship of Theseus "hesitated" between its possible historical identities, not settling on any of them, and in this way managed to function both as a marker of a great span of time (the history of Athens) and as a usable instrument in a living ritual (the annual votive mission to Delos).[5] To think "structurally," then and now, is to reject linear chronology as the inevitable matrix of experience and cognition.

Chronological time, flowing steadily from before to after, is an effect of its figurations: annals, chronicles, calendars, clocks. The diagrammatization of time as a series of points strung along a line allows one to speak of diverse events happening in different places as happening at the same time. This is not an obvious concept. The ancient Romans, Denis Feeney has argued, had no notion of linear time and therefore no notion of the date. Instead they saw the myriad interconnections among events and people.[6] Many societies have figured to themselves the ramification, the doubling, the immobilization of time: in the naming of planets and seasons; in the promise of reincarnation; in narratives of the rise and fall of worldly empires understood in cyclical terms; in the time travel of dreams and prophecies; in religious ritual; and, within the Christian tradition, in the mystical parallel between Old and New Dispensations, read between the lines of holy scripture. Such contrivances mirror the sensation, familiar to everyone, of time folding over on itself, the doubling of the fabric of experience that creates continuity and flow; creates meaning where there was none; creates and encourages the desire to start over, to renew, to reform, to recover.

No device more effectively generates the effect of a doubling or bending of time than the work of art, a strange kind of event whose relation to time is plural. The artwork is made or designed by an individual or by a group of individuals at some moment, but it also points away from that moment, backward to a remote ancestral origin, perhaps, or to a prior artifact, or to an origin outside of time, in divinity. At the same time it points forward to all its future recipients who will activate and reactivate it as a meaningful event. The work of art is a message whose sender and destination are constantly shifting. In the fifteenth and sixteenth centuries, it became increasingly common, in the West, to attend closely, perhaps more closely than ever before, to what it is that artworks do. Christians wondered whether the temporal instability of images made them more suitable for religious devotion, or less suitable. On the one hand, art with its multiple temporalities offered a picture of a meaningful cosmos woven together by invisible threads, of an order hidden behind the mere illusory sequence of lived moments. On the other hand, the references back to the meaning-conferring origin points that art seemed to offer—the god, the temple, the founding legend—threatened to collapse into their own historicity. The link back to the origin might turn out to be nothing more than a historical link, crafted by human hands, and therefore unreliable.

The art historian Aby Warburg (1866–1929), trying to explain the peculiar hold of ancient Greece and Rome on the European imagination right up to his day, spoke of the *Nachleben der Antike*, the "afterlife" or "survival" of antiquity. For Warburg, a painting or a court masque was a dense archive of cultural energies, a *dynamogram* that concretized and transmitted traumatic, primordial experiences.[7] Archaic stimuli were directly imprinted in matter and gesture, Warburg believed, giving figuration the power to disrupt an historical present tense. Warburg's cultural symbol was a token (*sumbolon*) that literally "throws together" past and present. For Warburg, the painter Sandro Botticelli was not only "assimilating" ancient art. Rather, his paintings *became* instantiations of ancient gestures. When Warburg described the mysterious continuity of life forces across far-flung chains of symbols, whereby pictorial form delivered, centuries later, the pitch and pulse of primordial emotions, he was describing nothing other than a real virtue of artworks.

With its power to compel but not explain a folding of time over onto itself, the work of art in the fifteenth and sixteenth centuries was able to lay a trail back to Europe's multiple pasts, to the Holy Land, to Rome — monarchical, Republican, Imperial, or Christian — and sometimes to Rome's Byzantine legacy. Historical treatises, philological glosses, sketchbooks, paintings, monuments, and anthologies of inscriptions notated the relics and events of disappeared worlds. Forms of life, ways of picturing or building, customs and costumes came to seem obsolete and yet retrievable, retrievable perhaps because they were obsolete. The differentness of the past made repetition an option. The figuring of succession in turn made reckoning possible, enabling a comparison of the present to the past, and bringing forth new worries about the inferiority or superiority of the present.[8] New systems for storing and recovering information, above all the printed text and the printed image, allowed for direct comparison of historical life-worlds. The commercial and colonial networks that were closing the globe, meanwhile, offered evidence of otherness across gaps of space rather than time. The two remotenesses, temporal and spatial, were confused, and from that moment onwards non-Europeans were condemned as non-synchronic, out of sync, trapped in states of incomplete development.[9] The hypothesis of cultural anachronism made it possible for Europeans to deny the synchronicity of other people they shared the world with, and so to refuse to engage with them in political terms.[10]

Artifacts played an indispensable role in the overall cultural project of time management, not simply as beneficiaries or participants, but as the very models of the time-bending operation. Non-artists aspired to imitate the artist's ability to conjure with time. Theologians, for example, read sacred texts as indications of a suprahistorical divine plan that suspended earthly time. The theology of typology identified formal rhymes between historical events that revealed the pattern imposed on reality by divinity.[11] One event was the shadow, the image, the figure of another. For the theologian, therefore, merely secular time was overcome through metaphors of figuration that invoked the powers of imagination and intuition.

In the fifteenth and sixteenth centuries, different models of the image's temporality came into conceptual focus, and nowhere more clearly than in works of art themselves. One powerful model proposed the perfect interchangeability of one image or work for another. Under this model, the work did not merely repeat the prior work, for repetition proposes difference, an altering interval. Rather, the work simply *is* its own predecessor, such that the prior is no longer prior but present. This model of perfect commutativity among works across time and space flies in the face of the empirical fact that works of art are created by specific people at specific times and then replaced for various reasons. Communities may well ask a mere artifact, image, or statue to stand in for an absent authority. They may well propose the work's perfect exchangeability, involving no loss of reference, with other works referring to the same source. This capacity to stand in for absent authority, however, comes to be doubted when too much is learned about how works are actually fabricated. The idea of the artwork as an effective substitute for another, absent work, which itself stands in for yet another work, is reasserted in the face of such doubt. The hypothesis of substitutability, conceived in this manner, is a mode of magical reasoning because it asserts the identity of like to like. "Magic" is nothing more than the name given to the attempt to manipulate the hidden paths and conduits that connect like to like, behind the deceptive screen of experience. Art, too, is a manipulation of the similarities and identities proposed by the substitutional model of production. Art, therefore, cannot be understood as an enlightened successor to magic.

According to Paul Valéry, in his essay on the "method" of Leonardo da Vinci, creativity is the perception of relations, or a "law of continuity," between things where others see none.[12] This formulation permits us to understand the chain of substitutions, one work standing in for the next, not as a historical reality but as a fiction that the artist and a viewing public create backward from present to past. The new work, the innovation, is legitimated by the chain of works leading back to an authoritative type. But the chain also needs the new work. It is the new work that selects the chain out of the debris of the past.[13] Valéry's phrase gives the model of a perfect substitutability among artifacts a new reality that poses a challenge to the materialist and literalist—one might almost say counterintuitive—model of an artwork securely moored in historical time, the model that dominates the modern scholarly study of art.[14]

With their temporal flexibility, artworks and other "structural objects" were the perfect instruments of the myths and rituals that knit present to past. The reforming humanist Erasmus homed in on the fiction of irreplaceability when he set out to discredit the custom of pilgrimage, the journey undertaken by hundreds of thousands in the late Middle Ages in hopes of a glimpse of or even contact with a relic. In a letter of 1512 Erasmus announced his intention to visit Walsingham, the pilgrimage target in Norfolk, England, and hang up a Greek poem in honor of the Virgin; a humanist scholar's wry parody of a votive offering.[15] Erasmus transformed his experiences at Walsingham into a dialogue, "A Pilgrimage for Religion's Sake," one of the *Colloquies* published in 1526. In that dialogue, the character Ogygius recounts his visit to a popular pilgrimage site. He is shown a shrine, a simple rustic hut, by a local guide. By legend the shrine at Walsingham was a building constructed by angels in the late eleventh century, a scale model of the Virgin's house in Nazareth.[16]

> *Ogygius*: Inspecting everything carefully I inquired how many years it was since the little house had been brought there. "Some ages," he replied. "In any event," I said, "the walls don't look very old." He didn't deny they had been placed there recently, and the fact was self-evident. "Then," I said, "the roof and thatch of the house seem rather recent." He agreed. "Not even these cross-beams, nor the very rafters supporting the roof, appear to have been placed here many years ago." He nodded. "But since no part of the building has survived, how is it known for certain," I asked, "that this is the cottage brought here from so far away?"
>
> *Menedemus*: How did the attendant get out of that tangle, if you please?
>
> *Ogygius*: Why, he hurriedly showed us an old, worn-out bearskin fastened to posts and almost laughed at us for our dullness in being slow to see such a clear proof. So, being persuaded, and excusing our stupidity, we turned to the heavenly milk of the Blessed Virgin.[17]

Erasmus's skeptical prolocutor does not accept the principle of continuity that holds together the shrine's identity across four centuries of rethatchings and replaced rafters. To Ogygius's jaundiced eyes the shrine has become, like Simone de Beauvoir's Imperial Palace, a mere "imitation of itself."

Erasmus derided the credulous Walsingham pilgrim. And yet that pilgrim was as justified in his or her attentiveness to the relic as any Athenian in the presence of the reconstructed Ship of Theseus, or any Roman in the presence of the statuettes that Galba made to replace the Penates destroyed by Nero. For the pilgrim, the identity of the shrine at Walsingham with an original eleventh-century structure, which was in turn homologous with the Virgin's house in Nazareth (which in the meantime had been transported by angels to Loreto, on the east coast of Italy; see section 18) was protected as such by the building's label.

This book is about European buildings, paintings, prints, drawings, sculptures, medals, pavements, and mosaics, mostly of the fifteenth and early sixteenth centuries, that moved between the two conditions marked out by Erasmus's satire: on the one hand, the shrine at Walsingham as understood by the devout pilgrim, on the other, the shrine as understood by Erasmus. For the pilgrim, the shrine is linked, no matter how often its timbers are replaced, to a primordial, meaning-conferring past through labeling and ritual. The shrine's reference to the dwelling of the Virgin Mary, ultimately to her body, is effective. For Erasmus, the shrine was drained of its meaning once it turned out not to be a literal, physical relic of the eleventh century (of course, it is not clear that Erasmus would be impressed even if the shrine really were old). Erasmus did not permit the shack to "deliver" the founding legend of the cult site. For him, the reference to the past is ineffective. The shrine on the site is evidence of nothing more interesting, in his view, than the capacities of its contemporary restorers.

The power of the image, or the work of art, to fold time was neither discovered nor invented in the Renaissance. What *was* distinctive about the European Renaissance, so called, was its apprehensiveness about the temporal instability of the artwork, and its re-creation of the artwork as an occasion for reflection on that instability. The work of art "anachronizes," from the Greek *anachronizein*, built from *ana-*, "again," and the verb *chronizein*, "to be late or belated." To anachronize is to be belated again, to linger. The work is late, first because it succeeds some reality that it re-presents, and then late again when that re-presentation is repeated for successive recipients. To many that double postponement came to seem troublesome, calling for correction, compensation, or, at the very least, explanation.

The work of art when it is late, when it repeats, when it hesitates, when it remembers, but also when it projects a future or an ideal, is "anachronic." We introduce this term as an alternative to "anachronistic," a judgmental term that carries with it the historicist assumption that every event and every object has its proper location within objective and linear time. From a historicist point of view, an artifact that has been unmoored from its secure anchorage in linear time and has drifted into an alien historical context is an "anachronism." Such an artifact can appear inside a representation: the Elizabethan clock that strikes the hour in Shakespeare's *Julius Caesar*, for example, or the "doublet" Caesar wears. The embedded anachronism creates a temporal tension between container and contained. An anachronism can also appear on the stage of life itself—but only when sensitivity to the historicity of form is so far developed that the entire visual environment is seen to comply with a stylistic "program." The anachronistic artifact then appears to be out of step with that program. Such an artifact is the sixteenth-century painting with a gold ground, for example the *Crucifixion* by Albrecht Altdorfer in Budapest (ca. 1520), a picture that reprises an iconographic type (the "Crucifixion with Crowd") and a non-naturalistic approach to space long out of fashion. Historical anachronism of this sort may be the product of naiveté or ignorance — with the possibility of historical accuracy comes the possibility of error — or it may contribute to a deliberately anachronistic cultural project such as neoclassicism or archaism. The anachronic artifact also moves freely in time, but unlike the anachronistic artifact, it does not depend for its effect on a stable conception of the historicity of form. The anachronic artifact is quite generally an artifact that resembles an artwork. It is the more global category: the anachronistic artifact is just a special case of the anachronic artifact.[18]

To describe a work of art as an "anachronism" is to say that the work is best grasped not as art, but rather as a witness to its times, or as an inalienable trace of history; it tries to tell us what the artwork *really is*. To describe the work of art as "anachronic," by contrast, is to say what the artwork *does*, qua art.[19]

Some images in the fifteenth century delivered remote realities and permanent truths, with the expectation that the accidents of time would not interfere with that delivery. Other works bore direct witness to the life-world that generated them. Some works refused to be pinned down in time, others derived all their meaning from their anchorage in time. Works credited to an author, an individual who "originates" or "founds" (Latin *auctor*, from *augere*, "to increase"), were most tightly tethered to a point in time. Such works testified to their own authors. The principle of continuity of identity across a succession of substitutions is in tension with a principle of authorship.

For Leonardo da Vinci, the basis for the principle of authorship was the mystery of the artist's talent, a gift that leaves its inimitable traces especially in the art of painting. The singularity of the person, the artist, underwrites the singularity of the work:

> [The painting] cannot be copied, as happens with letters, where the copy is worth as much as the original. It cannot be cast, as happens with sculpture where the impression is like the original as far as the virtue of the work is concerned. It does not produce infinite children, as do printed books. Painting alone remains noble, it alone honors its author (*onora il suo Autore*) and remains precious and unique and never bears children equal to itself. This

singularity makes painting more excellent than those [sciences] which are widely published.[20]

The painting, like its talented author, has one body that can never be duplicated. The painting's resistance to duplication allows it to dominate time. The author intervenes in time by performing a work. Leonardo's praise of painting, a medium that registers the traces of the hand and cannot be replicated by mechanical means, privileges manual execution. But under this model it is the entire process of creation, not only execution but also invention, that alters the given, that makes a difference. The author does not simply deliver a preexisting packet of information but generates something that did not exist before. The element of agency gives the work its punctual quality. The authorial performance cuts time into before and after. The artist who replaces the Marian icon or keeps the Imperial Palace in good repair, by contrast, makes no caesura in time.

Authorial agency is a performance in the sense that it is behavior carried out according to rules. The authorial innovation presents itself as a surplus added to reality, an increase. But the new is never truly new. The absolutely new would be incomprehensible. Rather, the work restages the given and creates an impression of novelty. The authored work must comply with conventions in order to be understood at all. Those conventions anchor the individual innovation in custom and fashion, that is, to supraindividual, collective norms. The performance is the adjustment of the conventions to the private project, to which the finished work of art will provide, for the rest of the world, the only access. To describe the authored work as a performance is to emphasize its punctual, time-sensitive quality. But performance involves an interaction between the individual and custom. Custom is the field that confers signification on the difference-making act that Leonardo valued. In the performative work, the past is therefore doubly present: first in the conventions that the artist must conform to, and second in the idea of the past, perhaps even of the meaning-conferring origin itself, formed in the artist's own imagination. It is that second processing of the past that has traditionally raised suspicions, simply because it happens, as it were, behind closed doors. In a traditional society, to admit an ideated object into the process of artifact creation is to hand over the crucial business of collective memory to an individual memory. For buildings and paintings and poetic texts, as much as rituals, are cables that hold a society together through time. The individual memory is unreliable and cannot be trusted with the past. The artist makes a double of a chosen model, but the double is imperfect, or simply idiosyncratic, and so falls away from its origin. This falling away was the basis for Plato's dissatisfaction with the image.[21]

Why should one trust what an artwork says? What sort of authority did an artist have? Plenty was at stake in this question, not only for society but also for art, because the artwork's relation to real power, to institutions such as church or state, depended on the persuasiveness of its referential claims. When the ties between the work and its referent, for example a divine personage, begin to fray, the model of mutual substitutability among works can compensate. So too can the myth of the acheiropoietic image, or the image not made by human hands: a direct impression of Christ's features on cloth, for example. The miraculously generated portrait and the chain of effective substitutions together function as an artificial memory, a system that archives a past and generates a future without recourse to the poor mechanisms of the human imagination.

We are not proposing simply that a substitutional model of production gave way, over the course of the fifteenth century, to an authorial model. Such an argument would reproduce a traditional account of Renaissance art as an emancipation of the artist from mindless submission to custom, an account sketched out already by the sixteenth-century historian Giorgio Vasari, who asserted that in the Middle Ages artists were content to copy one another and only with Giotto did they stop copying and begin attending to nature.[22] The substitutional model was not a primitive or superstitious creed, but a model of production that grasps, in many ways more successfully than the authorial model, the strange and multiple temporality of the artwork. Substitution and performance are not phases succeeding one another, but rather are two competitive models of creativity that are always in play. One defines and responds to the other. The authorial performance asserts punctual difference against repetition and continuity; substitution proposes sameness across difference. The idea that an artist might also be an author, a founder, was not invented in the Renaissance. Greek and Roman antiquity and the Western Middle Ages held strong conceptions of the singularity of the creative artist, evinced in the praise and honors meted out to artists and in conventions of signing and dating works of art, already highly developed by the twelfth and thirteenth centuries in Europe.[23] In the Renaissance, however, the artistic author was for the first time institutionalized, in the sense that he was enshrined as a protagonist in histories of art and theories of art. The idea that works of art merely substitute for one another then stood out in relief, with more clarity then ever, against the precarious model of authorship, which left the referential capacities of artifacts in so much doubt. The two models were coevolutionary.

Paintings, sculptures, and even buildings figured their own origins, although often in disguised fashion. The artwork emerged in the European

Renaissance as a place where two competitive models of the origins of art could be held in suspension. In addition to doing everything else it did — indicating real things like people or gods, proposing fictional worlds, gathering the scattered and the dissimilar under one roof — the artwork reflected on its own origins by comparing one origin myth to another. The work can represent itself either as a "structural object" or as a relic. It can represent itself either as a magical conduit to other times and places or as an index pointing to its own efficient causes, to the immediate agencies that created it and no more. It is finally the tension between the two models of the work's temporality that becomes the content of the work of art. The mark of the artwork was its capacity to test the models and at the same time to continue to function as a work underwritten by one or another of these models. This recursive or self-sustaining property of the work of art — its ability to question the conditions of its own possibility — distinguishes it from many other things.

The conception developed here of the artwork as a recursive structure stands in some contrast to the conception of art, developed especially in Anglo-American scholarship of the last two or three decades, as a form of material and symbolic wealth, even as a modality of luxury consumption.[24] Renaissance paintings or sculptures, in these accounts, functioned as adornments of person, home, and life; as investments in rare materials and rarefied craft and skill; as tokens of a capacity for discrimination as well as of social distinction. That is, they functioned not so differently from furniture, costume, jewelry, and other finery. No one would deny that paintings fulfilled such functions, and still do. But the painting, in addition to exploiting the straightforward appeal of materials and craft, also *comments* on that appeal. Rarity, talent, expense, and consumption become aspects of the work's content. The conflict between matter and reflection is factored into the work's value. The very ability of the artist to transform apparently intractable materials like marble, bronze, or pigments, to make them speak, is narrativized, symbolized. The muteness and mindlessness as much as the intrinsic agency, even the charisma, of the raw materials can be figured by a painting or a sculpture.[25] The capacities of jewelry and furniture to narrate, comment, reflect, and ironize are comparatively limited.

The historian who interprets the work of art as a token within a system of symbolic exchanges opens up a window onto the hidden mechanisms of social power in a remote, vanished society. But such an interpretation tends not to want to take up the possibility of the work's symbolic reach *beyond* the historical life-world that created it — its ability to symbolize realities unknown to its own makers. Only the idea of art can open up this possibility. "Art" is the name of the possibility of a conversation across time, a conversation more meaningful than the present's merely forensic reconstruction of the past. A materialist approach to historical art leaves the art trapped within its original symbolic circuits. It tends not even to notice that the artwork functioned as a token of power, in its time, precisely by complicating time, by reactivating prestigious forebears, by comparing events across time, by fabricating memories. The only time-bending agency made available to the historical work by a materialist approach is one that reproduces its token-like existence in the symbolic economy of luxury and taste: namely, as an absurdly overvalued heirloom of a modern, consumption-based society; a collector's item or museum piece, in other words. Such an approach will not help us interpret the messages about time or memory, about the gods or the creation, about first things or last things, phrased in the wordless plastic language or embedded in the material makeup of paintings, sculpture, prints, drawings, and buildings.

The ability of the work of art to hold incompatible models in suspension without deciding is the key to art's anachronic quality, its ability really to "fetch" a past, create a past, perhaps even fetch the future. These anachronic powers are not entirely accounted for either by the substitution model or by the authorship model. The artwork is more than the sum of its own origin myths. When the artwork holds substitutional and authorial myths of origin in suspension, it does not hesitate, like Simone de Beauvoir's Imperial Palace, between the state of the unaltered relic and the state of the repristinated relic. Rather, it hesitates between hesitation itself (the substitutional system's unwillingness to commit itself to linear time) and anchoring in time (the punctual quality of the authorial act). Art, a recursive system, is a hesitation about hesitation.[26]

This book is not meant to be an eccentric history of Renaissance art, but rather a road map to an obscured landscape. It maps a web of paths traveled by works and artists, mostly in the fifteenth century, that are difficult for us to perceive today, peering back as we do through the screen of the artwork as it was institutionalized between the late sixteenth and the eighteenth centuries by treatises on art and art histories, catalogues of collections, the emergence of professional art dealers, the establishment of art markets and art academies. The road map is presented in the form of a story, a sequence of interrelated episodes. The book is heavily dependent on recent research on the topic of the evidentiary or referential image, especially on the reception in western Europe of Byzantine images with special claims to authenticity.[27] It relies on recent work on the beginnings of an archeological scholarship in fifteenth-century Europe: the turn to the testimony of material artifacts as a supplement to the testimony of texts.[28] Our proposals were also inspired by research into the typological basis of medieval architecture,[29] and on ancient and medieval spoliation, that is, the recycling of building materials and other artifacts.[30] The twenty-eight sections of this book trace a conceptual model of some flexibility, bearing potentially on anything built or pictured between the fourteenth and sixteenth centuries. This book is not *the* story of the Renaissance, but nor is it just *a* story. It imagines the infrastructure of many possible stories.

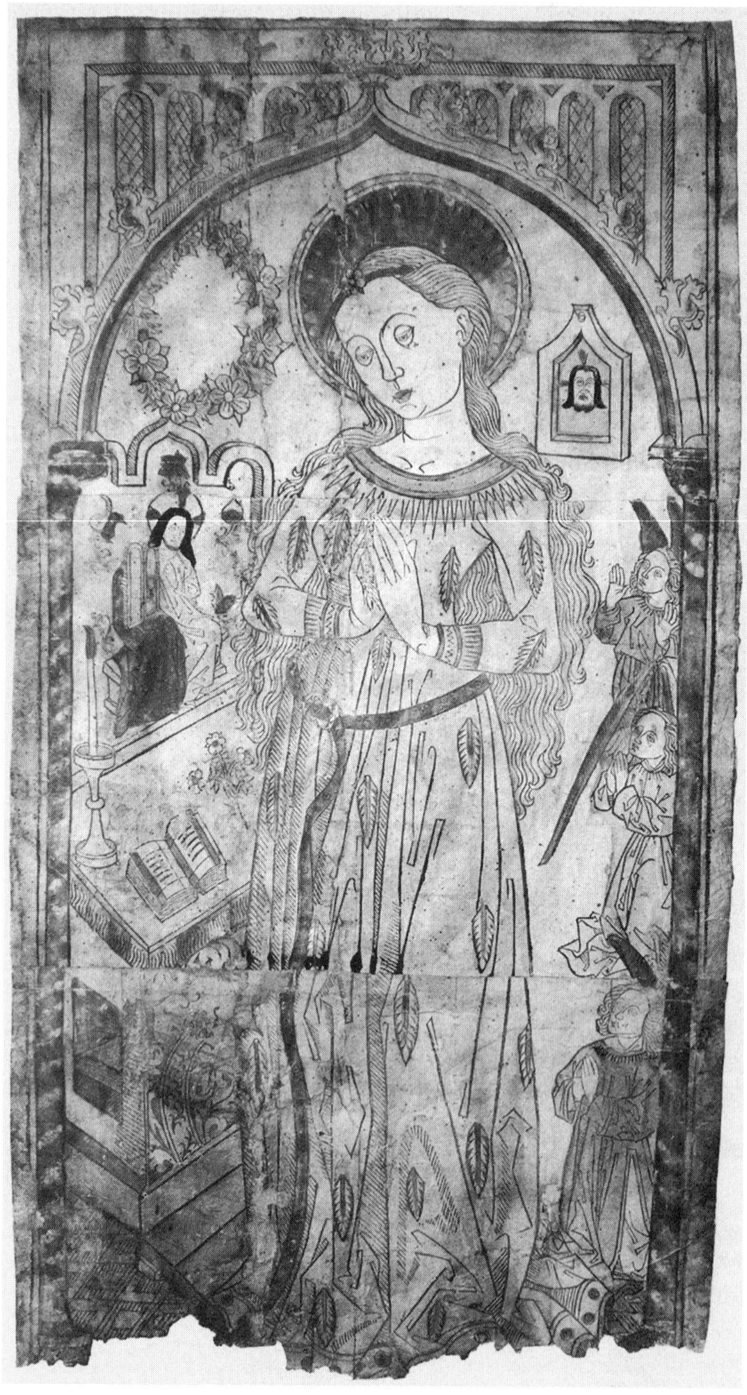

2.1 A celebrated cult image, recorded and amplified by print. *Madonna in the Robe of Wheat Ears*, hand-colored woodcut, 75.6 x 41.5 cm (south Germany, 1470s?). Copenhagen, National Museum. This print survives in only one impression, found pasted inside a cabinet in a church in Denmark a century ago. It depicts the Virgin Mary as a worshipper in the Temple of Jerusalem, just as she appeared in a venerable painting once preserved in the Cathedral of Milan, and now lost. The Virgin prays before an altarpiece depicting Moses, or perhaps God himself, displaying the tablets of the law. Behind her on the wall hangs a portrait of her son Jesus Christ, not yet born.

TWO

"The Image of the Image of Our Lady"

The figuring of the difference between models of origins comes into sharpest focus in differences between media. Medial switchings—transpositions of form and content from one system of communication to another—are an opportunity to glimpse the artwork at the moment of its resurfacing in another work.

This woodcut is one of the largest of all fifteenth-century prints (figure 2.1).[1] It was printed with black ink on three sheets of paper and then colored by hand. The only surviving impression is preserved in the National Museum in Copenhagen.[2] The print represents *Maria im Ährenkleid*, or Mary in the Robe of Wheat Ears, an iconographic type popular in southern Germany and linked to a no-longer-extant image—perhaps a statue, perhaps a painting—in a chapel in the Cathedral of Milan where the Virgin Mary had in the late fourteenth century performed certain miracles.

The sheet was found about a century ago pasted on the inside back wall of a sacristy cabinet in the so-called Cathedral of Dråby near the village of Mols, on the east coast of Jutland. The sacristy cabinet still survives, also in the National Museum in Copenhagen, and it is dated 1510–1520. The Copenhagen woodcut belongs to a family of woodcuts of this subject which betray some familiarity with Netherlandish panel painting of the mid-fifteenth century.[3] We do not know when and where this woodcut was designed and printed. The paper bears a watermark associated with French papers. But paper with that watermark was also used by a book publisher in Lübeck, in north Germany, in 1492. Stylistic comparison suggests that the block from which the Copenhagen woodcut was printed was designed and carved in the 1470s. The woodcut may have been printed only some years later, probably in the north of Germany, and still later pasted into the back of the cabinet in Jutland.

The relation of this work to prior works is spelled out in plain words on other woodcuts from the same family. A woodcut now in Munich bears a xylographic inscription around its outer edge that reads, "Das bild ist unser lieben frauen bild als sie in dem tempel war, ehe das sie Sankt Joseph vermahlet ward; also dyntten ihr die engel in dem tempel und also ist sie gemelt in dem tum zu maylandt" (The image is the image of Our Lady when she was in the Temple, before she was betrothed to St. Joseph; in this way the angels waited on her in the Temple; and in this way she is depicted in the Cathedral of Milan).[4] This print, like the one in Copenhagen, depicts the devout maiden described in apocryphal gospels and in medieval hagiographies, in a robe bedecked with ears of wheat and against an ornamental background. A woodcut in Zurich bears a similar but even longer inscription, describing miracles associated with the mentioned representation of the Virgin in Milan (figure 2.2).[5] In the Zurich print, the Virgin stands before an altar, and at the same time is standing out of doors: here the altar is as much her attribute as it is a real place. The Copenhagen woodcut evokes more vividly the historical setting, the Temple, by placing the Virgin in a built environment, a niche-like space with an altar backed by a painted retable.

The Copenhagen print bears no inscription, though it cannot be ruled out that there once was one since the bottom few inches are missing. The inscription on the Munich and Zurich versions explains the basis of the image's authority. Yet there is a hesitation in the statement that reveals a lack of certainty about the prehistory of the iconographic formula. According to the first part of the inscription, "the image is the image of Our Lady when she was in the Temple," the woodcut delivers the real aspect of the Virgin Mary as she looked when standing in the Temple. But in its second part the inscription undermines itself by admitting that the woodcut also notates another image: "in this way she is depicted in the Cathedral of Milan." The inscription is saying that the woodcut (*Bild*) is both the image (*Bild*) of the Virgin and a reliable notation of another picture, perhaps a painting, that in turn shows how she really looked in the Temple. With such a phrase, the print concedes its own mediality; that is, it concedes that it has fetched its information from elsewhere. When the second part of the inscription says, in effect, that we know this is how she looked because the picture in Milan tells us, it displaces the responsibility for authenticity to another picture. The second part of the inscription does not go so far as to claim that the woodcut is a direct copy of the image in Milan. Instead, it implies that it copies a picture that itself copied a picture, which copied yet another picture, and so forth, opening onto a sequence of pictures of unspecified medium all capable of standing in for each other and leading back to the ur-picture in Milan that preserves the true image of the Virgin. The beginning of the inscription, by contrast, did not mention any such notation, instead evading the medial problem altogether by using the same word, *Bild*, to cover two different meanings, "picture" and "aspect": *Das*

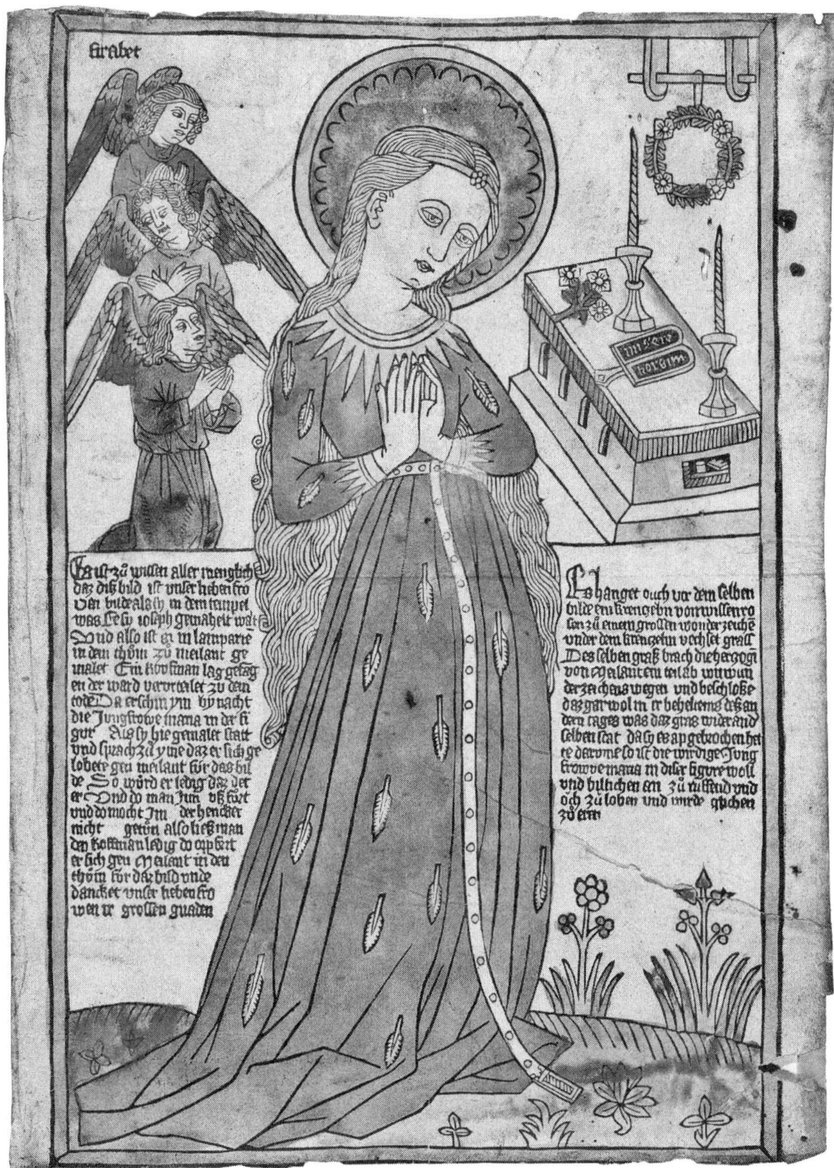

2.2 **The print explains its own relation to the prior image.** *Madonna in the Robe of Wheat Ears*, hand-colored woodcut, 39.7 x 26 cm, signed by the carver Ulrich Firabet (Switzerland, 1470s?). Zurich, Eidgenössische Technische Hochschule, Graphische Sammlung. The inscription refers to this woodcut as an image of the Virgin as she appeared in the Temple, but also mentions the cult image in Milan (see previous caption). It goes on to recount miracles credited to the Virgin, for example a wreath hanging near the cult image in Milan that instantaneously replenished itself with flowers. The identity of the altar in the upper right is ambiguous: is it located in the Temple in Jerusalem, or in Milan?

bild ist unser lieben frauen bild als sie in dem tempel war. The picture simply "is" the way she looked.

The ur-image in the Cathedral of Milan that the woodcut supposedly notates no longer exists and may never have existed. It is glimpsed, perhaps, in the several dozen surviving versions of Madonna in the Robe of Wheat Ears in paint, print, and sculpture.[6] The chapel in Milan was the home site, the site of efficacy, of an avatar of the Virgin known as the Madonna del Coazzone, or Madonna of Long Hair. The origins of the Milan cult are murky. The cult of the Madonna del Coazzone was held dear by the German community of Milan and by extension the devout of southern Germany. The Germans of Milan commissioned a silver statue of her in the later fourteenth century. It is not known when the Virgin's dress acquired its wheat-ear ornament, nor is the meaning of the motif agreed upon. There is no record of an early painting at all. According to a document, a painted panel was commissioned from an Italian painter, Cristoforo de Motis, in 1465, but that panel has not survived. By 1485 a marble statue by Pietro Antonio Solari was in place on its own altar in the cathedral; that figure is found today in the Castello Sforzesco in Milan. This skeletal sequence of cult images suggests that within the Milan cult, as far as one can tell, mediality was simply not an issue. The silver, painted, and marble images substituted for one another with no apparent diminution of meaning.

The woodcuts, by contrast, which all date from the 1470s or later, seem to feel compelled to explain their relation to prior images either through inscriptions or pictorially. Whereas in Milan the basic form of the Virgin was the crucial issue, the woodcuts, mobile images far removed from their notional origin points, thematize their own mediality. The woodcuts concede the possibility of a gradient between original and replicas, a stepped slope, a hierarchy measured in degrees. The most likely scenario is the one not mentioned by the inscriptions, namely that the print replicates not a painting but another print. That is, the woodcut replicates another woodcut equally alienated from the miracle site in Milan. The inscription admits nothing of the kind. The inscription skips over the chain of replications that got us from Milan, over the Alps, to southern Germany or to Switzerland, and finally, in the case of the woodcut in Denmark, to Lübeck and Jutland, and all by way of the Netherlands. In trying to downplay the possible loss of authenticity entailed by such a gradient, the woodcuts with their inscriptions actually create the gradient where none had existed before. By insisting on their own good relations with the past, the woodcuts raise the possibility that transmission might have been a problem. What if reference had broken down somewhere along the way? The broadcasting of the image through multiple painted copies and now woodcuts generated the desire for a single, original image with unimpeachable authority.

In the third and fourth quarters of the fifteenth century, the woodcut came to contain other media, and in this way the woodcut first became a medium. According to Marshall McLuhan, a medium acquires a "message" by delivering some content that had already been made available by another medium.[7] The "message" of any medium is the change of pace, scale, or pattern that it introduces to society by virtue of its re-mediation of an old content. In the first half of the century, the woodcut was not yet a medium. The very earliest woodcuts, from the beginning of the fifteenth century, never made self-justifying claims because they were not notating other images.[8] They never bore inscriptions that would link them to a place or to a particular cult image. The early woodcuts just delivered the real: the Virgin, Christ, the coronation of the Virgin, St. Sebastian, whatever it might be. They were images of holy personages, untroubled by their own mediality. Such pictures did not apologize for their fragility or modest cost, nor for switching from one material to another, stone to paper, wood to paper, glass to paper. A woodcut representing St. Sebastian did not say, for example, "This image is the image of St. Sebastian." Instead, it said, in effect, "This is St. Sebastian." The link it proposed to the real was copulative, in the sense that the image connected directly to St. Sebastian. The picture stood in for St. Sebastian. Such an image was in fact all one had of the divine personage, short of a corporeal relic. The images do not seem to imagine yet that anyone would judge them to be any less effective as substitutes for being printed with ink and colored with washes on paper.[9]

The woodcuts of the Madonna in the Robe of Wheat Ears, by contrast, do apologize for being prints. They hesitate between different possible theories or models of their own origins. According to the inscriptions on the Munich and Zurich versions, the woodcuts are still the direct, unmediated images of the Virgin, but they are also the notations of a picture in Milan that reliably archives the true image of the Virgin. The second claim diminishes the force of the first. The hesitation suggests that the ideal of a direct substitutional relationship is a phantom. The result of the substitutional ideal is stated in the first part of the inscription; the mechanism is explained in the second part. But the need to explain the mechanism signals a doubt. The model of a perfect substitution of one picture for another comes into view only in the moment of its dissipation. There was no "original," in other words, until someone tried but failed to replicate it. The original was the creature of the replica.

Although the inscriptions assert both the priority and reliability of the Milan painting, the woodcuts let that painting slip out of focus. For what exactly had the lost painting in Milan represented? According to the inscription, the painting preserved an image of the nubile Virgin as she was when she visited the Temple before, perhaps on the very eve of, her betrothal. Yet the wreath over the archaic altars in both the Copenhagen and Zurich woodcuts does not belong to the scene in the Temple but rather to the legend of the Madonna del Coazzone in Milan. According to this legend, which is recounted in the longer inscription on the Zurich woodcut, a wreath hanging near the image of the Virgin in Milan sprouted white flowers and grass which miraculously grew back one day after the Duchess of Milan had plucked it. What then does the woodcut reproduce? Does it represent the whole scenario in Milan: chapel, image, wreath? Or does it simply replicate a cult image in Milan, a painting that has already absorbed the wreath, the mere accessory to an earlier instantiation of the cult image, into its fictional space? The wreath has been imported from the modern devotional scenario in Milan into the supposedly historical image of the Virgin in the Temple. But which picture first collapsed the two events—the painting in Milan, the Copenhagen woodcut, or one of the predecessor woodcuts? And which picture first took the step of juxtaposing the Virgin with the small image, hanging on the rear wall, of her own son (the Holy Face or Vera icon), presumably a small, painted panel or even a hand-colored woodcut in a little, gabled frame? The collapse of the two events allows the devotions of the Virgin in the Temple to overlap mysteriously with the devotions in Milan (by the Duchess of Milan or others) to the Virgin, in such a way that the Virgin is both subject and object in the woodcut.

The print holds multiple temporalities in suspension, some punctual, some durational: the historical, prenuptial Virgin; the precise moment of her devotions on the eve of her betrothal; the time frame of the chapel in Milan and its accession to special status through the miraculous growth of flowers, whereby it is not clear whether the wreath is the wreath that flowered for the Duchess of Milan or just a symbolic wreath that always hangs there in memory of that event; the time of the lost painting in Milan, which presumably postdated the chapel and had, for all the artist of the woodcut knew, multiple identities (we know today it probably did have).

The Copenhagen woodcut registers its awareness of the multiplicity of time frames by constructing a complex internal skeleton that duplicates the frame, the exoskeleton. The edicule surrounds the Virgin like body armor. Inside, the woodcut weaves a rigid web of frames. The multiple, nested frames urge the viewer to take the external frame of this woodcut seriously, that is, as the boundary between sacred and profane realms. The woodcut replicates the multiple framing system that enveloped the

Madonna in Milan—the frame of the unknown image, the frame of the retable, the edicule she inhabited, the chapel, the Cathedral itself—all real frontiers between sacred and profane.

Everything in the Copenhagen image is touching everything else. There was a practical incentive to organize the picture this way, because it is easier to cut a block when line groups are contiguous. The paper was better supported by a dense web of ridges. But there is also a semantic dimension to the crowded, montage effect. The framed image of the Holy Face touches Mary's silhouette. The upper and lower angels also make contact with Mary. The wreath is overlapped by the arch and touches the retable below. The multiplication of internal frames keeps pace with the multiplication of potential origin points. In such a print, even the individual artist, the artist as author of the work, is on the horizon. That artist looms as a powerful rival to all the work's other possible origin points. Neither the designer, nor the cutter, nor the printer of the Copenhagen woodcut is identified. Fifteenth-century woodcuts were almost never signed. The signature of the woodcutter in the upper left corner of the print in Zurich, the single word "Firabet," is a rare exception.[10] Both woodcuts identify themselves closely with Netherlandish paintings whose authorship, or link to celebrated author-artists such as Rogier van der Weyden, was often a major component of their significance.

The Copenhagen woodcut, a picture which no longer delivers the real but mediates it, registers the presence of its viewer, the recipient of its message, in a new way. If this were a real glimpse into a chapel, all the overlappings and tangencies would shift the moment the point of view shifts, thus suggesting the contingency and momentariness of seeing.

By framing and reframing to excess, the work expresses a sense of its own distance from prior modes of art making that simply presented the real without explanation. But those earlier media and formats are present in the scene: the archaic altar with its image of Moses, or perhaps God himself, pointing to the tablets of the Law; the simple image of Christ's face, perhaps itself a woodcut pasted to a panel; the Temple in Jerusalem, the model for all Christian temples; the cult image in Milan, painting or statue, associated with a miracle. The Copenhagen woodcut is no longer simply a devotional target. It is also an antiquarian image, the notation of archeological data. It belongs alongside other contemporary prints that reproduced ancient artifacts and customs, such as the engravings after Andrea Mantegna's *Triumphs of Caesar* or Israhel van Meckenem's engraving of the mosaic icon of the Man of Sorrows in Santa Croce in Gerusalemme, Rome (see figure 26.5).[11] The Cathedral of Milan was, after all, an extremely old institution, housing mosaics that date to the fifth century. For all one knew in the late fifteenth century, the Madonna del Coazzone was a cult with roots in antiquity.

The simple and straightforward image that delivered the real never actually existed. It was only ever visible from a vantage point inside a later image, which worried about its own crafted and mediated nature. The later work is inhabited by imagined earlier modes of art making that were imagined precisely to be uninhabited, independent; imagined to be not yet art but simply images. Just as the artwork produced the phantom of its own superior opposite, the image, so too was "Renaissance art" a machine for the production of "medieval art."

THREE

What Is Substitution?

The Copenhagen woodcut with its embedded virtuous versions of itself—temple, Holy Face, altar with altarpiece representing Moses or God, angel—registered a desire for authentic, legitimate targets for devotion, the sort of targets that no one would think to interrogate with impertinent questions about production history. Whenever possible, people declined to ask such questions of the artifacts around them, not only paintings and statues but also buildings. Such artifacts were understood whenever possible to have a double historicity: that is, one might know that they were fabricated in the present or in the recent past, but at the same time value them and use them as if they were very old things. This was not a matter of collective naiveté or indolence, but rather a systematic self-delusion, a semidelusion, designed to extract from the artifact the maximum possible referential reach. The half lie of double historicity was abetted by relative ignorance about real production histories but was not simply a way of masking that ignorance. Rather, the hypothesis that an artifact "might as well be" very old was a way of exploiting ignorance. It was moreover a hypothesis true to the nature of artworks, which were adepts of time.

The image or building took up its multiple residencies in time by presenting itself as a token of a type, a type associated with an origin, perhaps mythical or only dimly perceived, an origin enforcing a general categorical continuity across a sequence of tokens. Under such a model of the temporal life of artifacts, one token or replica effectively substituted for another; classes of artifacts were grasped as chains of substitutable replicas stretching out across time and space. Modern copies of painted icons were understood as effective surrogates for lost originals, for example, and new buildings were understood as reinstantiations, through typological association, of prior structures. The literal circumstances and the historical moment of an artifact's material execution were not routinely taken as components of its meaning or function. Instead, such facts about an artifact were seen as accidental rather than as constitutive features. The artifact thus functioned by aligning itself with a diachronic chain of replications. It substituted for the absent artifacts that preceded it within the chain.

Tacitus described the restoration of the Capitoline temple in Rome under Vespasian as a triage between the essential features of the predecessor building, which had to be preserved, and the merely accidental, which could be altered.[1] The *haruspices*, the divinators, instructed the builders to remove the ruins of the old temple and erect the new one on the traces of the old (*templum isdem vestigiis sisteretur*). The gods were unwilling to see the old plan or "form" altered (*nolle deos mutari veterem formam*). In this way the identity of the old temple was transferred to the new. But the old temple was unimpressively low-slung, and so the builders were allowed to raise the new one higher—the only change that religious scruple permitted (*altitudo aedibus adiecta: id solum religio adnuere et prioris templi magnificentiae defuisse credebatur*).

Richard Krautheimer, in a seminal article of 1942 on the "iconography" of medieval architecture, made a similar point about medieval buildings.[2] He argued that the ground plans of many churches complied with a set of simple design principles embodied in a few prestigious and symbolically weighty early models. But Krautheimer carefully declined to push his thesis beyond a limited group of centrally planned churches dating from the ninth to the twelfth centuries. And yet it may be possible to extend the Krautheimer thesis beyond its original brief, to the paintings and the sculptures of the Renaissance.

To perceive an artifact in substitutional terms was to understand it as belonging to more than one historical moment simultaneously. The artifact was connected to its unknowable point of origin by an unreconstructible chain of replicas. That chain could not be perceived; its links did not diminish in stature as they receded into the depths of time. Rather, the chain created an instant and ideally effective link to an authoritative source and an instant identity for the artifact. The chains were not necessarily real. Hans Belting has pointed out that the earliest portraits of Christ made no claim to offer a true likeness. The chain of icons that ran backward to an authentic image of Christ was constructed only much later.[3]

Whereas under the performative or authorial theory of origins a given sequence of works is viewed perspectivally, each one with a different appearance, under the substitutional theory different objects stack up one on top of another without recession and without alteration. The dominant metaphor is that of the impress or the cast, allowing for repetition without difference, even across heterogeneous objects and materials. The idea that imprinting preserves identity was affirmed already in Byzantium in the wake of the iconoclastic controversy. The ninth-century theologian St.

Theodore the Studite compared the relation of image to prototype to the impress of a seal or engraved ring on different materials at different times:

> The impression is one and the same in the several materials which, however, are different with respect to each other; yet it would not have remained identical unless it were entirely unconnected with the materials.... The same applies to the likeness of Christ irrespective of the material upon which it is represented.[4]

This book argues that the apprehension of historical artifacts in the late medieval and early modern period, as well as the production of new images and buildings, was built on the following paradox: the possibility that a material sample of the past could somehow be *both* an especially powerful testimony to a distant world *and* at the same time an ersatz for another, now absent artifact. The interpretation of artifacts rested on two logically incompatible convictions, neither of which could be easily abandoned: on the one hand, that material evidence was the best sort of evidence; on the other hand, that it was very likely that at some point material artifacts had been replaced. Instead of allowing one conviction to prevail, people thought "doubly" about artifacts. Yet they did not think doubly about holy relics. A pig's bone was not an acceptable substitute for the bone of a saint. The falsification of relics was plainly seen to be wrong. Nor did they think doubly about nondocumentary verbal texts, which were obviously substitutable, handed down through time from one material vehicle to another without loss of authenticity. The force of an old poem did not depend on the literal antiquity of the page it was written on.

A political document, like a charter or a deed, or a material artifact, like an image, moved between these two poles, between the nonsubstitutability of the bone and the perfect substitutability of the linguistic text. The forgeries of documents so common in the Middle Ages can be understood, under a substitutional theory of artifact production, as the legitimate reproduction of accidentally misplaced facts.[5] Thousands of documents were fabricated and planted in archives by later scholars, both monastic and courtly, between the eleventh and the fifteenth centuries. Such documents were used to shore up the claims to antiquity or legitimacy of a monastic foundation or a bishopric or a ducal house. They attested to origins. If the crucial document did not exist, it was invented. Document and sacred image alike were grasped as something like relics and, at the same time, as something like poems.

The model of linear and measurable time was hardly foreign to the Western historical imagination before modern times, as many medieval chronicles attest. But to tell a story from year to year, from event to event,

was simply one way of organizing time. Artifacts and monuments configured time differently. They stitched through time, pulling two points
on the chronological timeline together until they met. Through artifacts
the past participated in the present. A primary function of art under the
substitutional system was precisely to effect a disruption of chronological
time, to collapse temporal distance. Such temporalities had something
in common, as we have noted, with the typological thinking of biblical
exegetes, according to which sacred events, though embedded in history,
also contained what theologians called a mystery, figure, or sacrament—a
spiritual meaning that lifted the event out of the flow of history. The
"omnitemporal" scheme of history presupposed by figural thinking was
an effort to adopt God's point of view, which grasps history all at once,
topologically, rather than in a linear sequence. To think this way was not
merely a privilege of the educated elite, for figural structures were embedded in every Mass ceremony and in virtually every sermon.[6]

Visual artifacts by their very nature were suited to the representation
of the figural dimension of history. The juxtapositions, stackings, displacements, and cyclical configurations found in countless medieval church
façades and altarpieces presupposed a competence for thinking through time
in flexible and associative ways. The advantages of figural disposition were
recognized in the medieval art of memory, which involved the construction of elaborate architectural configurations, as well as two-dimensional
compositional arrays, as a means of assuring secure storage and facilitating
random access to textual authorities. Texts themselves were not understood in strictly discursive and linear terms but were configured to facili-
tate the working of the mnemonic imagination. A well-honed memory saw
the verses of the source text as a line with many hooks on it connecting it
with other texts, so that in pulling on one of the hooks all the "fish" were
drawn in.[7] The figural approach to texts was reflected in the layout of the
glossed books that developed during the twelfth century in France. There
the comments were written all around the authored text, keyed into it
through red underlinings, heuristic symbols, and other punctuation. To
pull in one text was to pull in all the commentary, as well as other texts
that accorded with it. The "original" text and its author remained temporally unfixed. As Mary Carruthers put it, "A work of literature was not
taught in isolation, as an artifact produced by some person long dead whose
intention we must now 'recover,' but as an ever-rolling stream accumulat-
ing and adapting over time as it is 'collated' with its multitude of readers."[8]

But visual artifacts collapsed past and present with an ease and sudden-
ness that no text could match. Images proposed an unmediated, present-
tense, somatic encounter with the people and the things of the past.

They enacted a breaking through time and a raising from the dead. The difference between text and image as historical records was described in just such terms by Manuel Chrysoloras, a Greek scholar who emigrated to Florence in the fifteenth century:

> Herodotus and the other historians did great things with their works; but only in images is it possible to see everything as if in the time at which it happened, and thus this [image-based] history is absolutely and simply exact: or better, if I may say so, it is not history, but direct and personal observation [*autopsía*] and living presence [*parousía*] of all the things that happened then.[9]

The anachronic force of images and other artifacts was grounded in hopeful assumptions about the straightforwardness and instant intelligibility of figural representation. The image bent the linear sequence of events back upon itself, as if exerting a pull on time. This was a psychological fact that followed from the capacity of the figure to embody materially its own signified.

Erich Auerbach insisted that the figural or typological relationship was not allegorical, but real. The Old Testament type did not merely stand for the New Testament antitype. Rather, both were equally real events in the flow of history. The connection between the two events, indeed the *identity* of the two events, was perceptible to an exegete who saw them not in historical perspective, foreshortened, as a modern observer might, but instead saw their symmetrical subordination to a higher, ultimate truth. There is a mystical dimension to substitutional logic, a conviction of the real, and not merely symbolic, link between event and event, and between artifact and artifact. Identity across time was sustained by the substitutional hypothesis, only to be disrupted by modern historicist scholarship.

The figural alternative to linear and causal temporality is a permanent lure, a rhetorical, poetical, and political occasion. Figurality played a principal role in twentieth-century efforts to adjust the relationship between history and memory: in Sigmund Freud's identification of the psychic operations of condensation and displacement; in the art historian Aby Warburg's paratactic memory atlas, diagramming the coils of transhistorical pictorial reference; or in Walter Benjamin's adaptation of the principle of montage to history writing. For Benjamin, the "constellation" or configuration of images held a critical power, the capacity to shatter the order of things.[10] He saw in Surrealism the promise of the figural irruption or "illumination." Indeed, Louis Aragon had spoken of the critical productivity of stylistic clashes, violations of the historical logic of style, as "asynchronisms of desire" that would reveal the contradictions of modernity.[11]

In two recent books, Georges Didi-Huberman has pointedly confronted

the modern discipline of art history with its own chronographic complacency. In *Devant le temps: Histoire de l'art et anachronisme des images* (2000),
he identifies two modern modes of dialectical and productively anachronistic thinking about images, montage and symptom, associated in multiple
ways with Benjamin and Carl Einstein. In *L'image survivante: Histoire de
l'art et temps des fantômes selon Aby Warburg* (2002), he takes Aby Warburg
as his guide and unravels the obsolete evolutionary temporal schemas that
have structured the historical study of Western art. As an alternative to
a developmental, "biomorphic" conception of history, Warburg offered a
discontinuous, folded history in which time appears in the form of "strata,
hybrid blocs, rhizomes, specific complexities, unanticipated returns and
goals always frustrated."[12] Didi-Huberman brings Warburg's model of the
Nachleben, or survival, of antique pathos formulas into alignment with the
psychoanalytic mechanism of *Nachträglichkeit*, or "deferred action." Our
own project responds to Warburg's provocation, amplified in Didi-Huberman's exegesis, by attempting to draw a nonevolutionary metaphorics of
time from the historical works themselves, a temporality in structural
misalignment with, and therefore systematically misrecognized by, art
historical scholarship. The method will be a working from the artworks
backwards, by a process of reverse engineering, to a lost chronotopology
of art making.

FOUR

An Antique Statue of Christ

The only "modern" element in the woodcuts of the Madonna in the Robe of Wheat Ears (see figures 2.1 and 2.2) had been the medium itself, woodcut. Everything depicted was old. Yet the woodcuts were comparatively indifferent to, even oblivious of, the problem of historical style. They imagined an altar and, in one case, an altarpiece that looked much like the furnishings of a modern European chapel. The historicity of that altar and altarpiece—their belongingness to the distant world of Jerusalem at the end of the first century BCE—was marked only by the strange subject matter depicted on the altarpiece. But many other works in the fifteenth century pursued the possibility that style might be indexical to times and places, painting in particular discovering its own impressive capacity for citing style, that is, depicting style itself instead of just being "in" a style. Historical style, the "look" of a remote place or time, became one of the possible contents of painting. From this point on, any painting that stages past events in modern garb and surroundings has to be suspected of sophistication, that is, knowing exactly what it is doing, before it is accused of negligence or indifference.

Such a picture is the portrait of St. Augustine by the Venetian painter Vittore Carpaccio, where the saint is shown in the act of writing a letter to St. Jerome (figure 4.1).[1] Augustine is seated at a table in a roomy study, pausing, his pen raised from the paper. In his letter, Augustine will ask the older man for advice. But at that very moment, in distant Bethlehem, Jerome dies. Augustine looks up from his desk, as his room fills with light and an ineffable fragrance, and he hears the voice of Jerome. Carpaccio painted the picture around 1503 for the confraternity of San Giorgio degli Schiavoni in Venice, where it still hangs today. The picture recreates an incident narrated by Augustine himself in a spurious letter frequently published in late fifteenth-century Venice as a supplement to biographies of St. Jerome.[2] The fluttering pages of the open codices, the fall of the shadows, the alerted dog, the poised pen, all suggest the momentariness of that moment, the evening hour of compline, as the legend tells us. This is secular time, the time of lived

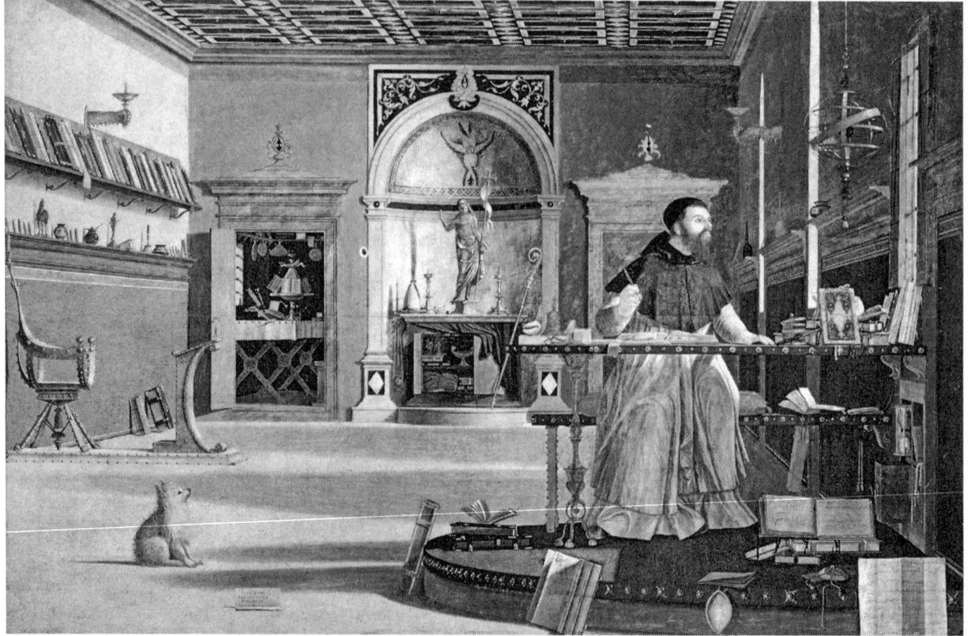

4.1 A clash of time-frames inside the scholar's study. Vittore Carpaccio, *Saint Augustine in His Study*, oil and tempera on canvas, 141 x 210 cm (ca. 1503). Venice, Scuola di San Giorgio degli Schiavoni. The fourth-century theologian is interrupted by the admonishing voice of the recently deceased St. Jerome. His study is populated by books, instruments, and furniture of modern design, as well as works of pagan art that the historical Augustine would never have owned. On the shelf to the left stands a bronze Venus based on a modern work by the sculptor Antico; or is it proposing Antico's ancient model, the *Venus Felix* in the Vatican?

experience, in which each moment repeats but differs from the previous moment. The modern and carefully described furnishings and objects enveloping Augustine vividly, paradoxically, convey the historicity of the moment. It was a *moment*: everything looked a certain way, and not another way.

In fact everything looks much as it might have looked not in North Africa of the early fifth century but in an Italian scholar's well-appointed study around 1500. At the left there is an elegant red chair with cloth fringe and brass rivets and a tiny lectern. A door at the back opens onto a smaller room with a table supporting piles of books and a rotating book stand. Carpaccio describes writing implements, pen holders, scientific instruments, an hourglass, and, on a shelf running along the left wall, under another shelf of books, still more bric-a-brac of the sort that scholars like to collect: old pots, statuettes, even prehistoric flint artifacts, misunderstood by the painter and his contemporaries as geological or meteorological curiosities, perhaps as petrified lightning.[3]

One sophisticated reason for transposing biblical and historical scenes into modern form was to disguise a reference to contemporary people or events. Carpaccio's Augustine may have been a screen for a modern portrait, a papal official in one scholarly account, in another, Cardinal Bessarion.[4] Such deliberate anachronisms, juxtapositions of historically distinct styles in a single picture and stagings of historical events in contemporary settings, fed back into the symbolic machinery of the pictures. Fifteenth-century Flemish painters, for instance, embedded samples of medieval architectural styles in their paintings as an iconographic device: the round-arched or "Romanesque" style as the signifier of the old covenant, "Gothic" pointed arches as the signifier of the new (for more on this topic, see section 14).[5] Rogier van der Weyden attached an anachronistic crucifix to the central pier of a ruinous Nativity shed, site of maximum condensation and redundancy of epochal time.[6] Botticelli dressed the characters of his *Primavera* in the costumes of contemporary festival pageantry, a blend of the still-fashionable and slightly out-of-date, creating a delicious tension with the literary premise of a primordial theophany, the invitation to the first spring of all time.[7] The staged collision between the visually familiar and the unfamiliar was one of the ways that modern paintings, to borrow a phrase from Alfred Acres, "customized the terms of their own perception."[8] Such works dared to make reference to a "here" and a "now" relative to a historical beholder, through perspective or modern costumes or hidden contemporary portraits. The "customized," contingent aspect of the work could then be folded back into the work's primary, usually non-local, aims. The internal dissonance between universal and contingent generated a whole new layer of meanings.

The condition of possibility for such complex feedback effects was the idea that form would be legible to the beholder as the trace of an epoch, a culture, a world—as a "style," in other words. Behind the idea of historical style stands a theory about the origins of formed artifacts. According to this theory, the circumstances of an artifact's fabrication, its originary context, are registered in its physical features. A clash of temporalities of the sort we find in Carpaccio comes about when patrons and artist and beholders all agree to see the artifacts "cited" in the painting, the buildings, statues, or costumes, as traces of historical moments. One can characterize this theory of the origin of the artifact—which is equally a theory of the origin of the artwork—as performative. The artifact or the work, according to this theory, was the product of a singular historical performance, the artist's performance. Any subsequent repetitions of that performance, for example, copies of the work, will be alienated from the original scene of making.

This theory of origins came into especially sharp focus over the course of the fifteenth century. An artist was now conceived for the first time as an author, an *auctor* or founder, a legitimate point of origin for a painting or sculpture, or even a building. The author, more generally the entire context of fabrication, leaves traces in the fabric of the work. By the third quarter of the fifteenth century, the image of the stylus or pen, the writing instrument that both in ancient rhetorical treatises and in modern Petrarch had come to stand symbolically for the individual author's peculiar, inalienable way of putting things into words, was carried over into the contemporary discourse on painting. The Florentine Filarete, in his *Treatise on Architecture* (1461–1464), wrote that "the painter is known by the manner of his figures, and in every discipline one is known by his style."[9] A character in Baldassare Castiglione's dialogue *The Courtier* (1528) says of Leonardo da Vinci, Andrea Mantegna, Raphael, Michelangelo, and Giorgione that "each is recognized to be perfect in his own style."[10] Since the late fifteenth century some version of this theory of origins is inscribed into every European painting.

There are thus several origin points visible in Carpaccio's painting, just as there were in the woodcuts of the Madonna in the Robe of Wheat Ears: the historical event, discerned, once the beholder is in possession of the right keys, as a narrative and as a psychological portrait; the painter's contemporary world, brought in through artifacts and furnishings to stand for worldliness in general, for temporal punctuality, for mundane or "fallen" time; Vittore Carpaccio the author, manipulator of styles, recognizable as an author through his distinctive style. The multiplicity of origin points is registered in the roster of objects and images vibrating anachronistically in the picture's background. One of the small statues on the shelf at the left is a representation of Venus, an object that a modern clergyman, a man of taste and liberal views capable of distinguishing a shelf from an altar mensa, might have prized, but that St. Augustine himself would not have owned.[11] St. Augustine was vehement in his condemnation of pagan statuary, as any of his Renaissance readers would have known.[12] On the rear wall there is a kind of private chapel, a wall niche framed by pilasters and faced with spandrels with inlaid vegetal ornament, and sheltering an altar (figure 4.2). The altar looks as if it is in use: the curtain is pushed aside and the doors on the front are open, revealing ecclesiastical equipment. Augustine has placed his bishop's mitre on the altar table and propped his crozier and a censer on either side. They are the costumes and the accoutrements that a modern bishop might have owned. The modern artifacts, even the modern chapel with its fashionable frame, had an *all'antica* flavor that connected them with the Roman past, with Augustine's historical world, more or less.[13]

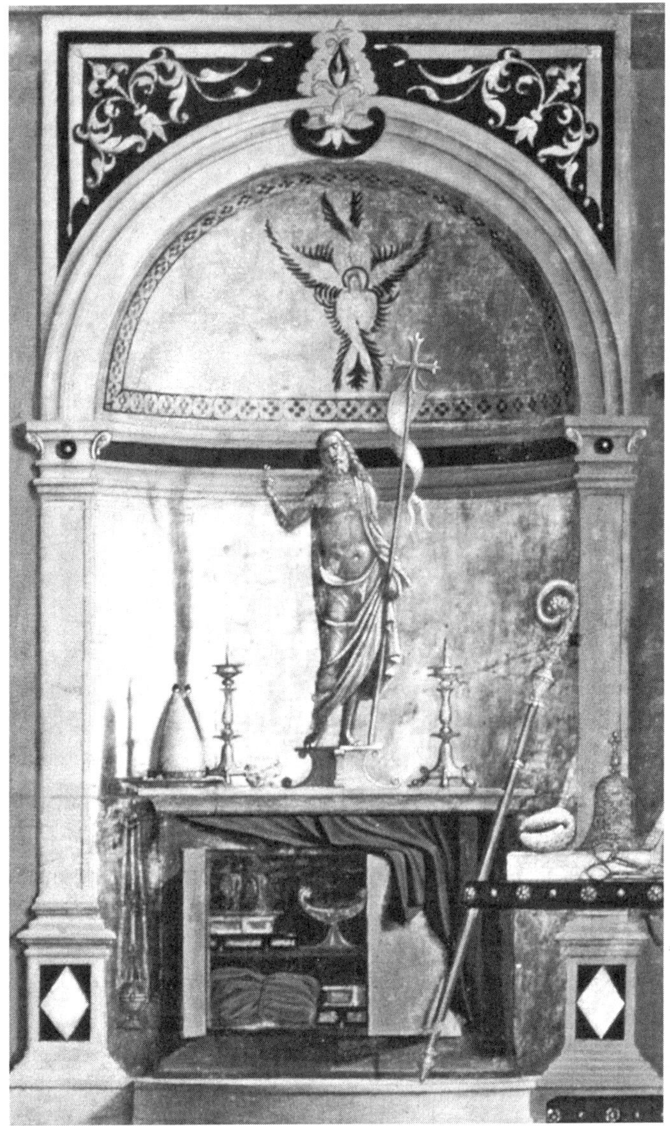

4.2 An anachronism at the heart of the painting. Vittore Carpaccio, *Saint Augustine in His Study*, detail. Venice, Scuola di San Giorgio degli Schiavoni. On the altar is a bronze statue of Christ resembling a modern work then in Venice (see figure 4.3). The mosaic in the apse above, representing a seraph, resembles those found in the thirteenth-century domes of the atrium of the basilica of San Marco in Venice.

The clash of temporalities grows more violent and mysterious deep inside the picture, inside the wall niche. On Augustine's private altar stands a statue of the resurrected Christ. Here Carpaccio has imagined an early Christian altar, adorned not by a carved and painted retable but by a free-standing bronze. No such work would have stood on a fifth-century altar. In fact, Carpaccio was describing a modern work, a bronze statue today in the Museo Poldi Pezzoli in Milan (figure 4.3). The work was made in the Veneto in the early 1490s and could be found, at the time Carpaccio painted his picture, on an altar in the Venetian church of Santa Maria della Carità.[14] It was commissioned, together with an elaborate chapel, by the wealthy jeweler and antiquarian Domenico di Piero.[15] It is significantly larger than a statuette, though less than life size.[16]

The Christ figure on the altar, a modern work, would appear to match the other anachronisms in the room, the modern furniture, the bound codices, the bibelots on the shelf. But it is not the same as these, for the bronze Christ stands on an altar; it is a cult image; in fact, it is a particular cult image attested in literary sources. Renaissance scholars had it on best authority that there had been ancient statues of Christ. One well-known account, preserved in the *Liber Pontificalis*, mentions silver statues of Christ made under the fourth-century emperor Constantine and donated to the Lateran.[17] Before Constantine, early biographers of Alexander Severus mention that he kept a statue of Christ in his *lararium*, together with statues of Apollonius of Tyana, Abraham, and Orpheus.[18] The idea of an ancient portrait statue of Christ or an apostle made perfect sense to Renaissance scholars and clerics: "The ancient founders of our illustrious Christian religion," wrote the Bolognese Dominican Leandro Alberti in 1521, "were no less wise than [the ancient Romans], since they too erected superb statues and images and built magnificent temples to those captains and first founders of our unsullied faith."[19]

The best-known legend of an antique statue of Christ originated in a report made by the early fourth-century church historian Eusebius, who described a bronze statue group in Paneas (present-day Banyas in the region of the Golan Heights) that showed a woman kneeling in supplication before a man with a cloak draped over his shoulder and with his arm outstretched to her.[20] Eusebius's account was retold and embroidered throughout the Middle Ages. Gregory the Great, at the end of the sixth century, mentioned the special glow of the statue's face.[21] In the thirteenth century the story acceded to the pages of the *Golden Legend*, one of the most widely read devotional texts of the later Middle Ages. In the *Golden Legend*, the bronze was no longer a two-figure group but a single statue of Christ.[22] The story was frequently invoked by iconophiles during the sixteenth-century image controversy as an example of the use of images in archaic Christian times.[23]

The bronze Christ cited in the painting was not merely, for Carpaccio, a modern work functioning as an ingenious hypothesis of a lost ancient work. The bronze Christ did not just "stand for" or refer poetically to

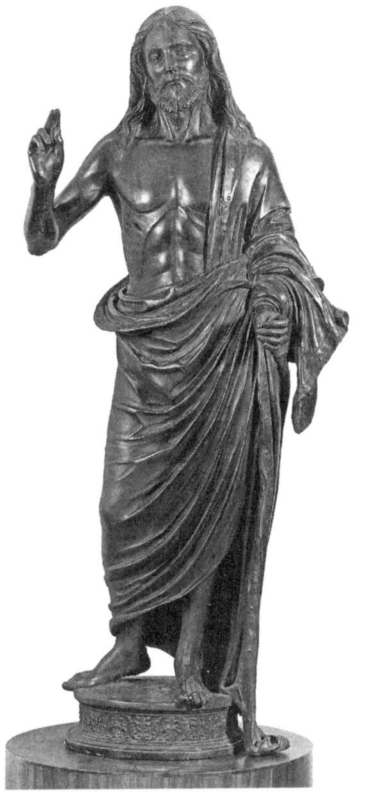

4.3 A modern antiquity. *Blessing Christ*, bronze, height 138 cm (ca. 1493). Milan, Poldi Pezzoli Museum. At the time Carpaccio painted his imaginary portrait of St. Augustine, this statue stood on an altar in the church of Santa Maria della Carità in Venice. It corresponds in basic form and in some details to an ancient statue of Christ reported by the fourth-century Church historian Eusebius and many other writers down to Carpaccio's time. The work is to this day unattributed; was it perhaps designed by its author to appear "authorless," a work linked by an invisible chain of copies to ancient times?

antiquity. Rather, the statue was for him an antique work. As, very likely, was the small bronze Venus on the shelf. It too renders a modern work, now in the Kunsthistorisches Museum in Vienna, by Pier Jacopo Alari Bonacolsi, called Antico.[24] This small bronze was itself a miniature copy of an antique marble Venus, the so-called *Venus Felix*, which had recently been discovered and set up in the Vatican. Thus Carpaccio quotes a modern work but not as a modern work.

In the literature on the ancient and medieval use of spolia some conceptual space has been cleared for artifacts like this. Patricia Fortini Brown, in her book *Venice and Antiquity*, identifies a "level of copying—the deliberate faking of an antiquity—in which the present virtually becomes the past."[25] Following a distinction drawn by Richard Brilliant, she describes such works as the thirteenth-century relief of *Hercules with the Cerynean Hind and the Lernean Hydra* on the façade of San Marco, or the thirteenth-century ducal tombs, as "conceptual spolia": artifacts filling gaps in the monumental record and made to look as if they might have been spolia.[26] One of the aims of the present book is simply to amplify and radicalize this argument. Not just a few but a vast range of works must be understood as virtual spolia or fabricated antiquities, whether they seem to our eyes to resemble real antiquities, or not.

The bronze Christ once in Venice and now in Milan did not actually belong to a chain. It was a philologically sensitive replica of the historical statue described by Eusebius and the *Golden Legend* and several other sources.[27] The modern statue preserves a peculiar detail of the legend. According to the texts, exotic plants that grew beneath the statue and came into contact with the sculpted hem of Christ's cloak took on miraculous powers and were used to cure illnesses of all kinds.[28] On the bronze statue now in Milan, the very work Carpaccio took as his model, the pedestal carries a dense motif of foliage and the hem of Christ's toga drops down sharply below the level of his feet (figure 4.4). The motif is strange and emphatic: the cloth pools up to the side of the pedestal as if to insist on the idea that it has come into physical contact with the ground. The vegetal ornament and the overflowing hem show that the patron of the bronze statue, Domenico di Piero, deliberately understood it as a replica of the original ancient statue of Christ recorded by Eusebius. The hem is like a scholarly footnote to the statue.

Once this detail is noticed other coincidences emerge. Eusebius speaks of a "double cloak" on the figure identified as Christ. The double cloak is the *diplois*, the garment worn by ascetics and Cynic philosophers who wore only the pallium, doubled in length, without the underlying tunic or any other undergarment. According to some, it was invented by the Cynic Diogenes. In his *School of Athens* (see figure 28.1), Raphael seems to make a point of showing him, in contrast to the other philosophers, sprawling on the steps in disregard of the world, clad in the pallium and nothing else. When Eusebius says the figure of Christ was clothed "decently" (κοσμιός, which literally means decorously) in the *diplois*, he is perhaps making the point that although the garment is slight, this figure wore it without looking half-naked and indecent. In the Milan statue, Christ is shown wearing a *diplois* without an undergarment (in the specific form of an *exomis*, without a fibula, leaving the right shoulder free). His torso is exposed and yet the overall effect is dignified and decorous: he does not look underdressed.

The simple existence of an artifact such as the bronze Christ in Santa Maria della Carità carried enormous validating power. Reflexively placing it within a substitutional mode of production, contemporary viewers looked past the local circumstances of its fabrication and instead concentrated on the referential target. Even a prototype otherwise unknown was in effect "retroactivated" by such a work. In the presence of the actual statue — especially one in bronze, a rare sight in churches at this time — the legend of an antique original immediately gained compelling concreteness.

The facial features of the bronze Christ now in Milan are smooth and uninflected, and the lines on the torso are highly abstract, in fact quite like the torsos on Greek icons.[29] "Authorlessness" may have been built into this work from the start, as part of its claim to antiquity. This may explain why even today connoisseurs are frustrated in their efforts to assign an attribution to this work. And yet just this authorless authority may also explain why the statue made such a significant impact in Venice after its appearance in the 1490s. Today the figure is virtually unknown, but around 1500 it carried great authority, as if it were understood to be much more than an imaginative fiction. It was often copied. In the church of the Carità in Venice where the bronze originally stood, the Christ from the Resurrection relief in the Barbarigo tomb, finished by 1501, is closely based on the statue. There were numerous freer emulations of the statue: Alvise Vivarini's *Resurrected Christ* of 1497 in San Giovanni in Bragora; Cima da Conegliano's figure of Christ in his *Doubting of Saint Thomas* of 1504; possibly the statue of Christ in marble by Giambattista Bregno in the De Rossi chapel in the Duomo of Treviso of 1501–1503.[30] Fra Bartolommeo, who visited Venice in 1508, registered the work in his Florentine altarpiece of the *Salvator Mundi* of 1516 now in the Palazzo Pitti. Carpaccio, as we have seen, copied it closely.[31] The reception history reveals that the Christ statue had come close to attaining the status of a true likeness.

Let us return to the Carpaccio painting by moving outward from the statue. The mosaic in the apse behind the statue renders an actual mosaic of a seraph from the Creation cupola found in the atrium of the basilica of San Marco in Venice.[32] Made in the thirteenth century, the mosaic

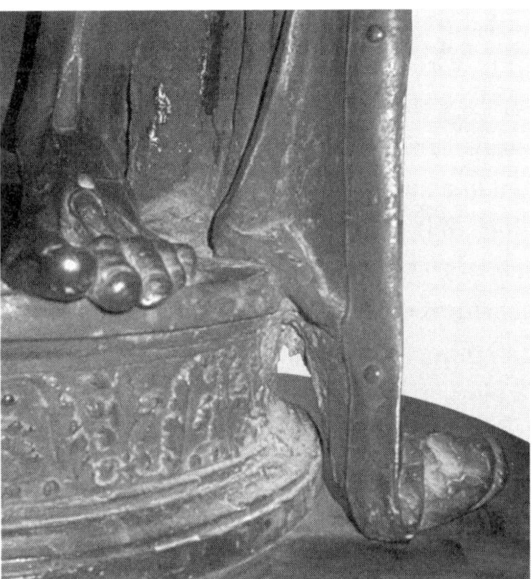

4.4 A footnote to Eusebius's Ecclesiastical History. *Blessing Christ*, detail. Milan, Poldi Pezzoli Museum. A piece of drapery falls to the side of the statue's base and gathers on the ground next to it. The hem of Christ's garment thus makes contact with the real ground beyond the confines of the work, a highly unusual feature in statuary of the period. Eusebius described the miraculous properties of herbs that had come into contact with the hem of the robe of a bronze statue of Christ known in his day. The falling hem links the Venetian statue to this legend.

is only two hundred and some years distant from Carpaccio's painting. Augustine in the fourth century never saw it, or anything like it. Perhaps Carpaccio simply did not know how to date the San Marco mosaic and in citing it meant to invoke the remote time of Christian antiquity, the time of the Church fathers. To put it in these terms, however, to speak of a "misdating," is to misunderstand the substitutional hypothesis. Carpaccio knew that San Marco and the mosaic were postantique, and yet at the same time he considered them substitutions for lost antiquities. Nothing was more reasonable than the hypothesis of a chain of replicas linking the mosaic in San Marco back to an origin. It has been shown that the mosaics from the San Marco atrium were, in fact, modeled especially carefully on illustrations like those of the fifth-century Cotton Genesis.[33] The principle of substitution was powerful enough to *make* the San Marco mosaic an antiquity.[34]

It is not enough to see Carpaccio's painting as a virtuoso manipulation of historical styles. Nor can it be described as an incompletely performative picture, with its historical vision of the past not yet quite in focus. Its interlocking anachronisms cannot be explained away as fancies of the artist or the peculiar preoccupations of the Venetians. Within the substitutional mode, anachronism was neither an aberration nor a mere rhetorical device, but a structural condition of artifacts.

Carpaccio's painting stages the statue's reinstatement of substitution against a foil of performativity, and in so doing diagrams a clash between two different versions of the time-artifact relationship. From one point of view, the painted statue is the lost and absent original, the nonexistent original, that the modern Italian statue reinstantiates. From another point of view, the statue is simply an anachronism, that is, a citation of a modern work that makes a bad fit in an historical scene. By holding both points of view open, the painting becomes something like an anatomical model, revealing the inner workings of picture-making. The painting proposes as the resolution of the predicament a new, or at least newly institutionalized, function for pictures: staging itself. Pictures like Carpaccio's become places where competitive models of the historicity of form can be juxtaposed, places of impossibility, of critical reflection and nonresolution. This staging operation is itself not in competition with the substitutional and performative modes. That is, a picture like Carpaccio's can itself maintain a particular substitutional relationship to the past, or a performative relationship to the past, or a combination of the two, and at the same time function as a diagram of the conceptual interference between the two modes. That simultaneity of operations becomes a fundamental feature of the work of art in the modern period.

FIVE

The Plebeian Pleasure of Anachronism

Today it is easy, almost too easy, to find "artistic" time—folded, misremembered—more interesting than merely linear historical time. The modern scholar willingly submits to what Jorge Luis Borges called the "plebeian pleasure of anachronism."[1] (Borges's fictional character Pierre Menard, too refined for the garden-variety anachronism of his day, deplored those facile modern novels that exploited the temporal freedom of art by situating Christ on a boulevard or Don Quixote on Wall Street. Instead, Menard elected to rewrite Cervantes's *Don Quixote* in its entirety, line by line, word by word; an exact repetition at a distance of four hundred years that achieved a more subtle and profound novelty. Menard's masterpiece is not so much anachronistic as anachronic.) The principle of substitution generates the effect of an artifact that doubles or crimps time over upon itself. The time of art, with its densities, irruptions, juxtapositions, and recoveries, comes to resemble the topology of memory itself, which emerged in the twentieth century in all its tangledness as a primordial model of historical understanding, a threat to the certainties of empirical historical science. In the substitutional mode, however, there is no human subject involved. The substitution of work for work produces a picture of history resembling a mnemonic topology without presupposing the workings of any actual memory. The commutativity of past and present is a memory effect generated by the substitutional machine.

It proves convenient to modern theorists of the strange folds of memory-based time to preserve the myth of a prosaically historicist Renaissance. That myth has its basis in Erwin Panofsky's celebrated definition of the Italian Renaissance as the period first capable of seeing historical art in perspective.[2] Panofsky had in mind the range of Donatello's interpretations of Roman sculpture, from impeccable pastiche to poetic *imitatio*;[3] likewise, Mantegna's fine-grained antiquarian reconstructions of Roman architecture or weaponry.[4] Such achievements are incomprehensible unless we admit that Donatello and Mantegna had a strong sense of historical style. That is, they must have believed that the look of an artifact registered the sensibilities and tendencies of the craftsmen or the culture that produced it, in the way that a pen responds to the movements of the mind of an author. The insight into the historicity and relativity of style, according to Panofsky, was the precondition for a rebirth of antique art, for not until ancient art was perceived as a corpus of works united by a common period style, clearly distinct from all the works made in the intervening "middle" period, could that corpus become the basis for a revival of the arts.

But such historical lucidity was scarce in the Renaissance. Renaissance artists and scholars could refer to no established chronology of artifacts, nor did anyone make much of an attempt to establish such a chronology. Historical chronology as developed by the chronographers of the sixteenth and seventeenth centuries was a sequence of *events*, and it was not at all clear—nor is it even today—that artifacts are best understood as events. When people in the Renaissance did measure out a "cognitive distance" to an historical work of art or building, this turns out to be a peculiar, con- trived aspect of the period's historical imagination, not more essential to the period than other aspects. That has seemed clear enough to historians such as Elizabeth Eisenstein, who wrote of the "amorphous spatio-temporal context" of fifteenth- and sixteenth-century humanist scholarship, and Lucien Febvre, who described the multiple temporalities that structured life in sixteenth-century Europe.[5] The researches of Frank Borchardt, Wal- ter Stephens, Anthony Grafton, and others force us to take seriously the vitality and persistence of old stories about races of giants locked in combat with Egyptian gods in the valleys of ancient Europe.[6] Fantastical myths of national origins were promulgated well into the seventeenth century.[7]

There is an incentive to overrate the clarity of Renaissance and Enlight- enment thought so that a delirious twentieth- and twenty-first-century modernity can stand out in relief. Likewise, for those who wish to believe in the lucidity of the Renaissance, either as the foundational moment of their own lucid modernity or as the foil for their own obscure modernity, it may be equally convenient to stress the confusion and irrationalism of medieval thought. In the 1969 postscript to his well-known article "Introduction to an 'Iconography of Medieval Architecture'," Richard Krauthcimer spoke of the "medieval pattern of 'double-think,' or, better, 'multi-think'"; and noted that multiple connotations and images "all 'vibrated' simultaneously in the mind of educated Early Christian and medieval men."[8] But Krautheimer had been careful to explain in the article itself that all this "vibration" settled down as the Middle Ages came to a close and the archeological vision of the artistic past came into focus. By the time of the Renaissance, "multi-think" was over. From that moment on, apparently, people were careful to think only one thought at a time. Krautheimer maintained this in all his writings, as Marvin Trachtenberg has pointed out. Krautheimer's Middle Ages were endlessly complicated and self-contradictory. The Italian Renaissance, by contrast, remained for Krautheimer an idealized "never-never land" insulated "from the complexities of facture and chronology, from the messy realities of Renaissance practice, and from…social context."[9]

The same schema is at work in the writings of Georges Didi-Huberman, although with the values reversed: here the "delirious" Middle Ages are prized over a rationalist modernity launched in the Renaissance. In imposing a mimetic function on the image, the Renaissance introduced a "tyrannie du visible," suppressing the indexical conception of the image that prevailed in the Middle Ages. The medieval image, in Didi-Huberman's histories, is not the site of mastery, adequation, and intelligibility, but of an opacity, a disruption of the coded operations of the sign, a disjunctive openness by which the image unfolds onto a dizzying series of figurative associations well beyond the logic of "simple reason." Didi-Huberman is interested in Renaissance art only insofar as it resembles his idea of the medieval image. This is an understanding of the image better served by the Freudian concepts of symptom and dream-work than by the interpretive procedures developed under the rubric of "iconology" by the self-designated inheritors of Renaissance humanism, in particular Panofsky.[10] Iconology stabilizes the artwork by coordinating it with the codes and conventions that surround it, moving outward from the work to the world in measured steps. Didi-Huberman's memory images, by contrast, will never settle down long enough to be decoded, and may never reconnect with the world.

In the end, all parties seem to agree that the Italian Renaissance imposed the contrivances of cognitive distance on the fluid, associative models of historical time that prevailed in the Middle Ages. The only point of dispute is the relative value placed on cognitive distance. Panofsky prized the distancing power of reason as one of the founding intellectual achievements of European civilization. He valued the contrivance of objectivity and saw it as a fundamental principle of a humane and liberal society. His many critics tend to repudiate the historical objectivity of the Renaissance and the succeeding "classical" epoch as a grand lie that needed to be unlearned in the twentieth century.

To continue the debate in these terms is pointless, because they are still the terms recognized already by Panofsky. Panofsky knew very well that cognitive distance was a cultural contrivance that overcame the subjective, "interested" distortions of memory. The tension between immeasurable memory and measured, historical chronology is contained within Panofsky's writings. For Panofsky, it was already implied in the system of linear perspective developed by the fifteenth-century painters. "The history of perspective," he had argued in his 1927 treatise *Perspective as Symbolic Form,* "may be understood with equal justice as a triumph of the distancing and objectifying sense of the real, and as a triumph of the distance-denying human struggle for control."[11] To continue discussing the Renaissance vision of history as a contest between, on the one hand, an invested and interested figural imagination and, on the other, the contrivance of disinterested cognitive distance is to repeat the error of those historians and critics of modern art who used to struggle interminably to overcome the legacy of Clement Greenberg by refuting him in terms that were already dialectically present in Greenberg's own writing. For both the formalist and the political or critical reading of modern art were contained within Greenberg's avant-gardism.

To transcend the dilemma we might ask, How was the question of historical time addressed by the *work of art*? Panofsky actually pointed to the answer. In the essays collected in *Studies in Iconology* (1939), which tracked the artistic fortunes of iconographical motifs such as "Father Time" or "Blind Cupid," he relaxed the historical schema outlined in the introduction to that same volume. In these studies Panofsky crossed the threshold of the sixteenth century and looked directly at the fully developed Renaissance artwork, supposedly purged of temporal confusion. Here he conceded that medieval attributes and features frequently "clung" to the new, archeologically correct image of the Renaissance.[12] To characterize such persistence of the medieval mismatch between historical form and historical content, Panofsky borrowed a term from Oswald Spengler, without actually naming Spengler: *pseudomorphosis,* a term that Spengler in turn had adapted from mineralogy.[13] Spengler had used it in his *Decline of the West* to denote the unwilling conformity of a new and dynamic culture to the forms and formulas of an older culture, for example when the early Christians adopted the pagan form of the basilica. The basilica "employs the means of the Classical to express the opposite thereof, and is unable to free itself from those means—that is the essence and the tragedy of the 'Pseudomorphosis'."[14]

Although Panofsky did not dwell further on the idea of pseudomorphosis, his practical iconological readings can be understood as demonstrations of the "unwilling" and incomplete character of the early modern artwork.[15] Silvia Ferretti has argued that Panofsky's artwork was temporally "antinomic," that is, it occupied two incompatible time schemes at once. On the one hand, the artwork was fixed within historical or absolute time, and on the other, it inhabited an ideal and immanent time structured by an artistic problem.[16] One could argue—in defense of Panofsky—that although this antinomy slips through the mesh of a strict periodization schema, it is brought out by the practical hermeneutic of iconological analysis.

Our approach, in effect, redescribes Ferretti's antinomic artwork as that work complying with the substitutional principle, according to which an image or a building was a token of a type, invoking and perpetuating an originary authority through participation in a sequence of similar tokens. The principle of substitution created conditions of real identity between one token and another, something like a magical bond. Such a work submits neither to an absolute or objective time that underlies all events and experiences, nor to an ideal time beyond human life, but to another temporality altogether, one structured by the real interrelations among images and artifacts.

We are not arguing simply that substitution was a medieval way of thinking about artifacts that persisted but was finally vanquished in the Renaissance. This is a familiar enough schema. Any number of modern histories of Renaissance art, since Vasari, have offered versions of this account. It is true that many medieval images tried to make their contents present by downplaying their historical fabrication and instead claiming magical, handless production. It is equally true that Renaissance works were, by contrast, often authored and therefore securely moored in this world, in the *saeculum*. According to the theory of artifacts as singularities performed under unique historical conditions, associated with the historical rise of artist-authors in the fifteenth century, copies can only be seen as repetitions, not substitutions. The two models of origins interfered with one another. But that interference was dynamic. Substitution and performance were two completely different theories of origins, but each had its uses. In every case it is a question of which conception of origins was in effect. Very often both conceptions were in effect at once.

The author-based theory of artifact production was neither a historical inevitability nor a form of enlightenment; it was not more true than the other theory. Nor can it be cleanly coordinated with other "progressive" developments like the rise of pictorial naturalism or the revival of antiquity. Indeed, it is possible to argue that the neoclassicism of the early sixteenth century, described by Panofsky as the product of self-conscious historical distancing, may equally reflect just the opposite trend, a deliberate reapplication of the substitution principle in the face of an emerging culture of artistic performance. In the same way, a case can be made that new conceptions of artistic authorship arose both *within* and *against* the highly substitutional tradition of painted icons—one thinks of the development of Jan van Eyck's authorial self-consciousness against the foil of the Byzantine icon. The disengagement in the fifteenth century of a few prestigious artifacts from their traditional functions and the establishment of non-labor-based and non-material-based criteria of value developed in a dialectical relationship with the substitutional principle of artifact production.

One effect of the interference between the substitutional and the authorial principles was the emergence of art forgery as a category. The art forgery was a historical novelty of the Renaissance. Until the late fifteenth century, when the market for art began to link value to demonstrable authorship, no one was accused of "forging" an artwork. This criminalization of substitution came about only when the two modes of production we have been outlining entered into their dialectic. What is an art forgery if not a substitution cruelly unmasked as a mere performance?

Archaism, aesthetic primitivism, pseudomorphic imitation, typology, forgery, misdating, citation, the deliberately "styleless" mode, ideal classicism: each of these temporal disturbances of the Renaissance image was an effect generated by conflict between the two theories of origins. The friction of mutual interference only brought out the contours of the competing theories with greater conceptual clarity. By 1500 the two principles, performative and substitutional, were defining one another. No sooner had the performative mode emerged than artists began to reinforce the substitutional mode in compensation. Many of the archaizing tendencies in Renaissance art, including the revival of ancient art, can be seen not simply as exercises in formal imitation but as quasi-theoretical efforts to reinstate the substitutional approach to artifact production. Works of art like Carpaccio's picture mobilized the principle of substitution deliberately, and thus revealed its workings. A painting might do such a thing for any number of reasons: to bend the expectations of a beholder, for instance, and so generate a peculiarly aesthetic effect; or to comment negatively on the competing, performative theory of origins.

Over the course of the fifteenth and sixteenth centuries, as prints sent pictorial ideas circulating all over Europe, and as published treatises and dialogues and ephemeral conversations created an independent culture of art, the dialectic between the two theories of production accelerated, and the cycles of response and counterresponse became briefer and briefer. Artistic authorship itself, which emerged in the early fifteenth century as a purely performative mode, later learned to manipulate substitution. Already by the beginning of the sixteenth century, one can almost define artistic authorship as the capacity to manipulate the two modes within the confines of an aesthetic field. It is just such a dynamic historical model, involving continual interaction between substitution, theories of artistic authorship, and self-conscious revivalism motivated by propagandistic or doctrinal principles, that has the best chance of making sense both of the density of the bronze Christ at the center of Carpaccio's anachronistic kaleidoscope, and of the restless, urgent disorder of the woodcuts of the Madonna in the Robe of Wheat Ears.

SIX

Architectural Models

Substitution is not the prehistory of Renaissance artifact production. It is a theory about making that cultures bring into focus when they need it. Building is a chaotic social process whose overall patterns are invisible from the inside. The substitutional theory of building—the idea that identity is preserved across long chains of restorations and replacements—imposes order on the process. One of the ways that cultures figure that orderliness to themselves is by making *models* of buildings. The ordinary sense of model is the maquette or mock-up that helps patrons and architects visualize a structure during the building process. Models, in the sense to be developed here, however, are not necessarily linked to a particular building, nor do they have to point forward in time, nor must they be small. Models are small by etymology; *model*, like *module*, descends from Latin *modulus*, a "small measure." Models also tend to be small because miniaturization signals the model status.[1] But a real, functional, nonminiature building can also model an idea about how buildings are made.

The Romans, around the time they began to build extensively in marble, perhaps the second century BCE, constructed a model of the city's very first building: a wooden hut, the Casa Romuli, dwelling of the city's founder. In fact, the texts mention two such huts, each provided with its own cult, one on the southwest corner of the Palatine, the hill of Cermal (this hut is attested by Varro and Dionysius of Halicarnassus), and another somewhere on the Capitoline (in Virgil *Aeneid* 8.654, the house is pictured on the shield of Aeneas, *Romuleoque recens horrebat regia culmo*, "rough and newly thatched").[2] It is not clear when the model huts were actually built, when the cults initiated, or how really knowledgeable the model-builders were about the earliest settlement of Rome. Today on the Palatine one can see post holes in the bedrock on a plateau just below the site of the Temple of Magna Mater.[3] Many archeologists consider the post holes evidence of Iron Age wooden huts. In the second century BCE, so the argument runs, the notional thatch-roofed hut of Romulus was reconstructed on the basis of the old post holes.[4] It is hard to imagine, however, that the second-century authorities possessed such archeological sense. Nor is the oral tradition likely to have preserved many details of the founding of the city.[5] More probably the tradition of huts on this site was a whole-cloth invention of the late Republican period. By that time, every material trace of Rome's historical origins had been effaced. If there was to be a trace, it would have to be created. The huts were artificial relics of an archaic wooden architecture embedded in a city of stone.

The model hut did not pose as the original dwelling of Romulus, for who could have believed that that structure's flimsy materials had survived seven centuries? The thatched cabin conspicuously depended on regular maintenance. Nor was it a reconstruction, serving merely as a sample of the rustic living conditions in Romulus's time. Instead, the hut created the fiction of a building chain leading back to the original hut. The hut modeled a proposition: the idea that this very hut had replaced an earlier hut on the same site, which in turn had replaced a still earlier hut, and so on through a multitude of generations back to the original dwelling. There is no need to ask whether any Roman actually believed in this chain. The hut stood for the idea of such a chain; it created a fiction, not an illusion. Like the bronze Christ pictured in Carpaccio's painting, it invented a tradition.

The Roman state treated the hut of Romulus as a relic, but unlike a true relic, the hut was also held to be substitutable. Dionysius of Halicarnassus, the Augustan-period historian of archaic Rome, reported that the Palatine hut was rebuilt every time it was damaged by weather or fire: "[the priests in charge] add nothing to it to render it more stately, but if any part of it is injured, either by storms or by the lapse of time, they repair the damage and restore the hut as nearly as possible to its former condition."[6] The priestly rebuildings were symbolic reenactments of substitutional practice. The rites of the hut and the periodic reconstructions stood for the idea of architectural continuity at a time when the city's temples were one by one being reconstructed in new forms and new materials. The consuls and emperors were replacing the original wood and terracotta sanctuaries from archaic times with marble temples on the Greek model, but without change of dedication. The temples looked different but retained their identity and antiquity. The Casa Romuli was a stabilizer in response to these changes in building practice. The rites of the hut in the early imperial period and the priestly maintenance schedule were dramatizations of the normal life of buildings, designed to reassure everyone that Rome was still bound together by sinews of memory. The hut pointed out that every building that survives does so through a process of successive substitutions—recognitions, replacements, and restorations as necessary—and yet retains its identity across those substitutions. Every significant building was a hut of Romulus, or could become one to prove a point.

The doubling of the memory of the hut into competing Palatine and Capitoline versions was a symptom of uncertainty, a reflexive marker of the purely mythic status of the hut.[7] The illogical fission of the sacred site into parallel cults allegorized the "double-think" of substitution, the hesitation at the core of the theory. If the Palatine hut was "really" linked to a point of origin, then the Capitoline hut, with its weaker claims to place specificity, could be understood merely to *represent* the primordial dwelling. The Capitoline hut defended the Palatine hut against the charge of excessive, implausible literalism; the Palatine hut defended the Capitoline hut against the charge of a merely symbolic arbitrariness.[8]

Like the cabin that Henry David Thoreau built at Walden Pond in Concord, Massachusetts in 1845, the hut of Romulus was the construction of an increasingly sophisticated, rationalized culture inventing pride in its humble origins. Thoreau's cabin was itself, in its time, a model of a simpler way of life. He built it only a few hundred feet from a railway line. In the late twentieth century, Thoreau's cabin was replicated on its original site and it is maintained today much as the hut of Romulus once was, effectively preserving its identity for tourists, who possibly ask themselves few questions about the substitution chain behind it.[9] Thoreau's cabin both is and is not the original cabin. Place, and some rough idea of what the ur-structure must have looked like, create the identity effect.

Some structures represent their own novelty and unprecedentedness: a bridge, for instance, a technical achievement; or a palace, an assertion of newly won power. But many other buildings derive their authority from a hypothesis of distant origins and depend on the principle of substitution to create the link. Christian churches were often built on top of and around prior churches. The earliest church on the site, remembered by local legend, was built on the ruins of a pagan temple, perhaps, or was itself a reconsecrated pagan temple. And that temple—probably mythical, never-existing—was in turn thought to occupy a site designated as sacred long before anyone undertook to build on it. The modern church on that site, for all its stylistic modernity—that is, no matter how vividly people recalled the last building campaign—stood in a substitutional relationship to all the previous structures below it, behind it, within it. The building retained its identity through all the additions, improvements, repairs, and even devastations that it was imagined to have experienced; preserved its identity, in some sense, even across the epochal threshold of conversion from pagan to Christian. No one in the Middle Ages or the Renaissance was actually capable of archeologically reconstructing such a building history; it is hard enough to do today. No matter, for the substitution chain guaranteed identity by designating any alterations or replacements that the building might suffer as mere accidents.

The principle of substitution is by no means peculiar to Europe.[10] A well-known example of ritualized architectural substitution is the Ise Shrine in Japan.[11] Every twenty years, stretching back as far as the late seventh century, the buildings of the main sanctuaries at each of the two Shinto shrine complexes at Ise, Naiku (inner) and Geku (outer), are ritually razed and rebuilt. The reconstruction of 1993 was the sixty-first (some cycles were missed in the Middle Ages). The cluster of temples is rebuilt on identical rectangular sites directly adjacent to the existing sites. The cult object at the core of the shrine is transferred and the old site is then left empty for twenty years. That empty plot, covered with white pebbles, models the natural, entropic destination of artifacts. The ritual dismantling is an accelerated acting-out of the catastrophic narrative of architectural history, the pragmatic tangledness of destruction, decay, and repair. The always-again new sanctuary, meanwhile, an ideal architecture that never decays, models an ur-sanctuary. The rebuildings at the Ise Shrine preserve obsolete techniques of wood construction of which no other examples survive. The Ise temples are simultaneously among the newest and the oldest buildings in the country. The rebuildings do not replicate the predecessor buildings precisely, down to the last beam. Nevertheless, they maintain the essential continuity of the sanctuary, that is, they are held to do so as an article of faith.[12] Half-sunk in the earth at the center of each site is a wooden post; this element alone is not replaced throughout the cycles of rebuilding, but rather is preserved as a relic. The meaning of the posts is not clear; they are perhaps fragments of ur-temples, perhaps symbols of a primordial, minimal cult architecture involving posts erected in sacred precincts.

Ideas about building are figured in models. But it is not so easy to distinguish models from non-models. The two categories blend into one another. Models can be building-sized or made out of stone; a functional or "real" building, contrariwise, can have a representational dimension. To grasp this interpenetration of model and non-model in the European context, one must address the problem of the replication of the rotunda and edicule of the Holy Sepulchre.

The rock-cut tomb of Christ was excavated by Bishop Makarios of Jerusalem, with the support of Emperor Constantine, in 325–326.[13] The tomb, Christians pretended to remember, lay buried under a temple of Venus erected by Hadrian in 135. Makarios had the temple leveled and, in the phrase of Eusebius, writing only a little more than a decade later, "against

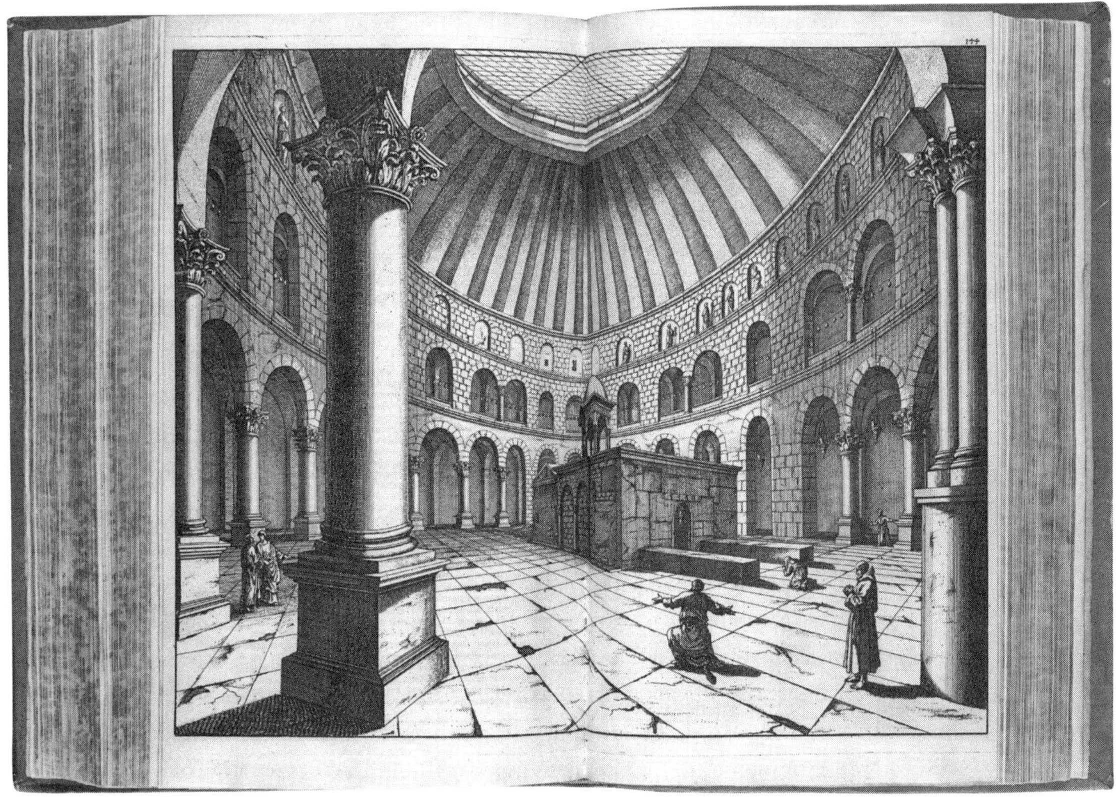

6.1 A scenic visualization of the edicule of the Holy Sepulchre inside the Constantinian rotunda. Repeatedly rebuilt, originally 326. Cornelis de Bruyn, *Reizen door de vermandste deelen van Klein-Asie* (Delft, 1698), plate 144. New Haven, Yale University, Beinecke Rare Book Library. Whereas medieval travelers described the Holy Sepulchre through words and measurements, this engraving by the Dutch traveler and illustrator de Bruyn renders the *experience* of seeing the tomb of Christ under the vast span of Constantine's dome.

all hope" fell upon the tomb chamber.[14] Once the rubble and surrounding rock had been cleared away, Constantine had the tomb encased within a ring of columns and topped by a conical roof. At some point the roof was crowned with a small, colonnaded lantern and cupola. The structure had a small rectangular porch affording a view into the tomb cavity. Over this edicule, Constantine built a vast hemispherical rotunda, the Anastasis, standing at the head of a courtyard, a long basilica, and an atrium. Our reproduction is an engraving from a traveller's account published in 1698, a wide-angle view that captures the sweep of the rotunda's arcade and the great dome dwarfing the edicule at its center (figure 6.1).[15] The seventh-century Muslim conqueror of Jerusalem, Omar, left the complex untouched. In 1009, however, the caliph Hakim of the Fatimid dynasty razed the structures to the ground. The Byzantine emperors, encouraged by Hakim's own mother, a Christian, immediately began the rebuilding process. The reconstructed rotunda and edicule were complete by about 1040, and these were the structures that the Crusaders found when they took the city in 1099.[16] The edicule was entirely reconstructed in 1555 by Boniface of Ragusa, Franciscan custos of the Holy Land, with the support of Pope Julius III.[17] Each time there was alteration of details but maintenance of the basic format of circular or roughly polygonal baldachin on columns, crowned by a cupola on colonettes, with a small rectangular forecourt. The overall size of the edicule remained about the same, approximately 13 meters front to back in the 1555 version. In the last reconstruction of 1809–1810, undertaken by the Greek Orthodox Church, the baldachin and the porch were combined into one nave-like structure.

Pilgrimages to the Holy Land in the early Middle Ages were rare and travelers' descriptions of both the rotunda and edicule were loose. Few physical traces remain of the Constantinian structures. Knowledge of the Constantinian rotunda, even today, is basically substitutional; that is, it is read through the successor structures. So, too, is knowledge of the three edicules preceding the current one, although here substitutional knowledge is supplemented by a surviving family of often contradictory, two-dimensional picturings (on coins, plaques, reliefs, paintings, and the like) and three-dimensional replicas, for example, the marble model in Narbonne dating from the fifth century and measuring 1.24 meters in length,[18] or the many reliquaries and ciboria that imitated the edicule, not always accurately.[19] One apparently reliable rendering is the drawing of the edicule reproduced in paint by Jan van Scorel in his group portrait of the Brotherhood of Jersualem Pilgrims of Haarlem (ca. 1528) (figure 6.2). Scorel himself had been to Jerusalem in 1520.[20]

Constantine's rotunda or Anastasis, along with the Mausoleum of Hadrian, the Pantheon, and the Lateran Baptistery in Rome, the basilica of San Vitale and the Mausoleum of Theoderic in Ravenna, and the Church of the Ascension (Imbomon) and the Dome of the Rock in Jerusalem, hovered in the background—in the imagination—of every medieval, centrally planned building.[21] But some structures explicitly replicated the rotunda and became the targets of what can only be described as virtual pilgrimages. One of the key examples, discussed by Krautheimer at the beginning of his fundamental essay on medieval architectural replicas, was the St. Michael chapel at Fulda of about 820, where a round ambulatory surrounded a tumulus-like edicule.[22] In such examples the resemblance of replica to original was often very weak. At Aquileia, for example, a

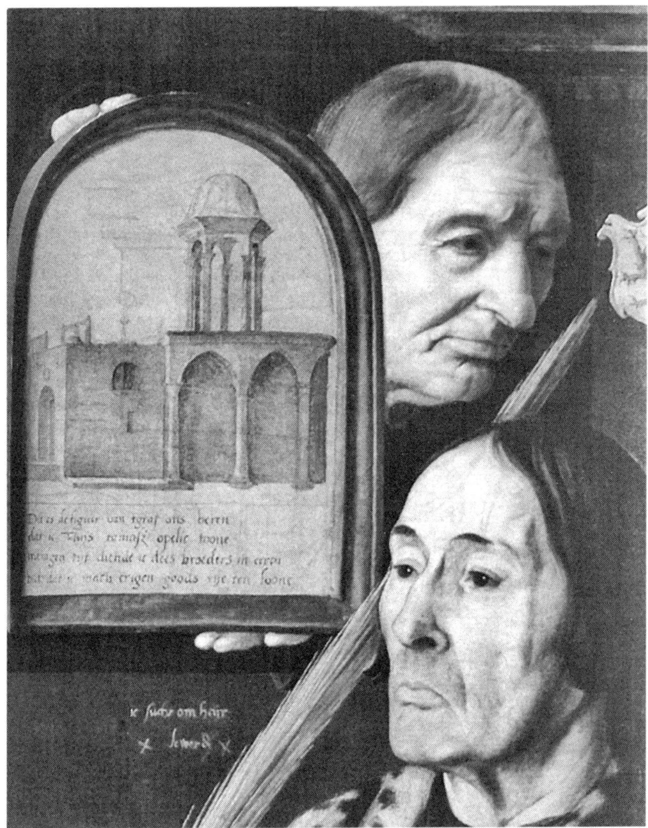

6.2 A depiction of the edicule of the Holy Sepulchre, transmitted by paper and archived in paint. Jan van Scorel, *Twelve Members of the Haarlem Brotherhood of Jersualem Pilgrims*, oil on panel, detail (ca. 1528–1529). Haarlem, Frans Hals Museum. A servant holds aloft a framed drawing or monochrome painting of the Sepulchre. The inscription reads: "This is the figure of the Holy Tomb of our Lord/ that I, Thijs Tomaszoon show./ For many years I have served these brothers with honor/ Bid that I may be repaid with God's glory." The experiential basis of the description is the key to the object's status as trophy and proof of the lay confraternity's visit to the Holy Land.

perfectly round imitation of the edicule sits inside the cathedral, whereas the actual edicule had both round and rectangular elements (figure 6.3).[23] But the labels on the buildings set everyone straight.

After the Crusaders took Jerusalem in 1099, the family of "topomimetic" replicas multiplied.[24] The relative ease of contact reactivated symbols and inspired updatings based on measurements. In Bologna, at Santo Stefano, a round chapel was erected next to a Calvary chapel, the distance between them matching the real distance in Jerusalem.[25] The Knights Templar sponsored many structures related genetically to the rotunda even if they were often called "temple" (London, Segovia, Metz).[26] Pisa, from

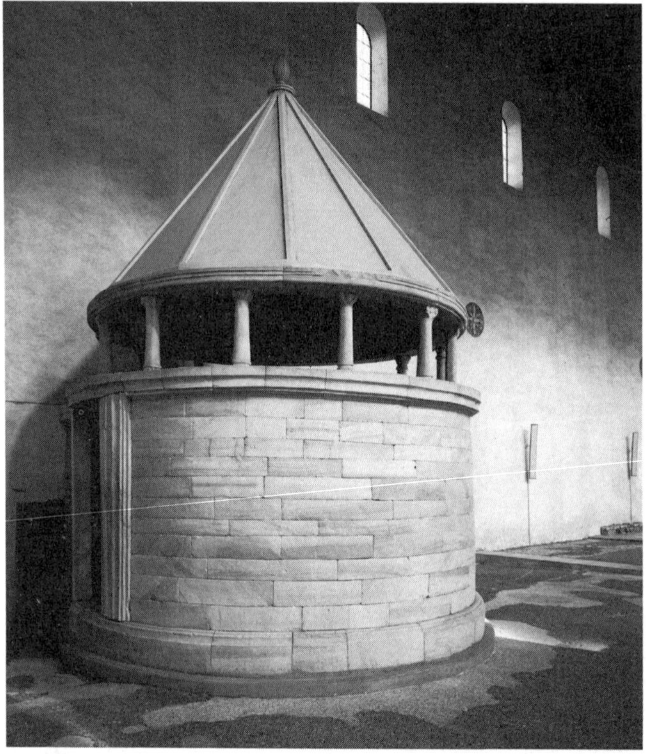

6.3 A medieval replica of the Holy Sepulchre, attentive to some features of its model but not all. Holy
Sepulchre, Aquileia, Cathedral (eleventh century). This object made the tomb of Christ present in a
northern Italian church. Based on a pilgrim's oral description, the structure preserves a memory of a
quasi-circular form and of a cupola on columns, but forgets the rectangular portion of the edicule.

the twelfth century, had a Holy Sepulchre chapel in addition to the centrally planned baptistery. The Holy Sepulchre was revealed in paintings,
for instance in Simone Martini's *Carrying of the Cross* (Paris, Louvre) —
a panel that was already in northern Europe by the late fourteenth century —
where it is pictured as a polygonal building with a pyramidal roof and a
small lantern. The dense sequence of copies extended into the sixteenth
century. Many more structures have vanished and are known only from
textual references.

Holy Sepulchre replicas often misunderstood the two nested structures.
An example is the chapel on the Weinmarkt in Augsburg consecrated in
1128 and possibly rebuilt in 1236, conjoining properties of both the edicule
and the rotunda.[27] The Augsburg structure was a round building about 18
meters in diameter topped by a pointed tower, thus apparently obeying a
description of the Church of the Holy Sepulchre as a tower-like structure

in a round chapel. The nested structures in Jerusalem were confusing to pilgrims because both structures, after all, were only frames surrounding the empty place where Christ had lain, the true target of the pilgrimage. The pilgrim arrived at the site—then as today—only to find that there were three ur-structures, not one: tomb, edicule, and rotunda (not to speak of the bewildering basilica attached to it with its various split-level and subterranean chapels). The collapsing of edicule and rotunda in some replicas follows from this redundancy. In other cases the confusion followed from the tendency to miniaturize the rotunda, for practical reasons and also because miniaturization is generally a powerful symbol of possession. It was difficult to distinguish the edicule clearly from the englobing rotunda, apparently, on the basis of verbal descriptions or depictions.

Without the skills or technology to fix the authentic form in analogue depictions, travelers measured. In effect, they digitized the edicule so they could carry it home as a list of numbers.[28] The numbers that preserved the dimensions of the tomb and the edicule were used as the basis for replicas in true scale or in true proportions. The proportional imitations of the edicule could then stand alongside such standards as the high, stone table preserved in the cloister of San Giovanni in Laterano that supposedly marked the true height of Christ.[29] Likewise, woodcuts that reproduced the almond-shaped wound of Christ,[30] or the lance that made the wound, in actual size, permitted comparisons between a person's experience and Christ's.[31] In 1498, Archbishop Johann von Baden marked out Christ's path from Pilate's house to Golgotha in the streets of Trier: the route ran from a pillar in the aisle of the cathedral, around the high altar, out the doors and across the main market, all the way to the church of St. Martin's, and was based on the latest measurements carried home by Jerusalem pilgrims.[32]

But the essential identity of the sacred building was crystallized in its centralized plan, and that identity flowed evenly through all the various performances all over Europe in various media, sizes, and ornamental garments. The centrally planned building *had* to remain exceptional in Europe—an exception to the rule of the basilica—in order to mark its own symbolic or model status.[33]

An intricate cross-referential network of centrally planned buildings emerged. This citational web was almost completely detached from its point of origin because the West knew the Constantinian buildings, edicule and rotunda, only through the magic lens of substitution, that is, only through the Crusader reconstructions. In this case, the substitution worked perfectly, because it seems that no one knew that the buildings had ever been reconstructed; or at least they never said that they knew. Observers of the Church of the Holy Sepulchre and its edicule after the Fatimid destruction of 1009 and the subsequent Crusader reconstruction never mention the rebuilding.[34] The reconstruction followed so quickly on the destruction that the gap was elided in collective memory. Moreover, and this is not much noted, medieval observers did not know that the edicule was Constantinian. Many people seem to have assumed that Constantine found the edicule and simply protected it with his rotunda. The basis for this assumption was perhaps the burial site of St. Peter in Rome, which was protected by an edicule as early as the second century.[35] Constantine later englobed the whole site, edicule and all, within his new Vatican basilica.

The Holy Sepulchre replicas would seem to clash with the essential meaning of pilgrimage. The pilgrimage asserts nonsubstitutability. The pilgrim travels at great expense and trouble because one experience is not so easily exchanged for another. The pilgrim visits a cult image that is never altered or moved, or a place that by definition cannot be moved. (The calculated defiance of this condition—the literally, that is, miraculously, movable building—is the subject of section 18.) And yet the cult images, the destinations of the pilgrim, were in actual fact not only restored and even repainted, but were also replicated and disseminated. The claims of authenticity attached to these far-flung replicas appear to undermine the premise of pilgrimage. Nevertheless, the pilgrimages continued. The institution of pilgrimage was a culture's way of acknowledging that it knew what authenticity really was, even if most of the time it chose to forget all that and instead make replicas. When Leonardo da Vinci argued that painting, unlike the other arts, is "inimitable," that is, exists only in unique, nonsubstitutable instantiations, he adduced pilgrimage to prove his point, for if a copy of the image were equivalent to the original then people would stay at home and not "go to tiring and dangerous places on pilgrimage, as one sees people doing continually."[36] Yet Leonardo knew perfectly well that most cult images had been repainted and that they were not at all like his own paintings, which he surely hoped would not be touched by anyone. The cult image provided the type of the untouchable image (the work of art authored by a singular individual), just as the pilgrimage is the type of aesthetic tourism. The replicas of the Holy Sepulchre, in the same way, would seem to undermine the real Jerusalem pilgrimage. The replicas pretended to move the absolutely immovable, defying the very idea of place itself. They created spaces that symbolized place.

The Holy Sepulchre models and the practices surrounding them opened up a whole gamut of possible relationships between original and replica. At one end, they were simply memorials, acting as physical reminders of places distant in space and events receding in time, both the Passion and the pilgrimages. They helped the mind close the gaps. At the other end, they shared the identity of the original site. They were treated as if they could reproduce the efficacy of the original site, independent of mind. Pope Innocent VIII institutionalized the concept of virtual pilgrimage when in 1491 he granted an indulgence, or time off from purgatory, to visitors to the Franciscan convent of Villingen in Swabia, where the abbess Ursula Haider had designed abstract replicas, basically labels painted on the wall, of 210 holy sites.[37] The pope lent similar support to the friar Bernardino Caimi at the Franciscan foundation of Varallo in Piedmont, the so-called Sacro Monte, which reproduces the sites of Jerusalem in over forty chapels.[38] Such replicas split open the space-time of normal experience, re-creating the power of the original site and transporting a visitor into a place and time shot through with biblical meaning. The fact of the indulgence made that supersymbolic claim forceful. The indulgence was a tangible corroboration of a strong, almost typological figuration.

"Substitution" names the possibility of identity that the virtual pilgrimage enacted. Substitution was the far end of the gamut of possible symbolic relationships between original and replica. It is in this sense that the architectural model was not just a representation of a particular building, or even an ideal building type, but rather a representation of the substitutional theory itself, a theory that adjusted the real history of building.

Virtual pilgrimages and the sequence of pedantic replicas of the holy structures intensified in the fifteenth century. The press of pilgrimages exerted creative force on the modalities of architectural representation, generating new mechanisms for translating the meaning of a site from one place to another. The proliferating families of reliquaries, sacrament tabernacles and ciboria, baldachins, edicules, microarchitectural retables, pyxides, censers, and *choroi* (lamps) maintained multichanneled, unsteady reference to the original tomb at Golgotha.[39] The model character of these artifacts ran parallel to the rituals that reenacted the sacrifice. The ornamental or supplementary character of art was predicted by these artifacts and their framework of ritual, itself an "ornamentation of time."[40] The nested families of fifteenth-century edicule models became simultaneously more intricately interconnected and more crudely literalizing and self-referential. Sacrament tabernacles, for example, often spelled out their function through small reliefs showing Christ in the tomb.[41] The overall structure of boxes nested within boxes signaled the fundamental redundancy of the model function. In all these ways the staggered, doubled structure of the rotunda and edicule on Golgotha was repeated in every Christian church.

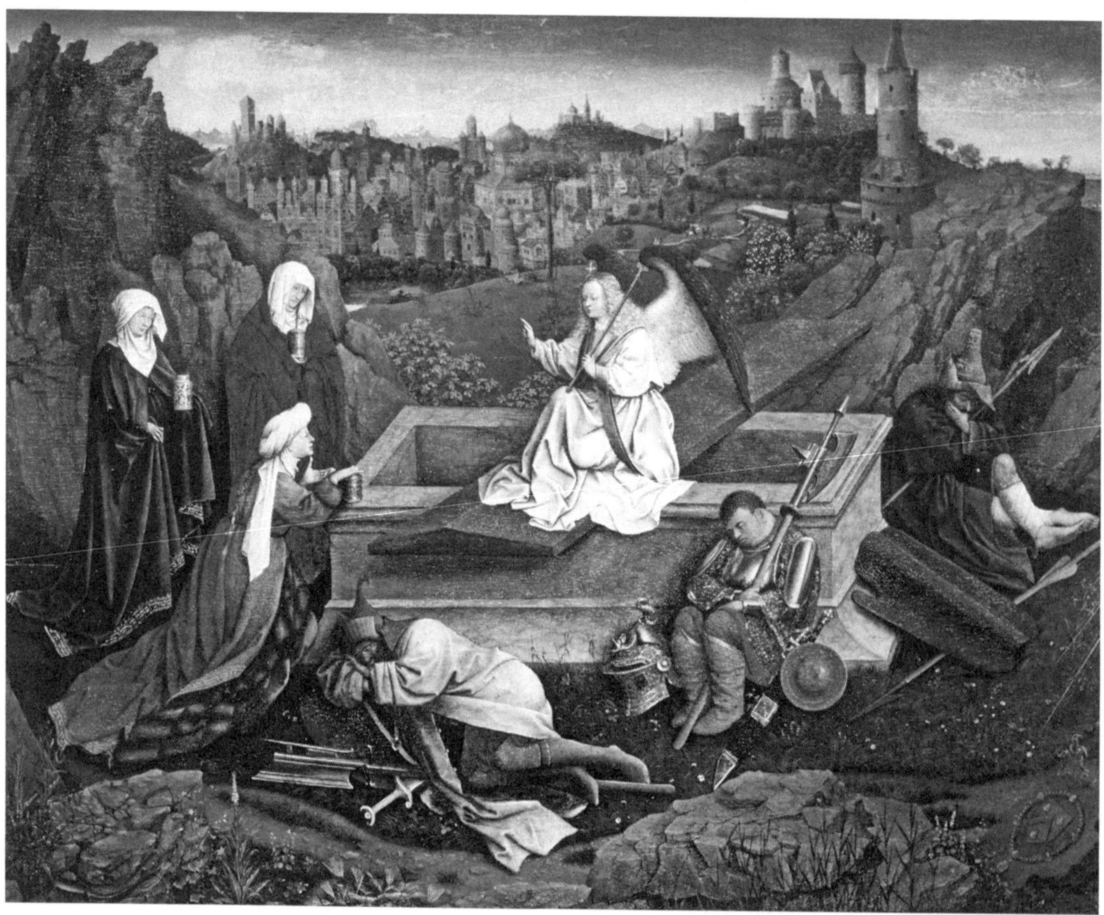

7.1 The first Christian pilgrimage. Jan van Eyck, *Three Marys at the Tomb of Christ*, oil on panel, 71.5 x 90 cm (ca. 1425–1435). Rotterdam, Museum Boijmans van Beuningen. The women made the short journey from Jerusalem to Christ's tomb on the morning after the Sabbath, intending to treat the body. They found an empty tomb and a mysterious messenger whose gesturing hand, in the painting, is precisely aligned with the polygonal Dome of the Rock above.

SEVEN

Double Origins of the Christian Temple

The hesitation at the origin point of Christian church building was staged by the arch-painter of the fifteenth century, the Netherlander Jan van Eyck. The painting *Three Marys at the Tomb of Christ*, now in Rotterdam, is datable with some (though not complete) confidence to 1425–1435 (figure 7.1).[1] On Easter morning, three women arrive at the burial site of Christ planning to treat the body with spices. "And suddenly there was a great earthquake; for an angel of the Lord, descending from heaven, came and rolled back the stone and sat on it. His appearance was like lightning, and his clothing white as snow. For fear of him the guards shook and became like dead men" (Matthew 28:2–4). The young man — in the accounts of Luke and John, two young men — tells the women that the corpse has arisen and that Christ is at that moment abroad in the world, on his way to Galilee. And indeed the women will soon meet the resurrected Christ.

The iconography is ancient. It is found already at Dura Europos before 235. In the Middle Ages the subject of the three Marys at the tomb was represented in every medium. Often the Resurrection itself, or the encounter between Christ and Mary Magdalene — the immediately preceding and following episodes — were depicted in the same frame. Van Eyck focuses on the dwarfish angel and his verbal exchange with the kneeling woman. With the steeply slanting tomb lid and the outstretched hand of the speaking woman, he cites the earliest examples, known to him through the manuscript tradition, perhaps also directly from ivories.[2] The severing of the scene from a narrative cycle and its promotion to physical independence are unprecedented (unless the panel was once flanked by hinged wings, as some scholars believe).

The painting isolates the moment when the grave of Christ loses its identity as the container of a corpse and instead begins its career as architecture, or representational building. From this point on, as we have seen, the empty tomb of Christ outside the walls of Jerusalem began to underwrite a whole range of symbolisms: it became the type of the box that contained relics; of the altar mensa focusing worship and supporting the sacramental repetition of sacrifice; and of the church itself housing the altar. The tomb fixes the code that will generate ritual. Van Eyck's painting figures that generative trajectory with a departure from the scriptural text: the women visit not a hollow in the rock, as the text demands, but a cleanly cut rectangular sarcophagus with moldings and a sloped base. This anachronistic upgrading of the tomb was even more dramatic in early Christian art, where the three women were sometimes shown arriving at the Constantinian edicule itself.[3] Just as every Christian altar mensa will represent the sarcophagus of Christ, so too will every church represent that original architectural frame mounted over the tomb, the edicule.

The three Marys, bearing salves in costly vessels, repeat the pilgrimage of the three Magi to the cradle of the Savior undertaken thirty-three years earlier. But unlike the three kings, the women arrive too late. They find not Christ, but his miniature double, a young man in white holding a standard (like the resurrected Christ), who tells a scarcely believable story. There will be no relic of Christ, the young man says, no corpse to stabilize the stories told about him, but rather a second, living body, not a phantom but a real body, briefly experienced by the women and men closest to him. The whole religion will rest on the accounts of these witnesses. The structure of the episode was later reproduced in the story of Veronica and the portrait of Christ, which begins to figure in panel paintings in these same early decades of the fifteenth century. According to the *Golden Legend*, the emperor Tiberius, gravely ill, learned of the healing powers of Christ and sought him out through an agent, Volusianius. But he came too late, for Pilate had already carried out the execution. Volusianius then met the pious woman Veronica, who owned an authoritative image of Christ, a direct imprint of his features on a cloth. He persuaded her to bring the portrait to the emperor, which she did, and the simulacrum of Christ immediately worked the healing magic.[4]

In van Eyck's picture, the belated arrival and bewilderment of the women rhyme with the beholder's own search for evidence of the origin of Christian building, for on arrival at this painting one finds not, in fact, a foundation, but again a repetition. In the Jerusalem panorama of the background, directly above the signaling hand of the angel, van Eyck portrays the Dome of the Rock, the octagonal Muslim shrine that to this day dominates the Old City (figure 7.2).[5] The Dome of the Rock was constructed from the ground up by the fifth Umayyad caliph, Abd al-Malik, in 691, on the site of the Abrahamic rock on the Temple Mount and the location, or so it was believed, of the Solomonic temple.[6] And in fact van Eyck's painting represents not the mosque but, *through* the mosque, Solomon's Temple, the scripturally sanctioned ultimate origin of Christian temple-building. At the same time it echoes, at a physical remove of less than a third of a mile, the Anastasis, the rotunda raised by Constantine over the Holy Sepulchre in 335. In its identity as mosque, van Eyck's building looks backward in time to the Constantinian rotunda, invisible in the painting; in its identity as Solomonic temple, it looks forward to the rotunda. At the same time, the polygonal shrine brackets and contests the rectangular archetype that is pictured below it, Christ's empty sarcophagus. The tomb and the temple are pockets of collapsed, absolutely dense signification, like the Christ statue in Carpaccio's painting—except that in van Eyck's painting there are two such pockets, not just one.

Van Eyck's temple defies scripture, which had described Solomon's Temple as rectangular. The dimensions of the temple were given in 1 Kings 6, and in Ezekiel 40 and the following chapters. In the Middle Ages these passages were thickly commented on and the temple reconstructed in pictorial diagrams. Every synagogue and, arguably, every basilical church remembered the biblical archetype.[7] Some medieval builders tried to reactivate it by matching the prescribed proportions, 6 : 2 : 3, and so fashioned their own princely patrons as new Solomons.[8]

Despite the authority of scripture and the exegetical tradition, which described a rectangular archetype, many Christian visitors to Jerusalem

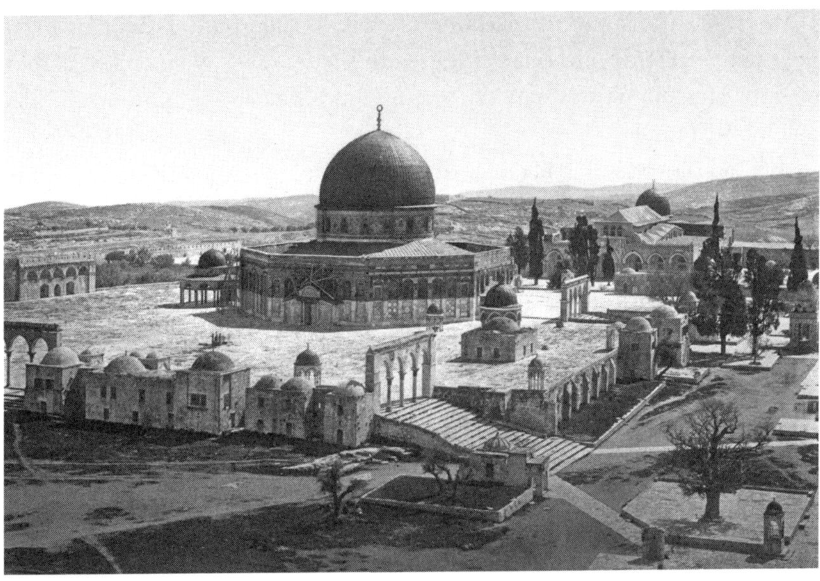

7.2 The "Templum Domini" of the Western imagination. Jerusalem, Temple Mount (photograph ca. 1910). The Dome of the Rock was built at the end of the seventh century by the Muslim conquerors of Jerusalem. One of its models was the rotunda that Constantine raised over the tomb of Christ in the fourth century. Yet throughout the Middle Ages, Christian travelers associated the structure, even identified it, with the Temple of Solomon.

described the Dome of the Rock with its cylindrical drum (erroneously polygonal in van Eyck's painting) and hemispherical cupola as the biblical temple. The French monk Bernard, for example, described the building around 870 as "the Temple of Solomon, which contains a Saracen synagogue."[9] The Crusaders took the city in 1099 and the Dome was for the first time open to Christians. In 1141 it was rededicated as a church. The Dome is usually described by Crusaders as Templum Domini, "Temple of the Lord," with reference to the Jewish temple as site of the Holy of Holies. The same sources, however, as if mindful of the scriptural account of the Jewish temple as rectangular in plan, will often identify the basilical Aqsa mosque, just 200 meters to the south and built in 705–715, as Solomon's Temple or Solomon's Palace.[10] During the Crusader occupation of Jerusalem, which lasted until 1187, the Dome of the Rock became a destination for Christian pilgrims and was advertised as the site of Christ's Presentation in the Temple, the Circumcision, the Dispute among the Doctors, the Scourging of the Moneylenders, and so forth. It *was* the site of these events, or at least the pilgrims had every reason to think so.[11] John Mandeville, or whoever wrote the book of travels that bears that name (the original text is in French and dates from the middle of the fourteenth century), identified the Dome of the Rock as a reconstruction undertaken by Emperor Hadrian (!) of the Jewish "temple in the same manere as Salomon made it."[12] Even Jews put the Dome into relationship with the temple.[13] Van Eyck was thus by no means the first to blur the distinction between the mosque and the Solomonic temple.

Behind the switching between mosque and temple stood the idea that the structure of the Dome of the Rock, despite the disaccord between rectangular and polygonal plans, somehow transmitted the temple. No one could deny that many reconstructions and replacements had intervened since Solomon's original edifice of ca. 960 BCE. That building had been destroyed by the Babylonians and rebuilt by Zorobabel in ca. 520 BCE. The temple was rebuilt in the second century BCE under the Maccabees and then again by Herod in 37–34 BCE. Everyone remembered the catastrophic destruction of the temple by the emperor Titus in 70 CE. In 361–363, Julian the Apostate allowed the Jews to launch a new temple, but this seems never to have been built. The Temple Mount became a wasteland, fulfilling the prophecy of Christ himself (Mark 13:2). The label "temple" that accrued to the octagonal Muslim shrine signaled a strong desire on the part of Christians, and some Jews, to imagine a chain stretching backward from the Dome. The Dome of the Rock was the most successful of architectural substitutions.[14]

To call the Dome of the Rock the "temple" was not altogether to misunderstand the building. For by building his own structure—not a temple but a shelter for the sacred rock—on the foundational platform of the Jewish temple, on the elevated sacred precinct built by Herod, the Muslim conqueror was acknowledging the regimes that preceded his own. The Dome of the Rock was the first major sanctuary of Islam. But the caliph was also building a "classical" building, true to the timeless principles of the triumphant architecture of the civilizations of the past. He could see for himself that the Christians had built a great dome to shelter the tomb of their martyred hero. His own cupola and the ring of columns beneath it imitated the rotunda over the Holy Sepulchre, perhaps as well the fourth-century Church of the Ascension (Imbomon) on the Mount of Olives.

The Dome of the Rock, before it did anything else, substituted for its predecessor buildings. The Dome generated a nonexistent tradition—a centrally planned building on the Temple Mount—by activating the substitution principle. In effect, the building argued, the Jewish temple had survived; only the signs, the theological references and dedications, had been changed.

The Christian *antonomasia* ("naming instead") of the Muslim structure—the sometime identification of the Dome as the temple—should be understood not as an error, but as a theory about the vertical structure of building history. The temple label stood alongside, and not in mortal competition with, other labels. Many travelers lucidly identified the Dome as a Muslim structure. Abbot Daniel, a Russian pilgrim of the early twelfth century, described the "church of the Holy of Holies" as "wonderfully and skilfully decorated with mosaics," with doors of gilded copper, only to concede that "nothing remains of the first building of Solomon except the foundations of the church" and that "the church which is there now was built by a Saracen chieftain called Amor."[15] The fifteenth-century Genoese pilgrim Anselm Adorno, who owned two paintings by Jan van Eyck, and whose father and uncle had founded the Church of the Holy Sepulchre in Bruges in 1427, wrote of "the first and most sacred Temple of the Lord constructed long ago by Solomon, now almost entirely destroyed. Whether anything of the original temple survives is not clear [*ambiguum est*]. Let it suffice that we know that this was the place where the Temple was first built."[16] Yet the twelfth-century German monk Theoderic asserted that "the present building we now see was constructed...by Queen Helena and her son Emperor Constantine. This, then, is the fifth renewal of the Temple."[17] Observers traveling together on the same pilgrimage left conflicting descriptions. The Dominican cleric and pilgrim Felix Fabri called it a Muslim building, while his companion Bernhard von Breydenbach, in the pilgrimage narrative he published in 1486, spoke of "Solomon's Temple, round, and built in the Greek manner with cut and polished or leveled stones; this Temple is high and broad and roofed with lead. The heathens have placed a half-moon on top of it, as if it were eclipsed, that is, darkened."[18] There is no point in distinguishing the observers who got the identification right from those who got it wrong. It is the sum of the statements that amounts to the truth about the Dome.

This is not to say that all labels were equal. The "temple" labels that cancelled the Muslim architectural and political achievement were colored by Christian despair about the Crusades. The "temple" label tried to undo the undoing of the Kingdom of Jerusalem in 1187. From that date on, until deep into the fifteenth century, many princes and popes stoked the crusading will. Philip of Burgundy, van Eyck's patron, actually owned the keys to the Holy Sepulchre.[19]

Van Eyck's painting depicts the very first Christian pilgrimage, and at the same time the very first Crusade. The three Marys on their Easter-morning trek meant to reclaim, with their attentions, the burial site of the Lord. Christ had been buried in haste, without proper preparation of the body, in order to meet the Sabbath deadline. Pilate had then posted guards to prevent theft of the body and spurious claims of resurrection (Matthew 27:57–58, 65). The Crusade launched in 1095 by Urban II was a violent repetition of that first pilgrimage. Like the three women, the Crusaders were belated: they arrived too late to protect the original Constantinian structures over the tomb, and then repressed that fact by accepting the eleventh-century reconstructions as their legitimate substitutions. Above all they arrived too late to permanently displace Islamic control over the Near East. Christian Europe, in disarray for four centuries after the fall of Rome, had failed to defend its own ur-sanctuary. Muslim force finally provoked them to muster an army. But the Kingdom of Jerusalem never took root and after only 88 years it was liquidated by Saladin. This painful reality put even more pressure on the repairing theory of substitution.

The Dome of the Rock entered into direct rivalry with the existing buildings of Jerusalem, and Christians could not keep their eyes off it.[20] The Constantinian Church of the Holy Sepulchre, by contrast, played a formidable role in the Christian imagination but was never grasped clearly in its form. The thirteenth-century liturgist William Durandus interpreted the tabernacle, the microarchitectural shelter for the Eucharist, as an imitation of the Ark of the Covenant, not of the Holy Sepulchre.[21] Unlike the Dome of the Rock, the rotunda was difficult to see from the outside, probably as difficult then as today, hemmed in as it is by later buildings. The church literally had no profile. The interior was hard to represent in words, and therefore hard to see; descriptions in word or image failed to convey the precise relationship between edicule and rotunda. Drawing and painting had not yet gone indoors.[22] Substitutional thinking, as we have seen, figured the external profile of building history and left the jumbled, confusing interiors in the dark.

Christian builders, seeking models, looked past the rotunda of the Holy Sepulchre and instead focused on the edicule nested inside it, on the Dome of the Rock, or even on the Pantheon. The rotunda was a mutilated body. In Constantine's original complex, the rotunda capped a long east-west sequence of atrium, basilica, and courtyard. The basilica had been entirely razed by Hakim in 1009. The Crusaders replaced it with a stunted, two-bay nave on the site of the old courtyard. The use of spolia from the old structures gave the new church a disordered, ugly appearance.[23] The rotunda played a scant role in Christian iconography because it postdated most of the stories, the stories about the martyred saints as much as the life of Christ. By the early fourth century, Western Christian history had effectively abandoned the Holy Land. The rotunda, like Constantine's Church of the Nativity at Bethlehem, was already a monument, a building that marked and remembered but did not itself need to be remembered. Constantine, it seemed, belonged already to modern, belated times. In the Holy Land, Constantine could not be an origin—at best the path to the origin could be routed through his buildings—whereas in Rome, his basilicas (St. Peter's, San Giovanni in Laterano) could in fact function as origin points.

Basilicas point to Jerusalem. The longitudinal plan, oriented toward an altar, acknowledges cultural off-centeredness and a distance from the origin. The spatial distance implied by the longitudinal plan is also the map of a temporal distance. In principle, the only legitimately centrally planned Christian temple is the Anastasis rotunda itself, directly over the tomb and therefore unoriented. The Constantinian basilica, or its Crusader replacement, is therefore the last basilica, the one not only pointing to the source, but contiguous with it.

That source could not really be replicated, because it was a mere place, in fact an emptiness. Instead, models were built which represented the *idea* of a substitution chain linked to an original, centrally planned building that framed that empty space. The models, standing just to one side of the real chains that held the history of building together, were free to make any sort of hypothesis about building and building history. The medieval pilgrims' strange statements about the Dome were matched by equally strange statements about the Solomonic origins of centrally planned churches like the Palace Chapel at Aachen (according to Charlemagne's biographer Notker) or Germigny-des-Prés in the Loire Valley (806) with its quincunx plan. Every centrally planned structure was a model, and none of them really belonged to a substitution chain.

The model becomes the attractor for a certain kind of statement that conflicts with knowledge, for instance, the statement that the Dome of the Rock *is* Solomon's Temple. That statement clashes with the awareness, more or less acute, that the Dome had been built from the ground up by the Muslims. The sometime labeling of the Dome as temple coexisted with the knowledge that the Dome was not the temple in the same way that the model coexisted with "real" or nonrepresentational buildings. Are there ever any such "real," nonrepresentational buildings? No, for it is only the model that creates the idea of the nonrepresentational building. Statements and counter-statements can coexist, and there is no need to force an artificial stability by insisting on a decision about where "belief" lies, or comes to rest. The identity between antitype and type—between an artifact and its origin—is asserted linguistically, and that is enough to bend the substitutional link closed. The model models that link. When the model is inadequate, through its inferior materials or small size, then the label, the merely asserted link, must do the work.

The space that the artwork clears out for itself is the space around the model. The artwork coalesces around the modeling operation. The artwork is a metamodel, the model of a model. It mimes the modeling operation. The artwork does not assert a link to an origin, rather it pictures the kind of assertion about origins that artifacts made, at least under a theory of substitution. Van Eyck closed in on the Holy Sepulchre in trying to make space for his paintings. He found that space in the trajectory between buildings and models of buildings. His *Three Marys at the Tomb of Christ* literally pictures the space, the stretch of landscape, between the doubles. The Temple/Dome is directly above the tomb, but the intervening landscape cuts across the interval on a diagonal. The soft slope, the low vegetation, the landmark tree, the peopled, serpentine path are invitations. From that moment on in the history of painting, increasingly, the portraits of the doubles will fade and paintings will come to picture only the path between them. Van Eyck portrays the two architectural models that exerted so much force on the European imagination, the Sepulchre and the Solomonic Temple. But now the space between them is so much more than a merely diagrammatic interval. It is a humanized, fictive space that visualizes a human time frame, which now threatens to trump all the other time frames. In the artificial pressure of the neo-Crusader moment, when European princes and builders— like van Eyck's patron, the Duke of Burgundy—were refusing to cut themselves free from their dreams of origins, van Eyck creates an image that at first seems to take its place within the sequence of plastic models. But the real import of his painting is the case it makes for the metamodel character of painting itself, that is, painting's capacity to frame and stage, to hypothesize, to adopt a perspective.

EIGHT

Icon Maintenance

European paintings were quite able to point back to prestigious origins in the same way that buildings did, through typological reference and labeling practices. But over the course of the thirteenth, fourteenth, and fifteenth centuries, paintings developed a representational flexibility that began to distinguish them from buildings and even sculpture or any other kind of artifact. The capacity of the painted image to conjure fictional worlds, to register the physical circumstances of its own fabrication, and to simulate optical experience interfered, potentially, with the task of reference. By projecting imagined realities with such ease, the painting undermined some of the impersonal referential authority it once enjoyed. By thematizing its own handmadeness, the painting, a planar archive of the manual trace, guided the beholder back into the physical circumstances of its own making, back to the person of the painter, who now possibly merited promotion to the status of an author. The very idea that a maker of mere artifacts might be an author comparable to a poet emerged first in the domain of painting. And by imitating the perceptible world, the painting turned the beholder's attention back upon itself, in a recursive loop. Van Eyck's works marked the culmination of a nearly two-century-long process in which European painted panels readjusted their own relationship to origins. Paintings, because they were often under the control of a shaping individual rather than a collectivity, implied authorship. Authorship produced its own countermodel, namely, the substitutional hypothesis, a compensation for the event-based nature of all artifact production. The countermodel came to be pictured in paintings by van Eyck and others. Such paintings thematized their own resistance to substitution by figuring substitution. Paintings not only became sites of highly visible performativity, but they also provided a place for reflection on the antagonism between substitution and performance as van Eyck did when he set his expressive, gesture-driven encounter between women and angel against the backdrop of the substituted temple.

Early panel paintings often display a fraught sense of their own vulnerability to time. Physically more fragile than buildings or sculptures, they needed frequent repair, replenishment, or even replacement. The cycles of maintenance were most highly charged in the territory of the icon, the holy portrait, for here theologians, habitually concerned with reference to the correct origin points and with the threat to reference posed by facticity, or handmadeness, were most vigilant.

Until the thirteenth century, in most parts of western Europe, painted panels were basically cheaper surrogates for artifacts carved, cast, wrought, or woven in more durable or precious materials. No parish or bishop preferred an antependium of painted wood to an embroidered cloth or a beaten silver relief panel, or a mere painted portrait of a saint to a statuette in gold with inlaid stones. The influx of Eastern icons after the Fourth Crusade in 1204 began to shift these attitudes. In that year the Crusaders, foiled by the Muslim reconquest of Jerusalem, turned instead on a more vulnerable Constantinople, a Christian city. Here the Crusaders did not liberate so much as plunder. Relics and prestigious icons were stolen and transported back to France, Germany, and Italy. Many icons, it was now recognized, were themselves relics, survivors from Christian antiquity. The icons offered a direct connection back to a primordial culture of painting. The panels from Constantinople, or from the Levant via Constantinople, were humble, fragile affairs beside the sleek silver-gilt and enameled ornaments of the well-endowed Western altar. But the lowly, hand-crafted character of the ancient icons was the mark of their virtue.

Ideally, one trusted in the absolute singularity, the relic status, of an Eastern icon. Yet everyone knew from experience that a painting deteriorates with time and requires periodic cosmetic improvement. Many of these icons, it was understood, were but replicas of their predecessors. Awareness of the probability of invisible substitutions stood alongside hopeful confidence in the lesser probability of singularity. An icon could have a double identity, at once substituting for its immediate predecessor in the replication chain and also retaining an attribution to St. Luke — according to legend, an amateur painter who painted the features of the Virgin Mary from life.[1] Other icons were connected with near-miraculous author-less image-making processes, such as the family of portraits of Christ descended from the veil of Veronica, a cloth that had been pressed against Christ's grimy and bloody face.[2] Precious few of these images pretended to *be* the Sudarium. But a panel that could pretend to be linked to the Sudarium by a chain of scrupulous copies was still impressive. Only under the sign of the more modern expectations of direct appeal to nature, or even of inventive creativity, would the very virtue of such an icon be converted into a demerit. In the phrase of Leonardo da Vinci, writing at the end of the fifteenth century, painters after the "Romans" did nothing but "imitate one another," with a constant decline in quality.[3]

Inspired by this reopening onto the Eastern cult of image relics, the city of Rome rediscovered its own household icons. A small number of painted portraits of Christ and the Virgin had survived the oblivion of the early Middle Ages and had been carefully preserved in Roman churches: the Pantheon, Santa Maria Antiqua, San Sisto, Santa Maria Maggiore, San Giovanni in Laterano, and Santa Maria in Trastevere (figure 8.1).[4] They were all painted, we now know, between the sixth and the eighth centuries, but in the Middle Ages they were simply considered ancient. There are records of processions and rituals involving the icons already in the twelfth century.[5] The Roman icons played the same role in the sacred life of the city that the huts of Romulus had once played. The icons stood for the idea of a material link back to a point of origin. No one really knew when they had been fabricated, but they were treated as if they were authentic. The Roman icons emerged as cultural focal points in the same centuries that inner European pilgrimage was gathering momentum. Jerusalem, in the best of times a distant goal, was from 1187 Muslim again, and so once more inaccessible except to the bravest travelers. In its place a network of surrogate pilgrimage targets emerged: Rome, Compostela, and dozens or even hundreds of lesser sites stretching from Walsingham to Czestochowa. Pilgrimage, we saw earlier, was a way of asserting the value of the true site and the authentic artifact, even as in practice one was always making do with surrogates and replicas.

In the thirteenth century most of the major Roman icons were reconditioned or updated. But from this point on, with one exception, they were handled like relics: no overpaintings, no alterations.[6] The logic of substitution that under normal circumstances licensed the periodic repainting or even replacement of panels was abrogated in favor of straightforward preservation of the original, material artifact and thus of that primal, ultrareliable reference to the divinity, which dispersal and interference in the transmission chain might threaten. This shift in restoration practices coincides with the growing interest in the performativity and historicity of painting generally.

Rome had its supposedly ancient portraits; practically every other town in Europe, unless it was lucky enough to share in Constantinople's plunder, had, at best, copies. The Tuscan cities Pisa, Siena, and Florence invested more and more cultural energy in panel painting in the thirteenth century, as churches and patrons competed to mount the largest or most splendid altarpiece or painted crucifix. The authority of the Roman icons, uncontestable and unattainable, loomed a few days' journey to the south. Tuscan altarpieces were associated, if not with the foundations of Christianity

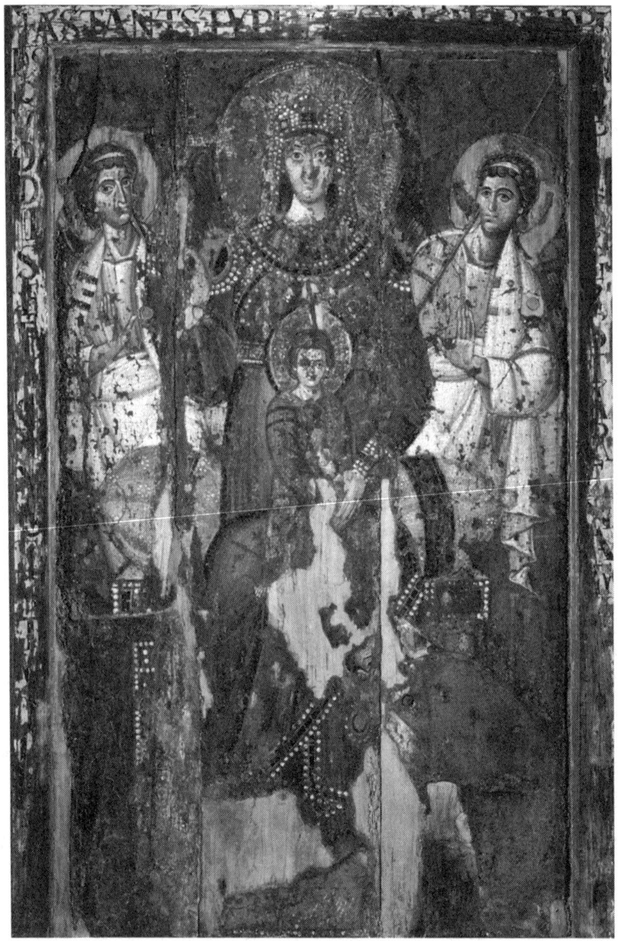

8.1 One of the family of ancient portraits of the Virgin Mary. *Madonna and Child*, tempera on panel, 153 x 105 cm, 164 x 116 cm with frame (eighth century). Rome, Santa Maria in Trastevere. The enthroned Virgin is flanked by a pair of archangels, identified by a fragmentary inscription on the painting as witnesses of the Incarnation. The inclusion of a (now partially destroyed) portrait of a pope kneeling at the foot of the throne is a context-sensitive feature, registering the historical circumstances in which the painting was made. Nevertheless another inscription on the painting refers to divinity "made by itself" (DS QYOD IPSE FACTYS EST), reinforcing the legend that the painting itself had been divinely produced or acheiropoietic, "made without hands."

itself, then at least with the foundations of local institutions or with signal events in local history. Authentic, relic-like portraits portrayed, if not Christ or the Virgin themselves, then the modern saints Dominic and Francis, who had died in 1221 and 1226 respectively. Paradoxically, the most revered images were the ones most frequently overpainted. The portrait of St. Dominic in the Fogg Museum in Cambridge, Massachusetts, possibly the oldest portrait of the saint, was painted shortly after the saint's canonization in 1233. In the 1260s the head was repainted, and then was painted over again in about 1280 by the school of Guido da Siena. The hands were repainted at least once, as well as the tunic. In the early fourteenth century the halo was redone.[7] The alterations of these panels early in their lives reflect a hesitation between two possible approaches: preservation of the relic as an irreplaceable link to a stable point of origin (even if relatively recent or local), and proliferation, with preservation of identity and efficacy, through carefully regulated replication processes.

The enthroned Madonna, or *Maestà*, of Guido da Siena, the largest painted panel of its time, and inscribed with the artist's name and the enigmatic date 1221, has long been a magnet for disputes about the origins of Renaissance painting (figure 8.2). The date, preceding by decades the births of Cimabue and Giotto, seems to contest Vasari's thesis of Florentine primacy. The painting is an origin out of focus, an anachronic composite. Temporal instability may even have been an aspect of its design.

The picture was painted for the church of San Domenico in Siena in the 1270s. Yet the inscription on the panel reads, "ME GUIDO DE SENIS DIEBUS DEPINXIT AMENIS: QUEM XRS LENIS NULLIS VELIT ANGERE PENIS ANO. DI. MI. CCXXI" (Guido da Siena painted me in the happy days; may the gentle Christ be willing to spare him all punishment, AD 1221) (figure 8.3). Technical analysis has shown that the inscription is original and intact.[8] As late as the 1950s, Cesare Brandi took 1221 to be the date of the authorship of the panel, a possibility that more recent scholarship has ruled out.[9] A now widely accepted explanation is that the date refers to the death date of St. Dominic, founder of the order for which the painting was made.[10] But it is not clear why this panel should have been linked retrospectively to Dominic's death.

A better hypothesis, one that makes sense in the framework of a theory of substitution, is that the date was inherited from an older work that Guido's painting replaced.[11] The diarist Sigismondo Tizio actually asserted in 1528 that Guido's painting had stood on the high altar of the church that existed on the site before San Domenico, which he calls San Gregorio.[12] Tizio was not right about this, for Guido da Siena was active as a painter only many years after San Gregorio became San Domenico, but the diarist may have correctly grasped the retrospective reference of the panel, even if he collapsed what was in fact a history of substitutions. For the first presence of the Dominicans in Siena goes back to the donation of the hospice chapel of Santa Maria Maddalena, made in 1221, the year recorded in the inscription on the painting.[13] The Dominicans were thus first stationed in Santa Maria Maddalena, outside the Porta Romana,

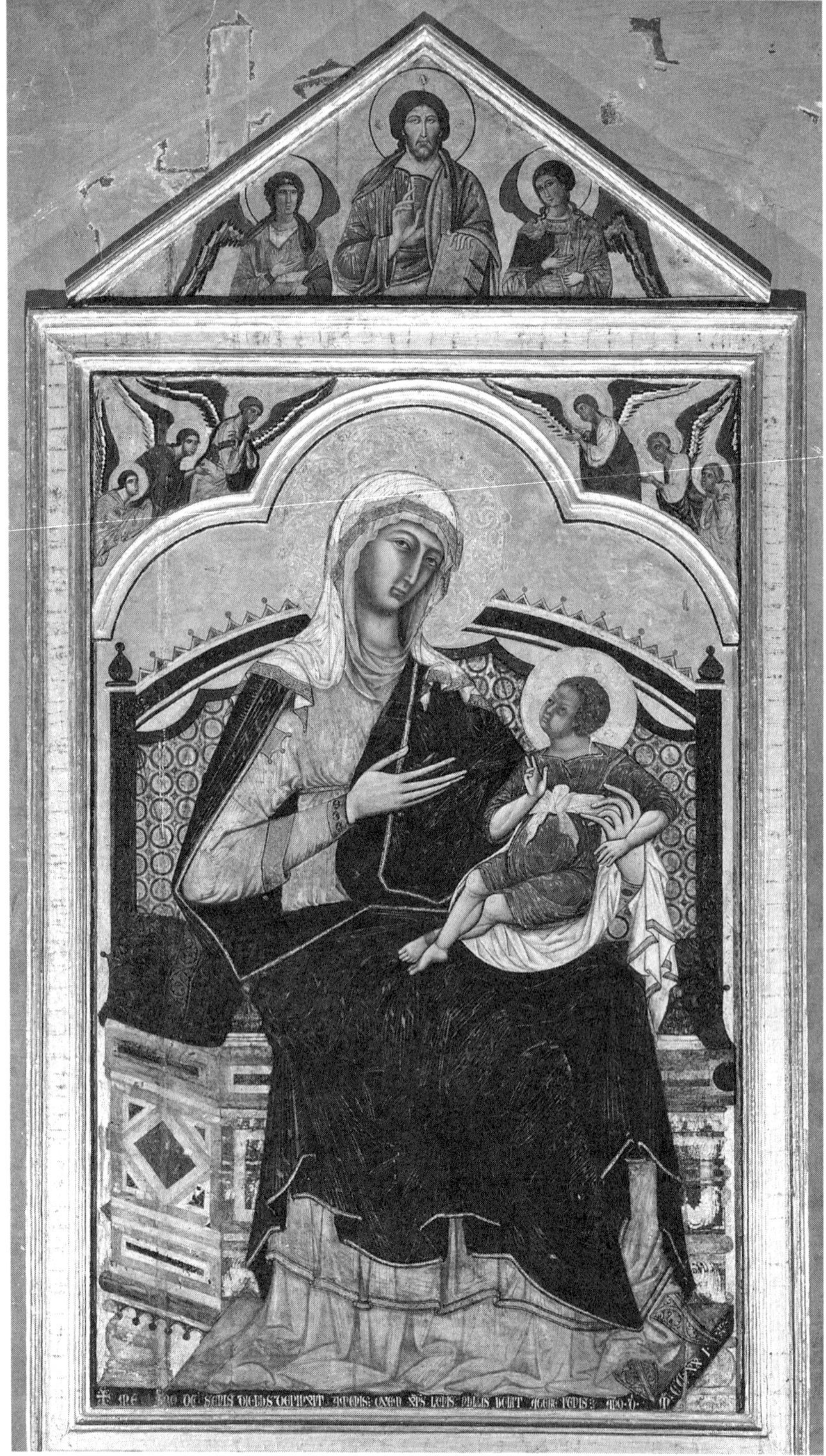

8.2 An origin point of Renaissance painting. Guido da Siena, *Maestà*, tempera on panel, 283 x 194 cm without gable (1270s). Siena, San Domenico. This massive panel, once the high altarpiece of the church of San Domenico, is one of the most ambitious Italian panel paintings of the thirteenth century and has long stood at the center of debates about where the revival of painting in Italy was launched.

then (in 1226) they were granted the current site, where Tizio says San Gregorio stood, and started building their new church there, which was then eventually replaced by the larger one that stands there now. Decades later, Guido painted his panel for this larger church. (It is still an unsettled question whether Guido's imposing altarpiece was made for the high altar of the church. The argument proposed here, though strictly independent of this question, lends support to the view that it was for the high altar and for this reason carried special "foundational" burdens.) Guido's panel thus comes at an advanced stage in the history of the Dominicans in Siena, which had been a typically complex history of replacements and substitutions. By Guido's time it may have seemed a good time to remember first foundations. Clearly *some* sort of commemorative impulse was at work in placing an early date on the panel, and the date given corresponds to the first foundation of all, the first foothold of the Dominicans in Siena, which was given to the order in 1221. Another example, from Treviso, suggests

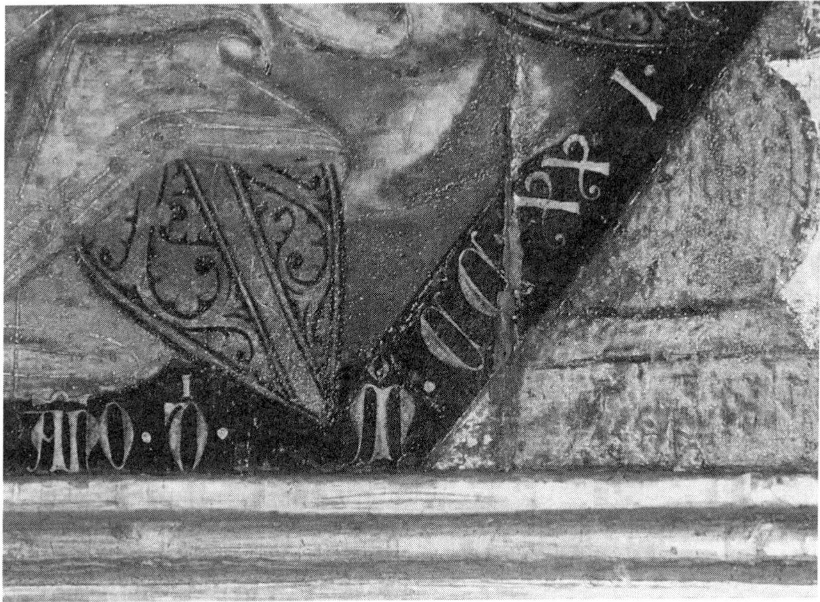

8.3 The date 1221 inscribed on a painting of the 1270s. Guido da Siena, *Maestà*, Siena, San Domenico, detail. The inscription reads: "Guido da Siena painted me in the happy days; may the gentle Christ be willing to spare him all punishment, AD 1221." On the one hand, a powerful claim to authorship, designating Guido as the work's maker and as the potential beneficiary of God's grace, on the other, a date that long precedes the artist's activity. 1221 is the date of the first Dominican foundation in Siena, thus casting this work as the substitution for a putative original altarpiece. The section of the inscription with the date bends around the corner of the throne's base, as if to figure the relationship, both continuous and discontinuous, between the authorial present and the institutional past.

that the idea of commemorating the first physical establishment was something of a Dominican pattern: an inscription in a trecento fresco cycle in the Dominican chapterhouse in Treviso also makes a point of commemorating the date of the order's first foundation in that city.[14] Like Guido's panel, the Treviso inscription records the name of the painter, Tommaso da Modena, but unlike Guido's panel it also gives the date of the painter's work, 1352. It thus measures the temporal distance between the foundation and the painting. In Guido's panel of eighty years earlier we have a much shorter inscription that has the effect of contracting that temporal distance. Guido's inscription gives the name of the painter but then only the one date, the more important date — the date of the foundation, not the date of the painting.

By carrying the date of the first Dominican foundation in Siena over onto his own panel, Guido submitted his painting to a larger institutional identity even as he was asserting, through his signature, his own authorship of the panel. The inscription proclaims, simultaneously, the two origins of the panel, institutional and authorial. Guido's prominent signature on the San Domenico altarpiece, with its appeal to mercy for his soul, should be placed within the tradition of inscriptions added to churches and chapels at times of significant restoration. Those inscriptions, which usually contain the name of the donor or the cleric in charge of the renovation, register pride in having served and preserved a venerable institution. Here Guido assumes something like the role of donor, in this case the artistic donor. In this class of inscriptions, the work is not exalted as the work of an individual; rather, the individual is exalted by affiliation with the monument.

Tuscan altarpieces often assumed the functions of earlier paintings that had stood on the same altars. The *Madonna degli Occhi Grossi*, a single panel of the early thirteenth century which originally stood on the high altar of Siena cathedral and still survives in the Museo dell'Opera del Duomo in Siena, was replaced on the high altar by Guido da Siena's *Madonna del Voto* in the 1260s (shortly before he produced the altarpiece for San Domenico just discussed). Then, in 1311, Guido's painting was replaced by Duccio's famous *Maestà*. In Florence, Bernardo Daddi's *Madonna* in Orsanmichele followed and replaced two successive earlier Madonnas.[15] Each substitution differed from the painting it replaced, indicating that formal resemblance was not the dominant criterion in the substitution.

In the case of Guido's *Maestà* for San Domenico, substitution continued in the form of art restoration. Around 1310 the panel was altered: the face of the Virgin, the flesh of the Christ child, and the faces of the angels in the gables and the lower part of the throne were repainted in a modern manner resembling that of Duccio, the outstanding Sienese painter of the new generation. Why was the panel repainted only a generation after it was created? The panel was surely still in good shape. It has been argued that the painting was repainted in order to bring it into compliance with the latest and most desirable painting manner, the contemporary style of Duccio.[16] Guido's old-fashioned style, according to this argument, was suddenly unacceptable and an up-to-date style was preferable. This view assumes that aesthetic criteria were paramount in the decision. We propose that the restoration was motivated instead by a desire to maintain the work's functionality. The old style had become intolerable not because, or not only because, it had come to look ugly or unfashionable. It had become intolerable because the stylistic obsolescence was interfering with the work of the panel. The restored painting, no longer distracting its beholders with stylistic unfamiliarity, recovered functional presentness. The result of this intervention was, necessarily, to update the painting style, but that does not mean that modernization per se was the goal. The point was not to make the picture look like a modern picture, but to make it look as splendid as it did the day it was first painted. This was not a new impulse. Inscriptions on repainted icons in the Byzantine tradition routinely refer to the repainting process as a form of "renewal."[17] The updated painting was not actually advancing any claim at all about the date of its own production. The overpainting restored the work not to its original appearance but to its original high degree of efficacy.[18]

Nonetheless, the situation was novel. Stylistic obsolescence had become a factor within the traditional approach to restoration, an obstacle to legibility almost as distracting as sheer decay. And that meant that a striking modernization, paradoxically, became a collateral and almost accidental effect of the restoration project.[19] The evidence suggests that the rhythm of restoration of Tuscan panels quickened in the late thirteenth and early fourteenth centuries. A well-known example is Coppo di Marcovaldo's *Madonna del Bordone* of 1261, in the church of the Servi in Siena, the faces of which were repainted in the early trecento.[20] Coppo's *Madonna* in the church of the Servi in Orvieto, also from the 1260s, underwent a similar intervention even before the end of the thirteenth century.[21] The *Saint Francis* by Margarito d'Arezzo in the Arezzo Pinacoteca was almost entirely repainted, with quite significant changes to the head, within twenty years of the original painting.[22] Modern art historians have postulated external conservation disasters to explain the apparently premature interventions. Coppo's panel in Orvieto, it has been argued, suffered "probable damage by fire"; Margarito's original painting was "perhaps ruined."[23] But this was the generation of Duccio and Giotto, a time when pictorial conventions were undergoing especially volatile change. A painting that adhered to obsolete conventions came to look unfamiliar; the pictorial signifier threatened to call attention to itself and distract from its representational or cultic functions. Conventional representations, like the Ship of Theseus, had replaceable parts. The face of the Virgin could be updated without impairing the representational success of the picture as a whole. The status of the panel as an *image*, a frictionless reflection of its object, thus came into conflict with its status as a *relic*. The pace of artistic change accelerated; the old Tuscan ways of painting were superseded within a generation, and restorers—that is, painters—were called in even before dust accumulated.

The history of Guido's *Maestà* epitomizes the array of possible approaches to the problem of transmission. Guido's painting of the 1270s, as we have seen, was itself very likely a substitute for an earlier image at San Domenico, or perhaps even for an image transferred from an earlier church, with identity theoretically carried over intact from panel to panel. The early fourteenth-century overpainting of parts of the panel was undertaken as a form of functional maintenance in the face of an increasing rate of stylistic change. The following centuries were the most dangerous for early panel paintings. Even the most famous of them fell so far out of step with the sequence of modern and ever more modern painting manners that they were routinely discarded. Only the most fortunate survived, and then often only out of neglect and oblivion. A still smaller portion of these survivors were honored as relics, venerable by virtue of their difference. By the time of the reinstallation of Guido's *Maestà* in the Venturini chapel, in the early eighteenth century, a modern theory of restoration was in place. The new installation was not a substitution or an updating but a form of relic exhibition, designed to preserve and stage Guido's *Maestà* as an artifact of the history of painting, and of Siena.

The perception of stylistic change threatened the smooth operation of the replica chain. The very notions that the look of a painting could be peculiar to its moment, and that old paintings might require stylistic updating, raised the possibility of an alternative origin point: not the divine referent itself, lost in time, or a mythical ur-painting, but the individual, modern artist. This disclosure of the painting's status as a mere artifact was exactly what theologians had always feared. The quickening pace of the restoration cycles framed stylistic change, indeed it helped create the idea of style. The stylistic updatings threatened the basic, categorical denial of the historical meaning of form that had driven the substitutional restorations in the first place. Paradoxically, in the short term, in the fourteenth century, the antidote to public perception of stylistic obsolescence was a kind of artificial, accelerated substitution: repair and replacement before it was strictly necessary, in the hopes of keeping the flow of identity moving.

It remained the same picture—as long as the label said so. But then this acceleration itself brought about a change in attitude.

Klaus Krüger has assembled numerous examples of deliberate archaisms and citations of historical styles—"retrospective semantics"—in trecento and quattrocento paintings.[24] Krüger argues that awareness of an image's age and place in history created a strong sense of the concrete, material fact of the panel that supported it. The panel's historicity thus entered into conflict with the image's theologically sanctioned function as the stimulus to an imaginative experience of divine reality. This conflict was in turn thematized by many fifteenth-century paintings.[25] Krüger's argument is compatible with the schema developed in the present book. The conceptual tension he describes between the image-as-medium and the image-as-object may be thought of as a special case, whose special terms are generated by the theological discourse on cult images, of the more general tension we describe between artifacts linked by referential mechanisms to their origins and artifacts whose reference is disabled by excessive historical anchoring.

Sensitivity to the historicity of pictorial form led to a complete reversal of restoration policy. In the mid-fifteenth century, old panel paintings were

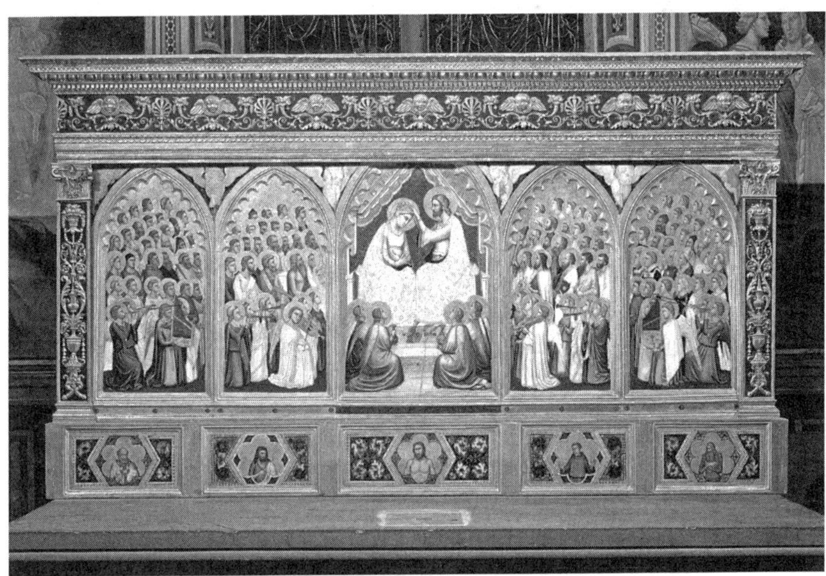

8.4 A famous altarpiece by Giotto, reframed in the fifteenth century. Giotto, *Coronation of the Virgin*, tempera on panel (ca. 1334). Florence, Santa Croce, Baroncelli Chapel. Giotto's polyptych was trimmed and adapted to a modern frame, with *all'antica* pilasters and entablature, in the 1480s. This was a transitional approach to conservation. In earlier centuries, altarpieces were simply replaced or overpainted; later, they were preserved as much as possible in their original state.

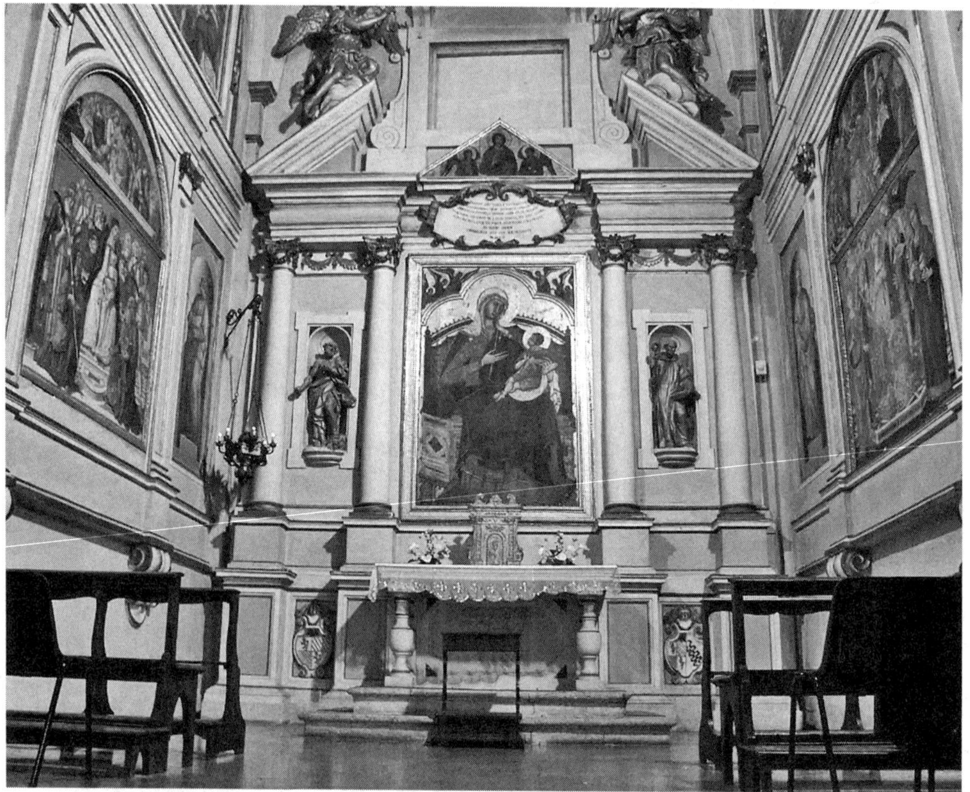

8.5 The chapel as a reliquary for a venerable Sienese painting. Guido da Siena, *Maestà*, tempera on panel, Siena, San Domenico (1270s) in Venturini chapel (installed in 1706). Taking the date of 1221 on the painting to be a record of the time of its making, the chapel patron Domenico Venturini enshrined this work as a monument to the antiquity of Sienese painting and "to lay to rest the false view of those who say that [the Florentine] Giovanni Cimabue was the rediscoverer of painting in Tuscany, as this image was painted fifty-nine years before he [Cimabue] was born, as one can see in the inscription at the bottom of this same painting."

for the first time preserved intact, embedded in modern framing elements and even juxtaposed to passages of modern painting that were surely meant to read as modern framing elements for a precious sample of old painting. In the late 1480s a member of Domenico Ghirlandaio's shop, Bastiano Mainardi, recuperated Giotto's *Coronation of the Virgin* in the Baroncelli Chapel even as he reframed it in a modern tabernacle frame with flanking pilasters and an entablature above (figure 8.4). The process required the removal of several elements of the original framework, especially the crockets and finials that would have risen up from between the gabled panels, as well as the original crowning gable with God the Father, which was recognized in 1957 to be the fragment in the San Diego Museum of Art.[26] Thus, not only was the central field of Giotto's famed altarpiece newly enshrined, but also a piece cut out from the original ensemble was preserved carefully enough to survive until the present day.

These hybrid objects emphasized a seam between old and new modes of painting. Just as with the updating of Guido's *Maestà* around 1310, the aim was to recover or even magnify the cult image's original effectiveness, except that now the modern painting manner was not allowed to seep into the interior of the image but was kept at bay, outside the frame or on the far side of a clear internal seam. This practice persisted until the eighteenth century. The framing devices were given the job of bridging the gap between the revered image and the worshipping public, and thus of bringing the old images into the cultic present. As a result, that gap itself became semiotically charged, and the visual unfamiliarity of the old image—palpable manifestations of antiquity, like gold ground or a strange way of rendering figures—themselves became meaningful to contemporary viewers as signifiers of venerability. As we have seen, Guido's *Maestà* was submitted to just this type of procedure by Venturini in 1705. When the painting was returned from the Palazzo Pubblico to San Domenico in the 1990s it was reinstalled in its early eighteenth-century arrangement (figure 8.5).[27]

From this point on, venerated images will be extracted from the substitution chain and treated like relics, which are by definition nonsubstitutable. Such relic-pictures are no longer credited with the capacity to collapse history, however. Instead, they *picture* history by pointing to a gap in the historical sequence of representational conventions. Reverence for them takes the form of a historical relationship to the image as artifact. Here, for the first time, we recognize the contours of the core principle of modern historical scholarship of art: pictorial form as index of history, that is, as *style*.

NINE

Fashion in Painting

By the early fifteenth century, the time-specific elements in contemporary painting were becoming increasingly insistent, and also more intently noted. Clerics began to deplore the new obsession with stylistic updating; vigilant eyes were struck by the intrusion of elements of modern life into religious paintings. The early fifteenth-century reformer Giovanni Dominici, for example, believed old and smoky images ("vecchie affumate") to be closer to "the figures, or to the truth represented by those figures," than the highly ornamented pictures of his own day.[1] The new, garish paintings refused to slide smoothly into the flow of replication and instead advertised themselves as sensitive responses to shifts in custom.

In 1423 the citizens of Thessalonica, under dire threat from the Ottoman Turks, threw themselves into the hands of the Venetian Republic, which took control of the city until its final capitulation to the Ottomans in 1430. During these seven years the city saw an influx not only of Venetian citizens but also of Western images. In his dialogue *Contra Haereses*, probably written at this time, the archbishop of the city, Symeon of Thessalonica, unleashed a scathing critique of the new "Latin" images:

What, then, has been instituted anew by these people [the Latins] contrary to the ecclesiastic tradition? Holy and sacred images [εἰκόνων] have been handed down for the honor of the divine prototypes [πρωτοτύπων], for the worship of the faithful that is relative to holy images [εἰκονισμάτων], and for the truth of the things reflected in images [εἰκονικῶς[2]]. For they mold into form [εἰκονίζουσι] the Word that was made flesh for us, and all of His deeds, sufferings, wonders, and mysteries; and yet they also mold into form the all-holy figure of His ever-virgin Mother, and the figures of His saints, and those very things that the evangelic history and the divine Scriptures say; just as if they were another alphabet [γράμμασιν ἄλλοις[3]], images teach with paint [χρωματουργία] and the rest of the materials used in images [εἰκονικῶς[4]]. These people, who are instituting all these things anew, as it has been said, often make sacred images [εἰκόνας] in another way — one which is in fact contrary to custom.

The next sentence of his diatribe brings Symeon to specific observations:

> Instead of the clothing and hair of images [εἰκονικῶν], they are embellishing [καλλωπίζουσιν] images with human hair and human garments. This is not the image [εἰκὼν] of hair and clothing, but rather they are the hair and clothing of some human being! And what results is not the image and model of the prototype [εἰκὼν τε τῶν πρωτοτύπων καὶ τύπος]. Thus, contrary to what is pious, they make and fashion [καλλωπίζουσιν] these things.[5]

When Symeon says that Western painters "make sacred images in another way" he is saying not only that they make unfamiliar images but also that they undermine a whole system of replication that was designed to ensure the faithful transmission of prototypes through copies. In Symeon's words, the holy images had been "handed down for the honor of the divine prototypes." According to the prototype theory he espoused, icons re-presented authentic and authoritative likenesses of Christ and the saints; they thus transmitted and shared in the power of the personages. As a result of this transmission, the worshipper's reverence before the image passed to the saint represented by it. In the wake of the iconoclastic controversy of the eighth and ninth centuries, the theoretical elaboration of this mechanism of transferences—from the image to the prototype, from the saint to God—was designed to safeguard image worship against the abuse of idolatry.[6]

Those transferences effected a series of topological and chronological dislocations. A legitimate copy—a true "image and model of the prototype"—was inherently anachronic: the painting was of recent manufacture, but at the same time reached back into antiquity. The patriarch Nikephoros, in the ninth century, said this about an icon produced in his own day: "the depiction of Christ is not a new invention. The picture has the authority of time: it is pre-eminent in its antiquity; it is coeval with the proclamation of the Gospels."[7] A legitimate substitution declared identity across apparent difference. The time of the prototype, impressed on the first portrait of Christ or a saint, was reactivated in its copies.

A coincidence that contradicts chronological remove—this was an idea that had something in common with the typological thinking of biblical exegetes. Sacred events, though embedded in history, also contained what theologians called a mystery, figure, or sacrament, a spiritual meaning that lifted the event out of the flow of history and connected it with other events and with divine truth. The *figura* represents a disruption of the logical flow of discourse: it both belongs to the chronological sequence and opens it to a series of supratemporal associations. These associations come as an effect of God's point of view, which grasps history all at once, topologically and not in a linear sequence.

Images were an occasion of Christian theology at work. The historical existence of Christ and the saints made their images possible, but the behavior of their images in turn reveals and releases their "supratemporal" virtue. Effecting a rift in secular time, the image not only represents but instantiates the operativity of the divine in temporal affairs.

In his meditation on time in the *Confessions*, St. Augustine argued that nothing passes away in the eternity of God and the whole is simultaneously present; the time of the *saeculum*, by contrast, is structured as a sequence where everything cannot be present at once.[8] God's eternal present is invisible to us; instead, we see only a succession of times, events following one upon another. Even past and future, for humankind, are strictly non-existent; we only have the present, and yet the present, under Augustine's withering analysis, turns out to have no extension whatsoever, disappearing continually as it passes from future to past.[9] We wander in the transitory passages of secular time, and only with effort might we be able to see through it and "glimpse the glory of that eternity that abides forever."[10]

The prototype theory of images espoused by Symeon was designed precisely to compensate for the distorting effect of human perspective. The image's rigid relation to its prototype was meant to guarantee duration without change, succession without difference. Participants in a substitution system were expected to look past the accidental, context-sensitive features that might attach to any given replication. And yet the danger of distraction was always present. Any sequence of replication—even one managed by direct imprinting, as imagined by the theologian Theodore the Studite (see section 3)—in fact ran the risk of drift. Already in the fourth century, St. Basil the Great complained that although artists made every effort to copy faithfully the older images, they nevertheless tended to wander away from the prototypes.[11] If the substitution mechanism failed, then the image was revealed as a mere fabrication, an artifact too obviously fashioned in the present tense. An elaborate biblical discourse of idolatry was available to any critic who wished to condemn the factitious "work of men's hands" (Psalm 115:4).

Symeon's diatribe, quoted in full above, was a direct response to a perceived break in the substitution chain. It also described the fault lines where the breakdown occurred and in that sense it is a penetrating early piece of art criticism: "Instead of the clothing and hair of images, they are embellishing images with human hair and human garments. This is not the image of hair and clothing, but rather they are the hair and clothing of some human being." Painters introduced elements of the world around them— in particular samples of what came to be called "fashion"—that advertised the moment of the artifact's production. The things observed by Symeon can be found in countless examples of late medieval and early Renaissance European art. The elaboration of architectural and interior settings, a new attention paid to the details and textures of materials and clothing, a new concern for anatomical accuracy and for the description of individual bodies and faces (and hair)—textbooks and art-history classes continue to echo Symeon on these points. To grasp what aroused Symeon's contempt, one need only think of the fat wine taster in Giotto's *Wedding at Cana* and his many descendants, or the countless stylishly armored and coiffed St. Georges of the International Gothic, or the aristocratically garbed St. Catherines of Alexandria, or the thugs in scenes of martyrdom in contemporary plebeian dress, or the costumes and weapons of the sleeping soldiers in van Eyck's *Three Marys at the Tomb of Christ*, not to mention the increasingly frequent appearance of actual portraits in religious scenes. For Symeon, these indexical intrusions were the imprint of secular time on the surface of the image.

The critical Byzantine cleric's attention was drawn especially to hair and clothes. And in fact nothing registers secular, successive change more sensitively than clothing and coiffure. Later in his diatribe, in fact, Symeon takes direct aim at the grooming practices of Europeans, in particular their predilection for shaving their beards, which he characterizes as a decadent departure from ancient and pious custom.[12] Western painters, in his view, had made the fatal secondary error of rendering the self-stylings of secular men in their pictures. Symeon was not the only one to notice hair and clothes in painting. Throughout the fifteenth and sixteenth centuries, viewing earlier art actually became an occasion to observe outdated fashions. These were the elements that most insistently cried out for attention and proclaimed the time of the artifact's production. The temporal advertisements of fashion provided the visual footholds for an early form of stylistic analysis and historical criticism.

During the fifteenth century, observers in the West became increasingly aware that the dress around them was subject to the most extreme variations over time. Some historians have asserted that beginning in the late Middle Ages modes changed with greater frequency than ever before—indeed, that a modern fashion culture emerged at this time.[13] Others have interpreted the new attention paid to dress—for example, in the burgeoning field of sumptuary law—as one of the effects of new forms of social mobility in the period.[14] On the level of cultural production, one of the most significant consequences of this new awareness was a fascination with the pageantry of historical costume, and with its arbitrariness, a fascination that constitutes a form of early ethnographic thinking. It became obvious to many that though climatic conditions do not vary drastically, modes of clothing do, continually exhibiting "an absolute indifference to the material standards of life."[15] Or, as Shakespeare put it, "If only to go warm were gorgeous,/ Why, nature needs not what thou gorgeous wear'st" (*King Lear*, II, 4).

Costume, it was observed, was supremely semiotic in its supplementarity and arbitrariness. The perception of arbitrariness entailed the perception that costume was meaningful as well as functional, that it said something about a place or a time. These interests produced, in the sixteenth century, a cascade of books devoted to the illustration of habits and mores—costumes, customs—arrayed both geographically and chronologically.[16] Art was directly implicated by these developments. In a concrete sense, people became aware of the vicissitudes of clothing over time through encounters with older works of visual art: coins, sculptures, tapestries, paintings. In fact, they concocted new fashions by plundering outdated fashions visible in images, as Shakespeare describes:

> *Borachio*: Seest thou not, I say, what a deformed thief this fashion is? how giddily a' turns about all the hot bloods between fourteen and five-and-thirty? Sometime fashioning them like Pharaoh's soldiers in the reechy painting, sometime like god Bel's priests in the old church-window, sometime like the shaven Hercules in the smirched worm-eaten tapestry, where his codpiece seems as massy as his club?
>
> *Conrade*: All this I see; and I see that the fashion wears out more apparel than the man. But art not thou thyself giddy with the fashion too, that thou hast shifted out of thy tale into telling me of the fashion?
>
> (*Much Ado About Nothing*, III, 3)

A "deformed thief," Shakespeare calls it: fashion takes from the past not to redress a lack, not to dress its naked body, but needlessly, excessively, and as a result emerges misshapen, a monstrous fabrication. The giddy "hot bloods" between the ages of fourteen and thirty-five seek out modes long out of style but useful now, in making the present unrecognizable. Fashion muddles times, and when it reaches into the past, it finds the deformed results of earlier anachronic collisions. Dismantling and remantling the present, fashion makes itself susceptible to revival: every moment in fashion is an anachronic time bomb, waiting to explode back into the now.

In one sense the schoolroom for an awareness of the historicity of style, fashion also confuses chronology. Art-historical thinking arose in the fifteenth century in part because observations of the intersection of fashion and art became more frequent, but fashion's instability was always to confound art-historical thinking even while enabling it. For George Kubler, fashion is a vanishing point of history, the "minimal boundary" of things that keep time. Fashions in dress are among the phenomena with the briefest duration, so short-lived and so quickly forgotten that they lie below the threshold of his "history of things," failing to give shape to time. Rather than belonging to a "connected chain of solutions," each fashion in turn constitutes, as he puts it, a class with only one member each.[17]

But fashion's temporal zoom—offering the image of a single moment that is like no other—is an irresistible lure to the historian, holding out the promise that it could provide the most sensitive seismograph of cultural change. The art historian Heinrich Wölfflin famously compared the finials and pinnacles of Gothic architecture to the fanciful pointed shoes of the time.[18] He believed that such visual manifestations expressed a "will," a "feeling of the *Volk*" that pervaded both the spirit and the products of the age. Transmitted primarily through the body—through the way people carry themselves and move—this feeling is clearly registered in costume.[19] As Frederic Schwartz has shown, Wölfflin's concept of style contested the disintegrating effects of modernity embodied in fashion.[20] Art-historical style—a visual uniformity expressing a spiritual unity—was one aspect of the organic, precapitalist unity of past societies, a unity no longer available to the modern age. "We no longer have any right to talk of styles," Wölfflin wrote, "but only of fashions, change that can no longer express an age."[21] In contrast to the Baudelairean painter of modern life, who loses himself to the ephemeral parade, the disciplined historian of art musters past styles, and the very concept of style, as a bulwark against the devalued spectacle of modern fashion.

If the concept of style was concocted as an antidote to fashion, it is of little surprise that the cure should taste of the poison: as it happens, the pointed Gothic shoes that Wölfflin saw as a "weighty" expression of their time were in fashion for a brief moment at the end of the twelfth century and then disappeared.[22] In the fifteenth century, fashion's secular disobedience—its insistent contemporaneity—provided an early working model for the history of art. By the late nineteenth century its temporal instability ripped through the art-historical project. Twentieth-century critics of historicism saw this, too, as a potent force. Walter Benjamin found in the chronic volatility of fashion a key to grasping the explosive temporal disruptions of revolutions. Like fashion, revolutionary thought reaches back into the past and releases the "now-time" [*Jetztzeit*], a "messianic" time, from history into the present.

> For Robespierre the Rome of antiquity was thus a past charged with now-time, a past which he blasted out of the continuum of history. The French Revolution regarded itself as Rome reincarnated. It quoted ancient Rome as

fashion quotes past costumes. Fashion has the scent for the contemporary [*das Aktuelle*] wherever it stirs in the thicket of long ago. It is the tiger's leap into the past.[23]

Fashion, like the revolutionary dialectic, carries inside it a powerful critique of chronological complacency. It disregards the logical progression of linear time, finding a contemporaneity in the past that breaks through to the present. Benjamin knows this is rash advice in urgent times. Under modernity, an embrace of the contemporaneous is the only way out of the progression of history. For medieval clerics, fashion worked the other way. Its claws were sunk deep in secular time and would not let go. The historical register may be essential to Christian theology, but too tenacious a grip on history gets in the way of temporal revolution. The now-time of fashion can blow history open, or it can be the shredder in the eschatological works.

"I have before my eyes a series of engravings of fashions beginning with the Revolution and ending more or less with the Consulate." Baudelaire begins his meditation on fashion and modernity by turning to a set of images already packaged into a history of fashions. The catalogue serves to bring fashion to the level of the symbolic, making it possible to see in the past modes "la morale et l'esthétique du temps."[24] Fashion is almost an image, almost a symbol, and that is why images rush to it, collect around it, in an effort to fulfill fashion's symbolic promise. In turn, that symbolic activity feeds back into fashion as it does its anachronic work. The endless quotation of past styles relies on a continual raiding of the visual record, and even some deep digging in the bric-a-brac of art history. Shakespeare makes this clear in the passage quoted above, where the hot bloods get themselves up "like Pharaoh's soldiers in the reechy painting, sometime like god Bel's priests in the old church-window, sometime like the shaven Hercules in the smirched worm-eaten tapestry." The fashion sense is drawn to the reechy painting and finds amidst the grime something it can pull into the present. In the process and by the way, it finds itself practicing an art history. Before there were art historians, there were hot bloods on the trail of the modern wherever it stirs in the thicket of long ago.

Erasmus, in his lashing dialogue *Ciceronianus*, published in 1528, explained the principle of the historicity of literary style by invoking the spectacle of historical fashions offered by old paintings. According to Erasmus, Cicero's language was appropriate to the age he lived in and thus was not to be reintroduced unthinkingly into the present. Erasmus finds an analogy in the domain of fashion, where "what was admired a hundred years ago wouldn't be acceptable now"—a statement that elicits the following exchange:

Nosoponus: No, indeed, everyone would laugh and boo. Just look at pictures that aren't all that old, painted, say, sixty years ago, and see what was being worn by those of the fair sex belonging to prominent families or living at court. If a woman went out in public dressed like that now, the village idiots and street-urchins would pelt her with rotten fruit.

Hypologus: Only too true. Who would put up now with a decent married woman wearing those huge horns and pyramids and cones sticking out from the top of the head, and having her brow and temples plucked so that nearly half her head is bald; or with men wearing those hats stuffed like a cushion with a great tail hanging down, coats with scalloped borders and enormous padded shoulders, hair shaved off an inch above their ears, tunics far too short to reach the knees, hardly covering their private parts, slippers with a long pointed beak sticking out in front.[25]

Erasmus here is not addressing the style of painting itself, but rather is using paintings as windows onto the past. He assumes, at least for the purposes of his dialogue, the representational transparency of painting. Paintings show us that clothing goes out of fashion, just as literary styles do. But do paintings themselves have a style, an overall formal concept independent of what they represent, a style that registers their historical moment? It was easy to see, around 1500, that the often arbitrary conventions of fashion shifted smoothly with the times, just as the pioneering art-historical formalists Wölfflin and Alois Riegl, around 1900, turned first to ornament to demonstrate the supersensitivity of form to history.[26] It was not so easy, in Erasmus's time, to see that a painting itself might have style, that is, that its overall formal principle might register historical change. We are far from anything like a robust conception of historical style, which postulates a change in the *way* the world is represented from period to period.

Artistic styles shift with cultural conditions: a self-evident truth to any modern art historian, but an extraordinary idea in this period. Nor is it clear that any such idea was articulated in antiquity. Indeed, it has even been argued the ancient Romans had no conception of period costume.[27] Pliny was attentive to changes in ways of art-making, but he presented such change as driven by technology and wealth. Vasari, too, attributes the strangeness and, in his view, the deficiencies of earlier art to lack of technological know-how and cultural sophistication.

Nonetheless, it was the capacity of painting to depict historicity of style in the world—in fashion, in architecture—that led fifteenth-century commentators step by step to the notion of the historicity of the art of painting itself. This is revealed in texts about historical anachronism in painting.

The concept of decorum in ancient literary theory referred to the appropriateness of expression and behavior, to character and situation; when it was applied to painting in the fifteenth century the criteria of decorum were expanded to encompass the problem of appropriateness of dress, weaponry, and so forth to historical time and place. The first comments were negative: admonishments to painters to eschew a mindless mirroring of the contemporary. In 1464 the theorist Filarete warned painters against dressing the figures of Caesar and Hannibal in modern costumes.[28] To learn to dress Caesar and Hannibal properly, the painters will need to study the sculptural reliefs of Roman antiquity. Leonardo da Vinci also advised fellow painters not to use contemporary dress in their works, but not, like Filarete, out of concern for historical accuracy. He was more concerned to avoid the fate of those old paintings looked on with (Erasmian) curiosity and bemusement by his own contemporaries:

> The garments of figures should be in keeping with their age and decorum, that is, an old man should be robed; the young man should be adorned with clothing that doesn't quite cover the neck down to the shoulders, with the exception of those who have professed religion. And avoid as much as possible the dress of your own day, unless they belong to the [religious] category just mentioned. Contemporary dress is only to be used in figures like the ones used on tombs in churches [for example, donor portraits]. In this way perhaps our successors will not be provoked to laughter by the mad inventions of men, but rather will be made to admire their dignity and beauty.[29]

A timeless notion of costume had been customarily observed for the figures of Christ and the saints, but here Leonardo appears to want to extend it to all figures. He exempts religious figures because clerics were, and still are today, distinguished among their contemporaries by wearing anachronistic robes that signal their independence from time and custom. He seems to say that it is permissible to depict historical clerics in costumes that may appear modern, because modern clerical dress is already emancipated from time; here, so to speak, the principle of decorum is built into the world. (This is the reason that Carpaccio could depict Augustine in modern but timeless robes.) The rest of us wear clothes—arbitrary, excessive, and vain—that are subject to history, to the *saeculum*.

The ambitious painter does well to disdain the merely "journalistic" reporting on his own time. Otherwise he will suffer the fate of the trecento paintings, many of which are interesting to later generations—according to Giorgio Vasari—only as records of their time, as historical documents. On several occasions Vasari defended trecento painting, "although it is not very beautiful," for its documentary value, and specifically as a record of period costumes—that is, "for the variety of clothing, grooming styles, and the differing armours of those times."[30]

The aim of the reforming theologians and anachronism-sensitive artists and theorists was to remove the signs of contemporaneity from religious images; the aim of the new antiquarianism, of the sort recommended by Filarete and practiced by Mantegna and others, was to construct an image of the past that matched the archeological evidence of ancient life. In either case we are far from a substitutional conception of the image's place in time. The substitutional painting is disengaged from this level of formal preoccupation altogether. In an effective substitution, context-reflexive features, those aspects of an artwork that belong to the time of its manu-facture, are in principle invisible. The traces of the present are simply over-looked. Reflection on painting's sensitivity to circumstances of fabrication, whether registered on the level of content or form, "what" or "how," was always at the expense of substitution. In this way the theorists' strictures against anachronistic costume were a rudimentary articulation of a theory of painting as an authorial, that is, temporally punctual, performance.

The key, finally, to any conception of "period style" was the beholder's ability to *abstract* from the representational content to a more general concept of the picture's form or structure. For the modern beholder who perceives historical style, a trecento picture is still a trecento picture, a quattrocento picture is still a quattrocento picture, and so forth, no matter what the costumes inside the picture look like. In the fifteenth and sixteenth centuries in Europe, the exercise in abstraction took two clear forms, neither of them matching a modern art-historical notion of the historicity of style. First, the substitutional premise presupposed an abstract principle that linked all the disparate works or buildings in a chain or network of replicas. Such a unifying principle overcame any naïve conception of painting as simple representation of the world, as transpar-ent, just as it overcame any conception of buildings as simple responses to local, practical needs. The second form that abstraction took was the project of idealism, that is, the attempt to bring a fabricated thing into conformity with a transhistorical principle of beauty, perfection, or grace. Idealism also elevates painting above any slavish, mimetic relationship to the experienced world. The noble draperies of the sort that Leonardo was recommending were the symbol of this escape from a mere aping of con-temporary experiential reality.

Both substitutional reference to an authoritative original and idealist compliance to a transhistorical canon of form would seem to represent the very opposite of the principle of painting's sensitivity to circumstance and history, a principle of style that would permit a history of art to be written. But the abstraction from mere representationalism entailed by both substitution and idealism was the operation that permitted thinking about the historicity of painting to move beyond the simplistic observation that historical paintings show us what the past looked like, to the more subtle observation that historical paintings show us how the past saw. For when modern art history recognizes "historical style," it recognizes a set of common formal and structural features that tether an entire diverse class of paintings to the historical life-world that produced them, regardless of whether they are "realistic" or "idealist" paintings. Moreover, expressions of preference in the Renaissance for a substitutional conception of the cult image, or a "return" to such a conception, as well as idealist and neoclassicist disdain for the contemporary, seem to signal the worry that pictures and other works of art of the day will in the future look too much like the products of their time. If so, then the idea of historical style, even if never clearly articulated in the Renaissance, was nevertheless present in the attempts to overcome it. When Leonardo and Vasari spoke of painting as a report on the costumes of the day, they were actually talking about the risk that painting itself might become another creature of fashion, subject to meaningless shifts in taste.

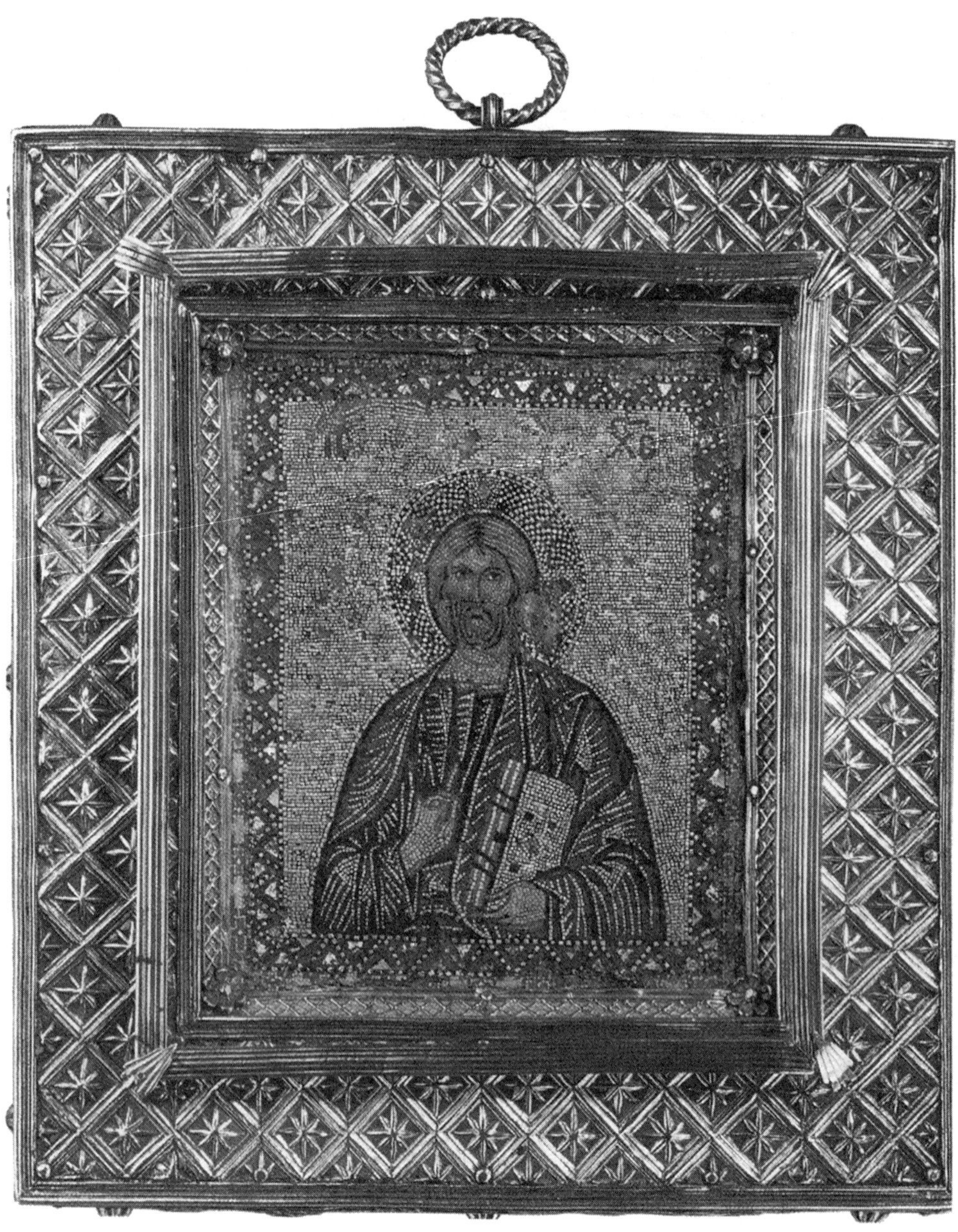

10.1 The value of the Byzantine icon was its overestimated antiquity. *Christ Pantocrator*, micromosaic, 12 x 10.6 cm (fourteenth century, frame added after 1475). Chimay, Parish Church of Saints-Pierre-et-Paul. This icon was given in 1475 by Pope Sixtus IV to Philippe de Croÿ, count of Chimay, who added the silver frame. In Chimay the image acquired fame as an *acheiropoieton*, or an image made without human hands.

TEN

Ancient Painting

The sacred icons exported from Byzantium to Europe in the thirteenth, fourteenth, and fifteenth centuries passed through a temporal looking glass on their way to the West.[1] These panels were not necessarily very old. Many are datable to the Palaiologan period (1261–1453), that is, they were contemporary works. And yet the Eastern panels were venerated by Europeans as antiquities. Several were ascribed directly to St. Luke, for example the icon of around 1100, painted over at least once before it arrived in Europe, and given by the della Scala family to the cathedral at Freising in 1440.[2] In 1475 Pope Sixtus IV gave to Philippe de Croÿ, count of Chimay, a micromosaic icon of Christ Pantocrator, dating from the fourteenth century (figure 10.1). De Croÿ took it home to Chimay and had a precious case made for it, and it soon acquired fame as an *acheiropoieton*, a work "made without hands," a miracle and automatically an antiquity.[3]

But the attribution to St. Luke, or to a direct imprinting from Christ's features, was historically improbable, and not all who spoke of "Luke" Madonnas or *acheiropoieta* necessarily meant it literally. As if in compensation for such ambiguities, propped up by pious lore and local pride, datings of some other icons took on a spurious exactitude. The connoisseurs responsible were typically humanist scholars, prelates, and princes. In the 1380s, a micromosaic of Christ as Man of Sorrows datable to around 1300 was taken from the monastery of St. Catherine at Mount Sinai and given to the church of Santa Croce in Gerusalemme in Rome (figure 10.2).[4] Throughout the fifteenth century it was held to be the very image that St. Gregory commissioned, eight centuries earlier, to commemorate a miraculous appearance of Christ on the altar during the saint's performance of the Mass. A fourteenth-century micromosaic of the Virgin Eleousa, now in the Metropolitan Museum in New York, bears a piece of parchment on the back with an inscription in a late fifteenth-century humanist hand claiming that this was the first Christian image gazed upon by the just-converted St. Catherine of Alexandria, thus placing the image in the early fourth century at the latest

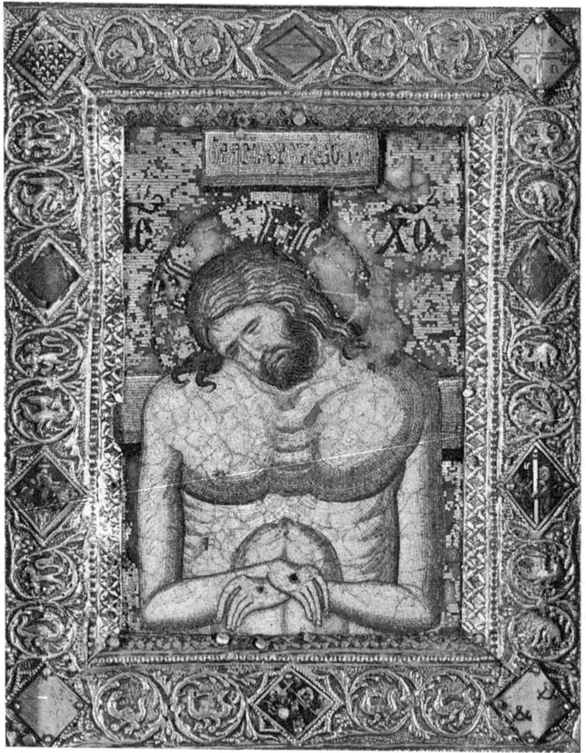

10.2 A product of a Constantinopolitan workshop, less than a hundred years old, becomes an antiquity in the West. *Christ as Man of Sorrows,* micromosaic, 13 x 19 cm (icon) (ca. 1300, frame added ca. 1380). Rome, Santa Croce in Gerusalemme. Raimondello Orsini del Balzo acquired this work in 1380–1381 at Mount Sinai and gave it to the church of Santa Croce in Gerusalemme in Rome a few years later. By legend, St. Gregory the Great, Pope from 590 to 604, was visited by Christ in the form of the Man of Sorrows. A later adaptation of the legend, propagated throughout the fifteenth century by the Carthusian order, the order attached to this church, maintained that the saint commissioned this very image as a record of the miracle.

(figure 10.3).[5] Another fourteenth-century micromosaic, representing St. Demetrios and now in Sassoferrato, was probably given by Cardinal Bessarion to his secretary, the noted grammarian Niccolò Perotti (figure 10.4). The silver revetment carries an inscription in archaizing letter forms and the now-lost inscription on the left side of the image was a prayer written in the voice of the emperor Justinian—antique associations that would have delighted Perotti.[6]

It is likely that a large ivory carving with an enthroned Christ, owned by Sixtus IV's nephew Cardinal Giuliano della Rovere, later Pope Julius II, was similarly assessed (figure 10.5). Cardinal Giuliano added a framework with gems and with niello roundels of the evangelists and Church fathers,

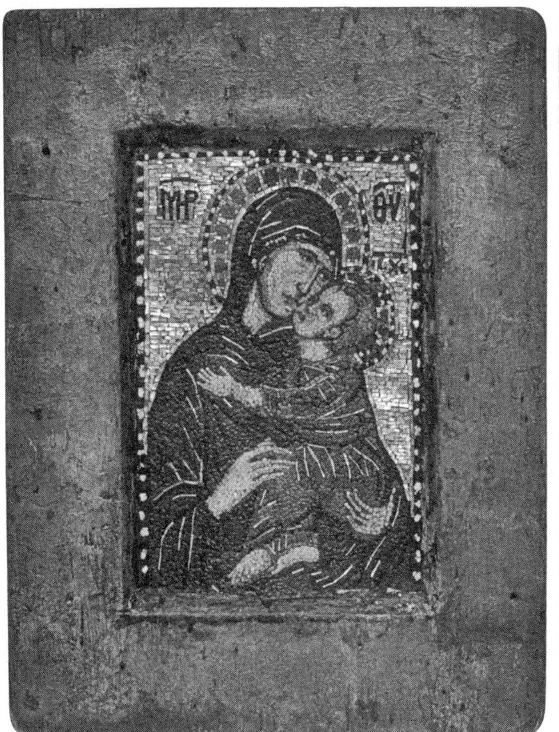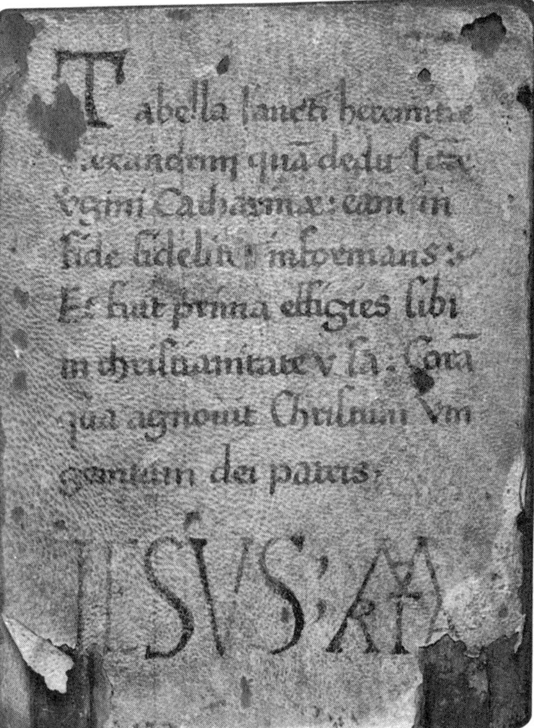

10.3 A work of the fourteenth century backdated at least to the fourth century. *Virgin Eleousa*, micromosaic, 11.2 x 8.6 cm (first half of the fourteenth century). Verso: inscription on parchment (fifteenth century). New York, Metropolitan Museum of Art. The label on the back, written in Latin in a fifteenth-century humanist hand, reads: "This is the little painting that the hermit saint Alexandrinus gave to the holy virgin Catherine [of Alexandria] as he was initiating her into her devotion to the faith. And it was the first image seen [by her] in her Christianity [i.e., as she was converted], in the presence of which she acknowledged Christ the only begotten son of God the Father. Jesus Mary." The association with St. Catherine implicitly dates the icon to the fourth century at the latest.

inscribing it with his initials and with the date 1500.[7] Today the ivory is dated to the tenth century, but Cardinal Giuliano would have had neither incentive nor means to think art historically about the object. Instead, this imposing figure in pallium and tunic, sitting like an emperor on a throne, would have struck him as an emanation from antiquity. In its general layout, the metal framework he added resembles those added to other icons that were invested with hoary provenances. The frame and the ivory together set up a network of temporal references. The gem arrangement, a form of decoration reserved for the most venerable objects, imitates the decorations shown within the ivory, on the throne, and especially on the book held by Christ. The book's contents are projected in the portraits of

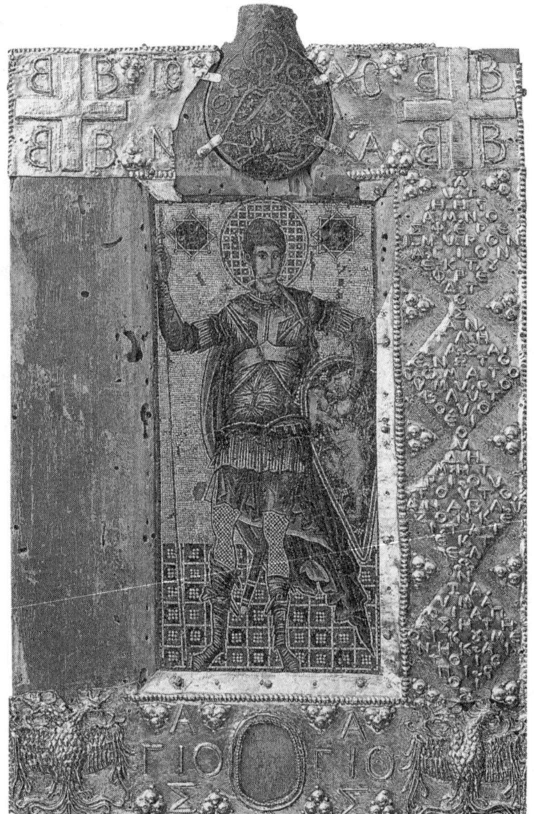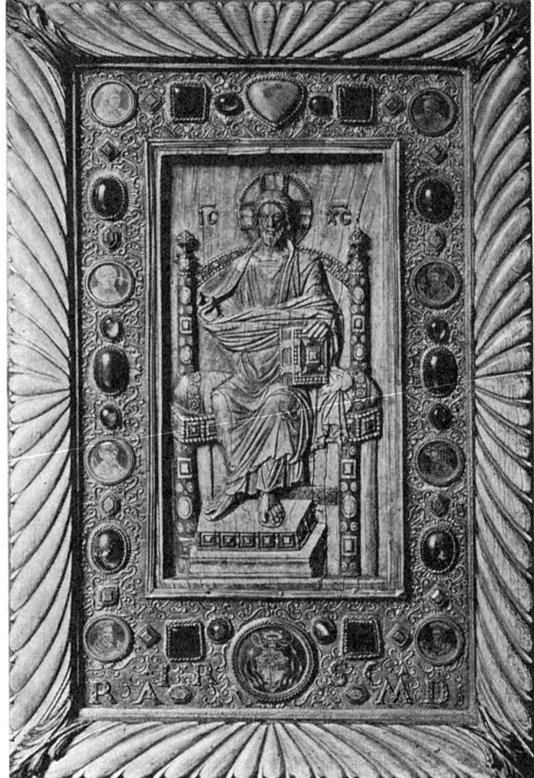

10.4 Another modern work endowed with ancient resonances. *Saint Demetrios*, micromosaic, 24.3 x 16 cm (probably fourteenth century). Sassoferrato, Museo Civico. Again the unfamiliar iconography and medium encouraged antiquarian-minded Italians to exaggerate the image's age. The silver frame, probably of the fifteenth century, carries embossed capital letters in archaic form. The flask or ampulla at the top bears an image of St. Demetrios and contained holy oil collected from his tomb, as the inscription on the right side of the revetment declares. The missing panel on the left, lost in the late nineteenth century, carried an invocation to St. Demetrios spoken in the voice of the sixth-century emperor Justinian. The empty cartouche at the bottom of the frame once carried a cameo bearing the image of a saint, an object that carried ancient associations.

10.5 A modern frame wraps a Byzantine ivory in ancient references. *Christ Enthroned*, ivory, 24.5 x 13 cm (tenth century); silver revetment with gems and niello roundels of the evangelists and Church fathers. Switzerland, private collection. The revetment bears the date 1500 and the coat of arms of Cardinal Giuliano della Rovere. As Pope Julius II (1503–1513), Giuliano was patron to Bramante, Michelangelo, and Raphael, among others. The engraved niello roundels of the evangelists and Church fathers embed this image of Christ in layers of early Christian references. It is likely that Cardinal Giuliano considered the precious central panel an antiquity.

the evangelists, the first Christian writers, and the Church fathers, their most authoritative early commentators. These *all'antica* roundel portraits thus gain an antique authority from their proximity to the ivory, and, conversely, form a tight-fitting envelope of early Christian resonances around the object, converting it into a relic of deepest antiquity.

In this case the artifact itself provides the evidence that the object was backdated to antiquity, and was indeed taken as a sample of ancient art. Most evidence of the reception of the Greek icons was "internal" in this sense, deriving from elements, usually framing devices, attached to the artifacts themselves. Only rarely did textual descriptions of artifacts comment on dating. One exception that explicitly affirms the antiquity of the Greek icons is Cardinal Jacopo Ammanati's description of the collection of Pope Paul II (1464–1471), which also contained Roman antiquities: Ammanati noted "images of saints of ancient workmanship brought from Greece, which they call icons."[8] We are confronted with the fact that the dating of such works was regularly off by a thousand years or more—a strange phenomenon that needs explaining.

The geographical removal of the empire to the new Rome initiated by Constantine and consolidated by Theodosius had produced a temporal loophole in the eyes of fifteenth-century Europeans. Byzantium, spared the tumult and waste of the Western Middle Ages, seemed exempt from time. Even people, visitors from the east, were treated like living relics, indeed like icons. No Eastern import was more significant than the person of the emperor himself, the very embodiment of the continuing existence of the Roman imperium. When the emperors from the East returned to the West in the fifteenth century in order to appeal for help in defending the empire against imminent Turkish invasion, the West saw antiquity as if preserved in amber. Describing the spectacle of the Ferrara-Florence Council of 1438–1439, intended to effectuate a reconciliation between the Eastern and Western churches and thus an alliance against the Turkish enemy, Vespasiano da Bisticci made a special note of the garments worn by the Byzantine officials, which seemed to resist the universal law of secular change in costume style: "Before going on I must say one thing in special praise of the Greeks. For the last fifteen hundred years and more the Greeks have never changed their dress; their clothes are of the same fashion now as they were in that time." He knows this because he can refer to the testimony of visual artifacts: "This may be seen in Greece in a place called the field of Philippi, where were found many records in marble in which may be seen men clothed in the manner still used by the Greeks."[9] Earlier, in the years around 1400, when the Byzantine emperor Manuel II and his retinue made the rounds of the European courts in an effort to raise money and troops for the defense of Constantinople, the unfamiliar costumes similarly made a great impression and were copied by artists attempting to portray ancient figures in ancient dress, for example in the illustrations for the manuscript

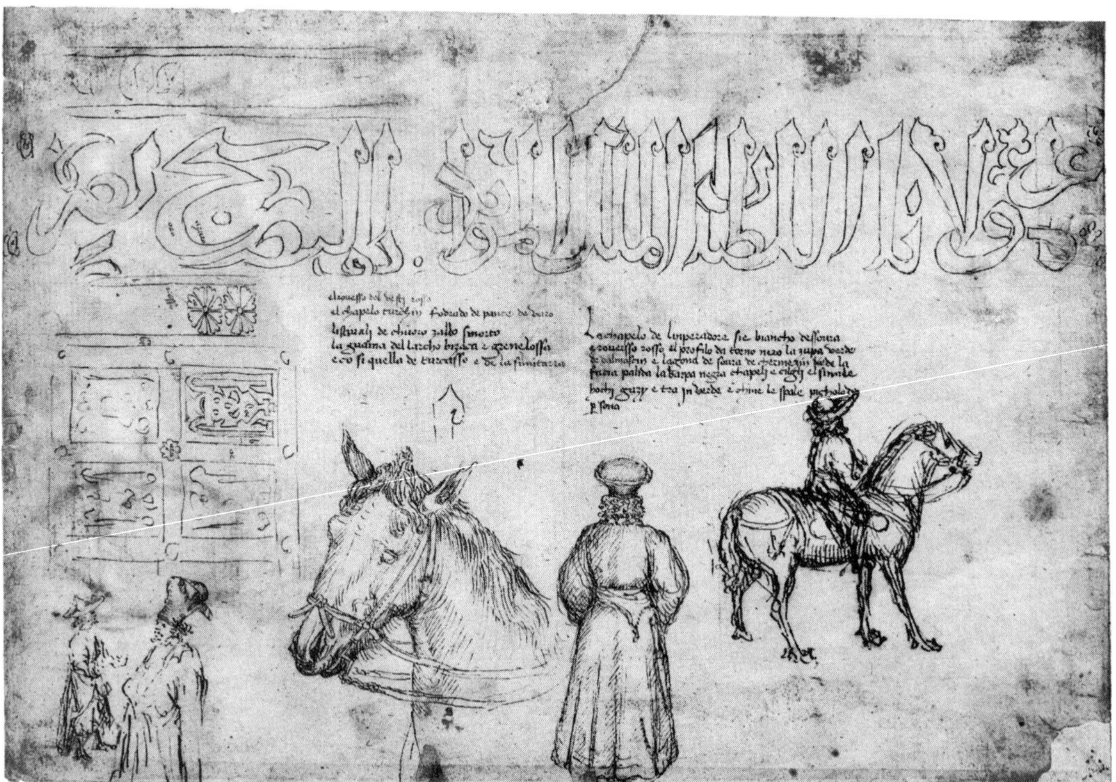

10.6 The Greek Emperor as a living antiquity. Pisanello, *Thuluth script within an ornamental border; John VIII Palaiologos on horseback and three other figures*, pen and ink on paper, 19.9 x 29 cm (1438–1439). Paris, Musée du Louvre. The artist Pisanello observed the visiting head of state either in Ferrara or in Florence in 1438–1439 at the time of the Council deliberating over the unification of the Byzantine and Latin churches. Beyond the drawing of the emperor, shown on horseback at right, from behind at center, and possibly also at far left, the drawing carries careful textual annotations recording the color and material of the clothing and headgear worn by the emperor ("the hat of the emperor should be white on the outside, on the reverse red, the border around it black, the doublet of green damask, and the gown on top crimson..."), thus extending the referential reach of the monochrome drawing. Across the top is an exceptionally accurate transcription of a passage of Arabic writing in the thuluth style, a dedicatory inscription invoking the Mamluk sultan who reigned in Egypt from 1412 to 1421. The bands of decoration above and below it suggest that Pisanello was observing a textile, probably given to the emperor by this or another sultan.

of Terence produced for Jean, Duke of Berry, before 1416.[10] The visit of John VIII Palaiologos in 1438–1439 made an even more powerful impact on artists. Pisanello examined the Byzantine emperor like an artifact, recording all his features in notes and drawings, even transcribing, as if from an ancient monument, the inscriptions that adorned his figure (figure 10.6).[11]

Not only Byzantine visitors were seen as living antiquities. The so-called gypsies (Roma), who arrived in western Europe in the first years of the fifteenth century, made a similar impression. The costumes of these wanderers, often involving stripes and outsized headgear, seemed to transmit the long-outmoded customs of the East, perhaps of Egypt. The costumes were immediately adapted by modern painters to scenes of Biblical antiquity.[12] The idea that costume from the East is unchanging persisted in the Christian imagination all the way to James Joyce: "O, Mairy lost the pin of her. Dressed up to the nines for somebody. Fashion part of their charm. Just changes when you're on the track of the secret. Except the east: Mary, Martha: now as then."[13]

The person of Emperor John VIII was susceptible to artistic commemoration in forms not used for contemporaries—that is, in the anachronic forms of the bronze bust and the bronze medal. The bronze bust attributed alternatively to Filarete and Donatello, now in the Vatican Museums, was probably made at the time of John VIII's visit to Florence in 1439 during the council (figure 10.7).[14] It may be the very earliest portrait bust of a living person since antiquity. Likewise, Pisanello's medal of John VIII was among the very first portrait medals of the Renaissance (figure 10.8).[15] These renderings of the anachronic person of the Byzantine emperor unlocked the formats for modernity. They also served as models for artists interested in depicting ancient personages in their works.[16]

It was the bust-length format that to Western eyes most immediately marked the Greek icons as antiquities. The bust format carried strong associations with pagan culture, where it was found in profile portraits on coins, reliefs, or *imagines clipeatae*, in which the head or bust appear in a circular frame; and in three-dimensional busts in marble or bronze. The bust-length painted portrait, meanwhile, was a format known primarily through Christian antiquities. Around 1211, Gervasius of Tilbury noted that the image of the Veronica kept in St. Peter's was an "effigies a pectore superius."[17] In his widely read manual on divine offices (*Rationale Divinorum Officiorum*) of 1286, William Durandus, bishop of Mende, explicitly associated the format with Greek painting and linked the feature to a greater moral rectitude: "The Greeks employ painted representations, painting...only from the navel upwards, so that all occasion for vain thoughts be removed."[18]

Early experiments with the bust format in the West were often directly tied to specific, highly venerable artifacts imported from the East. For example, a diptych showing heads of Christ and the Virgin given to Pope Clement VI at Avignon in the 1360s (now lost) made a great impact on art in the Provençal region and in the Netherlands in the early fifteenth century. Otto Pächt has shown how carefully the Master of René of Anjou,

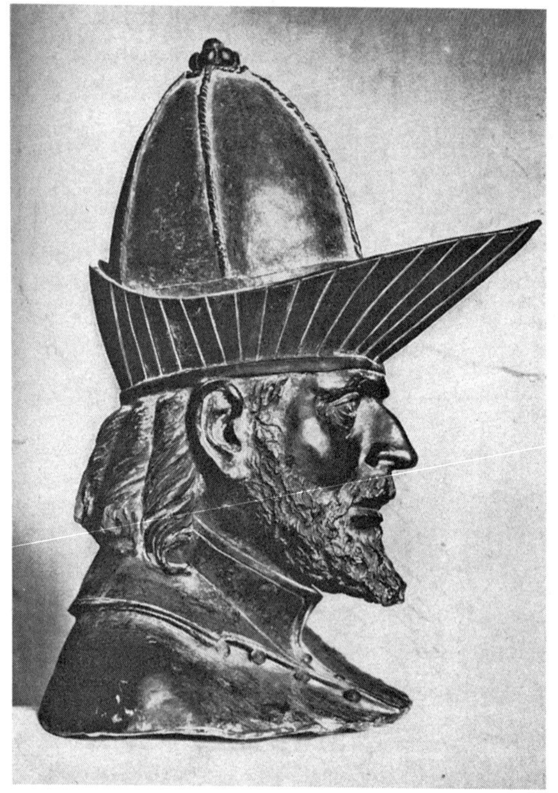

10.7 The Byzantine Emperor in an ancient medium and format. Antonio Filarete or Donatello, *Bust of Emperor John VIII Palaiologos*, bronze, 49 x 37 x 26 cm (1439). Vatican City, Musei Vaticani. The person and the costume of the emperor seemed, to Western European eyes, direct testimony of Roman antiquity. The visored hat was adopted by Italian painters after this visit as an attribute of emperors, Roman officials, and ancient personages of all kinds.

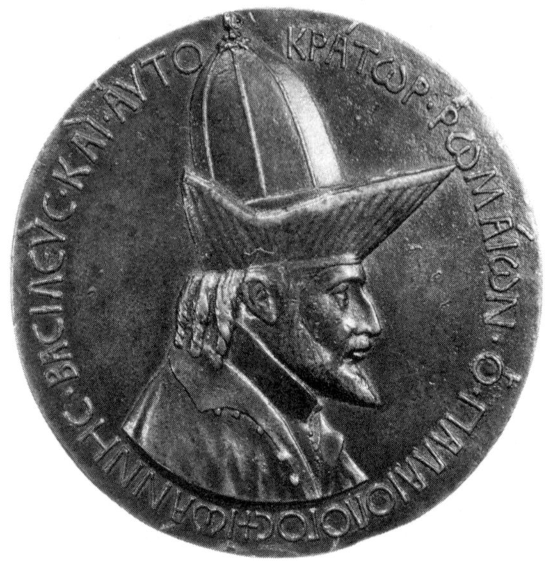

10.8 The prestigious visitor in a supposedly ancient medium. Pisanello, *Medal of John VIII Palaiologos*, bronze, diameter 10.1 cm (1438–1439). Paris, Bibliothèque Nationale, Cabinet des Medailles. The artist took the bronze images of emperors Constantine and Heraclius (see figure 23.1) as models for his portrait of John VIII. Very likely granting those earlier medals ancient authority, Pisanello accidentally invented a completely new format: the medal portrait.

Robert Campin, and Jan van Eyck emulated this model, which did indeed preserve a Byzantine prototype from the preiconoclastic period, that is, before the eighth century.[19] Another image type, a half-length Virgin and Child composition based on a Byzantine model, provoked a flurry of responses in the circles of Jean Malouel and the Limbourgs around 1400; Pisanello made careful studies of the French adaptations in producing the half-length Virgin and Child at the top of his Virgin and Child with St. George and St. Anthony Abbot in the London National Gallery.[20] The care with which he treated the French models suggests that he saw them as transmitters of a venerable and authoritative Greek image.

The teaching of Greek language and literature and the transmission of Greek manuscripts—the work of scholars such as Manuel Chrysoloras, Ambrogio Traversari, Guarino da Verona, Vittorino da Feltre, Giovanni Aurispa, Basilius Bessarion, George of Trebizond, and others—is a well-understood episode in the history of humanistic scholarship.[21] The Greek icons, imported, collected, and promoted by many of the same individuals, represent a visual equivalent to the story of textual transmission. They played a catalyzing role in the development of Renaissance art comparable to the role played by the Greek texts in the development of Renaissance literature and scholarship. The collecting of icons was continuous with the antiquarian and philological interests of fifteenth-century humanists. In the very decades when the Roman statues were extracted from the ground and ancient literary texts pried out of the monasteries, ancient Greek paintings were arriving in waves from the East, achieving similar fame and status. Antiquarian-minded artists were as attentive to the icons as they were to the remains of pagan sculpture.[22] And yet the importation of the icons has never been fully integrated into accounts of the art of this period. The picture has been confused by Vasari's account of Cimabue's and Giotto's innovations as rebellion against and liberation from the degraded conventionalism of Greek painting. Vasari had forgotten that the Greek manner had not always been there; that the most advanced innovations in late dugento Italian painting were an effort to rise to the challenge posed by the Greek icons imported in increasing numbers during and after the Latin occupation of Constantinople from 1204 to 1261. He had forgotten that the art before Cimabue, which he decried, was merely Western work that fell far short of matching the sophisticated art emerging from Byzantium.

The mingling of Byzantine icons and Greco-Roman statuary in fifteenth-century collections prompts a reconsideration of the period taste for ancient sculpture. The most admired features of icons—authoritative design, a sovereign and styleless appearance, an overall effect of temporal immunity—were perhaps not so different from the qualities contemporaries valued in antique statuary. Did not the superiority of ancient sculpture follow pre-cisely from its transcendence of mere style, of local custom or individual manner? The names of many ancient Greek sculptors were remembered, but more for their surpassing skill and ingenuity than for their distinctive, personalized manners. Greek and Roman works somehow "cleared" the level of authorship. There was little sense in the Renaissance of a contesta-tion of styles within ancient art. The ancient works were both perfect and styleless—"classic," as they later came to be called.

The true difference of the Greek icons was that they were Christian.[23] The fragments of antique pagan sculpture hailed from the far side of a caesura created by the rise of Christianity itself. Their headless bodies and severed limbs were overinterpreted as the lurid evidence of early Christian iconoclasm.[24] Their physical fragmentariness exacerbated an inherent dif-ficulty in thematic decipherment, providing irresistible occasions for erotic projections and poeticizing fiction-making on the part of their Renaissance interpreters.[25] In contrast to Christian images, which could be inserted into existing social and religious structures and institutions, the recuper-ated pagan statuary opened a new space of aesthetic experience, a realm where motifs migrate independent of context and art emerges as the main preoccupation of art.

The Greek icons were at once foreign and originary. Their strangeness only measured the distance of the modern Western church from a pure and primitive Christianity. They offered Christian history as a history of diva-gation and forgetting, a pattern now lamented by reformers hoping that the process could be reversed.[26] Whereas the modern European religious image was scorned by Byzantine visitors and some reform-minded Western clerics as a fiction, the Greek icons seemed to bear authentic relations to the people they represented. The consciousness of lost continuity governed the Western response to the icons. The arrival of the icons prompted rein-vigorated assertions of an ideology of succession and reinstatement, giving rise to a new generation of images, modern icons, claiming to restore their own referents, the ancient prototypes. The icons achieved, finally, what had always been asked of images, no more than the reliable transmission of prototypes. The substitutional chains implied by the icons were reacti-vated and extended. By this strategy, the total population of icons would increase and the gradient between ancient and modern work—both tokens of a common type—would be leveled.

Whether as originals or copies—the principle of substitutability left this question open—the unfamiliar image types were propagated Europe-wide. This process had begun in the thirteenth century but accelerated in the fifteenth, especially after the fall of Constantinople in 1453.[27] In the later fifteenth century, icons were collected and promoted by prominent—and interconnected—personages all over Italy and Europe. In 1457, twenty-three mosaic icons and thirteen painted and sculpted icons were listed in the collection of Pietro Barbo, later Pope Paul II, none of which has been identified.[28] Cardinal Bessarion donated seven mosaic icons to St. Peter's in 1462 and 1467.[29] An inventory of 1489 indicates that Bessarion gave further icons to St. Peter's, presumably mostly painted.[30] Upon Paul II's death, in 1471, a portion of his collection passed to Lorenzo de' Medici. These may or may not have included the eleven mosaic icons listed in the inventory of 1492, six of which are described as "teste."[31] Cardinal Francesco d'Este possibly acquired icons from Barbo, and commissioned copies of Greek manuscripts borrowed from Bessarion.[32] The trend also had a mass-market dimension. In 1499, two dealers in Venice placed an order for seven hundred icons of the Virgin with three painters in Candia, present-day Heraklion in Crete. They specified the models to be used, the colors for the Virgin's garments, and whether the icons were to be in Western style or in Greek style (*in forma greca* or *in forma a la latina*)— and demanded that the whole order be filled within five weeks![33] In the sixteenth century this demand seems to have petered out, revealing the brisk trade in icons to be a fairly restricted phenomenon of the decades around 1500.[34]

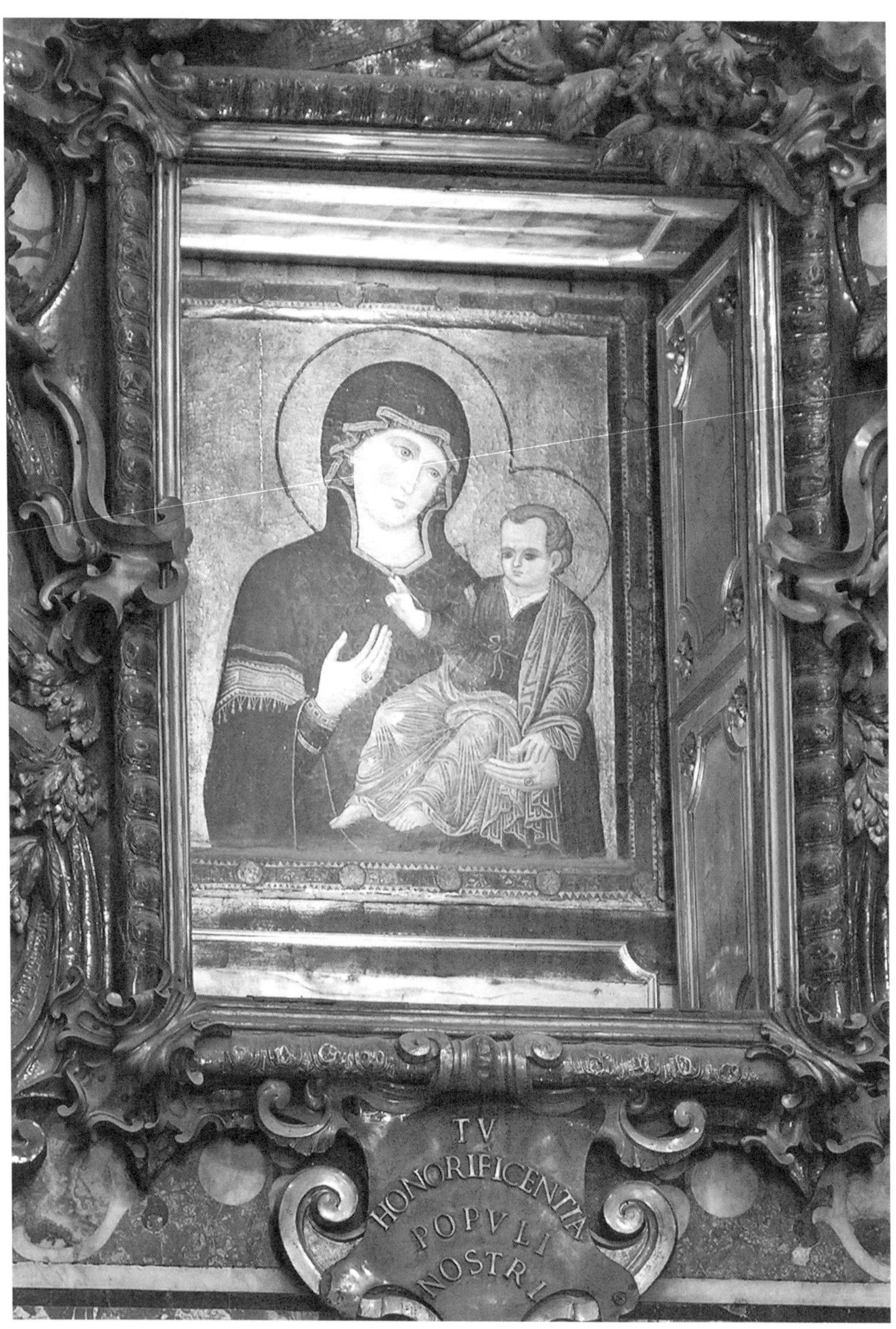

11.1 One of the most frequently reproduced images of the later Middle Ages. *Virgin and Child*, tempera on panel (ca. 1300 with later repaintings). Rome, Santa Maria del Popolo. This panel was treasured as an authentic portrait of the Virgin by the hand of St. Luke, who according to legend was a painter. In 1472 Pope Sixtus IV issued an indulgence to those who would visit the church on a feast day associated with the Virgin. Copied countless times, the image was propagated throughout Europe in paintings and prints.

ELEVEN

Substitution Symbolized

The icon vogue of the later fifteenth century prompted a rediscovery of old icons that were already in Italy, repeating and amplifying the thirteenth-century rediscovery of the Roman icons. Most of the attributions of the Italian icons to St. Luke are not in fact inveterate traditions but rather fifteenth-century inventions, registering the radiating effects of the new enthusiasm for Byzantine icons.[1] Communities debated the origins of their local cult images.[2] Partisan clerics penned quasi-scholarly treatises asserting the greater antiquity or efficacy of their own icons, selecting from a plethora of disparate, fragmentary accounts, identifying types to which modern performances and painting could serve as antitypes. In 1464, a canon of Santa Maria Maggiore in Rome, named Giovanni Baptista, dedicated to Cardinal d'Estouteville a treatise on the icons of St. Luke, naming four paintings in churches in or near Rome: Santa Maria Maggiore, Grottaferrata, Santa Maria in Aracoeli, and Santa Maria del Popolo.[3] The icon of the Virgin at Santa Maria Maggiore, the so-called *Salus Populi Romani*, had played a prominent role in the life of the city of Rome at least since the twelfth century. But not until Giovanni Baptista's treatise were the threads of local lore braided together into a coherent story, clarifying the icon's provenance and powers for the first time, above all its claim, superior to that of the Aracoeli Madonna, to be the very icon wielded by Gregory the Great in 590 against the plague. The treatise explicitly compared the icon to the other Roman and Tuscan icons.

Giovanni Baptista in effect wrote an art-historical monograph on the Santa Maria Maggiore icon, and in so doing reactivated it. On the basis of such local scholarship, rulers commissioned copies and inaugurated pilgrimages. In Rome, over the course of the last third of the fifteenth century, the leading local painters helped build a subclass of modern icons, replicas of prestigious Marian icons that were themselves in turn expected to stoke the cycle of entreaty and gratitude between worshippers and the Virgin. The augmented copy by Antoniazzo Romano of the Byzantine icon at Sant'Agostino, for instance, painted in 1486, was offered as a votive gift acknowledging the delivery of the city of Velletri from the plague. It

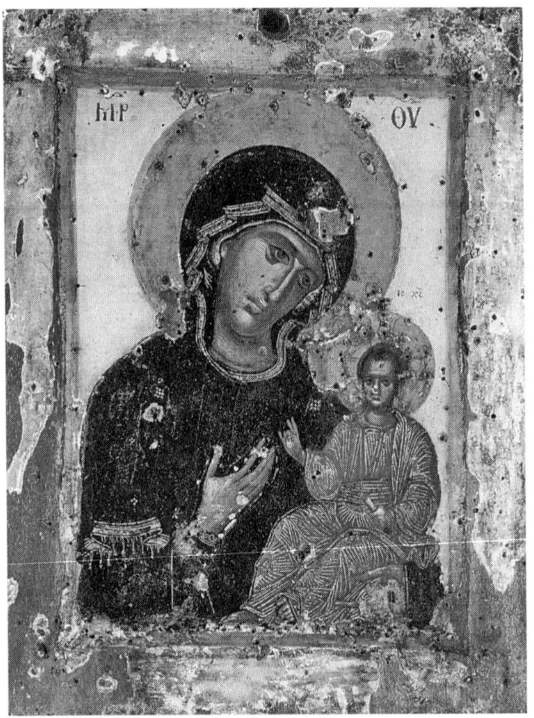

11.2 A model for the icon at Santa Maria del Popolo. *Virgin and Child*, tempera on panel, 112 x 95 cm (thirteenth century). Siena, Carmine. This Greek icon, kept in Siena from the thirteenth century, impressed contemporaries as an object of venerable antiquity, for it complied with an iconographic formula derived from an icon attributed to St. Luke and brought from the Holy Land to Constantinople in the fifth century. The Roman copy (figure 11.1) scrupulously replicated the Virgin's costume and the disposition of the two right hands at the center, but not the relation of the hands to the body behind them.

immediately itself became a votive target. In the 1460s Cardinal Bessarion had Antoniazzo Romano make a copy of the Greek icon in Santa Maria in Cosmedin, the church of the Greek community in Rome, for his titular church of Santi Apostoli.[4] The lord of Pesaro, Alessandro Sforza, who was on friendly terms with Bessarion and with the avid icon collector Pope Paul II, arrived in Rome in 1469 and commissioned copies of the St. Luke icons in Santa Maria Maggiore and Santa Maria del Popolo by Antoniazzo and Melozzo da Forlì, respectively.[5]

Modern, Western copies of the Eastern icons routinely acquired the status of their prototypes. The icon in the church of Santa Maria del Popolo in Rome (figure 11.1) was a copy, made around 1300 by a local artist, of a mid-thirteenth-century Byzantine icon in the church of the Carmine in Siena (figure 11.2).[6] It was the Roman copy that achieved European fame in the later fifteenth century through dissemination in prints, paintings, and prayer book miniatures.[7] In 1478 Pope Sixtus IV affirmed the authenticity of the Santa Maria del Popolo icon in order to raise money for the rebuilding of the church, through the sale of indulgences. In 1440 the Flemish canon Fursy de Bruille returned to Cambrai from the Ferrara-Florence Council with a small painting of the Virgin and Child on gold ground (figure 11.3).[8] The exotic panel was installed in Cambrai cathedral and soon

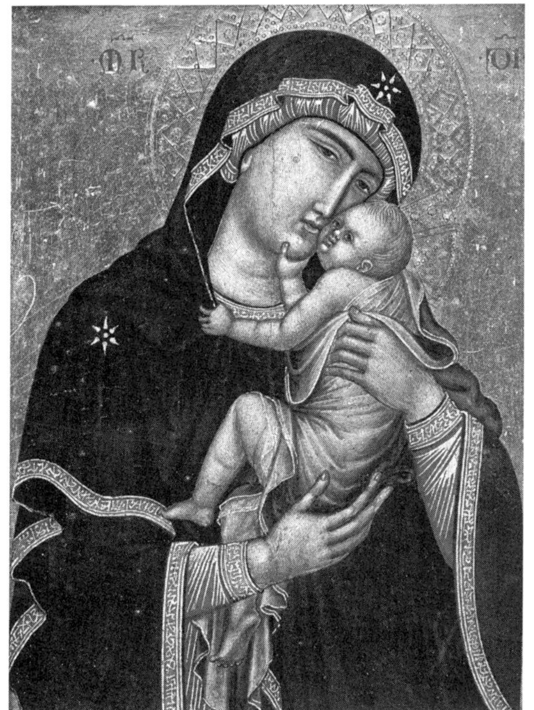

11.3 A modern Italian painting achieves fame in northern Europe as an antiquity. *Virgin and Child*, tempera on panel, 35.5 x 26.5 cm (ca. 1340). Cambrai, Cathedral. This Sienese painting was painted by an Italian artist close to the brothers Lorenzetti, but in the exotic eastern manner. When it arrived in northern Europe it was hailed as an original work by St. Luke.

became famous in its new setting: recognized as a portrait of the Virgin painted by St. Luke, it began attracting thousands of pilgrims. In fact, the picture had been painted only about 100 years earlier in a Byzantine manner by an Italian, probably Sienese, painter. It conforms to a type invented, according to legend, by St. Luke, the Virgin of Tenderness or Virgin Eleousa. The Cambrai Madonna in turn generated further iterations: fifteen copies by Petrus Christus and Hayne de Bruxelles were ordered in the mid-1450s (figure 11.4).[9] These copies were not exact, no more than were the French copies from Byzantine prototypes studied by Pisanello or the Santa Maria del Popolo copy of the Carmine icon in Siena, or for that matter the Cambrai Madonna itself. All these iterations bear the traces of their modern fabrication, in some cases even altering the figures and facial features. And yet the type held, or was seen to.

The strangeness of the Eastern icons read in the West not as conventional, but as truth itself. Otto Pächt argued that the archaizing features in the Western copies should be understood less as an effort to simulate a remote, hieratic style than as an effort to comply with what were deemed historically accurate likenesses. When Jan van Eyck, in the *Head of Christ* preserved in copies in Berlin, Bruges, and elsewhere, adhered closely to the appearance of the frontally portrayed Christ in the Avignon diptych, he was thinking like a portraitist: "Since a study from life was not feasible in this case he based his picture on what was believed to be the most authentic likeness of the Saviour, recording its particularities with 'historical' accuracy."[10] Likewise, as Pächt noted, the apparently archaizing copy of the Virgin panel of the Avignon diptych by the Master of René of Anjou retains a feature charged with particularity and evidentiary power—a wart with hairs growing out of it. This feature can be found in later copies of the image as well, for example in two late fifteenth-century miniatures attributed to Georges Trubert, who had himself worked for King René, one now in the Morgan Library in New York and one in the J. Paul Getty Museum.[11] The discipline of art history has learned to understand the pictorial naturalism of the fifteenth century, involving the simulation of optical impressions of light and texture, as a style in its own right, a symbolic form. But naturalism in its time expressed a dream of escape from style, of liberation from all the acquired devices and conventions of the picture-maker's craft. The density and clarity of van Eyck's images suggested that the painter was attending so closely to what was in front of him that he had forgotten everything he had learned. The personalized temporality of direct experience overcame the communal, shared temporality of custom and pedagogy.

At the same time, the reception of the icons generated some of the most dynamic experiments in fifteenth-century painting.[12] The icon's authorlessness paradoxically did not derail, but rather stimulated the authorial imagination, which in the middle decades of the fifteenth century was moving in the space between the affective, rhetorically fortified devotional image, often a close-up from a narrative scene, and the secular portrait. The comments of Gervasius and Durandus, noted in the previous section, reveal that the bust-length format attracted attention and even demanded explanation: the icons struck the thirteenth-century theologians as truncated figures, fragments of a witnessed whole. Although often described by modern commentators as rigid and hieratic, the icons delivered to European eyes an intimate "zoom" effect. The fascination with the half-length format of the Eastern icons provoked experiments, both in the Netherlands and in Venice, with the "dramatic close-up," whereby the painting is understood as an intimate view excerpted from a larger narrative whole.[13] For Rogier van der Weyden, for example, the model of the Cambrai Virgin spurred an exploration into the tender contact between the Virgin and Child viewed from close up, a solution that in turn became an influential type in northern Europe during the fifteenth century. The Italian counterparts of these works are the half-length images of the Virgin and Child by Michele Giambono, Jacopo Bellini, Andrea Mantegna, Antonello da Messina, and, most prolifically of all, Giovanni Bellini (figure 11.5).[14]

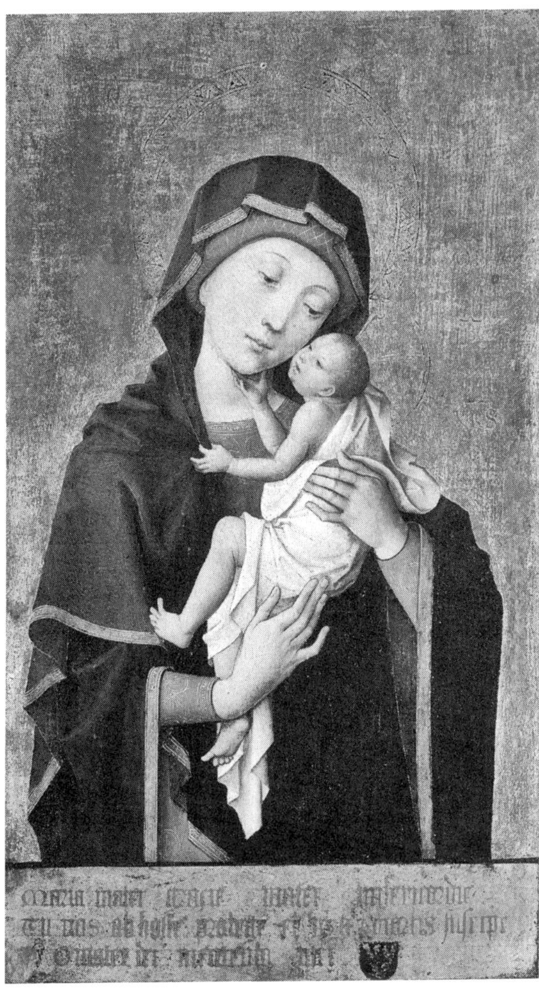

11.4 One of many Netherlandish copies of the Cambrai Virgin. Hayne de Bruxelles, *Virgin and Child*, tempera on panel, 61.9 x 36.2 cm (1454–1455). Kansas City, Nelson Atkins Museum of Art. The copy respects the iconographic type of the Eleousa or tender Virgin and preserves the gold ground, but does not hesitate to translate the figure style into a more familiar local idiom. This was one way of performing the triage between essential and accidental features in the transmission from model to copy.

In a brilliant challenge to the assumption that fifteenth-century painters were obsessed with authoritative prototypes, Amy Powell argues that works of art were more likely to enter into "horizontal" communication with other modern works than to forge "vertical" links with the past.[15] The very idea of an "original" work that might guide future production, she suggests, was generated by the web of modern copies: the original did not precede its multiples. A reflective artist such as Rogier van der Weyden, in Powell's view, had no interest in replicating a supposedly ancient icon such as the Cambrai Madonna.[16] Instead, in works like his *Deposition from the Cross* in Madrid, Rogier thematized the paradoxes of creativity within a tradition of Christian images, comparing through visual repetitions and rhymes the two modes of production, on the one hand fidelity to the prototype (which offers a referential link to divinity), and on the other a

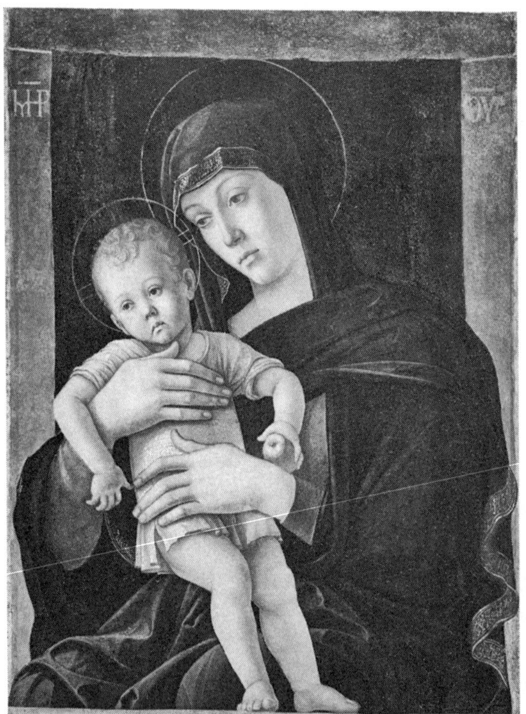

11.5 The logic of substitution extended by modern painting. Giovanni Bellini, *Virgin and Child*, tempera on panel, 82 x 62 cm (ca. 1470). Milan, Pinacoteca di Brera. Like many other painters of the fifteenth century, Italian and Netherlandish alike, Bellini repeatedly adopted the half-length format of the eastern icon. In the Christ child's pose and even in morphological features such as the elongated face of the Virgin, this work follows fairly closely the model of a Byzantine icon now in the Hellenic Institute of Venice and already in Venice in the fifteenth century.

"self-divided, nonclassical repetition" that never arrives at a fixed point of meaningfulness. Rogier worked within a field of alternatives; his most ambitious works took the field itself as their subject.

The process of adapting and updating the old models was a natural extension of the logic of substitution, indeed the process was driven by the substitution impulse. Yet the very extension exposed the substitutional principle to scrutiny. How much could one adjust and invent before the connection to the origin point, the prototype, was dissolved? The creative adaptations by Rogier van der Weyden, Giovanni Bellini, and others generated the opposite approach, the archaizing copy. An archaizing copy abandons contemporary conventions and instead attempts to adhere to the model. Antoniazzo Romano, the Roman painter who specialized in copies after authoritative icons, alternated between the adaptive and the archaizing modes. His copy of the Santa Maria Maggiore icon for Alessandro Sforza, mentioned above, does not survive, but the corresponding panel by Melozzo da Forlì, after the Santa Maria del Popolo icon, has been identified with a panel in Montefalco that is clearly in the archaizing mode (figure 11.6).[17] The very option of an archaizing mode suggests that the question of the distance between copy and model was at issue. Epigrams were attached to Melozzo's and Antoniazzo's copies, inscriptions meant to

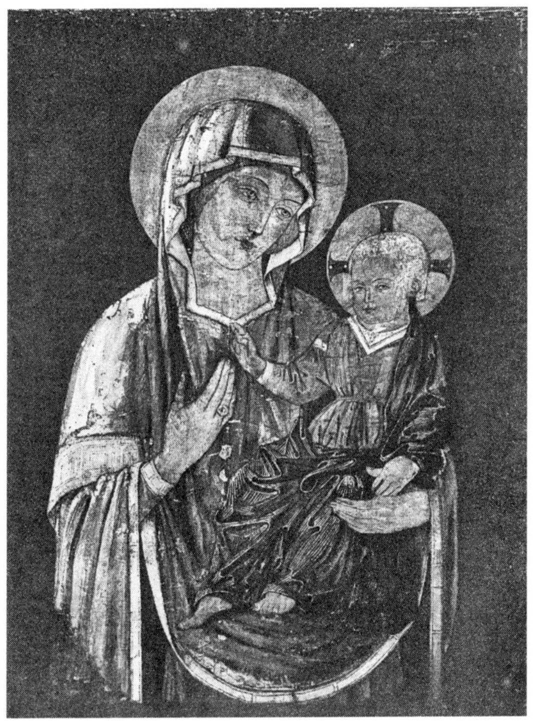

11.6 A copy of the icon at Santa Maria del Popolo. Melozzo da Forlì, *Virgin and Child*, tempera on canvas (ca. 1470). Montefalco, Museo Civico. An epigram appended to this copy of the Santa Maria del Popolo icon reads: "This was painted by St. Luke after the Virgin from life/ This is the authentic portrait of the Virgin/ Alexander Sforza commissioned it, Melozzo painted it/ Luke would say it was his own work." The text, like the inscription on the contemporaneous woodcut of the Madonna in the Robe of Wheat Ears (figure 2.2), registers hesitation in the face of multiple agencies.

reassure but that instead speak symptomatically to this problem. Substitution is affirmed, even explained, in the face of authorship, and in the process it is opened to question.[18] The epigram to Melozzo's copy affirms that the painting was made by St. Luke after the Virgin from life and that it is the authentic portrait of the Virgin, only to state that it was commissioned by Sforza and painted by Melozzo. The final statement—"Luke would say it was his own work"—turns the evangelist-painter into an author endorsing a forgery. The epigram to Antoniazzo's copy instead reflects doubt about the "original" image in Santa Maria Maggiore and thus about its status as a model for a modern painter. It is an image of the Virgin painted by St. Luke, and "who could imagine his image to be an error?"

Despite the new wave of substitutions, or because of them, a split opened up between modern painting and authentic icon. This awareness produced a second set of responses. Even as they spawned a new generation of copies, the ancient icons were being isolated and collected, cordoned off as a privileged but deactivated class. They were offered sanctuary within a fallen modern system. Sandro Botticelli's portrait of a youth holding an icon illustrates and glosses the new conceptual framing of icon painting (figure 11.7).[19] The youthful figure is shown presenting a round, gold-ground image of a saint to the viewer. This roundel of an unidentified saint is not a quotation but an actual relic of gold-ground painting that has been physically inserted into the panel, in an excavated cavity, like a jewel in a setting. It is not a Byzantine icon but rather an Italian painting not much more than a century older than its host, probably excised from an altarpiece by the fourteenth-century Sienese master Bartolommeo Bulgarini.

Did Botticelli himself, on instructions from the patron, insert the trecento fragment into the portrait? We believe he did.[20] Other scholars are skeptical. Keith Christiansen agrees with Roberto Longhi that the icon embedded in the portrait amounts to "*un antistorico* nonsense," in other words an anachronism for the late quattrocento. He believes that the icon was inserted in the late nineteenth or early twentieth century, though he is not sure what it replaced.[21] Ulrich Pfisterer argues that the portrayed youth, in the original arrangement, was much more likely to be presenting the portrait of a lover than an old icon.[22] We are not persuaded by these arguments and see no reason not to date the marriage of the icon and the portrait to the 1480s.[23] The venerable icon, or the altarpiece it came from, may have had some significance to the family of the sitter.[24] Or perhaps the sitter was a precocious antiquarian and collector.[25] The patterns of icon collecting brought forward in this section and the next provide a historical context for the panel's assemblage and make it seem less strange than it did to Longhi and to connoisseurs after him.[26]

The secure dating of the roundel by modern scholarship to the mid-fourteenth century does not resolve the problem of the temporal relationships staged by this portrait. The anachronic behavior of all the objects discussed so far, their tendency to slip back to the time of their ancient prototypes, compels us to ask whether the roundel in Botticelli's panel did not also function in this way. In embedding a fragment of a trecento panel in his portrait, Botticelli remembers an episode in the replication of Greek icon types. Like the Cambrai Madonna or the Madonna del Popolo, the Bulgarini fragment was a fourteenth-century panel that ventriloquized the language of much older icons, and thus the language of antiquity itself. To frame an icon within a modern painting, as Botticelli did, was to give symbolic expression to its predicament. The framed icon was made to stand not for a living possibility of image production, but for an entire system of image transmission, now understood *as* a system. Earlier in this book we described how the bronze statue of Christ, a virtual antiquity, entered into both these layers of response. The statue generated modern replicas, but at the same time it was itself regenerated, through Carpaccio's pictorial embedding, as a symbol of an increasingly strange theory about the temporality of objects.

The European response to the icons was the mirror image of Symeon of Thessalonica's reception of Western art. If in Symeon's eyes Western

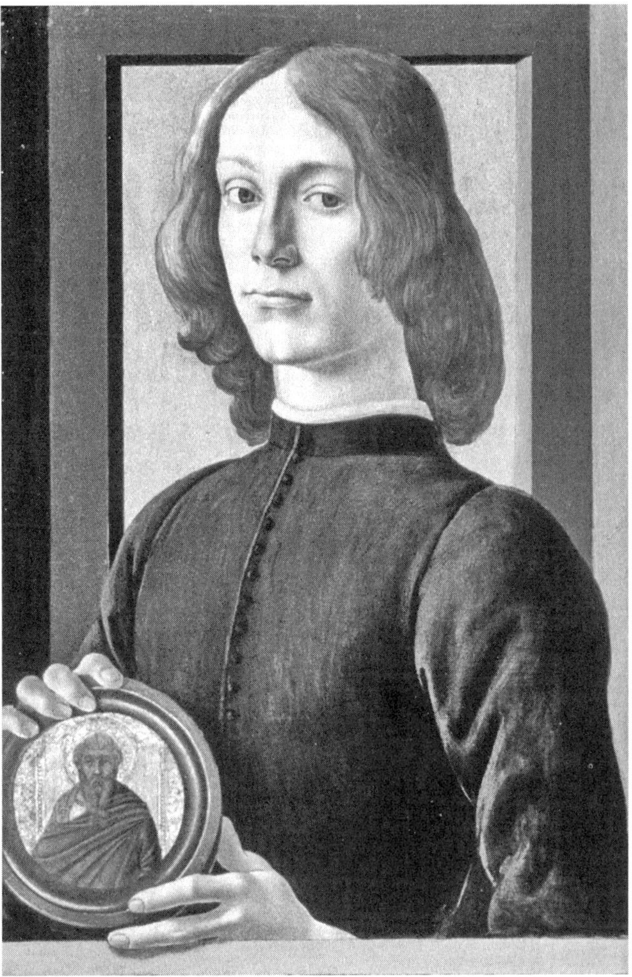

11.7 Substitution symbolized in the form of a painting-relic. Sandro Botticelli, *Portrait of Youth Holding an Icon*, oil on panel, 58.4 x 39.4 cm (ca. 1480). Solow collection, on loan to the National Gallery of Art, Washington. The round panel in the man's hands is a real fourteenth-century painting, embedded in a cavity in the modern panel.

art was the art of context sensitivity, advertising the time of its manufacture through the depiction of up-to-date hair and dress—an art whose secular interferences jammed up the works of substitution—in Western eyes the Eastern Church was the realm where not just individual images but substitution as a process had been preserved intact. The icons' arrival brought into the open a mutually defining encounter between models of image making. In contrast to the fashionable Western paintings of the day, the icons seemed authorless and therefore authoritative. But at the same time, the collecting, reframing, and publicizing of the icons staged them as autonomous and charismatic objects, portable objects with "careers," and in the clamor the claims of substitution were almost lost. The icons were both like and unlike works of art, and in the comparison the two categories, "work of art" and "cult image," were clarified. The isolation of the icon as a special category of image produced a quasi-anthropological view of religious images as a subset nested within art making. To adapt the terms but adjust the schema developed by Hans Belting: *Bild* (the cult image) did not cede to *Kunst* (art); rather, *Bild* was a retrospective myth invented by *Kunst*.[27]

Botticelli, within his artwork, presents an "image"—or rather, his surrogate does, the portrait's youthful subject. The re-presentation of the "icon" within this portrait creates an association with ancient painting. The pattern of the punch holes in the gold ground, extending vertically off the top and bottom edges of the icon, reveals that the portrait of the saint was not originally round. The portrayed collector, or the person from whom he acquired the picture, cut it down to the roundel format. The painting may have become a roundel, a format resonating with associations to ancient coins and *imagines clipeatae*, only when it was inserted into the modern painting. In its new form and setting the icon gathers authority and venerability. In contrast to modern painting, that is, in contrast to the portrait by Botticelli that surrounds it, the trecento fragment lives, for Botticelli and his patron, in a *natural* relation to antiquity. It was easy to see the saint's exotic beard, the pallium, and the arcane hand gesture as neither the inventions of a modern (fourteenth-century) artist nor the fruits of antiquarian research, but instead as the attributes of the saint himself, reliably transmitted across the centuries from work to work.[28] In the new assemblage, the icon appears not merely as a portrait of a saint but as a symbol of a whole class of paintings, and as an example of how a substitutional system works.

The dramatic staging of the icon alters the meaning of the enveloping work. A notionally normal fifteenth-century painting, one that wished to be like a fourteenth-century work, would simply "deliver" its contents. Instead, because it literally contains a fourteenth-century work, one which is substitutionally linked to even older works, the painting by Botticelli appears deficient and self-conscious. It invites reflection on its own mediality. The portrayed sitter holds and presents the sacred portrait, now for the first time clearly identifiable as the historical prototype of the profane portrait enveloping it. It is often observed that religious pictures in this period were attentive to innovations in secular portraiture. The history outlined here and in the previous section suggests a development in the other direction. Throughout the Middle Ages, painted portraits of living people had appeared as attendant, marginal figures of larger scenes, with only a few exceptions in the category of ruler portraits. To extract the portrait of a living individual from such a scene and make him or her the sole subject of a panel painting was a radical step. The Greek icons, prized as faithful reports on encounters with a physical person, became a major model for portraiture, the modern genre that to moderns symbolized art's ability to resist mortal temporality. In the opening paragraph of chapter 2 of *Della pittura*, Leon Battista Alberti celebrated painting for its capacity to "make the dead after many centuries almost come to life," a power that he relates directly to the central function of portraits in religious cults.[29]

It is easier to grasp this connection if one sets aside the prevailing notion of the icon as the emblem of mystical remove from earthly reality. In this period icons were understood primarily as examples of ancient portraiture, visual records that brought one face to face with the earliest personalities of Christian history. The art of portraiture was revived precisely in the half century between Alberti's treatise and Botticelli's portrait of a man holding an icon. Half-length and bust formats for portraits, no longer in profile but in frontal or three-quarter view, flourished in European art in the very years of the intensified importation of icons, after the Ferrara-Florence Council of 1438–1439 and especially after the fall of Constantinople in 1453. Portraiture came into being as a genre, as if to match the neologisms introduced to fifteenth-century inventories to describe Eastern icons: *dal petto in sù, demy-image, mezza fighura*.[30] The artists most interested in the Eastern icons—the Limbourgs, Robert Campin, Jan van Eyck, Rogier van der Weyden, Jacopo Bellini, Antonio Pisanello, Giovanni Bellini, Antonello da Messina—were also the artists that contributed most significantly to the early history of modern portraiture.

In both their icon-based religious pictures as well as in their portraits, Western artists elaborated formal devices such as parapets or windows in an effort to articulate and rationalize the half-length format of icons.[31] The entwined relation between the two types of image is made manifest in Netherlandish diptychs showing on the one side a half-length image of Christ or the Virgin, and on the other, a corresponding portrait of the donor. One such case is the diptych by Rogier van der Weyden for Philippe de Croÿ, the French nobleman who received a micromosaic icon as a gift from Sixtus IV (figures 11.8 and 11.9).[32] Rogier paired the portrait with a half-length Virgin and Child that seems to belong to a different realm, as indicated by the gold ground, a feature by now almost obsolete, used here perhaps to suggest that Rogier was only "reporting" on a venerable image.

And yet in other ways the two halves of the diptych are not so remote from one another. Technical analysis has revealed that originally the background of de Croÿ's portrait was not dark, as it is now, but was made up of a thin green glaze over a silver ground, now almost invisible under layers of overpaint.[33] The combination of gold for the sacred figure and silver for the secular one is not in the end very different from what we see in the Christ icon owned by de Croÿ (see figure 10.1), where the mosaic shimmers with gold but the framing added by de Croÿ shines decorously and

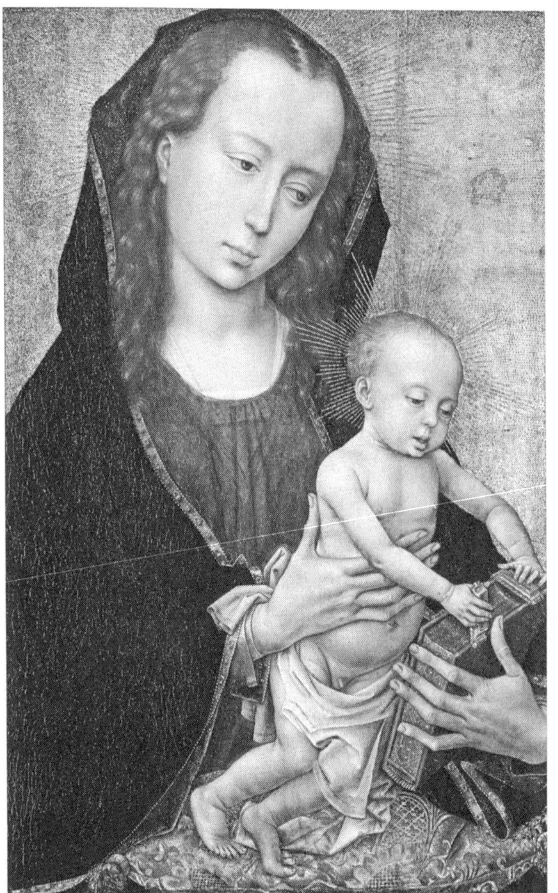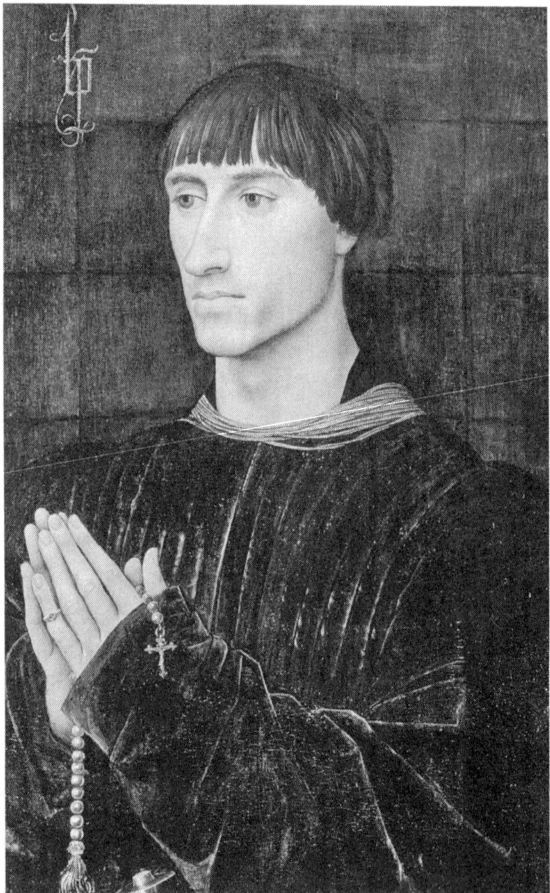

11.8–11.9 The common program of icon and modern portrait. Rogier van der Weyden, *Virgin and Child*, oil on masonite, transferred from canvas, originally on panel, 50.8 x 33 cm (ca. 1460), San Marino, California, Henry E. Huntington Library; and *Portrait of Philippe de Croÿ*, oil on panel, 51.5 x 33.6 cm (ca. 1460), Antwerp, Koninklijk Museum voor Schone Kunsten. The ambitious and self-aware artist van der Weyden takes the prestigious ancient type as a starting point and no more. The modern experiments with the forms of the Marian icon supposedly established by St. Luke now enter into a mutually reinforcing relationship with the half-length portrait of living people, at this point still a relative novelty.

deferentially in silver. The diptych thus observes the differences in status between the two figures, and yet at the same time links them through a medium, precious metal. On the one hand, de Croÿ is shown as if praying before an icon of the Virgin, clearly distanced from her. On the other hand, he has acceded to a privileged plane of communication precisely by inhabiting a physically parallel image. The portrait format here is undergoing dramatic changes on both sides. The icon is being modernized and the secular person is being elevated—elevated precisely through accession to the realm of the independent portrait, which for centuries had been reserved for royalty and religious figures. The diptych reveals the portrait format in a historical moment of extreme flexibility. The boundaries of the portrait are being extended, and yet this extension is consistent with the original function of portraiture as established by the icon, namely to distribute the appearance of a historical person across time and space.

The bust format represented a fragment of a person, implying selection from a whole and therefore an adaptation of experience to the rhetoric of witnessing. The bust format reiterated and clarified the synecdochic structure of portraits as a class, which make a given moment in the life stand for the life and make an external, physical description stand for the whole person. The reading of the icon as fragment of a larger whole was in part determined by the larger context in which they were acquired: as survivors from the wreckage of a crumbling empire, they assumed the burden of standing for a lost cultural unity. The reception of Greek icons and relics was overshadowed by the loss of the Holy Land and the impending fall of Constantinople and the Eastern Empire. These objects were traces of a long history of loss and attempted recovery: they had been retrieved or looted by pilgrims and crusaders or offered as diplomatic gifts by Eastern princes in need of Western succor. They acquired the status of fragments, of relics, on their way to the West.

The other significant source of the modern portrait, beside the painted icon, was the ancient sculptural bust. Just as ancient portrait painting survived in the form of the icon, the bust portrait persisted throughout the Middle Ages primarily in the form of the reliquary bust.[34] Like icons, reliquary busts also lived an unstable temporal life: the presence of the saint's relic inside them forced an association with the time of the saint, a more or less remote antiquity. Of less interest to most beholders were overly precise questions about when the sculptural "shell" was produced. Irving Lavin noted that whereas ancient Roman busts are generally rounded at the bottom and hollowed out at the back, medieval reliquary busts are usually cut straight across the chest and are modeled fully in the round.[35] The ancient bust is presented as a complete and artificial whole, whereas the reliquary bust is conceived as a fragment, a part of a human being. The fragment conception, which insists on the portrait as a synecdoche, recapitulates the semiotic claims of the relic itself, which is also a part of a whole, a remnant of a body that carries something of the force of the living person. The fragment conception was taken over in the early Renaissance portrait bust. The first modern sculpted portrait bust, the bronze likeness of Emperor John VIII, is cut off at the bottom like a bust reliquary (see figure 10.7). The work is thus similar to nearly contemporaneous bust portraits associated with Donatello, to whom the John VIII bust has at times been attributed: the *San Rossore* in Pisa, for example, which is a reliquary bust that takes on some of the qualities of portraiture by endowing the long-dead saint with highly characteristic features; and the *Bust of a Youth* in the Bargello, whose oval relief in front of the breast resembles the jewels or openings often seen in that position in bust reliquaries.[36]

The circularity of the molded frame of the false icon embedded in Botticelli's portrait articulates the new closure that attends the conceptual shift from functional cult image to collectible art work. The youth rests the roundel directly on the parapet, another framing device. The icon is placed at the very level of the youth's body, the waist, where the figure of the saint—in its original, unmutilated form—would very likely have been truncated, suggesting a relationship of succession between venerable icon and youthful portrait. Like the saint in the roundel, the figure of the youth is also starkly isolated, the strips of dark and light that make up the embrasure around him reiterating the work of framing that went into his portrait.

The portrait does more than simply offer the icon as a model for portraiture. It is what the icon has become in this refined youth's hands that matters. The youth props the roundel on the parapet, a contact of edge with edge that makes us feel this icon's objecthood. It is tilted slightly up; we see the bottom of the icon's round frame and appreciate its portability. This is an object that needs to be held and presented, a work whose real frame now is the hands of its owner and the polite or learned conversation that begins when it is picked up and held out for someone to admire. The youth tilts the roundel towards the source of light, upper left, which dramatically picks out all of these framing elements—the repeated ridges of the molding, the youth's delicate fingers, carefully kept just clear of the relic's surface. The portrait stages the transformation of an excerpt into a self-sufficient "work," glossing the process of framing and reframing that goes into making a work of art, and in this sense it tells its own prehistory. But it also marks the differences, the gap between the image of the venerable saint, whose frontal and ancient appearance express his alignment with noncontingent truth, and this attentive but somewhat arch youth, who turns to a viewer who might not know him. In effect, the objectification of the old panel, its reframing and presentation as a relic, releases in it an uncanny quality of animation. The saint looks up in the direction of the light, as if in this newly mobile condition his image must maintain, compass-like, an active relation to this immutable source. The "image" (Belting's *Bild*) comes into being in the hands of "art" (*Kunst*), and seems to say, "I am real, the rest is fiction."[37]

TWELVE

Author and *Acheiropoieton*

Botticelli's portrait of a youth holding an icon is in many ways a singular work, and yet in its comparison of the two modes of production, substitutional and performative, and in its nested structure, it is not alone among works of this time. Another programmatic statement, much more public, was the Monument to Giotto on the south wall of the interior of Florence Cathedral, perhaps the first monument ever erected in honor of a visual artist (figure 12.1). This pioneering exercise in art-historical myth-making was carried out in 1490, a century and a half after the artist's death. It comprises an epitaph composed by Angelo Poliziano and a relief portrait of Giotto by the Florentine sculptor Benedetto da Maiano. The inscription expresses supreme artistic self-consciousness:

> I am he through whom painting, dead, returned to life
> and whose hand was as sure as it was adept.
> What my art lacked was lacking in nature herself.
> To no one was it given to paint better or more.
> Do you admire the great belltower resounding with sacred bronze?
> This too on the basis of my model has grown to the stars.
> After all, I am Giotto. What need was there to relate these things?
> This name has stood as the equal to any long poem.
> Deceased 1336. Erected by the citizens 1490.[1]

Rather than simply extolling Giotto's accomplishments, the epitaph has the artist speak, post-mortem, in the first person. *Ille ego sum*: the first three words render the first person's intrusion into the third-person account, almost as if Giotto has awakened from the dead to take over his own epitaph. The formula was well known in the epigrammatic tradition and was especially frequent in those epigrams appended to *imagines* or portraits. The formula *ille ego sum*, for example, is used by Martial 9.53 for an epigram referring to the image on the tomb of a prematurely deceased chari-oteer.[2] Several other examples of "speaking epigrams" can be found in the *Carmina Latina Epigraphica*, all referring to tombs and monuments.[3]

Poliziano's epigram is more than simply an application of this tradition. The speaker of the lines is no ordinary commemorated person but specifically an author claiming responsibility for his work. The epigram adopts a well-known device, known as the *sphragis* or "authenticating seal," in which the author of a poem directly addresses his audience to give autobiographical information and proclaim his accomplishments. A sort of embedded signature, both belonging to the poem and branding it as if from the exterior, the device was not a late literary development but was used already by the sixth century BCE poet Theognis. The *sphragis* may have been a corollary of the move from orality to literacy that was occurring at the time of Theognis: the device proclaimed what was most clearly expected in committing poetry to writing, namely a new notion of textual stability and literary property.[4] The *sphragis*, in that case, arose with writing. It is not surprising, therefore, to find it invoked whenever notions of authorship are newly at stake.

To take a few examples that would have been known to Poliziano: Ovid introduces a *sphragis* at book 4, verse 8, of the *Tristia*, in which he addresses the posthumous reader and describes his birthplace and his work as a poet of love.[5] He includes another at the end of book 2 of the *Ars Amatoria*, in which he encourages the lover to use the weapons he has provided and enjoins him to inscribe on his trophies the words "Ovid was my master."[6] Perhaps the best-known example was to be found in the opening to the *Aeneid* as transmitted by Donatus and Servius:

> I am he [*Ille ego*] who once tuned my song on a slender reed,
> then, leaving the woodland,
> constrained the neighboring fields to serve the husbandmen,
> however grasping —
> a work welcome to farmers: but now of Mars's bristling
> [arms and the man I sing][7]

The verses are now generally considered to be spurious later additions and modern editions of the poem begin with the famous next line: *Arma virumque cano*.[8] Fifteenth-century editions of the poem, however, carried the incipit beginning with the words *Ille ego*.[9] Apart from the obviously similar opening, these famous Virgilian verses form an especially strong parallel to the Giotto inscription in that they offer an account of the artistic corpus in more than one genre (bucolic, pastoral, and now epic), just as the Giotto epitaph describes the artist's work both as painter and as architect.

The combination of *sphragis* and speaking epigram was especially well chosen for an epigram celebrating a painter. As we have seen, the speaking epigram was used especially in association with images. The insistent

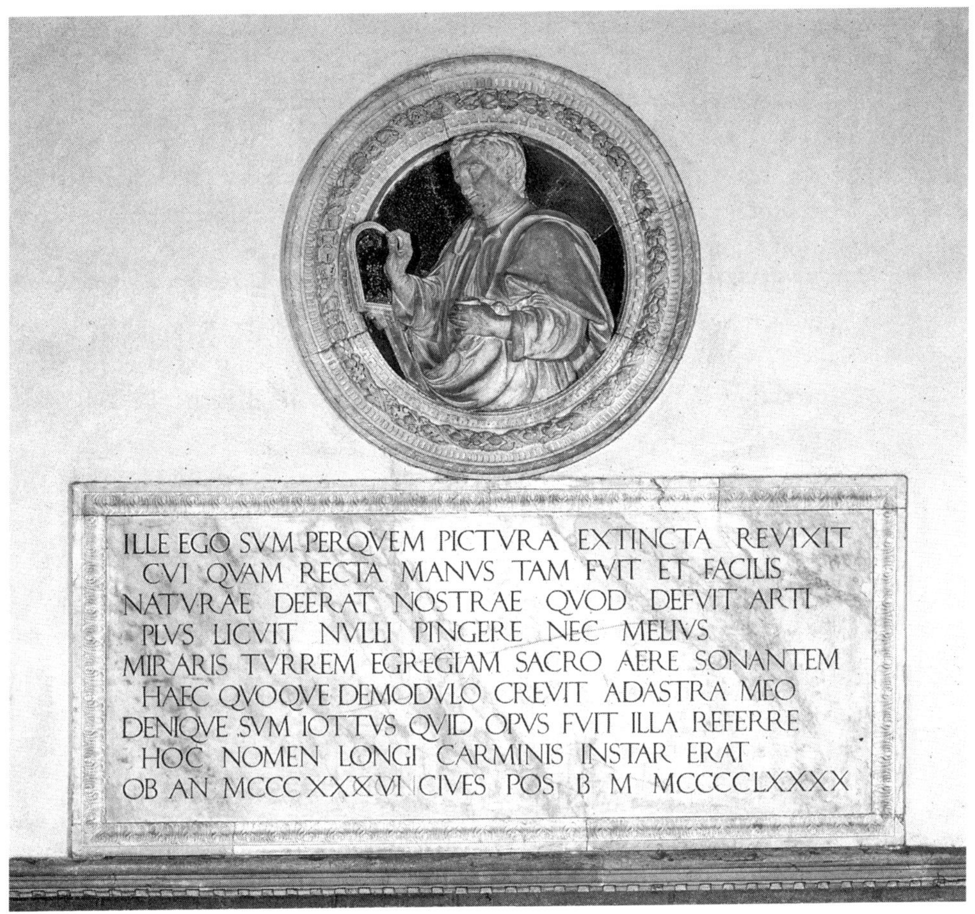

12.1 The first art-historical monument? Benedetto da Maiano, Monument to Giotto, marble and mosaic (1490). Florence, Cathedral. In the inscription, written by the humanist Angelo Poliziano, Giotto gives voice to his own achievements in the fields of painting and architecture. The inscription says the monument was erected by the citizens of Florence but in fact this act of commemoration was engineered by Lorenzo de' Medici, then de facto ruler of the city.

present tense of the image opens a widening rift between the "then" of the speaking subject's life and a succession of "nows," into the future. The represented person speaks about the past but from a permanent present tense. Giotto recalls his achievements from a vantage point after his own death, from the position of the retrospective monument; it is as if he has awakened from the dead to speak his own epitaph, again and again. In a sense, every image carries off this magical overcoming of time by introducing a fragment of a past reality into a permanent presentness. The spatial presence of the image "reads" as a temporal present tense. It is just the

125

paradox that a literary mind such as Poliziano's would want to invoke when celebrating a painter.

In literary texts, as we have seen, the *sphragis* introduces a highly visual moment, an authorial self-portrait in which the author reveals himself and brands his text with a proprietary mark. This effect assumes a special force in the case of an author who is also a visual artist. What is implicit in the convention of the speaking epigram—that the image makes the dead person speak in the present—is made explicit by the device of the *sphragis*, in which the artist-author gives an account of his work. In Poliziano's epigram for the Giotto monument, the account begins, suitably, with a reflection on resurrection, not of the painter but of painting itself: "I am he through whom painting, dead, returned to life."

Although the *sphragis* and the speaking epigram are highly image-like moments within a text, they are still established literary devices. This epigram, applying the devices to a painter, must go one step further. As if to dramatize the difference between the visual artist and the writer, the impatient painter *interrupts* his own epigram: "After all, I am Giotto. What need is there to relate these things? This name has stood as the equal to any long poem." The gesture stages a topos of word-and-image confrontations. Within the linguistic context of the epigram, the name *Iottus* is a stand-in for the image that renders words superfluous, a parallel brought home by the use of the word *instar*, which resonates with references to visual modeling. In fact, the name *Iottus is* painted on some of the painter's works and thus as brand or logo functions both as word and image.[10]

The epitaph inscribed in marble is itself an intermediary entity, between word and image, both text and monument. The epigram thus takes as its subject matter the basic nature of monument-making, an event by which a name is transformed into an image, the event by which the name Giotto becomes the logo IOTTUS. Only the names of the greatest artists can assume this kind of iconic force, capable—like the painter's works themselves—of summoning a whole series of images and a whole history before one's eyes. Beyond extolling Giotto's various achievements, the monument also celebrates and confirms the gathering of these achievements under the artist's name. It marks the historical fact that in Florence, at least, a quasi-literary notion of authorship has been successfully transferred to the work of a visual artist. The name is a fixed point that anchors fame. The name raises a protest against the powerful and perhaps finally irrefutable thesis that agency can never really be localized but is instead always dispersed across a field of persons and events.

Almost inevitably, the principle of substitution exerts a counter-acting pull here, in a monument whose brief is to suggest that not only princes

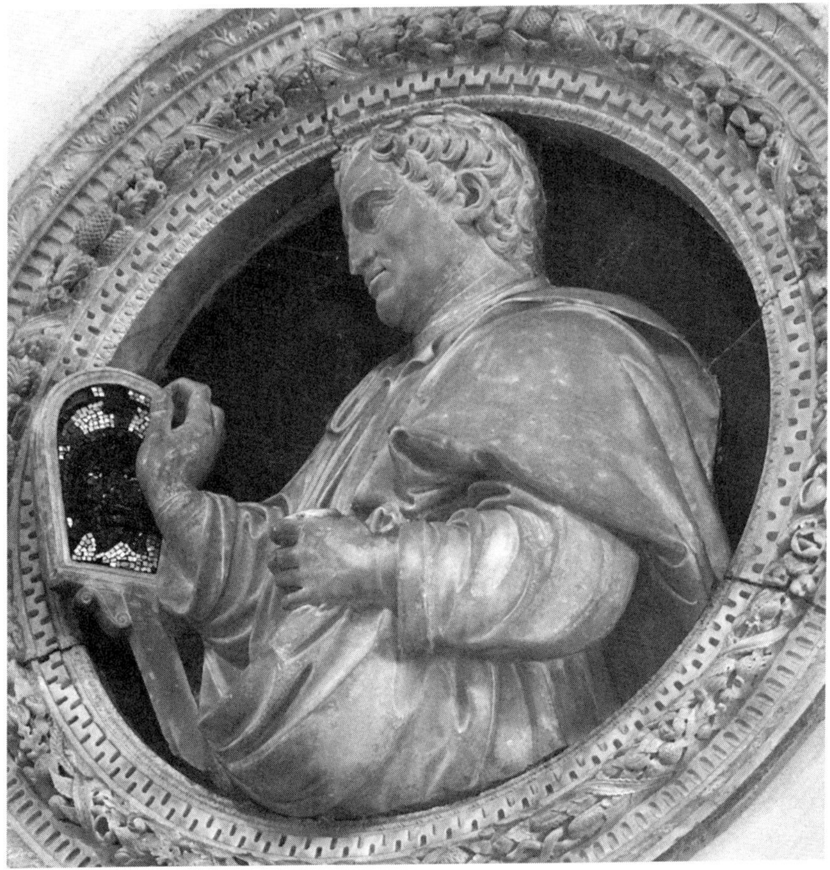

12.2 The artist as relay. Benedetto da Maiano, Monument to Giotto, detail. Florence, Cathedral. The celebrated artist, dead for more than 150 years, is shown making an icon of Christ—and not a painted icon but a mosaic icon. Moreover, the icon is clearly shown to be of the type of the Mandylion (figure 18.4), the towel on which Christ's features were directly impressed. It is an image invented by no one, but continually refashioned by Christian artists through the centuries, including Giotto, who is adding a tessera to the still unfinished icon.

and writers but also artist-authors deserve a monument. The model of work-for-work substitution, which spreads production out across a chain of mutual equivalency, had the merit of being true to the principle of distributed agency, in contrast to the model of authorial production. The antiauthorial element in the monument comes through, not surprisingly, in the part of the monument that deals in images. The tondo by Benedetto da Maiano, portraying the artist at work, stands in a paradoxical relationship to the inscription below. Whereas the inscription celebrates Giotto's work as painter and architect, the relief shows him at work as a mosaicist (figure 12.2). This may be seen as a reference to Giotto's authorship of the Navicella mosaic in St. Peter's, the only modern work of art mentioned by Alberti in his treatise *On Painting*.[11] However, here Giotto is shown at work on an icon, a bust of Christ.[12] The bust of Christ was the image type most detached from association with individual authorship. Any images of the Holy Face carried associations with the most famous nonauthored image of all, the towel on which Christ's face had been "mechanically" impressed, a legendary image that came down as the Veronica in the West and the Mandylion in the East and was transmitted through innumerable icon panels. One of the most authoritative busts of Christ was the mosaic in the apse of the Lateran basilica in Rome, where Giotto had once worked.[13] In his own monument, then, the great author and founder transmits a nonauthored image in a nonauthorial medium.

Here, just as in the Botticelli portrait of a man holding an icon (see figure 11.7), tensions between substitutional and performative theories of the artifact's genealogy are figured as a relationship of embeddedness. The distinction between the two theories reads as a differential between contained and container. The holy portrait, with its rhetoric of remote origins, is surrounded by fabricated modern things, things less ancient. Those enveloping objects (other pictures, liturgical apparatus, buildings) might well claim their own substitutional connections to the deep past. But once contrasted to an internally nested icon, the artifact with the strongest claims to authority, the surrounding objects re-emerged as merely modern. The relationship of enclosure permitted the nested image to define itself against the nest, and vice versa. For it was the piling up of context-reflexive costumes and stylistic signatures in the parergal zone surrounding the auratic core, the traces of modernity deplored by conservative theologians, that helped create the icon as icon.

In Benedetto's portrait, Giotto works on a small mosaic panel. His right hand is raised and between his thumb and forefinger, where one expects to find a brush, there is a mosaic cube (figure 12.3). As we saw in section 10, one of the prized categories of Eastern icons was the portable mosaic, often called micromosaic on account of the extremely small tesserae. The origins and meaning of these objects are not at all clear. Only fifty micromosaics survive, of which some are partially destroyed or restored beyond recognition. Thirty-four of them date from the latest, or Palaiologan, period. They were produced in Constantinople, but almost all the surviving examples are in the West, suggesting that they were an especially prized export item.[14] Lorenzo de' Medici, who sponsored and probably conceived the Giotto monument, was himself an enthusiastic collector of micromosaic icons. All of the eleven Greek icons in Lorenzo de' Medici's collection

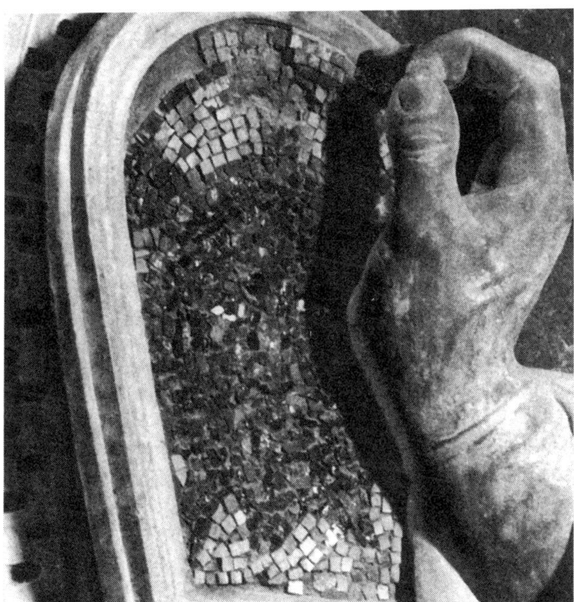

12.3 **The artist as relay.** Benedetto da Maiano, Monument to Giotto, detail.

were in mosaic.[15] Part of the attraction of these works was that mosaic was an ancient technique largely lost in the West. The mosaic medium was in itself a strong advertisement of antiquity. Although classical sources spoke of wall and panel painting, there was almost no sense in the Renaissance of what those works had looked like.[16] Ancient mosaics, by contrast, could easily be seen first-hand—for example the fifth-century mosaics in the chapels of Santa Rufina and St. John the Evangelist at the Baptistery at the Lateran, the fifth-century mosaics at Santa Maria Maggiore, and the remains of plenty of earlier Imperial Roman mosaics at the Baths of Caracalla and elsewhere—and so became by default the automatically imagined medium of two-dimensional ancient images. The fifteenth-century physician Michele Savonarola, for example, speaks of Giotto as "the first to make from ancient and mosaic images modern ones, in marvelous fashion."[17]

Mosaic also displayed, for fifteenth-century Western Europeans, a lesser degree of time-sensitivity than painting. Mosaic translated painting into durable and repairable form. The tesserae did not fade; and if they fell, they could easily be replaced one by one by a moderately skilled craftsman, with no impairment of the image's reference to origins. Mosaic lifted images away from the real-time process of their production. In painting, the pigments are finely ground and mixed with a medium, resulting in minimal friction between the movement of the artist's hand and the work that results from it. Every stroke on the painting's surface becomes an index, in effect a signature, of the artist. In mosaic, the material building blocks of the image do not disappear into the medium but remain integral, introducing a remove between author and image. That gap is filled by the inherent properties of materials—resplendent stones, reflecting glass, shining gold—that involve another register of creative forces and that open the image, abyss-like, onto multiple origin points and temporalities. In contrast to the analogue condition of painting, mosaic is a digital medium. Mosaic subsists in a substitution-ready state. Vasari perceived this property of mosaics and described it with recourse to a metaphor of reignition:

> It is certain that mosaic is the most durable painting there is, for the other [ordinary] kind of painting is extinguished over time, but this kind of painting in being continually made is always ignited. And whereas painting on its own is consumed, mosaic due to its long life can almost be called eternal.[18]

To believe that a recently-made mosaic was somehow also an antiquity was therefore no foolish delusion.

With its power to resist time, the medium itself had maintained the chain leading back to the ancient sources. The arrival of the Greek icons, painted and mosaic alike, beginning in the thirteenth and accelerating in the fifteenth century, confronted Western Europeans with the realization that their own art may have lost this capacity. But by 1490 mosaic was a lost technique, at least in Tuscany and Rome (not to mention transalpine Europe).[19] Lorenzo de' Medici, not content simply to collect the Greek icons, was spurred into action and set about promoting a mosaic revival, a challenging enterprise in the absence of any local tradition. He directed two sets of brothers, Domenico and Davide Ghirlandaio and Monte and Gherardo di Giovanni, to learn and practice the craft.[20] This is the immediate context for the Giotto monument in Florence Cathedral. Lorenzo had plans to decorate the interior of Brunelleschi's cupola with mosaics.[21] In 1490, the same year in which Lorenzo engineered the erection of the monument that shows Giotto as a master mosaicist, he contracted Domenico Ghirlandaio and Gherardo di Giovanni to provide mosaic decoration for the chapel of St. Zenobius, patron saint of Florence, also in Florence Cathedral.[22]

These efforts, if they had been successful, would have produced powerful anachronic effects. Zenobius was the first bishop of Florence; his chapel, in the subterranean vault underneath the high altar of the cathedral, was a symbolic kernel of the cathedral itself. To decorate it in mosaic would have been to give it, retroactively, the character of a primitive Christian sacellum. If the cupola had also received mosaic cladding the entire cathedral would have come out of these renovations newly retrofitted with ancient resonances, more like the Florence Baptistery, which although built in the eleventh century managed to convince later observers for centuries to come

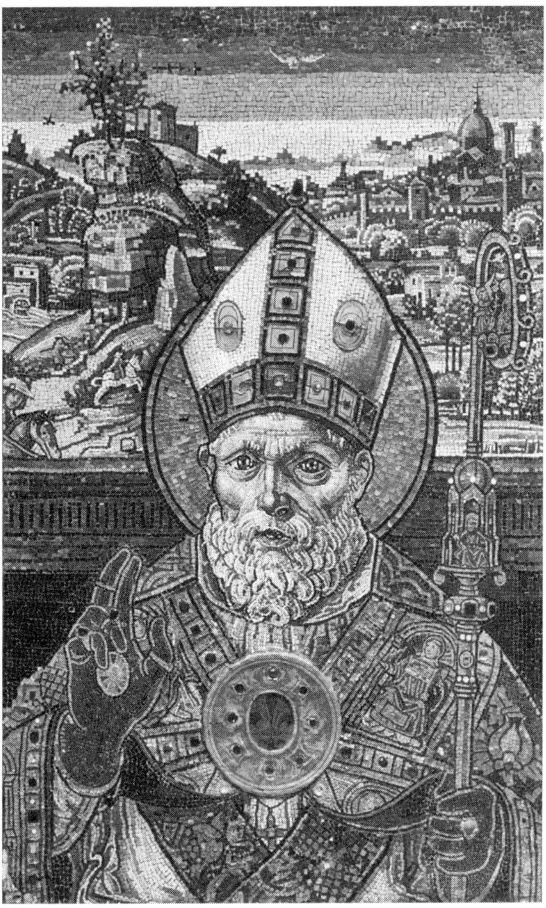

12.4 The mosaic revival in Florence. Monte di Giovanni, *Saint Zenobius*, mosaic, 60 x 91 cm (1505). Florence, Museo dell'Opera del Duomo. In the 1490s Lorenzo de' Medici launched a mosaic revival in Florence, planning mosaic decoration for the interior of the cupola and for the chapel of St. Zenobius in the Duomo. This portrait, a test panel, is one of the few relics of that incomplete experiment.

that it substituted for a Roman building. Very little came of these initiatives, but in 1505 Monte di Giovanni did produce a sort of test panel, a mosaic icon of Zenobius himself now in the Museo dell'Opera del Duomo (figure 12.4).[23] To render the saint in mosaic was a time-bending gesture, instantly associating the image with the antiquity of the early Christian bishop. In the background one sees a view of Brunelleschi's cupola and Giotto's bell-tower. Pixelated and defamiliarized, these structures become temporally unstable, as if they had been landmarks of Florence from time immemorial.

The mosaic revival spurred by Lorenzo de' Medici returns us to Florence Cathedral, where the Monument to Giotto stands. Here the founder

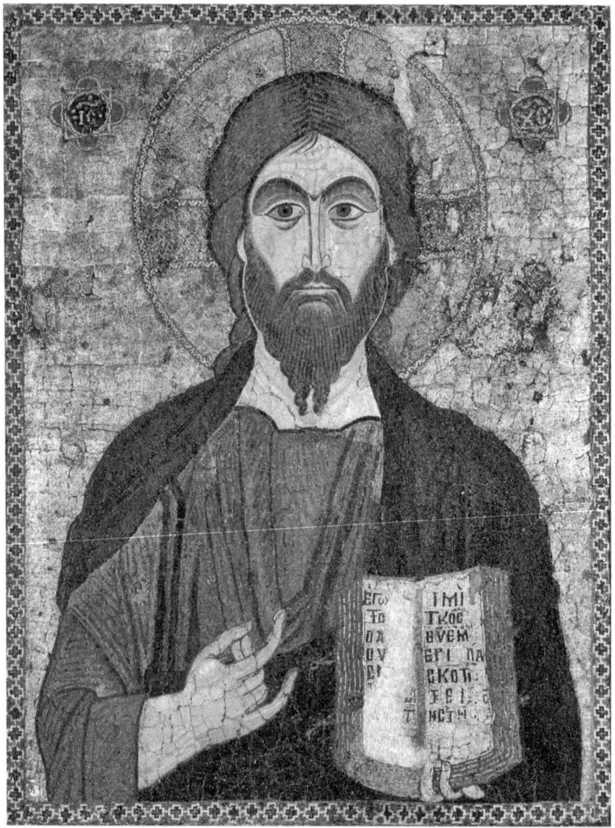

12.5 A mosaic icon once in the collection of Lorenzo de' Medici. *Christ Pantokrator,* micromosaic, 41 x 54 cm (twelfth century). Florence, Museo del Bargello. This large icon, composed of vanishingly tiny tesserae, was one of eleven Byzantine micromosaic icons owned by Lorenzo de' Medici. It remained a prized object in the Medici collection and in the sixteenth century was given an ebony frame.

of Florentine art is shown as already, or rather still, a master mosaicist, a tessera held deftly between his fingers. Giotto was not only the first great modern painter, he was also the last great artist with a living connection to antiquity. Turning him into a master of the art of mosaic confirmed this linking role. In the words of the theorist Antonio Filarete,

> This art [mosaic], as is said, is lost, and from Giotto until now has been rarely used. He did some: in Rome one can see by his hand the *Ship* [the Navicella] in St. Peter's in Rome. And a certain Roman Pietro Cavallini also made works in the art in his time, and he was a very good master. I have also seen it done in a small panel in Venice, which came from Greece, done very solemnly and with very minute pieces, which they say are made of eggshells.[24]

The painters of circa 1300 were still in touch with ancient traditions. The monument in Florence Cathedral gathers together all these associations by showing Giotto working as a mosaicist within the oldest image tradition of Christian art, the portrait of Christ.[25] The one Greek icon that can still be traced back to Lorenzo de' Medici's collection is, in fact, a micromosaic bust of Christ, now in the Bargello Museum in Florence (figure 12.5).[26] In the monument, Giotto acts as a relay between this "antiquity" and the present. He is the master author whose acquired expertise in the non-authorial medium of mosaic ensures the faithful transmission of the original and authorless Christian *imago*. He grasps neither brush nor stylus, index-generating extensions of the artist's hand, but the tessera, the particle of color that offers no information until it is joined to a hundred others. Giotto did not physically produce the piece of stone he holds in his hand and he did not invent the image before him; instead, he will expertly patch the tessera in and so preserve the face of Christ. The implication of Benedetto's relief is that such an icon is never made but always restored.

This is an unfamiliar twist on *rinascimento dell'antichità*. The Giotto monument gives us not a lucid reconstruction of a historical style associated with Greco-Roman antiquity, but instead a structural lesson in the time-collapsing efficacy of images. The image of Christ within the monument is a special assertion of this efficacy, not only because it is the Holy Face, but also because it is a mosaic. It is not a fictional mosaic, of the sort one sees in paintings of the time that reproduce, say, mosaic apses (see Carpaccio's *Saint Augustine in His Study*, figure 4.1), but an actual mosaic made up of real tesserae. It is a sample of the mosaic art safely embedded within the modern fiction, partly deactivated by its oblique disposition within the relief tondo and the occluding hand of Giotto. The mosaic in Benedetto's representation is what it purports to be; in its reality it breaks through the temporal layers that make up the monument. It is an advertisement and first product, one of the very few, of the mosaic revival of circa 1490.[27] It also demonstrates the time-resistant virtue of the art. The mosaic reports back to the originary portrait of Christ and yet it is also plainly of the time of Giotto, who holds one of the tesserae that would complete it. And it is a product of 1490. It belongs to each of these moments simultaneously, threading them together. Giotto is not, therefore, merely commemorated as the restorer of ancient art; he is celebrated as the restorer of art's capacity to make past really present. The wording of the inscription is, in fact, well chosen, calling him the one *through whom* painting returned to life. Giotto revealed that art had never died, that its capacity for self-generation had been kept alive all along in the channel of icons. He was the author who restored authorless authority.

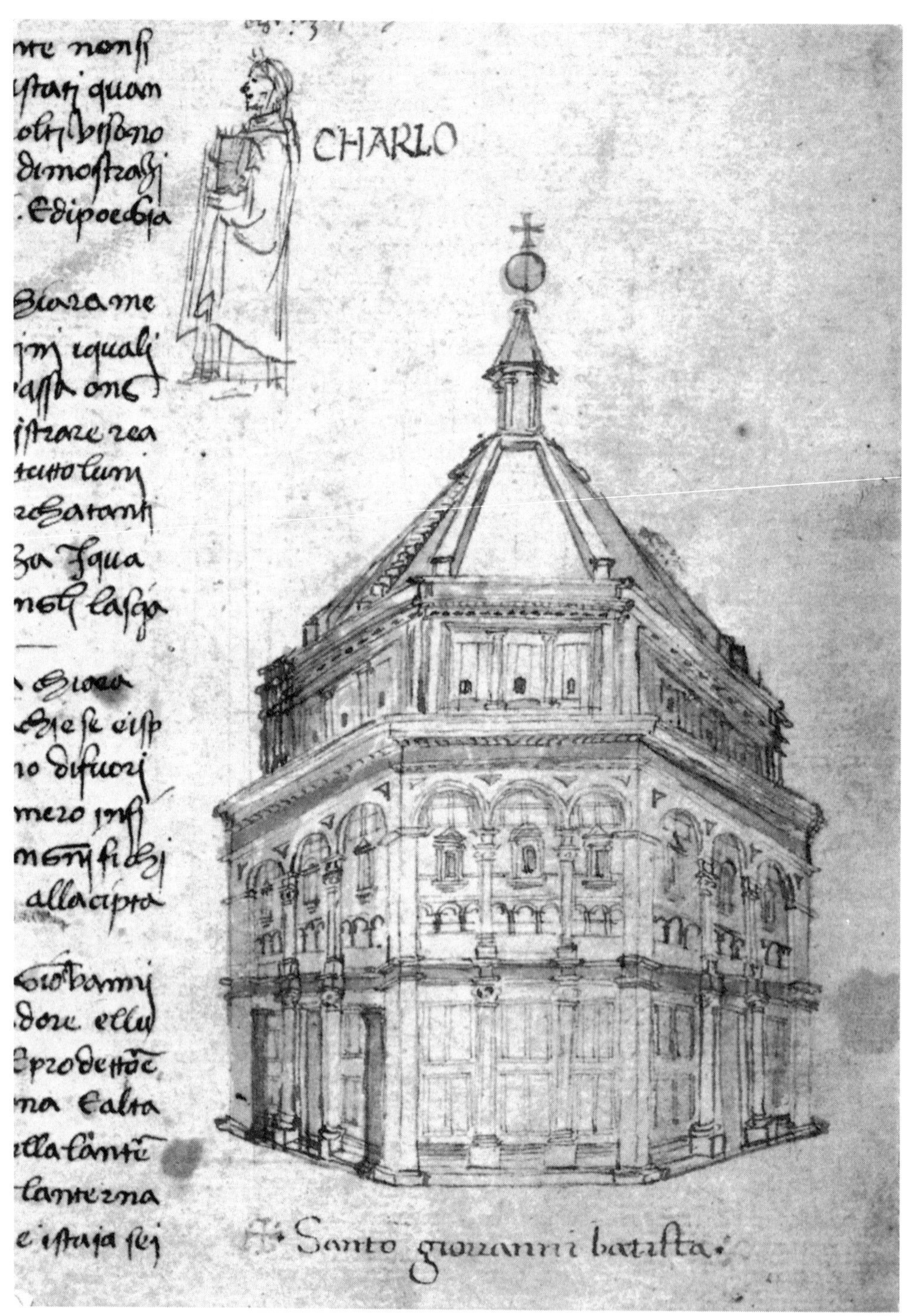

13.1 The most famous case of Renaissance misdating. Marco di Bartolommeo Rustici, *View of the Baptistery in Florence,* pen and ink (mid-fifteenth century). Florence, Seminario Arcivescovile, Codex Rustici, vol. 1, fol. 8r. In his *Zibaldone* or book of commonplaces, Rustici, a Florentine artisan, says that the Baptistery was built in the time of the emperor Augustus. The building was universally believed to be a temple of Mars—refurbished and repaired, no doubt, but still essentially an ancient Roman structure. In fact, it was built in the eleventh and twelfth centuries.

THIRTEEN

Antiquity of Buildings Overrated

Through the retroactivating art of mosaic, Lorenzo de' Medici attempted to affirm the antiquity of Florence Cathedral, the seat of Florence's first bishop, the fourth-century St. Zenobius. Lorenzo was linking the cathedral to the powerful substitutional efficacy of the Baptistery of San Giovanni in the facing square. Yet when Filippo Brunelleschi painted the Baptistery in correct perspective, probably in the second decade of the fifteenth century, or when it was drawn in pen and ink on the pages of the Codex Rustici, the building was barely four hundred years old (figure 13.1).[1] Yet the Baptistery enjoyed the status of a Roman antiquity. Precisely those scholars and architects most interested in identifying, measuring, and drawing the real relics of ancient Rome, like Brunelleschi, were asserting the great age and exemplarity of the Florentine Baptistery. The architects quoted the Baptistery in their own modern buildings. Texts described the Baptistery as "antique." The Codex Rustici reports that the building was "made in the time of the emperor Octavian." In the middle of the sixteenth century Giorgio Vasari, justifying the stylistic choices of Brunelleschi and other fifteenth-century Florentine architects, was still describing the Baptistery as a "most ancient temple."[2] One could almost conclude that the Renaissance — the recreation of the cultural achievements of the ancients — was built on false premises.[3]

The paradox is acute and not easy to explain. How could the Florentines have misdated their own Baptistery? Did they not know that this perfect structure had been consecrated by Pope Nicholas II in 1059? They *did* know; and at the same time they thought beyond this knowledge. For the scholars and patriots of the fifteenth and sixteenth centuries were also aware that the eleventh-century octagon was not the first building built on that site. The original Baptistery, whose traces were in fact invisible to fifteenth-century eyes, was erected perhaps around 500; another one succeeded it a century later.[4] For Brunelleschi and Vasari the existing building was simply the last link in a vertical chain stretching back to Florence's pagan origins. The Baptistery substituted for its own predecessors.

An art historian, following Erwin Panofsky, might describe the creative cross wiring surrounding the Baptistery as a pseudomorphosis, that is, an investment of historical form with meaning that it had not possessed in the past (see section 5). Or, following Panofsky's teacher Adolph Goldschmidt, the art historian might recognize an episode of *Formenspaltung* or "formal disintegration": a profitable misunderstanding and dismantling of an earlier artistic formula that in the end generates new formulas.[5] But the Florentines were thinking completely reasonably about the Baptistery. There were no misunderstandings. The observers of the Renaissance, who had no access to modern art-historical libraries stocked with comparative material, had little capacity to "parse" a building—that is, to say with any certainty which aspects of the building's form or even which columns or capitals derived from the predecessor structures. Neither architects nor scholars were practicing a philology of architecture that might distinguish building fabrics and serve as the basis for a reconstruction of building histories. They had little interest in doing so. The label "antique" left unresolved—deliberately unresolved—the distinctions between *being* an old building, *replacing* an earlier building, and *altering* an earlier building. And after all the Baptistery in Florence shared many features, in structure and in detail, with the Pantheon in Rome.[6] The hypothesis of substitutability allowed Brunelleschi and Vasari to *look through* the eleventh- and twelfth-century buildings of Florence to the true meaning hiding behind them, namely, the normativity of the ancient Roman building manner.

The overall pattern of credulous reception of old artifacts, especially of the cynosural objects associated with national or civic origins, was scarcely disrupted, and was in some ways reinforced, by Renaissance scholarship. A small company of fortunate statues, the *mirabilia* or wonders, had been salvaged from the wreckage of antiquity and displayed throughout the Middle Ages.[7] Everyone remembered from Pliny what monuments had once meant in the public life of Athens and Rome. The *mirabilia* were almost always misidentified. The Dioscuri or *Horse Tamers* on the Quirinal in Rome were interpreted by the author of the *Marvels of Rome*, a standard guide for pilgrims composed in the twelfth century and many times copied, as a pair of naked philosophers called Phidias and Praxiteles.[8] From the mid-sixteenth century through the eighteenth the best opinion held the Quirinal horsemen to be portraits of Alexander and Bucephalus, in duplicate.[9] The equestrian statue of Marcus Aurelius at the Lateran, meanwhile, was believed to be a portrait of the Emperor Constantine; or Theodoric the Great; or a Roman knight, riding bareback, who had defeated a dwarfish king. In the fifteenth and sixteenth centuries the identity of the statue switched from Septimius Severus, to Commodus, to Lucius Verus before settling on Marcus Aurelius.[10] Scholars were dissatisfied with these not very adhesive labels and yet were themselves incapable of dating statues by internal material criteria. When Leonardo da Vinci visited Pavia in the company of Francesco di Giorgio in 1490, he admired the ancient equestrian statue known as the *Regisole*, probably in origin a late antique statue of Theodoric. This artifact provoked him to his most trenchant pronouncement about the superiority of ancient art: "to imitate ancient things is more laudable than to imitate modern ones."[11] And yet the statue he was admiring had been heavily restored, and in relatively recent times. The Milanese destroyed the statue in 1315 and took the pieces back to Milan, from where they were rescued by the Pavians and used to recompose the statue in Pavia in 1335. Among other alterations, the restored statue substituted a little dog for the barbarian originally shown underneath the horse's front hoofs.[12] Because the statue was destroyed in 1796, we cannot know how deep the restoration went, but it is clear that Leonardo's words of appreciation addressed a significantly remanaged late antique work, hardly a classical antiquity.

Local experts routinely misdated and misidentified old buildings. Enigmatic towers or round or polygonal structures were almost automatically assigned pagan pedigrees.[13] Such fictions were not only the stuff of ill-informed *campanilismo* and popular lore. The Renaissance scholar's new-won knowledge of pagan cults and iconographies did not necessarily disrupt the architectural conversion narratives. The church of San Lorenzo in Milan was for a long time described as a temple of Hercules founded by Emperor Maximianus in the late third century. The Romanesque church of San Fedele in Como was described until the seventeenth century as an ancient temple of Hercules. The eleventh-century Duomo Vecchio of Arezzo was still described by Vasari, a native of the city, as a fourth-century structure.[14] Santa Costanza in Rome, the mausoleum of Emperor Constantine's daughter, was on the basis of vineyard imagery in the vault mosaics identified as a temple of Bacchus.[15] Shapeless architectural remnants were even harder to date. The Biblical scholar, theologian, and cardinal Egidio da Viterbo believed the ruins of a Langobard fortress to be precious remains of Etruscan architecture.[16] In Trier—a city described by the antiquarian and historian Hartmann Schedel as "a city so old that it was founded 1,947 years before the birth of Christ, in the time of Abraham, by Trebeta the brother of King Ninus, who had been driven by Queen Semiramis out of Assyria"[17]—the fourth-century ruins of the imperial baths, three-quarters the size of the Baths of Caracalla, were interpreted by scholars, including the historian Beatus Rhenanus, as a palace dating back to the very origins of the city.[18] The archeological ambitions of sixteenth-century scholars could create confusion as easily as dispel it. The humanist

Caspar Bruschius, intrigued by a reference in a medieval chronicle to a *centifanum*, or temple to multiple gods, near the Roman bridge in Trier, rashly identified it with the ruins of the so-called "Barbara" baths, a structure of the second and fourth centuries re-used as a palace in the twelfth century.[19]

It was common to link a city's ruins with its most ancient origins, or an old church with a putative pagan predecessor. Such ascriptions claimed no great chronological precision: they were associative, symbolic, true in spirit. The architects and scholars of the early Renaissance, ironically, began to make real dating errors because they were now aiming, for the first time, for historiographical precision. They produced accounts of the architectural past at once more fine-grained and less true. The Florentine chronicler Giovanni Villani explained in 1330 that the Florentine Baptistery had once been a temple of Mars and that Christianization had brought only minor changes to the building.[20] The original temple, according to Villani, had been open above like the Pantheon and had lacked the present vault and the crowning ball and cross, which, he correctly states, were added after the re-edification of Florence in 1150. By producing facts about the building, facts based only partially in reality, Villani converted a relative antiquity—a building that merely dated from before "our own time"—into an absolute antiquity. Whereas the age of a building had once been unspecified, even unquestioned, now, at the moment of philology and historical taxonomizing, scholars began to interrogate the typological, substitutional identities of buildings, but without adequate preparation. The antiquarian "fell into careless habits of accuracy."[21] The art-historical precision of the early fifteenth-century humanist Coluccio Salutati, who described the structure as a "temple neither in the Greek style nor in the Etruscan style but rather simply in the Roman style," masks his fundamental ignorance of those styles.[22] Salutati had an idea of a progression of styles, but a confused idea. He had little to look at. There was hardly any visible record of a Roman past in Florence beyond the grid layout of the streets in the city's core. About the Greek building manner Salutati knew exactly nothing. But as a writer and a scholar, he felt increasingly compelled to make accurate statements. To picture a succession of mutually substitutable regimes, pagan and Christian, was to outline something like an historical anthropology of religion. Antonio Manetti in his life of Brunelleschi of the 1480s conceded that some medieval Florentine buildings appeared to anticipate the classicizing innovations of his hero. He decided to date those buildings to the Carolingian era, in effect pushing them back a few centuries until they practically merged with antiquity itself. This was intellectually ambitious history writing. But the drive to model history was running ahead of the gathering and publication of knowledge.

Architects could array plans and elevations from different eras on the same page without saying what it all meant, or gather diverse citations under a single roof. Writers, however, were compelled by writing itself to make statements about origins already resembling the statements that modern scholarship would later make. Buildings with model status, as we saw in section 6, became attractors for a peculiar class of statements that clashed with what was actually known.

The most archeologically minded and antiquity-oriented Florentine architects were as attentive to pre-Gothic churches as they were to ancient Roman ruins. Simone del Pollaiuolo, called Il Cronaca, carefully recorded details of the Pantheon, the Septizodium of Septimius Severus, the Florence Baptistery, Santi Apostoli, San Miniatio al Monte, as well as of Andrea Bregno's Piccolomini altar in the Cathedral of Siena, a completely modern structure. Giuliano da Sangallo combined on a single page a plan of Bramante's Tempietto, two other centralized plans, studies of a capital from the theater of Marcellus, and a vault from Hadrian's Villa.[23] In his many drawings of centralized buildings, meanwhile, Leonardo da Vinci returned continually to the eighth-century church of San Satiro in Milan, a reference bolstered by the church's associations with the Holy Sepulchre. Richard Schofield has pointed out, however, that Leonardo's studies of San Satiro appear to reflect Donato Bramante's alterations of the 1480s.[24] Leonardo sought the archetypal form, the true form, the essence of the centralized plan. He found that form not in an old building, but in an old building intelligently completed by a modern scholar-architect. Bramante— so Leonardo's studies imply—was simply bringing the building into alignment with its own origins. Architects and artists alike, intrigued as they were by the fragmentary relics of early imperial architecture, were fundamentally interested in whole buildings, complete buildings; they were interested in the *telos* of a building, which was always its origin.

Maria Fabricius Hansen has explained the backdatings of medieval buildings—the will to assign remote origin points to early medieval buildings—by arguing that the quattrocento visual appetite was not satisfied by the disjointed bases, capitals, and sculptural reliefs salvaged from the wreckage of Rome, perfect and exemplary though such fragments may appear to the schooled modern eye capable of projecting the part back onto an architectural whole. An image of an ancient Roman architectural totality, of basilica, temple, or forum, was not yet available in the quattrocento. Instead, Brunelleschi and his contemporaries were drawn, so argues Hansen, to the late antique and early medieval structures of Rome and Ravenna that were whole, standing buildings: the Lateran Baptistery, Santa Costanza, Santo Stefano Rotondo, the Mausoleum of Theodoric, San

Vitale. The fifteenth-century architectural imagination was fired by centralized plans, elaborate, multimedia decorative schemes, colored marble paneling, the "light-reflecting, plane-camouflaging" effects of mosaic, and combinations of arcades and columns.[25] The distinction between "late antique" and "Romanesque" buildings, between Santa Costanza and the Florentine Baptistery, a distinction crucial to all modern models of European art history, was simply not meaningful in the fifteenth century.

European admiration for the building projects of the Ottoman sultans, who controlled Constantinople from 1453 on, did not clarify matters. The sultans understood Justinian's tremendous multidomed temple, Hagia Sophia (532–537), completely reasonably, as the culmination of the ancient Roman building tradition. There was nothing like it in Rome itself. The Greek scholar Manuel Chrysoloras, living in Rome in 1411, struggled to describe Hagia Sophia: "For just as it amazes us that the heavenly sphere revolves by itself, so we are at a loss to understand how this inimitable and heavenly vault and ceiling was built and continues to stand."[26] The Ottoman architects took up the thread of ancient Roman architectural history, constructing a series of nuanced interpretations of Hagia Sophia, beginning with the Fatih Mosque constructed by order of Sultan Mehmet II a decade or so after his conquest of Constantinople (1463–1470) and culminating in Sinan's Süleymaniye (1548–1559) and Selimiye (1568–1574) Mosques. Western European builders' awareness of Hagia Sophia throughout the Middle Ages was dim. But in 1486 the Fabbriceri of Pavia cathedral, local patricians in charge of the construction, made efforts to secure plans of Hagia Sophia. In 1487 Bramante proposed a design for Pavia influenced, apparently, by these plans.[27] The Ottoman and the Italian architects were turning almost simultaneously to centrally planned structures. The evolving conceptions of the elevation of the new basilica of St. Peter's by Bramante and his successors are hard to conceive without awareness not only of Hagia Sophia but also of the modern mosques of Mehmet II and Bayezid II. It is easy to see how Italian observers understood the Ottoman mosques as resuscitations and extensions of ancient building traditions. Cardinal Francesco Gonzaga, in a letter dated March 16, 1473, appraised the new church of San Sebastiano in Mantua, based on a design by Alberti: "Beware that as the edifice has been done in the antique manner, not dissimilar from the fantastic prospect of Signor Battista Alberti, I was at a loss to understand if it would turn out to be a church, a mosque or a synagogue."[28]

Ottoman architects were, for their part, equally attentive to the latest Italian projects. Mehmet II destroyed the Byzantine Church of the Holy Apostles, a quincunx church which had served as a model for San Marco in Venice, and then erected his own mosque on the site (1463–1470). That mosque and the axially planned complex of mausoleums and madrasas flanking it were apparently inspired by the Ospedale Maggiore in Milan by Antonio Filarete, who visited Istanbul in 1465. Pope Julius II may have been emboldened in tearing down Old St. Peter's by Mehmet's example.[29]

The builders of the fifteenth century, many of whom were themselves scholars, sought with increasing ingenuity their lost archetypes. Buildings began to model a history of architecture. Archeological attentiveness to the historicity of the built environment pushed the architect's world into a slow rotation, opening up new referential and citational sightlines. The substitutional confusion generated new architecture. When designing his own church of San Lorenzo (1422–1425), Brunelleschi looked to Santi Apostoli, an eleventh-century basilica, for the plan as well as the Romanesque device of arches resting directly on columns. He derived the entablature blocks interposed between capital and arch, here and at Santo Spirito (1428–1434), from the exterior of the Florence Baptistery—unless it was from Taddeo Gaddi's *Presentation of the Virgin* in the Baroncelli Chapel in Santa Croce, Florence (1328).[30] The combination of major Corinthian and minor Ionic forms in the Barbadori Chapel, also used in Masaccio's *Trinity* fresco and in Donatello's Parte Guelfa niche at Orsanmichele, is a system not found in Vitruvius or in any Roman building, but can be found in the Florence Baptistery and other Romanesque monuments.[31] Brunelleschi's Old Sacristy is modeled closely, both in plan and in elevation, on the Romanesque baptistery in Padua. These strong relationships to postantique models occur throughout his work; according to Howard Burns, "there is not a single major work of Brunelleschi for which a plausible and specific post-antique source (or sources) cannot be suggested."[32] In fact, it is difficult to identify Brunelleschi's antique sources. Leon Battista Alberti, meanwhile, modeled the squares on the attic of his addition to the façade of Santa Maria Novella (begun ca. 1458) on those of the Baptistery attic, while the basic articulation of his second story strongly resembles the façade of the twelfth-century basilica of San Miniato al Monte.[33] Such examples are suspended between the anachronic assumption that allows artifacts to collapse temporally one upon another, and the sensitivity to anachronism that lucidly perceives the discontinuities of time. In the long run, historical scholarship will aim to dispel anachronic confusion. But in this early stage, the historical perception of old buildings invites the architects to repair the disruptions of time; to stitch time back together again; to recreate, in effect, the anachronic collapse of like upon unlike.

The Italian artist most interested in manipulating time through targeted historical citations—and in this respect he was the match of Jan van Eyck—was the sculptor Donatello. For Cosimo de' Medici Donatello designed a pair of bronze pulpits for San Lorenzo in Florence, left unfinished at the artist's death in 1466.[34] The pulpits invoked the long obsolete custom of reading the Epistles and the Gospel from a pair of ambos, a liturgical configuration familiar from medieval Roman churches such as San Lorenzo fuori le Mura. One of Donatello's pulpits was adorned with a relief of the three Marys visiting the tomb of Christ. To find comparable renderings of the scene taking place within an architectural setting, one had to look back to Tuscan painted crucifixes of the thirteenth century. Donatello's series of paired apostles and martyrs on the bronze doors of the Old Sacristy (1434–1443) were guided by the Romanesque door jambs of the baptistery at Pisa, by early Christian ivory diptychs, and by Byzantine manuscript illuminations.[35] At San Lorenzo, the patron Cosimo had his architect Brunelleschi place the choir not in the nave or crossing, as was customary, but in the apse behind the altar, again just as it was in the early medieval basilicas of Rome. Moreover, the altar was apparently placed at the edge of the raised presbytery in such a way that the priest faced the congregation, an archaism reversed in the seventeenth century.[36]

Brunelleschi and Alberti understood the meaning of buildings to be a referential quantum preserved across an invisible chain of intermediary buildings. Any knowledge they possessed about the particular or local circumstances of the buildings' fabrication, or their absolute position within sequences, was not allowed to interfere with the referential linkage and the presumption of substitutability. Brunelleschi and Alberti knew one or two things about their models, about the real histories of their models.[37] But that knowledge was overridden by their desire to make those models stand in for the missing ancient models that they really wanted. The identity of a building was its *meaning*, not its physical being, which distended in complex ways across time and was for any practical purpose unreconstructible.

Santa Maria del Popolo in Rome was rebuilt in the 1470s under Sixtus IV. The architect looked not only to remnants of ancient buildings but to round-arched Romanesque models, which were scarce in Rome. The immediate models for its round-arched arcades resting on piers with semicolumns and pilasters seem to have been thirteenth-century Lombard churches. The arches of Santa Maria del Popolo cannot have been meant as references to Lombardy; Sixtus's builders, in search of a true Roman style, had no interest in invoking northern lands or cities. The Lombard models permitted the Roman builders to break out of local custom, by this time ossified and all too familiar.[38]

Fifteenth-century philologists mastered the Greek language; antiquarians meanwhile divined the ancient Greek manner in Olympian sculpture, Christian painting, and manuscript illumination. What did they know of Greek building? The ancient Roman architect Vitruvius, author of a miraculously preserved treatise on building, had much to say about Greek architecture, but his comments were difficult to interpret and no illustrations had been transmitted with the text. Few scholars and architects had been to Greece other than the learned traveler and amateur draughtsman Ciriaco d' Ancona. The Greek buildings transmitted by Ciriaco's drawings, Deborah Howard has shown, were anyway apt to be credited to the Romans. Giuliano da Sangallo copied Ciriaco's elevation of the Parthenon, but gave it a Composite order, which is an exclusively Roman form.[39]

The leading edge of the substitutional chain leading back to a true Greek architecture, or so it seemed in the fifteenth century, was the Byzantine church. Especially appealing were churches with quincunx or cross-in-square plans, a type established in Byzantine territories in the eighth century. The type is attested in the West by the late eighth and early ninth centuries, for example at Santa Maria delle Cinque Torre at San Germano near Cassino and at Germigny-des-Prés in the Loire Valley.[40] The design was also found at San Satiro in Milan, San Vittore delle Chiuse, Santa Croce in Sassoferrato, and Santa Maria delle Moie near Jesi, to name a few examples near Urbino that were probably known to Bramante.[41] The quincunx, in the architectural imagination of the fifteenth and sixteenth centuries, was the distinctive feature of ancient Greek building.[42] In the mid-fifteenth century the architectural theorist Antonio Filarete took the quincunx, as exemplified by the Venetian church of San Marco, as the basis for the cathedral of Sforzinda, his ideal city. He represented a similar structure on the reverse of his medal of the treatise's patron Francesco Sforza, placing medal and patron under the imprimatur of the antique.[43] Venetian architects, too, inspired by San Marco and San Giacomo in Rialto, both churches understood as transmitters of ancient forms, reactivated the quincunx plan in their own projects.[44] It was only left to Cesare Cesariano, the Milanese architect and theorist, to assert the direct philological association of these Greek-derived forms with actual Greek temples from antiquity. In his 1521 translation and commentary of Vitruvius, Cesariano illustrated the ancient architect's discussions of the prostylos and amphiprostylos temple forms with woodcuts of quincunx plans, despite the fact that these plans openly conflict with Vitruvius's descriptions.[45]

Behind many neo-antique architectural visions of the end of the fifteenth century, both built and unbuilt, hide the forms of the medieval church. Bramante, before he knew Rome, studied not only the quincunx churches of the Marches but also the Romanesque structures of Pavia and Milan.[46] When Giuliano da Sangallo provided a corrected version — in quincunx form — of Bramante's plan for St. Peter's, Bramante responded immediately with sketches of plans of the Duomo and of the church of San Lorenzo in Milan.[47] Bramante specifically wanted to include in the St. Peter's plan ambulatories such as those found in both those churches, elements that modern architectural historians recognize as typically "medieval," but that he evidently considered to be of great antiquity.

The phenomenon is thus in many ways analogous to the treatment of Greek icons and can be observed in other media as well. The frontispiece of a Greek *Iliad* manuscript prepared for Cardinal Francesco Gonzaga in 1477, with facing page translation in Latin, is a clear demonstration of this pattern of thinking. Whereas the Latin side shows marginal ornamentation composed of elaborate quotations of Roman antiquities drawn from monuments such as Trajan's Column, the Greek side shows an equally careful citation of "ancient" Greek ornament, but in this case the patterns are drawn from tenth- and eleventh-century Byzantine manuscripts.[48]

The fields of ornament and lettering were, in fact, the most susceptible to anachronic thinking. Italian scholars of the first decades of the fifteenth century developed a lucid and elegant alphabet, the so-called humanist minuscule, perfectly matched, so it seemed, to the classical texts they were discovering and editing.[49] They had found this alphabet in old manuscripts. The initial letters in those same manuscripts were graced with flat thickets of coiled, white vines. The humanists then instructed painters to adorn the initial letters and page borders of their own books with crawling, interlocking growths of vine, curling white stems and shoots, just like those they had seen in the old books.[50] An initial E from a Bolognese manuscript of Suetonius, datable to the middle of the fifteenth century, adorning a text written in a round humanist hand, is a good example (figure 13.2).[51] But the white vine scroll and the minuscule alphabet were born of a chronological misconception, for the ancient models that scribes and painters looked to were not so ancient. Their models were actually twelfth-century Italian manuscripts, which in turn transmitted interlaced forms developed in transalpine monasteries, such as St. Gall, between the ninth and eleventh centuries. An example is the initial C from an Italian homiliary of the early twelfth century (figure 13.3).[52] There can be no mistake about the derivation, for the fifteenth-century white-vine ornament—our example is no exception—duplicated even the blue, green, and red color scheme of the intervals between the vines found in the medieval sources.[53] The scholars were reviving not ancient Roman but early medieval and northern European forms.

In the fifteenth century the substitutional hypothesis emerged out of the background of consciousness and became, for the first time, a cultural program, a strategy. Antiquarians in quest of a chimerical antiquity were

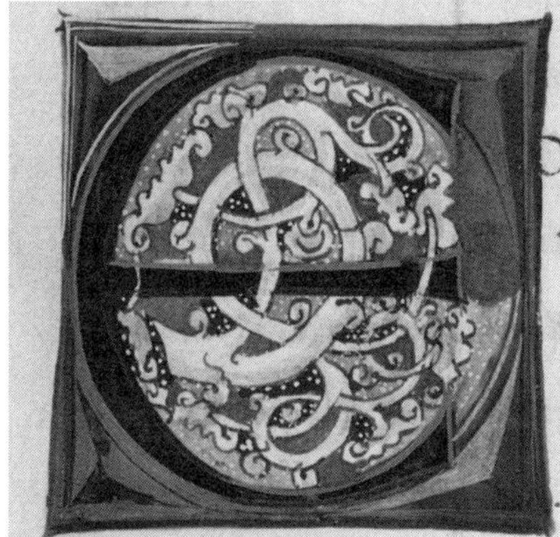

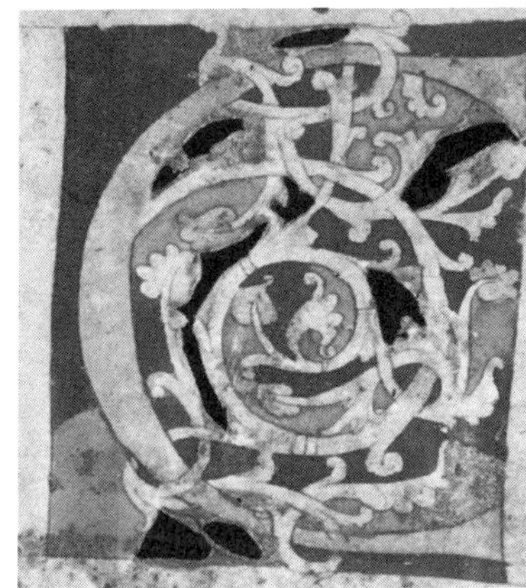

13.2 Renaissance ornament supposedly based on the best ancient models. Initial E, Suetonius, *Works* (Bologna, mid-fifteenth century). New Haven, Yale University, Beinecke Rare Book Library, Marston MS 52, fol. 119r. Such tangles of white vines, coiled about large initial capitals, were much favored by fifteenth-century illuminators of manuscripts of classical texts.

13.3 The model for the antiquarian-minded illuminators. Initial C, *Homiliary* (Italy, early twelfth century). New Haven, Yale University, Beinecke Rare Book Library, MS 481.35, fol. 1r. White-vine interlaced ornament was not an ancient Roman convention at all, but a legacy of the Carolingian era. A manuscript such as this served as the model for the initial reproduced in figure 13.2. It was taken by fifteenth-century painters and scribes either as a book much older than it really was, or as a reliable record of ancient forms.

now prepared to mobilize substitutional terms when they needed them. Scholastic exegetes had analyzed the proportional systems for tabernacle and temple encoded in Genesis and Ezekiel. In the Renaissance this material was reactivated with a new literalism. The philologist Lilius Tifernas, in the introduction to his translation for Sixtus IV of Philo's *Life of Moses* (c. 1480), asserted that the basilica of St. Peter's in Rome "appears certainly

to have been built on the model [*ad exemplar*] of the original oblong tabernacle erected on columns by Moses. The basilica resembles the tabernacle
and seems derived from it; thus we learn that this temple was erected in
accordance with a divine prototype. Many churches on earth have been
built in imitation of this church."[54] Such an idea could—and in the case
of St. Peter's, did—become the justification for building programs. Once
the backward-stretching chain of buildings came into historical focus,
the temptation to intervene, extend, and manipulate increased. Whereas
buildings used simply to be maintained, now they were "restored." Restoration was in effect an artificial substitution, an assisted substitution.
Many Romanesque portals and bell towers in northern Europe, at least,
have survived not by accident but because they were restored, sensitively
restored, in the Renaissance, and with an eye to form, their worn fabrics
no longer simply replaced in the style of the day, as they would have been
under the old medieval system, described by Krautheimer, of nonvisual
substitution, before stylistic concordance mattered. This care in preserving earlier forms corresponds to the contemporaneous efforts to produce
archaizing copies of old icons or to preserve them through embedding (see
sections 8 and 9).[55]

The preservation of early medieval form, the mimicry of ancient form,
and the fabrication of the new all converged. In 1513 Cardinal Giovanni de'
Medici became Pope Leo X and in that same year undertook a restoration
of the ninth-century church of Santa Maria in Dominica, matching the
forms in his new clerestory, façade, and portico to the system developed by
Paschal I, itself an ingenious imitation on a small scale of Constantine's St.
Peter's. In front of the church stood a sculpted ship, from which the church
takes its sobriquet Navicella. To this day scholars cannot decide whether
the ship is the ancient Roman original or a copy ordered by Leo.[56]

When Vasari described the Florentine Baptistery as ancient, he was well
aware of the disharmony between substitutional and performative accounts
of architectural time. His history is about that disharmony. Vasari did not
commit the error of backdating the eleventh-century basilica of Santi Apostoli to antiquity; he dated it only to the time of Charlemagne, an interesting error. For Vasari still described it, despite its supposed ninth-century
date, as "a work of such good manner that it approaches the good and true
ancient manner" and in this way able to serve as a model for Brunelleschi.[57]
Vasari offered Santi Apostoli as an exemplum not simply of ancient architectural principles, but of the reliable transmission of ancient principles.

FOURTEEN

Non-Actual Histories of Architecture

The French painter Jean Fouquet (1415/20–before 1481), when illustrating a French translation of the *Jewish Antiquities* of the first-century historian Flavius Josephus, pictured Solomon's Temple as a rectangular Gothic pile, a massive block, gilded and encrusted with statuary, baldachins, niches, trilobate pinnacles, and deep pointed portals (figure 14.1).[1] The temple's construction is in full swing: an artisan on a scaffold at the right applies the gold; a winch hoists stone to the roof; stone carvers bend over emergent forms in the foreground; the faithful, wearing not hard hats but turbans, stream in through the portals. Later in the book, when the temple burns at the hands of the Babylonians, Fouquet shows us the completed structure, topped by a low rounded roof and surrounded by a symbolic wall, a *temenos*, keeping the profane realm at bay.[2] The portals of Fouquet's temple are quite accurate portraits of the portals of the west façade of the cathedral of Tours, Saint-Gatien. The nearby palace, where Solomon gestures within a corner baldachin, is modeled on the archepiscopal palace in Tours. Fouquet has "actualized" ancient history. In this he was not unique. By this time, around 1470, the portrayal of the local townscape as a setting for sacred narratives was a well-established conceit among Netherlandish, French, German, and Italian painters.

The architectural portrait emerged in parallel with the human portrait. As soon as there were portraits, they were used in such riddling ways. The earliest "disguised" portraits of people — projections of the features of modern individuals onto the representations of historical characters in paintings — were those of Emperor Charles IV and King Charles VI of France, depicted between 1360 and 1380.[3] The architectural portrait was first introduced anachronistically into sacred scenes in illuminations of the *Très Riches Heures* of the Duke of Berry, by the brothers Limbourg, around 1400. The three Magi meet at a crossroads, for example, not far from the city of Paris with its cathedral and the Sainte-Chapelle. In the features of the Magi some have seen the portraits of Charles VI of France and the Byzantine Emperor Manuel II.[4] Jan van Eyck introduced portraits

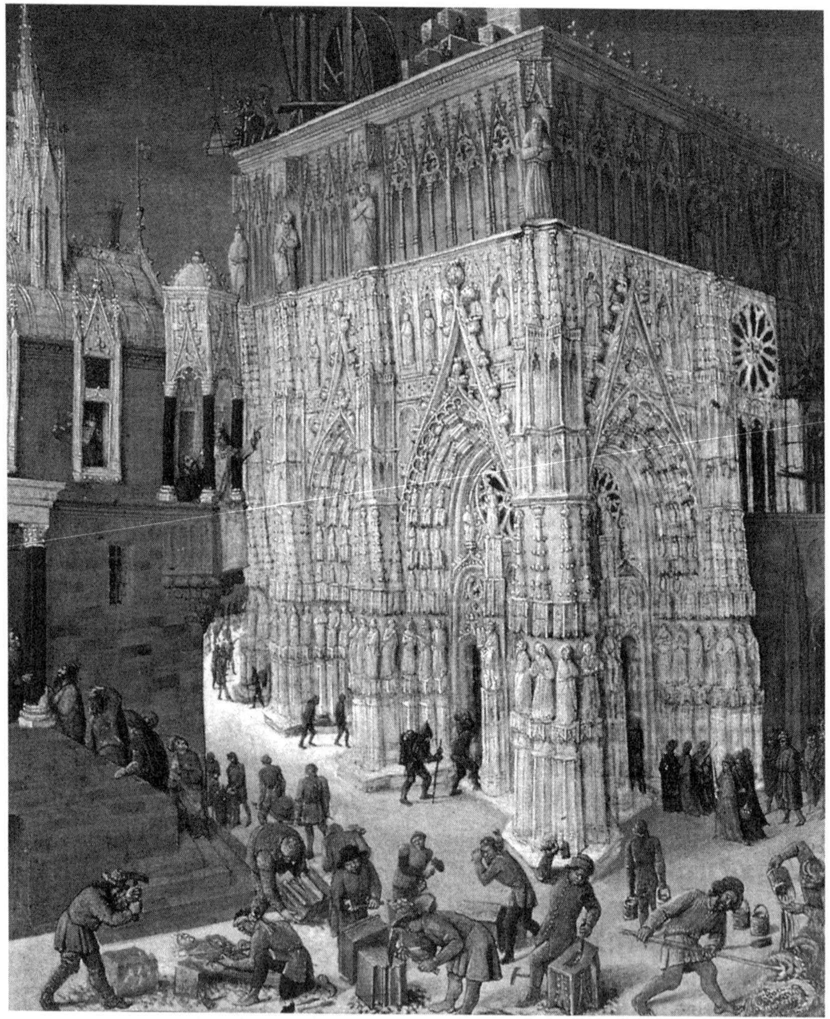

14.1 The Temple of Jerusalem as a Gothic pile. Jean Fouquet, *Construction of Solomon's Temple* (ca. 1465), Josephus, *Jewish Antiquities*. Paris, Bibliothèque nationale de France, ms. fr. 247, fol. 163. Fouquet respects the biblical description of the Temple as rectangular but gives it a modern surface. Solomon supervises the construction from a balcony on the left.

of contemporaries among the celebrants at the Adoration of the Lamb in the Ghent Altarpiece (1432). Visible through the round-arched window in the panel just to the right of the annunciating angel on the exterior wings of the same altarpiece are the spires and steeply pitched roofs of a modern, northern European town, perhaps recognizable to contemporaries as an exact portrait of a street in Ghent.[5] In his Nativity altarpiece, now in Berlin (ca. 1445), Rogier van der Weyden portrayed Middelburg, a town built from the ground up by the financier Pieter Bladelin. Middelburg appears behind the kneeling patron as his emblem or attribute. Its presence is no more surprising than Bladelin's own presence, in full scale, at the side of the Virgin Mary at Bethlehem.[6] The encounter between St. Martin and the beggar is placed by Jean Fouquet, in his book of hours for Étienne Chevalier, on the quayside in modern Paris.[7]

The architectural portrait was especially favored in Bruges. The Master of the St. Lucy Legend depicted in his panels ten different monuments of that city with such accuracy that the documented construction history of the bell tower between 1480 and 1500 allows us to date the works of the painter.[8] Hans Memling, meanwhile, in the late 1480s, painted two portraits of the skyline of Cologne, from different angles, on the side panels of the St. Ursula Shrine, an updating in oil paint of an earlier medieval type, the reliquary chasse (figure 14.2).[9] The panels narrate events that took place, if they took place at all, in the fourth century, or perhaps the third, or the fifth; yet the portrait of Cologne in the *Arrival of Saint Ursula and the 11,000 Virgins in Cologne*, the left-most and central scenes on this side of the shrine, describes the churches of St. Maria Lyskirchen, St. Severin, and Gross St. Martin as well as the torso of the cathedral, all structures of the twelfth and thirteenth centuries.[10]

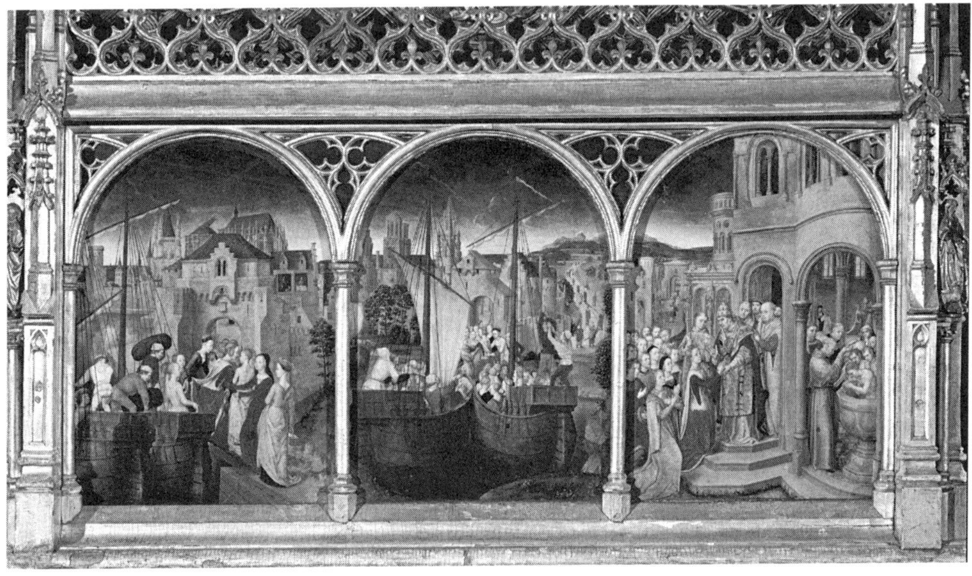

14.2 **Portraits of the Romanesque and Gothic churches of Cologne.** Hans Memling, *Shrine of Saint Ursula*, gilded wood and oil on panel, 87 x 33 x 91 cm (late 1480s). Bruges, Sint-Jans Hospitaal, Memling Museum. The modern skyline on the left is the setting for Memling's rendering of St. Ursula's arrival in Cologne—in early Christian times.

German painters were attentive early on to the crisscross between here and there, now and then, cultivated by the Netherlandish painters. In the *Flight to Egypt* in the altarpiece of the Schottenstift in Vienna (1470s) the Holy Family avoids the modern city of Vienna.[11] Michael Pacher set his *Circumcision* on the St. Wolfgang altar (1477–1481) in a long basilica with a flowing network of rhomboid-forming rib vaults, an interior that could not have been read by contemporaries as anything but ultramodern. There are also many Italian examples of embedded, anachronistic architectural portraiture: the mosaic portrait of St. Zenobius with Giotto's bell tower and Brunelleschi's cupola (see figure 12.4), for example; or the buildings of Florence in Domenico Ghirlandaio's Sassetti chapel frescoes.[12]

When Fouquet paints the cathedral of Tours transformed into the Solomonic temple, he means to compare past and present. The technique of accurate description, producing confidence that an unlabeled description of a singular entity would be recognizable, opened up this window of meaning.

Fouquet's Jewish cathedral says several things at once. It says, for instance, "The events recorded by Josephus and pictured here are still relevant. Royal building projects and religious persecution are still very much with us. The patterns of history are deep and permanent." The dissonance that Fouquet creates between the ancient story and the modern architectural style gives the clue. The beholder who is irritated by the friction between old and new, who doubts that Solomon built in the Gothic manner, will be forced to seek the hidden consonances between past and present. The image proposes, for example, that "it is easier to grasp the meaning of Solomon's ambitious building project if we compare it to a modern cathedral. Today, in the third quarter of the fifteenth century, we see such long-term construction projects still underway, all around us. The construction of great piles is much the same everywhere; the technical challenges are the same. In this way civilizations are linked across the gulfs of time and faith."

But the anachronism may be suggesting something stranger still: "Modern Tours, or Paris, is the legitimate successor to Jerusalem; history, even sacred history, is happening here, now." Europeans spoke of their cities as symbolic repetitions of the heavenly Jerusalem—*ad similitudinem paradisi*.[13] The town of Borgo San Sepolcro styled itself a "New Jerusalem" on the basis of a collection of stones carried back to Tuscany from the Holy Land in the tenth century and a cathedral that pretended to be the replacement for the Church of the Holy Sepulchre, which was destroyed in 1012.[14] Piero della Francesca, in his fresco cycle at Arezzo, portrayed Arezzo as the setting for the *Invention of the Cross*—portrayed Arezzo as Jerusalem, in other words. The center is "hard to get to," as Mircea Eliade put it, and so people find ways "to extend the hierophanization of the World *ad infinitum*, to keep finding duplicates, substitutes." Every dwelling becomes a center of the world; "easy substitutes," according to Eliade.[15] If the built city was sacralized by such typological intentions, then to portray it in a religious painting was simply to feed the sacred back into the sacred.[16]

Fouquet's picture reveals the contours of a thesis about the origins and meaning of the Christian temple: "The modern cathedral," it proposes, "is linked to the Solomonic temple in multiple ways. The basic structure of Christian worship—the focus on an altar, symbolic site of sacrifice, guided by liturgy and priesthood—was inherited from the Jews." True or not, this was the historical theory advanced by innumerable paintings representing the interior of the temple. "Synagoga was the type of ecclesia," these paintings seem to say. The dimensions of the Solomonic temple were recorded in scripture and this formula was preserved, even if sometimes disguised, by generations of Christian masons. It is preservation of the underlying structure of the temple that locks the cathedral into a substitutional relation with its own origin. "True, the modern cathedral is pointed in style. But who knows what the temple itself looked like? We know that the arches of the Saracenic temple in Jerusalem, the successor to the Solomonic temple, are pointed. In any case, the distinction between pointed and round arches is insignificant; it is the proportions that matter, the underlying patterns."

The pictorial overlap between temple and cathedral makes a proposition about the real identity of origin point and end point. It does not decide the matter but rather leaves it open. The recipient can either accept the literal identity of temple and cathedral, or simply reflect on the possibility of such identity, on the possibility that the relentless linear sequence of events that humans experience masks a hidden sameness.

The precondition for such calculated anachronisms was a reasonably well-developed sense of historical style. Unless artists and beholders share an idea of the coordination between the age of buildings and the way they look, the device will not work. The building has to be seen to possess an overall style that is linked to a historical moment, to the circumstances of its fabrication. Only then can that link be dramatically undone by the hypothesis of substitutional identity across a variable sequence of styles.

A sense for the historicity of architectural form was the precondition, for example, for the conceit of mapping the round and pointed building systems onto the historical and theological diptych of Old and New Dispensation.[17] This conceit was introduced already in French book painting in the early thirteenth century. A *Bible moralisée* dated 1220 juxtaposes a domed temple of Solomon and Christ's Gothic ecclesia.[18] Admittedly

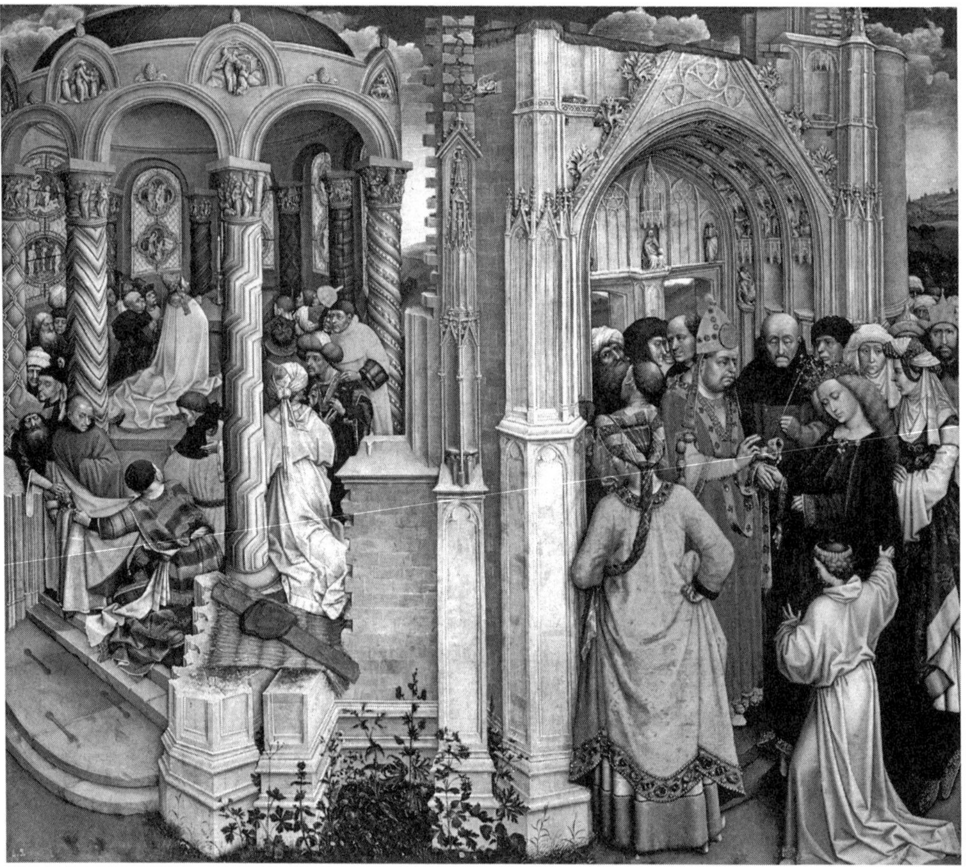

14.3 Old and New Dispensation. Robert Campin, *Betrothal of the Virgin*, oil on panel, 77 x 88 cm (ca. 1428). Madrid, Museo del Prado. The round and pointed building systems mapped onto the historical and theological diptych of Old and New Testaments. On the left, under the cupola, the suitors, dressed in ancient robes and turbans, compete for the hand of Mary. Joseph, an older man, retreats in embarrassment. He will unexpectedly win the competition. On the right, before the unfinished portal of a Gothic church, the couple is married.

the contrast here is not between a "Romanesque" structure and a Gothic structure, but between a fantastical, exotic church and a familiar western European church; between "them" and "us," in short.[19] French and Netherlandish painting of the early fifteenth century developed the model. Here, too, the Jewish temple in Robert Campin's *Betrothal of the Virgin* (ca. 1428) is fantastical, a virtually freestanding octagon, a green (metal?) cupola perched on extravagantly carved columns supporting depressed round arches and pine-cone acroteria, perhaps observed on colonial Roman mausolea (figure 14.3).[20] But the porch at the right sheltering the betrothal itself, an architectural fragment, still under construction, is in a straight-forward Gothic style.[21] The event taking place in the temple, at left, the Miracle of the Rod, is still remote, outlandish; with the immediately suc-ceeding episode, the betrothal, we are again at home, in the here and now, amidst the familiar forms of everyday life.

On the two panels between the angel Gabriel and the Virgin Mary on the exterior of his altarpiece at Ghent (1432), Jan van Eyck represented, on the left, as we have noted, a view through a round-arched, biforate window onto a cityscape and, on the right, a wall niche with finials and a pointed, crocketed gable housing a ewer and laver. The panels are among the proto-types of the independent landscape and still life, staples of modern art. Here the contrast between the two building modes is more nuanced. Van Eyck's two vignettes communicate, through the simple binary code of round and pointed, left and right, the historical passage from Old Dispensa-tion to New. The conceit is stranger than we might at first think, because the pointed arch had been introduced to western European architecture less than three centuries earlier and therefore was not an obvious marker of the passage from Mosaic Law to Christian Grace. Many European churches, constructed in phases over several centuries, exhibited both building man-ners side by side. Why would one coordinate the round-pointed distinction with the historical succession of religions? There is more than one way of interpreting the device. The juxtaposition of round to pointed in a painted building remembered the historical shift in building styles that took place in many parts of Europe in the twelfth and thirteenth centuries—a shift that no one in the fifteenth century could date any more accurately than "the time of the fathers of our fathers"—and represented it as if it were the final, belated phase in the passage from the ancient to the modern world. The device depends on an understanding of the round-pointed distinction as a shift, singular and real, rather than as an arbitrary choice. The device models an evolutionary and unidirectional account of architectural history.

Painting itself, by translating the built world into two dimensions, generated consciousness of the distinction. The pointed manner, once painted, became a foil for the round manner, setting it off and creating it as an integral mode of building that knitted together the long run of time from pagan antiquity to the almost-present. The Gothic style created the image of its own opposite, the round-arched style which the ancient pagans had developed and bequeathed to Christians. The round-arched system could now be understood as the old, traditional way of building that linked Roman antiquity to the recent past.[22] In his St. Ursula Shrine, in the right-hand scene on the same side that represents, on the left, the *Arrival of Saint Ursula and the 10,000 Virgins in Cologne*, Hans Memling pictured the

Roman church (presumably St. Peter's?) where Pope Cyriacus greeted the saint with round-arched doors and, in the second story, biforate windows flanked by engaged columns (see figure 14.2). It is basically a twelfth-century church. But then the very existence of Pope Cyriacus, Ursula's host and fellow Briton, is unattested outside the legend (the legend even explains why this is so). The building elements pointed to the way of building before the present time: this was the way churches used to be built, the picture says; in our own time, that is, as far back as living memory reaches, we build differently. The image of the round style was the image of the past itself. Thus to picture it was to symbolize the possibility of a break with the past. To build in a non-round manner was simply to be modern.[23] In studying the local built environment the Netherlandish painters were conducting their independent revival of antiquity.[24] Northern painters cited archaic motifs found in local medieval structures, not only round arches but also post-and-lintel construction.[25] Such references are best understood not as archaisms but as attempts to connect with antiquity.

The fifteenth century wrote a history of architecture by embedding buildings in painted narratives. Sacred painters rendered dream-exact portraits of vanished buildings, never-built buildings, buildings with purely textual existences: the temple in Jerusalem; the ruins of King David's palace at Bethlehem, site of the Nativity (imagined by Rogier van der Weyden and others as a Romanesque structure, for example in his Columba altarpiece, now in Munich); the praetorian palace of Pontius Pilate. Some of their fabrications were chimeras, looking like nothing ever seen and so signifying pure distance and alterity. Pictures commented on the life of real buildings by depicting the traces of non-actual architectural histories. As the descriptions came into sharper focus, the accumulated architectural history of Europe, real and virtual, opened up as a semantic field.

Inside a painting, the binary distinction between round and pointed architecture took on a meaning that it had not possessed in the real built environment. Until this moment, the concept of a building as a singular, datable event was underdeveloped, and understandably so, since everyone could see that buildings grew in time, slowly, and little by little fell apart and had to be patched up.[26] Buildings were difficult to see as events, but paintings of buildings were definitely events, and in turn prompted a rereading of buildings themselves as events, or as traces of events. When the substitutional theory of building was pictured within a pictorial regime capable of exact portraiture; when modular and typological thinking about buildings met interference from an event-based, archeological conception of time; when an idea of a building was remade as an image; then the result was a new set of distinctions and a new interest in differentiation as such.

The old buildings, such as St. Peter's in Rome or the oldest of the local basilicas, had been tightly controlled by typology, or so it seemed to modern builders whose enthrallment to type was broken. In our time, the paintings argue, the substitutional, anachronic building has given way to the building that responds more sensitively to circumstances, that attends to function or fashion. The painted portraits of round-arched buildings were models of buildings that themselves had model-status, in contrast to the free buildings of modernity, no longer bound to type. The round manner was timeless, a nonstyle. Such paintings were therefore offering not only a history of architecture, but also a theory of the history of architecture. When nested within a modern painting, the round manner set the two modes of production, substitutional and performative, into tension, exactly as did the icon inserted into the Botticelli portrait. Such a painting set off a type-governed, anachronic building manner against a performative building manner. From this point on, the architect's reengagement with once typologically controlled building modes — central-plan modes, above all — was no longer innocent. The nontypological invocation of type is now nothing more than anachronism, whether understood as survival (classicism) or revival (neoclassicism).

Such an account equally permits reversal of the sequence to make a mystical point. Jan van Eyck did just this in his Washington *Annunciation* (ca. 1435) (figure 14.4).[27] Here the older styles, a round-arched clerestory and a trabeated triforium, sit on top of the more modern style, the lightly pointed or Gothic arcade — an unlikely stacking.[28] The device marks the building as celestial, beyond all physics and experience; it is as if God himself had built the structure from the top down, as he well might. The Virgin's response to the angel, *Ecce ancilla domini*, is written upside down, as if to be read from above. Did not God build history itself from the top down, starting with the end, the meaning, and then planting symbols or foreshadowings of that end throughout the span of time? A symbol that precedes the reality it symbolizes, such as a prophecy or van Eyck's upside-down church, can only appear to the human mind as a mystery.

One might understand the juxtaposition of round and pointed styles in paintings as an encoded message about sacred history that exploits the real world as a "key." The painter can count on the beholder knowing some facts about the world, about how buildings look and how they were constructed. The painter then lets the historical shift from round to pointed style stand for the succession of covenants between man and God, even though one shift has nothing to do with the other. The near arbitrariness of the key provides for the encryption.

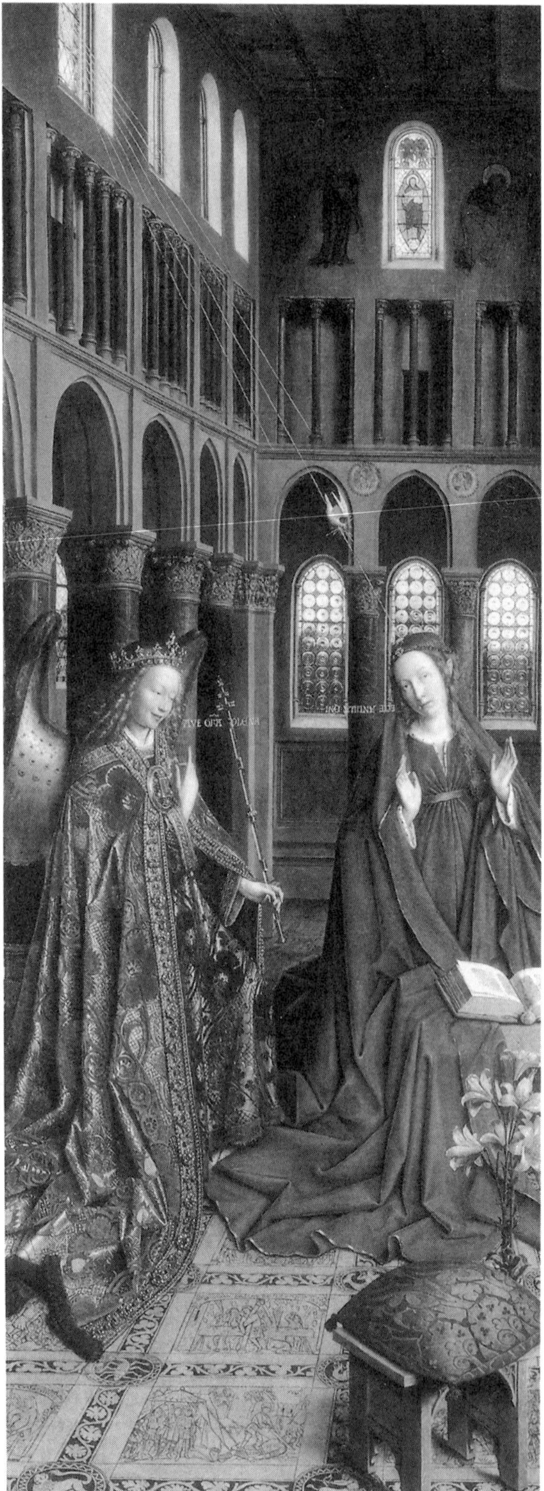

14.4 Architectural history in inverted perspective. Jan van Eyck, *Annunciation*, oil on canvas, transferred from panel, 92.7 x 36.7 cm (ca. 1435). Washington, National Gallery of Art. Here Gothic is on the ground floor and Romanesque is above, an unlikely sequence in a real church. Inside a painting, the binary distinction between round and pointed architecture could take on a meaning that it did not possess in the built environment.

The device of mapping sacramental history onto architectural history did not survive into the second half of the fifteenth century. Campin and van Eyck were recovering an older conception, glimpsed in the contrast staged in the *Bible moralisée* of the thirteenth century, of a symbolically meaningful distinction between an apparently undisciplined and sensationalizing "foreign" architecture and a rational and liturgically governed "home" architecture. That distinction could not be drawn so clearly in the context of the antiquarian and classicizing ambitions of the later fifteenth and sixteenth centuries. Once the antique building manner was reinterpreted as an ideal manner, worthy of studied emulation — even if the historical style now known as Romanesque was often "standing in" for that of antiquity[29] — the round arch could no longer simply symbolize the superseded. The round arch now also stood for what was to be recovered. It became modern.[30]

We have seen buildings themselves model histories of architecture. Brunelleschi and Alberti introduced citations of exemplary medieval buildings, half-aware of the buildings' real ages. A substitutional theory of architectural history suited them because it allowed them to see ancient building principles in medieval Florentine churches. A performative theory of architectural creation appealed to them because they wanted to be strong authors, on the model of contemporary painters, sculptors, or poets. Their claim to authorship was in part based on their ability to select from the menu of historical styles. In this way performance and substitution produced each other. Alberti and Brunelleschi were generating with their antiquarian measurements, their drawings, and their own built buildings a history and a theory of form as subtle as that of van Eyck or Memling.

Once painting seized the possibility of reliable portraiture, the exchanges between the real built environment and representations of buildings became dizzyingly rapid. The painting duplicated the city, and the city then learned from the painting. The history of form accelerated and pursued a looping path that ran from three dimensions to two dimensions and back again to three. The city reentered itself, after having been routed through the painting. This process began already in the early fourteenth century, when the Florentine mural painters staged sacred narratives in carefully described buildings, schematically reduced and cut away for clarity.[31] A century later, Brunelleschi drew on these paintings for ideas. In his buildings he cited capitals that he saw in Giotto's frescoes at Santa Croce. The arcades of San Lorenzo and Santo Spirito, as we saw in the last section, are dependent on Taddeo Gaddi's *Presentation of the Virgin* in the Baroncelli Chapel in Santa Croce.[32] Already in the fourteenth century, the commune of Florence began to conceive the layout of the city itself in pictorial terms, as an urban "scene": the prehistory of the perspectival painting.[33]

This pattern of exchange between real and painted cityscapes was matched in the north. The oldest surviving buildings held powerful, positive associations for Germans, who saw their own emperors as the successors to the Caesars and so, unlike Italians, recognized no caesura intervening between antiquity and modernity.[34] In Augsburg, for example, the wealthy southern German commune with trading ties to Venice, the Gothic building manner that had dominated for more than two centuries was challenged in the 1510s by a new, triple attentiveness: first, to the local Romanesque; second, to sacred paintings that represented a fantastical, round-arched cityscape; and third, to fashionable modern Italian building styles, disseminated mostly by prints.[35] The recovery of ancient forms, whether descended directly or indirectly from peninsular antiquity, came to be known as the "Welsch" or Italian style.[36] Whereas in Italy the recovery of pre-Gothic building manners was driven by drawings of Roman (and Romanesque) buildings made on site by artists and protoarcheologists, in the north this role was assumed almost exclusively by the circulation of panel paintings and prints. North and south found their way back to the ancients along different paths.

The implication of such adjustments and corrections of the real world was that by the late fifteenth century painters could no longer use the world as a stable "key" for encrypting messages about history or theology. Round could no longer be counted on to precede pointed—just as van Eyck had predicted in his Washington *Annunciation*. Reality itself was confused when the round arch, processed through pictorial figuration, reemerged into the built environment. The orderly succession of styles was garbled by the idealizing "restorations" of ancient round buildings undertaken especially in Rome, beginning in the mid-fifteenth century. Pope Nicholas V hired the Florentine Bernardo Rossellino to restore the early medieval church of Santo Stefano Rotondo in 1453. In the same year he had San Teodoro, the sixth-century round church at the foot of the Palatine hill, outfitted with a cupola. This was perhaps the very earliest cupola of the Roman Renaissance, very likely inspired by the domes of Brunelleschi in Florence.[37]

The revival of the round in turn elicited a counter-revival, a reasserted or reinvented Gothic that in many ways dominated the architecture of northern Europe throughout the sixteenth and into the seventeenth century.[38] The moment one could no longer count on the round-arched style being read as an old style, the device of the staged comparison between round and pointed to make points about law and grace, the "Campin" device, lost its effectiveness. The world, mutable, dynamic, could no longer be used as an encryption key.

FIFTEEN

Temples Painted, Printed, and Real

Jean Fouquet, as we saw in the previous section, represents the tenth-century BCE temple of Solomon as a Gothic building (see figure 14.1). He invokes a way of thinking about architecture unfamiliar to modern, historically sensitive viewers. Fouquet asks us to identify the Jewish Temple on the basis of its size and shape, and by the quantity, not the quality, of ornamentation. Fouquet's temple is a solid block, as the Bible seemed to say it was; and it is splendidly carved and gilt. That was enough to establish identity—so said Fouquet's painting. Buildings, according to that theory, are congruent merely on the basis of broad typological correspondences— on the basis of matches within rough categories such as plan type (centralized or basilical) or function (tomb, baptistery, or temple). The typological approach to architecture was sustained by the sheer lack of reliable information about old and distant buildings, not only about the vanished Temple and the Holy Sepulchre in Jerusalem, but also about local buildings. Buildings that look wildly dissimilar to modern eyes, schooled by travel and photographs, were in the past capable of standing in for other buildings. Conversely, features that might vary across a continuum, features hard to capture in words or numbers, the experiences of space or aspect, were effectively factored out of any discourse on architecture. The builders knew one building from another, but one wonders who else did.

Fouquet, by the same principle of commutativity that governed his rendering of the Solomonic temple as a pointed cathedral, also converts pointed buildings into round ones. In his illustrations to the *Grandes Chroniques de France* (1450s), he rounds the arches of real Gothic churches, known first-hand to all his beholders, as if to stress their substitutional roots in the deep history of Europe. Fouquet stages the coronation of Marie de Brabant, for instance, queen of Philippe III the Bold, in 1274, in a Sainte-Chapelle—the royal chapel built by Philippe's father Louis IX in the 1240s—outfitted counterfactually with a wide, round-arched door. It is as if Fouquet were correcting the history of recent architecture, dismissing the pointed style as a mere fashionable garment, superficial and meaningless. Fouquet's most remarkable comment on the ambiguity of the pointed arch—its dubious relation to antiquity and possible threat to ideal substitution-driven continuity—is his miniature in the *Grandes Chroniques de France* representing the burial in 1314 of Philippe le Bel in the choir of the abbey church at Saint-Denis (figure 15.1).[1] Here the tips of Abbot Suger's early twelfth-century arches, slightly pointed, the incunabula of the Gothic style, are discreetly masked by six ceremonial banners elevated on poles.

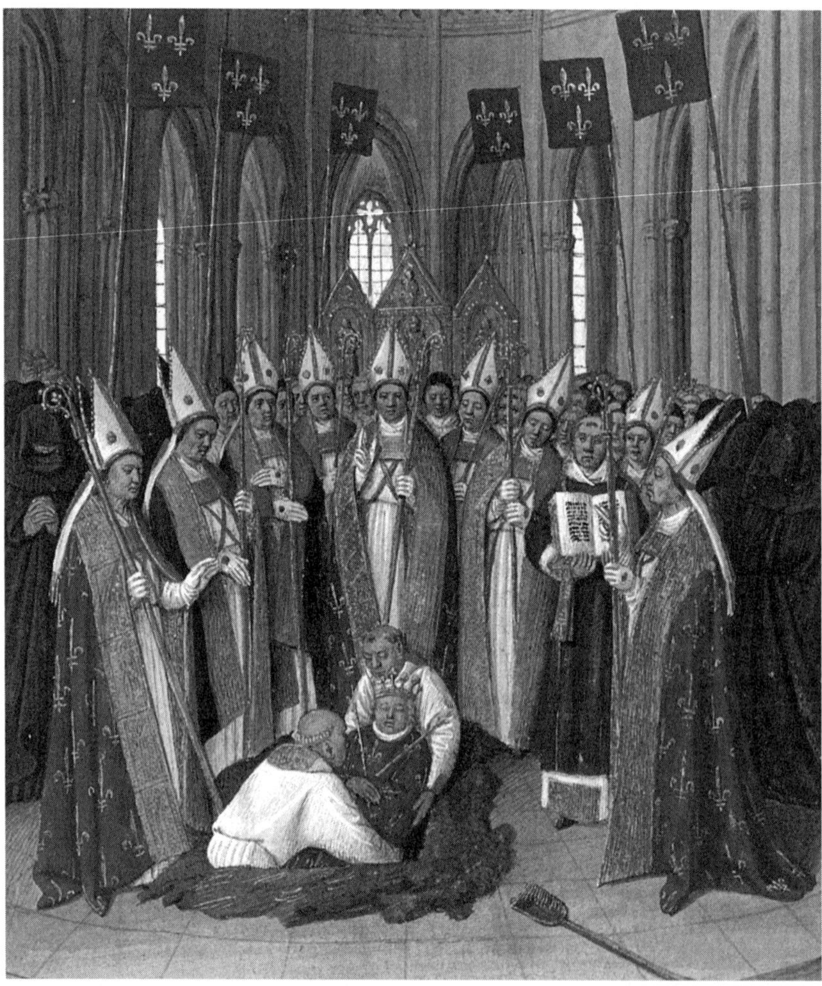

15.1 The pointed arches of Saint-Denis strategically masked. Jean Fouquet, *Burial of Philip IV* (ca. 1460), *Grandes Chroniques de France*, Paris, Bibliothèque nationale de France, ms. fr. 6465, fol. 323. The miniature represents an event that took place at the abbey church of Saint-Denis in 1314. The summits of the arches, pointed in the actual building, are concealed here by banners and perspectival distortion, leaving open the possibility that they might be round and therefore older than they are.

The contemporary beholder knew perfectly well that the arches behind the banners were not round, but the picture refused to concede the point.

From a typological point of view, a Gothic building could even serve as a guide to the lost building manner of the ancients. While one builder was looking to the twelfth-century round-arched basilica as the template for a reengagement with Roman imperial architecture, another was exposing the substitutional infrastructure of the Gothic cathedral, the basis for *its* peculiar "romanity." Alberti, unlike Vasari, said nothing explicitly derogatory about Gothic architecture. It is not even clear that he had any language at his disposal capable of isolating or characterizing the Gothic. In fact, many of Alberti's desiderata for a revival of good architecture seem derived from his experience of Gothic. He compares the three types of arches, semicircular, depressed, and pointed (*compositus* or *acutus*), evenhandedly, well aware of the virtues of the pointed arch even though the ancients did not employ it.[2] Or had the ancients after all employed a pointed arch? Many buildings in the Holy Land far preceding the Latin Crusades carried pointed arches. The Dome of the Rock, with its ring of pointed arches, was, as we saw in section 7, routinely taken to be the living face of the Jewish temple. The earliest Gothic architecture itself emerged in the mid-twelfth century during the period of the Latin occupation of Jerusalem and in an intensive dialogue with Holy Land architecture; indeed, the Crusader additions to the church of the Holy Sepulchre are among the earliest examples of Gothic architecture.[3]

In harmony with Alberti, Aeneas Silvius Piccolomini, Pope Pius II, praised the lofty naves and spires of Cologne, Strasbourg, and Vienna in his pamphlet on the Germans (1458, published 1496).[4] The church in Aeneas Silvius's own model city, Pienza, with its raised side aisles and free-flowing interior space, designed by Bernardo Rossellino, imitates a late Gothic German hall church (figure 15.2). Admiration for the volumes of Gothic architecture was continuous with admiration for the massive Romanesque structures of the Rhineland: Aeneas Silvius was no less awed by the vast interior of Speyer, the basilica of Emperor Henry II (early eleventh century). Aeneas Silvius had to concede that few Italian buildings of the thirteenth or fourteenth centuries rivaled the regularity and technological achievement of the great northern piles. He glimpsed in their light-bathed interiors the sublime *claritas* that the buildings of the Romans, reconstructed in his mind from a handful of standing piers and walls, must once have had.[5]

Fifteenth- and sixteenth-century eyes sometimes saw proximity to antiquity where modern eyes, schooled by thousands of reproductions, see distance and difference. Where we see a clash, say, between the plain, sober manner of the Netherlandish devotional image and the copious,

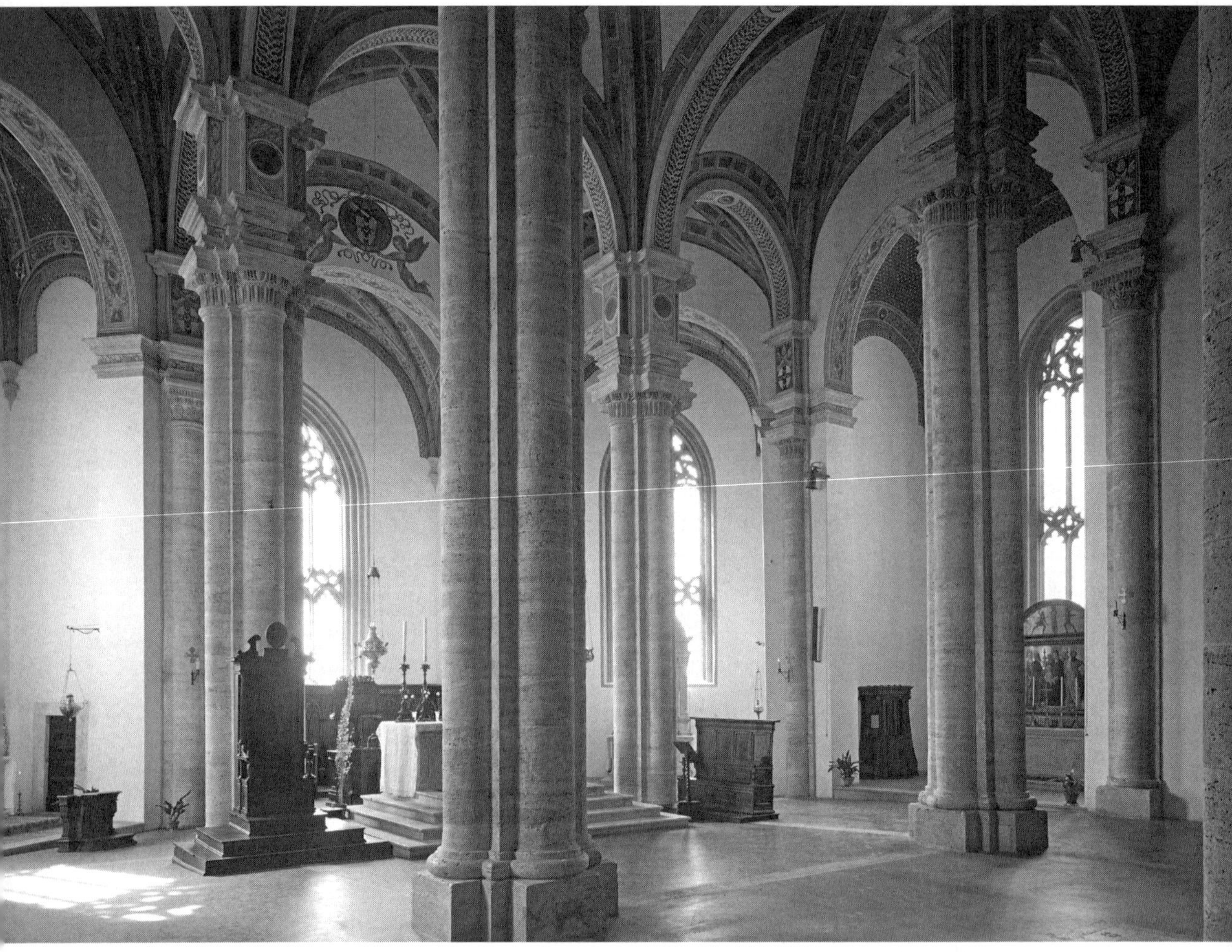

15.2 The German hall church enlisted into the *all'antica* project. Bernardo Rossellino, Pienza, Cathedral (1462). Aeneas Silvius Piccolomini, Pope Pius II, was impressed by the light-infused interiors of the Gothic churches he saw in Germany and Austria, with their elevated side aisles and wide-open spaces. He took these churches as the model for the cathedral of his own ideal city, a reconstruction of the town of his birth according to the timeless, classical principles of urbanism and architecture.

learned stylishness of Italianate ornament, contemporaries may well have seen two modalities of the antique. An intriguing example is a small Madonna and Child perhaps by a Ghent illuminator, perhaps by Simon Marmion, pasted into an Italian manuscript and surrounded by an elaborate painted frame in the latest and fanciest *all'antica* style. That frame is attributed to Attavante Attavanti and dated to about 1510.[6] A family of late fifteenth-century Italian plaquettes, meanwhile, featured a Pietà derived

162

from a painting close to the southern German master Hans Multscher and dated 1457. The German image was adopted by the Italian artists as if it were a venerable cult image. The motif was translated into the medium of bronze relief and, like the Netherlandish miniature just discussed, framed in an *all'antica* tabernacle.[7] This is the equivalent of the enshrining of plain cult images within Bernardo Pinturicchio's antiquarian-flavored della Rovere chapels at Santa Maria del Popolo in Rome. Where an art history sees conflict between the plain, iconic Madonna and Child and Pinturicchio's sophisticated adaptations of mosaic, relief, and baluster, involving grotesque ornament based on direct study of pagan work, contemporaries may have seen no essential clash—a clash in style, to be sure, but everywhere reverence for the ancient, the inveterate, the authentic.[8]

In 1521 the Milanese architect and scholar Cesare Cesariano reproduced in woodcuts the plan, section, and elevation of the cathedral of Milan as an accompaniment to his commentary on Vitruvius, book one, chapter two (figure 15.3).[9] Cesariano was well aware that the cathedral of Milan was a late Gothic building, *germanico more*, displaying *germanicam symmetriam*. And yet he was confident that the projections of the modern building would serve to illustrate the point he was making, namely that the rationality of the system of the orders recommended by Vitruvius was best represented in elevation. The "style" of the cathedral of Milan was different from the temples known to Vitruvius, as Cesariano clearly saw, and yet the building's structure made it possible to demonstrate the *eurythmiam proportionatam* that the Vitruvian system of representation both demanded and demonstrated. Cesariano did discreetly adjust some elements of the modern building, for example, adding moldings to the arches in order to bring the vaults into correspondence with the grid he had superimposed on it.[10] And yet he interprets not only the larger geometry but also the parts of the building as counterparts to the elements of ancient buildings, seeing the high socles of Milan cathedral, for example, as equivalent to the stylobates of temples described by Vitruvius.[11] Cesariano held a capacious, flexible view of architectural history typical of the pre-print era. It was only his decision to publish and illustrate his insights in movable type and woodcut, mechanical media carrying strong connotations of precision and authority, that created an effect of chronological paradox. The creative imitation of the ancient Roman building manner stabilized as a program only when the Roman forms, proportions, and system of orders were fixed by print, both by the printed treatise but especially by its woodcut and engraved illustrations.[12] Once the architectural treatise began to be illustrated by printed images, square Milan no longer fit into round Vitruvius.

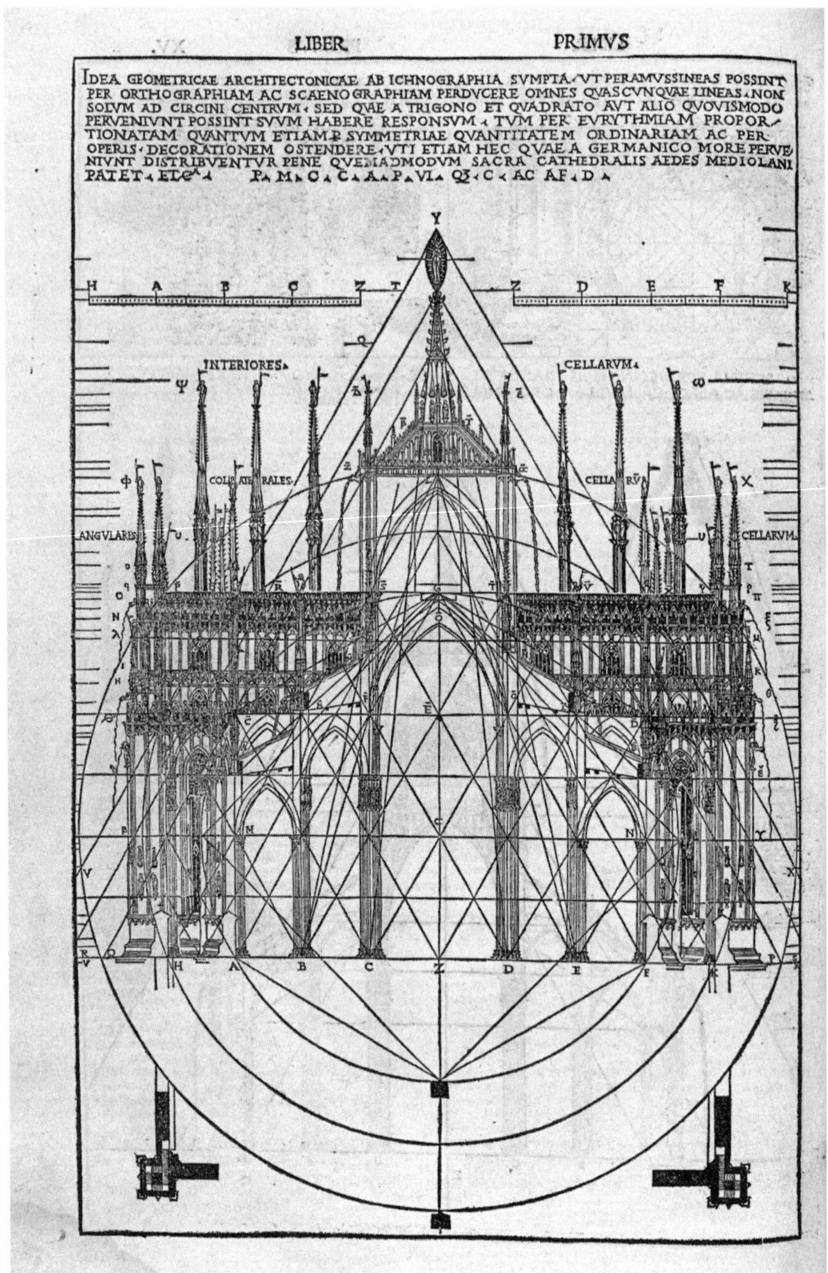

15.3 The elevation of a modern church used to demonstrate Vitruvian "eurhythmic proportion." Cesare Cesariano, *De architectura libri dece* (Como, 1521), fol. 15v. New Haven, Yale University, Beinecke Rare Book Library. The cathedral of Milan was constructed in the late fourteenth and early fifteenth centuries, mainly by German architects. Cesariano conceded that the style of the church was modern, but felt that the underlying structure was sufficiently connected to ancient building practices that it could serve as an exemplar of Vitruvius's principles.

Lorenzo Ghiberti, in his *Meeting of Solomon and Sheba*, one of the bronze reliefs on the doors of the Florence Baptistery (1430s), posed the protagonists on the threshold of a (cutaway or cross-sectioned) cross-vaulted basilica with pointed arches; exactly the profile of the arches of the Duomo of Florence.[13] The Florentines were excavating a substitutional dimension of Île-de-France Gothic that has been difficult for modern art-historical scholarship to perceive. For is it not possible that Alberti understood the pioneering architecture of Saint-Denis, Chartres, and Reims not as a cancellation of the preceding round-arched tradition but as a completion and clarification? Were not the Gothic architects simply generating a more lucid vision of antiquity?[14]

Erhard Reuwich in his fold-out woodcut view of Venice, a woodcut illustrating the published pilgrimage narrative of the Mainz patrician Bernhard von Breydenbach (1486), emended a Gothic structure by converting the pointed arches into round arches. Reuwich, who obviously studied the Venetian cityscape carefully, nevertheless endowed the fourteenth-century doge's palace with a portico of round arches (also reducing the quantity from seventeen to nine) and rounded off the upper-story windows.[15] Reuwich's point in making these small adjustments was that some arches were really round even when they looked pointed. He was correcting the history of architecture. And yet, in the end, there is little evidence that anyone saw the move to pointed arches as an outright violation of antique building principles. The Muslim builders had done it, after all, and early Muslim building practices, as we have seen, were understood as continuous with ancient Roman building practices. This is why the Dome of the Rock was so easily accepted by Crusaders and pilgrims as a substitution for the temple.

Paintings modeled a virtual history of architecture, an ideal and multi-channeled flow of building. Paintings, behind the mask of art, revealed history as a morphology, in speeded-up time. The virtual history of architecture beside the real one publicized the principle of substitution. In paintings of the fourteenth and fifteenth centuries, two families of images of the Temple of Jerusalem flourished in parallel, the one rectangular in plan, the other with central plan. This binarism of plan cut across the binarism of round and pointed. The hesitation between the rectangular and the centrally planned temple, sustained inside the pictorial tradition, permitted the substitutional myth to survive. Origin myths, as we saw with the Hut of Romulus (see section 6), thrive when they are doubled, and then left suspended in a doubled state.

The rectangular or basilical temples descended from images of the Temple of Jerusalem in narratives of the Presentation of the Virgin, the Betrothal of the Virgin, the Circumcision, the Expulsion of the

Moneylenders, and so forth.[16] An influential example was Taddeo Gaddi's *Presentation* in the Baroncelli Chapel in Santa Croce, Florence (1328), with its skeletal, cut-away, attenuated temple mounted high on a podium. The temple in Botticelli's mural painting of the *Temptations of Christ* in the Sistine Chapel (1481–1482), the site of one of Christ's ordeals, is a basilica with a temple front perforated on the ground floor by round arches and above by Gothic tracery framed in rectangular apertures (figure 15.4).[17] Ghirlandaio's *Betrothal of the Virgin* in the Tornabuoni Chapel at Santa Maria Novella in Florence (1486–1490) is set in a square temple, a kind of courtyard enclosed by heavy round coffered arches. The *Circumcision* by Marco Marziale, the high altarpiece of San Silvestro in Cremona (London, National Gallery, 1500), is set inside a nave, under a sequence of vaults coated with gold mosaic. The *Expulsion of Heliodorus* by Raphael in the Stanza d'Eliodoro in the Vatican (1511–1512) also envisions the temple as a nave of gold domes.

In this sequence of images of the temple, the ideal plan, the score that guided the performances — the biblical account of the building of Solomon's Temple — was divinely dictated and could be read by anyone. The paintings corroborated the scriptural account and underwrote the actual history of Christian temple building, dominated as it is by basilical plans. The rectangular lineage of temple representations was also cross-checked with real buildings, especially Old St. Peter's and San Marco (for the mosaics in Marziale's *Circumcision*). But the sequence of painted temples is essentially a self-contained flow, running from picture to picture. The flow is not a simple repetition but a morphology, a repetition with a difference. Each painted temple differs from its predecessor in the sequence. And no matter how little one temple resembles another, they are still all temples. For substitutional identity carries over from painting to painting. Thus the sequence of painted temples represents the *idea* of identity across a substitutional chain. In reality, in the world, sequences of buildings are morphologies. The model of substitutional production, whereby stylistic variation does not interfere with identity, was nothing more or less than the denial of that morphological reality.

The other, competing family of temple pictures was guided by the central plan. Here the scriptural authority was ignored. The temple took its form instead from pilgrims' eyewitness accounts of the Dome of the Rock and was thus founded on a substitutional conflation, or what we would today call a misdating. The polygonal cupola in the background of Duccio's *Christ's Entry into Jerusalem* (1308–1311), with finials and pointed-arched, biforate windows, is surely based on travellers' descriptions of the Dome of the Rock. But the main sequence of painted centrally planned temples

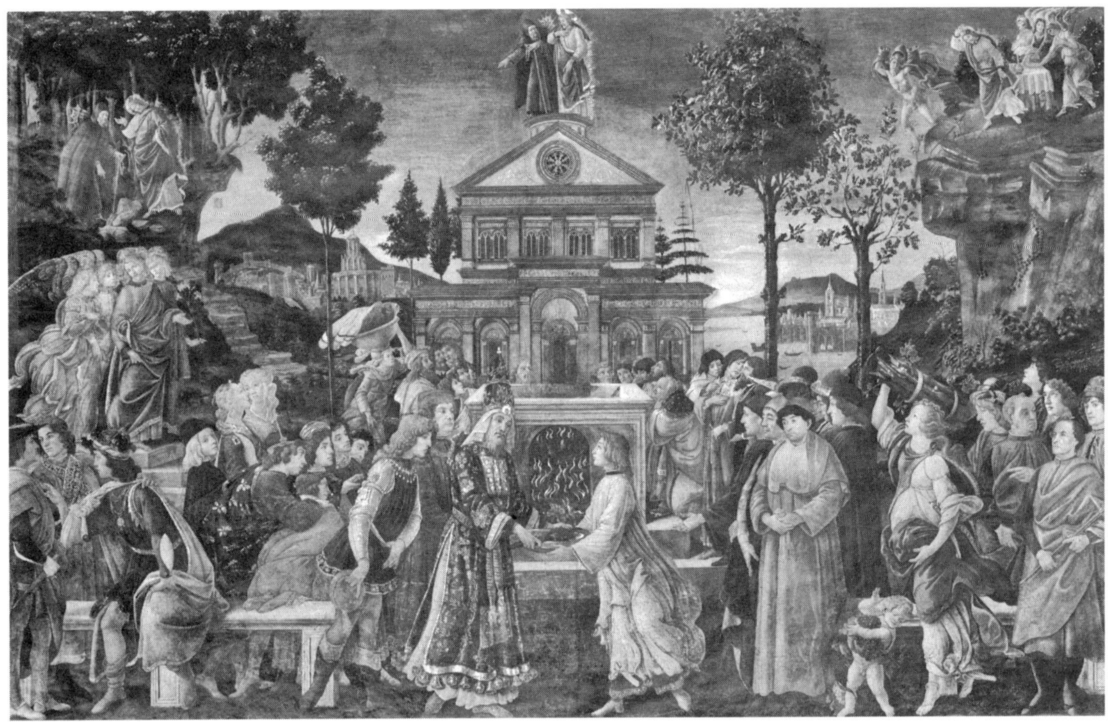

15.4 A portrait of the hospital church of Santo Spirito as the Temple of Jerusalem. Sandro Botticelli, *Temptations of Christ*, fresco, 340 x 540 cm (1481–1482). Vatican City, Vatican Palace, Sistine Chapel. Christ is escorted by the Devil to the "pinnacle of the Temple" (Matthew 4:5). Botticelli endorses the scriptural account of the Temple as rectangular by taking a modern Roman church as his model—and thus provides the Christian basilica with a genealogy.

was Netherlandish. Most attentive to the Muslim structure on the Temple Mount are the representations in the Eyckian *Crucifixion* in the Turin Hours[18] and, as we have seen, in the Rotterdam *Three Marys at the Tomb of Christ* (see figure 7.1). Van Eyck's views of Jerusalem with the polygonal Dome of the Rock, along with the very earliest accurate portrait of the Church of the Holy Sepulchre (ca. 1435), in a manuscript report on a visit to the Holy Land by an official at the court of Burgundy, are clearly based on on-site drawings.[19]

But information about the Dome of the Rock was scarce and mostly unreliable, and it was exactly the interference in the east-to-west flow of data that sustained the substitutional myth with all its formal flexibility. It was no different with the replicas of the edicule of the Holy Sepulchre. Patrons wanted exact replicas. But in the event, they were content with reproducing the dimensions, or even simply the proportions, of the actual object sheltered by Constantine's rotunda in Jerusalem. Giovanni Rucellai reputedly sent an expedition to the Holy Land to obtain "il giusto disegno e misura" of the edicule.[20] From Leon Battista Alberti he commissioned a replica of the structure for a chapel in the church of San Pancrazio, near his palace in Florence.[21] Alberti's structure, dated 1467, was about half the actual size of the edicule (figure 15.5). With its clear stereometric forms, marble and inlaid cladding, and cornice adorned with a row of trefoils, however, it did not very closely resemble the edicule in Jerusalem. The cladding was derived instead from the Florentine Baptistery. Alberti did not imitate the edicule itself, but only its dimensions. The edicule was not, after all, a Constantinian structure; it had been replaced and restored over and over again. Alberti was attempting to imagine the Constantine original, which the extant edicule was believed to reproduce in no wise except for the all-important dimensions. What did the edicule of the Holy Sepulchre look like in the fifteenth century? Images and replicas of the structure from the twelfth to the sixteenth century differ considerably; some have round arches, others pointed.[22] And yet Alberti's archeological fiction immediately assumed exemplary status. A painted wooden box from the period, a reliquary, imitates Alberti's model in the chapel at San Pancrazio.[23]

The first reasonably accurate printed images of the Dome of the Rock and of the Holy Sepulchre were the woodcut illustrations that accompanied the pilgrimage report of Bernhard von Breydenbach, published in German and Latin in 1486.[24] Breydenbach had traveled with a skilled artist, Erhard Reuwich. Painters and architects alike seized upon Breydenbach's images with their technologically conferred authority. A patrician couple in Augsburg, Georg Regel and Barbara Lauinger, built an oval sepulchre for their funerary chapel in Santa Anna (1508), an image of "the tomb of Our Lord Jesus Christ in the very dimensions and form that one is said to find in Jerusalem" (*die begrebnuss unsers lieben Herrn Ihesu Christ in mass und form, wie es in Iherusalem sein solle*). The microarchitectural fancy was guided both by Breydenbach's illustration and the accurate written account of the Nuremberg patricians Sebastian Rieter and Hans Tucher, who had been to the Holy Land in 1479.[25] The newly precise descriptions introduced uncertainty into the tradition. The woodcut view of Jerusalem in the printed *World Chronicle* (Nuremberg, 1493) portrays the Dome of the Rock labeled clearly as the temple of Solomon. Yet the author of the text of the *World Chronicle*, the humanist Hartmann Schedel, reports the rectangular Biblical proportions (fol. 47v), contradicting the illustration. Pilgrimage and travel, accurate descriptions and reliably reproduced images, began to edge Jerusalem out of abstraction and into the realm of experience, threatening the preeminence of the typological approach to architectural history. Paradoxically, the substitutional relation of one structure to the next, copy

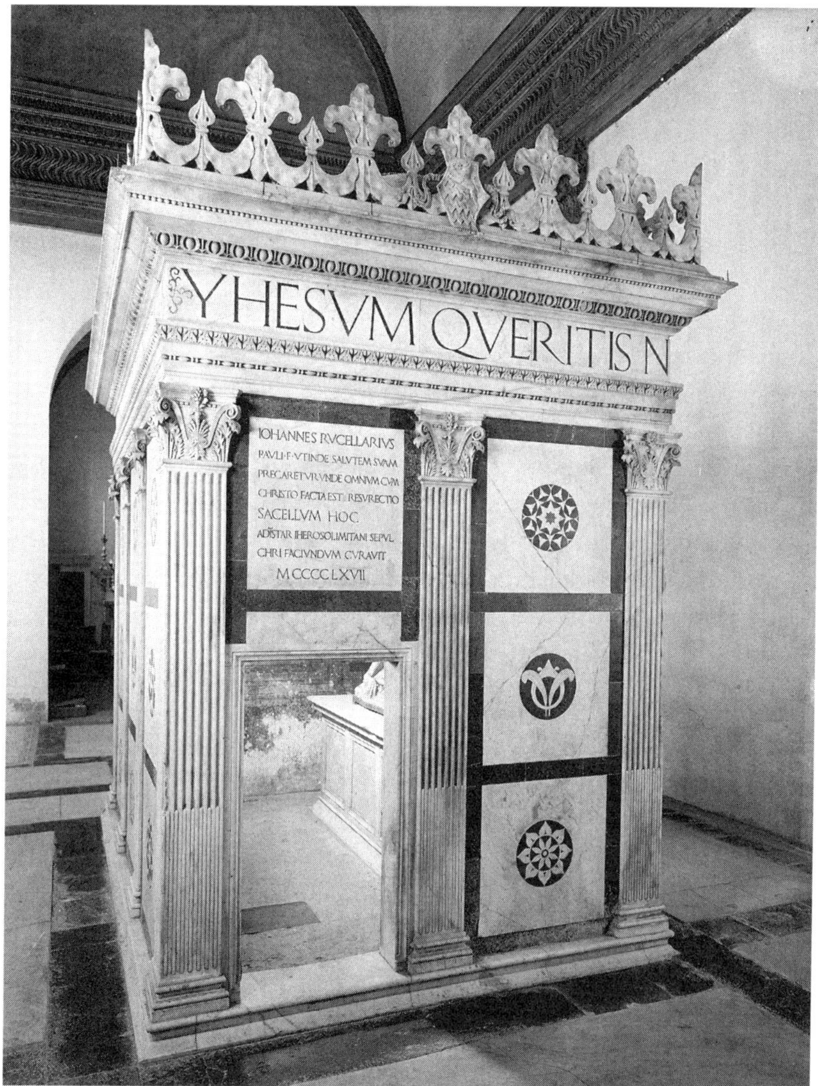

15.5 An abstract replica of the Tomb of Christ. Leon Battista Alberti, Chapel of the Holy Sepulchre, Florence, San Pancrazio (1467). Giovanni Rucellai had Alberti build a half-scale replica of the Holy Sepulchre, based on on-site measurements. Alberti's self-assured performance in Florence does not closely resemble the original in Jerusalem.

to copy, *lost* force as it was more accurately rendered.[26] The principle of substitution began to crumble under the weight of excess precision.

The typological approach to architectural production worked best when type and token, model and copy, did not resemble one another too closely. The virtue of the typological and substitutional principle of building was that identity across sequences of buildings was maintained in theory even as builders enjoyed in practice considerable room for variation. The project of literal formal repetition, legislated by accurate printed renderings of authoritative models, was not appealing to all builders and patrons. The situation was similar in the realm of sculpture. Here, too, the project of replication came to an end just as it approached the possibility of perfection. To make an impeccable sculptural replica was to invoke a force perhaps too powerful, the magic of mimetic doubling. In sculpture, the perfect replica emerged as a suddenly attainable ideal in the later fifteenth century. The Paduan and Florentine sculptors were able to cast faces and animals that generated perfect replicas in clay or bronze.[27] Only a generation earlier, such ambitions had still seemed compatible with the aims of art. Donatello had cast forms from life and integrated them into his works. But at the moment of technological fulfillment, the indexical representation quickly lost its charm. From that point on, few artists counted exact replication either of natural forms or of other works among their ambitions. The divorce between replication and representation was later ratified by Vasari, whose historical narrative awarded little credit to the technicians of printing, imprinting, and casting.

In architecture, multiple antiquities flourished side by side, noncompetitively, until the moment that prints and illustrated books created the possibility of direct visual comparison and forced private notions about form out into the public domain. At that point decisions had to be made. The project of the recovery of ancient architecture could no longer take both the Pantheon and the Dome of the Rock, both the Basilica of Maxentius and the Gothic cathedral, as its models. The intermittent fifteenth-century admiration for the great Gothic structures did not survive long into the next century. The illustrations of Cesare Cesariano's Vitruvius edition of 1521 (see figure 15.3) were a great exception.[28] At this point the "false" image of the temple—the one grounded not in scripture, but in the traditional identification of the temple with the Dome of the Rock—submerged itself deeply into painting, as if seeking protection under the palladium of the imagination. Painting protected the marvelous error by displacing it from the realm of fact to the realm of fiction. In the late fifteenth and early sixteenth century, a sequence of ambitious Italian paintings pictured the temple as polygonal. Pietro Perugino painted an octagonal temple in the background of his *Christ Handing the Keys to Saint Peter* in the Sistine Chapel (1481–1482) (figure 15.6); on the same wall, three bays away, Botticelli was working on his basilical temple (see figure 15.4). At Spello in Umbria, Pinturicchio painted a *Christ Among the Doctors* (1501) before a temple with a six-sided dome and four projecting chapels (figure 15.7). The

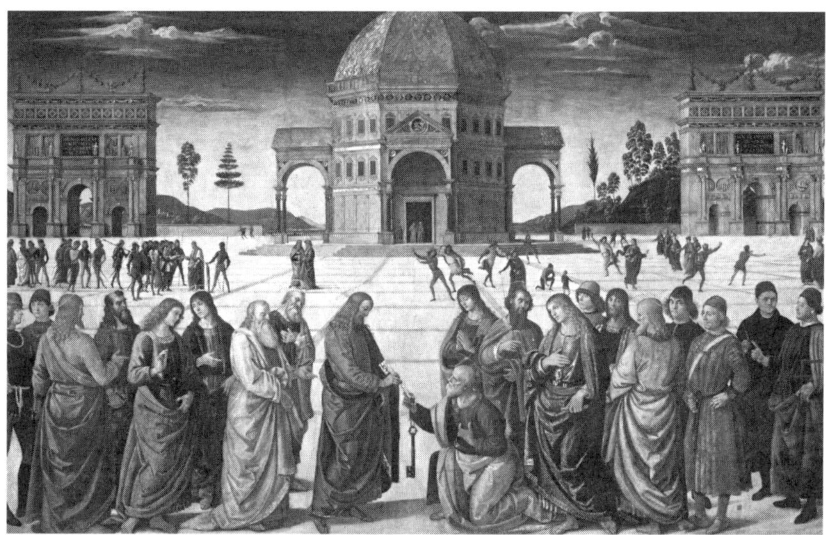

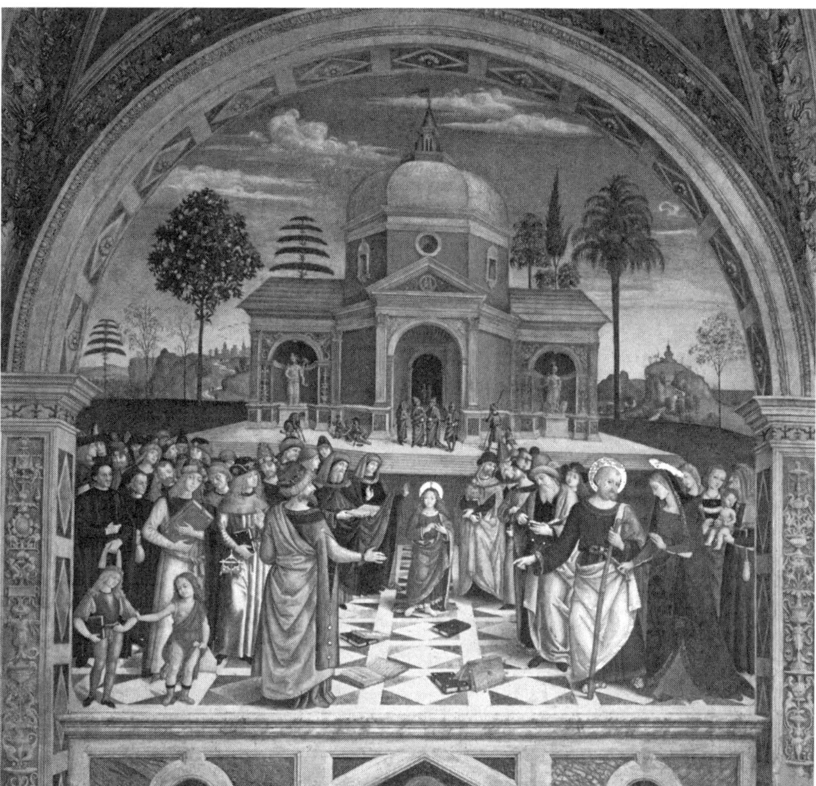

15.6–15.7 The marvelous error of the centrally planned Solomonic Temple, perpetuated and protected in fifteenth-century painting. Pietro Perugino, *Christ Handing the Keys to Saint Peter*, fresco, 340 x 540 cm (1481–1482), Vatican City, Vatican Palace, Sistine Chapel. Bernardo Pinturicchio, *Christ Among the Doctors*, fresco (1501), Spello, Cappella Baglioni, Santa Maria Maggiore. These depictions propound the other theory about the Temple, based not on scripture but upon the archeological evidence of the Dome of the Rock, which was understood as the Temple's successor in Jerusalem. Perugino's interpretation clashed directly with Botticelli's painting on the same wall of the Sistine Chapel (figure 15.4).

temple in Raphael's *Betrothal of the Virgin* (Milan, Brera, 1504) is sixteen-sided. Antiquity, as so often for the Italian painters, was routed through the Netherlandish tradition, which with its archaisms—less authentic and more contrived than admirers perhaps realized—struck the Italians as a living link to an older way of painting. Such images figured an alternative ancestry to polygonal baptisteries like that of Florence, not a pagan ancestry but Jewish.

The sources of the new generation of painted temples were many. Again the forms were threaded in and out of cities and pictures, across the frontier between real and imagined. Buildings were extracted from pictures and actualized in the cities. Many architects around 1500 attempted to pull the central plan out of its character as a model, and out of its picturesque representational identity, and into reality.[29] Some new churches, often associated with miracles or prestigious cult images, complied with the ideal of the central plan.[30] More often the ambition of centrality was only partially realized, in chapels and tribunes. Those buildings in turn became the models for further pictures, thus reentering the realm of fiction, as it were, after a passage through the realm of matter.

The structure that most perfectly realized the central-plan dream was Donato Bramante's Tempietto, a round peripteral structure (figure 15.8). The Tempietto, although consecrated, was a symbolic building placed in the courtyard of an adjoining church. It was the marker of a place—the site of Peter's crucifixion—that no one was quite sure about; a martyrium without a body; a building to be seen and not used. The immediate models of the Tempietto were the pagan round temples at Tivoli, source of the Tempietto's round stylobate, and on the banks of the Tiber, at the Forum Boiarum, source of its three steps. But many of Bramante's ideas cannot be traced to ancient architecture. As a matter of fact, the first mention of the building, in 1517, did not call it a temple but a "large ciborium of marble" (*magnum marmoreumque ciborium*), thus linking it to the tradition of sacramental shelters, baldachins and tabernacles, often in small scale. On this view the source of the building lay not in pagan monumental architecture but in Christian microarchitecture. It was a ciborium brought back up to full size.[31]

Another nonancient feature of the Tempietto is the encircling parapet with its balustrade. The baluster, a kind of miniature Doric column, was known from ancient furnishings and candelabra. The form was adapted by Florentine architects already in the 1450s as supports for benches and altars. The balustrade as a parapet or a crowning element on a building was introduced at the latest in 1479 by Giuliano da Sangallo, at the Villa Medici at Poggio a Caiano.[32] A balustrade, this one constructed out of spolia, was

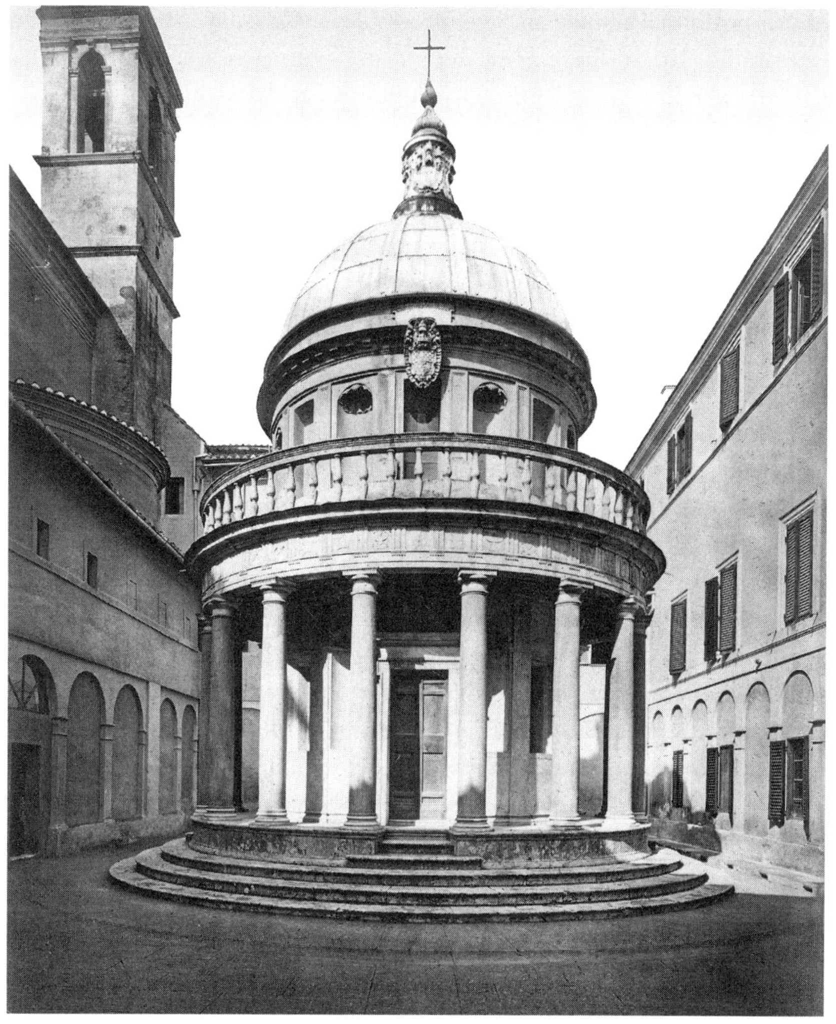

15.8 Model of models. Donato Bramante, Tempietto (after 1502). Rome, San Pietro in Montorio. Bramante combined features of surviving Roman buildings with modern elements to create a completely unprecedented structure. Nevertheless the Tempietto was cited in countless later paintings as if it possessed the authority of antiquity, and was included by Andrea Palladio among the illustrations of ancient temples he published in the fourth book of his *Four Books of Architecture* (1570), for "it seemed to me reasonable that his work should have a place among the ancients."

used in the chapel by (probably) Pinturicchio for Girolamo Basso della Rovere at Santa Maria del Popolo (mid-1480s);[33] at Santa Maria delle Carceri in Prato, at the inner vault gallery and cupola gallery, by Giuliano da Sangallo (1485); and at Giuliano's Palazzo Strozzi (from 1489). Balustrades quickly entered into modern paintings, for example along the cornice of the polygonal temple in Perugino's *Christ Handing the Keys to Saint Peter* in the Sistine Chapel (1481–1482) (see figure 15.6), or Pinturicchio's *Coronation of Enea Silvio* in the Piccolomini Chapel at Siena (1502–1508).[34] Reuwich's woodcut of the Holy Sepulchre introduced twin balustrades (1486).[35] Carpaccio in his *Sermon of Saint Stephen* (Louvre, 1514) gave his Jewish temple, modeled on the Dome of Rock, a balustrade.

Why did Bramante introduce the balustrade, a feature of modern architecture, into his archeological synthesis on the Gianicolo? In fact the confusion had already set in with Giuliano da Sangallo's antiquarian drawings. Giuliano had included balustrades on his descriptions of real ancient buildings, for example the round temple on the Tiber.[36]

Once the Tempietto was in place, any painter interested in picturing ancient temples had the option of quoting Bramante, an authority. One could assume that Bramante, so attentive to archeological detail, knew the secret genealogy of the balustrade. The Tempietto became a "paradigm," discussed and illustrated by all sixteenth-century students of the principles of ancient building, including Palladio, as if it were an on-site reconstruction of—a substitution for—a real vanished temple.[37] Raphael in the *Sermon of Saint Paul at Athens*, a cartoon for a tapestry destined for the Sistine Chapel (ca. 1515), depicts a pagan round temple that closely resembles Bramante's Tempietto, complete with its Doric order. The balustrade on Raphael's painted temple appears strangely provisional, fragile, as if made of wood. Perhaps this was Raphael's way of signaling his doubts about the ancient pedigree of the motif, his loss of confidence in the substitutional mechanisms that used to knit together the infinity of forms into a meaningful history.[38]

SIXTEEN

Citation and Spoliation

A complex commentary on architectural substitution was Leon Battista Alberti's Tempio Malatestiano at Rimini (1450s).[1] Here Alberti worked with an earlier church, the conventual church of San Francesco, a single-aisled, thirteenth-century structure outfitted with side chapels in the fourteenth and fifteenth centuries. He did not allow the older structure to vanish inside the new, however, but rather left it visible by encasing it in a perforated shell. To the front of the building Alberti attached a façade with elements derived from ancient triumphal arches, much as he would at Santa Maria Novella in Florence a few years later. Unique, however, is his treatment of the flanking walls at Rimini. Here the architect designed a pair of arcades, heavy arches on pillars, perhaps under the influence of the Mausoleum of Theodoric at Ravenna; and he placed them at a slight distance from the side walls (figure 16.1). The building inside remains visible through Alberti's marble arcade, half-hidden, as if by a screen, like a relic glimpsed through the grill of a reliquary. Those inner walls, the exterior walls of the side chapels, were in part constructed by Matteo de' Pasti in the 1440s; Alberti may even have been involved in their planning. But they are completely unlike the outer shell, brick rather than marble, and with Gothic windows.[2] The difference between the building's two skins is stressed by the variable rhythm of the apertures: Alberti's arches are not in step with the existing windows, which anyway were irregularly spaced.[3] The irregular spacing of the chapel windows, once dramatized by Alberti's regular arcade, comes to symbolize—again, even if those brick walls were in fact not so very much older than the neoclassical shell—an older way of building, a way of building governed by convention and custom, a conception of building as pragmatic, organic, emergent. Alberti's arcade, by contrast, was a designed intervention requiring the guiding intelligence of an architect. It was an architecture shaped both by timeless principles and by the architect's creativity. Alberti's supplements marked a rupture in a substitutional chain. Alberti's façade and arcade were no slavish imitations of ancient models but rather an independent synthesis born

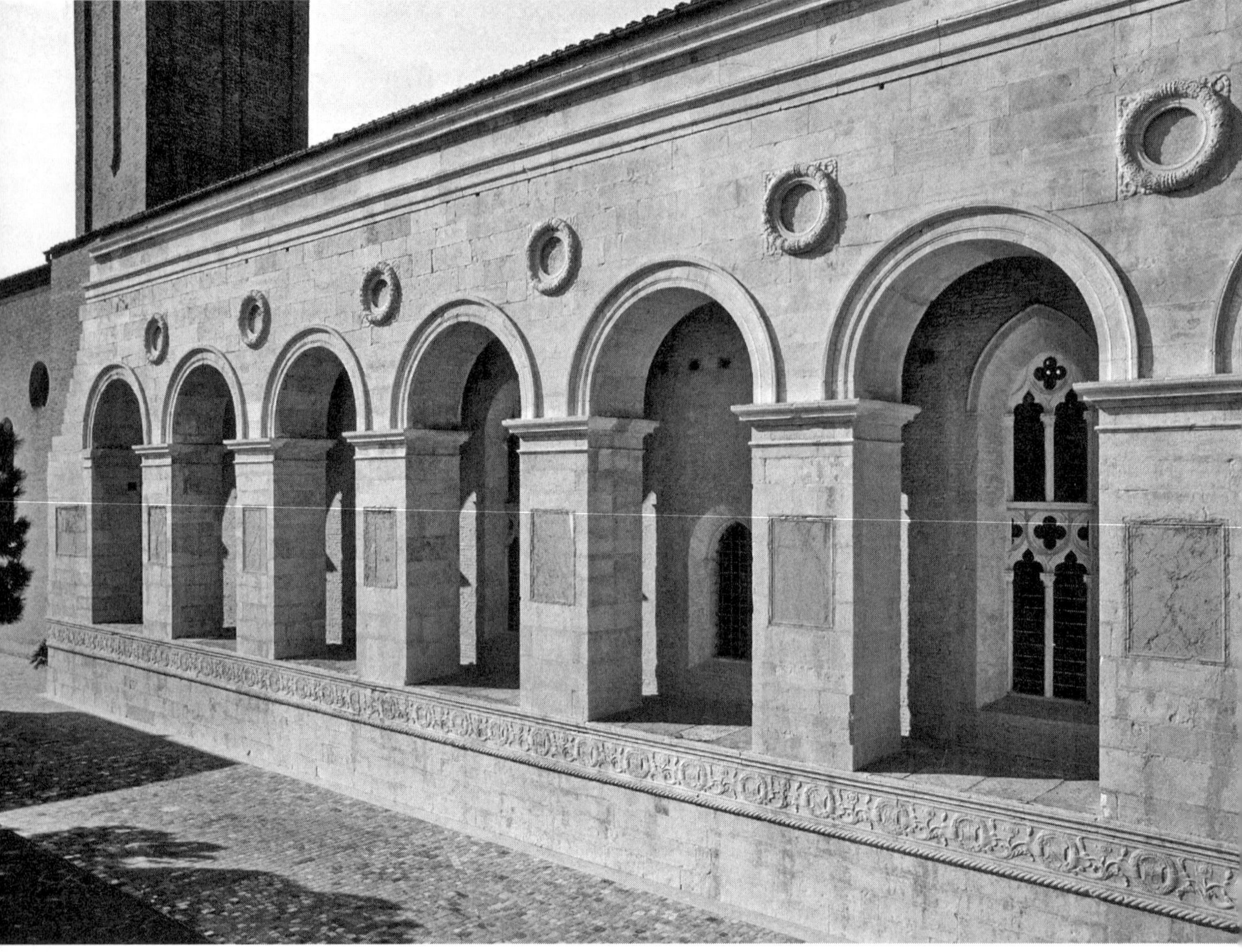

16.1 Sheathing rather than substitution. Leon Battista Alberti, Tempio Malatestiano (1450s), Rimini. Behind the screen of Alberti's neoclassical arcades we glimpse the brick walls of the older Gothic church. The pointed style of the windows, rendered historical by Alberti's stately revetment, is not replaced but preserved, framed as if on display.

of Alberti's mind, once and for all; a performance, in short.[4] The Tempio Malatestiano is a building that diagrams its own construction history and its own epochal placement within a new and ideal history of architecture driven, from this point on, by authorial will.

Alberti's screen isolated an earlier phase of the building's life, extracting it from the flow of time and recreating it as an independent object. The few inches of space he left between the core and the shell, between the relic and the reliquary, symbolized the distinction between a building that simply existed, fulfilling its functions, and a new kind of building capable of conferring intentional meaning. With his architectural supplement Alberti reconfigured his own activity as one of framing and commenting. Instead of trying to mask the earlier life of the building, he enshrined it.

Alberti's modern temple, a three-dimensional diagram of the mechanisms of architectural history, did not so much choose between substitutional and performative origin myths as hold them both in suspension. The two origin myths needed each other. The substitutional myth — the principle that buildings or artifacts replace one another, perfectly, across time and space — was not simply a description of the traditional way of building. Rather, the myth of substitution was developed in order to diminish the significance of the obvious facts that fabricated things are internally heterogeneous, that their identities are multiple, that the flow of creation is always stopping and starting. Alberti's new myth of strong authorship — the principle that the form of a building sprang from the synthetic imagination of the architect — was a way of recovering the antisubstitutional reality of punctuated, disorderly, pragmatic building histories. Alberti was conceding, in effect, that buildings are really built, by people, at one moment and another, and do not unfold mysteriously across time as the substitutional myth would have it. He was proposing to take control of that historical process.

Alberti offered a new way of understanding a building by fashioning a new way of looking at the building, literally. At Rimini, the eye easily reconstructs the building history simply by peering across the screens and moats on its own and seeing diachrony written on a continuous, three-dimensional structure. Without the sort of didactic help that Alberti provides, the curious beholder of a building is reduced to the poor resources of mnemotechnics, like the poet Simonides who, in the fable recounted by Cicero and Quintilian, is able to identify the crushed victims of a collapsed roof by remembering the seating plan at the dinner table.[5] Under a substitutional system, only the newest instantiation of a building matters. The beholder who is unsatisfied with this arrangement will need to remember what it was that the new replaced in order to fill the new with its full quotient of meaning. Alberti helps the viewer remember by leaving a gap. Later, reproductions, archeology, and historical narratives will serve the mnemotechnic function, permitting every building to be, in addition to whatever else it might be, a document of architectural history.

The comparison that Alberti staged at Rimini between older and newer ways of building was not so different, structurally, from the comparison that Robert Campin staged in his Prado *Betrothal of the Virgin* thirty years earlier, where he thematized the passage from Old Dispensation to New by a passage from Romanesque temple to Gothic portal (see figure 14.3). In each case, the outer building "needs" the inner building. At Rimini, in an environment where neoclassicism had come to prevail, the signs are simply reversed: now the pointed-arched building is the type, and the round-arched shell is its antitype or fulfillment. For by 1450 the real world, in the person of Alberti, had reembraced the round arch, complicating any notion of building history as a linear flow. The round arch was now no longer the old term but the modern term.

Painters and sculptors would soon learn to reflect on the production histories and origin myths of their own media, and not just those of architecture, by staging comparisons inside their own borders between old and new ways of making images, between the referential and the fictional image. (Sections 11 and 12 pointed to examples of such juxtapositions: Botticelli's *Portrait of a Youth Holding an Icon*, figure 11.7, and the Monument to Giotto in Florence Cathedral, figure 12.1.) Such comparisons would take the form of managed contrasts between container and contained, marked by visible seams.

Alberti's comparison achieved with real materials what Campin's comparison had achieved on a virtual level. Campin's staged comparison was an easier trick because the frame and the flat picture plane brought all the elements of the picture to a common denominator. The picture plane, symbolizing the control of the single author, signals that everything you see is meaningful. Total meaningfulness is the criterion of the pictorial text, which gathers the time of the work into a single plane. On the surface of a painting, difference reads *as* difference, and not merely as adaptation to pragmatic circumstances.

The mechanism of comparison remains the same, however, whether the materials are real or virtual. The physical recontextualization of an artifact, whether a painting or a building, is conceptually continuous with the practice of citation, or the transfer of parcels of coded meaning from one text to another. In the one case, the reused element is material; in the other case, the transferred element is only a representation, a virtual relic. Virtual reuse repeats a form or combination of forms; or brings to life again a fictional character. An original shaping labor is valued and preserved. In both modes, real and virtual, recycling is able to generate meaning if a perceptible hierarchy, a comparison, is established between the alien element and its new host, its container.

All production of artifacts; all art making, meaning making, and manipulation of codes; all histories of building and painting are histories of reuse. In fact, the true rarity is the opposite of reuse, namely, pure creation *ex nihilo*. Artistic creation *ex nihilo* may not exist at all, for an expression without any ties to the past would be incomprehensible. One could say that citation, the *imitatio* of prior models, is the basic condition of expression; whereas citation by means of literal, physical transfer of materials is the special case. Physical citation is an eloquent version of ordinary citation.

Ensembles of shrine and enshrined, of reliquary and relic, of building and spolium, of text and citation, are meaning-making machines. Meanings are set in motion by the perception of the seam between shrine and enshrined. The enshrined fragment of the past—whether a fragment made of stone or a fragment made of code—now stands out in conceptual relief against its container. Such meanings become available once histories of making can be visualized; that is, once form or materials are seen to have historical coordinates. The icon in Botticelli's portrait, a relatively indifferent piece of trecento painting showing a still unidentified saint, becomes in the new ensemble a symbol of icon painting, that is, a sample of a mode of image making now recognized *as* a mode of image making. Campin's, Alberti's, and Botticelli's reframings are the prehistory of the later practice of conservation. In his account of the life of Perino del Vaga, Vasari describes an elaborate episode of enshrinement and bricolage. Remarking, probably around 1540, that a Madonna by Giotto in St. Peter's in Rome was to be destroyed during the rebuilding of the church, Perino and his friend, the scholar Niccolò Accaiauoli, "had the wall cut around it" and moved the fragment underneath the organ, where there was no altar or liturgical furnishing. Then, interpreting the kneeling figure at the Madonna's feet as a portrait of the poet Petrarch, they added to the fragment another monument, the memorial to Orso dell'Anguillara, the Roman senator who crowned Petrarch on the Capitoline hill in 1341. Thus two preexisting pieces in the church were brought together into a historicizing ensemble, framed by "ornaments and stuccoes and paintings" by Perino's hand.[6]

This possibility—the historicist reading of the earlier artifact—was latent in the medieval practice of architectural spoliation, or the translation of already worked materials into a new context.[7] Spoliation, the carting off and display of the artifacts of the vanquished as a form of trophy, is a military metaphor. The metaphor has survived because the elements of violence and of the reassignment of meaning as the perquisite of cultural dominance are so often present in the history of European architecture, well beyond a strictly military context. Military looting is an apposite metaphor also because it implies an ambiguous attitude of mixed contempt and admiration on the part of the victors. The vanquished are in disarray; the fine products of their workmanship, displaced and displayed, take the measure of the triumph. The shields and arms of the vanquished, rendered useless through defeat, mark the neutralization of the enemy.

Not all reuse of previously worked materials carries meaning. Many buildings contain blocks, columns, capitals, or other material taken from some older building, sometimes from the same site, sometimes transported considerable distances. If the seam between container and contained is invisible, or visible only to modern scholars, then we are faced simply with a pragmatic recycling of scarce materials. Any reuse that breaks down the original form of the used material does not signify, or does so only weakly. Ancient Roman structures were crushed and burned to make lime, and so erased from memory. Bricks were carted away from the old buildings and reassembled in new form. Such reuses are well described as *ecological*. Materials are broken down so that they can reenter the life cycle of things. The bits of stone come without memories. The condition for their reincarnation, their second life, is a forgetting of the first life. When a reused element is treated as a modular unit and simply reinserted into a new system, it is easily absorbed. The bronze horse that the bronze Marcus Aurelius rides on the Capitoline Hill was once riderless, a horse monument perhaps of the first century. A century or so later the emperor (or at least his legs and upper body) was added. Not until quite recently did it occur to anyone to question the synergetic pair.[8] The recycling of the horse was effectively masked. In this case, the container succeeded in "colonizing" the contained. The container or frame—the body of the emperor—flooded the recycled horse with meaning such that its original state and context were completely overwhelmed.

The heavy use of columns and capitals stripped from pagan buildings in early medieval Italy was a matter of thrift, more than anything else, and severe shortages of materials and skills. The popes between the fifth to the thirteenth centuries were trying to sustain the architectural momentum initiated by Augustus and perpetuated by Constantine. But the great imperial marble quarries along the edge of the Mediterranean were all shut down by the sixth century and never reopened until modern times, if at all.[9] All medieval precious marbles are spolia. Monolithic columns and the largest and most finely carved ashlar blocks and capitals, not to mention the prestigious colored marbles from Egypt, Tunisia, and Asia Minor, had to be extracted from local temples and palaces. The Christian basilica of the Italian Middle Ages, not only in Rome but also in Milan and in Campagna, was unable to conceal its patchwork quality. Sets of columns and capitals were cobbled together from diverse sources. Capitals were used as bases, cornices as lintels; smaller bits of colored stone that could not be used for larger elements were reset as pavement. Any ashlar or straight-edged block was valuable and was employed in a wall even if it bore an inscription.[10]

The basilicas were unable to conceal their patchwork quality, but also perhaps unwilling to do so. Early Christians sometimes turned a functional necessity into a semantic virtue. They had the authority of Constantine's triumphal arch, after all, which displayed recut, spoliated reliefs from second-century sources, not out of dire necessity but to make an effect. When the seam between old and new is visible, it is possible to place the different elements, present and past, here and there, into a figural or typological relationship: the triumphant building, the container, completes or fulfills the spoiled building just as the New Testament had fulfilled the Old. Maria Fabricius Hansen, radicalizing Alois Riegl's paradoxical apologia for the late antique and early medieval *Kunstwollen*, has unfolded the semantic dimensions that soon accrued to the heterogeneous, irregular aspect of the early medieval Roman churches, beginning with the basic meaning of simultaneous continuity with and triumph over paganism.[11] She characterizes Christian reuse of building material in the first millennium as "appropriation," in effect a milder, theologized version of the military spoil.

Rome's obsession with spolia was exceptional. Still, spoliation was more common in the rest of the continent, indeed in the entire Mediterranean basin, than is often realized. Many medieval structures incorporated building material from their own prior incarnations or from nearby abandoned structures. Some potentates went far afield in search of the best materials. Charlemagne brought columns from Rome and Ravenna to his palace chapel at Aachen.[12]

The Gothic building system as it was developed north of the Alps had little use for spolia. Valuable material such as colored marble or monolithic shafts was in any case scarce in the north. Gothic architecture was strictly modular and the incorporation of nonstandard parts would spoil the effect, not to mention risk destabilizing the building. In the Gothic system, every stone had to be custom cut. The French, German, and English builders had the skill and wherewithal to do that.

Yet during a post-fire rebuilding of Magdeburg Cathedral in the 1230s, columns that had been carted from Ravenna by Emperor Otto I in the tenth century were, understandably, not only preserved but reinstalled in the new choir.[13] Spolia could "backdate" a building, as at Saint-Rémi in Reims, where spoliated columns at the portal with statues of St. Peter and St. Remigius recalled the historical role of those saints in the Christianizing of France and registered the building's great antiquity.[14]

Spoliation ought to have appealed to the fifteenth-century builders. Part of the project of the new architecture was simply the restoration of ancient splendor, the base-level indicator of cultural prosperity. Spolia were "stones reborn," *rediviva saxa* in the phrase of the late fourth-century

Codex Theodosianus.[15] They could have become a symbol of the Renaissance. Fifteenth-century eyes were wide open to what was left of the oldest Roman buildings, pagan and early Christian, including such putative relics as the Baptistery in Florence, with their polychromy, precious monoliths, and variegated aspect. Quattrocento eyes were pleased by aggregation and bizarre piling on of architectural elements.[16]

To disassemble and then reassemble the built world into new forms was less to make the world function as the key to a hidden code, as the Netherlandish artists did when they portrayed real modern buildings in their historical paintings, than as a *palette*. If one wanted colored stone, then it had to be recycled stone. The exception was Lombardy, where brick was used, in effect, as an ersatz for red marble. In the north of Italy a wildly creative polychrome architecture flourished. Such fantasies as the Certosa di Pavia, Santa Maria delle Grazie in Milan, the Colleoni Chapel at Bergamo, the Portinari Chapel at Sant' Eustorgio in Milan, Santa Maria dei Miracoli in Venice, and the church at Crema in turn captured the imagination of a wide range of painters, including Giovanni Bellini, Cima da Conegliano, and Albrecht Altdorfer. Architects of the late fifteenth and early sixteenth centuries did not share the painters' freedom. There just were not enough stones left on the ground. The stones had found their homes and they were not permitted to keep circulating. The medieval churches, repositories of the best ancient building stuff, were by now off-limits as quarries, and therefore the fifteenth-century architects had few opportunities to use real ancient material. Already in 1436 Pope Eugene IV had issued an edict prohibiting theft of valuable church furnishings including colored stones, and in 1439 he took "protective action" on the Colosseum.[17] Admittedly, Eugene's successor Nicholas V went to great lengths to obtain spectacular materials such as monoliths and colored marbles, for example the four massive monolithic columns from the Baths of Agrippa near Santa Maria sopra Minerva, carted to St. Peter's in 1451–1452 at the cost, according to the German observer Nikolaus Muffel, of 1600 ducats. This was a severe technical challenge, for the columns, if the dimensions reported by Muffel can be credited, were even larger than the huge columns of the porch of the Pantheon. Later, Popes Innocent VIII and Alexander VI installed colossal columns, perhaps from the Baths of Diocletian, in the triumphal arch at San Giovanni in Laterano.[18]

Ancient and medieval displacement of building material was a topic of intense interest in the Renaissance. Raphael in his letter to Leo X carefully described the patchwork effect of the Arch of Constantine.[19] The new St. Peter's of the sixteenth century relied heavily on spoliation, and for clear reasons: the builders needed to assert the continuity, as vividly as possible, between the destroyed Constantinian basilica and the modern pretender. Thirty-eight of forty-four 30-foot columns from the old structure can be identified in the present basilica.[20] Bramante used columns from the central nave of St. Peter's in the Tegurio, the temporary shelter for the high altar that he built among the ruins, and he may have planned to use spolia in the new cupola.[21] At St. Peter's the comparison between container and contained took the form of a comparison between past and present: the *spolium* or the citation recreated the past as a figure against the ground of a present. The past is assigned a form, a form distinct from the form of the past. The point at St. Peter's was to symbolize continuity. The use of spolia preempted the substitution principle's healing of heterogeneity by producing heterogeneity artificially. The visible spolium was a kind of homeopathic remedy for discontinuity. The spolium compensates; it is the building's resort to the rhetoric of assertion. Visible spoliation either explains that the building has been repaired but its identity is stable, or insists that the building stands in an effective referential relationship to much older buildings. The mechanisms that fastened artifact to artifact, monument to monument, were at once perceived and perceived to be failing. The spolium expresses the fear that because we cannot any longer count on the legibility of referential links, such links must be literalized by the physical insertion and display of relics.

At Rimini or St. Peter's there was no mistaking the identity of the architectural relic. The host building became the reliquary of the spolium. But once transported from one site to another, the architectural relic was in danger of losing its identity. The relic was often physically contiguous, even continuous with its container. Potentially the container furnished a spectacular, public foil for the inlaid relic. But if the relic was not clearly marked as such, and had to depend for recognition on the sharp eyes and art-historical memory of beholders, then there was a risk that the relic would blend into the host building and become invisible. Such spolia were half visible, half invisible—in effect, "screened." The screen protects, obstructs, and captures, but it also permits a degree of transgression.

To identify a column as a spolium was to acknowledge its historicity. But that historicity might only be loosely coordinated with chronology, with historical events and persons. Plainly, the spoliated marble had been quarried somewhere far away; someone fetched it; someone cut and polished this column. The spolium established a real connection with the labor, indeed the body, of another maker, not the builder of the present tense but the body of another artist or builder or even a whole community, elsewhere, and in the past tense. That labor was extended by the reach of the spolium. The ancient column or capital reused by a medieval builder, even if the builder knew which ancient structure it came from, might carry a reference not to that one structure but to classical or pagan culture in general, or simply to empire. It is like the distinction between architectural portraiture and a more general invocation of an obsolete building manner.

As we have seen, quattrocento architects had limited access to spolia. There was plenty of recycling of material, especially columns, in sacred and domestic architecture. But even when the quattrocento builder uses a readymade component, it is very hard to tell whether he meant to make an historical point, or was simply grateful to have interesting materials. Ambiguous are the sixteen columns of the peristyle of Bramante's Tempietto (see figure 15.8). They have been described as spolia on account of small differences in size and other irregularities that presumably would not have been acceptable in a custom-made set of columns.[22] On the other hand, is it likely that Bramante would have been able to find, anywhere in Rome, a complete set of sixteen unbroken columns of exactly the size and proportions he wanted for his little masterpiece? Perhaps Bramante found the columns but customized them to fit his own structure. One might finally wonder whether Bramante had the columns prepared in such a way as to suggest the possibility of their being spolia.

On the whole, fifteenth-century architects were more interested in physical continuity than in heterogeneity. When they did recycle ancient columns, they were apt to endow them with brand new capitals to produce a unified effect. Bramante used old columns but always designed his own capitals and other ornament. Most significant new structures used no spolia at all.[23] Fifteenth-century Italian architects tended to fashion imitations of ancient capitals or moldings, possibly meant as virtual spolia, or simulations of material relics.[24]

The architects therefore moved between the possibilities marked out by Botticelli's antiquarian-flavored spoliation of a trecento altarpiece and Carpaccio's painterly embedding of a virtual antiquity, the bronze statue of Christ. Architecture rediscovered representational dimensions that it had forgotten, touching off a subtle semantic interchange between spoliation and citation. The architectural citation represents spoliation, in the sense that it symbolizes the literal fact of material continuity that sustained buildings through their life in time. At the same time, spoliation comes to represent citation, in the sense that it literalizes a typological or intertextual relationship between buildings. Speaking most generally, the flow of building history was perceived in the fifteenth century to have broken down, and the response was the preparation of two parallel tracks, or possibilities for meaning: citation and spoliation.

SEVENTEEN

Neo-Cosmatesque

The sharpened eye of the fifteenth century rediscovered, on the floors of the churches of Rome, a prestigious form of ceremonial mosaic pavement composed of grid, interlace, and whorl patterns built up from small square and triangular fragments of white and colored marble as well as larger disks. But like the manuscripts that yielded the minuscule script and the vine scrolls, the Roman floors were not quite as old as their admirers hoped. The fifteenth-century pavements imitated the flooring of the churches of the twelfth and thirteenth century in Rome and in the surrounding province of Latium, work in the so-called "cosmatesque" manner. Once assigned a false pedigree, the cosmatesque floors could stand in for the ancient imperial way of paving, about which little was known.[1]

The system of small square and triangular fragments of white and colored marble patterned in grids had indeed been developed in early medieval Rome and therefore did bear a genealogical relationship to ancient pavement design. The distinctive guilloches, whorls, and disks that appealed to the imagination of the Renaissance, however, were not Roman but middle Byzantine patterns, introduced to Italy in the late eleventh century, for instance by Byzantine workmen hired by Abbot Desiderius of Monte Cassino, 80 miles south of Rome.[2] The eastern system was adopted in Rome and Lazio over the next two centuries by the well-documented network of workshops known as the Cosmati on the basis of a family of masters who dominated the craft for four generations.[3] The Cosmati also designed church furnishings, pulpits, thrones, portals, and plutei on the same system. In the twelfth and thirteenth centuries most major churches in Rome were paved or repaved with such a floor. In many cases these floors replaced earlier inlaid floors that perhaps date from the ninth century or earlier but had fallen into disrepair.[4]

The stones employed in the medieval tiled pavements were all spolia. The Cosmati reused many of the tiles from the predecessor floors, as well as bits of stone left over from the larger pieces of Roman-era marble. And so in a real material sense the floors were linked to Roman antiquity. Cosmatesque

floors were the opportunistic products of what might be called microspolia-
tion. The large disks favored by the Cosmati were slices of massive columns.
But most of their tesserae were the exiguous remainders of previous spoliations, bits of colored marble too small to be re-used in any other way. Before
they were completely trampled underfoot, before they became gravel or
dust, the fragments were put back into circulation, arranged into geometric
patterns, pushed back toward meaningfulness.[5] The whorled patterns of the
twelfth- and thirteenth-century cosmatesque floors were the near end of
a long and tortuous replica chain winding through the east but ultimately
grounded in Roman antiquity. Some patterns deployed by the Cosmati,
for example in the interval areas, were in fact modeled directly on ancient
Roman pavement designs.[6] The cosmatesque work was thus a creative synthesis of two traditions, metropolitan Roman and Constantinopolitan, a
whole greater than the sum of its parts, in the end matching nothing that
the ancients had done. To thirteenth-century eyes, cosmatesque work was
the timeless and most splendid approach to interior decoration, the one
naturally preferred in antiquity as it was in heaven above. The Sancta Sanctorum, the papal chapel believed to have fourth-century origins, was rebuilt
and repaved, by the Cosmati, around 1280.

The chain of Roman pavement making broke in the fourteenth century.
No Roman workshop any longer produced cosmatesque work. The cosmatesque patterns had to be relearned in the fifteenth century. In the quattrocento the inlaid floors of the Cosmati were only a century and a half to
three centuries old, and yet they might as well have been a thousand years
old. The real origins of the floors of the old Roman churches had slipped
into oblivion. It was not so unreasonable to assume the great antiquity
of a polychrome floor, given that the twelfth-century cosmatesque pavements were themselves derived through multiple channels from ancient
pavements. The process was slow and uneven, for it was really only popes
and a few other grandees who had the power to rip up old floors and reassemble their tiles in new patterns. The key episode was the restoration
of the floor of the Lateran basilica by Pope Martin V in 1425. In that year
Martin hired two artisans to collect marbles and stones from abandoned
buildings and sites with a view to a new pavement at San Giovanni.[7] The
floor restoration at the Lateran basilica is hard to reconstruct because it
is not clear what was there before. It may have been largely a repair job
involving substitution of broken tiles and the like. Such repairs were easy
to do, for there were plenty of odd bits of colored marble lying about; in
the churches of Rome they are carried out by local artisans, rather casu-
ally, to this very day. Martin's recovery or reinterpretation of the old floor
of the Lateran inspired in the 1480s a series of neo-cosmatesque floors in

Roman chapels: the Bufalini (figure 17.1) and Crucifixion Chapels at Santa Maria Aracoeli (both 1480s) and the Carafa Chapel at Santa Maria sopra Minerva (ca. 1488).[8] The fifteenth-century floors are not copies of their twelfth-century models. Rather, they extract the key motifs, especially from the main axes of the floor, and redeploy them in a new system.

The recovery of the twelfth-century floor patterns was a joint project involving Roman and Florentine patrons and craftsmen.[9] The interest of the Medici in ancient colored marbles was the context for the earliest neo-cosmatesque floor in Florence, at the chapel of the Cardinal of Portugal at San Miniato al Monte (mid-1460s).[10] Cosimo de' Medici's grandchildren installed a marble slab over his tomb in front of the high altar of Brunelleschi's San Lorenzo in 1467. With its quatrefoil design in inlaid red and green porphyry the tomb slab recalls medieval cosmatesque designs and tries to share their ancient referential force. The tomb slab in San Lorenzo, designed by Andrea del Verrocchio, was only one element in a total revivalist program at San Lorenzo, the liturgical unfolding of the architect Brunelleschi's formal references to Santi Apostoli and the Baptistery. Donatello's bronze pulpits, noted already in section 13, were oblong in form rather than octagonal and were attached to piers on either

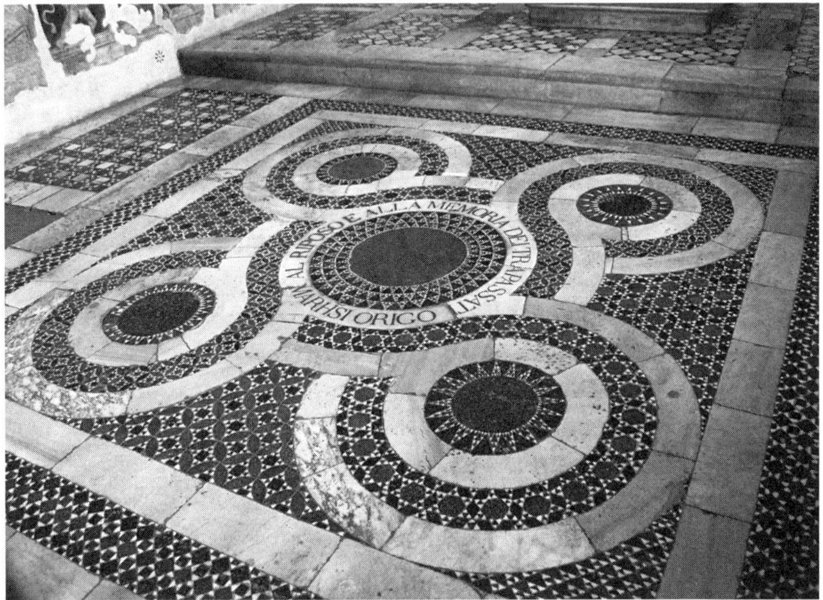

17.1 Antiquarianism in chapel design. Pavement, Bufalini Chapel (1480s). Rome, Santa Maria Aracoeli. One of several Roman chapels of the 1480s that revive an approach to floors believed to be ancient: small tiles of colored marble arranged in interlocked whorls.

side of the nave, specifically recalling early Christian double pulpits *a cornu Evangelii* and *a cornu Epistoli*.[11] The backward references at San Lorenzo in Florence do not reach back all the way to Constantine, however; some of them indeed only go back a century. The bronze pulpits recovered the form of early fourteenth-century Tuscan pulpits and altars. In 1532 Michelangelo, extending the by now seventy-year-old project of Cosimo, proposed a reliquary ciborium on four columns for the high altar of San Lorenzo not unlike the fourteenth-century example at San Giovanno in Laterano.

The recovery of cosmatesque ornament in the fifteenth century is easily situated within the intertwined contexts of the archeologically-minded revival of pagan antiquity and the reengagement with the Byzantine icons. Like the icons (see sections 10 and 11), the cosmatesque pavements and church furnishings were twelfth- and thirteenth-century artifacts with presumed ancient pedigrees; like the icons, they were reassessed and imitated in the fifteenth century. These projects anticipated the more scholarly restorations of the Roman Counter-Reformation, for example the redecorations of San Cesareo and Santi Achilleo e Nereo by Cardinal Cesare Baronio.[12] Indeed, the measure of the substitutional effectiveness of the cosmatesque floors is that they were taken to be ancient floors not only in the fifteenth century but well beyond. In the later sixteenth century, in the context of the archeologically self-conscious revival of ancient Roman arts, the twelfth-century floors were still valued as relics. In 1562, fragments of the cosmatesque ornamentation of Old St. Peter's — a pair of marble panels from the nave — were preserved as relics and installed in the Casino of Pius IV. The last portions of the old floor were inventoried around 1600. Twenty years later Giacomo Grimaldi, in his *Descrizione* of Old St. Peter's, assessed the pavement in Old St. Peter's as *fortasse Constantiniani*, "perhaps Constantinian."[13] But Grimaldi could have read in the *Liber Pontificalis* that Pope Callixtus II furnished the basilica with a new pavement in 1123, at the very moment when the Cosmati workmen were renewing the floors of San Clemente and Santi Quattro Coronati.[14]

The pavements of the most prestigious monuments of the Roman Renaissance are imitations of medieval cosmatesque floors: the pavements of the Sistine Chapel, of Bramante's Tempietto, and of the Stanza della Segnatura.[15] This surprising fact is not so much misinterpreted by modern scholarship as simply ignored.

The Sistine Chapel was restored by Sixtus IV between 1477 and 1480. Its length is 40 meters, its width 13, and its height 20, the very proportions of the most venerable of prototypes, the Temple of Jerusalem, whose dimensions, according to 1 Kings 6, were 60 cubits long, 20 wide and 30 in height.[16] The dimensions seem to have been fixed by the original Palatine

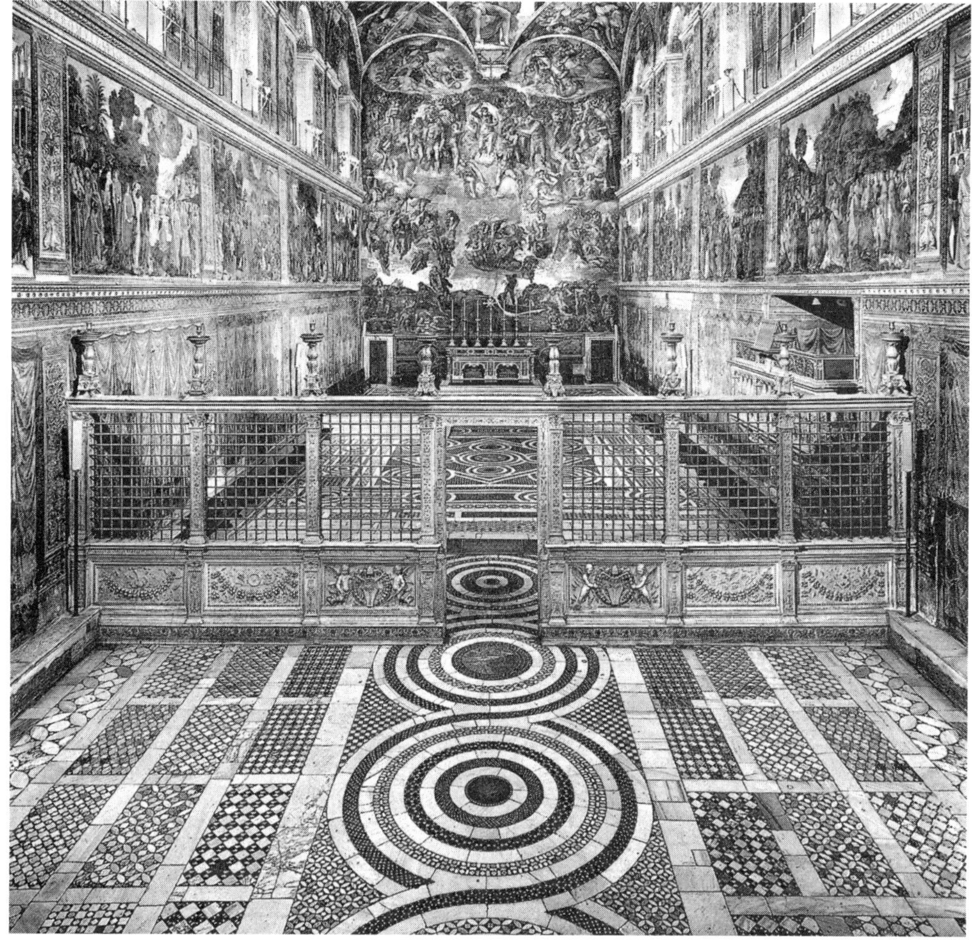

17.2 A papal commission recovers the obsolete conventions of medieval Rome. Vatican City, Vatican Palace, Sistine Chapel (late 1470s). Pope Sixtus IV creates a marble carpet of disks or guilloches leading toward the altar of his private chapel, below frescoes by Botticelli and Perugino (figures 15.4 and 15.6).

chapel of Pope Nicholas III (r. 1277–1280). Nicholas V's new floor of 1450, accomplished with the help of Florentine craftsmen, may have adapted elements of that earlier chapel's floor. Sixtus IV's restoration, finally, was based on the 1450 floor, though to what extent it is impossible to say (figure 17.2).[17] With its huge porphyry disk just inside the entrance, Sixtus's neo-cosmatesque pavement also referred to the nearby floor of St. Peter's. The six interlaced disks leading like a marble carpet to the *quadratura* or seating area for the cardinals recalled San Clemente. The pavement divided the space according to liturgical functions. Floor and fixed furnishings—choir-gallery (*cantoria*) and screen (*cancellata*)—together achieved a scholarly recovery of the decoration of early medieval Roman churches.[18] It is crucial to understand that these models were *ancient*. There was no clash, in the Sistine Chapel, between the pavement, derived from twelfth-century models; the screen and other furnishings governed by medieval liturgy; and the palmettes, acanthus, garlands, candelabra, and vases carved in low relief on all the surfaces of the *cancellata*, derived directly from the best pagan models, the Arcus Argentariorum (204) at San Giorgio al Velabro and the Ara Pacis itself (13 BCE).[19] The neo-cosmatesque floor resonated within this substitutional field.

The pavement of the Stanza della Segnatura, the room designed by Julius II in 1508 and decorated with murals by Raphael, is dominated by a massive quincunx pattern (figure 17.3). The keys at the center may be a generic papal symbol, but here more probably they refer to the coat-of-arms of Nicholas V, who built this wing of the palace around 1450.[20] The floor is related to the floor of the Vatican library of Julius's uncle Sixtus IV. Julius II was partial to cosmatesque floors: he had one installed in 1482 in the piano nobile of the apartment he built at Santi Apostoli when Cardinal, a room corresponding in several ways to the Segnatura at the Vatican.[21] The rare coincidence of two secular rooms decorated with neo-cosmatesque floors suggests that the Segnatura floor was also a Julius II commission, and indeed it carries an inscription with his name (figure 17.4).

Bramante's round temple on the Gianicolo, meanwhile, marked an ancient site, the traditional location of St. Peter's crucifixion. The structure's earliest commentator, Fra Mariano da Firenze, insisted on its special relation to its site, writing in 1517 that the height of the Tempietto was determined by the amount of the hill taken away to build it: *ad magnitudinem ablati collis.*[22] Whether or not this statement is true, it provides the conceptual rationale for the treatment of the floor. The building was in principle subterranean, nestled into the site, as if an archeological dig and a construction project were collapsed one onto the other. The Tempietto's neo-cosmatesque pavement offers itself as a primordial floor, the footprint of the building in antiquity (figure 17.5).[23]

The twelve liturgical implements and symbols, depicted four times each on the 48 metopes on the Doric entablature of the Tempietto's peristyle, a Christian translation of ancient frieze decoration, are based on the colored inlays on the arcades of the fifth-century Roman church of Santa Sabina.[24] The idea had a modern intermediary. The Christian metopes of Santa Sabina were already imitated in paint by Filippino Lippi in the ornate frieze of the Carafa chapel in Santa Maria sopra Minerva—above a neo-cosmatesque floor. Bramante translated the metopes back into stone. In both Lippi's and Bramante's friezes we see incense boat, mitre, candle

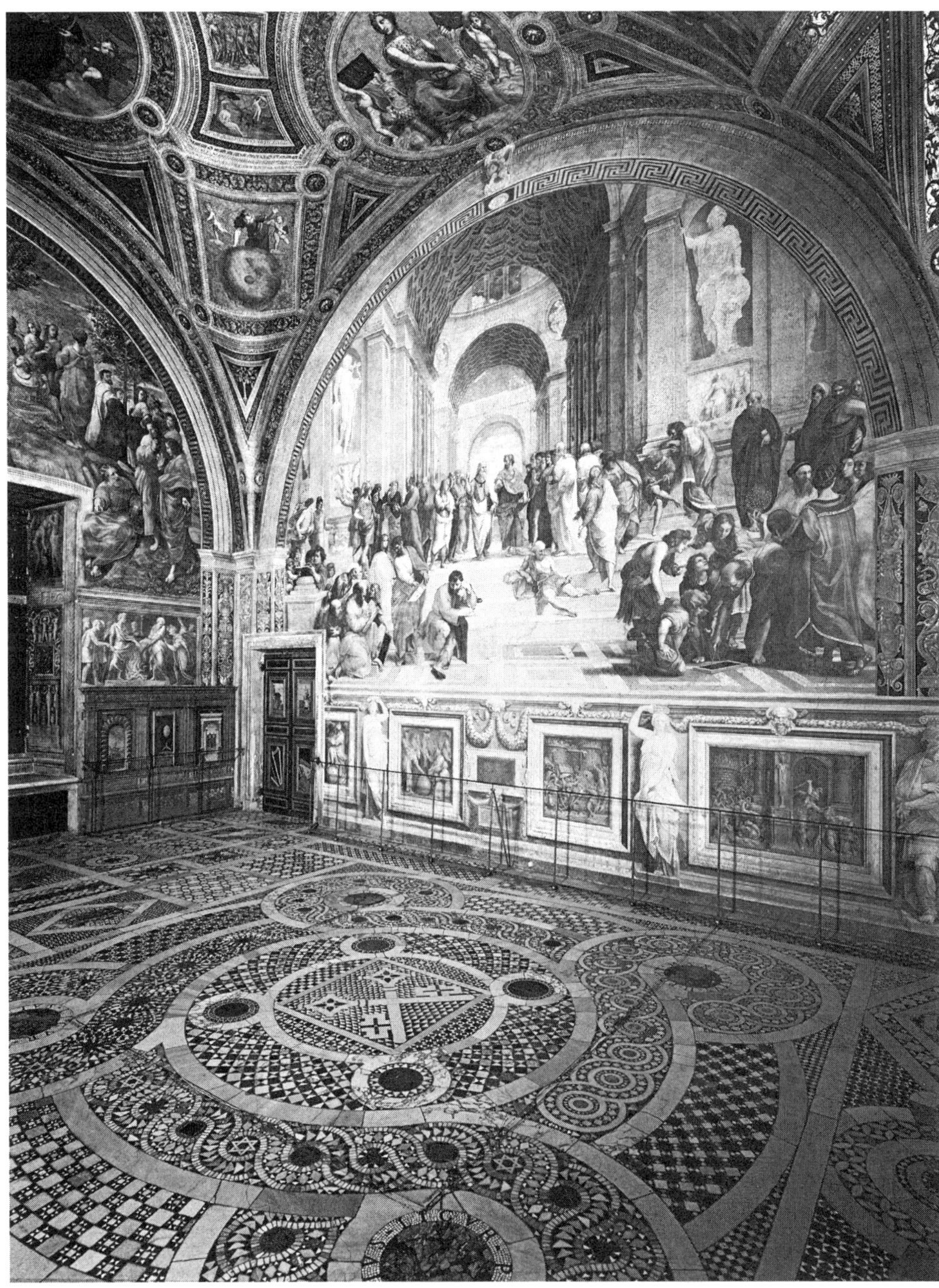

17.3 Pope Julius II, nephew of Sixtus IV, extends the revival of cosmatesque ornament. Vatican City, Vatican Palace, Stanza della Segnatura (ca. 1508). In the twelfth and thirteenth centuries such floors were never found in profane spaces, but Julius II employed it here in his library, and even earlier when he was a cardinal in his apartments at Santi Apostoli, Rome, perhaps suggesting that he considered it a mode of paving that long preceded its churchly uses.

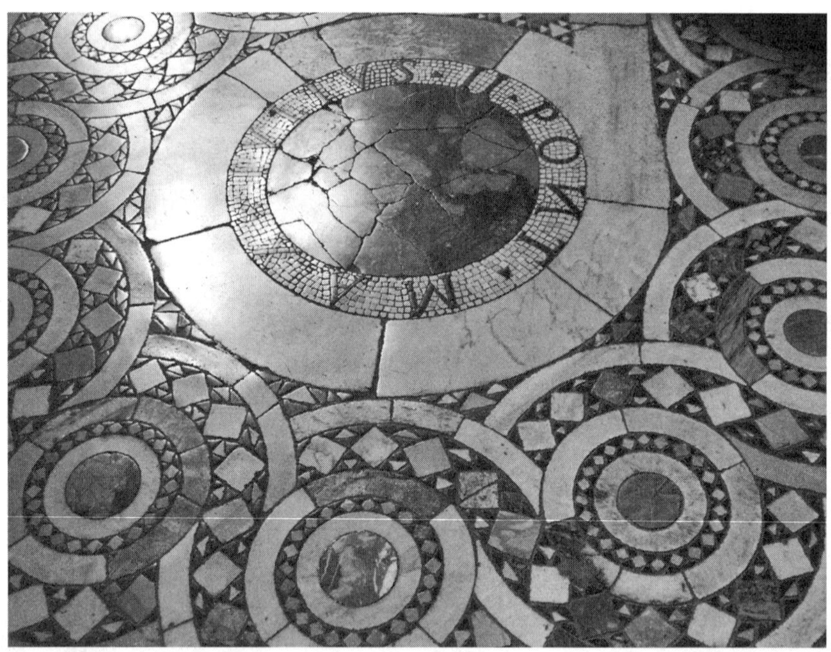

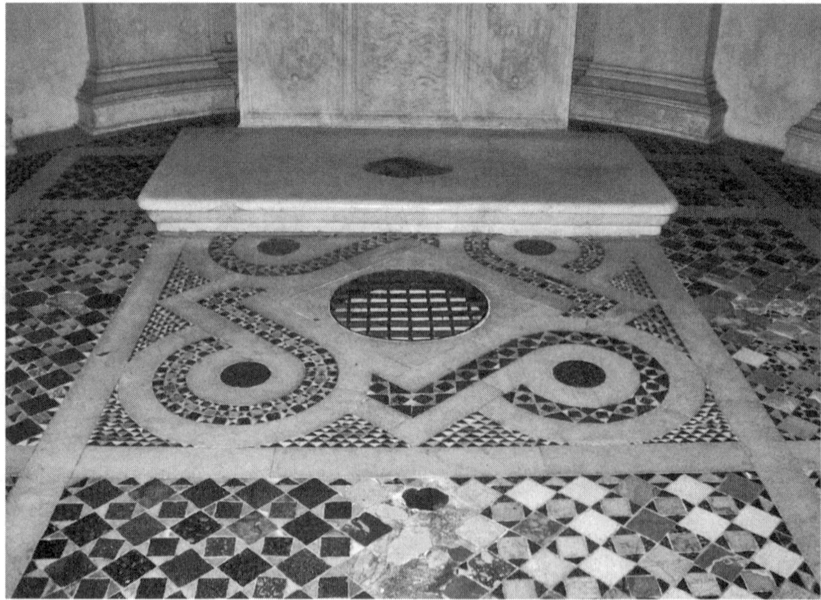

17.4 Julius marks the floor with his name. Pavement, Stanza della Segnatura, detail.

17.5 Bramante, too, studies the floors of the medieval Roman churches. Pavement, Tempietto (after 1502). Rome, San Pietro in Montorio. The cosmatesque pattern reinforced the thesis of the site's ancient significance, as it was held to be the location of St. Peter's Crucifixion.

snuffer, books, chalice, crucifix, candelabra, and the like. But there is one element on Lippi's frieze that Bramante omits: a ciborium. Perhaps Bramante felt that the symbol was redundant, for as we recall Fra Mariano described the Tempietto itself as a "large ciborium of marble."[25] The Tempietto was a building generated by a process of modeling. It translated into full-scale architecture conceptions that had been elaborated in miniature form in countless Tempietto-like tabernacles and in pictorial elaborations of ideas about round buildings. Fra Mariano seems to have grasped that the Tempietto was the architectural realization of miniature forms such as the one glimpsed in Lippi's frieze.

The Tempietto is marked by the hesitation about the site of Peter's crucifixion.[26] That site is the Roman counterpart of Golgotha, the site of Christ's crucifixion. But Rome already had a virtual Golgotha, the so-called Chapel of Helena in the basilica of Santa Croce in Gerusalemme. St. Helena, the mother of Constantine, transported earth from the foot of the cross at Golgotha and packed it into the flooring of this chapel, repository of the principal relic of the True Cross.[27] The Chapel of Helena, known throughout the Middle Ages as the Jerusalem Chapel, was a place

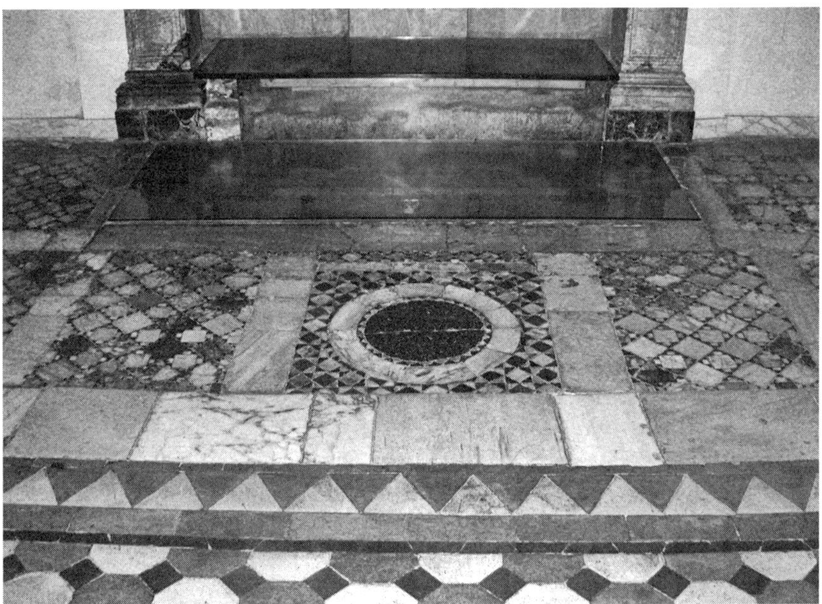

17.6 An architectural pseudo-relic. Pavement (twelfth century?). Rome, Santa Croce in Gerusalemme, Jerusalem or Helena Chapel. When the chapel was remodeled in the later sixteenth century, a patch of medieval floor was preserved in front of the altar, as if Helena herself might be expected to have trod on it.

of maximum spatio-temporal ambiguity, a patch of holy ground in Rome. And here too one treads on a cosmatesque pavement, or at least the battered and discolored remains of one, dating probably from the twelfth century (figure 17.6).[28] This pavement was misunderstood in the Renaissance as an ancient floor. The rest of the current floor of the chapel was installed in the sixteenth century or later.[29] But a few sections of the cosmatesque pavement, near the altar, were left untouched as a relic of Helena's original floor, the floor that covered the bloody earth of Golgotha. The patch of preserved cosmatesque pavement is near the altar (today the altar is partly removed in order to reveal, through plexiglass panels, the blood-soaked soil shipped from Jerusalem by Helen). The asymmetrical placement of the *serpentino* disk with respect to the altar is significant, as this irregularity could easily have been corrected at any point in time. It was instead preserved in order to signal the relic status of the floor.[30]

The Vatican chapel of Sixtus IV; that same chapel as updated by Julius II; Bramante's archeological conceit on the slopes of the Gianicolo; the Chapel of Helena at Santa Croce; and Julius's ceremonial room in the Vatican Palace not far removed from the Sistine Chapel, whose mosaic ceiling was based on that of the Chapel of Helena, amount to a sequence of symbolic projects linked by the red thread of their historically attentive floors.

EIGHTEEN

Movable Buildings

One of the theaters of the artifact's crisis of legitimacy was the pilgrimage site, where nonsubstitutability was dramatized. Pilgrimage, the temporary but long-distance displacement of the individual—such displacement, on any pretext, was highly exceptional in premodern times—is an assertion that a replica would not suffice. There was no substitute for being there. Pilgrimage was one of the few opportunities for non-elites to deliver opinions on these issues, in the first instance by the fact of their participation or non-participation. The individual's decision to go or not to go was the equivalent, in another "medium," of the antiquarians' disputes about the dating of old buildings.

A revealing, if still mysterious, episode is the hypertrophy of the cult of the Virgin at Loreto in the second half of the fifteenth and beginning of the sixteenth centuries, involving the dubious legend of a flying house: an emblem of the increasing vulnerability of the substitution model if there ever was one. For if a replica were really just as good as an original, there is no need to send in the original by airlift. Here the desires and performances of elite and nonelite were most intricately interlaced.

The legend is dubious not because houses cannot fly, but because, although there was a Marian cult at Loreto since the early fourteenth century, there is actually no secure evidence of a fable about the miraculous transportation of her house, to Italy all the way from Nazareth, before the mid-fifteenth century. This suggests that the story was invented to gloss the reputation of an existing devotion to a more modest cult object, perhaps an image or a simple hand-carried relic.

The Santa Casa or Holy House at Loreto, a town in the province of Recanati in the Marches, on the Adriatic coast of Italy, is allegedly a relic of the Virgin Mary. The house was carried to Italy by angels after the fall of Acre in 1291. The Santa Casa is a rectangular structure in brick and stone incorporating, in its lower masonry courses, a number of apparently non-local stones marked with graffiti in Greek and Hebrew.[1] Someone, perhaps the bishop of Recanati, may have brought these stones from the

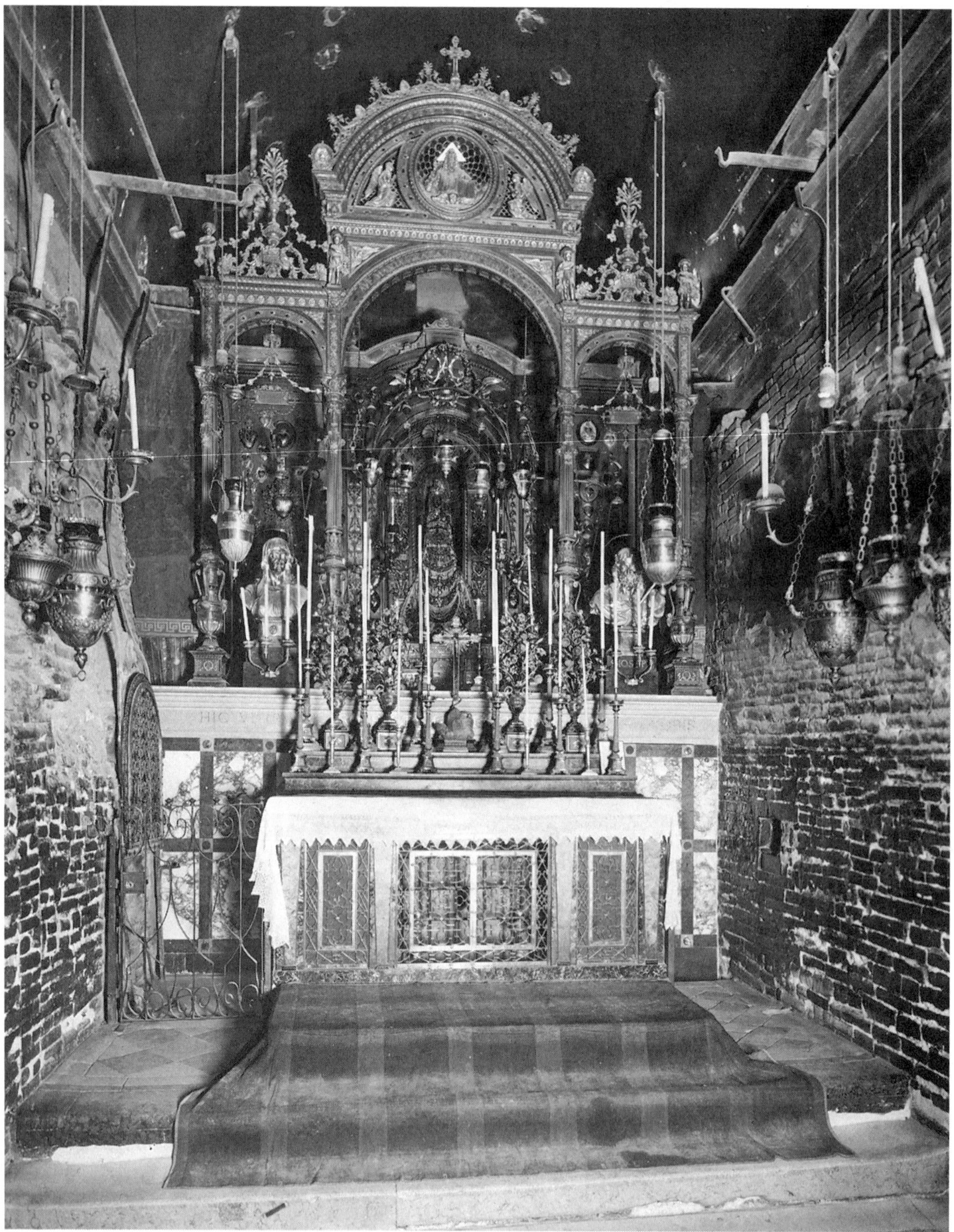

18.1 The space shared across time by the Virgin Mary and the millions of Loreto pilgrims. Holy House of Loreto, view of the eastern wall of the interior of the shrine. Loreto, Basilica. This photograph, taken after the installation of the iconostasis in 1896 and before the fire of 1921, shows the shrine congested with candles, lamps, vessels, and images. The bare brick walls are the relic itself, the shell of the house reputedly carried over the Mediterranean by angels.

Holy Land to Loreto in the late thirteenth century believing that he had rescued pieces of the house where the Virgin had been born and had received the Annunciating Angel. The present walls, whose inside surfaces alone are visible (the relic is encased in a decorated marble sheath), were constructed on and around these spolia following, perhaps, a verbal or pictorial description of a structure in Nazareth (figure 18.1).[2] The Holy House has no foundation, which meant that the walls had to be sustained by lateral reinforcement or buttressing. The missing foundation also sent the message of the house's status as a nonfunctional model.

There is archeological evidence of a Marian cult in Loreto and a pilgrimage, involving a panel or a statue, or both, as well as the house, already from the beginning of the fourteenth century. Not much is known about the early cult of the Holy House at Loreto, or what exactly pilgrims thought they were seeing.[3] Did they realize that only a portion of the building blocks were authentic? How was the presence of the Holy House in Italy explained? There is no surviving textual tradition to turn to, only a sequence of pictures which appear to refer to a story about a flying house. In a manuscript painting of the *Annunciation* in a Book of Hours by Jean Pucelle from around 1325, the Angel greets the Virgin Mary inside an edicule supported from below by a flying angel. The image was adduced by Panofsky as the oldest trace of an oral tradition of the miraculous transportation by a chorus of angels of the Holy House over the waves.[4] Pilgrims' badges and paintings of the late fourteenth and early fifteenth century represent the Virgin under a baldachin or an edicule with thin columns clutched by angels, perhaps interpretable as a highly abstract house, but nothing like the rough cottage-like building actually in Loreto.[5] It is not at all certain that the earliest of these images referred to Loreto at all. They may well have simply represented the Virgin enshrined in a three-dimensional frame and were linked to the legend only retroactively. The motif of a Virgin on a throne supported by angels can be traced back to Cimabue's Uffizi *Maestà* of the 1280s.[6] The Parisian Bible of Philippe le Bel (c. 1310) represents an initial I as a tower supported from below by two angels; the angel hefting the Marian edicule in Pucelle's miniature may simply be a stylized caryatid of this sort, with no connection to Loreto.[7] The earliest textual reference to a Loretan legend of transportation, by an English pilgrim, William Wey, not later than 1462, mentions the angels' abduction not of the house of the Virgin but rather of a "stone chapel of Blessed Mary…built by St. Helen in the Holy Land."[8] It appears that the ambiguous iconography of the edicule supported by angels informed the legend of the flying house rather than the reverse. By the 1460s, the date of a recently discovered engraving by the Master of the Vienna Passion, the hexagonal baldachin with four slender pillars hugged by angels with powerful wings surely does refer to the legend of the flying house (figure 18.2).[9] By the 1490s the standard iconographic formula for the Madonna of Loreto was a half-length Virgin no longer under a baldachin but on or above an airborne gabled house. The images of the flying edicules and houses were poetic figures for the more prosaic—and yet perhaps not so prosaic!—reality that the structure in Loreto was little more than a full-scale model of the Nazarene original built on top of a sample of authentic architectural relics. The model in Loreto had been generated from a single cartload of spoliated building modules.

The Holy House of Loreto was simply a more precisely targeted version of the many referential Roman churches that, in effect, had been generated by the spolia they contained. Santa Maria in Trastevere in Rome, to name a celebrated case, inserted itself into a chain of substitutional building practice reaching back to the Constantinian basilica of St. Peter's basically by throwing a roof over a double set of trabeated colonnades made of materials plundered from the Baths of Caracalla.[10] The twelfth-century church *became* old by virtue of the parts it had englobed. The creative work of the spolium was so powerful that it lost its identity as spolium; it vanished into the building. The frontier between old and new was effaced and the entire building became a relic. The Holy House at Loreto had begun in the late twelfth century as the humble reliquary of a few authentic stones lugged across the Mediterranean in a ship. Eventually those stones succeeded in converting the entire reliquary, by contagion, into a relic. The stones were the relics of another sort of reliquary, for what was the house of the Virgin if not the reliquary of a forever absent relic, the Virgin's body itself? And the body that carried Christ was in turn the type of all Christian reliquaries.

Conceptually the generation of the house relic from a few authentic stones is no different from the absorption into a painting of a fragment of an old panel or fresco. Unless the seam between container and contained is clearly signaled, the embedded relic has the power to colonize the whole image. Another conceptual equivalent from the period is the *Tunica domini* or Holy Robe of Trier. According to legend, Helena, mother of Constantine, had bequeathed to the city of Trier a relic of the robe worn by Christ and recovered by the soldiers at the Crucifixion. The relic was kept in the east choir of the cathedral but since 1196 no one had seen it. In 1512 Emperor Maximilian remembered the robe and persuaded Archbishop Richard von Greiffenklau to find it and display it, first secretly then publicly. These events on April 14, two days before an Imperial Diet in Trier, and on May 3, 1512, unleashed a massive pilgrimage and dozens of books and broadsheets. The scene of Maximilian's discovery of the robe

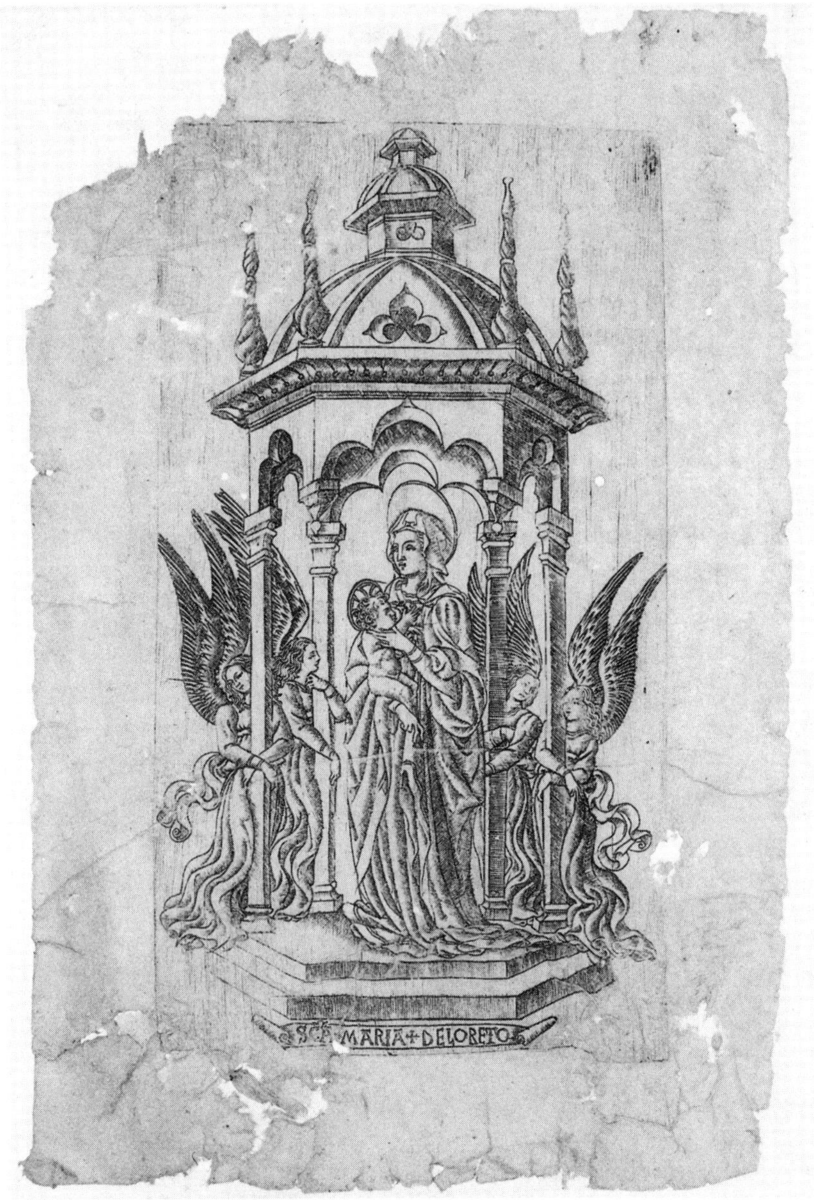

18.2 The Virgin in her airborne shelter. *Madonna of Loreto*, engraving, 19.5 x 11.1 cm (Italian, 1460s). Whereabouts unknown. This print, surviving in only a single impression, reflects the consolidation of the myth of the flying house in the third quarter of the fifteenth century.

was immediately memorialized in Albrecht Dürer's woodcut in the lefthand tower of the emperor's monumental paper Triumphal Arch (figure 18.3).[11] The relic was displayed for twenty-three days and then again in

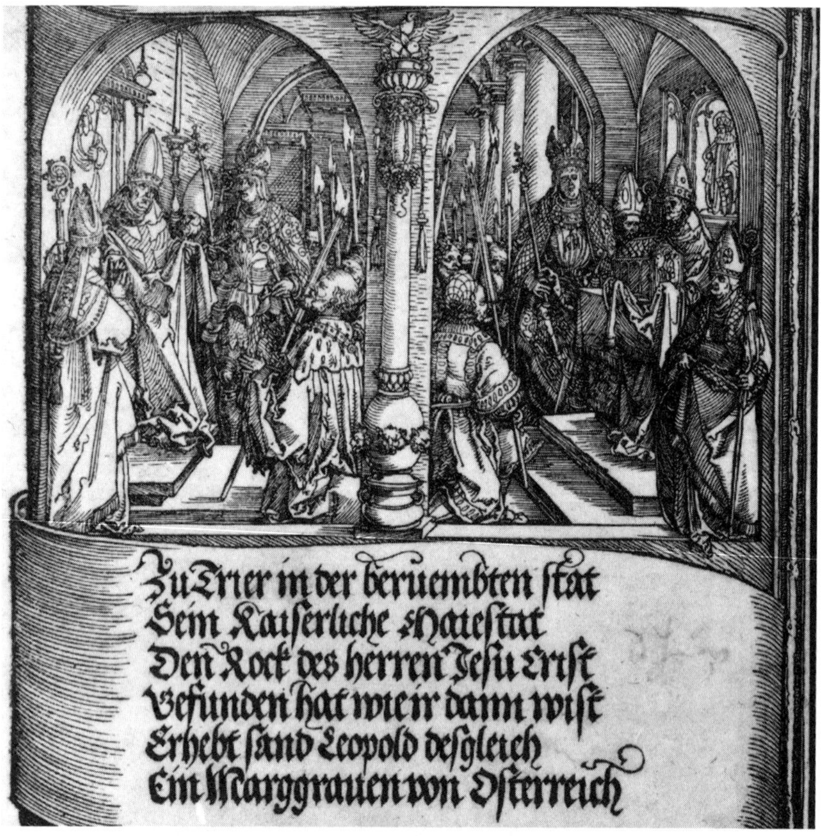

18.3 The generation of a relic by contagion. Albrecht Dürer, *Emperor Maximilian and the Holy Robe of Trier*, woodcut from Triumphal Arch (1515). Berlin, Staatliche Museen, Kupferstichkabinett. "In the famous city of Trier his Imperial Majesty found the Robe of the Lord Jesus Christ." The relic preserved in Trier was really only a small fragment of cloth, extended by tailors into a complete robe. Maximilian's sponsorship of the relic's rediscovery and public display is recounted in one of the many scenes on the gigantic paper Arch.

subsequent years.[12] The robe published by Dürer's woodcut was a whole robe. The archbishop lifts the garment by its two sleeves while Maximilian looks on attentively. But the relic itself was only a small swatch of cloth. At some point, possibly at the time of Maximilian's propaganda campaign, the swatch was attached to a larger stretch of cloth, so creating a complete robe — discreetly, one assumes, since the robe of Christ was meant to be seamless (John 19:23–24). The integral robe was, in effect, the reliquary for the patch of real cloth sewn into it. Yet no one could perceive the seam between container and contained and so the swatch colonized the entire robe and converted it into a relic.[13]

The Scala Santa or Holy Stair, an architectural relic, was very likely not a relic at all. Leading to the Sancta Sanctorum at the Lateran Palace, the pope's private chapel, is a flight of twenty-eight marble stairs.[14] An anonymous source of 1375 connects the Roman staircase to the Praetorian palace of Pontius Pilate in Jerusalem.[15] On a painted plan of 1414 the site of the Sancta Sanctorum is labeled "Scala St.p.q.Xps. ad Pilatum."[16] Chroniclers of the 1450 Jubilee described it as the stairway ascended by Christ at Pilate's palace and from then on the relic was installed in the imagination of every Roman pilgrim. Understandably, there was confusion about how it got to Rome. It was said that the stairs had been transported perhaps by Helena in the fourth century, perhaps already by Vespasian and Titus in 70 CE. The staircase acquired its importance probably because the popes used it to climb to the Sancta Sanctorum. There is no evidence that it really contains any stones from the Holy Land. It is plausible that a fragment of a ruin thought to have been Pilate's palace had been transported to Rome at some point and in effect generated the rest of the stairway. Here, too, just as at Loreto and Trier, the container, the reliquary, would have been converted by contagion into a relic, the seam between contained and container effaced.

In some cases the imported material was so humble, even intrinsically worthless, that only its origins in contiguity with a sacred source could have conferred relic status and value. Holy Land pilgrims commonly brought home stone memorabilia, chips, fragments, rubble.[17] The author of *Mandeville's Travels* (fourteenth century), purveyor of clichés, described zealous pilgrims breaking the Holy Sepulchre "in peces or in poudre," until the Sultan erected a protective wall.[18] The town of Borgo San Sepolcro in Tuscany was built on just such rubble broken off from the tomb and imported by pilgrims. Borgo San Sepolcro styled itself the new Jerusalem.[19] Such relics, like the bones of saints, were nothing without their labels. Shapeless bones of Holy Land sites, bits of stone, cloth, and wood bearing the labels "Mount of Olives," "Bethlehem," etc., rest in a bed of hardened earth, undisturbed since the sixth or seventh century, inside a box long housed in the Sancta Sanctorum in Rome.[20] Stones and bits of hay from the Nativity grotto at Bethlehem were worshiped at Santa Maria Maggiore in Rome perhaps as early as the seventh century.[21] The less serviceable the relics were as building material, the less likely they were to be converted into use and thus disappear. But at the same time, the intrinsically meaningless relic, ineloquent about its own origins, was the purest relic, for there was no other visible reason for transporting it other than its former contiguities and location. Formlessness was the sign of value. The limit case of formlessness was dirt. Between 1189 and 1192 the archbishop of Pisa, Ubaldo Lanfranchi, acquired earth from the presumed site of

Calvary and transported it back to Pisa, supposedly in fifty-three galleys. By 1203 he had set aside land beside the cathedral to enshrine the earth.[22] But he was only following the example of Helena herself, who packed earth soaked in the blood of Christ into the foundations of the chapel she built at the Sessorian Palace, the Jerusalem Chapel (now called Helena Chapel) behind and below the high altar of the basilica of Santa Croce in Gerusalemme in Rome (see figure 26.1). By building on that earth, Helena was building in two places at once.

The structure in Loreto, meanwhile, began to generate its own copies.[23] Chapels and churches were dedicated to Santa Maria of Loreto at San Pietro di Pusterola in 1404, at San Angelo di Pontano near Macerata in 1408, at Castelbuono near Palermo in 1453, and at San Domenico in Cremona. This new network of virtual holy houses all over Italy had the effect of devirtualizing the Loreto structure. The status of the house as a referential model of the original house, incorporating a few relics and a cult image, gave way finally to the idea of a house relic. The hypothesis of the simple identity of the Loreto structure with the birth house of the Virgin—a hypothesis which of course depended on a miracle story involving airborne transport of the house—materialized in both the pictorial tradition and, now for the first time, a literary tradition, in the middle of the fifteenth century. We saw something similar in the case of the St. Luke images. The medieval icons in Rome became ersatz originals at the very moment when they began to be intensively copied. The copying created them as originals. Until then they had been nothing more than models.

In 1464 Pope Pius II visited Loreto in the company of Pietro Barbo, Cardinal of Venice, who would succeed him as Pope Paul II later that very year. In 1464 and again in 1470 Paul issued indulgences associated with Loreto. These documents mention only an *image* transported by angels, however. The papacy seems to have wanted to replace the emergent legend of the flying house with a slightly more plausible legend of a flying image. In the contemporary written accounts of the cult at Loreto, however, this "image" never quite comes into focus. It is not certain whether it was a statue or a painting. This is typical of fifteenth-century cults and pilgrimages, which normally target a place, marked by a church or chapel, and not a particular image.[24] The pilgrimage site was a place where the Virgin (or another intercessory holy personage) was known to have brought about a miracle or made herself accessible to human entreaties. The pilgrim was visiting the site of a documented epiphany. The prospect of the pilgrimage was the hope that the Virgin, having manifested herself in this place at least once, or having proven herself willing to listen to her devotees at this place, might do so again. An image was often physically present at such a target to serve as a place marker and experiential focal point. But the image at the pilgrimage site was not always, in fact was seldom, credited with power. Neither the treatises, nor the chronicles, nor the miracle books recording votive offerings speak of the images at pilgrimage sites as sources of power or even as objects of devotion. The painting or statue, even for the pilgrim, was just a representation of the Virgin, easily reproduced on metal badges, prints, and panels, though without particular attention to accuracy. This basic premise was complicated at Loreto, however, by the attempt of the papacy to create a myth of an image (not a house) miraculously transported from the Holy Land. In such a case, the image at the pilgrimage site would be no mere representation or place marker but the object and relic of the miracle itself, and so quite powerful and worthy of worship. But this version of things seems not to have taken hold. It is hard to say today what the key image there might have been. Loreto is a complex nesting of frames where no one is ever quite clear about what is being framed.

The frame, in such a system, points to a place where substitutional slippage stops. We saw how in the woodcut of the Madonna in the Robe of Wheat Ears (see figure 2.1) a multiplication of internal frames and a stiffening of the external frame registered worries about a possible loss of origin, or a losing track of the origin. The message spoken by the frame is the same message spoken by the reliquary: "what is contained here is, finally, nonsubstitutable." The papal indulgence invoking the miraculously transported image was trying to point to the image as a relic and thus as the stable element in the Loreto system. But an image, painted or carved, is a labile, unreliable target. No one really knew for sure whether the Marian icons in Rome had been painted by St. Luke, any more than they knew what the original image of the Madonna in the Robe of Wheat Ears was. The cult image appears always *as* its own replicas in metal badges, prints, and panels. When you seek an origin, you find multiple origins. In the end, at Loreto, it was the place that mattered, and a building was a better way of marking a place than an image.[25] At Loreto, the building was both the reason why the place was significant, and the marker of the place.

In 1469 Niccolò delle Aste, bishop of Recanati, announced a plan, sponsored by Pope Paul II, to build a church over the Holy House.[26] In 1476 Sixtus IV formalized the adoption of the cult by the papacy by linking Loreto administratively to Rome.[27] By now the story of the transportation of the house was crystallizing into fact. Two treatises dating from around 1470 provide full textual accounts of the house and its origins, *Virginis Mariae Loretae Historia* by Giacomo Ricci, a canon of the cathedral of Brescia,[28] and *Translatio miraculosa* by Pietro Giorgio Tolomei (il Teramano).[29] Until this moment, as far as we can tell, the relationship of the structure in Loreto to the birth house in Nazareth had never been spelled out. It had all been left substitutionally vague. Ricci and Tolomei are the earliest of a series of commentators in manuscript and print who will insist with a new and painful literalness on the authenticity of the Holy House. The transportation of the cult image was not enough, evidently. The shift in stress from the image to the house, between the papal indulgences of 1469 and 1470 and the treatises of Ricci and Tolomei of the 1470s, tracks a resistance to the "power of images" thesis. The precise nature of the link between an image and the Virgin was insecure; it was better to have her literal housing, her reliquary.

The pamphlets of Ricci and Tolomei are representative of the more general trend, all across Europe, towards historicization and publicization of relics and cult images in the 1460s and 1470s, a construction of tradition through the medium of the quasi-scholarly treatise. The encouragement of pilgrimage repeats this movement on another cultural plane. The participation of great numbers of people in pilgrimages, the convergence of strangers on a place singled out from the infinity of places by the presence of a single relic, gave a sense of the vertical depth hiding below the surface of lived life. The patterns of repetition and convergence that emerged over the life span of a pilgrimage were another form of publication.

The latter half of the fifteenth century busies itself with recording, narrating, memorializing, and marking. The famous cult images only really became famous in the fifteenth century. In this period and not earlier they are first seen in relation to one another; understood as a class of objects. The differences noted in the new treatises among the celebrated cult images lent the array of icons the specificity and texture of a catalogue. In the 1460s and 1470s, all over Italy, such texts created traditions backwards by identifying the prototypes of modern portraits of the Virgin and of Christ. The icon of the Virgin at Santa Maria Maggiore, the *Salus Populi Romani*, had played a role in the life of the city of Rome since the twelfth century. But not until the manuscript treatise of 1464 written by a canon of Santa Maria Maggiore known as Giovanni Baptista were the threads of legend braided together into a coherent story (see section 11). That treatise, and the competition with the other Roman icons, activated the Santa Maria Maggiore icon. The St. Luke icon in the church of the Madonna del Monte in Bologna also came alive in the middle of the fifteenth century. The first procession of the image from its hilltop sanctuary to the city dates to July 1433, during the bishopric of the Blessed Niccolò Albergati, imploring the Virgin to bring a halt to rains that had fallen without interruption for three months, thus damaging the harvest and threatening famine. The procession was undertaken at the urging of Graziolo Accarisi, a member of Bologna's Council of Elders who was in close contact with the Greek Cardinal Basilius Bessarion. Later, in 1454, the icon was taken in procession for the wedding of Sante Bentivoglio and Ginevra Sforza. In 1459 Accarisi wrote an account of the legendary origins of the icon, attributing it to St. Luke.[30]

The Holy Robe in Trier was forgotten throughout the entire fifteenth century. The cult of the Scala Santa in Rome was knit together in the mid-fifteenth century. A Marian icon preserved in the Alte Kapelle in Regensburg, painted by a Byzantine or Italian artist in the early to mid-thirteenth century and related to the icon at Santa Francesca Romana in Rome, is mentioned in no document before 1451. According to local tradition the panel was a gift from Pope Benedict VIII to Emperor Henry II in 1014.[31] The origin myth of the miraculous chapel at Walsingham, supposedly built in 1061, does not figure in any textual source before 1496.[32] All these examples, even if their roots ran deep, were re-recognized and publicized in the middle and later fifteenth century, during the very decades of the antiquarian rediscovery of ancient temples, statuary, and icons. Legends about origins were gathered and collated in treatises, as if in immediate response to the massive opening up of opportunities for publicization — for truth creation — represented by movable type, which was invented in Germany in the 1450s and disseminated throughout Europe in the 1460s and 1470s. But the project of publicization did not depend on print technology. Print only accelerated and reinforced the trend, stabilizing records and fixing visual forms.

In some cases, it was not until the sixteenth century that a legend about a cult image coalesced. The Mandylion, reputed to be a direct impression on cloth of the features of Christ, was the most prestigious acheiropoietic portrait. The original Mandylion came to Constantinople from Edessa in Mesopotamia in the tenth century. After the fall of Constantinople in 1204, the portrait resurfaced in Rome and Paris at the same time. And then in the fourteenth century, a third portrait claiming to be the true Mandylion found its way westward from Constantinople to Genoa, where it still is venerated in the church of San Bartolommeo degli Armeni (figure 18.4). Strangely, however, there is as far as we know no documentary reference to the presence of the Mandylion in the city, not a single mention of the icon in any local source, until 1537. In that year, the arrival of the icon in Genoa in the fourteenth century is attested for the first time in a chronicle written by Agostino Giustiniani, who reports that the Doge Leonardo Montaldo had received the Mandylion as a gift from the Eastern Emperor in payment for military services, and that upon the doge's death in 1384 he had willed the icon to the city of Genoa. The chronicler Giustiniani also

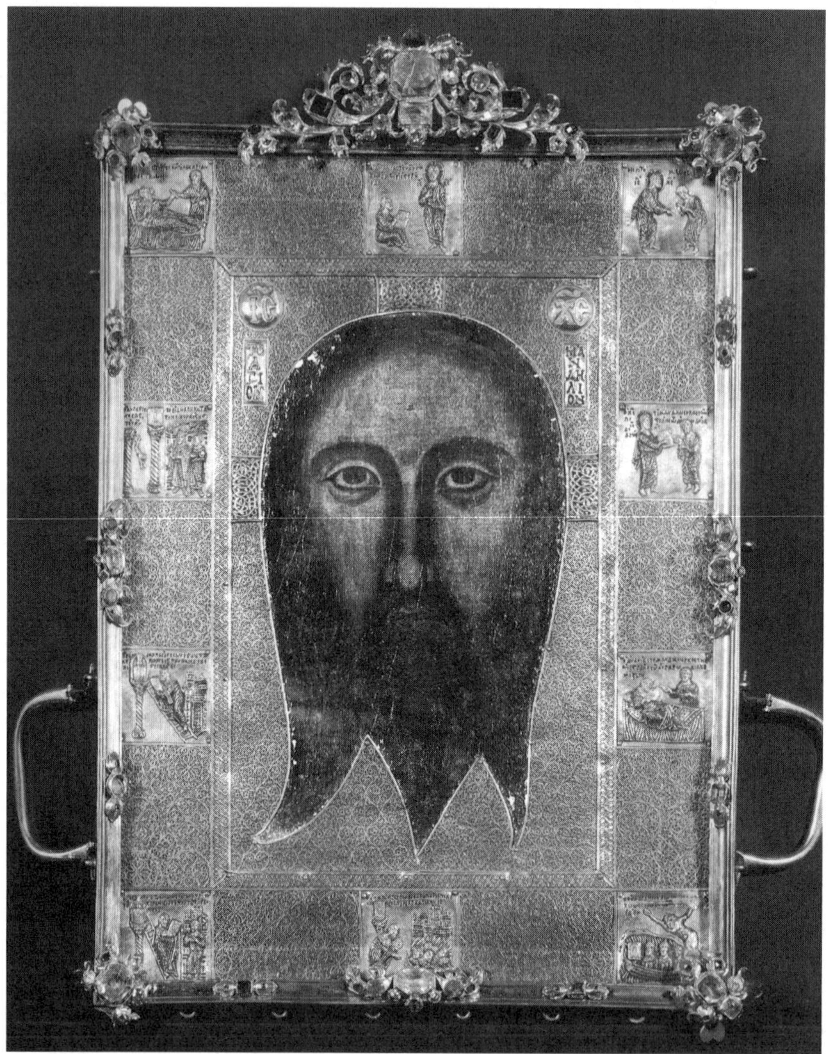

18.4 Late recognition of a true portrait of Christ. Mandylion, cloth on panel, 28.8 x 17.6 cm (panel: thirteenth century [?]; gold revetment: fourteenth century). Genoa, San Bartolommeo. This image, tightly framed in its perforated box, is one of several exports to the West with some claim to be a portrait of Christ made by direct impression on cloth. It came to Genoa in 1384 but is not mentioned in any document until 1537.

described the theft of the prestigious portrait by a French army in 1507. The French took it all the way back to Paris, says Giustiniani, but upon negotiation restored the Mandylion in the following year to the Genoese.

This singular artifact, which supposedly came to Genoa accompanied by extravagant claims of authenticity, resided for a century and a half in that city, from 1384 to 1537, without once being mentioned in a contemporary document. It was never described in any of the lists of the city's key relics, never invited, apparently, to participate in civic or ecclesiastical ritual, never referred to by any city chronicler before Giustiniani. The fifteenth-century chronicler Giorgio Stella recounts the death of Montaldo in 1384 without mentioning his gift of the relic.[33] Stella's silence about the Mandylion is striking in light of his own comment on the lack of secure documentation for the provenance of the Holy Grail relic in the Treasury of the Cathedral of Genoa: Stella noted that the twelfth-century Annali di Caffaro did not mention the object.[34] St. Vincent Ferrer delivered a sermon in Genoa in 1406 or 1407 listing the city's prestigious relics: the ashes of John the Baptist, Cross relics, the Holy Grail, but no Mandylion.[35] The sensational French kidnapping of the Mandylion in 1507, finally, is unattested by any independent witness beyond Giustiniani; no mention in either the French or the Genoese archives, for example.[36] The only textual record of the Mandylion's presence in Genoa before 1537 can be found in the travel diary of Anselm Adorno, the Genoese merchant living in Bruges whose description of the Dome of the Rock we cited in section 7. In 1471 Adorno visited his home town and paid his respects to the image at San Bartolommeo before departing for the Holy Land.[37]

To all appearances, the cult of the Mandylion in Genoa was a fabrication of the second half of the fifteenth century, a fabrication that was intensified in the next century, perhaps in response to the installation of the Shroud of Turin in its chapel in Chambéry in 1502.[38] Another late-developing cult was that of the Madonna Nicopeia, the eleventh-century Constantinopolitan icon which once served as the palladium or protective talisman of the Byzantine emperor and was subsequently acquired by the Venetians as booty in 1204. The picture is mentioned in inventories of the treasury of San Marco in the fourteenth century; it is first attributed to St. Luke in an inventory of 1463. But only in 1559, in the writings of the geographer and humanist Giovan Battista Ramusio, was the Madonna Nicopeia outfitted with a proper legend describing the icon's imperial provenance. This legend became the basis for the prominent role the icon played in the life of the city in the later sixteenth and seventeenth centuries.[39]

In the late sixteenth century, in the era of the Counter-Reformation, icons and architectural relics were again reframed, often elaborately, and republicized. The eighth-century icon in Santa Maria in Trastevere (see figure 8.1) was mentioned in no written source prior to the mid-sixteenth century; it was ignored by Onofrio Panvinio in his guide to the churches of Rome (1570); and was finally promoted at the end of the century by Cardinal Altemps.[40] The Scala Santa and Sancta Sanctorum were given a new building of their own on the Lateran piazza. In 1590 the chapel containing the Presepio or Holy Crib at Santa Maria Maggiore, which on the basis of metonymic contagion spreading outward from the relics it contained had been identified simply as the Presepio, was moved into the same church's Sistine Chapel and rebuilt in grand style.[41]

In the late 1560s the buildings surrounding the diminutive chapel of St. Francis at Portiuncula near Assisi, a pilgrimage target since the saint's death in 1226, were removed by Pius V. The chapel itself, spared, was englobed in a basilica designed by Vignola where it sits directly under the cupola. The model for the three-dimensional framing at Portiuncula was Loreto.[42] The room at the Dominican convent in Rome where St. Catherine of Siena had died in 1380 soon became a pilgrimage target. In the late fifteenth century Antoniazzo Romano painted its walls with sacred scenes. In 1637 the entire room — the walls together with the frescoes — was transported to the nearby church of Santa Maria sopra Minerva and rededicated as a chapel.[43] The sacred spoliations of the Counter-Reformation aimed only to sustain venerable traditions of relic handling and relic publication, traditions that had culminated in the fifteenth century. But many of those traditions had effectively been created in the fifteenth century.

This is the context for the curious turn that the legend of the Holy House at Loreto took in the 1460s and 70s. The Brescian cleric Giacomo Ricci reported that the house had to leave the Holy Land under threat of desecration by "barbarian infidels." He seems to have been referring to the fall of Acre, last bastion of the Crusader kingdom, in 1291.[44] Ricci says that the house was first transported by a choir of angels to Tersatto in Illyria where the locals sadly did not accord it sufficient respect. After "a few years" the angels lifted it again and carried it across the Adriatic Sea to a forest near Loreto belonging to a noblewoman. The local people were amazed to find one day the house together with its portrait of the Virgin by St. Luke, which had been installed by the Apostles, who already in the first Christian century had converted the house into a shrine.[45] In this way Ricci synthesizes the legends of the flying image and the flying house: the image came as a passenger! However, the house's second landing place — the forest — proved dangerous to pilgrims and after some time the structure was moved again to its present site on a hill near Loreto.

Ricci's step-by-step tracking of the house's journey compensated for a perceived insufficiency of the substitutional version of things. There had been no need for such a detailed narrative in the early fourteenth century, when it was enough, apparently, that a shrine to the Virgin had been built using a few auratic stones carried in the hull of a boat all the way from the Levant; enough to establish a cult and a pilgrimage. Nor was there any need for such a narrative at Walsingham in Norfolk, where a replica of the Virgin's house in Nazareth, in the true dimensions as recorded by a Holy Land pilgrim, seemed to have sufficed.[46]

Ricci, and a series of writers surrounding and following him, pulled the conceit of the angel-borne edicule out of the realm of poetry and into the written record. The transition from orality (and pictoriality) to literacy triggered a hypertrophy of explanation. Hoping to publicize a straightforward, authoritative account of the house's origins, Ricci found himself forced to describe, as if it were historical fact, an unbelievable supernatural event. He could have simply given the plausible explanation of a transport of relics that served since the fourteenth century as the basis for a substitutional model of the original house. But the substitutional relationship to the original house now no longer sufficed. That relationship begged analysis and legitimation. In order to stress the greater reasonableness of his own account, Ricci describes the initial reactions of the local populace to the arrival of the house as a confused misunderstanding. In their ignorance they imagined that the house in Loreto had been constructed as shelter for the cult image, itself a miraculous gift. Foolishly, they failed to grasp what a later chronicler called *l'ordine della cosa*, namely, the simple fact that this was the house of the Virgin that had been carried over the sea by angels.[47] The miracle is no longer suspended in the poetic state. Ricci now tries to assimilate the miracle to a rhetoric of factuality, producing awkward contortions. He sets his own supernatural but learned account against the foil of the untutored responses of the locals.

The pressure brought to bear on origins produces a hesitation, and thus a doubling. In the *Mirabilia urbis Romae*, the medieval pilgrims' guidebook, the spolia that Constantine installed in the Lateran and Vatican basilicas are given double origins: four gilded columns were brought first by the consuls from the Campus Martius to the Temple of Jupiter, and from there by Constantine to the Lateran. Twelve twisted columns were brought from the Temple of Apollo at Troy to Greece and from there, again by Constantine, to St. Peter's.[48] Another paradigmatic case of doubling is the hut of Romulus, with one on the Capitoline and one on the Palatine hill, discussed in section 6. In Ricci's account, the Holy House does not come directly to Italy but rather makes a meaningless stop in Illyria. The function of the staggered journey in Ricci's narrative is to contrast the Loretans' receptivity to the house to the disrespectful treatment of the Illyrians. But the legend of the two-legged journey must predate Ricci's narrative and conforms to a deeper, older pattern of mimetic doubling as the marker of a fundamental, insuperable uncertainty about origins. In fact there is a further subdivision of the journey even after the landing in Italy.

The house first appeared in a forest but that site proved too dangerous. After a time it was hauled once again by the angels to a nearby hill where it stands to this day.[49]

A similar pattern of hesitation and staggered movement appears in the contemporaneous foundation narrative of the shrine at Walsingham in Norfolk. The shrine is attested from the twelfth century and attained national significance by the late fourteenth century. But, as we have noted, there is no trace of an origin myth until 1496, when the printer Richard Pynson published a ballad dating the chapel to 1061.[50] A lady pilgrim is instructed by an angel to take the measure of the Virgin's house in Nazareth and "another lyke thys at Walsingham thou sette." This she undertakes to do, but

> Whan it was al fourmed, then had she great doute
> Where it shold be sette and in what maner place,
> In as moche as tweyne places were founde oute
> Tokened with myracle of Our Ladyes grace.

The lady chose between the two sites, but the carpenters soon found themselves unable to fit timber to timber and in sore frustration abandoned the task; "They went to reste and layde all thynge on syde." At this point the Virgin herself took over the construction

> with heuenly mynystrys,
> Hirsylfe beynge here chyef artyfycer,
> Areryd this sayd house with aungellys haudys,
> And not only reyrd it but set it there it is,
> That is, two hundred fote and more in dystaunce
> From the fyrste place bokes make remembrance.

The Virgin finished the construction job and then moved the house to a site little more than two hundred feet away. The Virgin offered the patroness a choice of sites, and both were sacred; but only one place was right. In order to establish the shrine the building had to be moved, miraculously and by night. Why all the trouble? It was in the interest of the narrative to create an effect of the mystery of place. It must be *this* place and no other.

The literary insistence on the miraculous translation of the house at Loreto, by Ricci and the series of subsequent authors, was a response to negative cultural pressure on the institution of pilgrimage. Pilgrimages in the fifteenth century were increasingly "managed." Print technology invited sponsors to publicize cult sites and founding legends. Print also publicized the skeptical, debunking attitudes of humanist scholars and reform-oriented clerics.[51]

The supernatural transportation in Ricci's account was basically a literary device. The purpose of the text was to supplement the substitutional assumptions that once would have sustained, all by themselves, the reputation of the site. Substitution was a theory about origins that operated without recourse to miracles. When substitution came to seem merely poetic and not sufficiently historical, the author was put in the paradoxical position of invoking a supernatural event to secure his otherwise rational narrative. Miracles were an effect generated by miracle books. The paradox here is registered by Ricci's embarrassed wriggling at the crucial point of the text: "But why do I say 'supposed to have been transported'? In fact, an immobile thing cannot be transported. Why, therefore, do I refer to incredible things? Do I speak or remain silent? But it is good to reveal the works of God."[52]

Ricci and the other early sources each dealt with the transmission problem in a different way. Ricci defensively explains why there are no earlier accounts of the miracle: the story "was once exalted and described by many," but in our time "works about it either do not exist or they come to us so corrupt and ruined that we can hardly read the Latin and we understand very little."[53] Pietro Tolomei, meanwhile, author of the *Translatio miraculosa*, also composed around 1470, attested to the reality of the miracle by invoking the chain of oral tradition. Tolomei says he knows someone whose grandfather's grandfather witnessed the event:

> Et dictus Paulus dixit mihi quod avus avi eius (*his grandfather's grandfather*) vidit quando angeli duxerunt predictam ecclesiam per mare et posuerunt eam in dicta silva, et ipse pluribus vicibus cum ceteris personis ipsam ecclesiam visitavit in dicta silva.[54]

Tolomei literalizes oral tradition as a pair of conversations that link four generations. The two conversations reach back to 1294, 170 years — the time of his grandfather's grandfather — just about the maximum span of time, by customary reckoning, before the chain snaps and the event falls into legendary status. Just as the miracle books produce miracles, so too does literacy generate the myth of a foundational orality.

Still another early author rejected orality and invented an archeological source. The humanist and poet Giovanni Battista Spagnoli (il Mantovano or Mantuanus), in his text *Redemptoris mundi Matris ecclesiae lauretanae Historia*, published in 1489, reports that he saw a *tabella* in the church at Loreto on which the story was inscribed.[55] This report overlaps confusingly with the fact that Tolomei's account was inscribed on a tablet and mounted on the wall of the church. It is possible that Mantuanus mistook this tablet, only a decade or two old at that point, for a much older document. With time and growing skepticism ever more details are invented. None of these early accounts mentions any dates. Not until around 1530, in the account of Girolamo Angelita, are the landings in Illyria and Loreto dated, and then not only to the years (1291 and 1294, respectively) but also, with extravagant precision, to the days (May 9 and December 10).[56]

The treatises of Tolomei and Ricci, themselves efforts to explain what had not needed explaining, namely, substitution, created the desire for an impossible certainty, for proof. Instead of stabilizing the history of the cult site, they exposed it to ridicule. Only a few decades later, as discussed in the opening pages of this book, the scholar and skeptic Erasmus, who had visited Walsingham in 1512, took deadly aim at the *topos* of the miraculously transported Marian shrine.[57]

Surrounded by the newly assertive treatises of Tolomei, Ricci, and others, struggling to assume the force of inveterate authority, the Holy House of Loreto took on a more intense and demanding identity as a relic. Not only the form of the house, not only the schedule of its journey, but also its precise position on the ground became an aspect of its authenticity. In the myth the house is constantly moving, in briefer and smaller stages, from Nazareth to Tersatto to Loreto forest to Loreto hill. Finally, once and for all, the moving is arrested. This is the stability that everyone has been waiting for. In the ambitious basilica at Loreto initiated in 1469 by Pope Paul II, the house sits under the crossing, more or less on axis with the presbytery but out of alignment with the nave. The misalignment signals the authenticity of the relic. No doubt there were structural or topographical factors that kept the builders of the basilica from aligning nave with presbytery, rendering impossible the perfect alignment of the house relic. The designers of the marble sheath attempted to correct this irregularity, as an early sixteenth-century plan reveals (figure 18.5).[58] This plan shows the inner house twisted sharply clockwise inside the sheath. Before the encasing of the relic in marble, the misalignment would have been emphatic. Even today the misalignment of the house in the basilica is clearly visible. The skewing of the house reminds the visitor that the relic had been moved three times. But when a last adjustment, a matter of a few feet, would have brought it into smooth alignment with the basilica, when a move would have been *least* disruptive, the moving had to stop. The message of the misalignment is: "the Holy House landed exactly here, and it must not be moved. Under no circumstances can the House be moved again."[59]

The desire to maintain an old structure in symbolic misalignment to a new building is well attested in ancient Rome. In the late sixth century BCE, when the last king of Rome, Tarquin the Proud, built the temple of Jupiter Optimus Maximus on the Capitoline Hill, according to the ancient

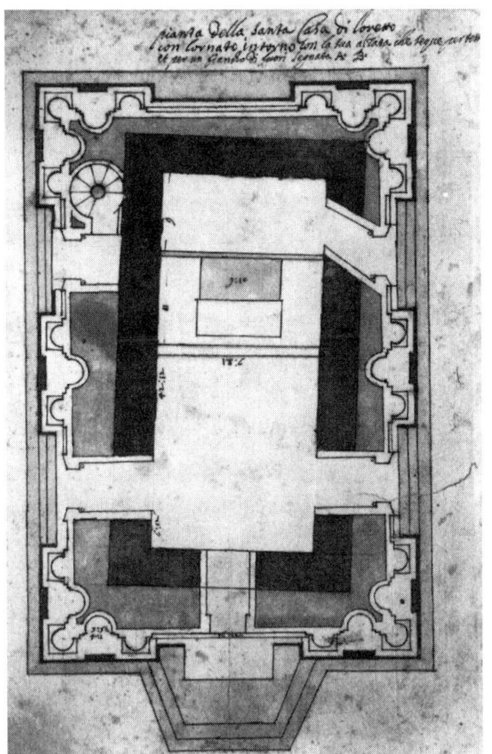

18.5 The misalignment of the new sculptural sheath and the house relic. Holy House of Loreto, plan, drawing (early sixteenth century). Vienna, Albertina Museum. The Holy House and the basilica raised over it in the fifteenth century are not in alignment with one another. This irregularity signaled that the transported walls, once landed in Loreto, could not and would not ever be moved. The sculptural cladding applied to the Holy House in the sixteenth century, the outer perimeter in the drawing reproduced here, partly corrects for the misalignment but not fully: the sheath is still not in alignment with the basilica.

historians, the preexisting altar to the archaic god Terminus was left just where it was found, untouched. The augurs did not permit the builders to deconsecrate this shrine or to "move it from its seat." Since Terminus's cult could only take place under the open sky, a hole was opened in the roof of the temple. Another such arrangement occurred in the Capitoline temple of Cosa, near the Etruscan territory of the Vulci, of about the year 160 BCE, where an earlier altar was maintained at an angle of 45 degrees to the new temple building.[60] A memory of this tradition, and not only liturgical considerations, may have fuelled the outrage of Julius II when Bramante dared to propose that the orientation of St. Peter's be rotated 90 degrees, moving the tomb of Peter around with it.

At Loreto, there had been no "native" house, no house with a claim to the land. The misalignment does not express the noncontingency of an original foundation but rather the fact of the house's miraculous *landing*. The skewed placement of the Holy House of Loreto, paradoxically, is the symbol of its absolute stability as a target.[61] The staggering decelerated to a mere tremor before coming to a permanent halt; the slight obliquity is the afterimage of that tremor; the nesting structure is the perfect screen for that afterimage.

Once the house was accepted by everyone as a relic—everyone except those who considered it a complete fraud, that is—it needed a new reliquary. In the sixteenth century the house was completely encased in the marble sheath designed by Bramante and decorated on the outside with reliefs by Andrea Sansovino and others (figure 18.6).[62] This sheath, described in documents as the *ornamento*, had the effect of conceptually integrating the stones of the house inside, creating the rough rustic walls as a relic, once and for all, by effacing their internal fault lines. The marble casing improved upon the framing accomplished by the fourteenth-century wall, the *muro bono et grosso*, except with a stronger, this time unmistakable, differentiation between container and contained. The sheath completed the blending of spolium and constructed container. Then the container was newly contained. Over the house rose a vast basilica, the superreliquary initiated in the previous century by the Tuscan architects Giuliano da Maiano, Baccio Pontelli, and Giuliano da Sangallo.[63] The treatment of the house relic at Loreto repeats the fourth-century treatment of the Holy Sepulchre, which because Constantine got his agents to Jerusalem in time, and because the Sepulchre was (mostly) respected by the Muslim rulers of Jerusalem, did not have to be transported. The international career of Mary's birth house at Nazareth, after all, became necessary only because the Crusades had failed. The basilica at Loreto is the true reliquary, for the marble sheath—the shifter that is contained by the basilica but itself contains the house—in fact performs a more complex function. The sheath with its splendid classicizing reliefs, impossible to confuse for a humble relic from Palestine, was nevertheless still physically contiguous with the relic, as if—at least notionally—it were a completion of the house and not merely a container. The sheath invokes a different, unrealized approach to the house, the substitutional approach: the option of simply rebuilding or replacing it. It figures that function without actually replacing the house. The principles of substitutability (a neoclassical structure) and nonsubstitutability (an architectural relic) now exist one inside the other, surface to surface, just as at Alberti's Tempio Malatestiano at Rimini (see figure 16.1). If the house *had* simply been rebuilt, the gesture would have acknowledged doubts about the miraculous transport, reconceiving the house merely as a virtual relic, like one of the replicas of the Holy Sepulchre. In Loreto both approaches to originality—spoliation and citation—are held in suspension. Whereas at Rimini one looked through the sheath and saw the relic building inside, at Loreto the sheath masks the crude walls of the house and with its beautiful carved surfaces shows how effective a proper substitution might have been. The sheath brings the house to you, forward in time. But once you are inside (see figure 18.1), the sheath's substitutional mechanism

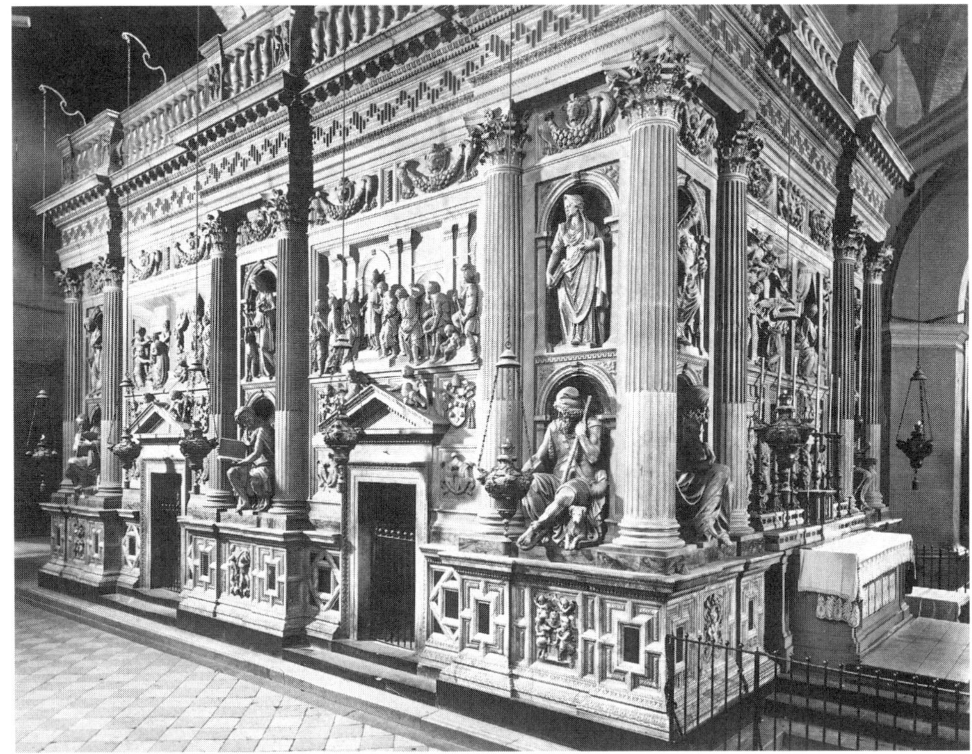

18.6 The exterior walls of the Virgin's house disappear inside a grandiose reliquary. Donato Bramante, Andrea Sansovino, Antonio da Sangallo the Younger, and others, marble sheath for Holy House of Loreto (1507–1538). The splendid ornament in the modern style marked the contrast between the artificial architectural frame and the rough brick courses of the relic within.

is forgotten; the house becomes a relic again in the fullest sense and you yourself perform the mystical time travel.

The Alpine counterpart to Loreto was the chapel of St. Meinrad at Einsiedeln in the canton of Schwyz.[64] In the tenth century a small church was constructed on or around the humble cell that Meinrad had occupied a century earlier, for Benedictines already a precious relic. In 948 that chapel was consecrated, miraculously, by Christ himself who appeared in a company of angels. Although the monastic church was burnt and reconstructed several times over the next centuries, the ancient cell contained within seemed to have remained unharmed. In 1465 a new basilica was raised following yet another fire, again over and around the original cell of Meinrad. Three engravings by the Rhenish printmaker known by his initials E. S. mark the reconsecration of the basilica and at the same time remember the original, miraculous, angelic dedication, which was celebrated every seven years

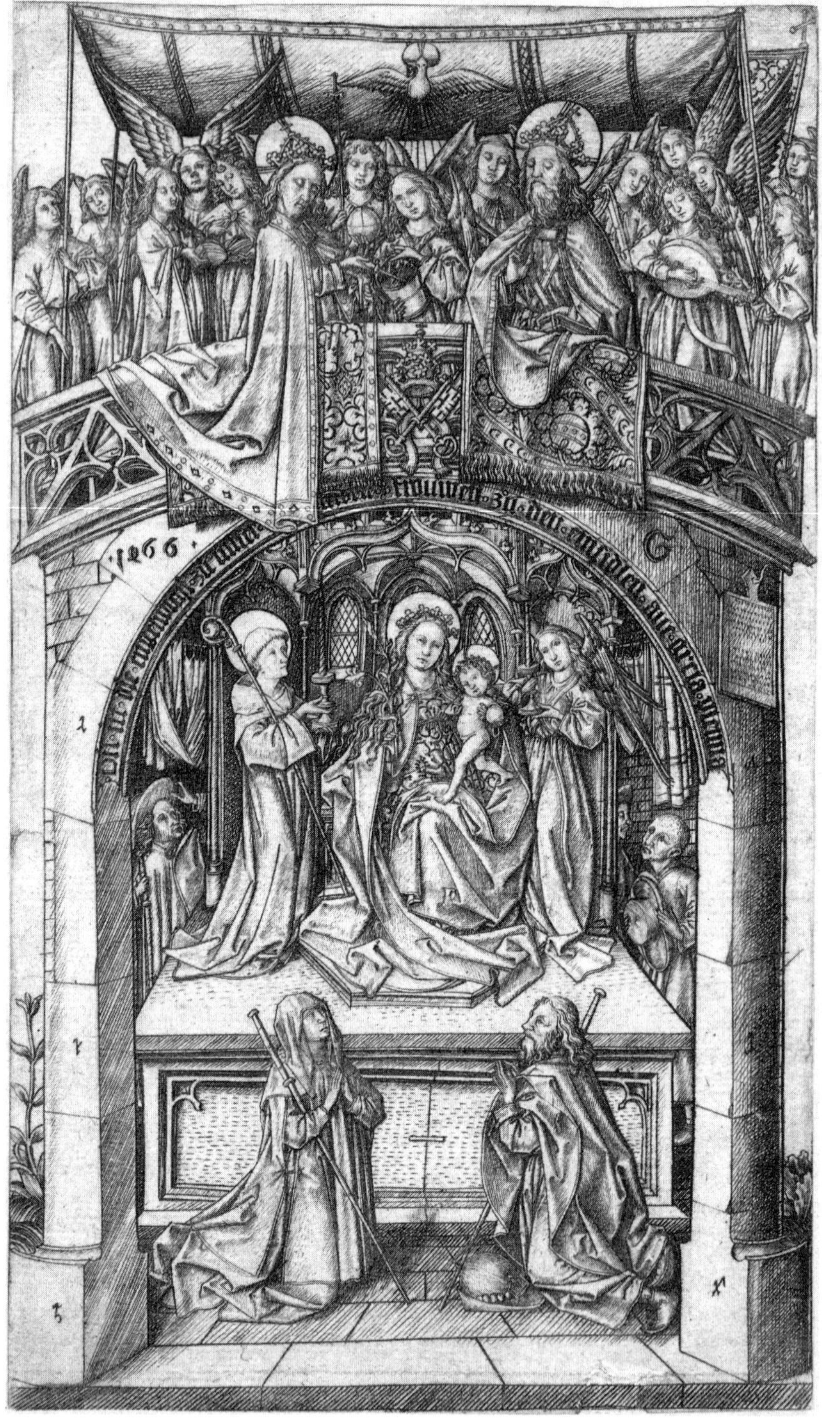

18.7 The earliest print associated with a pilgrimage. Master E.S., *Miraculous Chapel at Einsiedeln*, engraving, 20.6 x 12.3 cm (1466). London, British Museum. An eighth-century hermit's cell was consecrated a century later by the Holy Trinity accompanied by angels. Successive basilicas rose up over the cell-relic. The miraculous dedication was celebrated in regular pilgrimages. This engraving represents pilgrims worshipping an image of the Virgin and Child inside the cell.

(figure 18.7). The prints are dated 1466. They are the very first prints associated with a mass pilgrimage.[65] Around the same time the legend of the chapel's miraculous angelic dedication was stabilized in a new text and publicized in a block book (a way of reproducing texts not from movable type but from carved wooden blocks). The precise situation of the chapel in the new structure of 1466 is unknown to us but may not have differed much from the view of the fifth basilica (following yet another fire, in 1577), as depicted in an engraving of 1606–1609.[66] According to this publication the primordial chapel, dwarfed by the new rib vaults, sat in the nave of the church — slightly off axis, like the house at Loreto.[67] The chapel itself is hard to decipher but was evidently a combination of original stones and subsequent reinforcing, containing, and framing elements, another relic-cum-reliquary.

According to the documents the ancient cell was reinforced with buttresses and vaulted after the fire of 1465. But that vaulting was then capped by a simple wooden roof, perhaps to hide the structural improvement and preserve the primitive aspect. Another source points out that the poor quality of the masonry, so needful of reinforcement, was proof that the chapel really had been built by the pious but unskilled hands of the early monks, Meinrad and his tenth-century successors Eberhard and Gregor.[68]

The reconsecration of 1466 at Einsiedeln triggered or revived a pilgrimage, or was meant to, as the Master E. S. shows us. Yet once again the cult image itself does not quite come into focus. The image in the chapel today, the so-called Black Madonna of Einsiedeln, predates the fire of 1465 yet does not resemble the Madonna and Child enthroned on the altar in this engraving. In precise accord with evidence suggesting that pilgrimages were not focused so much on images as on places where the Virgin manifested her power, the engraving does not make it clear whether the kneeling pilgrims in the engraving are worshipping the Virgin herself or a carved image of her. Like any artwork, the engraving collapses time, representing all at once the miracle; the cult image erected to mark the miracle; St. Benedict, who lived some centuries before the time of the miracle; and the modern pilgrims. The engraving reproduces the cult image already framed, in fact three times framed: first by the vaulted chapel, second by the round-arched aperture in the building, and third by the date 1466 and the monogram of the artist — that is, by the engraving itself. The print offers the cult image as *mise-en-abyme*, an analogon of the entire work embedded deep within itself. One of the features of the modern artwork is its capacity to model itself. Here it becomes possible to see the entire cultic system, with its multiple interlockings of building and image, with its reflexivity and recursivity, as already an artwork in a full sense, capable of interpreting itself. "Einsiedeln," like "Loreto," was an art theory performed by an entire culture.

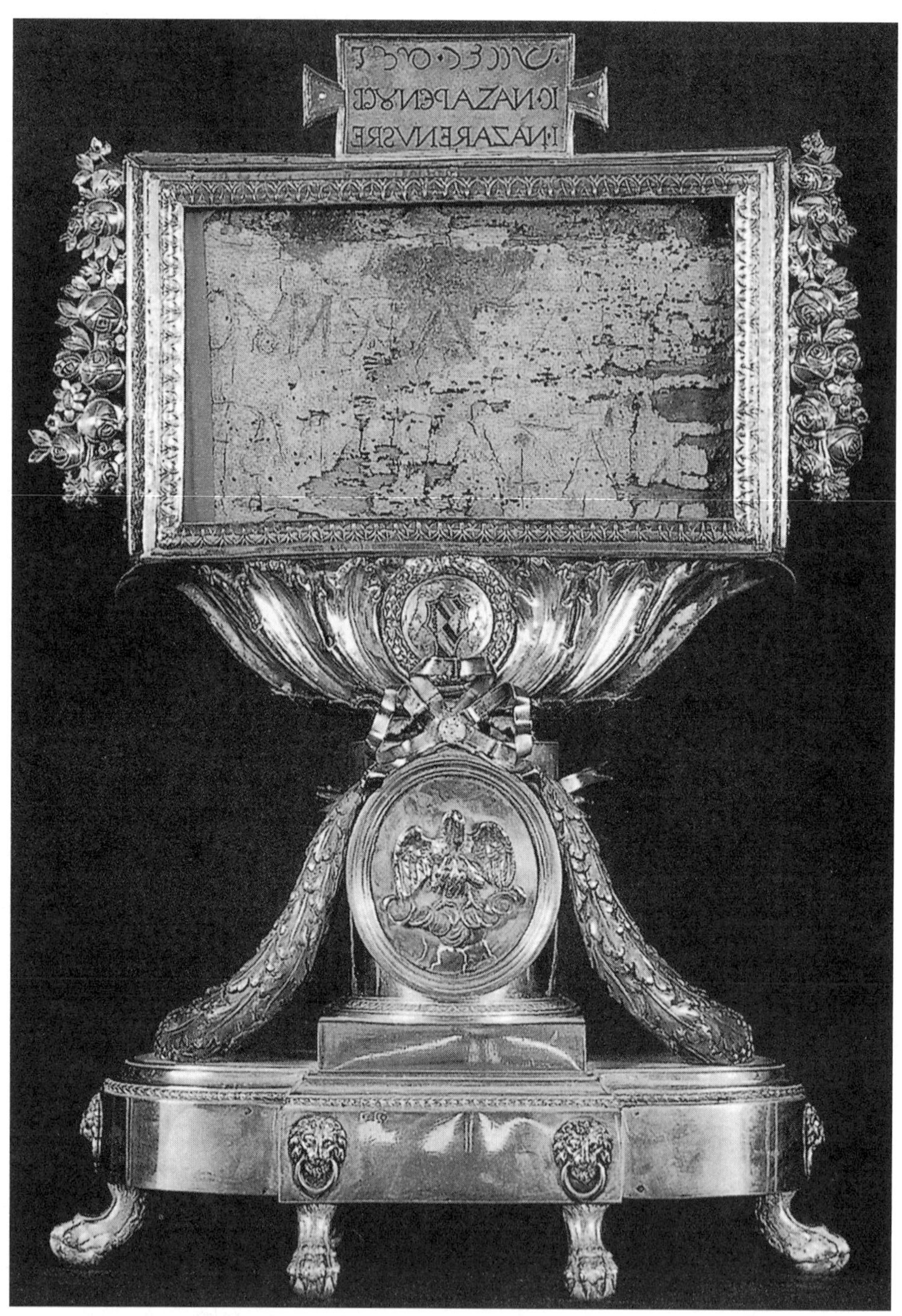

19.1 **The trilingual label attached to Christ's cross, supposedly recovered by St. Helena in 325 and carried back to Rome.** Titulus Crucis, walnut panel, 25.3 x 14 cm (twelfth century), silver reliquary frame (early sixteenth century). Rome, Santa Croce in Gerusalemme. The inscribed tablet, a portion of the original label, was found on February 1, 1492, inside a walled-up niche high on the tribune arch of the basilica of Santa Croce.

NINETEEN

The Titulus Crucis

In the winter of 1492, workmen carrying out restorations at the Basilica of Santa Croce in Gerusalemme in Rome found a sealed lead capsule inside a walled-up niche above the triumphal arch, near the ceiling. The capsule contained a sizeable fragment of the Titulus Crucis, the inscribed wooden tablet that Pontius Pilate had mounted on the cross. The Titulus belonged to the trove of artifacts—including a nail, a large share of the True Cross, and blood-bathed earth from Golgotha—that St. Helena, Constantine's mother, was supposed to have excavated in the Holy Land in 324–325. Once transported to the Sessorian palace, her residence in Rome, these objects converted the palace into the sanctuary that was later to become the Basilica of Santa Croce in Gerusalemme. During a twelfth-century rebuilding campaign, the Titulus was immured above the triumphal arch. In the ensuing centuries everyone forgot where the relic had been hidden; or so the powerful primate of Spain, Pedro González de Mendoza, the titular cardinal of the church, would have had people believe in 1492. The mosaic inscription identifying the wall niche had deteriorated and was by the late fifteenth century illegible from floor level. Cardinal Mendoza publicized the rediscovery as a divine coincidence, as it occurred on the very day—February 1— that the news of the reconquest of Granada by the Spanish monarchy reached Rome.[1] The rediscovery of the Titulus was a pure publicity stunt, since Mendoza knew exactly where to find the relic; or rather, his agents in Rome knew where to find it, for Mendoza himself, archbishop of Seville and later Toledo, the chancellor of Ferdinand and Isabella, never actually visited Rome. The German pilgrim Niklas Muffel, in his diary of his visit of 1452, had reported that the Titulus was kept in a "window" above the altar.[2] It is difficult to believe that the clerics at Santa Croce were ignorant of the location of the relic only forty years later.

The relic is a rough wooden panel, 2.6 centimeters thick (figure 19.1).[3] There are traces of white paint on the board and red coloring in the incised letters. Today it is encased in a silver reliquary in the treasury at Santa Croce in Gerusalemme, dimly visible through thick glass. The panel appears to corroborate the report of the Gospels, which tell, all four of them, of a superscription on the cross identifying the executed man as "Jesus of Nazareth, King of the Jews." According to John 19:19–20, "Pilate also had an inscription written and put on the cross. It read, 'Jesus the Nazorean, the King of the Jews.' Now many of the Jews read this inscription, because the place where Jesus was crucified was near the city; and it was written in Hebrew, Greek, and Latin" (*hunc ergo titulum multi legerunt Iudaeorum quia prope civitatem erat locus ubi crucifixus est Iesus et erat scriptum hebraice graece et latine.*)[4] The inscription is maladroitly carved. The Hebrew text is almost entirely missing except for the bottom of some of the letters; the Greek and Latin lines are incomplete. The Greek and Latin lines are written backwards, from right to left, not only letter by letter but also in mirror script.

It is tempting to take this battered plank with its enigmatic letters for a true relic of the Crucifixion. The clerics and scholars who examined the object in 1492 had every reason to believe in it. Tablets of this sort, naming criminal and crime, really were used in Roman executions. Admittedly, the fourth-century historian Eusebius, in his account of Helena's visit to Jerusalem, made no mention of the discovery of an inscribed tablet. The Spanish pilgrim Egeria, on the other hand, writing about her journey to the Holy Land of the 380s, reported that the Titulus or at least a portion of it was indeed preserved in Jerusalem. And in 395 St. Ambrose said that it was in Rome.[5] But in the end the Titulus is too good to be true. The wooden panel has recently been dated by radiocarbon analysis to the eleventh or twelfth century.[6] It is a fabrication undertaken probably in the early 1140s at the behest of Gerardo Caccianemici, archbishop of Bologna and titular cardinal of Santa Croce, the future pope Lucius II (1144-1145), whose seal adorned the box found in the wall niche in 1492.[7]

One context for the rediscovery of the Titulus was the resurgent public cult of relics. In the late fifteenth century, all over Europe, clerics were learning how to convert their relic collections into revenue. One only needed to read the old chronicles and saints' lives to be reminded of once-buried but now forgotten remains of local saints. A few strokes of pickaxe and spade could bring the past to life again. A spectacular and exactly contemporary example in Augsburg was the rediscovery (and like the rediscovery of the Titulus, an "accident") of the relics of St. Simpertus, a ninth-century bishop.[8] Simpertus had been reburied below the floor of the choir of the abbey church of Sts. Ulrich and Afra in the eleventh century and again in the twelfth century. The precise site of the burial was forgotten and in the fall of 1491 the abbot and bishop decided to dig for them. The discovery of Simpertus's bones set in motion months of public ceremony involving processions, the fashioning of a new sarcophagus, and reburial in the presence of the emperor. A new life of St. Simpertus was written and published. Local myth was fitted to a grid of history. Here and elsewhere in the last decades of the fifteenth century, long-neglected relics and images reemerged as evidence of prestigious episodes in the life of church and city.

The Titulus was not only a relic but also a vehicle for information. The ordinary relic of the holy personage, a fragment of a body, was uninformative, perhaps even formless. The historicizing imagination had to project a body and a physiognomy, indeed a personality and life known from the hagiographies, onto the bones. At Augsburg, the sculptor devised a full-length supine portrait of Simpertus, complete with invented but realistic physiognomy, to adorn the new tomb. The Titulus was a different sort of relic, for it had form—maybe too much form. Scripture said nothing about the size of the panel, the shape of the letters, whether they were carved or written, the puzzling right-to-left script. Until this moment, Christians had no information at all about the Crucifixion except through the spare words of the Gospels. Now here was a piece of material evidence that supplemented and even contradicted scripture, calling attention to the disparity between one evangelist and another and thus to the possibility of their fallibility.

The second context for the rediscovery of the Titulus was the new antiquarian fascination with ancient Roman inscriptions. Humanistically trained scholars, since the early fifteenth century and with mounting intensity in the last decades of the century, especially in Italy and Germany, were hunting, transcribing, and collecting inscriptions. The corpus of inscriptions ballooned as scholars copied each other's finds into their own notebooks. Scholars learned to decipher the puzzling abbreviations. The inscriptions, together with other tangible remains, opened up dimensions of ancient life unavailable to the mere reader of literary prose and poetry.[9]

The Titulus Crucis occupied a position at the intersection of these two contexts, the cult of relics and the historical study of inscriptions. The Titulus at Santa Croce was a wooden plank more or less the size of an icon. But it resembled even more an epigraphic inscription. Scholars around 1500 were increasingly thinking about the overall look of inscriptions and not merely decoding them. The earliest collections of inscriptions, or sylloges, gathered by scholars betray indifference to the visual aspects of the lettering. With the advent of print and the attendant possibility of perfect replication of letter forms scholars began to focus on the formal features of epigraphic texts.

The Titulus was an object oscillating between two identities, medial and sacral. This panel, if genuine, was an extremely reliable witness to the historical event of the Crucifixion. At the same time, the Titulus was an object that once upon a time had been in direct physical contact with the cross itself, and so by one degree of remove in contact with Christ's body, and to that extent an object whose value to worshippers was inestimable, even if nothing at all had been written on it.

The Titulus was like one of the sacred icons that played a role in some miracle stories, like the mosaic icon supposedly commissioned by St. Gregory in the sixth century, also housed at Santa Croce in Gerusalemme since the late fourteenth century (see figure 10.2), or the icon that the just-converted St. Catherine gazed upon (see figure 10.3). Such icons were not merely reliable transmitters of pictorial information like ordinary icons, but also relics of Gregory and Catherine, independent of their iconographic content.

The medial approach and the cultic approach to the Titulus each handle doubts about the object's authenticity in different ways. For even if the Titulus at Santa Croce were not the Titulus itself, but rather only an old copy of the original plank, it would still transmit valuable testimony. It would still function medially. A Titulus that was never mounted on the cross, however, a fake Titulus, was in no way a holy relic.

An inscription may well be a relic, but relic status will only make it a relatively more reliable witness. A good copy can provide all the information required. The whole institution of scholarship as a social phenomenon depends on this principle. The very point of an inscription is to transcend the trivial circumstances of its own material fabrication. An inscription on wood or stone or bronze, in the ancient world, was a device designed to do just that, exactly as does publication with ink stamped on paper in the post-Gutenberg world. The capacity to transcend the contingent circumstances of its own material nature is the basis of the power of the inscription (or publication) in political and juridical contexts.

The Titulus was a lens that focused all the paradoxes of the anachronic artifact. For the artwork, too, around 1500, was suspended in the minds of its admirers between two identities: *relic*, an object whose value depended upon impeccable credentials, a birth certificate that moored it in history; and *inscription*, an object whose function was to deliver a message and which could be replaced if necessary by another object bearing the same message.

The reader of messages who asks too insistently after the historical credentials of the message's physical vehicle—the reader who interrogates the messenger—is naïve. The scholarly epigraphers of Rome, Padua, and Augsburg learned to trust the content of the stones. In epigraphy, the distinction between original and copy is usually irrelevant. The Titulus Crucis, an ancient inscription that had survived not by accident but only because it was a relic of Christ, could not be read this way. As a relic, it invited a new attentiveness to form and material beyond what was customarily trained on inscriptions.

Several features of the Titulus demanded that it be read as a relic with specific attributes. First, as noted, the Greek and Latin lines are written backwards. The most plausible explanation for this strange feature, the one that the twelfth-century forgers must have had in mind, was that the scribe of the Titulus was a Jew who could not write Greek or Latin any other way than right to left as he was accustomed to do. But no one in the late fifteenth or sixteenth centuries seems to have proposed this explanation. The papal master of ceremonies Johann Burchard only noted that all three texts were written "backwards, in the manner of the Jews" (*ordine retrogrado, Judeorum more*).[10] Another explanation offered was that the retrograde script was a form of linguistic obeisance, the "later" languages conforming themselves to the more venerable Hebrew.[11]

A second notable feature of the inscription is the sequence of the languages on the relic, top to bottom: Hebrew, Greek, Latin, as the Vulgate has it. But modern textual scholarship finds that Hebrew, Latin, Greek is actually the sequence most strongly supported by the preponderance of manuscripts of the book of John. Hebrew, Greek, Latin is a later development in the textual tradition, perhaps simply meant to register a historical movement from east to west. Thus the Titulus, if genuine, ought to read Hebrew, Latin, Greek. But the philology of the Gospel passage is inconclusive. It would be difficult to discredit the Titulus on this ground alone.[12] The trilingual inscription, even if attested by scripture, clashed with the pictorial evidence, including such prestigious images as the mosaic icon at Santa Croce representing Gregory the Great's vision of the crucified Christ, where the inscription is only in Greek (see figure 10.2).

The Titulus Crucis was a creation of the twelfth century undertaken surely not entirely in bad faith but rather in a spirit of imaginative supplementation of the historical record.[13] The prestige of the Basilica of Santa Croce in Gerusalemme, once lofty on account of the relics brought to Rome by Helena, had declined sharply since the seventh century. The Titulus was an additional relic that Santa Croce really ought to have possessed.[14] The twelfth-century forgers were clever enough to have fabricated only a partial relic, perhaps remembering accounts, like that of the pilgrim Egeria, of a titulus relic in Jerusalem. Egeria had said that the relic was contained in a small box, implying that the panel had been cut in two, divided between Jerusalem and Rome. The forgers were clever enough to mask their own ignorance of Hebrew by cutting the top line of text horizontally, leaving only a few almost meaningless strokes, reconstructible as a good Hebrew text only by a sympathetic viewer. Although the Latin and Greek texts on the Titulus diverge from the biblical texts, the forgers made no grievous linguistic errors.[15] It is even possible that the rough, formless quality of the letters was contrived as a trace of the violence of the event, simulating an authentic "front-lines" quality. Twelfth-century clerics and craftsmen were certainly capable of such an ingenious confection. One is reminded of the excellent eleventh-century forgeries of a set of inscribed clay tablets, involving obsolete letter forms, which clinched the claim of the bishop of Regensburg to possess the true relics of St. Denis.[16]

No one in the 1490s discredited the discovery at Santa Croce, at least not in any written text that has survived. And yet the relic, which might have been expected to compel a revision of the conventions governing depictions of the historical Crucifixion, exerted a minimal impact. The discovery at Santa Croce delivered the very object that scholars and artists supposedly sought: the evidentiary image, the material trace of a vanished moment, both evidence of the moment and an iconographical datum, to be assimilated into any representation of the crucifix or crucifixion. But questions were asked, it seems, about the true origins of the artifact, questions of agency that quietly marginalized the relic. The anticlimactic reception of the Titulus signals a new literalism, around 1500, in thinking about origins. The implications for a public cult of relics were catastrophic.

A newly active media network broadcast the sensational news of the discovery of the Titulus across Europe. Diarists recorded the event and news of the finding was sent to princes and scholars. The discovery prompted a reengagement with the iconography of the true cross, in the apse of the Basilica of Santa Croce itself (see section 26), as well as in Venice, where the nobleman and scholar of Greek, Girolamo Donato, had a jasper reliquary, now lost, made for a fragment of the Titulus that Cardinal Mendoza gave him, and at the same time founded an altar of the cross at the church of the Servi.[17] The altar was decorated with reliefs depicting the Finding of the Cross, the Proof of the Cross, Constantine's Vision of the Cross, and Constantine's Victory at the Milvian Bridge by Andrea Riccio, as well as a tabernacle; all are now in the Ca'd'Oro in Venice.[18]

The form of the Titulus was propagated by German prints. A pair of woodcuts printed in Nuremberg survive in a single impression each. They were pasted by the Nuremberg scholar Hartmann Schedel into the last pages of his copy of his own *World Chronicle* (published in 1493) and in this way rescued from destruction.[19] One of the two gives the trilingual text in its correct right-to-left orientation (figure 19.2), the other reverses the texts (figure 19.3). Both reproduce the forms of the letters and offer explanatory captions: "This is the breadth, length, and size of the panel and with the same letters and forms as are engraved in the board, as I have seen with my own eyes; and it is hard to read because worms have eaten through it."[20] On the pages of the book Schedel added his own reverent captions—"Miserere mei," have mercy on me—in majuscule letters, and a further account of the discovery in Rome. No doubt there were other prints reproducing the Titulus, as well as drawings, which have not survived.[21] No ancient Roman inscription on stone was treated with comparable attentiveness. Prints sometimes reproduced the texts of Roman epigraphic inscriptions but not the special forms of the letters.

On the basis of these prints some contemporary painters reinserted the tablet in its proper historical context in scenes of the Crucifixion, Deposition from the Cross, and Lamentation under the Cross. Such scenes, traditionally, depicted a Latin-only titulus, in fact most often simply the acronym INRI. Apart from the precocious trilingual titulus in Giotto's Santa Maria Novella crucifix, real Hebrew letters do not appear in European painting until the early fifteenth century.[22] Now, after the rediscovery of the Titulus relic, the tablet could assume its proper form. Some few artists responded immediately to the discovery. A German sculptor, Master Thomas, must have had a reproductive print before him when he carved a titulus in sandstone, complete with reversed letters, above a crucifix dated 1493, in Worms.[23] Fascinated by the discovery of the Titulus was the artist known as the Master of the St. Bartholomew Altarpiece, active in Cologne; arguably the most significant painter of the Renaissance whose name has not been preserved. The trilingual titulus in his Crucifixion altarpiece in Cologne followed a woodcut that gave the Greek and Latin texts in conventional left-to-right direction, possibly the Nuremberg woodcut on Schedel's fol. 334v (figure 19.3).[24] The painter preserved the truncation of the texts at the right edge—nonsensically, since the relic found in Rome was obviously (pretending to be) a fragment of the original titulus. The Hebrew text at the top, unintelligible on the titulus and in the woodcut, is conveniently obscured in the painting by a trompe l'oeil carved frame. In a small painting of the Deposition from the Cross in Philadelphia, the Bartholomew Master followed the other Nuremberg woodcut (on Schedel's fol. 334r, figure 19.2), correcting his own Cologne painting by giving the texts in their proper right-to-left sequence, and this time allowing the frame to cut off the troublesome Hebrew entirely (figure 19.4).[25]

A Crucifixion painted by Benozzo Gozzoli or his shop for the Pisan church of San Domenico shows a trilingual titulus with the first line, the Hebrew text, cut off at the top edge just as it is on the Titulus relic.[26] The titulus on the crucifix of the high altar at Miraflores, commissioned by

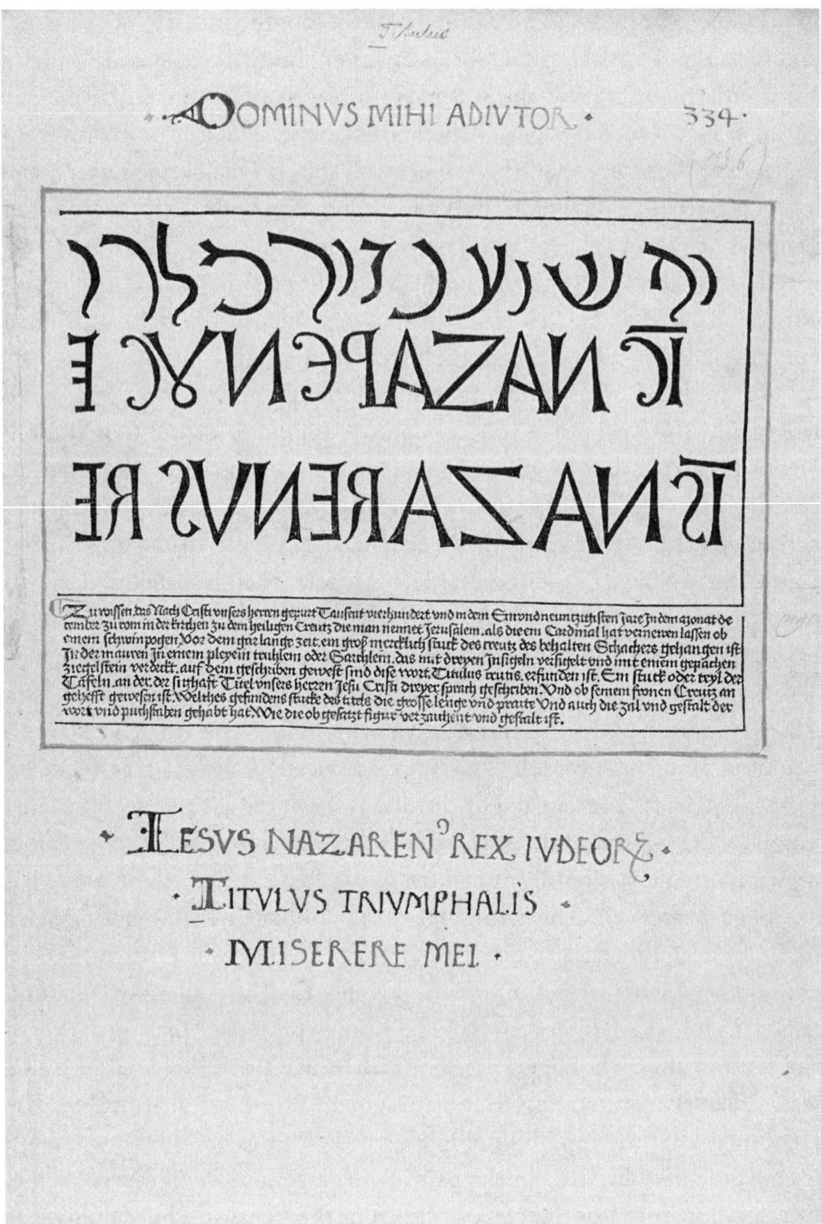

19.2 Publication of the relic. Titulus Crucis, woodcut, approx. 20 x 27 cm (Nuremberg, after 1492). Munich, Bayerische Staatsbibliothek, Rar. 287, fol. 334r. This print reproduces the Titulus fragment found at Santa Croce with the lettering running right-to-left, as in the relic, and provides an eight-line explanatory text. The incomplete marks on the relic's top register have here, however, been formed into real Hebrew letters, rough-hewn but legible. The scholar Hartmann Schedel pasted the print into a book and wrote conventional prayers above and below in his own hand. This print bears a watermark associated with Nuremberg.

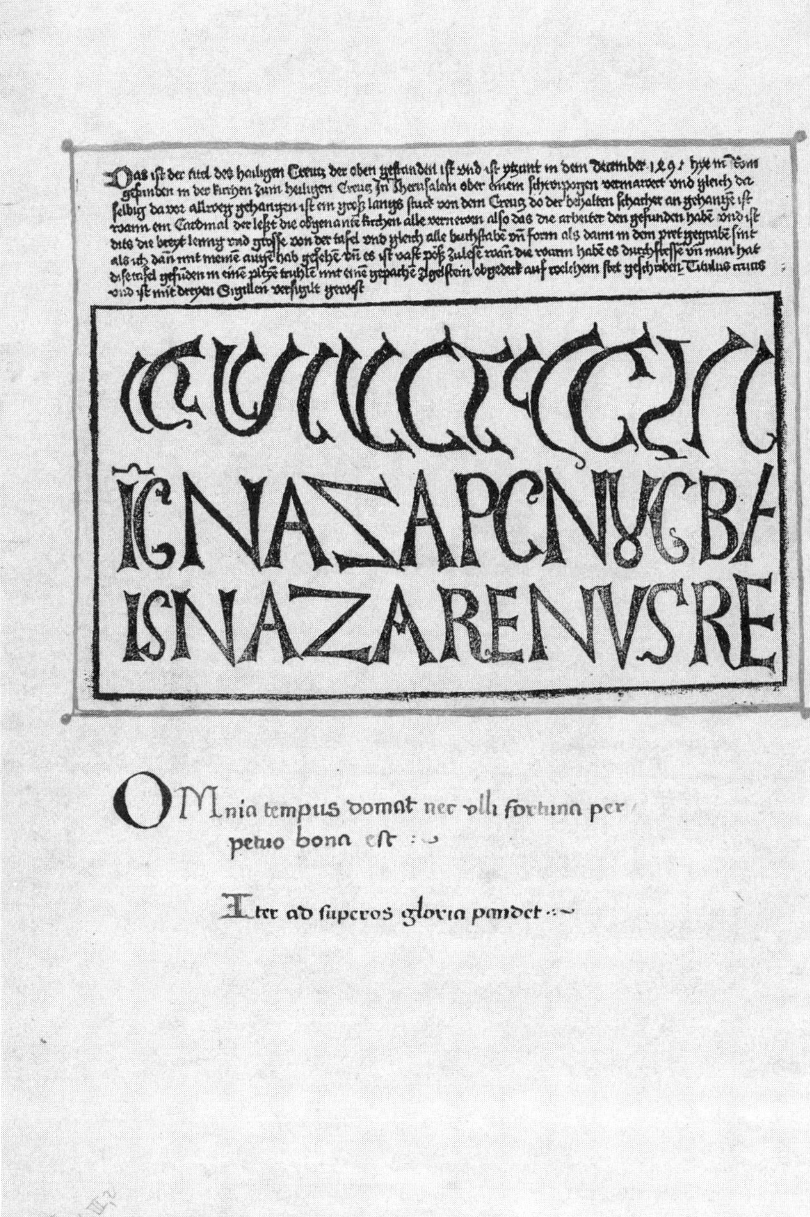

19.3 A different interpretation of the inscription. Titulus Crucis, woodcut, approx. 20 x 26 cm (Nuremberg, after 1492). Munich, Bayerische Staatsbibliothek, Rar. 287, fol. 334v. A second woodcut, possibly by the same printmaker, but also possibly by an imitator, reverses the orientation. Why was this done? Perhaps the information from the other print was mistrusted, or perhaps the letters were reversed to their normal orientation for purposes of clarification, or perhaps this print was following a different source drawing that had already reversed the lettering of the relic. The Hebrew has been carefully preserved, but the letters now run left to right. As if to bolster its claims, this print adds a letter to the Greek line and in general presents a more embellished inscription. The eight-line text above the facsimile of the relic recounts the discovery of the tablet "here in Rome" and assures the beholder that this is really what the letters look like.

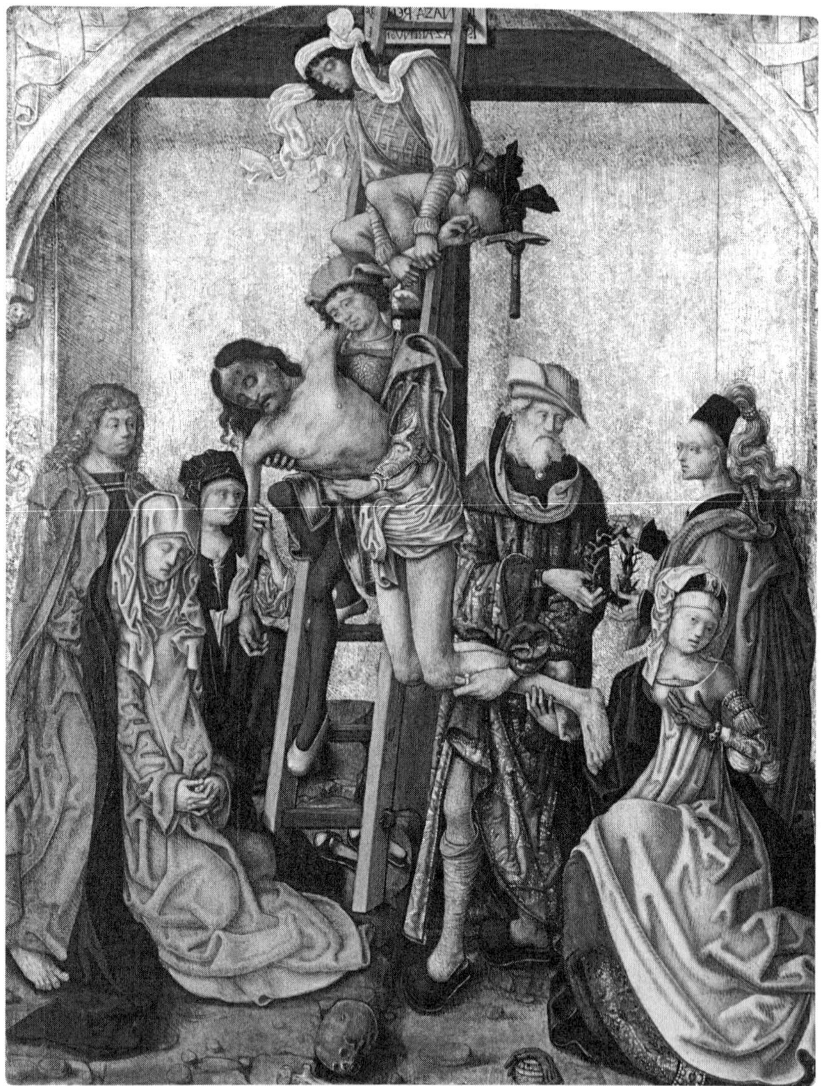

19.4 Incorporation of the new data from Rome into an historical painting. Master of the St. Bartholomew Altarpiece, *Deposition from the Cross*, oil on panel, 51.3 x 39.5 cm (after 1492). Philadelphia, Philadelphia Museum of Art. This brilliant but anonymous artist, who worked in Cologne, struggled to align his renderings of the *Deposition* with the evidence of the relic. For this version he appears to have studied a print very like our figure 19.2. But evidently he did not have confidence in the Hebrew text, and conveniently allowed it to be cut off by the top edge of the picture.

Ferdinand and Isabella from the sculptor Gil de Siloe (1499), complies with the relic discovered in 1492.[27] An early sixteenth-century German painting in Munich, meanwhile, represents the Man of Sorrows seated in a church interior with a trilingual titulus suspended on a tablet over his head. Here, too, the lettering closely follows the right-to-left scripts in the Nuremberg woodcut on Schedel's fol. 334r.[28]

Another possible registration of the news of the discovery is a drawing of the Preparations for the Crucifixion now in the Pierpont Morgan Library in New York, one of a small group of late fifteenth century German images that represent a scribe carrying out Pilate's instructions (figure 19.5).[29] The scribe sits in the lower left of the scene and supports the scroll on his knees. He is assisted by a crouching henchman holding an ink pot. The drawing is attributed to the Master of the Herpin Manuscript, a work dated 1487. Several other contemporary German works picture such a scribe, always writing on a scroll with pen and ink: a drawing associated with Martin Schongauer, two simple woodcuts, and a large panel painting in Frankfurt.[30] Only in the Morgan drawing, however, does the scribe write backwards—after a fashion (figure 19.6). The result will be the acronym INRI, in the correct sequence, but the scribe, according to the drawing, has begun writing from the right edge. The final I is invisible, curled below on the right edge; then comes the R; and now the scribe starts the downward stroke of the N.[31] Perhaps the discovery of the Titulus encouraged artists to reflect anew on the circumstances of its fabrication.

The informational value of the Titulus relic was potentially immense. Along with the Holy Lance, the nails, splinters of wood from the cross, and a fragment of Christ's seamless robe, the Titulus was a rare surviving element of the event of the Crucifixion. The inscribed panel was an indispensable component of any depiction of the Crucifixion. To possess the Titulus relic was to have a patch of the painting ready-made. If the relic were genuine, it should have cut through the chain of copies, all the pictorial conventions, and "corrected" the tradition. Any claims that Christian painting made to historical reliability depended on faith in the chain of substitutions that carried information from picture to picture, across centuries. The icons that had been filtering into western Europe since the thirteenth century, and had captured the imagination of scholars, patrons, and painters in the fifteenth century, were valued precisely because they seemed to leap across this chain and give access to a much earlier point in the transmission, perhaps the very origin point. The Christian painter ought to have taken advantage of any available evidence about how things looked. Certainly news about the discovery of the Titulus was not lacking.

The same principle applied to the iconic portraits of Christ and the Virgin. If the Mandylion and the Luke icons were really documents from the lifetime of the Virgin, eyewitness testimony to her appearance, then modern images of Christ and the Virgin ought to have stabilized, around

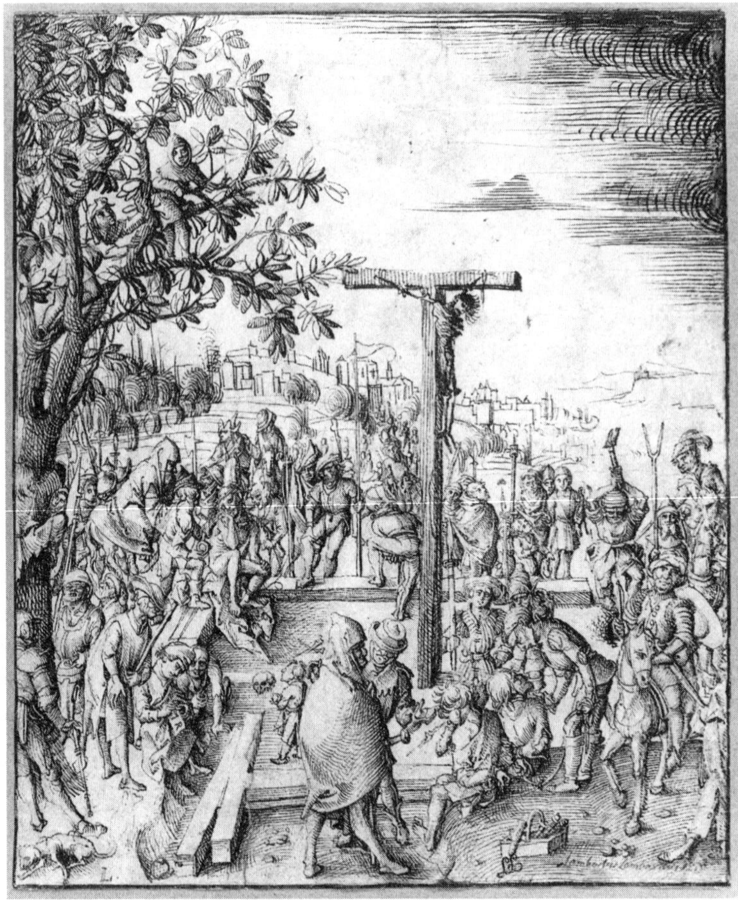

19.5 How the fabrication of the Titulus Crucis was imagined. Master of the Herpin Manuscript, *Preparations for the Crucifixion*, drawing, 23.4 x 19.8 (ca. 1490). New York, Pierpont Morgan Library. In this encompassingly descriptive rendition of the event, we see a figure seated lower left who is in the act of inscribing the mocking title, one of the rare representations of this action. The drawing is attributed to a German artist, possibly Franconian, who illustrated a prose translation of a French courtly epic, *The Story of Herpin and His Son Lewe.*

those portraits, into a Buddha-like consistency. But that did not happen. Nor did the authentic medal portraits of Christ, as we will soon learn, fix the image of the Savior as they ought to have done. The documentary authority of the icons was left undecided. Doubts about their relic status were allayed by a substitutional hypothesis. But this hypothesis was not strong enough to enforce pictorial compliance.

The problem of the Eastern icons—their antiquity, their challenge to the Western cult image—unfolded into the more general problem of the

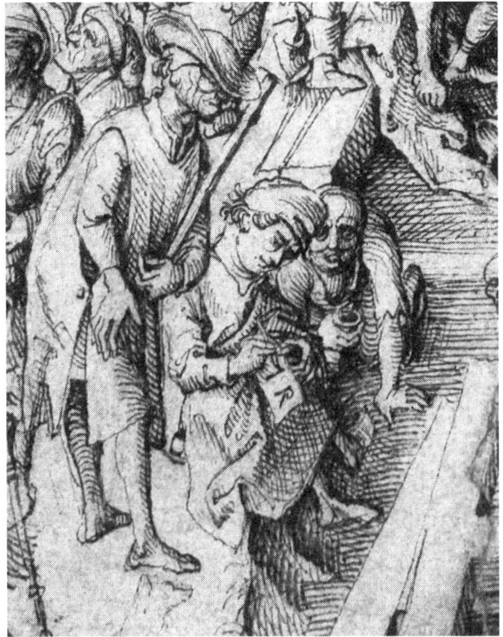

19.6 The Titulus written backwards. Master of the Herpin Manuscript, *Preparations for the Crucifixion*, detail. New York, Pierpont Morgan Library. The scribe, accompanied by a servant holding an inkwell, appears to be writing backwards.

evidentiary image. The European engagement with the icon in the fifteenth century should not be misunderstood as the mere persistence of an older, substitutional conception of transmission. To repaint, reframe, imitate, and write the biography of an icon was to display the substitutional system and to some extent to interrogate it. The fact of the icons' long east-to-west journeys lent them an aura of singularity. But the cult of imported icons in the West was structured by doubt about whether the panels really did date from early Christian time, or whether they were just effective stand-ins for lost originals—whether they were relics or inscriptions, in other words.

Inscriptional or substitutional logic works perfectly as long as an artifact is not being asked to function as historical evidence, that is, as the unmediated witness of a past event. To ask that of an artifact is to apply pressure on the substitutional model. According to that model, the material vehicle is irrelevant and only the information transmitted matters. The antithesis of such a trusted artifact is the nonsubstitutable relic. The relic does not transmit information, but rather communicates by virtue of being a piece of the material world once contiguous with an absent object or present at a past event. The icon reemerged in the fifteenth century as a possible new basis for the authority of the art of painting. But it ran up against new expectations for evidence. The icon was asked to be a relic and, despite the late fifteenth-century enthusiasm for images by St. Luke, in most cases that was too much to ask. Under the archeological paradigm, authority is tied to relic status (nonsubstitutionality) rather than to a link to the origin by a chain of copies that no one had ever seen (substitutionality).

The Luke icons were never really put on trial; the Titulus, however, was subjected to forensic scrutiny. The Titulus was well-suited to stand as a test case of the usefulness of substitutionally transmitted information because the story of the trilingual tablet thematizes authorship and the problem of the source of utterance. The rough, unprofessional carving is a powerful index of the utterance, returning the reader to the historical fact that the person—a Jew, possibly, for why else would the Greek and Latin texts be written in reverse?—who carved these words into the wood did so ironically, that is, without believing in their referential function. According to the source of this utterance—the Roman state and the carver working in the name of the state—Jesus was *not* king of the Jews; he was a criminal for having claimed to be such. This reminder would only sharpen the crucial second irony, for a Christian, that the words meant in mockery were the least of his titles. He was much more than merely King of the Jews. Indeed, John 19:21–22 already alludes to the possibility of a misreading advantageous to Christians: "So the chief priests of the Jews said to Pilate, 'Do not write "The King of the Jews," but that he said, "I am the King of the Jews."'" The priests wanted the words "he said" because they worried that onlookers would understand the label as a generally true statement, a statement without a source, as it were. But John reports that Pilate refused to append such a framing device, an attributive phrase that would reduce the universally true statement to the status of a mere local utterance. "Pilate answered, 'What I have written, I have written.'" Probably Pilate's decision to leave the inscription tablet's text elliptical was no more than a bit of sardonic humor at the expense of the Jewish leaders (as if to say, "You Jews deserve such a 'king'").[32]

"King of the Jews" is the *aetia*, the *causa poeniae*, the explanation for the punishment. But it is archly truncated. The real cause for punishment was that "he claimed to be King of the Jews." As it stands, the label introduces the shadow of a possibility more deeply alarming for Jews, namely, that this is how the Romans would deal with a legitimate King of the Jews. The still darker humor behind Pilate's "what I have written, I have written" is the thought that Pilate might actually have half-believed that Christ was who he said he was, and that he nevertheless was cynical enough to let the punishment be carried out (and on the heads of the Jews themselves).

John's report is also a parable on the relative inarticulateness of artifacts and images: the limits on how many layers of nesting are possible. Pilate stipulated that the text appear without discursive framing, that it provide no "return address" for the utterance—other than the Roman state itself, of course—and in doing so he made the Titulus an inscription, a non-contingent statement, rather than an utterance, which carries the memory of its source. In trying to convert Pilate's Titulus into an utterance, the protesting Jewish priests were insisting that Christ's crime was after all a speech act, a proclamation that he had made about his own identity. The Gospel account, by revealing that Pilate authored it, undermines the force of his decision to leave the tablet as a label rather than as quoted speech. In the light of *quod scripsi scripsi*, "what I have written, I have written," the Titulus becomes an inscription between quotation marks, and an inscription that raises the general question, "What is an inscription?"

For Tertullian and other Church fathers engaged in biblical hermeneutics, Pilate had dictated the text of the Titulus prophetically, under the direction of the Holy Spirit.[33] Within this tradition of interpretation, which tried to see things not from a historical but from a divine perspective, the Titulus was a metastatement about the ironic nature of relics generally: what was meaningless and incidental turns out to have enormous significance. A humble sign turns out to be a glorious emblem, and a mockery turns out to be a prophesy.

John's account, which is only interested in what Pilate said, reveals that for Christians the relic of the Titulus has zero additional value as evidence. The Bible already tells Christians all they need to know about the incident. A philological analysis of the inscribed text at best helps to validate the relic status of the object, that is, its proximity to Christ's body.

The Titulus, if genuine, did also validate the Gospels, if validation was needed. For to believe in the relic of the Titulus was to see it as the only preevangelical textual source, the source, indeed, for the text on the tablet as given in the Gospels. The three languages affirmed the transmissibility and translatability of textual reference. For the sixth- and seventh-century theologian and grammarian Isidore of Seville, the Titulus was proof of the sanctity of these three languages and of the need for interpreters of the Bible to know all three, so as to cross-reference one against the other in problems of decipherment.[34]

The relic quality of the object would be secured by interrogating noninformational aspects of the text, the material and formal remainder beyond the substitutable textual content: the rough carving, the backward lettering, the tablet's fragmentary condition. The relic would thus become evidence of itself. This is exceptional, for most relics—a bone, a rag, a fragment of the cross itself—were formless, mute, dependent on labels. The Titulus was a relic that was also a label and so could testify on its own behalf, like a painting. The querying of the Titulus was like a rehearsal for art history. It was subjected to multifaceted scrutiny, as evidence and as medium, well before anyone had thought of giving an extended description of the material and formal qualities of a work of art. Johann Burchard and the diarist Stefano Infessura both noted that letters were missing due to the mutilated and dilapidated condition of the tablet.[35] Burchard, commenting on the quality of the inscription, introduced a drawn copy of the "forms of the letters" into his diary. A letter of February 4, 1492, from Leonardo da Sarzana to the papal nuncio in Florence, Giacomo Gherardi, described the find and noted the backward lettering, which he interpreted as a sign of "the greater faith and religion that attaches to this object, as they did not want to contravene the primary way of writing proper to Hebrew letters." In a letter to Gherardi ten days later da Sarzana added that he had sent a full report to Lorenzo de' Medici, containing "everything that is to be found on this most venerable wooden tablet," including the characters in their proper measure and in backward order "ut Hebrei solent."[36]

Da Sarzana's explanation makes little historical sense, for why would anyone carving this crude tablet amidst the tumult of the Crucifixion have thought it necessary to encode a gesture of reverence for the Hebrew language? But perhaps da Sarzana's reasoning was not strictly historical, but rather hermeneutical, like that of the Church fathers who read the words as prophecy and not merely as a document of an accusation. Now that we are in a position to see the tablet as something holy, as a sacred relic, da Sarzana seems to say, then everything about it must be meaningful. According to da Sarzana, the retroscript is an intralinguistic admission by the Latin and Greek tongues that they are mere mediations, "fallen" languages that can only dream of finding their way back to the purity and authenticity of Hebrew. And in finding their way back to that pure state, in taking the reverse path, they actually reveal that the original statement *is* encoded, that it needs to be unpacked: that its literal meaning (Jesus of Nazareth, King of the Jews), though meant ironically, in a double negative proves true. The backward script is a figure for that irony; the words must be read "in reverse"—twice—in order to be understood correctly. (The straightforward reading of the tablet is: "He is King of the Jews." A first layer of ironization, urged by the priests, would have given us the text: "Christ says that he is King of the Jews." The second layer of ironization is provided by Pilate's statement: "I am not going to alter the tablet so that it reads 'Christ says that he is King of the Jews,'" which leaves open the possibility that Pilate thinks Christ might be who he says he is and that therefore the initial straightforward reading that we started with is true.)

The Titulus, both text and image, contains information, like the curious form of the lettering, which the Johannine text (written in Greek) alone did not provide. All Christian interpreters knew that the biblical text was encoded, that, for example, a statement meant in irony can in a double irony turn out to be true. But the artifact, which shows the texts running in reverse, does something more: it *figures* the text's encoding. Reverse writing is a figure of figuration, an acknowledgment that the words will reveal their meaning only when read back from the present—that they are written for the present but will only be understood in the present when the present understands itself to be spoken to by the past, and thus that it was in a sense already present in the past. The inversion of normal (chrono)logical order, figured in the reverse script, expresses this recognition of temporal inversion.

These features that belong to the Titulus as an artifact, as visual image, reveal the deep structure of every Christian image. Works of Christian art, representations of the Crucifixion for example, do not only depict. This image, the later figuring of the event, *is* the future predicted by the event. The fact that the episode is now being remembered, in ritual and image, proves the efficacy of the event, proves that it was never merely an historical event that belongs to the past. The Crucifixion is a picture of the event, but it is also the recognition of the event's "figural" life. The image reveals that the event already contains the principle of its own depiction. The time of the image, therefore, is not merely the time of the event or the time of the event's depiction, the moment of the making of the image. Its time is the crossing of the one by the other. It depicts not only the event, and not only the fact that the event is more than an event; it also inevitably carries the acknowledgment that the present knows itself to have been predicted by the event. This temporal cat's cradle was the implicit structure of all Christian images.

In European art around 1500, that structure was itself undergoing intensive analysis amidst rising concerns over the reliability of visual evidence across the board. Christian images, as we have seen, had themselves entered into an intensive phase of self-analysis, performing internal examinations of their own temporal interlacings. Works of art became spaces in which modes of image making could be conceptualized and compared. This anatomization was a rehearsal, within the register of art making, for the real and sometimes brutal dismantlings and displacements that would occur in the Protestant Reformation.

Once da Sarzana's report on the Titulus reached Lorenzo de' Medici's hands, the artists in his circle started to respond. In the letter of February 14, da Sarzana had asked Gherardi to remember him to Pico della Mirandola and Poliziano, among others; it is likely that these scholars played a role in the transmission of the new information to the artists.[37] The unusual titulus in three languages with Greek and Latin written in reverse appears atop Michelangelo's crucifix for Santo Spirito, which was likely completed in 1492, shortly after the news of the find reached Lorenzo de' Medici (and probably before his death in April 1492) (figure 19.7).[38] It also appears above the cross in Luca Signorelli's 1494 *Crucifixion* banner in Urbino.[39] But the two artists responded differently to the information. Signorelli treated the Titulus like a relic, but only in part: for the Greek and Latin text, his inscription stops where the fragmentary relic stops, even if it does not precisely reproduce the layout. His partial Latin text reaches the edge—in fact it illogically establishes the width of the tablet—but the partial Greek text stops far short, leaving an empty gap in the tablet. This makes no more sense than the tablet depicted in the Philadelphia *Deposition* of the Bartholomew Master, for why would the historical Titulus have cut off the inscriptions in mid-word?

One might conclude that the two artists were interested not so much in reconstructing the historical event as in using their own paintings as frames or pretexts for publishing the newly discovered archeological evidence. Signorelli restored a full Hebrew text, a transliteration from the Greek text of the Gospel, just as did one of the German prints preserved by Schedel. Michelangelo, for his part, was clearly inspired by the discovery of the relic at Santa Croce to give his Crucifix a full trilingual titulus, and with Latin and Greek texts in mirror writing. Yet he made no effort to reproduce the letter forms. The rough script of the relic clashed with the artist's strong sense of decorum. Michelangelo completed the text and corrected the Greek to bring it into conformity with the Johannine text. The Titulus relic reads ναζαρενγς β; the Johannine text reads ιησους ο ναζωραιος ο βασιλευς των ιουδαιων, exactly the text that we find in reverse on Michelangelo's titulus.[40] His Hebrew, finally, is independent of the relic, and beautifully inscribed. Michelangelo's Hebrew text is linguistically perfect, except for the fourth word, which should read *ha-yehudim*. The first letter should be *heh*; instead the letter has been closed and so turned into a *mem*, producing the statement Jesus Christ King *from* the Jews (rather than *of* the Jews). This could be a simple error in transcription, or (less probably) a deft détournement on the part of a Hebrew adviser.[41]

The dubious Greek of the Titulus relic had put Michelangelo and his counselors, perhaps Poliziano himself, on guard, and they gave themselves the license to complete and correct the text of the tablet. And yet they still valued the tablet as formal evidence and not merely as a textual vehicle, for they preserved the reversed lettering. Even a learned humanist may have persisted in believing in the relic, attributing the linguistic pecularities of the tablet not to the medieval forgers but to the original, ignorant henchmen who carved the letters. Michelangelo, like some modern scholars, especially in the wake of the radiocarbon dating, may have understood

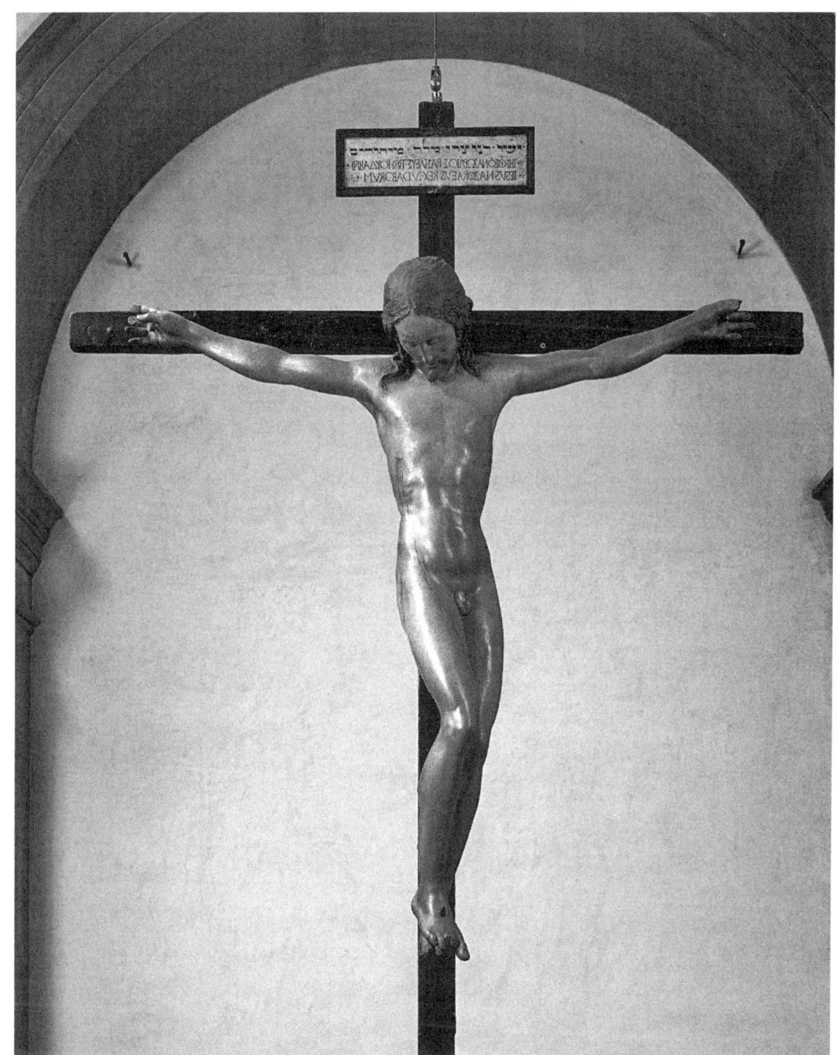

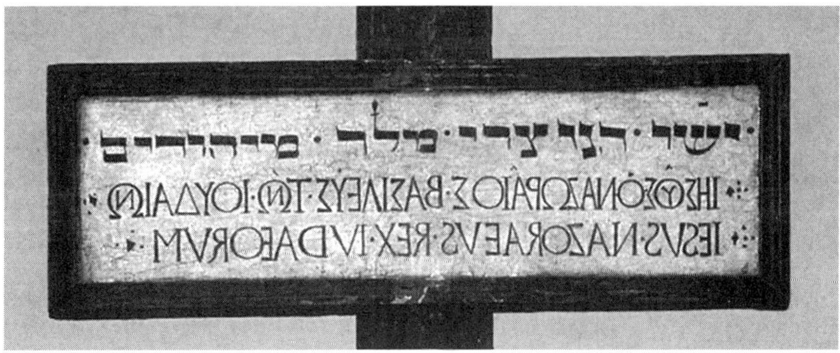

19.7 Limits of antiquarian respect for the Titulus relic. Michelangelo, *Crucifix*, polychromed wood, 139 x 135 cm (early 1492). Florence, Santo Spirito (in deposit at the Casa Buonarotti). Michelangelo was not yet seventeen years old when the Titulus was discovered. Here he adopts the backwards script of the relic found at Santa Croce but—with the help of a scholar—polishes the letter forms, alters the spelling of the Greek, provides the Hebrew, and completes the lines, which were truncated in the fragmentary relic as re-discovered in early 1492.

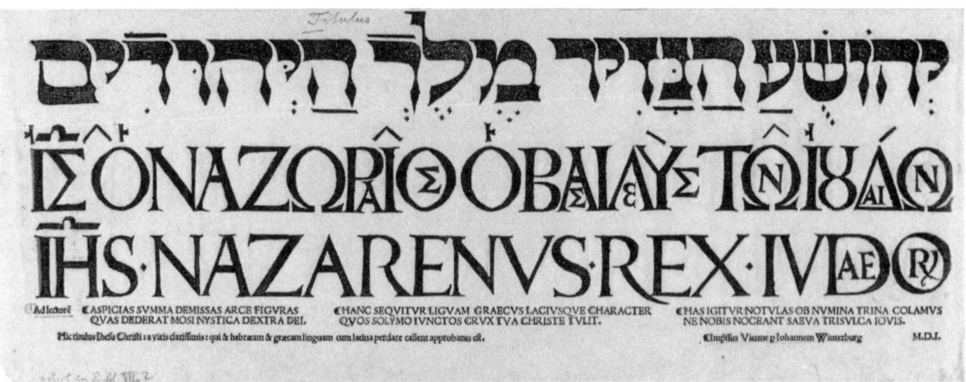

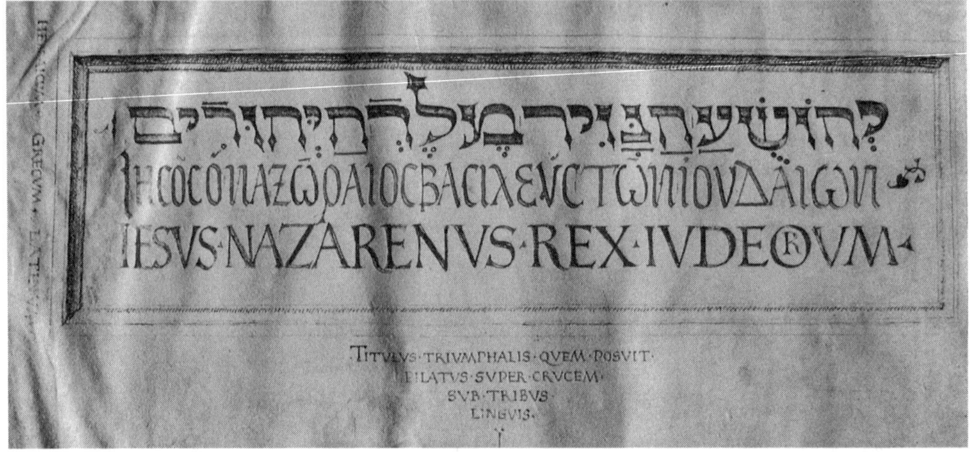

19.8 The philologists correct the relic. Titulus Crucis, woodcut and type, approx. 16 x 42 cm (Vienna, Johann Winterburger, 1501). Munich, Bayerische Staatsbibliothek, Rar. 287, fol. 333v. This woodcut, too, was preserved by Schedel in the back pages of his own copy of the *World Chronicle* he published in 1493. The report makes no effort to reproduce the look of the Titulus found in Rome. Instead it offers clean texts, prepared by scholars.

19.9 The Titulus relic recedes into the distance. Leonhard Wagner, Titulus Crucis, pen and ink on parchment (1507–1517), from *Proba centum scripturarum*. Augsburg, Archiv des Bistums Augsburg. A slightly different approach to the philological problems raised by the relic, presumably based on still another print. Wagner was a fanatical calligrapher, staving off the printing press by inventing and recording new letter forms.

the tablet as a substitution for a lost authentic relic. He felt himself free to choose which features to imitate and which to ignore.[42]

The scholars reconstructed the texts and soon left the physical Titulus relic behind. A third woodcut preserved by Hartmann Schedel, published by Johann Winterburger in Vienna and dated 1501, gives three complete lines of text, with the latter two in normal left-to-right format (figure 19.8).[43]

The inscription below avers that "this Titulus of Jesus Christ has been approved by renowned men who clearly understand not only Latin but also Greek and Hebrew."[44] One can compare the trilingual titulus copied out by the Augsburg scribe and calligrapher Leonhard Wagner, a Benedictine, who between 1507 and 1517 composed a model book of one hundred sample scripts, *Proba centum scripturarum*.[45] Wagner began his entire anthology of scripts with a rendition of the Titulus, perhaps based on still another print (figure 19.9). Neither the language nor the form of Wagner's transcription has much in common with the object at Santa Croce. The discovery kindled an interest in the historic Titulus that quickly diverged from the relic itself.

Although no one publicly discredited the Titulus at the time, its reception was, as we have seen, ambivalent and inconsistent. The Titulus hovered between the status of a relic and that of an inscription. It is not hard to imagine that some late fifteenth-century scholars recognized the Titulus relic as a fabrication of the Middle Ages and saw the few nearly meaningless strokes of the Hebrew inscription as a dodge by twelfth-century forgers with deficient knowledge of the language. In 1496 Pope Alexander VI declared the Titulus an authentic relic. But the Titulus was never really accepted. Despite the initial agitation, the object did not establish itself in the figural record. The implicit charge against the Titulus was that it was a mere performance, that is, an artifact fashioned by some person at some point in time, almost surely not the time of the Crucifixion. The Titulus receded into an ambiguous middle status, revered as a relic yet disrespected as evidence.

This was a crucial moment, for relics as much as for Eastern icons. Questions about the referential claims of the icons had for a long time been deferred. It is as if the Titulus, at its "trial," stood in for the painted icon. The Titulus "took the rap." The icon, meanwhile, persisted, even as sophisticated painters increasingly ignored its existence. Eventually the icon, too, would recede from the scene of art. Vasari was completely uninterested in Byzantine icons, authentic or not. Christian paintings from this point on will increasingly be content to generate fictions, out of the tradition and out of the imagination, and so liberate themselves from concerns about referentiality and authenticity; though not from concerns about doctrinal legitimacy or affective power, concerns that would reemerge in the second half of the sixteenth century. The trial of the Titulus represented the high water mark of the reception of the Eastern icons and the beginning of their long eclipse.

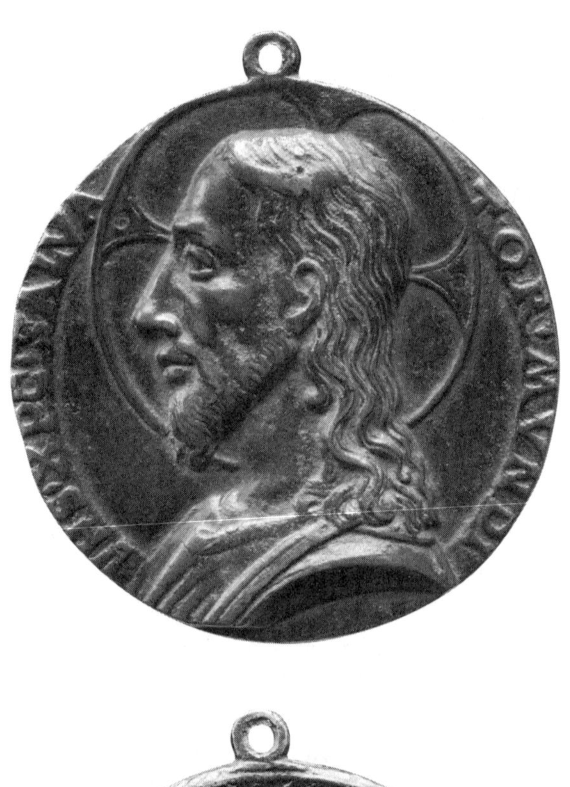

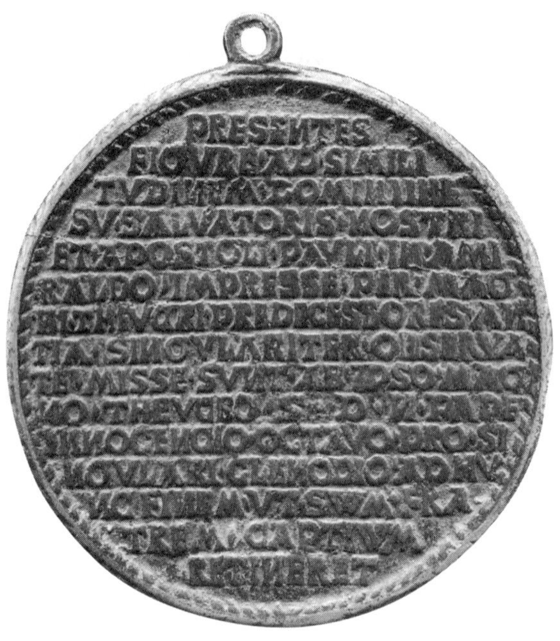

20.1 Evidence of Christ's appearance. Obverse: Profile of Christ; Reverse: Provenance legend of the likeness. Bronze medal, diameter 8.5 cm (Florence, ca. 1500). London, British Museum. The long inscription on the back of this medal claims that the likeness on the front reproduced the true features of Christ as transmitted by an emerald found in the Treasury at Constantinople and given as a gift to the Pope.

TWENTY

The Fabrication of Visual Evidence

A bronze medal circulating around 1500, probably Florentine, portrayed the features of Christ himself, in profile. The distinctive facial features made for a strong reality effect: long sloping forehead, full lips, short upper lip (figure 20.1).[1] One of the several versions or "editions" of the medal bears an inscription on the reverse averring that the profile is based on a portrait of Christ engraved on an emerald found in the Treasury at Constantinople and given by Sultan Bayezid II to Pope Innocent VIII as a gift in thanks for keeping his brother Djem, a pretender to the throne, prisoner in Rome.[2] This emerald, according to the inscription, was "impressed" with a portrait of Christ and one of St. Paul and had been "kept with special care by the predecessors of the Turks," an allusion to the Byzantine Empire as the repository of authentic early Christian relics. Such an emerald has never been found, nor is there any other record of its existence.[3] Bayezid II did send a legation to Rome in 1490 with rich gifts in order to encourage the Pope to keep his brother in captivity, and in 1492 he offered to Innocent the tip of Longinus's lance, a relic preserved to this day at St. Peter's. The arrival of the Holy Lance relic raised a good deal of publicity. The inscription on the medal in effect "appended" the otherwise unattested emerald to the gift of 1492.[4] The modern medallic portrait of Christ made the case for its own reliability as an historical document by adducing as its own model a prior, apparently unimpeachable image — an image in stone, possibly not made by human hands, and of Eastern provenance.

The capacity of an image to convey information was by no means well established. What sort of evidence was an image? The written document, charter, privilege, or letter, played a crucial role in medieval public life and thus was subject to critical testing. Everyone was alert to the possibility of forgery. Even inscriptions carved in stone were doubted, and indeed, were faked.[5] But in the Middle Ages no such tests were applied to pictures or statues, and no one articulated the concept of a forged image.[6]

The problem of the authority of the image was framed clearly in a letter of 1525 written by the professor of Greek at Padua Niccolò Leonico Tomeo, who had been offered an ancient bust of Socrates by a friend. Leonico asks: How do you know this is a bust of Socrates? On what authority? The statues of the Roman emperors and indeed of certain Greeks, he points out, can easily be identified on the basis of coins, which carry identifying labels in the form of inscriptions, "[b]ut since we have never seen a coin struck of Socrates which could convey his features (*qui illius referre faciem possit*), I do not see how we can confirm that it is him."[7]

And yet, for all the doubts, an image remains a compelling monument. To some scholars, a sequence of copied images seemed more trustworthy than sequences of copied texts. Medals and coins were routinely adduced as the very best sort of historical evidence. The scholar Fulvio Orsini in 1577 explained why coins and inscriptions were so valuable: "Because they were issued to the public and by the public magistrates of the people of Rome, nothing in them could be embellished or falsified, without it being immediately apparent."[8] Lorenzo Valla, in his treatise exposing the fraudulent *Donation of Constantine* (1440), had wondered why the evidence produced by the Papacy in favor of the *Donation* was merely textual and why there was no corresponding, clinching material evidence: "I should have expected you to show gold seals, marble inscriptions, a thousand authors." Or elsewhere: "This donation of Constantine ... can be proven by no document at all, whether on gold or on silver or on bronze or on marble or, finally, in books, but only, if we believe that man, on paper or parchment." Valla's protests are ironic. He does not really consider the absence of material evidence decisive proof of the *Donation*'s falsity. Nevertheless his remarks reveal his assumption that evidence transmitted by metal or stone is better than evidence transmitted by paper. At another juncture he points out that

> gold coins, of which I own many specimens, were in circulation ... bearing an inscription in Latin letters, not Greek, from the time of Constantine, already a Christian, and of almost all the Emperors after him: CONCORDIA ORBIS, with this legend normally placed below a representation of the cross.[9]

Valla trusted coins and inscriptions even though they were replicas and often hard to date. Three quarters of a century later Leonico Tomeo, with a will to believe, did in the end acquire the bust of Socrates.[10]

Leonico's doubts, the ones he might have expressed to Lorenzo Valla, were about transmission: Could one really count on the reliable delivery of information across an unfathomable chain of copies and substitutions? Or was the family of familiar Socrates portraits merely a retrospective invention without a real source? How fine grained was the informational package delivered by the bust? How much was lost en route? Could a bust portrait stand up to a "philology" of artifacts comparable to the battery of tools and tests developed by humanist scholars to draw distinctions among texts?

Doubts about the authenticity of pictorial information grew acute in the fifteenth century. Awareness of the hazards of transmission prompted concerns over the inscription of context-sensitive features such as costume (section 9) and altered approaches to the restoration of artifacts (section 8). Such concerns were only sharpened by the reception and staging of Byzantine imports (sections 10–11). The renewed influx of relics and icons from the East in the later fifteenth century put new pressure on the evidentiary status of images. The medallic portraits of Christ were modern products that met the demand for a philologically reputable pictorial document.

The medallic portraits of Christ were not allowed to circulate innocently, however, providing delectation, but rather were drafted into evidentiary service. Like the Titulus relic, and like the bronze statue of Christ installed in the church of the Carità in Venice in the early 1490s, the medals served for a time as templates for artists, the modern portraitists of Christ, *as if* the profile they bore carried authority. Scholars who wanted to press the question could see that features of the Venetian statue's posture, the specific type of garment, even details about the fall of the drapery, were corroborated by textual records from Eusebius's fourth-century *Ecclesiastical History* down to the thirteenth-century *Golden Legend*. These features were the artist's para-scholarly confirmation of what would have been a natural, uncomplicated assumption about a bronze, free-standing statue of Christ, namely that any such statue *must* render an ancient prototype. Just as humanist scholars were convinced that there must have been a statuary portrait of Christ in antiquity—he deserved such a tribute!—so too were they ready to believe in the possibility of a medallic portrait. Christ was an ancient personage of high stature. Many were his learned and powerful followers. Christ and his followers participated in an international classical culture. Some moderns still believed in the authenticity of the series of letters exchanged between St. Paul and Seneca.[11] If the modern medals were not copies of ancient medals, then surely they transmitted Christ's features as they had been preserved in another medium; if not an emerald, then perhaps a cameo or a carved relief, or even a painting made from the life. This was no harder to accept than the story of a portrait of the Virgin descended from an original painted by St. Luke.

In 1492 Cardinal Mendoza's team uncovered an eloquent artifact whose true age he could not possibly have known. The Titulus was reframed and fortified with philology. From here it was a short step to the fabrication of evidentiary images. In a recursive process, the knowledge of what needed to be done in order to convince readers of the antiquity of a modern text

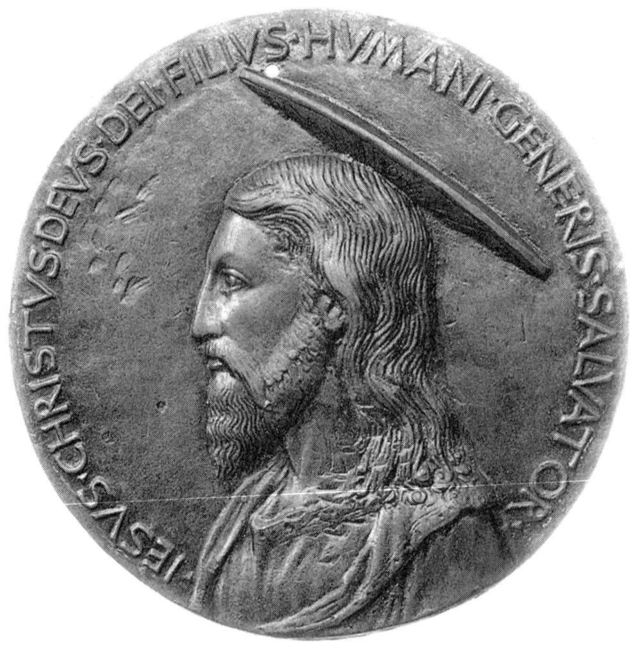

20.2 One of the earliest of all medal portraits. Matteo de' Pasti, Profile of Christ. Bronze medal, diameter 9.3 cm (1440–1450), Washington, National Gallery of Art. The medal portrait of Christ follows the portrait of John VIII (figure 10.8) by a decade or less. This image was accompanied by no metadata; it does not tell us how it knows what Christ looked like.

became more refined as criticism became more alert, and vice versa.[12] Now artists, with help from humanists fascinated by the capacity of artifacts to link directly back to deepest antiquity, began to claim that power for themselves.

The earliest experiments with this desirable but missing category of a profile portrait of Christ occurred more or less with the birth of the medal in Italy. Pisanello's medal of John VIII (see figure 10.8), a modern antiquity in its own right, was followed in the 1440s or ca. 1450 by a medal with a profile of Christ by the Veronese medallist Matteo de' Pasti (figure 20.2), which may derive from a drawing close to Pisanello in the Vallardi Codex in Paris.[13] Here Christ appears in profile with a flat, foreshortened nimbus. The reverse shows Christ as Man of Sorrows and bears Matteo's signature. Both the profile format and the replicable medium carried strong connotations of authenticity, proposing an authoritative set of features, not for a contemporary prince or merchant but for a holy man who had been dead for a millenium and a half.[14]

Later in the fifteenth century, as we have just seen, one of the redactions of a new family of medallic portraits of Christ was linked to a portrait engraved on a precious emerald—obviously an antiquity. A broadsheet published in 1500 by the Augsburg printer Erhard Ratdolt linked the same profile to a famous textual account of Christ's appearance, a letter sometimes attributed to Pilate, sometimes to a Roman soldier, sometimes to Publius Lentulus, a fictitious Roman official who had seen Christ.[15] Ratdolt printed the Latin text of the letter, here credited to Pilate, alongside a woodcut by Hans Burgkmair portraying a full-length image of Christ as Salvator Mundi with features drawn from the medal, and with a German translation below (see figure 21.5)[16]:

> This letter was written by Pilate from Jerusalem to the Emperor Tiberius and to the entire Senate in Rome. There has appeared in our times, and there still lives, a man of great power, called Jesus Christ. He raises the dead, and heals infirmities. The people call him prophet of truth; his disciples, son of God. He is a man of medium size and admirable in appearance; he has a venerable face, and his beholders can both fear and love him. His hair is of the color of the unripe hazelnut, straight down to the ears, but below the ears wavy and curled, with a bluish and bright reflection, flowing over his shoulders. It is parted in two on the top of the head, after the mode of the Nazarenes. His brow is even and most serene with a face without wrinkle or spot, embellished by a slightly reddish complexion. His nose and mouth are faultless. His eyes are changeable and bright. His beard is abundant, of the color of his hair, not long, but divided at the chin. His hands and arms are beautiful to behold. He is terrible in his reprimands, sweet and amiable in his admonitions, cheerful without loss of gravity. He was never known to laugh, but often to weep. His conversation is infrequent, and modest. He is the most beautiful among the children of men.[17]

The letter is a text and thus subject to philological interrogation, like the Titulus Crucis. It is better evidence than an image engraved on an emerald. The source text of the letter of Pilate with its compelling description of Christ is very probably a devotional text dating from the late thirteenth or early fourteenth centuries. It is related to mystical devotional works like the *Revelations of Saint Bridget* (ca. 1370). In the fourteenth-century manuscripts of the passage, the text is presented without any framing devices; at most it is said to be "from the Roman annals."[18] For many readers, the problem of the text's "origin" was not a problem at all: it was a received text; it appeared in various and mutually corroborating manuscript contexts; its reliability seemed to be confirmed, more or less, by many old paintings.

In the fifteenth century the letter began to acquire a more elaborate apparatus. One manuscript reported that the text was discovered in the year 1421 by a certain Jacopo Colonna, a scholar otherwise unknown. Another named an early fifteenth-century jurist, Antonio di Budrio, as the discoverer. Anxiousness about the authenticity of the text provoked responses both critical and creative. Skeptics were increasingly alert to the performative character of verbal texts—their connection to an author, a place and moment of origin, their status as utterance, *before* their inscription into an entangled skein of manuscripts. Those who believed in the text, and texts like it, were equally alert to this performative dimension and furnished their texts with fabricated provenances to make them more competitive. Evidentiary fictions were being reconstructed as fast as they were being dismantled.

The name "Lentulus" (supposedly an official in the province of Judaea who delivered a report on Christ to the Roman Senate; in fact, the name of a Roman patrician family) was attached to the text for the first time only in 1440, by Lorenzo Valla himself, in the course of his debunking of the *Donation of Constantine*. In the late fifteenth and early sixteenth centuries, Valla's treatise was widely distributed and debated. And yet in these very years, unperturbed by Valla's rejection, the Lentulus letter was growing in fame; the text was copied in a wide range of contexts, including in scholarly compendia. There is reason to believe that many learned readers saw the text as an historical document with at least partial claims to authenticity. The family of modern profile portraits of Christ, in a range of media, appeared to corroborate the letter.

Although the Lentulus letter and the various profile portraits were supporting each other, the two kinds of evidence, textual and pictorial, did not enjoy equal scholarly prestige. The authority of the letter was highly suspect; the medals by contrast were simply not submitted to criticism. This fault line between textual and iconic evidence ran straight through Valla's treatise. Valla's dismissal of the Lentulus letter came in the context of a discussion of a painting: "Similarly, although there are ten thousand instances of this kind at Rome, among the sacred objects are displayed the portraits of Peter and Paul on a panel which Sylvester put on show, when those apostles had appeared to Constantine in a dream, as a confirmation of the vision." Valla doubts the legend of the miraculous origins of the painting. But, significantly, Valla does not doubt the portraits themselves: "I do not say this because I deny those portraits of the apostles exist. I wish that Lentulus's letter about the image of Christ were as authentic.... But I say what I say because that panel was not shown by Sylvester to Constantine. In this matter I cannot restrain my astonishment."[19]

The "philological" criticism of material evidence—coins, sculpted portraits, carved inscriptions, panel paintings like the one discussed by

Valla—was less sophisticated than the criticism of linguistic texts and remained so for a long time afterward. Even learned scholars had trouble dating images on the basis of internal stylistic clues. Scholars were often paralyzed in front of images. And yet they could not fail to recognize the persuasive power, the eloquence, of images; and they saw how useful images could be in building a public argument.

A whole series of paradox-generating tests of substitutional logic unfolded in the very years of the fame of the medallic portrait of Christ and the Titulus relic. The poet and humanist Conrad Celtis (1459–1508), touring the Bavarian forests probably in 1492, discovered portrait statues of Druid priests, evidence of the primordial pagan and sylvan roots of the German religion.[20] These were simply jamb figures on the portal of an abbey church, apostles or prophets, but Celtis managed to convince himself, and others, that the figures portrayed the prehistoric founders of the cult site. In 1492 or 1493 the Dominican historian Giovanni Nanni, or Annius of Viterbo (ca. 1432–1502), announced, by way of a manuscript treatise, the discovery of a cache of "vases, bronzes, and marbles incised with old letters" near Viterbo.[21] Scholars frequently invented inscriptions and introduced them to the manuscript record, but not many took the trouble to have spurious inscriptions actually carved. Annius's faked Etruscan antiquities became the archeological basis for Annius's extravagant theses, which he published only a few years later—in the form of counterfeited texts attributed to the Chaldean sage Berosus—on the earliest history of Europe, involving the postdiluvian movements of Noah and his progeny and the Egyptian gods. In this way Annius provided the text that corroborated his artifacts, setting up a mutually reinforcing circuit between visual and verbal document.

Three of Annius's finds survive in the Museo Civico in Viterbo. The Tabula Cybelica Maeonica is a round tablet 40 centimeters in diameter inscribed with Greek characters.[22] The Decree of Desiderius, King of the Lombards, 42 centimeters in diameter, is inscribed with archaic-looking Beneventan characters, which Annius called *littera longobarda*.[23] The epigraphic text was of immediate interest to humanists and Angelo Poliziano mentioned it in a letter shortly after Annius's manuscript treatise appeared.

But the most intriguing of Annius's archeological fabrications was the so-called *marmo osiriano*—not a forgery, in fact, but a found object, or at least an assemblage of ready made materials (figure 20.3).[24] The object was not part of the phoney "excavation;" rather, it could be seen by anyone, Annius reported, in the Cathedral, which naturally was once a Temple of Hercules: "Our forefathers…in order to keep the eternal memory of the antiquity of this city before our eyes, placed before the pulpit a *columnula*,

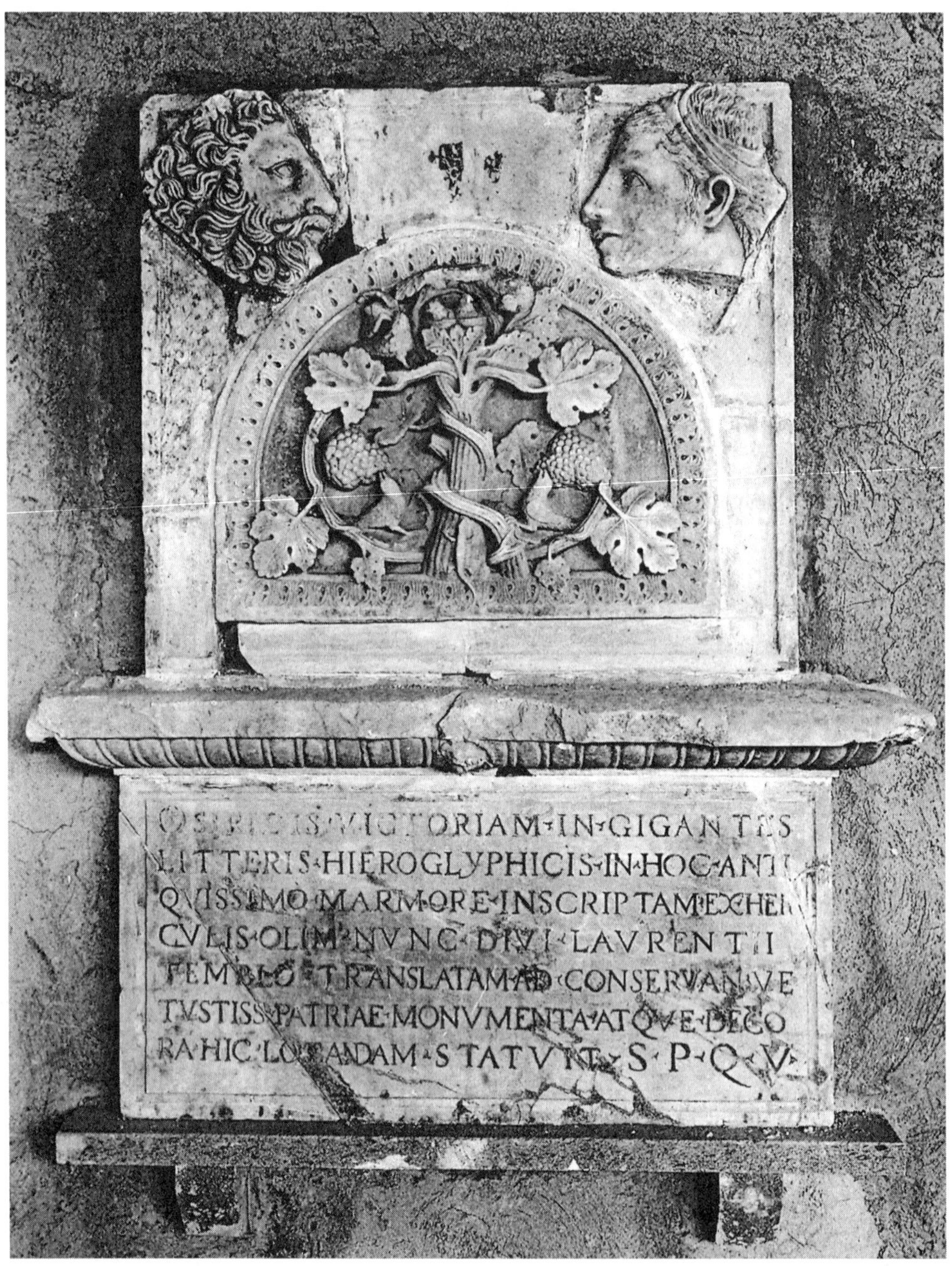

20.3 A pretended relic of postdiluvian Tuscan history. *Marmo osiriano* (marble stele of Osiris). Twelfth to fifteenth centuries? Viterbo, Museo Civico. This object, a medieval lunette framed by a pair of profile heads of uncertain date, was interpreted by the historian Annius of Viterbo as a monument erected by the Egyptian god Osiris in his own honor. Annius read these natural and human images not merely as enigmatic representations but as a hieroglyphic text with a clear message. The explanatory inscription dates to the late sixteenth century.

that is, an alabaster tablet, monument to the triumph of Osiris."[25] The *marmo osiriano* is a semicircular lunette, with vines, birds, and a lizard, mounted in a rectangular frame with two classical-looking profile heads in the corners. Annius interpreted the monument as a fragment of a triumphal column left in Viterbo by Osiris, the Egyptian god. He argued that the profile heads in the spandrel represented Osiris and his cousin Sais Xantho, a muse. This was proof that Osiris really had been to Italy. The birds and other objects in the vines in the lunette were sacred Egyptian letters symbolizing the historical encounter between the Italians, the Giants, and the Egyptians.[26]

Annius can be forgiven for mistaking the lunette with its twisted vines and animal symbols for an antiquity, for modern scholarship judged it a late Roman artifact until 1927, when Pietro Toesca dated it to the twelfth century. The frame with the profile heads, meanwhile, belongs to more modern times; presumably a century or two before Annius's time, just beyond the threshold of living memory.[27] The profiles were a magnet to his imagination. They seemed to await identification. It was by no means unreasonable for Annius to mistake the frame, even if no more than a hundred years old, for an antiquity. The whole ensemble was strange looking and hard to assimilate to any contemporary iconography or function. And as with the Celtis finds, there is no evidence of any doubt on the part of contemporaries. Even Giorgio Vasari two generations later adduced "the statues found at Viterbo" as evidence of the high quality of Etruscan sculpture.[28]

Annius was an inspired archeologist. Annius believed in inscriptions, artifacts, and names rather than authorities: things, rather than what people said about them.[29] He was all too aware of the ideological biases and the rhetorical gifts of the ancient textual sources.[30] Annius simply fabricated the missing archeological evidence that he needed in order to convince everyone else of what he already knew to be true.

"Retroactive" monuments like Annius's *marmo osiriano* and the Christ medals are best understood in the context of medieval document forgery.[31] The fabricator of charters and statutes was simply publishing a legal precedent known to be true, by oral tradition, for example, even though all original material traces and proofs had somehow gone astray. The forger produced documents substituting for absent documents that must have once existed. Sorting out the textual record of the earliest history of Europe was no simple task. The mosaic of sources had a number of author-sized gaps in it. Why not fill them, Annius reasoned, with characters like Berosus?

Annius put extreme pressure on the *marmo osiriano*, demanding it do intense referential work. He wanted it to be the perfect artifact, bedrock testimony of the most ancient events. In the process he had to explain how an artifact could endure so long, and so was prompted to articulate a theory of substitution. Annius admitted the possibility that the *marmo osiriano* was only a replacement of a lost original: "Whether this is truly the tablet," he wrote in his *Commentaries*, "or a substitute for it—the original having collapsed through age—we cannot yet be certain. Either way, we consider the tablet to have survived." (*An vero haec illa sit, an ei vetustate labenti, ad eius exemplar suffecta, nondum compertum habemus. Existimamus tamen eandem permanere.*[32]) Walter Stephens calls this a "doctrine of congruence": any inscription no matter when fabricated could be defended as a substituted copy of a lost original. It is the spelling out of a principle that until now had been left unstated.

TWENTY-ONE

Retroactivity

Annius of Viterbo might have had more success if he had published images of his monuments. Although he did publish his spurious source Berosus, he nonetheless mistrusted print, believing that movable type only multiplied the errors of the scribes, whom he already mistrusted. Print only made things worse, in his view.[1] Annius failed to see that the modern project of the evidentiary image was sustained by the replication technologies: casting, molding, impressing, stamping; coin, seal, medal, typographic page, woodcut or engraved image. These technologies offered—really, or by suggestion—reliable indexical links to their referents, so promising to eliminate the element of drift in the copy chain. They extended the range of the cult images.[2] The results formed a class of images to which, in the realm of prints, Peter Parshall has given the name *imago contrafacta*, the image not merely resembling its model but "made from" it, directly impressed.[3] Printed artifacts organized in chains made literal, tangible, the mysterious operations of substitutional transmission. This was the old substitutional mechanism, but now operated deliberately, driven, mimicking the rhythms established by typology and other confusions of "secular" temporality, but no longer observant of typology.

Ancient coins were copies without originals, and to publish images of them was simply to extend their reach across space and time. Early sixteenth-century scholars prepared editions of the corpus of coins, vivid source material that supplemented the written lives of the Caesars. In 1517 the Roman printer Jacopo Mazzocchi published an album of woodcut portraits of the kings and emperors, the *Illustrium imagines*, prepared by Andrea Fulvio, a humanist and antiquarian in the circle of Raphael.[4] In Augsburg, meanwhile, the historian and collector Conrad Peutinger enlisted Hans Burgkmair to prepare woodcuts of the emperors based on his own extensive collection of coins.[5] The woodcuts were meant to illustrate a history, never completed. The images on ancient coins, in their time, were the indexes of state authority that guaranteed the exchange value of the bits of metal that bore them. In 1500 the value of a Roman coin had a completely different basis. The disk of silver was valued as a relic, to be sure, by the likes of Peutinger. But now the image possessed a documentary value. Publications of the coins like Fulvio's and Peutinger's separated the information, the profile, from its vehicle, in effect discarding the metal disk. When a model was lacking, the reproduction was simply produced. The reproduction invented its own model. Circular patterns of mutual reinforcement, cycles of proof and creativity, masked the incompleteness of the material record. Not all of Fulvio's illustrations were based on real coins: some were simply invented. One of the coins that Burgkmair copied, the portrait of Julius Caesar, was actually a modern artifact.[6]

One prominent later fifteenth-century group of medallic portraits of Christ was also modeled on a proximate and modern source, the bronze statue of Christ with the doubting Thomas installed by Andrea Verrocchio in the niche of the Mercanzia (formerly of the Parte Guelfa) at Orsanmichele in 1483.[7] Like the statue that stood in the Carità in Venice, quoted by Carpaccio in his *Saint Augustine in his Study*, this free-standing statue of Christ in "eternal bronze" appears to have exerted an irresistible attraction for artists around 1500. The fact that it was a free-standing statue in bronze appears to have granted it, automatically, authoritative status as a likeness of Christ. Moreover, the head of Christ in particular seems to have attracted admiration; the diarist Luca Landucci said, on the day of the statue's unveiling, that it was "the most beautiful thing imaginable and the finest head of the Saviour that has as yet been made."[8] Artists such as Agnolo di Polo and Pietro Torrigiani literalized the referential power of the statue by restating Verrocchio's Christ in the overtly antique format of the portrait bust. And Niccolò Fiorentino, or whoever designed the more particularized type of Christ medal, adapted it to the antique format of the bronze medallion (see figure 20.1). The key move was the translation of the three-dimensional Verrocchio to the two-dimensional format of the medal, where the profile could convert physiognomy into evidence.

The point of such overtly *all'antica* iterations was not to canonize Verrocchio's Christ but to "retroactivate" its relation to an antique prototype. The medals in effect reversed their chronological relation to Verrocchio's statue, which was well known to everyone as a public work by a famous modern artist. The medals offered themselves as documents of the source for the modern statue, evidence of Verrocchio's dependence on an ancient prototype, forcing the statue, too, into a substitutional chain extending back to an originary portrait of Christ.

The inscription on one version of the medal connecting the portrait to an emerald from Constantinople reveals the medal maker's worry that beholders would need more evidence, a stronger connection to Christ himself. The emerald was introduced arbitrarily, ex post facto, as confirmation of the authority of the medal. From that point on, the medal could be understood as a publication of the emerald. But the series of medals in fact predates the story about the emerald. Not only that, but the series of medals was understood to be carrying reliable information even before the explicit tale about the provenance was hauled in. The proof is that every medal in the sequence faithfully preserved the meaningless detail of a fold in the collar of Christ's tunic, an "effect of the real" implying strict compliance with an authoritative model. In reality, the fold in the collar was introduced in the medals attributed to Matteo de' Pasti around 1450, well before the emerald had purportedly arrived in Rome. Here we might remember that the image of a Madonna in a baldachin supported by angels predated the legend of a house flying across the sea to Loreto.

As in the case of the misdatings discussed in section 13, learned observers—perhaps especially learned observers—were taken in. Teseo Ambrogio, the philologist of oriental languages active in Rome in the 1520s and 1530s, believed that the bronze Christ medals carried an antique portrait.[9] This is not the only case in which a humanist scholar took an obviously modern medal to be a carrier of ancient information. A parallel case is the discovery by Conrad Celtis of "antique" medals while traveling in Austria. Petrus Apianus and Bartholomeus Amantius in their anthology of antiquities, *Inscriptiones sacrosanctae vetustatis* (1534), published woodcuts of the artifacts and reported in captions when and where Celtis had found them. A circular image represents a nude man seated in a rocky landscape and accompanied by a winged child and a skull. The man holds his head in his hands as if anguished by contemplation of the skull. The caption reads: "Found by Conrad Celtis not long ago on a lead plate [or coin] in Styria, on the hill with the church near St. Andreas, in the year 1500."[10] The woodcut in fact reproduces an allegory of mortality found on the reverse of a self-portrait medal by the Venetian medallist Giovanni Boldù (d. before 1477).[11] Whatever traces of modern fabrication the Italian medals bore, Celtis believed that the medal reliably transmitted the content of an antique gem or relief. He felt licensed, or even compelled, to assign the work its "correct" iconographic label.

In northern Europe, a proliferation of mechanically made copies of the profile portrait of Christ corroborated the Florentine medals. A papier-mâché relief found in a German convent was apparently made by direct impression from the medal.[12] A Netherlandish engraving of around 1500 reproduced the entire medal, including the inscription.[13] Hans Burgkmair, finally, as noted in the previous section, introduced a new layer of proof by connecting the medal portrait to the description of Christ in the spurious letter by Pontius Pilate describing Christ's appearance (see figure 21.5). The

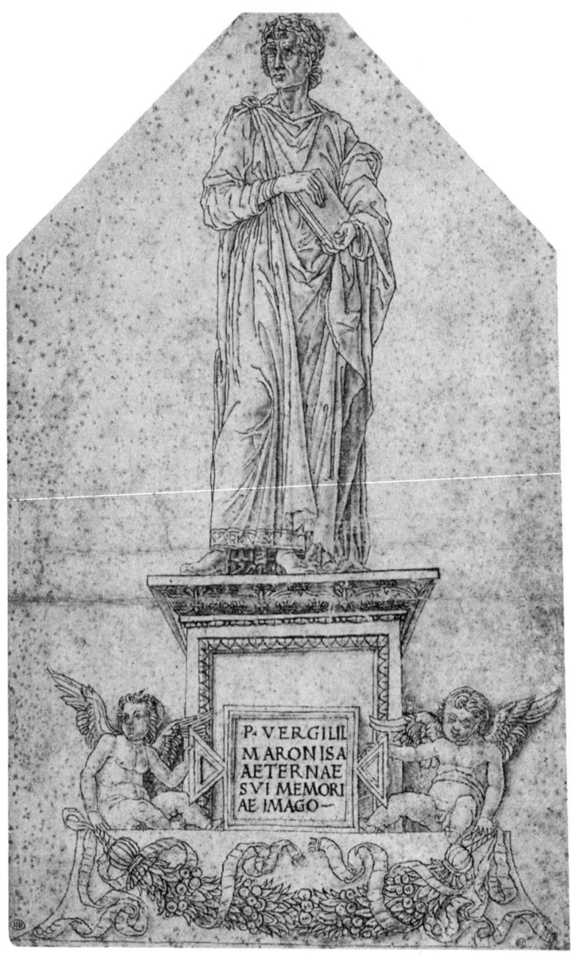

21.1 A modern memorial to the ancient poet, planned but never carried out. After Andrea Mantegna, Monument to Virgil, pen on paper, 33.9 x 21.4 cm (ca. 1500). Paris, Musée du Louvre. The likeness was supposedly guaranteed by an authentic portrait of Virgil identified by the humanist Battista Fiera.

confrontation of text and image revealed the special rhetorical force of the image. The pictorial portrait contained much more information than the textual portrait. Every detail, every feature of the physiognomy, took on an undeserved authority. The replicable media of print and bronze encouraged copyists to preserve those details. The characteristic or singular physiognomy functioned as proof of the good faith of the copyist. The physiognomy was proof of nothing at all, but it looked like proof. Now the image came with its own authenticating papers: the very peculiarities of its form.

The Christ medals are one instance of a larger trend. Plans were drawn up for a public portrait of Virgil, dead for nearly a millennium and

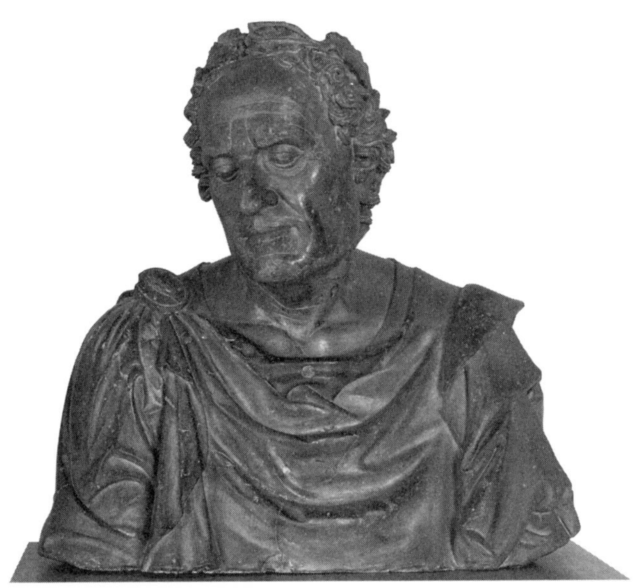

21.2 The countenance of the poet, with furrowed brow and downcast eyes. Portrait of Virgil, terracotta, height 74 cm (ca. 1514). Mantua, Museo della Città. This bust was owned by Battista Fiera. It must replicate the unknown portrait that in his view transmitted Virgil's likeness.

a half, in the ancient poet's native Mantua. A letter of March 17, 1499 to the marchioness Isabella d'Este from her agent Jacopo d'Atri in Naples reported the views of the humanist Giovanni Pontano, who proposed a free-standing figure in the antique style on a pedestal.[14] Though Pontano, d'Atri says, considered bronze the nobler material, marble was preferable since bronze is always at risk of being melted down to make bells or armaments. The figure, Pontano added, should be dressed in the ancient style, down to the sandals, as the painter Andrea Mantegna would know how to do, and should carry neither book nor any other attribute. When Pontano expressed concern about the statue's resemblance to Virgil, d'Atri assured him that an authentic likeness of the poet had been found by the Mantuan humanist Battista Fiera.[15] The monument was never completed and the project is recorded only in a drawing after Mantegna now in Paris (figure 21.1).[16] As no authentic Virgil portrait from antiquity has ever been found, one might well ask: What image did Fiera possess? In 1514 Fiera mounted a series of three terracotta busts on the ancient archway that adjoined his house on Via Stabili (and now visible in the Palazzo Ducale). They portrayed the marquis Francesco Gonzaga, the friar and poet Battista Spagnoli, and Virgil. The Virgil portrait is highly individuated, with deeply grooved cheeks and a characteristic curved nose (figure 21.2).[17]

Strangely, the high cheek bones, curly hair, and rugged features bear a strong resemblance to the figure in the Mantegna-school drawing of the Virgil monument, as if the same person had been portrayed, now some years later. The closed eyes suggest the bust's derivation from a body cast—not a death mask but an impress taken from a living person, as was often done. In other words, everything indicates that this bust, like those of Gonzaga and Spagnoli, is a portrait of a contemporary. In the place of a fiction, the portrait, and perhaps the portrait intended for the monument planned in 1499, offered a highly particularized likeness underwritten by replication technology. Like the Christ medals, it offered high informational density together with the signs of indexicality as a guarantee of authenticity.

Modern portraits of Christ or Virgil complied with one of the formulas devised by Umberto Eco in his "typology of falsifications," a systematic breakdown of the phenomenon of forgery: "Oa = Ob, or is interchangeable with it, where Oa doesn't exist."[18] That is, the fifteenth-century bronze medallic portrait of Christ (Ob) is an antiquity (Oa), or can for all meaningful purposes stand in for an antiquity, even though that antique portrait of Christ may never have existed.

A similar tactic was used some decades later in Padua, when in 1547 a monument to the Roman historian and native Paduan Livy was erected in the Palazzo della Ragione, complete with a bust portrait (figure 21.3).[19] The bust, now attributed to Agostino Zoppo, a pupil of the medallist Giovanni Cavino, had been provided by Alessandro Bassano, an antiquarian who occupied what was reputed to be Livy's house in the city. The bust on the monument likely derives from a bronze bust now in Warsaw, and probably served as the model for another head in the Museo Civico in Padua and one now in the Kunsthistorisches Museum in Vienna (figure 21.4),[20] all of them associated with Zoppo. Agostino Zoppo was a pupil of Andrea Riccio and a friend of the medallist Giovanni Cavino, who was himself a friend of Bassano and with Bassano executor of Riccio's will. Bassano belonged to a dense network of antiquarian sculptors and was thus in a position to understand how artifacts could serve to bolster an antiquarian argument. Rather than undermine credibility, the fact of a cluster of busts all bearing a close resemblance to one another actually reinforced the notion, first, that replication was reliable, and, second, that a stable prototype was controlling the restricted range of difference. This effect would have been only further reinforced by the propagation of the portrait across media, for example in a medal that was produced around the same time, offering a profile version of the same head seen on the bust, and in a fresco showing a version of the same portrait by Domenico Campagnola in the Bassano palace, the so-called Casa degli Specchi. A corroborating network of images stabilized an invented portrait.

The portrait of Livy existed only in its publications; the source image was missing but everywhere referred to. As in the case of the Virgil portrait in Mantua, the source was in fact quite contemporary. All of the Livy busts that appeared at this time, and especially the bronze bust, bear the characteristic marks— sunken cheeks, pressed mouth, thin lips—of the death mask. The Paduan sculptors frequently used death masks as the basis for portraits.[21] The device was rhetorically effective: Montaigne, after having seen the portrait of Livy in Padua, which he called an "ancien ouvrage," wrote that one could see that Livy was "un home studieus et malancholicq."[22] That a portrait based on a death mask could have made a successful claim to be an antiquity is a paradox for modern scholars,[23] and yet the bust of Livy conforms to the pattern established by the other cases discussed so far. The authenticity of the portrait did not consist in the claim that any of these artifacts was physically an antiquity; all of these busts were self-professed copies. Instead, the demand for authenticity was met by a combination of a high degree of particularity and an insistence on reliable replication, a combination that both delivered informative content and advertised the means by which that content could be transmitted across a series of tokens. This was a combination typical especially of the Paduan tradition of bronze sculpture, and an essential feature of its antiquarian culture.[24] As Dagobert Frey observed, the "antique" had not yet been classicized, defined by a set of stylistic features; instead, especially in Padua, it was thought to consist in works of great naturalism executed in bronze and marble.[25] On these criteria, the Livy bust was an excellent sample of ancient portraiture.

In his woodcut of 1500, discussed already in section 20 and mentioned again a few pages ago, Hans Burgkmair tried to synthesize the data delivered by the medallic portrait with the evidence of Pilate's letter (figure 21.5). The medal filled in the verbal text's syntactic gaps. The letter described not only Christ's face but also his stature and bearing. Burgkmair created a full-length portrait of Christ by rotating through 90 degrees the iconographic type known as the Salvator Mundi. The Salvator Mundi, a figure of Christ holding an orb and making a gesture of blessing, was an invention of northern European artists and was usually depicted half-length.[26] Burgkmair could have seen one of the few full-length or standing versions of the type on the first page of the *Plenarium nach Ordnung der christlichen Kirchen* published in Augsburg by Günther Zainer in 1473 (figure 21.6).[27] Burgkmair rotated the Zainer image and projected onto it the data from the medal: the high hairline, fleshy lips, forked beard, and

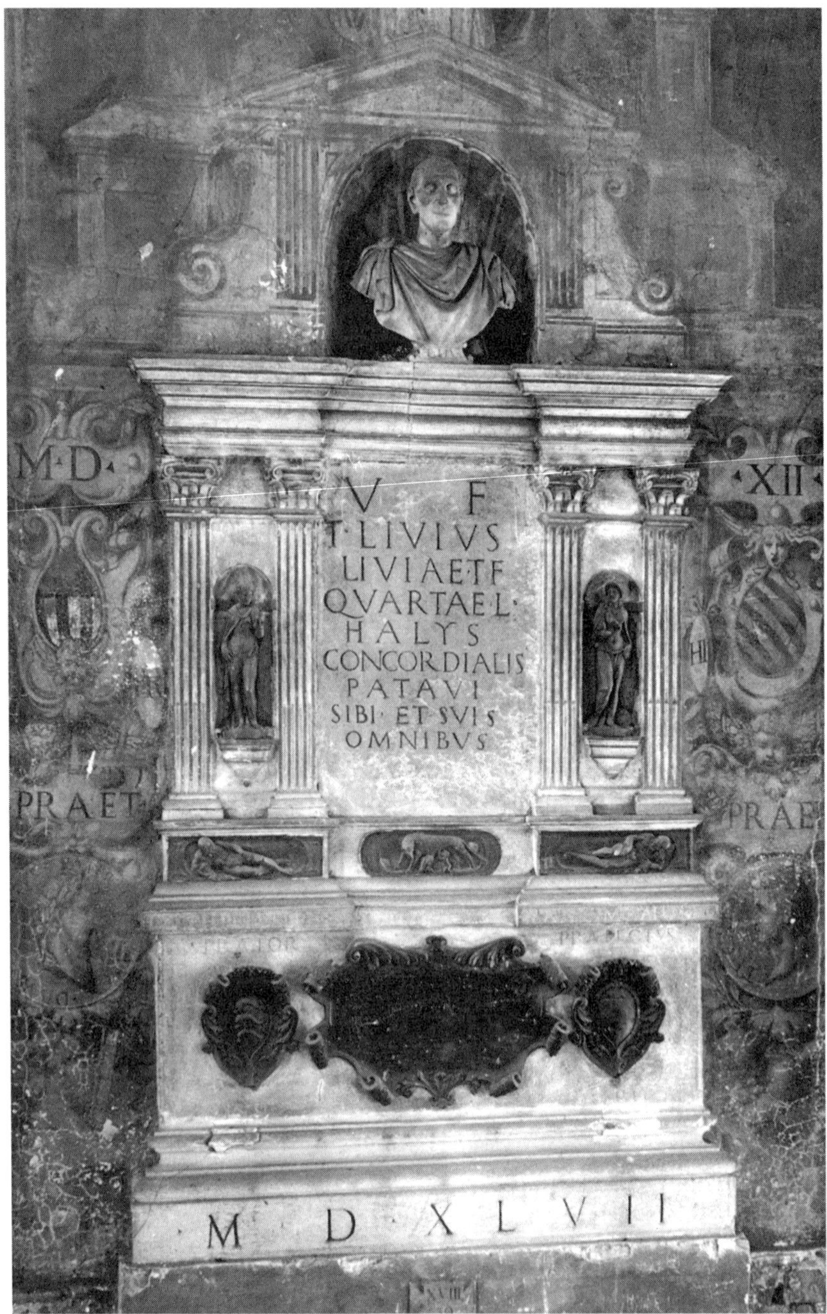

21.3 Livy remembered by the citizens of Padua. Monument to Livy, marble (1547). Padua, Palazzo della Ragione. The likeness of the ancient historian, here presented to the citizens of Padua, was probably based on a cast of an actual man's face. The French sixteenth-century essayist Michel de Montaigne found this portrait so credible that he used it as the basis for a physiognomic analysis of Livy's character.

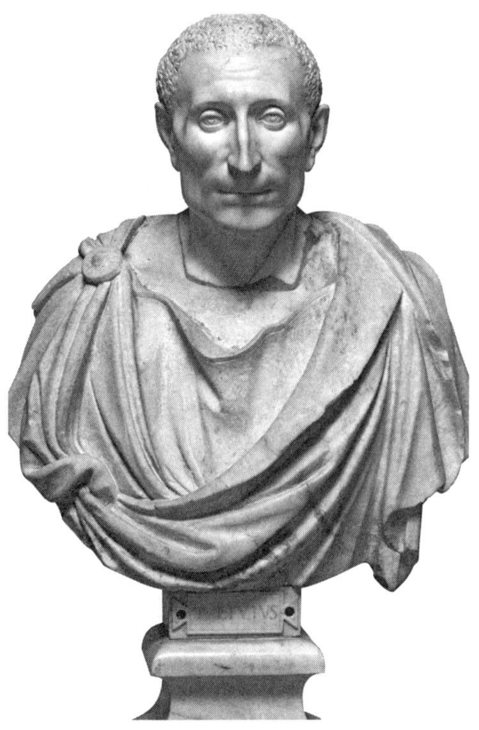

21.4 A network of replicas creates credibility. Attributed to Agostino Zoppo, Portrait of Livy, marble, height 67 cm (ca. 1550). Vienna, Kunsthistorisches Museum. This bust and several others in bronze or marble create a "portrait-class" that serves to corroborate the physiognomy enshrined in the monument. In fact we have no idea what Livy looked like.

the looped fold at the hem of the robe. Burgkmair and Ratdolt's broadsheet does not mention the medal, however.

A later broadsheet, undated but perhaps ca. 1510, connects a slightly different physiognomy to the letter from Pilate (figure 21.7).[28] The letter is again printed in both Latin and German. Here the profile is placed in a circular frame but against a shallow recessed panel with black ornamental vines and the initials "H. B." Again, however, the broadsheet makes no mention of a medal. In fact, Burgkmair "corrects" the medal derived from Verrocchio, perhaps by reference to the Matteo de' Pasti medal—for this profile, with its straight nose, thin lips, and protruding, angular beard, is closer to the medal type established by Matteo in the 1440s (see figure 20.2)—and certainly by reference to the letter. Burgkmair seems to attend closely to every point of positive physical description offered in the letter that can be transmitted in a black and white medium. The nose, "faultless" in the letter, is made straighter and higher; the hairline is moved higher, giving space for his "even and most serene" brow; the beard is shown, as the letter

Hanc Epistolam scripsit pilatus a hieru/
salem in Romam Tyberio et toti senatui.

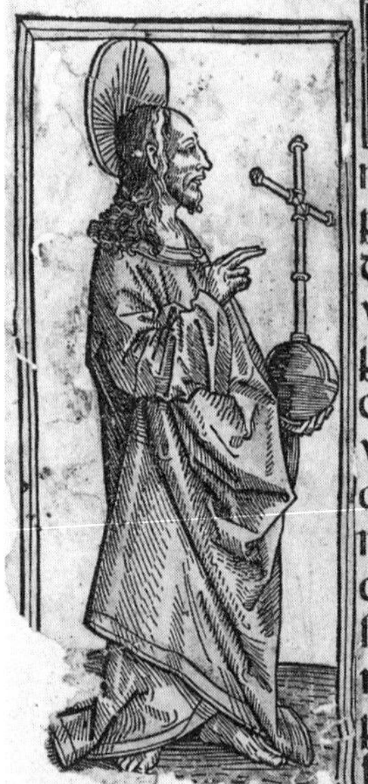

Aparuit temporibus nostris et ad/
huc est Homo magne virtutis: cui
nomen est christus Jesus: suscitans
mortuos: z sanas languores. Qui dicif pro/
pheta veritatis: que discipuli eius vocat filiu
dei: Homo quide statura pcer⁹ z spectabilis
vultum habes venerabilem: quem intuentes
possut diligere z formidare: capillos habes
coloris nucis auelane pmature z planos fere
vsqz ad aures: ab auribus vero crispos ali/
quantum z ceruliores et fulgentiores: ab hu/
meris ventilates: discrimen habes in medio
capitis iuxta more nazarenoru. Facie habes
sine ruga aliqua et macula: qua rubor mode/
ratus venustat: nasi et oris nulla prsus est re/
prehensio: oculis varijs glaucis z claris exi/
stentibus: barbam habens copiosam et non
longa: scilicet capillis cocolo   et impubere
sed in medio bifurcata: manus habens z brachia vi.d delectabilia:
in increpatione terribilis: in amonitione placidus et amabilis: hy/
laris seruata grauitate: qui nunq visus est ridere: flere autez. Sic
in colloquio rarus z modestus: speciosus inter filios hominu:.

Mccccc.E.R.Augusten.

Dysen brieff vnd Epistel schrayb Pilatus von Hierusalem gen Rom dem kayser Tiberio vnd
gemeyncklichen den eltisten senatoribus vnd der gantzen maysterschaft des Römischen volcks.

Zu vnsern zeyten erschinen vnnd noch ist ein mensch grosser tugent der genennet ist christus Jesus:
erkückend die todten vnnd hailmachend die kranckheyt: der da gehayssen wirt eyn prophet der
warheyt: welhe seine iungern nennen gotes sun. Nembtwar ein mensch langer masse vnd gar lieplichen
anzusehen: habend eyn erwirdigs angesicht: welhes die die es ansehen liebhaben mügen vnd fürchten
har habend varb eyner überzeytigen haselnusz: vnnd schlecht nahend bys auff die oren: aber von der
en kraus eyns teyls: vnd gelbleter vnd krechter bys auff die achseln sich wendet: habend eyn scheytel
im mittel des haubts nach gewonheyt der nazareischen: habend eyn angesicht on eynicherlay runtzel
vnd mackel welhes eyn mässige röte gezieret: der nasen vnnd mundes ist gäntzlich keyn vngestalt: mit
gezierten augen praunen vnd klaren wesend: habend eyne dicken part vnd nit lang den haubtes haren
geleich genar iüngklichen gestalt vnd zwyszlaten. hend vnd arm habend lieplich anzusehen: in der straff
erschrockenliche: in der vermant s geuallig vnd lieplich: frölich: doch mit behaltung der tapfferheyt:
der ny gesehen ist lachen: besund eynen: im gespräch seltzam vnd mässiger: vnd der allerwolgestal/
ist vnder den sünen der menschen.

21.5 **The medallic portrait of Christ backed up by an ancient text.** Erhard Ratdolt and Hans Burgk-mair, broadsheet with portrait of Christ, 15.8 x 6.8 cm (image) (1500). Munich, Staatliche Graphische Sammlung. This publication delivers the true likeness of Christ, as preserved by the Florentine med-als, accompanied by a description of the Savior's appearance widely believed to have been written by an eyewitness.

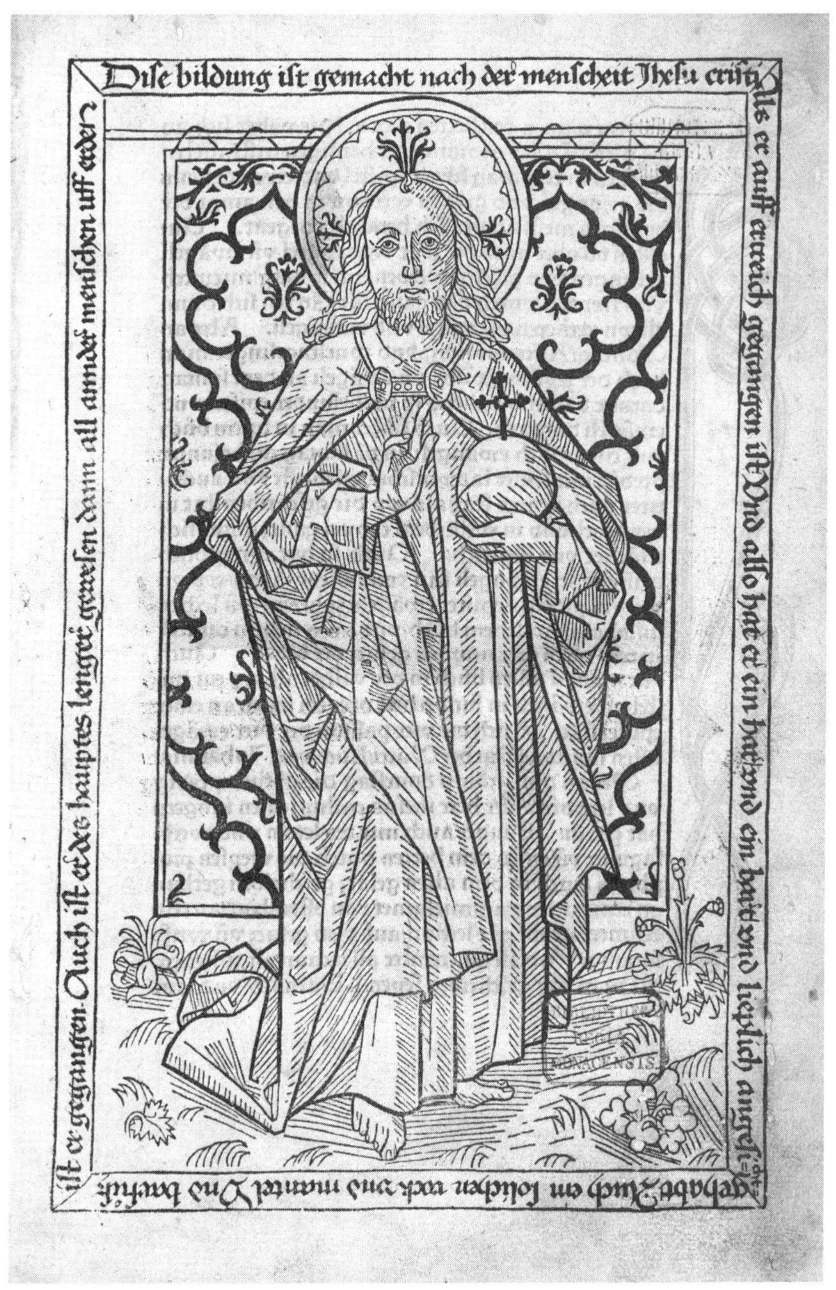

21.6 Christ as transmitted by custom. Salvator Mundi, woodcut, *Plenarium nach Ordnung der christli-chen Kirchen* (Augsburg: Günther Zainer, 1473), p. 1. Munich, Bayerische Staatsbibliothek. Burgkmair took this figure type, Christ presented frontally as the Savior of the World, as the basis for his own woodcut (figure 21.5). He rotated the figure ninety degrees so that he could apply the authentic profile and thus endow the image with evidentiary status.

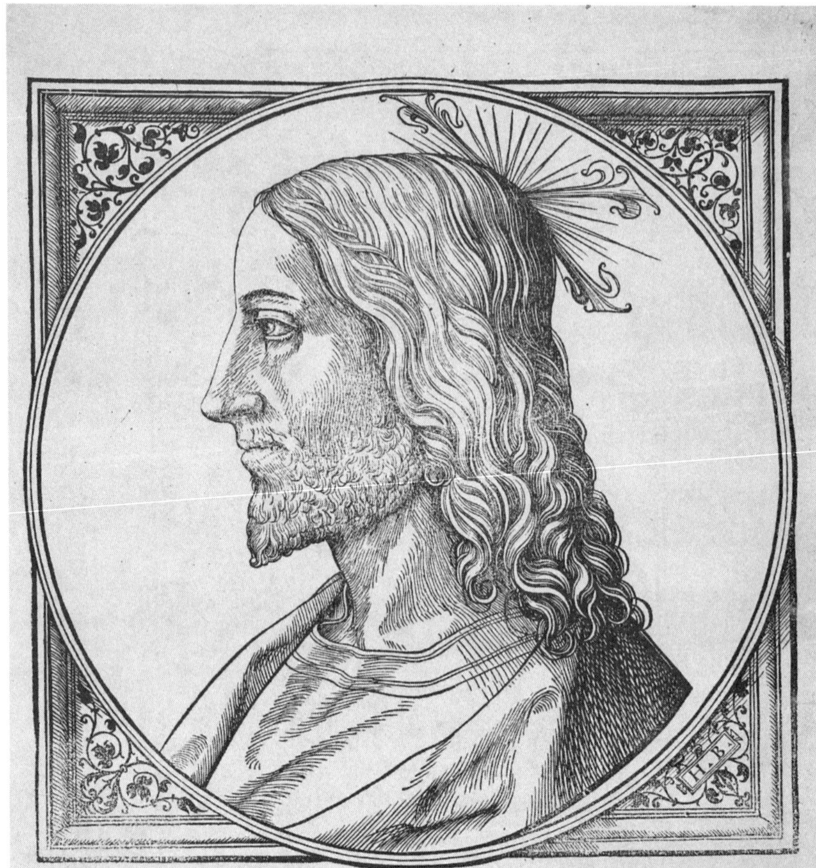

¶ Hanc Epistolam scripsit pilatus a jherusalem in Romam Tyberio et toti senatui

Apparuit temporibus nostris et adhuc est Homo magne virtutis:cui nomen est cristus jesus:suscitans mortuos:et sanans languores. Q̃ ui di-
tur propheta veritatis:quem discipuli eius vocant filium dei:Homo quidē statura procerus et spectabilis:vultum habens venerabilem. ere
intuentes possunt diligere et formidare:capillos habens coloris nucis auelane premature planos vero vsq̃ ad aures: ab auribus vero crispo
aliquantū et ceruliores et fulgentiores ab humeris ventilantes:discrimen habens in medio capitis iuxta morem nazarenorum: faciem hebē
sine ruga aliqua et macula:quam rubor moderate venustat:nasi et oris nulla prorsus est reprehensio:oculis varijs glaucis et claris existit ... ue Barba ā ha
bens copiosam et non longam:salicet capillis concolore et impuberem sed in medio bifurcatā manus habens et brachia visu delectebilia:in increp ati
ne terribilis.in ammonitione placidus et amabilis:hylaris seruata grauite-qui nunquam visus est ridere:flere autem:Sicin celle quie rare et medē fiu
speciosus inter filios hominum:

¶ Disen brieff vnd Epestel schraib pilatus võ Jherusolem gen Rem dē kaser tiberio vnd
gemaincklichen den eltisten senatolibus vnd der gantzē maisterschafft des rumischen volcks
Zū vnsern zeiten erschinen vn noch ist ain mensch grosser tugent der genenet ist Christus Jesus:erkuckt die toten vn hailmachend die kranck el hait: der
gehaissen wirt ain prophet der warhait:weliche seine jungern sein essen gottes sun:Nempt war ain mensch langer masse vn d gar lieplich an anzūsehen
haben ain eerwirdiges angesicht:welches die:die es ansehen lieb habē miigen vnd furd ten:hat habent varb ainer überzeitigen haselnuf: vn und schlee
nahend biß auff die oren:aber von den oren kruaß ains tails:vnd gelbleter vn liechter biß auff die achseln sich wendent:ebund ein schoeitel in mittel d
haubts nach gewonhait der nazareischen:habent ain angesicht en ainich erlay runtzel vn mackel welchs ain mässige röte gezieret:der nasen vn mu
des ist gentzlich kain vngestalt:mit gezierten augen praunen vn klaren varben hat er d ainen dicken part vnd nit lang den haubtes haren glich gar
jungklichē gestalt vn zwyslater:hend vnd arm habend lieplich an zūsehen:in der straff erschrecklich:in der vern ain gar gedullig vn lieplich:
doch mit behaltung der tapfferhait:der nye gesehen ist lachen:besunder wainen:im gespräch seltzam vnd mässiger:vnd der aller welgestaltigst vn an
den sünen der menschen

¶ Diese ... vnden getruckte linie:so ... alarogen essen ist die leng rpi jhesu

21.7 **The medal portrait adjusted on the basis of the text.** Hans Burgkmair, broadsheet with profile portrait of Christ, woodcut and type, 22.6 x 23 cm (image) (ca. 1510). Rostock, University Library. The letter about Christ's appearance, sometimes attributed to Pontius Pilate himself, is printed in both Latin and German. The portrait above adjusts the visual evidence of the medals in accordance with details gleaned from the letter.

specifies, "not long," a cropped version of the luxurious beard that drops from Christ's chin in the medal; the hair, which is shown in the medal curling back directly from the part, is here shown closer to the letter's description of it as "straight down to the ears, but below the ears wavy and curled." The broadsheet's concern for authenticity is intense: at the lower edge a line of text states that "the line printed here below [presumably a simple straight line, now missing] measured ten times is the length of Jesus Christ."[29]

In a third broadsheet, also datable to about 1510, Burgkmair took a straightforward documentary approach to the later, "Verrocchio" medal type (figure 21.8).[30] In this woodcut Burgkmair relies again on that highly characteristic portrait of Christ, with its sloping forehead, full lips, modeled cheek bones, and bushy eyebrows. Whereas Burgkmair's previous broadsheet had placed Christ's bust in a roundel far larger than any existing medal, the roundel on this sheet measures 11 centimeters in diameter: the medal itself supplemented by a framing ring with an inscription (the inscription on the reverse of a medal of this type). Without the framing ring, the inner roundel, corresponding to the front face of the medal, measures 9 centimeters, exactly the same as the medal from which it was "drawn." This portrait is thus a facsimile, not an adaptation or a translation. It is as if the medal itself had pushed up through the paper from behind, leaving its imprint. Again Burgkmair printed the text of the letter, now attributed to Lentulus, not Pilate, below the image, as a corroboration of the data on the medal, and now only in Latin—like the image, untranslated—conveying the new philological and archeological ambitions of the print. No doubt the broadsheet was prepared with the assistance of the humanist Conrad Peutinger, who owned a copy of the *editio princeps* of Lorenzo Valla's treatise on the *Donation of Constantine* (Strasbourg, Johann Grüninger, 1506).[31] We recall that Valla was the first to ascribe the letter to "Lentulus." And Peutinger very likely owned the medal portrait of Christ, too: he had one of the most extensive collections of coins and medals in all of Europe.[32]

This print distances itself from the earlier German prints that reproduced the profile of the medal but for merely devotional purposes, for example the woodcut published in 1507 by the Pforzheim printer Thomas Anselm, accompanied only by a prayer to the countenance of Christ.[33] The outer ring of the roundel transmits the text found on the reverse of some versions of this medal type, preserving even the triangular interpoints and the odd presentation of the words INHUNC in unseparated form.[34] Other versions of this type carried on their reverses the inscription telling about the Byzantine emerald.[35]

Above the image, Burgkmair offered not that tale but a completely new account of the image's provenance, now with a German slant, involving a

Conia vel effigies vere faciei domini nostri Jesu christi redemptoris generis humani: queadmodū tunc cū humana carne circūseptus terre incola cū hominibus familiariter cōuersans apparuit: a proprio ipsius vultu per quosdā plurimū denotos christicolas subtili gracilicꝗ pictura eo (vt supra dixi) seculo rectissime extitit effigiata. Que postea cū ꝫ numerus ꝫ denotio christicolaꝫ ob stupendoꝫ miraculorū crebrescentiā indies mirūimmodū magnū caperet incrementū: pro indelibili immortalicꝗ memoria facienda fuerat rursus erea aureacꝗ tabella mirabili sculptura excussa: pene ad modum nūmismatis huiusce proprie speciei ac quantitatis (vt hic oculis coram facile intueri poteris) multo ingenio arte ꝫ sagacitate (nullum denicꝗ a prototypo discrimē preseferens) diligentissime fabrefacta. Sicꝗ vt cū deinceps in diuersis Asie regionibus diu circumlata fuisset ꝫ ostensa: magnam intuentibus admirationem ingesserat ꝫ denotionem: ab vniuersiscꝗ per magnum temporis cursum in magna fuit habita veneratione. Quouscꝗ et nomen et christi religio ab oibus Asie climatibus a perfida Turcarum gente exul effecta: cum omnia sancte nostre religionis preciosa in profundis terre canenis absconderētur: fuit hec sancta effigies cum reliquo thesauro in secretis latibulis recondita: donec postea hec et alia sacra volente deo a denotis rursus inuenta fuere et cognita. Denicꝗ fertur a nonnullis genere ꝫ nobilitate prestantissimis viris probatecꝗ fame ac perinde fide dignissimis hanc sacro sanctam Jesu christi iconiam in erea tabella sculptam: cum aliis tribus numinis aureis in quibus illaipsa prefata effigies erat incussa: in cuiusdam Turcarum regis erario quondam fuisse reperta: fuissecꝗ data dono cuidam nobili Germanie magnati: qui cum (ex huiusce gentis ritu) sacro sanctū dominicū sepulchꝫ Jerusalē visitasset: rogatuscꝗ a quodā Turcarū primati de diuerso ꝫ Europe ꝫ christianoꝫ principū statu ꝫ potētia percūctanti aliꝗd differeret. qui cū benigne ad singula respōdisset: inter cōfabulandū hec ab eo munera humaniter elargita cū gꝛarū actione leta fronte accepit. Sicꝗ ad has europe prouincias delata: fuit a quodas antigrapho in arte pingendi experto opifici iterum perfectissime repicta. Insuper vt facilius tibi persuadeam hanc imaginem vere similitudinem habere cum christi facie corporali: pro testimonio sequentem proconsulis Zentuli (viri patriti Romani) epistolā fac legas amice denotissime.

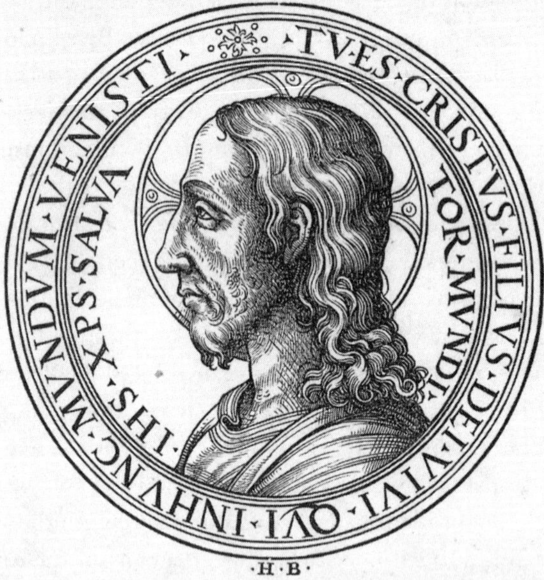

☙ Incipit epistola Zentuli de dispositione et qualitate faciei Jesu Christi.

Zentulus senatui Salutem. Apparuit temporibus nostris ꝫ adhuc est homo magne virtutis nominatus Jesus christus: qui dicit a gentibus propheta veritatis: quē eius discipuli nominant filium dei: suscitans mortuos ꝫ sanans languores. Homo quidem stature procere medioris ꝫ spectabilis. Vultum habens venerabilem: quem intuentes possunt diligere ꝫ formidare. Capillos habens in modum nucis anelane: et planos vsꝗ ad aures: ab auribus vsꝗ ad humeros cerinos ꝫ crispos aliquantulum cerulinos ꝫ fulgentiores ab humeris: discrimen habens in medio capitis iuxta morem nazarenorum. Frontem planam ꝫ serenissimam. Faciem sine ruga et macula aliqua: quam rubor moderatus venustat: nasi ꝫ oris eboris nulla prorsus est reprehensio: barbam habens copiosam in similitudinem capillorum: non longam sed in medio bifurcatam: aspectum habens simplicem ꝫ maturum: oculis glaucis ꝫ varris claris existentibus. In increpatione terribilis: in admonitione placabilis et amabilis: hilaris seruata grauitate. Qui nunquā visus est ridere: flere autem sic. in statura corporis propagatus ꝫ rectus: manus habens ꝫ brachia visu delectabilia: in colloquiis gratus rarus ꝫ modestus. Speciosus forma pre filiis hominum.

21.8 A facsimile of the medal. Hans Burgkmair, broadsheet with profile portrait of Christ, woodcut and type, 25.4 x 16.8 cm (ca. 1510). Munich, Staatiche Graphische Sammlung. This print reproduces, in actual size, the Florentine medal type we illustrate in figure 20.1. The letter describing Christ's appearance remains, at the bottom of the sheet, but the text above reinforces the evidentiary authority of the medal by providing a completely new provenance for the likeness.

carefully explained fable of substitution. The text reports that a painted portrait was made of Christ when he lived among men "as one of them." Eventually, "in order to preserve an indelible and immortal memory [the portrait] was in its turn cast in bronze in a tablet, gilt like a marvelous sculpture, in something close to the form of a coin"—that is, a medal. The text is careful to describe the quality and accuracy of the transfer from painted panel to bronze relief: "respecting the figure's proper appearance and size (as you can easily see before your eyes), the image was forged in the most accurate way, with great artistic genius, skill, and understanding (so that it was in no way distinguishable from the prototype)."[36] That bronze image, obviously an object of the type of the Florentine medal, was carried according to Burgkmair's inscription back to western Europe by a noble German pilgrim.

The process of substitution, already adduced in the story about the emerald, is here spelled out with didactic clarity. Bronze is explained as the medium to which the fragile painted likeness is transferred, as it were, for safekeeping. In bronze the image can endure over vast stretches of time and through the persecutions of the "perfidious Turks," and now it is succeeded, as the substitutional medium par excellence, by paper, durable in its relative inexpensiveness and therefore endless proliferation. The text on Burgkmair's woodcut gives a plausible historical context, with the fall of the Holy Land and the Byzantine Empire providing the scenario for a narrative of loss and retrieval. In a characteristic hesitation between Constantinople and Jerusalem, the text says that the medal, together with three others with the same image impressed on them, were found in the treasury of the Turkish sultan and given to a noble German merchant on pilgrimage to the Holy Sepulchre, who brought them back to the West. The text goes on to say that it has been newly and perfectly copied (*repicta*) by an *antigrapho* (literally, a transcriber) of great expertise, that is, Burgkmair. Preserved in its bronze form through the centuries, the image could now be released again, propagated through print, and in fact it was, in further copies on paper, as well as in copies in paint and stone based on prints. The print, which puts image and text on the same plane, provides a textual apparatus that explains the process of substitution and justifies the role of the print medium as an extension of its logic. Burgkmair's Christ broadsheet was an occasion for the print medium to forge its own prehistory.

We recall that Lorenzo Valla extended the same critical indulgence to the Peter and Paul panels: he did not interrogate the transmission process that brought them to the present. Valla may well have doubted the physical antiquity of the Lateran panels, but he did not doubt the portraits themselves, that is, the information about the physiognomies of the saints that the panels transmitted.

Confident in the initial transfer of data from original likeness to the medal, Burgkmair expended much effort in preserving the distinctness of the face, if anything exaggerating the facial peculiarities given by the medalist. Once there is Burgkmair's woodcut, the bronze medal is no longer the last link in the substitutional chain. The medal is no longer simply a copy; it has now become a model in its own right and so gains a new legitimacy. The medal itself, which had been designed to broadcast and preserve an accurate impression of a more authentic original painted portrait, recedes back into an unspecified antiquity. The print is now the most recent link in the chain. The medal as a category is presented as an ancient phenomenon, for the parenthetical explanation "something close to the form of a coin" implies that the medal is an unfamiliar format and needs to be explained, with reference to a modern format. In fact, just the opposite is true: the medal, a purely celebratory, nonmonetary numismatic portrait, is a modern invention and there was no ancient Latin word for it.

Burgkmair's efforts reveal the contradictions at the heart of his enterprise. Burgkmair published two broadsheets with unprecedented claims to accuracy and documentary reliability, and yet the sheets presented two completely different physiognomies for Christ. Once again we meet a hesitation at the point of origin, this time within the oeuvre of a single artist; the same hesitation that produced two tombs of David, two Temples of Solomon, two huts of Romulus, two authentic frontal images of Christ—the Veronica and the Mandylion—two sites of the Last Supper, two sites of the Praetorium, two houses of Caiaphas, two Via Dolorosas, and two places called Emmaus.[37] The pressure to produce accurate copies led Burgkmair to respect the differences between the two medal types, and the result was an explicit exposé, in two nearly contemporary broadsheets, of the fact that there were not one but two likenesses. The bifurcation within the medal tradition in a sense did not exist before this point. Until then it was a single image tradition with the usual variation from copy to copy, held together symbolically by the obsessive preservation of the detail of the fold in Christ's collar through all exemplars. But now the bifurcation was defined, and broadcast, at the very moment that the tradition was given its most rigorous documentary presentation. The effect was to undermine the physiognomic authority of the entire class of images. The *imago contrafacta* collapsed virtually at the instant of its birth.

The Italian medals and Burgkmair's woodcuts did not become the authoritative models for subsequent images of Christ—indeed, the face of Christ they offered no more succeeded in entering the visual record than did the backwards lettering of the Titulus. Only later were a small trickle of portraits of Christ made on their model. When artists did avail themselves of the medallic portrait, they often reverted to the simpler Matteo de' Pasti version, or even a more generic profile type based on no model in particular. They pulled back, in effect, from the brink of high informational density, instead reasserting the basic impact of the profile form as a documentary imprint. A marble relief with the portrait of Christ, associated with the Venetian sculptor Tullio Lombardo, recently acquired by the Kimbell Art Museum, copies no single source (figure 21.9).[38] The portrait resembles one version of the medal but also Burgkmair's broadsheet with the roundel inside the square frame (see figure 21.7). The sculptor straightens the line running from forehead to nose and generally smooths over the articulations of the models. Perhaps the artist was trying to emulate the low information density of the letter of Lentulus. Other works by Tullio Lombardo show curly locks beginning in waves right from the top of the head.[39] Here, however, the hair is shown straight at the top, in conformity with the Lentulus letter's description of Christ's hair as "straight down to the ears, but below the ears wavy and curled," perhaps also explaining why the ear is so insistently revealed.

Other artists translated the medal portrait back into three dimensions, into the sculptural bust, for example, a form equally imprinted with antique associations. A marble bust in San Pantalon in Venice, sometimes ascribed to the Milanese sculptor Cristoforo Solari but more likely made by a Venetian artist, bears a family resemblance to the profile portraits.[40] It even includes the telling detail from the medal tradition, the hairpin fold in the collar of the tunic at the center of the chest. A painted bust by Benedetto Diana in the London National Gallery distinguishes itself by showing Christ not quite frontally and with the head slightly tilted (figure 21.10).[41] These off-kilter elements within the bust format produce powerful reality effects, as if a living likeness had been recorded. Here too the painting relies on a prototype that had antique authority in its day, an equivalent to the Christ medals: the bronze statue of Christ then in the church of the Carità, copied by Carpaccio into his portrait of St. Augustine and discussed near the beginning of this book (figure 21.11, and see figure 4.3). Besides the pose, the painting retains the statue's abstract sharpness of features, a compromise between informational density and frictionless substitution. The statue was copied as an authoritative likeness by many artists around 1500, but all of the other cases render the full, statuesque figure. By adapting the figure to the bust format and to painting, this panel in a sense restores the prototype of the statue itself, the living Christ on which the statue was based.

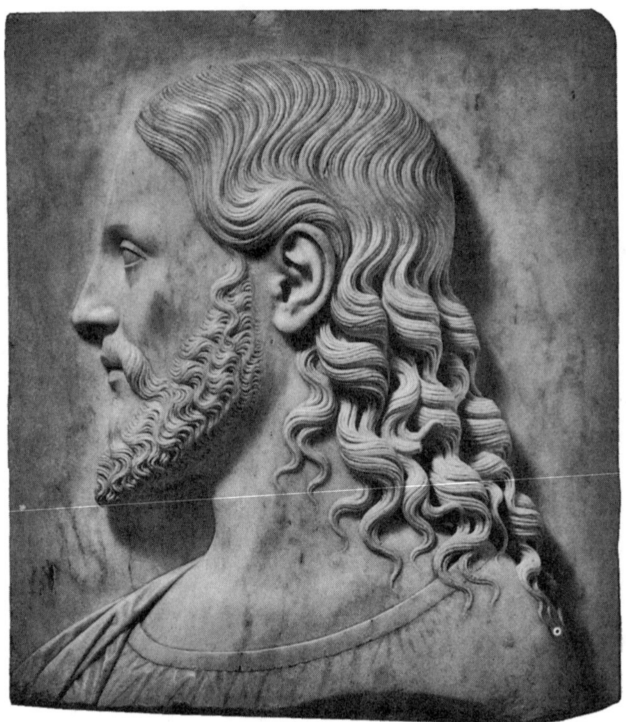

21.9 The artist resists the authority of the medal. Attributed to Tullio Lombardo, *Christ in Profile*, marble, 33.5 x 31 x 9 cm (ca. 1510). Fort Worth, Kimbell Art Museum. Just as with the Titulus Crucis, some artists insisted on a margin of freedom in interpreting the transmitted data.

A similar case is the painted portrait of Christ, once attributed to Giovanni Bellini, in the Academia de San Fernando in Madrid. This painting dispenses with any rigid adherence to the obvious indices of documentarity, such as the profile view, showing a highly descriptive rendering of the face in three-quarter view. And yet here too, perhaps because of the absence of any other evidentiary peg, a documentary basis in the form of the Lentulus letter was attached to it. A seventeenth-century inventory of the Vendramin collection presents this painting as the first item, immediately preceded by a transcription of the Lentulus letter.[42] It is unlikely that this association was an inspiration of the inventorist. Indeed, the linking of this document with this painting, rather than with the painting of the same subject attributed to Giorgione in the same collection, suggests that the text and the image had been associated for some time.[43] Perhaps the text had been originally attached to the panel in some way, to its cover or to its reverse.

The Belliniesque painting bears some resemblance to a painting of 1503

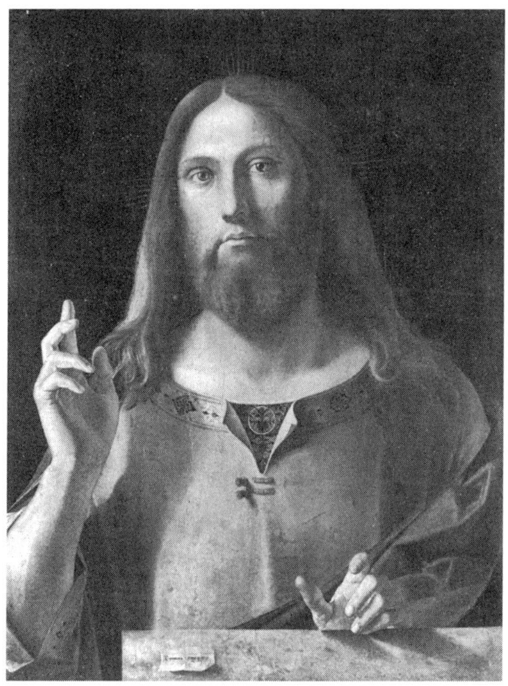 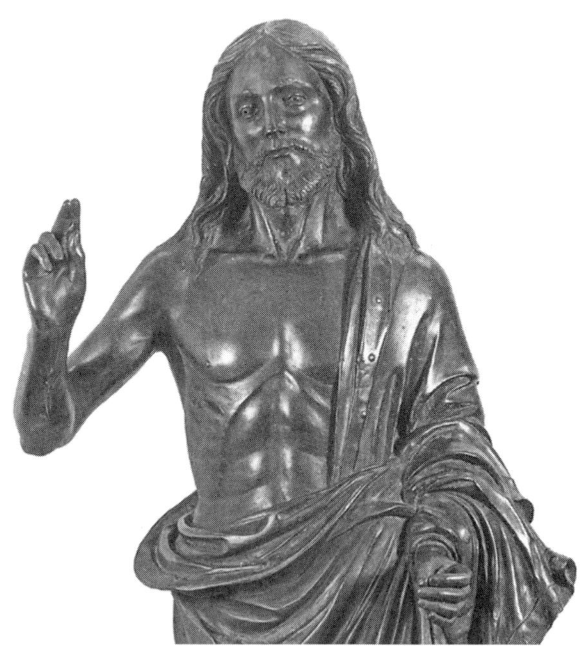

21.10–21.11 Sculptural evidence brought to life. Benedetto Diana, *Blessing Christ*, 76.2 x 59.1 cm (ca. 1510), London, National Gallery. *Blessing Christ* (ca. 1493), detail, Milan, Poldi Pezzoli Museum. The painter bases his living portrait of Christ on the bronze statue in the church of the Carità (see figure 4.3 for the full statue). Diana became a member of the Scuola della Carità in 1482, a decade before the statue made its appearance in the associated church.

by Jacopo de' Barbari now in Dresden. That picture, which was owned by Lucas Cranach the Elder, served as the model for a woodcut portrait by Lucas Cranach the Younger dated 1553. The younger Cranach, titling his woodcut *The Form of the Body of Our Lord Jesus Christ*, seems to have taken the half-century-old painting as reliable evidence for the appearance of Christ. Still, he supplemented the image with a descriptive text attributed to a certain Nicephorus, a preacher from Constantinople.[44]

Painted reproductions of the medal portrait were especially rare, as if painters recognized that the translation of the type to painting conflicted with the authorial claims of the medium. But framed citations did occur. The medal of Christ was quoted as a roundel in a frieze depicted in Bartolommeo Montagna's altarpiece *Madonna and Child Enthroned with Saints* (1498).[45] A diptych from Roermond in Limburg, now in the Catherine Convent Museum in Utrecht, probably derives from Burgkmair's more particularized woodcut.[46] Here the text of the Lentulus letter is written on the left wing of the diptych. The painting no longer shows the profile in the roundel format. Just as the second origin myth retailed by Burgkmair's print had asserted, in effect, that the medal was a preservation mechanism for the original portrait in paint, so too does this painting discard the medal format and "restore" the original likeness of Christ.

The profile portraits of Christ may have prompted new efforts to endow the hieratic, front-facing image of Christ with a comparable documentary status, a sculptural pedigree, even stronger than the miracle stories associated with the painted Veronica and the Mandylion. Here the presence of Byzantine sculpted reliefs of the Pantocrator type must have helped, for example the ivory Pantocrator owned by Giuliano della Rovere (see figure 10.5) or the mysterious frontal relief of the Blessing Christ in Genoa, a work of the thirteenth century, it seems, of either Constantinopolitan or Italian origin.[47] It stood to reason that such an image, as deeply rooted in the Byzantine tradition as were the painted icons, would carry ancient authority. It was a category of portraits of Christ that should have existed.

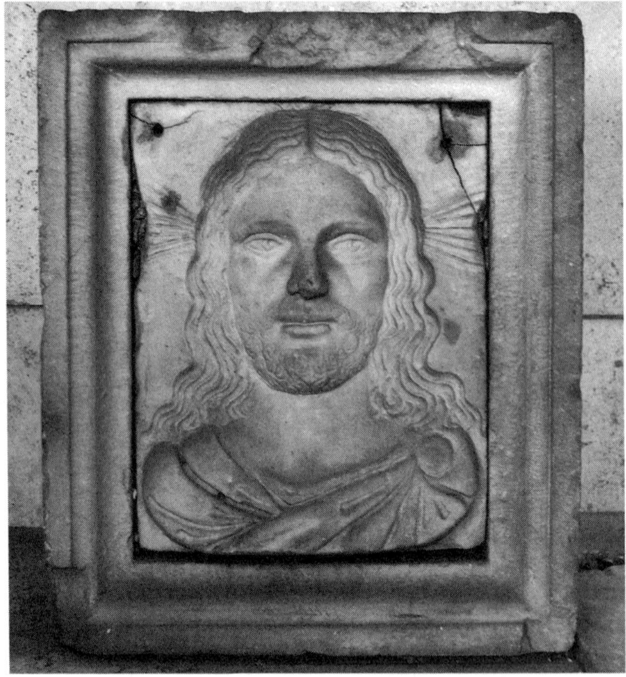

21.12 What an ancient Roman relief portrait of Christ would have looked like. Head of Christ, marble, frame: 54.5 x 46.3 x 18 cm (ancient Roman?); relief: approx. 40 x 32 cm (late fifteenth century?). Rome, American Academy. The modern relief is embedded in an ancient frame. The carving of the drapery at the bottom appears to be late antique, suggesting that this is a reworking of an actual ancient portrait.

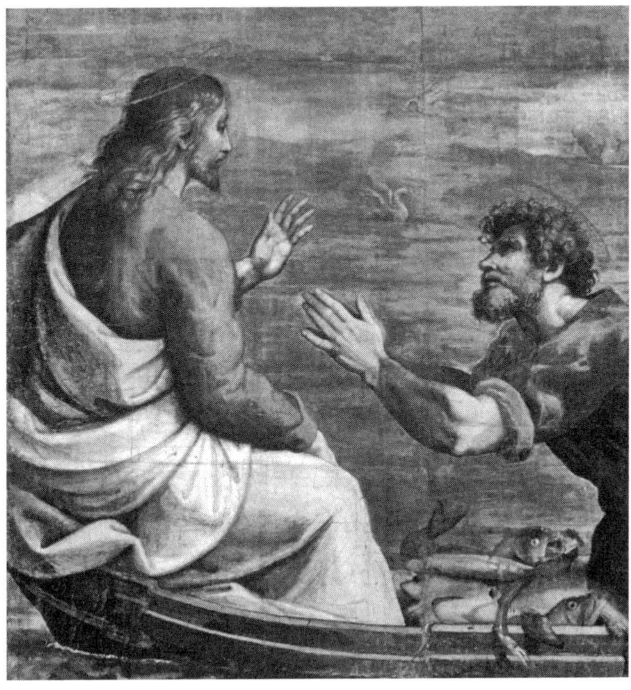

21.13 The authentic features embedded cameo-fashion in a modern work of art. Raphael, *Miraculous Draught of Fishes*, tapestry cartoon (1515–1516), detail. London, Victoria and Albert Museum. In the woven tapestry the profile will face left just as it does on the medals.

A frontal image of Christ at the American Academy in Rome, a marble relief dating probably from the end of the fifteenth century, represents a kind of *all'antica* version of the traditional Veronica type (figure 21.12).[48] With his toga falling in thickly cut folds and fastened by a brooch, Christ resembles a Roman portrait subject. The relief is lodged in an ornamental frame that very likely is a recycled Roman piece.[49]

Was the American Academy relief a forgery? Was there any intent to deceive? The image did fill an evidentiary gap. Yet many beholders would surely have recognized it, immediately, as a fiction, as a harmless "mystification."[50]

Raphael, like other ambitious artists, did not always obey the evidence.[51] But the documentary portrait of Christ did appear in his cartoon for the *Miraculous Draught of Fishes* tapestry at the Sistine Chapel (figure 21.13). Here Raphael modeled the profile of Christ on the medal type.[52] It is turned in the opposite direction to the model so as to appear in the correct orientation in the tapestry.[53] Raphael was introducing the profile head into

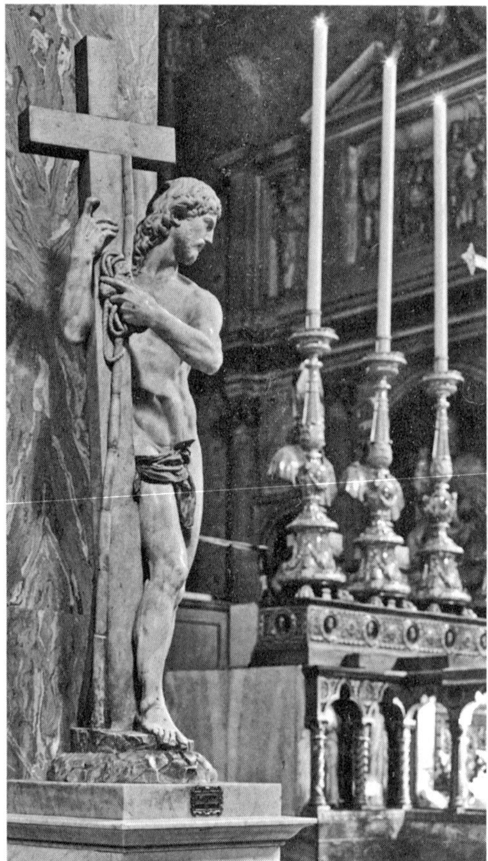

21.14 Even Michelangelo acknowledges the authority of the medal. Michelangelo, *Risen Christ*, marble (1520). Rome, Santa Maria sopra Minerva. From the correct angle the beholder spies the profile familiar from the medal. The third dimension allows Michelangelo to respect the historical data and at the same time depart from it.

a larger context replete with erudite biblical scholarship and associations to the ancient ceremonies and decorations of the Vatican. Michelangelo, too, invoked the medal portrait by stressing the profile view in his *Risen Christ* at Santa Maria sopra Minerva (figure 21.14). Michelangelo may have been aware of the medal tradition already from his Florentine years, at the time when Verrocchio's Christ for Orsanmichele was being adapted into busts by Torrigiani (Michelangelo's colleague from the days of the sculpture garden at San Marco) and into medals by Niccolò Fiorentino. The Minerva Christ would thus have made a double claim to antiquity, both in the allusion to the profile portrait preserved in the medals and in the antique form of the nude free-standing statue. This double claim was evidently honored by contemporaries. A sixteenth-century medal shows the profile portrait of Christ on the obverse and on the reverse a standing, statue-like figure of Christ modeled on the Minerva Christ.[54] The existence of the medal was more than corroboration: since the medal as a type purportedly carried ancient iconography, it inserted Michelangelo's Christ into a lengthy substitution chain. It provided retroactive evidence of an antique source not only for the head of Christ, but for the statue as such. Thus even this statue, made by the most renowned modern artist, came under the pull of the substitutional logic newly mobilized by the new documentary images. Like the medals, like the Verrocchio Orsanmichele Christ, like the bronze statue in the Carità, it too was something more than a work in an *all'antica* style—it read as a powerful substitute for an antiquity even as it was obviously a Michelangelo.

Fabricated evidence was not always taken as good evidence, or evidence of anything. But in some cases it really did work. According to Vasari, Andrea Sansovino produced a colossal terracotta portrait of the semilegendary sixth-century BCE king Lars Porsenna for the citizens of Montepulciano.[55] The bust alone survives, measuring 46 centimters in height (figure 21.15).[56] It would be unattributable to Sansovino, and hard to date, without the notices by Vasari and others. Sansovino did not conceal his authorship, nor was it forgotten; still, the artist chose a prestigious and rare

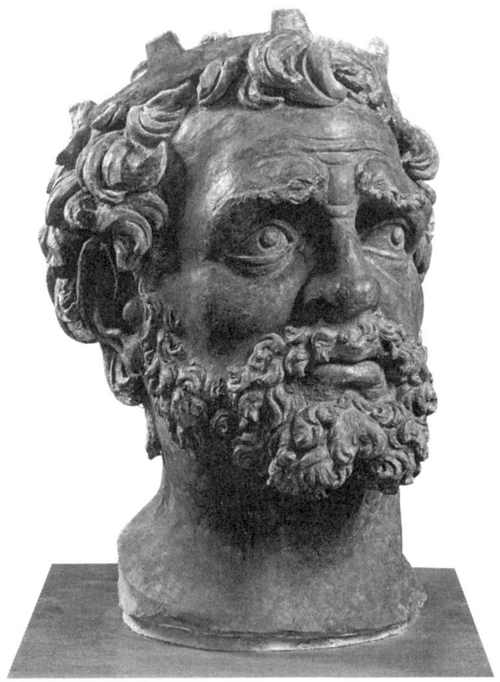

21.15 The colossal monument that the Etruscan king deserved. Andrea Sansovino, Lars Porsenna, painted terracotta, 46 cm in height (ca. 1516–1520). Private collection. Vasari explained that the work was made for the city of Montepulciano by the artist. Nevertheless, the portrait retained an aura of evidentiary authority into the seventeenth century.

format, the colossus, and an unconventional medium for such a colossus, terracotta, lending the figure an archaic flavor. The colossal portrait participated in the interurban Tuscan rivalry that for some decades had hinged on claims to Etruscan origins. The sepulchre of Lars Porsenna at Chiusi, involving the supposed ruins of a labyrinth and several pyramids described by Pliny, was discussed by Alberti, Filarete, and Vasari and reconstructed in drawings by Antonio and Giuliano da Sangallo and Baldassare Peruzzi.[57] The Florentine cleric Lorenzo Dati composed a fanciful chronicle, the *Historia Porsennae*, posing as a translation of an Etruscan text by one Caio Vibenna.[58] In 1492 the Sienese presented the funerary urn of Lars Porsenna, inscribed conveniently in Latin, to Lorenzo de' Medici.[59] The fifteenth century knew Etruscan civilization mainly through the textual accounts of the Romans, and everyone wanted more.[60] The Montepulcian colossus intervened in this story, filling a portrait-sized gap in the monumental record. It was still judged an antiquity by Luigi Lanzi in the late eighteenth century. The statue had already been reduced to a bust when Spinello Benci, secretary to the Medici, cited and reproduced it in woodcut as the frontispiece to his history of Montepulciano of 1641.[61] Benci knew that Sansovino was the author of the statue; he describes it as a "memorial" erected by the town to its founder. And yet the work figures in his account almost as if it were contributing to the claim, dear to him, of an ancient Etruscan presence in Montepulciano. It was as if the fact that the citizens of Montepulciano had commissioned a memorial in the early sixteenth century rendered the myth of Etruscan origins a little more plausible, just as the fabrication of a bronze statue of Christ made reports of an antique sculpted portrait of Christ more plausible. The folk of the sixteenth century, after all, were just that much closer to antiquity; the old traditions were perhaps still intact then, the invisible lines of communication to the deepest past still open. Modernity, by contrast, our own mid-seventeenth century, Benci seems to be saying, is forever cut off from the living past and has to make do with mere scholarship. Activating the magic of figuration, the three-dimensional "forgery" like Sansovino's was—perhaps still is— more effective than Lorenzo Dati's obviously fictitious chronicle.

TWENTY-TWO

Forgery 1: Copy

Around 1496 Queen Isabella of Castile ordered an exact copy of a sixty-year-old painting by Rogier van der Weyden. Isabella's father Juan II had given the original work, a triptych representing the Adoration of the Infant Christ, the Lamentation, and Christ Appearing to His Mother, to the Carthusian monastery of Miraflores in 1445. The work had been painted a decade earlier and was possibly a gift to Juan from Pope Eugenius IV. That original painting by van der Weyden is now in Berlin (figure 22.1).[1] By the time Isabella conceived her desire to have the exquisite forms before her own eyes, every day of the week, the artist van der Weyden had been dead for thirty years. She very likely required one of her own court artists to make the copy, perhaps Juan de Flandes, a Flemish painter who made his career in Spain. The three panels of the later triptych, the copy, are now divided between the Royal Chapel in Granada and the Metropolitan Museum in New York (figure 22.2).[2] The copy is a little smaller than the original but otherwise so similar, stroke for stroke, that no scholar, unaided by technology, was ever able to say for sure which was the original and which the copy. Most considered the Berlin version the copy.[3] Now dendrochronological analysis has dated the Berlin panels, once and for all, to about 1435 and the New York and Granada panels to the mid–1490s. Not only that, but the New York and Granada panels were hewn from the same tree as panels painted for Miraflores by Juan de Flandes, who was working in Spain from 1496 on.[4] And yet the surfaces of the two triptychs are still virtually indistinguishable, even to the eye of the expert.

For Umberto Eco, "a perfect replica of Michelangelo's *Pietà* which rendered each nuance of the material texture of the original with great fidelity would also possess its semiotic properties. Therefore the value accorded to the 'authenticity' of the original statue has more relevance for a theory of commodities, and when given undue importance on the aesthetic level it is a matter for social scientists or critics of social aberrations. The lust for authenticity is the ideological product of the art market's hidden

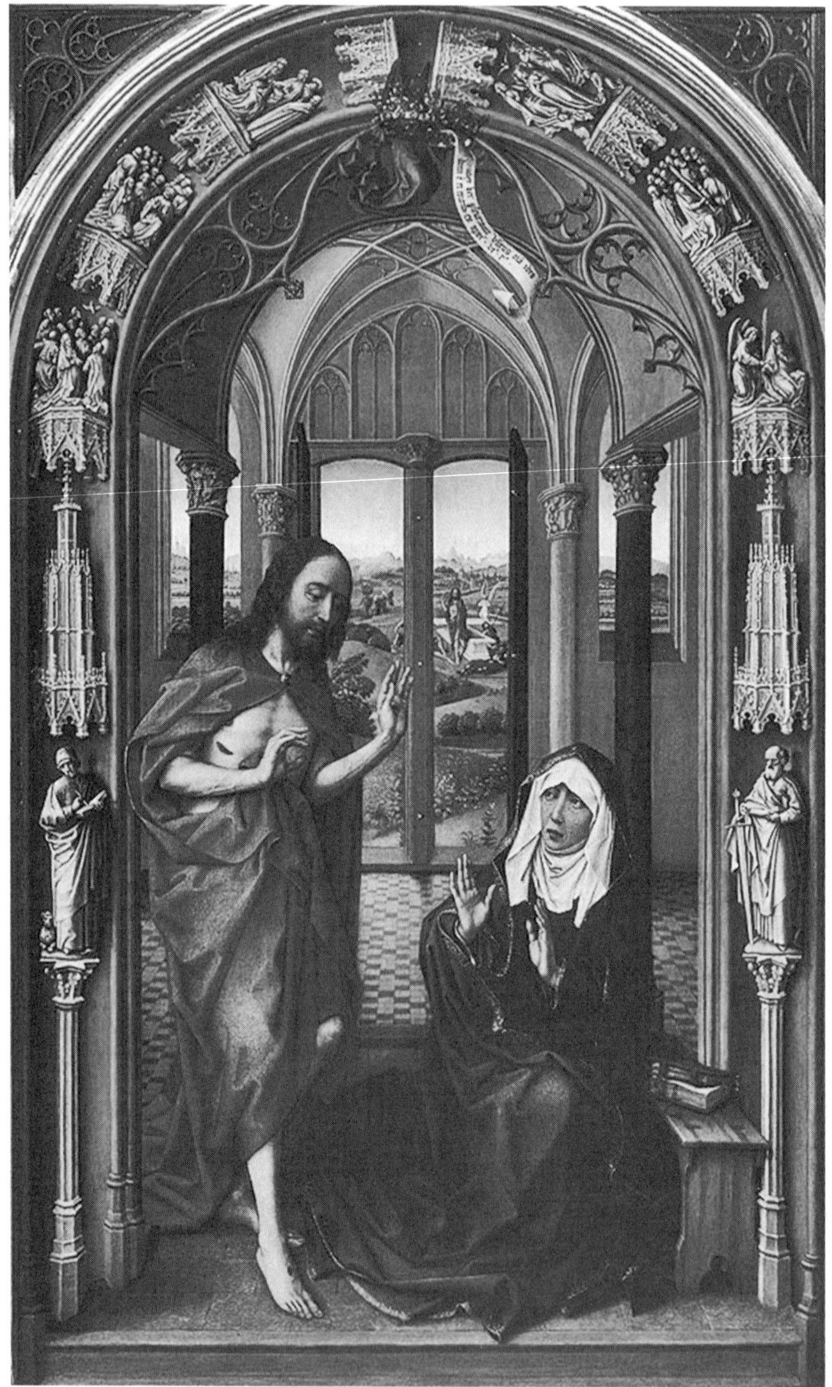

22.1 The gift in motion. Rogier van der Weyden, *Christ Appearing to his Mother*, oil on panel, 71 x 43 cm (ca. 1435). Berlin, Gemäldegalerie. The panel belongs to an altarpiece given perhaps by the Pope to Juan II of Spain, and in turn by Juan to the monastery of Miraflores in 1445. His daughter Isabella of Castile had a copy made half a century later. Twentieth-century scholars were unable to tell whether this painting, or the slightly smaller panel in New York (see figure 22.2), was the original or the copy.

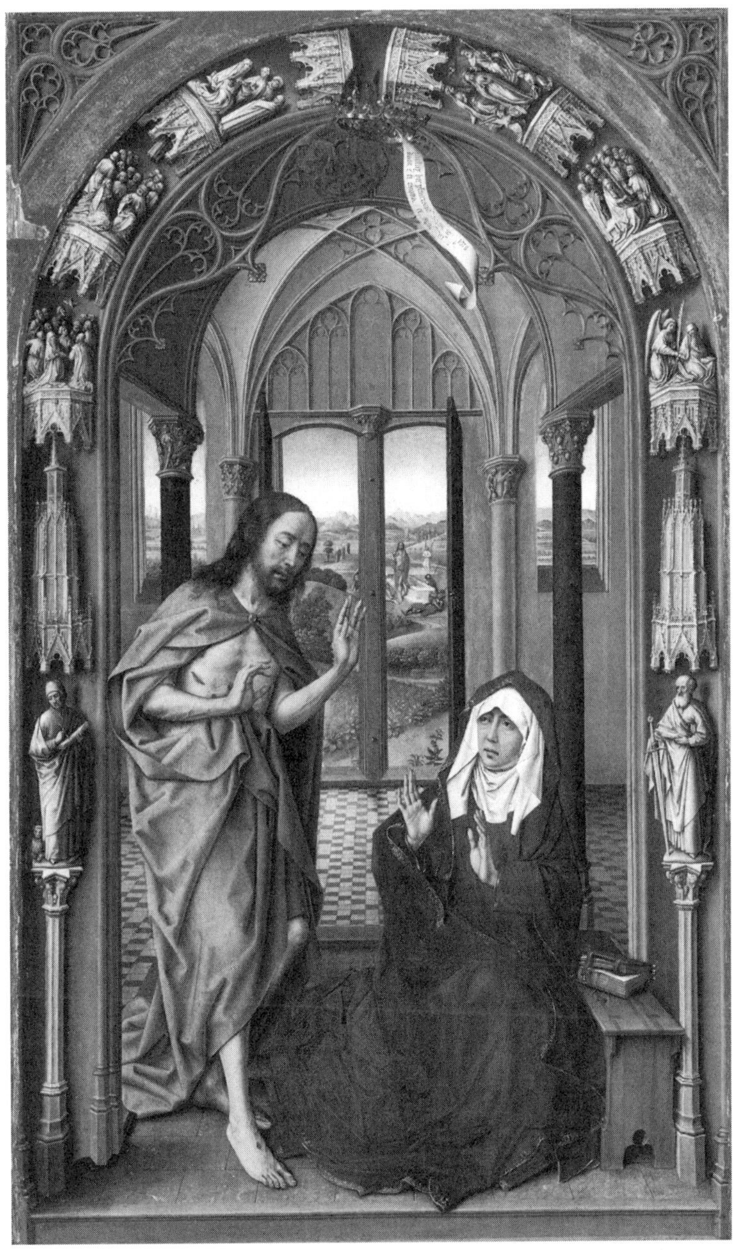

22.2 The gift replicated. Juan de Flandes (?), copy after Rogier van der Weyden, *Christ Appearing to his Mother*, oil on panel, 63.5 x 38.1 cm (ca. 1496). New York, Metropolitan Museum of Art. Long believed to be a work either by Rogier van der Weyden himself or by his workshop, dendrochronological analysis has now revealed it once and for all as the copy made for Isabella.

persuaders."[5] Those persuaders had not yet reached the orbit of Isabella of Castile.

Already by the late fifteenth century, Rogier van der Weyden and Jan van Eyck were fixed points, classics. They were known by name even to Italian art collectors. Some painters, not only Juan de Flandes, learned to make exact replicas of Jan's and Rogier's panels. In the 1520s Jan Gossaert made a copy of Jan van Eyck's *Virgin in the Church* (1437–1439) that deceived the Venetian connoisseur Marcantonio Michiel, who described it thus upon seeing it in the Vendramin collection only a few years later: "El quadretto in tauola della nostra donna sola cun el puttino in brazzo, in piedi, in un tempio Ponentino, cun la corona in testa, fo de mano de Rugerio da Brugies [here Michiel seems to have conflated van der Weyden and van Eyck], et è opera a oglio perfettissima."[6] Gossaert had learned, in effect, to unlearn the style of his own day, and then to unlearn his own personal style, and instead adopt—provisionally—the manner of another painter, long dead: a revered manner of painting, to be sure, but a half-century out of date.

The desire for copies is the very criterion of a culture of art collecting. Ernst Gombrich found it "astounding" that in ancient Greece

> copies were ever made at all to be displayed in the houses and gardens of the educated. For this industry of making reproductions for sale implies a function of the image of which the pre-Greek world knew nothing. The image has been pried loose from the practical context for which it was conceived and is admired and enjoyed for its beauty and fame, that is, quite simply within the context of art.[7]

The Roman collector of the first-century CE who acquired a "Praxiteles" was by no means the victim of a deception. If the collector had any sophistication at all, he understood perfectly that Praxiteles was long dead and that there were precious few original works by that master to be had. The collector was happy with his copy, and since the copy delivered so many of the desirable attributes of the original—the ingenious posing of limbs, the nuanced modeling of the body, the luster of marble—it could in a meaningful sense bear the label "Praxiteles." The replica substituted more than adequately for the original. Zeuxis's portrait of Helen was taken by Pyrrhus from Athens to Rome, but the late Greek source that describes the replica left behind in Athens seems unconcerned by its copy status, calling it simply the "Helen by Zeuxis."[8] Lucian, in an account of a visit to a private sculpture gallery, speaks of copies as "Myron's work" or "Polycleitus's work."[9] Longinus, in his treatise *On the Sublime*, is careful to distinguish the "good" imitation of Homer from plagiarism; to make his point he compares "good" imitation to taking impressions from statues, presumably involving casts but also some free interpretation, "as it is acceptable to do."[10] The interpretive copy was acceptable to all parties: to knowledgeable beholders capable of distinguishing between the artistic qualities of the original preserved by the copy and the supplementary qualities added by the copyist; to somewhat less knowledgeable beholders who simply considered the copy equivalent to the original; and to beholders who had no idea they were looking at a copy or who had no interest in the concept of the original.[11]

Some sophisticated ancient beholders had a clear sense of the inimitability of the hand of the master, especially of the painter. Pliny says of Apelles's last painting, the Aphrodite at Kos, that "when only a part was finished envious death interposed, and no one was found to finish the outlines already traced."[12] Yet no ancient writer ever articulated a concept of art forgery. This is because painting and sculpture were not considered liberal arts, "free" arts like poetry or music. Ancient writers were quite alert to the possibility of literary forgery.[13]

Many false claims were surely made in the ancient world, by dealers and perhaps artists themselves, about the production histories of paintings and statues. But it was not clear what the implications of such deceptions were *except* for the buyer who paid large sums of money for an old work that was really new, or for a work by Zeuxis that was really a copy.

The willingness to accept replicas of marble or bronze statues persisted well into modern times. Collectors of Greek and Roman antiquities between the sixteenth and nineteenth centuries contented themselves for the most part with modern replicas of the ancient works they admired. Since the prototypes themselves were mostly copies, the modern collectors had every reason to be content with their secondary copies.[14] The copies *were* antiquities, just as most photographs by Walker Evans in the collections of major museums *are* photographs by Walker Evans, even though they were printed from negatives after Evans's death in 1975. (The Metropolitan Museum of Art recently contested this convention by mounting an exhibition consisting mostly of so-called "vintage" prints, that is, photographs printed by Evans himself.[15]) Modern copies of antiquities were often so good that even modern scholars have been unable to perceive the difference. The *Youth of Magdalensberg*, the largest ancient bronze ever found north of the Alps, was excavated near the ancient settlement of Virunum, modern Maria Saal, in Carinthia in 1502. The figure now in the Kunsthistorisches Museum in Vienna was believed by every scholar to be that very artifact, a Roman work based on an earlier, perhaps fourth-century, Greek model. But technical investigations undertaken in the 1980s proved that the statue in Vienna was actually cast in the sixteenth century.[16] According to a document, Archduke Ferdinand, the grandson of Maximilian of Habsburg, had a copy made in 1551.[17] The original has disappeared.

Painting was another matter. It is not so easy to make painted replicas that will satisfy the eye of an expert. Pliny, writing in the first century CE, described the painting of Venus Anadyomene, Venus emerging from the sea, by the fourth-century master Apelles. Augustus brought the painting to Rome and donated it to the Temple of Divus Julius. Pliny reports that "when the lower portion was damaged (*corruptam*) no one could be found to restore it, and thus the very injury redounded to the glory of the artist." The unrepaired damage remained as a symbol of Apelles's inimitability. Pliny's account suggests that for a time, at least, the picture was valued as a relic of Apelles. But "in the course of time," Pliny continues, "the panel of the picture fell into decay, and Nero when emperor substituted for it another picture by the hand of Dorotheos" (*aliamque pro ea substituit Nero principatu suo Dorothei manu*).[18]

It seems that the copy by Dorotheos was not considered a completely adequate substitute, as a sculptural copy might have been. It was adequate but only from certain points of view; evidently not from the point of view of art experts or from the point of view of the keepers of the temple, or else Pliny might never have been aware that Dorotheos (an uncelebrated painter, unattested beyond this passage) was involved. For if the work by Dorotheos had successfully substituted for the work by Apelles, without remainder, Pliny would simply have gone on thinking of the painting as a work by Apelles, as many less well-informed citizens no doubt did.[19]

In the fifteenth century, the copying skills that eventually came to serve the culture of collecting were first honed in the context of the replication of cult images. Infinite was the demand for images of the holy personages. This was true in antiquity as well: iconographical types, avatars of the gods, embodied in famous cult statues, were replicated in many media and dimensions and disseminated into private spaces. But in antiquity as much as the European Middle Ages, precision copying of the sort delivered by Isabella of Castile's court painter was not so important. When it came to images of the gods, compliance with essential iconographic features was usually sufficient as the wide variations among the "copies" of Praxiteles's lost Aphrodite of Cnidos show. Substitutional chains carried the worshipper back, unperturbed by contingent variation, to the stable origin point, god or saint.

The cult did not require precise copies, and yet over the course of the fifteenth century the replica emerged as an idea and as a possibility. The oil painting technique developed early in the century by van Eyck and others permitted and even invited precision. Some workshops seem to have experimented with assembly line production of paintings. The reliable mechanical replication of images by woodcut, engraving, or bronze casting, which promised to eliminate the element of drift in the copy chain by virtue of their indexicality—these were artifacts physically and causally linked to their referents—put pressure on the comparatively error-prone handmade image. Imported samples of the supposedly static corpus of Byzantine cult images made an impression. The few glimpses of authentic portraits of Christ or the Virgin placed a new premium on exactness. When historical authenticity was at stake, the expectations of picture-to-picture matching were raised.

A Marian image by Jan van Eyck, not a copy but a free adaptation of a Byzantine type, took on special authority, as if van Eyck by virtue of his position as a pioneer and inaugurator of a modern painting tradition had enjoyed privileged access to the ancient traditions.[20] Van Eyck's painting, signed and dated 1439 and now in Antwerp, combines the Byzantine type of the Madonna Eleusa, who embraces the Christ Child, with the Western medieval Virgin of the Fountain. Several later painters took the trouble to copy the picture, in some cases attentively, in others more liberally. But even the freer interpretations of the picture, by such significant early sixteenth-century masters as Gerard David and Bernard van Orley, had the effect of making van Eyck's panel only look more stable, more authentic. The copies and interpretations created the original. This was the context for the intriguing description of a (lost?) Marian image by Jan van Eyck in an inventory of 1523 as "fort anticque."[21]

The Netherlandish panel painters introduced a level of informational density, an accretion of detail, and an insistence on maintenance of just those surface features that were traditionally overlooked or freely adapted in substitutional transmission. An obviously paradigmatic or merely structural relationship to a presumed prototype no longer satisfied developing criteria of visual authentication. The image's content at a precise visual level—distinguishing facial features, peculiar treatment of drapery—was now recruited into the referential work of the image and elaborately justified. The exact copy is a monstrous parody of the substitutional imperative. It crawls over the surface of the work, imitating with obsessive care the appearance of the original, and where the original is missing it offers a rich texture of surface features to produce the effect of an original.

The substitution was thus transformed into an artifact open to the accusation of forgery. The forgery is an object whose production history—the history it claims for itself, or which someone has claimed for it—turns out not to be true. In the Middle Ages, many artifacts made claims about their own origins that we might now consider false but which at the time troubled no one. It was the art market that eventually created the category of the forged work of art. Society, protecting purchasers of pictures or statues, began to designate some origin myths as criminal, actionable. Worries about forged documents, texts, or holy relics, or counterfeit coins, were rampant in the Middle Ages.[22] But not before the fifteenth century, in the context of a well-developed market for antiquities as well as for original products by the hands of modern masters, did anyone connect the concept of forgery with a painting or a sculpture.

Many artifacts make no claims at all about their own origins. Some others come accompanied by metadata or framing information—a label. Still others are given production histories by their owners. When the story of the object is told by a label, or by a narrator, then there is no sense that the object itself is telling a lie. The false production history attached to a work by an unscrupulous dealer is a matter best left to the sociology of art. More interesting in our context is the image that points to its own origins. Once the image offers a version of its own production history, we face the possibility that the image itself is telling a lie. Since images are relatively ineloquent and cannot really narrate or explain but only point, such internal signals are easily misunderstood, pushing the image into the realm of imitations, emulations, hoaxes, idolatries, fictions, and other deceptions, some harmless, some less so, before it ever arrives at the clear, market-defined category of the forgery.

Art collectors wanted copies, especially when the original was not to be had. But some copies were not honest about their status as copies and so before long it all went bad. Eventually the collectors required connoisseurs in order to distinguish the desirable from the undesirable copies. Marcantonio Michiel browsed the patrician collections of Venice in the 1520s and 1530s, smoking out fakes and misattributions. But even his practiced eye could not tell a Gossaert from a van Eyck, an Antonello da Messina from a Hans Memling or, at times, a modern carved relief from an ancient one.[23] Connoisseurship was a monster created by a new culture of art. Just as a substitutional transmission system does not require exact copies—on the contrary, typological identity thrives on flexibility and approximation—so too was copying incompatible with the aims of art. Or rather, it became incompatible, eventually. In the decades around 1500, art makers and collectors lived between systems.

In Italy, the exact copying of drawings was highly developed, a foundational skill that permitted masters to accumulate a stock of usable forms and to train their apprentices. A culture of collecting coalesced around drawings, apparently among those patrons, aware that artists themselves preserved drawings, who first asked for souvenirs or samples. No doubt some collectors were happy with copies, others perhaps not so happy. When Isabella d'Este was asked by Vittoria Colonna for her painting of the Magdalen (we don't know by whom), she replies that she would be happy to send it but asks only for time to have a good copy made. The wording clearly indicates that Isabella herself will keep the copy.[24] Michelangelo's presentation drawings regularly circulated in copies, so that Vittoria Colonna herself, applying more stringent criteria, had to ask specifically for one by his hand.[25] Others were less concerned. When Reginald Pole, a friend of Michelangelo, was asked for his drawing of a *Pietà* by the master, he replied that he would be happy to give it away since he could get another one from Vittoria Colonna.[26] To this day scholars debate the attribution of several highly finished Michelangelo drawings that exist in copies.[27]

The Italian painters, ever the students of Netherlandish painting technique, proved themselves more than able copyists. In 1523 Andrea del Sarto made an exact replica of Raphael's portrait of *Leo X with Two Cardinals* (Palazzo Pitti, 1517–1518). Federico Gonzaga, then Marquis of Mantua, had asked Pope Clement VII for the Raphael portrait as a gift, and here as elsewhere it was only natural to offer the painting.[28] But in Florence Ottaviano de' Medici, "a great connoisseur of art," not wanting to part with the painting, bought time with the Marquis by explaining that the frame was in poor condition and needed to be replaced. He then secretly contracted Sarto to make the copy which was offered as the original to Federico; it is now in Naples. Andrea del Sarto's activity as a copyist in this scenario is in many ways a traditional one, only now it became more intensive under the pressure of the deception. Indeed, it extended even to copying the imperfections that belonged to the painting *as an artifact*: Vasari says Andrea went so far as to copy the smudges on the original. The result was a copy so good that it deceived even Raphael's pupil Giulio Romano, who had lived in Mantua for decades with the copy, despite the fact that Giulio may have even assisted his master with the original.[29]

Portraits were copied because they carried information. Many fifteenth-century portraits exist in multiple copies.[30] The portrait asked to be copied. The rise of the portrait in the first decades of the fifteenth century developed in tandem with the fine-grained painting of the Netherlanders and the practice of close copying.

The portrait was often described in contemporary texts as a *counterfeit*, in no pejorative sense. Forgery and counterfeit are both words that started out with positive connotations and over time acquired bad connotations. The counterfeit is "made from," usually with the reassuring implication that the image was created by direct imprinting. To forge is simply to *fabricate*, as the late fifteenth-century poem about the replicated house at Walsingham reminds us: the patroness "called to her artyfycers full wyse,/ this chapell to forge as Our Lady dyd deuyse" (see section 18).[31] The forged is the constructed as opposed to the given, the natural. Skill in making was usually valued, but not always, as the theological discourse of idolatry reveals. In the fifteenth century the problem of the copied image is never far from the biblical discourse of idolatry, which offered the idol as a bad image, a "little image" (*eidolon*), a factitious product of merely human artistry and therefore an unreliable guide to divinity. The Christian defence of images was refined through a succession of battles with iconoclasm and through the looming examples of the two other monotheistic religions, one older and one younger, that held a far stricter line on this issue. Christians had to insist on the historical authenticity of at least some images. Images of Christ and the saints were linked to prototypical likenesses founded in encounters with the living personages.

The claim, originating in the iconoclastic controversy of the eighth century, that St. Luke doubled his function as evangelist by working as a visual artist, making images of the Virgin and of all the events of the Gospels, was an effort to put images on the same evangelical footing as the Gospels. Illustrated bibles could be understood to disseminate original sacred illustrations together with the sacred text. The result was a branching network of consistent iconographical formulae transmitted to an array of different media, from monumental to miniature scale. Substitution was the mechanism that explained how authentic information could be transmitted over vast stretches of time and through a succession of frangible physical vehicles. What transcription did for texts, substitution did for images and buildings. The maintenance of such fictions of legitimacy demanded the occasional purging of outlaws, illegitimate images that were considered to have dropped out of the substitution chain and thus were stripped of their authority. These were already forgeries, in effect, objects that masked their true, all-too-human production histories; mere fabrications with no link to an authoritative source: "gods made with hands are not gods" (Acts 19:26). Both the forgery and the idol are artifacts exposed as fabrications of a maker and in that sense raise the threat that *all* images are forgeries, that is, that images might not in the end be especially well suited to serve as reliable bearers of referential content.[32]

What is the difference between the copy of Rogier van der Weyden commissioned by Isabella of Castile and the copy of Raphael painted by Andrea del Sarto? The only difference is that in the latter case there was deception involved, false pretenses, and that is the criterion of forgery. Would the recipient Federico Gonzaga have cared if he had learned that he possessed only a copy, a replica identical to its model beyond the discriminating capacity of even the expert eye? Probably he would have cared, for there *was* a difference between the two; that is the point of the anecdote. Vasari and everyone else in Florence remembered well which one was the original: it was the relic of Raphael, the painting that he had made with his own hands. This was the moment when body relics of celebrated artists were first prized. A lock of hair was cut from the head of Albrecht Dürer, for instance, two days after his death. It was kept by his pupil Hans Baldung and indeed survives to this day.[33] In Greek and Roman antiquity no one ever thought to preserve a body relic of an artist.

A painting painted by a brush held by the hand of a celebrated artist—here the distinction between original and copy was clear. Most cases were not so clear. A concept of art forgery was slow to coalesce because not everyone agreed where in an image might be found the "art-like" qualities, the qualities that a proscription of forgery was supposedly protecting. A well-known example is the grievance against the printmaker Marcantonio Raimondi brought by Albrecht Dürer before the Venetian Signoria.[34] Marcantonio had published several engravings that closely imitated woodcuts by Dürer, even copying Dürer's monogram or signature, the famous nested A and D recognizable, since the publication of the *Apocalypse* woodcuts in 1498, to anyone in Europe interested in art. Dürer considered Marcantonio's works to be forgeries, that is, objects that pretended to a production history that was not their own, for the purpose of profit. Marcantonio was profiting not only from Dürer's artistic ideas, which he was able to reproduce with more than reasonable skill, but also from the allure of the monogram, which to some purchasers, at least, would have implied that the scenes had been engraved by Dürer's own hand and not merely invented by Dürer. Marcantonio, one imagines, argued that monograms on prints were understood as reference points for the invention of the forms and not for the execution. The Venetian Signoria probably felt that anyone who, like Dürer, staked his artistic reputation on a mechanically produced image such as a woodcut or an engraving, was running a risk and did not deserve much protection from the law. They delivered a Solomonic judgment, allowing Marcantonio to publish copies of Dürer's prints but preventing him from using Dürer's monogram. Marcantonio was liable insofar as he copied a form—Dürer's monogram—whose function, or one of whose functions, was to signify Dürer's control over the physical execution of the artifact. A monogram guaranteed the production process *after* the forms had been invented or stolen. The Signoria's understanding of the monogram was consistent with the function of ancient or medieval artists' signatures. Earlier artists who signed copies with their own names—Greek sculptors or fifteenth-century printmakers—were not attempting to deceive; they were simply claiming responsibility for the technical execution of *this* work.[35]

The earliest systematic treatment of art forgery was offered by the medallist Enea Vico in his treatise *Discorsi sopra le medaglie degli antichi* (1555). That the problem should have been identified clearly for the first time in the context of numismatics is not surprising given that there was a well-established and constant alertness about forgery in the realm of currency.[36] In order to take financial advantage from passing off coins made of debased metal rather than authentic bullion, the counterfeiter of currency had to reproduce effectively the visual appearance of coinage, including the portraits and the figurative reverses. Here the counterfeit coin pretended to bear a value-endowing relation to a central authority, the state. But in the context of antiquarian studies in the sixteenth century, the copied coin took on a second kind of value: now no longer as currency, for the institutions and regimes that had produced the original coins were no longer in existence, but as historical relics. Coin collecting was a well-established hobby. Thomas More owned 800 coins. He and other humanist scholars did not excavate these coins with their own hands. They received some as gifts, others they purchased from dealers. The historical coin was a special kind of relic that came in multiples. Just as it was for the engraving or the pilgrim's badge, membership in a class of identical replicas was part of the coin's identity.

But there was another reason that humanist scholars valued coins: they offered extremely reliable evidence that allowed one to put a face to history. As the Paduan scholar Niccolò Leonico Tomeo remarked in the letter discussed in section 20, coins were the best documents of the visual appearance of ancient personages since they combined the portrait with a clear identifying label in the form of an inscription.[37] Portraits of those ancient personages of great interest who never had coins struck with their likenesses on them—primarily the poets and philosophers—will, he laments, always remain somewhat dubious. It is noteworthy that in this letter, in which Leonico is considering purchasing a marble bust of Socrates, he is only interested in the authenticity of the referred likeness, and never once worries about the date of the object. The antiquarian preoccupation over true likenesses cropped up in the years around 1500, at the very moment that it had became an urgent concern in the realm of religious images.

In assembling a series, as collectors do, it can make a certain kind of sense to fabricate the missing items, for instance the numismatic portraits of the minor Roman emperors. Both Andrea Fulvio and Hans Burgkmair did it, as we saw. The artists learned to fill lacunae in the visual record of antiquity by sharpening the appearance of a worn ancient coin, by restrik-ing the old coin with a new die, by casting replicas of known coins in order to complete a series, or by inventing a completely new die; to name the various practices of forgery outlined by Enea Vico. What begin as a scholarly and creative exercise became a temptation for unscrupulous dealers. Vico added a section entitled "imitatori" to his chapter on frauds, and it is here that he listed the modern artists who counterfeited ancient dies. He was evidently not sure where to draw the line between fraudulent and normal artistic practice. Even later in the century, when the language of forgery was in common use, the scholar and archbishop Antonio Agustín identified Giovanni Cavino as one "who counterfeits the best surviving antique medals," and yet only to say with admiration, "they are done so well, that it is a great pleasure to look at them." His only objection is that occasionally Cavino does not forge *well enough*, making mistakes in the inscriptions and in the rendering of the objects depicted in the authentic coins.[38]

TWENTY-THREE

Forgery 2: Pastiche

The pastiche, the invention of a new work in a plausible past style, presupposes an advanced conception of the historicity of art. The creator of the pastiche studies a class of real historical works and grasps their essential style, as an abstraction.[1] The term pastiche is often used to designate a fanciful synthesis of styles, a hodgepodge of borrowed forms from diverse sources. A different sense of the term was introduced by Marcel Proust, who used to write stories in the manner of Balzac or Maupassant, as an exercise. In Proust's usage, the pasticheur is not combining the styles of different authors, but rather producing a story that Balzac did not actually write, but might have. This is the sense we are using here. When a sixteenth-century artist invented a nonexistent Roman coin that could pass stylistic muster in a humanist's collection, he was making a pastiche. So too was the successful twentieth-century art forger, such as Han van Meegeren, the inventor of Vermeers that deceived experts, and Elmyr de Hory, the ingenious fabricator of drawings by Matisse. In modern times the pastiche, the nonexistent but plausible work by the master, is the ambitious forger's best option, for there is no profit in simply copying an existing Vermeer.

The poet Phaedrus (ca. 15 BCE – 50 CE), in the prologue to book 5 of his *Fabulae*, a Latin versification of Aesop, makes a quip about profiteering artists. Phaedrus says that he refuses to pass off his work as Aesop's own, in the manner of those artists of his day who are not above affixing the signatures of Praxiteles, Mys, and Zeuxis to their works in order to increase their value:

> ut quidam artifices nostro faciunt saeculo,
> qui pretium operibus maius inveniunt novis
> si marmori adscripserunt Praxitelen suo,
> detrito Myn argento, tabulae Zeuxidem.
> adeo fucatae plus vetustati favet
> invidia mordax quam bonis praesentibus.

(Just as certain artists in our time manage to get higher prices for their new
works if they inscribe the name of Praxiteles on their marbles, Mys on their
worn down silver, and Zeuxis on their panels. So much greater is the favor
that biting envy bestows on tricked up antiquities than upon good modern
productions.)[2]

It is possible that the unscrupulous artists disparaged by Phaedrus could
count on buyers who knew the names of old artists but had no idea what
their works looked like. In that case it was necessary only to create false
signs of age and wear. Such buyers simply preferred an antiquity, if possible
in a semi-dilapidated state, to a modern work. But not all first-century
collectors were credulous. To deceive the experienced eye, the fake had to
look like an old work by Praxiteles or Zeuxis, and not just like an old work.
The signature alone would not do the trick, nor would the rubbed surface
of the silver. The artists described by Phaedrus may have been obliged to
mimic old styles, in other words, to fashion pastiches. The invention of a
new work in an old style is a sophisticated tactic. The imagined antiquity
is an artifact generated by an art-historical consciousness.

In the modern West, the inaugural and in some ways still the most
impressive exercises in pastiche were the medal portraits of Emperors
Heraclius and Constantine purchased by the Duke of Berry in 1401 and
1402 from Italian merchants together with portraits of Octavian and
Tiberius.[3] The reliefs the Duke purchased were gold and mounted in jew-
eled frames and no longer exist; he had copies made in gold; several further
copies of the Heraclius and Constantine medals in bronze survive, including the one reproduced here (figure 23.1). These were imagined antiquities, projections backward designed to fill a gap. With their outlandish
look, disguised citations of classical works, mysterious iconography, and
strange, antiquated lettering, they were learned and fanciful *jeux d'esprit*
devised by a scholar and a clever artist. No one at the time seems to have
questioned the antiquity of these medals. It is possible that some scholars
doubted their antiquity so thoroughly that they did not think it necessary
to make an issue of it. And yet they were still being discussed as antiquities
throughout the sixteenth century, even toward the end of the century, by
scholars as distinguished as Johann Cuspinian, Jacopo Strada, and Hubert
Goltzius. It seems likely that antiquarians did not know even how to begin
asking critical questions about the origins of such artifacts.

A tour de force of fifteenth-century sculpture was a bronze horse head,
a *protomo*, now in Naples, a gift of Lorenzo de' Medici to Count Diomedes
Carafa (figure 23.2).[4] The work closely resembles an antique bronze horse
head in Florence (Museo Archeologico) once in the Medici collection, a
work of the second century CE. The quattrocento work was not a replica,

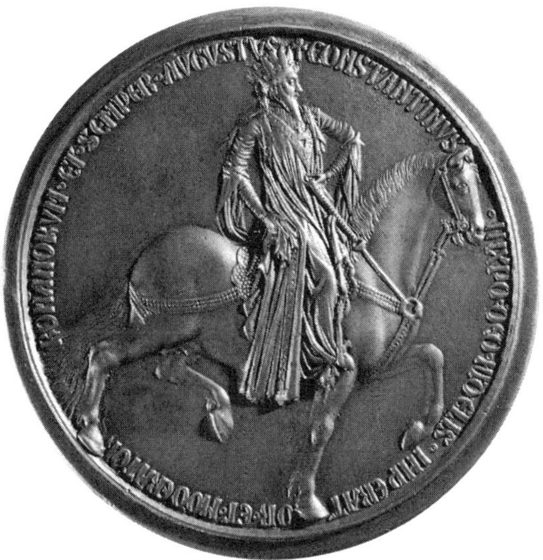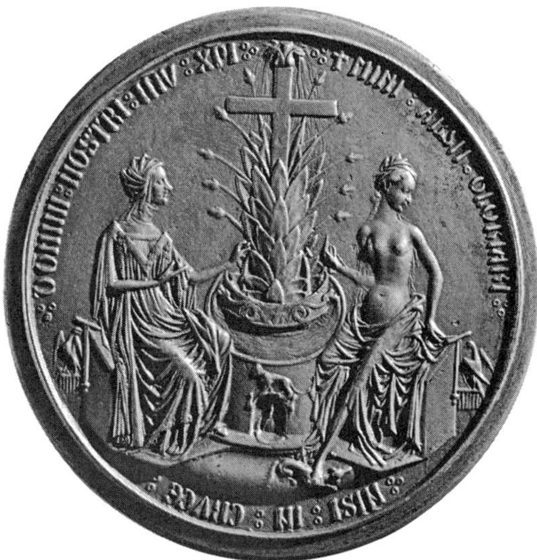

23.1 **A modern medal believed to be an antiquity into the seventeenth century.** Obverse: Emperor Constantine; Reverse: Two allegorical figures, possibly of Nature and Grace. Bronze medal, diameter 8.8 cm (Paris, ca. 1400). Vienna, Kunsthistorisches Museum. This is a copy of a medal portrait of Constantine sold by an Italian merchant to the Duke of Berry in 1402. Even today we are unsure who designed the images and where.

however, but an interpretation, twice as large as the original. Although the head in Naples was attributed early on to Donatello,[5] most modern scholars have not admitted it into his oeuvre. Vasari in 1550 believed that it could not be by Donatello, then in 1568 said that it was, but "so beautiful that many assume it is antique."[6] At the moment of the initial gift, at least, authorship seems not to have been an issue. A letter from the Count to Lorenzo of July 12, 1471, expressed gratitude and admiration for the gift of the horse's head without characterizing it either as an antiquity or a modern work.[7]

For Ulrich Pfisterer, the confusion about the horse head is a parable of Donatello's ability to confound a modern style-based criticism; as if Donatello in his relationship to antiquity had exceeded some hitherto unapproached threshold of nuance and intimacy.[8] Pfisterer's overall point is that Donatello was the first artist to propose, not in writings but through his works, a systematic coordination between artistic form and such constants as individual, place, or historical period. That coordination is no more or no less than what is meant today by the term "style." The individual artist has a style, the city or region has a style, the period has a style. The availability of the concept of style, or the relativity of form, entails the possibility of artistic choice. The work of art in the Renaissance detaches

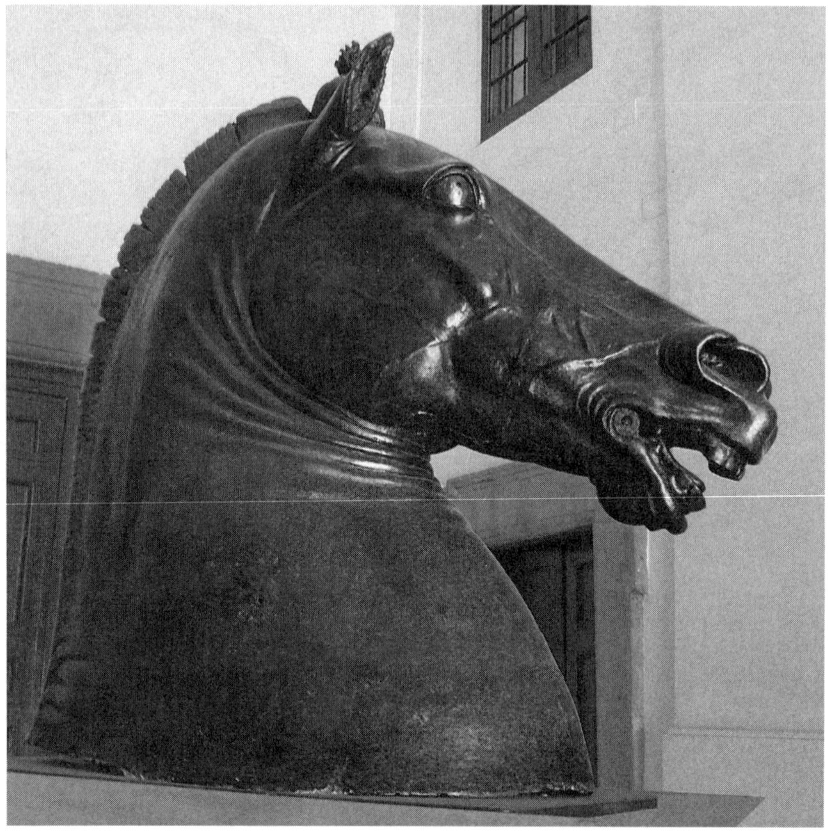

23.2 A modern work that was (and is) nearly indistinguishable from an antiquity. Donatello, *Horse Head*, bronze (ca. 1460). Naples, Museo Nazionale Archeologico. This mighty head was a gift from Lorenzo de' Medici to Count Diomedes Carafa in Naples. It emulates without precisely replicating ancient bronzes like one preserved today in the Archeological Museum in Florence.

itself from the moment of its making—achieves "anachronicity"—by citing historical works. The principle of the relativity of style permits the artwork to assume a transhistorical identity by simulating a historical identity that is not its own.

The slight swerve that Donatello introduced between the original horse head and his own copy was in fact consistent with ancient Roman practice. The possibility of variation between copy and original was built into the traditional substitution system. Few statues were as famous, and inspired as many copies, as Praxiteles's Cnidian Aphrodite, and yet the copies are so various that it is impossible to establish the appearance of the original. What was the difference between the second century CE and the fifteenth century? Perhaps nothing more than the intensive commentary and theorizing that enveloped Donatello's performances, as documented by Pfisterer, much of it soon extended, compounded, and archived on the printed page.

Again, one of the nurseries for the imitative skill and freedom of Donatello and his successors was the cult of old coins. Vasari said that Lorenzo Ghiberti delighted in "counterfeiting" (*contraffare*) the dies of ancient coins.[9] The implication is that the context for such exercises was basically ludic and creative. Ghiberti had no expectation of profiting other than perhaps to score a point against a cocky self-styled expert. Vasari uses the verb *contraffare* or *contrafare* primarily to speak of the artistic imitation of nature. On the occasions when he uses the word to speak of the imitation of art objects, there is no imputation of forgery but only admiration of the skill of the artist in imitating great models.[10]

Already the Shroud of Turin, the blood-stained cloth that once enfolded Christ's body, was a pastiche. This most impressive of fake relics is now securely dated by forensic tests to the fourteenth century. Whoever made it, perhaps challenged by the influx of Eastern panels with their claims to authenticity, hoped to trump the icons by manufacturing a really secure link back to the true origin. If Rome's Vera icon, the Sudarium of Veronica, was the double of the Byzantine Mandylion, then the Shroud of Turin in turn doubled the Sudarium. The ingenious forgers, whoever they were, may even have used blood as paint, justifying as true Sixtus IV's later comment that it had been "painted with Christ's blood." Skeptical clerics even at the time dismissed the shroud as a forgery. They were able to speak of forgery at all because they were treating the shroud as a relic and not as an image, as a painting.[11]

The true school for pastiches was the forgery of documents and epigraphic inscriptions, the many medieval charters, testaments, and tombstones that pretended to be much older then they were.[12] Here the forger had to imagine the linguistic text as it was supposedly composed, and the vehicle, parchment or stone, as it would look now.[13] These forgeries sometimes involved impressive imitations of obsolete handwritings or alphabets.[14] Pastiches of written documents are obviously problematic—in fact, they are criminal, because a document has no function *other* than to bear witness to an event or fact beyond itself. The pastiche in the realm of art, by contrast, poses no difficulties *unless* someone asks the artifact to be a document (evidence, relic, nonfungible trace of a singular event).

By the end of the fifteenth century, imitations of obsolete styles were becoming impressively convincing. In 1491 Pier Maria Serbaldi, working in Florence in the circle of Lorenzo de' Medici, put an intaglio gem of his own making into the hands of a dealer "to experiment if it could pass as antique" and so test the expertise of collectors. He claimed that his true clients were informed in advance, thus insuring that it was all a game.[15] The artifact was, in fact, identified by the dealer Giovanni Ciampolini as a modern gem, or if ancient at least recut. Another recipient, outside this tight circle of connoisseurs, might not have worried about these distinctions. The recutting of antique gems was, after all, standard practice and even today connoisseurs have no easy time assigning dates to this class of objects.[16] Around 1500, different parties applied different standards of authenticity. A forgery for one collector was an acceptable copy or restoration for another. On another occasion Ciampolini miscalculated when he sent a copy of a gem to Lorenzo de' Medici, perhaps hoping Lorenzo was in the latter category of collector. But Lorenzo, as the pranks of his artist Serbaldi suggest, was as interested in the distinction as Ciampolini. Interestingly, however, Lorenzo did not simply accuse Ciampolini of fraud, and to maintain good relations made sure his associate in Rome gave another explanation for his rejecting the gem. For Ciampolini's move was not necessarily fraudulent. As Lorenzo's agent in Rome put it, by way of defending Ciampolini's motives, "actually when something is good, even if it is modern, we should not let it go."[17] In fact, the Medici had profited by such a variance in criteria earlier in the century in the case of Donatello's horse head. They were not going to permit themselves to be fooled in the same way.

Marcantonio Michiel identified as a modern work a porphyry cup he saw in the collection of Francesco Zio, indeed attributed it to "Pietro Maria the cutter of gems, Florentine," the same Pier Maria Serbaldi mentioned above.[18] Sometime around 1495 the cup had been buried by Serbaldi and rediscovered as an antiquity. The analogy with the archeological ruses of Annius of Viterbo is striking: the unscrupulous and creative archeologist as well as the dealer stages decontextualization in order to fake a provenance. Forgery begins when works are unearthed and extracted, when they start to move. The hoax of the Heraclius and Constantine medals, if such it was, also depended on the involvement of Italian middlemen, dealers.

Also in the 1490s, Michelangelo simulated drawings of the old masters. Vasari said that he imitated the styles of the old masters (*maestri vecchi*) so effectively that no one could tell the difference between the copy and the original. Accuracy in imitation came with an awareness of the status of the drawings as relics: Vasari says of Michelangelo's copies that he "tinged them and aged them with smoke and various other means, making them look dirty so that they appeared old."[19] And yet these cannot be considered full-blown forgeries, for there are no indications that they were bought and sold under false pretenses. The market for drawings, especially for shop drawings as these probably were, was undeveloped at the time. Michelangelo could hardly have been counting on big profits in prospective sales. It appears that the artist made these documentary copies as a kind of *capriccio*, a bravura performance to impress fellow artists and admiring patrons. Vasari suggests that Michelangelo did it in order to keep the originals, but also says that the artist "acquired a great name" from his feats of imitation, suggesting that the trickery was meant from the start to be disclosed. Rather than exploiting an existing drawings market, Michelangelo's decision to copy the drawing not for its content but *as an artifact*, stains and all, contributed to the conceptual reframing of the drawing as a collectible antiquity, and so the creation of a completely new market.

Michelangelo's *Sleeping Cupid*, probably carved in 1496, reveals the other ingredients that went into the formation of the category of the art forgery. In this case, the work was not a copy of an existing ancient sculpture but, like the Constantine and Heraclius medals or Serbaldi's gem, a pastiche, although one fitting into an established iconographic type. In Vasari's 1568 recounting of the episode, which largely incorporates Condivi's 1553 account, Michelangelo made the statue simply in emulation of the antique. It became a forgery only through the machinations of Baldassare del Milanese (or, alternatively, Lorenzo di Pierfrancesco de' Medici), who saw the potential for profit and arranged to have the work buried, "distressed," and passed off as an antiquity to Cardinal Raffaelle Riario.[20] Within a few years the piece was snapped up by one of the great art collectors of the day, Isabella d'Este, and displayed henceforth as a famous work by Michelangelo. In fact, she set it alongside a Roman copy of a famous *Sleeping Cupid* by Praxiteles and so staged a mini-exhibition on the subject of copies and forgeries, modernity and antiquity.[21] The public conversion of Michelangelo's work, within the space of ten years, to the status of a forgery famous *as* a forgery helped consolidate the very notion of art forgery.

Forgery was a category that a work might move in and out of, depending on the claims made about it. Many bronzes and marbles, especially statuettes and busts and small-scale reliefs, emulated with brilliant skill the forms and subjects of Roman antiquity. Not all were produced with intent to deceive, or intent to profit from deception; but many were surely furnished with false labels.[22] The bronzes of Andrea Riccio, like the *all' antica* vases or statuary described in the engravings of Agostino Veneziano and Marcantonio Raimondi, could be described as virtual antiquities, even "honorary" antiquities.[23] Jörg Muscat's bust portrait of the emperor Probus (ruled 276–282), cast around 1510, was mistaken by scholars for an antiquity until 1933.[24] In her correspondence with the sculptor Pier Jacopo Alari Bonacolsi, known as Antico, both Isabella d'Este and the artist describe his copies after antiquities as "antichità"[25] However, on another occasion Isabella rejected certain bronzes, asking for her money back when she found they were modern.[26]

In the mechanical media, bronze, coin, and print, the play between transmission and creativity, between delivery of evidence and fabrication of evidence, was most subtle. The very content of Marcantonio Raimondi's engravings after the coins of the emperors, Madeleine Viljoen has shown, was their insistent slight variation from the models. Marcantonio framed one replicable medium (stamped or cast coin) inside another (copper engraving). He does not allow the beholder to decide whether his interpretations of the coins are failures as evidence, or successes as creative works.[27]

The refined relief portraits in marble of Roman emperors by Desiderio Settignano (Julius Caesar in the Louvre) or Mino da Fiesole (Marcus Aurelius) also hovered between the states of missing evidence and modern artwork.[28] The Venetian sculptor Tullio Lombardo, meanwhile, restored an ancient work known as the *Muse of Philiskos*, which he took to be a Cleopatra, by combining elements from various ancient styles: the round face and soft skin of classical Greek art, the incised pupils and iris from Roman art, the intense facial dramatism of the Hellenistic style. If this combination was willful—and not precisely the opposite, that is, the result of a lack of awareness of the difference between the styles—then this is a pastiche in the common sense of recombination of a variety of sources, a *pasticcio*.[29] A Venetian relief from the Este collection, now in the Kunsthistorisches Museum in Vienna, datable to about 1525–1535, quoted both an Attic relief and a pair of figures by Michelangelo, the David and the Christ of Santa Maria sopra Minerva; an art-historical puzzle for the cognoscenti, perhaps.[30]

In the mid- and late sixteenth century, market-driven art forgery was sufficiently conspicuous to attract commentary in writing. Authorship and age had become factors in every work's value. The dominant fables about art shifted from substitutional to performative. The physician and collector Giulio Mancini wrote a pamphlet describing the methods of fakers, including using old panels, and the Venetian painter and writer Marco Boschini warned against "smoked" paintings.[31] The imminent threat of forgery intensified the pleasurable rituals of art—the close looking, the drawing of fine distinctions—to the point where they ceased to be pleasurable. Sometimes it is hard to see where connoisseurship ended and surveillance began. The fabrication of historical evidence, meanwhile, had begun to meet with disapproval. Enea Vico may have admired the inventors of fictive ancient coins, but he also criticized them for giving historically unfounded titles to emperors and for suggesting inaccurate construction dates for the buildings they depicted on their reverses.[32] In contrast to Fulvio's printed gallery of 1517, which contained several fictive portraits, Jacopo Strada set a new standard in a publication of 1553 by leaving blank placeholders for portraits where no historical original was available.[33]

Certainly there had been art fraud in the Middle Ages. Pictures and sculptures were consumer goods like any others, subject to expectations and laws preserving commercial probity. Any commercial good can be faked. There will be fraud, involving concealment of true production histories and invention of false ones, as soon as there is value. A master agrees to paint the altarpiece with his own hands, but who will be watching when the work is actually executed? This is why there were contracts, hallmarks, and forms of expertise.[34] What changed in the fifteenth and sixteenth centuries? What was different—still is different—about modern art fraud is that a new factor was reckoned into the work's value: its place within a historical sequence of artistic performances. A modern bronze, even if identical in form and content to an ancient bronze, was now less valuable simply for having been fabricated later—for being dependent on prior works. When Riario rejected Michelangelo's *Sleeping Cupid* upon learning that it was not an antiquity but a modern work, his position was consistent with his principles. Vasari mocked him and other collectors for caring more about the "names" attached to works than about the "deeds" themselves.[35] If the work is beautiful, Vasari reasoned, why dismiss it merely because it is modern? Vasari was, however, subscribing to a normative, ahistorical conception of art, whereas the fastidious collector saw that art had a history. That collector wanted a real antiquity, not necessarily because it was more beautiful, but simply because it had been first.

The sixteenth-century theorists of poetry had another name for pastiche: *imitatio*, or the transformation of text into text. The literary text of the Renaissance was understood to be the altered double of a predecessor text. Acceptable doubling was literary creation itself; unacceptable doubling—duplicitous doubling—was plagiarism. Some fifteenth- and sixteenth-century writers, including Leon Battista Alberti, Pier Candido Decembrio, and Eobanus Hesse, explored the middle ground between doubling and duplicity by crafting pseudo-antique poems, dialogues, or letters.[36] Such hoaxes or exercises have proved to possess little enduring literary worth. Yet they share with the most ambitious poetic texts of the period both the desire to narrow the gap between the source text and its modern interpretation, and the desire to maintain that gap. The trivial pastiche and the mighty modern epic poem are just two modalities of the historical imagination. The distinction between them is one of degree not kind. Thomas M. Greene characterized such contentious struggles with subtexts as "dialectical imitations": "[w]hen it truly engages two eras or two civilizations at a profound level," the dialectical imitation involves a conflict between two *mundi significantes*. The text comes to terms most effectively with its own humanistic problematics, its own incompleteness, by measuring its own signifying habits with those of the subtext. The text is the locus of a struggle between two rhetorical or semiotic systems that are vulnerable to one another and whose conflict cannot easily be resolved. In this dialectic, I think, one reaches the heart of the mystery of acculturation and perhaps its key. Anachronism becomes a dynamic source of artistic power.[37]

In visual artifacts the enabling effects of anachronism would take different forms. The gap between the source and the modern imitation is on the one hand more evident, simply because images are material things and not so easily sewn together as texts are. On the other hand, confusions between the source and imitation were more common because visual artifacts, as we have seen, were by nature loosely anchored in history. The emphatic physical presence of the artifact made it difficult to place it historically. This double condition of remoteness and availability was compounded by the condition of fragmentariness, for the material artifact that surfaced into the present from the remote past was almost always incomplete: relic fragments, sculptures in pieces, buildings in ruins, and parcels of painting. The bust format of most icons, as we have seen, recapitulated the fundamental fact that the icons were relics, excerpts of a life-world that had somehow made it through to the present, permitting a face-to-face encounter with the past in the here and now. Leonard Barkan has explained how the discovery of fragmentary artifacts became an occasion for artistic fiction making in the fifteenth and sixteenth centuries, complicating and clouding the elegiac visions of the Renaissance poets, who had made a "lost" antiquity a tabula rasa on which to project their own poetic fictions. The surfacing of figural artifacts instead made antiquity palpably present, enacting something like a raising of the dead. The *Bed of Polycleitus* and the *Spinario*, enigmatic and antique works that cast a spell over generations of Renaissance artists and connoisseurs, became emblems of withdrawal and self-absorption, as Barkan has shown, in which an erotic undercurrent thematizes the viewer's engagement with intractable and ambiguous aesthetic experiences. These engagements unfolded on the near side of function, referentiality, narrative, and symbolization.[38]

The creative response to the problem of imitation, in artifacts as much as in texts, makes a virtue of indeterminacy, discovering an entire aesthetic project in the gap between source works and modern works. Still, that was only one aspect of the practice of imitation. Others attempted to repair the broken chain, to reinstate referentiality, to close the gap between source and imitation. And here we are once again in the realm of forgery and pastiche. The forgery of a document or an evidentiary image, like the forgery of an ancient work of art, will want to simulate the processes of aging and wear, at least if it hopes to convince. More puzzling and not so easy to account for is the pastiche that *does not bother* to invent fictive signs of aging. Such an artifact is a Netherlandish copy of the Cambrai Madonna (see figure 11.4); the bronze statue of Christ that appears in Carpaccio's historical painting (see figure 4.3); the bronze medal portrait of Christ (see figure 20.1); the marble relief of Christ by Tullio Lombardo (see figure 21.9); the neo-cosmatesque pavement of the Sistine Chapel (see figure 17.2); the round temple on the Gianicolo by Bramante (see figure 15.8). Such an artifact is temporally ambiguous. It will be apprehended differently by different recipients. A beholder who sees plainly that the artifact is new may yet trust in an invisible transmission process and so find in it some evidentiary value. Another beholder may be sufficiently indifferent to the transmission process to accept the pastiche as if it were a relic of a past moment. Both these beholders are still operating under the assumptions that artifacts are more or less interchangeable across time and that they can be relied upon to deliver packets of information across great spans. Still other beholders will see the artifacts as modern performances that merely remember the substitutional mechanisms that once governed the meanings of paintings, sculptures, and buildings. Still others, like Erasmus at Walsingham, will see the modern elements as clues that claims to venerability are spurious. All these objects were generated by the interaction of substitutional and performative models of artifact production. They constitute an elusive and apparently marginal class of objects. But these objects posed the question that this book has tried to answer. With their unstable temporality—they are brand new, and yet they make claims on antiquity—they have never been assimilable to ordinary art-historical narratives. And yet at the same time are they not completely familiar to us? For what is an artwork if not a forgery—an invention of a nonexistent form, fetched perhaps from the past, perhaps from the future—which does not take the trouble to conceal its own real origins in the present.[39]

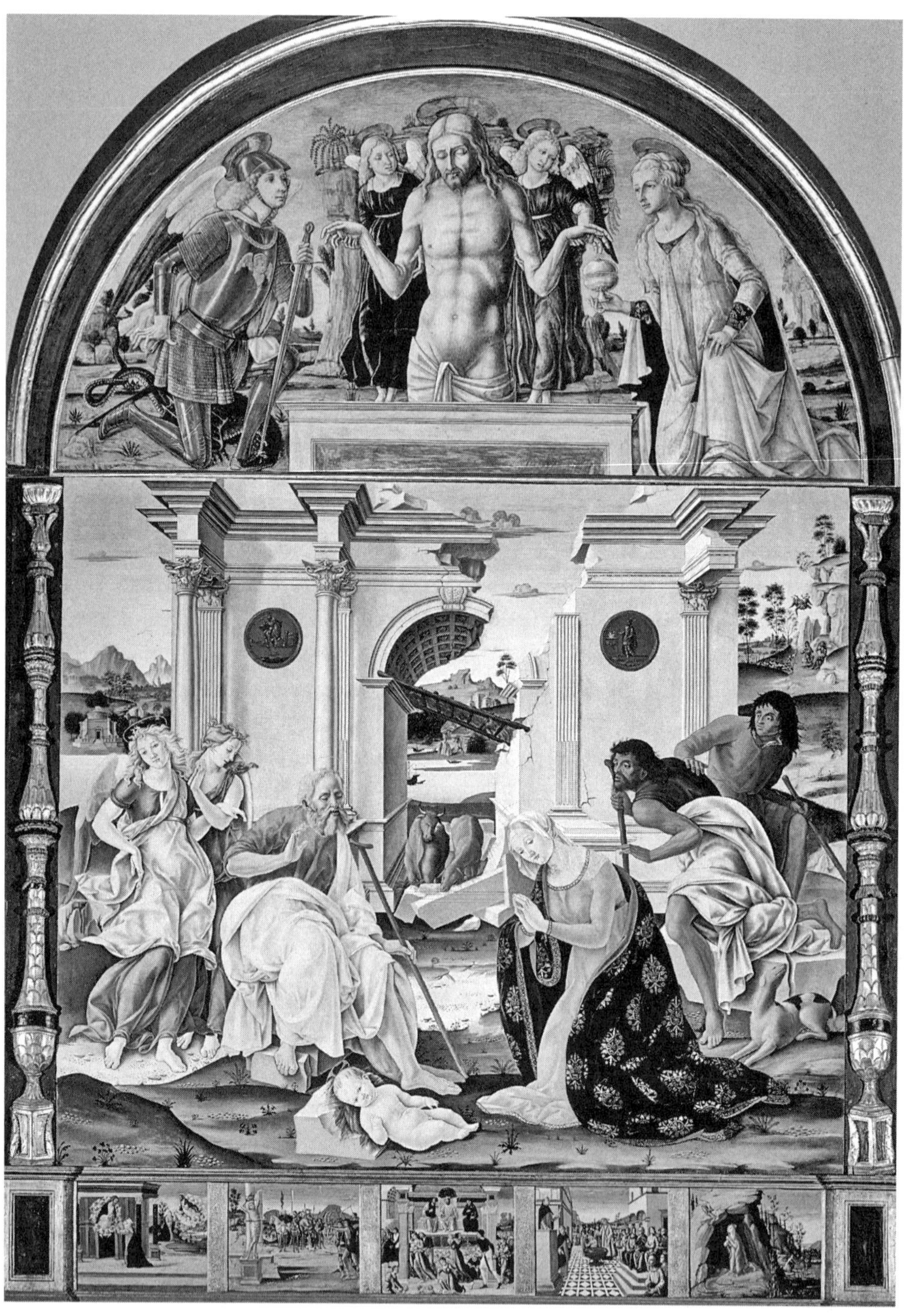

24.1 Historical time disrupted by eschatological time. Francesco di Giorgio Martini, *Nativity*, oil on panel, 239 x 209 cm (1490s). Siena, San Domenico. The imposing structures of pagan antiquity are threatened by the birth of a new king. According to the *Golden Legend*, the Temple of Peace in Rome collapsed on the night of Christ's birth. Here a triumphal arch is blown apart. Advanced architecture is brought low, and the history of architecture reverts to its beginnings in sheds, huts, and lean-tos.

TWENTY-FOUR

Anti-Architecture

In the *Nativity* altarpiece by the Sienese architect and painter Francesco di Giorgio Martini, datable to the 1490s, a triumphal arch in ruins looms over the Holy Family (figure 24.1).[1] The clean breaks in the masonry and the single, violent breach suggest that the building has been destroyed by a sudden blow. And yet there is a method to the destruction. On the left side of the arch the architecture remains intact; on the right side it is broken down, analyzed.[2] A pilaster with staved fluting is missing its capital. In front of it is an empty pedestal and further to the right a projecting entablature, each of them implying a missing column.

Triumphal arches translate a momentous event in time, usually a victory, into a processional shaping of space. They ensure the commemoration of the event by creating an artificial threshold, a passageway that repeats in ceremonial terms the movement from before to after. Occasionally they mark triumphs for which they were not intended. In Domenico Ghirlandaio's *Adoration of the Shepherds* in the Sassetti chapel in Florence, painted roughly ten years earlier than Francesco di Giorgio's altarpiece in Siena, the Magi pass through a triumphal arch in the background on their way to the Child, a new triumphal procession that spells the end of the civilization that built the arch. The overtaking of architecture by time is Francesco di Giorgio's theme as well. Painting steps out of the ranks of the cultic arts, momentarily, to reflect on the efforts of the other arts to manage time. In the Sienese panel, the triumphal arch, through a pair of fictive bronze medallions on its face, proclaims the time-conquering capacity of constructive civilization but also intelligently presages its own demise. The medallions represent, on the right, Mucius Scaevola, holding his hand in a flame in a demonstration of Roman valor, and on the left, Marcus Curtius, leaping mounted and in full armor into a chasm that had opened in the Roman Forum by an earthquake.[3] An oracle had promised that the chasm would not close until it had swallowed that which was most valuable to Rome. The martyr Marcus Curtius reasoned, successfully, that nothing was more valuable to Rome than its valorous citizens. This arch, therefore, commemorates no event in particular. Rather, by pairing the two heroes it offers a more general celebration of the acts of self-sacrifice that helped build the greatness of Rome, whose index is the magnificence of the arch itself. Francesco di Giorgio's arch stands for the general category of the triumphal arch, epitomizing the symbolic work done by such monuments, namely the redemption of blood and destruction through the achievements of civilization.

But now, in the painting, a higher power literalizes and extends the arch's message about destruction, with ironic and devastating effects. Celebrating the idea of the momentous event as passageway, it has blasted open the opening; honoring the call to sacrifice, it has cut the structure itself down. In its cloven state the arch is now truly a symbol of a break in history, an eloquent anti-monument, a mockery of the efforts of high civilization to maintain symbolic control over history. In the foreground a fragment of the cornice, a crowning element of the arch, has been thrown to the ground, where, humbled and upended, it serves as support for the softly resting Christ Child. We can almost follow the block's trajectory from the breach in the architecture to the place where it now lies. In direct line with the opening in the archway, the child looks out at us guilelessly but knowingly, as if to signal that *he* is the meteor that has broken through this proud monument on the way to earth.

A story reported in the widely-read thirteenth-century hagiographical compendium *Golden Legend* recounts that at the founding of the Temple of Peace in Rome the Oracle of Apollo declared that the building would stand until a virgin should conceive a child, a pronouncement taken by all as a guarantee of the building's eternal life.[4] The Temple of Peace was the traditional but erroneous name for the Basilica of Maxentius on the Roman Forum. Upon Christ's birth, inevitably, the building came crumbling to the ground. Christian artists adapted this story in various ways, expanding the reference to embrace the ruination of Roman buildings of all kinds.[5]

Scenes of the Nativity reveal a history of architecture under pressurized conditions. In representing the legend of the Temple of Peace they telescope the normal process of decay into a moment at Christ's birth; when they allude more generally to the ruins of pagan civilization they present the spectacle emblematically, as a charged symbol of the workings of secular time viewed, as it were, from the outside. On earth, buildings undergo ruin and destruction and then are built up again, only to undergo further destruction. In biblical tradition, a principle of anti-architecture is assigned a role, an agency as an equal and necessary counterpart to architecture, at least until secular time is superseded in the heavenly Jerusalem, where there is no physical temple (Revelation 21:22, "I did not see a temple in the city, because the Lord God Almighty and the Lamb are its temple"). Babylon's opulence is destroyed at the end of the world (Revelation 18), but already within the biblical narrative its earlier version, Babel, was disrupted in mid-construction by God. After that, Sodom and Gomorrah were destroyed by fire and brimstone raining from heaven (Genesis 19:23–26 and Luke 17:28), from which point onward the righteous lived in tents, with no permanent dwelling even for their God.[6]

Ruins represent time, but it proved easier to see this when the ruins were inserted into fictions, for example, into paintings (or later, in the eighteenth century, into fictive landscapes in real space — gardens). The painter of the ruined building in the late fifteenth century was the colleague of the sophisticated forger, for like the forger he fashioned a non-existing artifact in a plausible historical style, and then artificially aged it.

In fifteenth-century paintings of the Nativity and Adoration the process of architectural substitution, the succession of buildings, was submitted to analysis through self-reflexive representation. These scenes focus on a crucial juncture in the secular cycle, one that points to the real possibility of a total breakdown of substitution. Advanced architecture has been laid low, and the history of architecture is cycled back to its beginnings in sheds, huts, and lean-tos — essays in provisional, archaic wooden building of the kind described by Vitruvius in his disquisition on the origins of architecture in book 2 of *De architectura*. The clock is stopped and restarted. The Nativity shed is the reverse image of the hut of Romulus (see section 6): not surrounded by the masonry that has superseded it but propped on the castigated ruins of a whole era's worth of stone architecture. The pictures ask: Will the process begin again, or has the occasion for substitution been missed?

Francesco di Giorgio's painting stages the contrast in the starkest terms. The beautiful coffered barrel vault, now blasted, has been replaced by a thatched lean-to, the most primitive form of architecture of all. On one side the wooden lattice is propped on an intact cornice and on the other it is fitted into a fresh crack in the architecture, a tilted, makeshift arrangement that clashes with the ordered symmetry of the stone structure. The lean-to is the image of pure functionality, a shelter whose slant, though here an adaptation to circumstance, is the angle that repels the elements. It is architecture stripped of its representational dimension. The triumphal arch is the opposite, an exclusively symbolic building, almost a capriccio. The two poles, function and fiction, bring out in the starkest terms a contrast that was growing more acute in the arena of visual art in these years. The contrast is not far from those staged in the monument of 1490 showing the great inventor Giotto at work on the unauthored Face of Christ (see

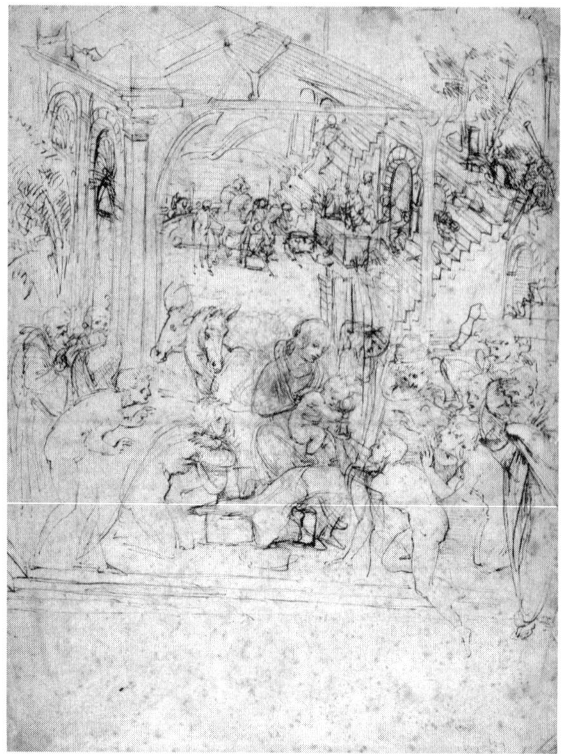

24.2–24.3 Vitrivius in reverse. Leonardo da Vinci, *Adoration of the Magi*, pen and ink over leadpoint, 28.4 x 21.3 cm (ca. 1482). Paris, Musée du Louvre. Sandro Botticelli, *Adoration of the Magi*, oil on panel, 70 x 104.2 cm (ca. 1480). Washington, National Gallery of Art. In these two almost contemporary renditions of the theme, architectural history is thrown suddenly into reverse. If the ancient architectural theorist Vitruvius described a progression from wooden architecture to stone architecture, here wooden architecture reappears in an architectural emergency. The wooden architecture, rudimentary in Leonardo and more substantial in Botticelli, relies on what remains of the stone constructions and at the same time changes their forms, or rather returns them to more primitive gabled structures.

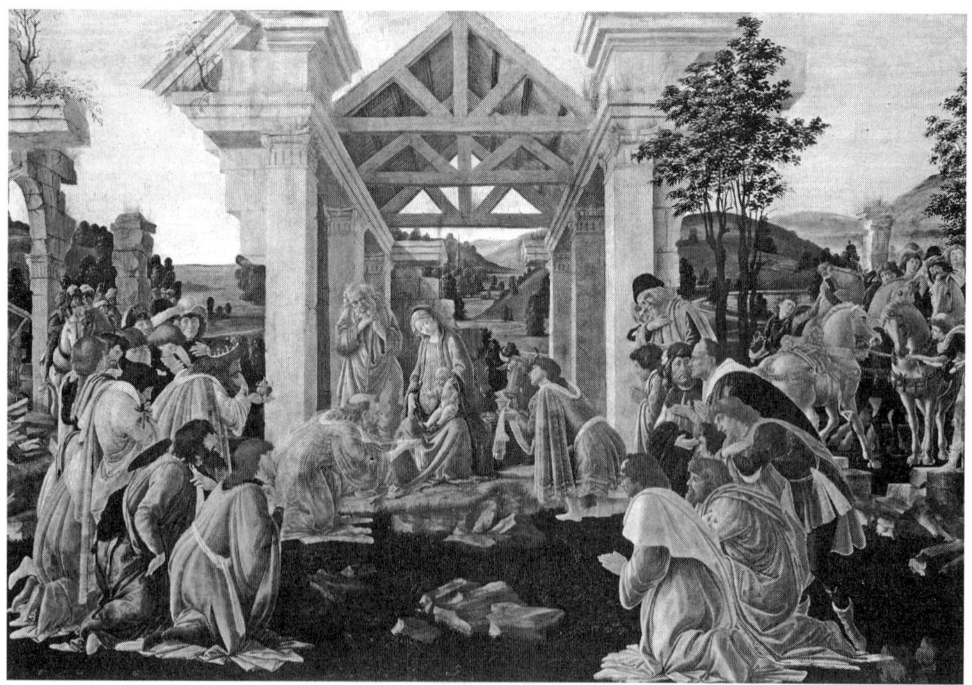

section 12) and in the painting by Botticelli showing the youth holding the icon roundel (see section 11).

Earlier, Leonardo da Vinci had imagined a more consonant relationship between stone and wood architecture. In a drawing for his *Adoration of the Magi*, the wooden shed picks up where the destroyed architecture leaves off, completing the building more or less as it was, but now in primitive form: the corner pilaster on the left finds its response in the Y-shaped tree trunk on the right, and the interrupted cornice is continued by a rough cross beam (figure 24.2).[7] We thus see a paradoxical reversal of the normal sequence from wood to stone, which the drawing manages by presenting the wooden elements almost as if they were the skeleton of the stone architecture, now again revealed. In Botticelli's *Adoration of the Magi* in Washington we see a similar process of reverse engineering (figure 24.3).[8] In showing a Doric temple in ruins, Botticelli appears to be illustrating, in reverse, the translation from wooden to stone architecture in Doric structures described by Vitruvius (4.2.1–6): his shed is complete with Vitruvian rafters (*cantherii*), tie beams (*transtra*), joists (*tigna*), and braces (*capreoli*). It is as if the primitive wooden architecture, a makeshift structure meant to compensate for the loss of the stone, has been caught up in a process of automatic regeneration; as if it were the incipient form of a future stone architecture that will return to the shape it once had.

In other cases, the disruption is more radical and the wooden architecture seems to go awry, turning away from the course of earthly architecture altogether. In Sodoma's *Adoration of the Magi* in Sant'Agostino in Siena, for example, the broken stone arches are dripping with vegetation and the provisional wooden beams reach for two standing, living trees (figure 24.4).[9] It is not clear whether this is architecture starting over again in natural forms, or simply architecture returning to nature. In Domenico Beccafumi's *Nativity* in the church of San Martino in Siena, stone architecture is left behind, moldering in the darkness and overgrown by vegetation (figure 24.5).[10] One of the columns has, in fact, been replaced by a twisting tree, a dissonant reversal of the normal evolution from tree to column.[11] From the cornice fragile lattices are impossibly cantilevered into the air in two directions, and then remain suspended amidst the angels. Bringing to life a metaphor used in the figural decoration of Byzantine domes, the angels come together to form an oculus—a perfect architecture, animated and ethereal. The circle of this angelic oculus is absolute, without perspective; it is pure light, in contrast to the dark, heavy, earthly architecture below. Primitive, provisional architecture leads away from false permanence altogether, offering an improbable bridge to an eternal, immaterial architecture.

As Joseph Rykwert has shown, the myth of the primitive hut recurs as

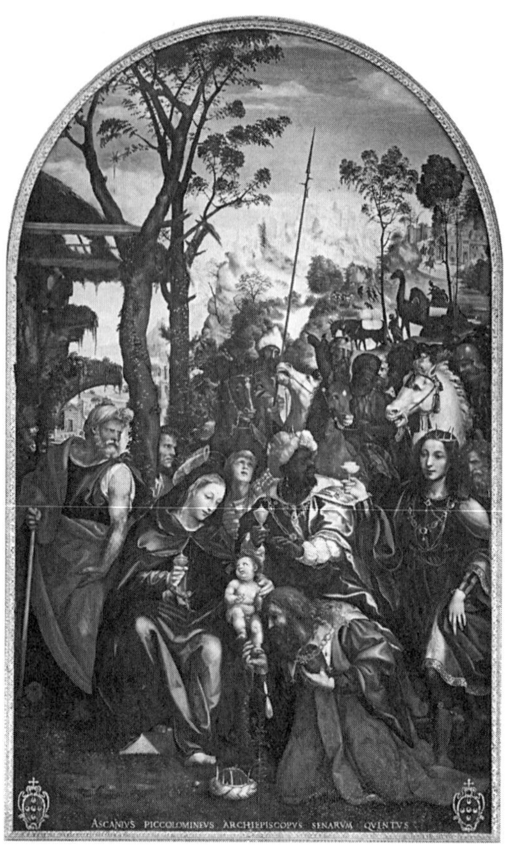

24.4 Nature as architectural crutch. Sodoma, *Adoration of the Magi*, oil on panel, 206 x 328.7 cm (ca. 1530). Siena, Sant' Agostino. Two standing living trees, presumably less old than the stone building now moldering in ruins next to them, fortuitously provide well-placed support for a highly makeshift wooden structure extending from the broken stone remains. Is this the end or the beginning (once again) of architecture?

a persistent preoccupation and point of reference throughout the history of architecture, a preoccupation that intensifies at times of architectural renewal.[12] The hut is installed in the imaginary of any advanced culture of building. The Roman priests continually rebuilt the primitive house of Romulus throughout imperial times as a reminder of the humble origins of the city and the empire (see section 6). Vitruvius points to the Romulus hut in the midst of an ethnographic excursus on primitive architecture in barbarian lands: "Likewise, on the Capitol the house of Romulus shows us—and calls to mind—the ancient ways; so do the wattle houses in the Citadel precinct."[13] Roman writers were well aware that beneath the archeological skin of their grand buildings were the ghosts of thatched

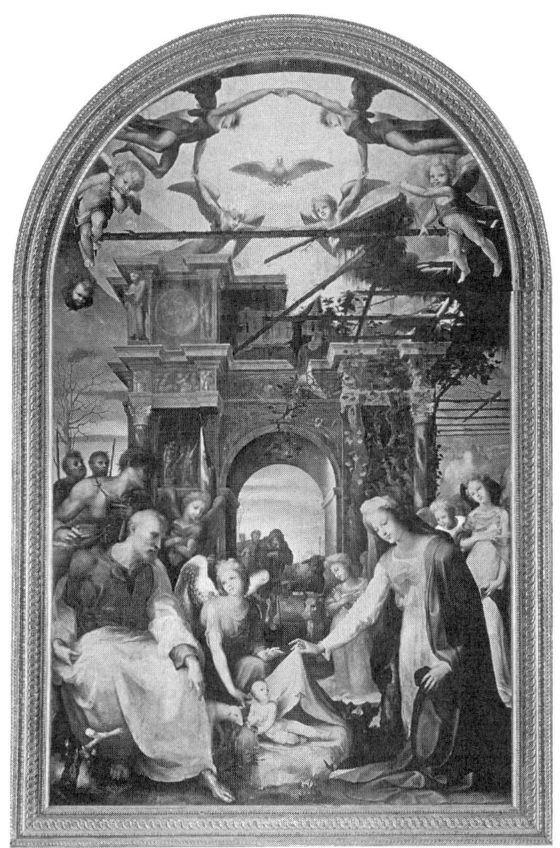

24.5 The sublimation of architecture. Domenico Beccafumi, *Nativity*, oil on panel, 390 x 235 cm (ca. 1522). Siena, San Martino. The history of architecture runs backwards: the proud triumphal arch is in ruins and one of the columns has been replaced by the trunk of a tree, normally the organic precursor for the architectural column. Below, the Virgin lifts a cloth both to reveal and to protect the Christ child, as if rediscovering the first form of the baldachin-tent; or is she offering the New Testament fulfillment of the Old Testament figure of the Tabernacle in the desert? Above, a provisional architecture becomes increasingly implausible until it is released from earthly contingency in an oculus composed of angels, a form seen both in perspective and in geometrically absolute terms as a circle.

huts: "Where you now see bronze, you would once have seen thatch, and walls plaited with the tough willow," says Ovid of the Temple of Vesta in the Forum (*Fasti* 6.691). In the Judeo-Christian tradition, the passage from wood to stone, from impermanent to permanent architecture, was directly invoked in the history of the temple in Jerusalem, which stabilized in durable materials the Tabernacle in the Desert.

In fifteenth-century Europe the primitive hut, the degree zero of architecture, became a focus of pictorial representation as never before, and these projections fed back into architectural practice. The wrinkled temporality of the Nativity scenes, with archaic sheds sprouting out of advanced architecture, is a dream-like, anachronic configuration. The primitive hut and the grand architecture of the ancients do not simply occupy two distant moments on a timeline; they are mutually necessary fantasies, knitted together repeatedly in the projections of Renaissance art and architecture. This work of projection was bound up with the reconstruction of the architecture of antiquity, which became a collective scholarly enterprise in the fifteenth century, an effort motivated by the dream of seeing the ancient Roman buildings rise again from their ruins in their "perfect" form. In the fifteenth century a consuming interest in Vitruvius arose among a new class of author architects and architectural cognoscenti who read the treatise as a guide for reconstructing ancient architecture but found themselves stranded between, on the one hand, the elliptical and in part incomprehensible text and, on the other, the fragmentary material evidence. The response was a recursive process of projective reconstruction: readers turned from the garbled ruins to the text, which in turn prompted reconstructive visualizations of the ruins that might serve as illustrations of the text. Francesco di Giorgio, the painter of the Nativity in San Domenico, described his own heroic efforts to match "nomi et vocabuli" with "antiche vestigie": "making a concord between sign and signified (*el signo cum il significato concordando*), in such a way that it is almost like discovering [architecture] anew, and not with little effort...."[14] The architecture that was discovered anew out of this process was, needless to say, in significant ways different from ancient architecture, and not primarily because mistakes in the reading of Vitruvius continued to be made right through the sixteenth century. It was rather that the procedures of mediation, through text and image, produced a different conception of architecture, more systematized and also more virtual. The classic instance of what Francesco di Giorgio would have called "architecture discovered anew" was the definition and prescriptive visualization of the orders with a rigor and systematicity far beyond what could be seen in ancient theory or architectural practice.[15]

The Nativity scenes thematize the problems posed by the process of projective reconstruction. The architecture shown in ruins, subject to divine castigation, is the architecture most admired by the artists who painted them and by the discerning viewers to which they were addressed. It was the architecture they most wanted to see built.[16] It is easy enough now to see that in fact this architecture is not very classical at all. Francesco di Giorgio's arch has an insubstantial attic, much lower than those on the arches of Constantine and Septimius Severus, and it carries no inscriptions. To say that the paintings show ancient architecture in ruins is misleading, for it is the artists' own fantasies of ancient architecture that are shown as having been destroyed. As soon as the reconstruction fantasy is produced it undergoes a dismantling. The process of construction and destruction that occurred in historical time is here, on the virtual level, rehearsed with no time lapse at all. These images are therefore emblems of the fantasy: they show fragments combined into fragile compositions that then undergo quick dismantling and supersession. The idea that the ancient building was ruined not by slow disintegration but by a sudden blow is a projection onto the historical register of this logic of accelerated repetition on the imaginary register.

The engraving by the Milanese goldsmith Bernardo Prevedari, dated 1481, reproduces a drawing by the architect Donato Bramante, as we are informed by an inscription at the base of the candelabrum at its center (figure 24.6).[17] At that date Bramante had still built very little. It is a prospective visualization of architecture that is extraordinary for the period and yet indicative of a widespread shift in architectural practice: from now on the work of architecture was not only a matter of technical know-how but of an architectural vision elaborated by an architect-author in an arena of two-dimensional projections. The "ancient" temple shown here is actually an amalgam of elements from medieval Christian architecture, according to a well-established pattern of anachronic thinking: the plan is based on Byzantine quincunx types and their adaptations in Romanesque architecture.[18] The high plinths and overall spatial unity recall hall churches, such as San Fortunato in Todi, which Bramante had studied before arriving in Milan. The basket capitals, alluding to the legend of the origins of the Corinthian style as recounted by Vitruvius (4.1.9), are based directly on those of the ninth-century ciborium in Sant' Ambrogio in Milan.[19] The temporal instability extends to the architecture's surface appearance, which gives the impression of being simultaneously ancient and new, ruinous and yet proleptic, model-like. The building is evidently in a state of advanced disrepair, with archways fallen, a hole in the vaulting, and plants growing from the exposed masonry—the keystone in the archway to the right is slightly dislodged, as if with one move the structure could come right down—and yet the dismantling looks willed, diagrammatic. It is like the planned destruction in Francesco di Giorgio's painting: a negative moment that thematizes rather than interferes with the projection of an ideal, prospective architecture. The evident fragility of the structure seems conceptual rather than historical, a self-referential marker of the house-of-cards quality of the fantasy itself.[20]

The draughtsman has reconstructed a pagan temple on the basis of the design of medieval churches. That temple is then shown having been

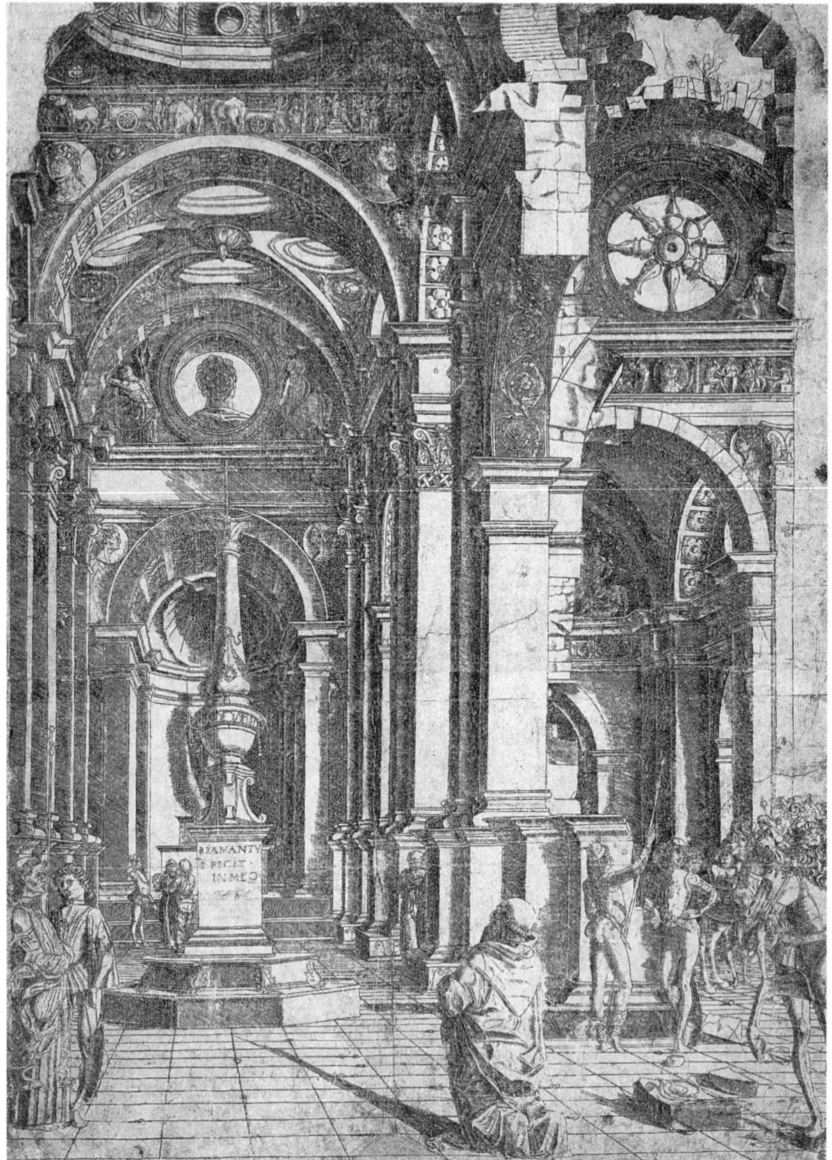

24.6 Plural architectural time. Bernardo Prevedari, after Donato Bramante, *Interior of a Ruined Temple*, engraving, 70 x 51 cm (1481). London, British Museum. The print records a fantastical synthesis of architectural ideas, a lamination of ancient, modern, and medieval form. The scene is enigmatic: a church seems to have been established among the ruins of a pagan temple.

baptized as a church. The print's "subject matter," which is at least at one level the Christianization of a pagan world that has fallen into ruins, provides a historical context for the building's formal instability. The anachronic reverse-engineering that the artist performed in arriving at the form of the fictional building is recapitulated—"remembered," as it were—on the level of content. In the niche in the background, a colossal statue—evidently still standing but at the same time occluded, rendered invisible—casts a shadow, and throughout there are Roman busts and elements of pagan iconography, such as centaurs, nudes, and processions. The only Christian sign amidst this exuberant paganism is an exiguous cross, placed on top of the candelabrum on the central axis of the perspectival construction, perhaps an allusion to the crosses that Constantine erected on columns in the place of statues throughout the Roman empire.[21] A monk has fallen to his knees before the column, his long shadow sharply pointing to it as the centerpiece of the image and the building. To the left a prelate is seen in profile, looking across at soldiers on horseback who are making a boisterous entry into the church/temple from the other side. Christianity arrives as something contingent, actual, and recent. The thin cross on the column is as yet the only sign of the Christianization of the space, its slightness pointedly raising the question of how much is required to transform the identity of a building. The monk responds to the cross's efficacy as if he had become the instrument of a cosmic magnetism. He seems suddenly struck, his needle-like shadow directed to this new focus like the shadow of a sundial.[22] The cross in the Prevedari print relabels and so "fulfills" the pagan building, invoking a figural or typological conception of architectural history: the pagan temple as the shadow-like type that is realized, made substantial, by its antitype, the Christian church. The mending of the broken arches and vaults in the print, such a theory implies, will restore the temple's true identity, an identity that had been locked inside it all along. The typological version of architectural history is perhaps the most theorized application of the substitution model. In that version, the links in the building chain succeed and repeat one another without visible difference; instead it is the label, the dedication, the tiny cross mounted on the column, that makes the difference.

Christian builders were ambivalent about this model. On the one hand, the idea that Christian temples were destined to succeed pagan temples was reassuring. On the other hand, a proto-anthropological perspective that envisioned an endless succession of regimes threatened to relativize Christianity as just another mode of belief. The substitutional chain is a version of history that cedes terrific power to labels. Christian church building was not necessarily prepared to subscribe to such a relativizing model of historical change. As a matter of fact, few early Christian churches literally occupied pagan temples, even in Rome. In the very earliest Christian times, such an occupation was obviously not even an option.

But even after Constantine, it was an opportunity seldom seized.[23] The late medieval Florentine myth of the origins of the Baptistery in a Temple of Mars sketched a scenario not only false but also unrealistic.

Spoliation in the early medieval churches may have referred to the idea of Christianity's typological fulfillment of the past. Yet in practice the spolium rhetorically interferes with the model of a smooth succession of regimes, of human history as a mere matter of strategic relabelings, for the spolium disrupts the invisible, mechanical operations of architectural history. Spoliation, the repurposing and sometimes deliberate framing of reused material, is an authorial intervention. It fends off doubt that the pagan temple is still somehow active within the church, even after reconsecration. The author of the spolium leaves a trace of a performance fixed in time and in this way symbolizes the singularity and irreversibility of Christianity. Medieval spoliation was often associated with strong authors ("founders"): Constantine, Charlemagne, Otto the Great (see section 16). The visible spolium asserts that it is the author, not the blind system, that permits the historical building to become what it was meant to be. The author may even decide that the predecessor building was meant to be destroyed, without afterlife. The two models of building history, substitutional and performative, were compared again in the fifteenth century, this time on the public stage provided by prints and altarpieces, which were discovering their capacity to gloss with ever-increasing narrative and symbolic eloquence the intertwined histories of cultic art and architecture.

TWENTY-FIVE

The Primitive Hut

Amidst the Ruins of St. Peter's

At the end of the fifteenth century, the primitive hut made a forceful reentry into the architectural imaginary. Just as in the late republican period of Rome, the hut resurfaced at a time of new and energetic building activity. The hut was reproposed in order to stabilize the idea of an origin point and to reaffirm that the new constructions, despite their apparent novelty, retained ancient identities. The hut was an ambivalent sign. On the one hand, it reassuringly preserved continuity across apparent difference. On the other hand, the hut in its artlessness expressed diffidence about progress. The hut measured out the gap between the simplicity of the past and the complexity of the present. The hut had the power to expose the most splendid modern buildings as nothing more than exhibitions of Babel-like hubris.

At Loreto, as we saw, the primitive hut was stabilized as a relic only in the context of the reconstruction of the basilica at the beginning of the sixteenth century. The solution at Loreto produced new definitions in both directions: the preserved building became a relic when it was sheathed by Bramante and Sansovino, set off as a cult object, within a framing architecture; the architecture, meanwhile, was defined as something new, designed, *authored*, against the foil of the relic—for better or for worse. Bramante's intervention at Loreto, in this sense, was a rehearsal for the protracted, agonized building campaign at St. Peter's in Rome, where the contention between relic-function and substitution-function was put on stage for the whole world to see.

Any rebuilding project might provoke expressions of concern about continuity and the maintenance of traditions, but the rebuilding of St. Peter's was from the beginning a most spectacular controversy. No project focused anxieties about rebuilding more intensively than this one, and none provoked more articulate debate about the nature and process of substitution. The humanist Paolo Cortesi, in his *De Cardinalatu* of 1510, reported widespread and sharp resistance to the reconstruction.[1] In 1511 the papal master of ceremonies Paris de Grassis noted how Julius II contemplated the "ruins and buildings that had been destroyed by his architect Bramante, called Ruinante because of the ruins and destructions he perpetrated both in Rome and elsewhere."[2] In the comedy *Scimmia* of 1517 Andrea Guarna has St. Peter refuse Bramante entrance to heaven for having destroyed his church, although he leaves open the possibility of eventual admission upon the completion of the new church.[3] Some scholars, indeed, maintain that Julius II had not planned total destruction of the old basilica when he began the demolition of the choir area of the old structure.[4]

The most important part of the ancient basilica, the part that could not be moved or changed, was the tomb of Peter and the altar over it. These, together with the ancient apse, now stood at the core of the new building, in the center of the crossing, surrounded by the massive new piers but as yet without any vaulting over them. One of the very first architectural interventions made by Leo X after being elected Pope in March 1513 was to provide a sort of house for the altar of Peter, a perimeter designed to allow papal masses to continue to be performed there. Described in the documents as a *tegurio*, it was Bramante's last work, built in less than a year in cheap peperino stone.[5] This small Doric arcaded structure, three bays wide and one bay deep (originally without a roof!), was put up between the destruction of the old building and the completion of the new, and expressed a phase in which the building was preserving the building's identity as it moved from one phase of its material history to another. During the many decades that it stood, the enclosure produced by the conjunction of the new *tegurio* in front and the ancient and crumbling apse behind became the capsule where the basilica's ritual life continued uninterrupted. It was the Noah's Ark of the basilica's identity during difficult times.

Like the sheath Bramante designed to house the Holy House of Loreto, or his Tempietto on the Gianicolo, the *tegurio* at St. Peter's has an intermediary status, hovering between full-scale architecture and microarchitecture. It is at once real architecture and an image of architecture. The *tegurio* functioned both as a model of the new architecture going up and at the same time as a stand-in for what was being replaced. William Tronzo has observed that the *tegurio* remembered the pergola-choir screen that projected out in front of the apse in the old basilica, specifically in the form given to it by Pope Gregory the Great in the sixth century, the form in which it had survived until the fifteenth century.[6] These altar enclosures are a signal instance of architecture in a state of shifting identity. Like a baldachin, they translate the idea of the sacred tent, the prototypical desert tabernacle. Even when translated into stone such structures hover under the register of full-scale architecture. In its metaphorically susceptible state, the *tegurio* functions as a place of communication between the ample and advanced architecture of the current church and its primitive and sacred origins, figuring that relationship as one between container and contained. It is the memory of the Tabernacle in the Desert within the magnificent Temple.

Bramante's *tegurio* took over the function of the ancient pergola, but now its references coalesced around the idea of the hut. The word *tegurio* is a direct adaptation of the Latin word for hut, *tugurium*, the very word Vitruvius used when speaking of primitive huts in his famous passage on the origins of architecture.[7] Between the destruction of the old basilica and the completion of the new basilica, the church returns to the degree zero, figured by this *tegurio* in "primitive" Doric. In 1526 the tegurio received a pitched wooden roof, described in the documents as a "tecto rustico," and so literally came to resemble a hut. In that form it was drawn repeatedly by Maarten van Heemskerck in the 1530s. One sheet depicts the *tegurio* from the nave, the principal view with its three bays (figure 25.1).[8] Another shows the structure from the side, revealing its one-bay depth (figure 25.2).[9] Heemskerck's renderings of the gabled structure amidst the fragmentary masses of the new basilica resemble the shed amidst ruins seen in the scenes of the Nativity discussed in the previous section. In the wake of the Sack of Rome, especially, the sardonic parallel between the great building under construction and the great building in ruins would have been all too easy to draw.

The whole complex of associations was visualized in diagrammatic form already by Raphael in the years immediately after the *tegurio* was built. A drawing by Gian Francesco Penni of the 1520s, based on a Raphael design, shows a Nativity scene with the Holy Family assembled with the shepherds under a stable shed (figure 25.3).[10] But in this Nativity the shed is not built or propped on ruins. In fact, there are no ruins anywhere in sight. Instead, the design assembles three pristine exhibits, pages from an encapsulated history of architecture. In the center is the shed, a humble structure but endowed with a basic correctness, its upright elements exactly the height of a man. To the right of the shed is a Doric structure made out of wood, a step beyond the hut but still a step short of architecture in stone. Rising behind to the left is full-blown advanced architecture in stone with arches, projecting entablatures, and disengaged Corinthian columns. This grand structure has been associated with the new St. Peter's, a proposition that remains uncertain given the unsettled state of the designs themselves at this stage.[11] In fact, it looks more like what remained then of the Basilica of Maxentius. Perhaps it is a projective amalgam of the two.

What has not been noticed is that the Doric structure in this drawing—the "middle" building, standing between the grand marble architecture

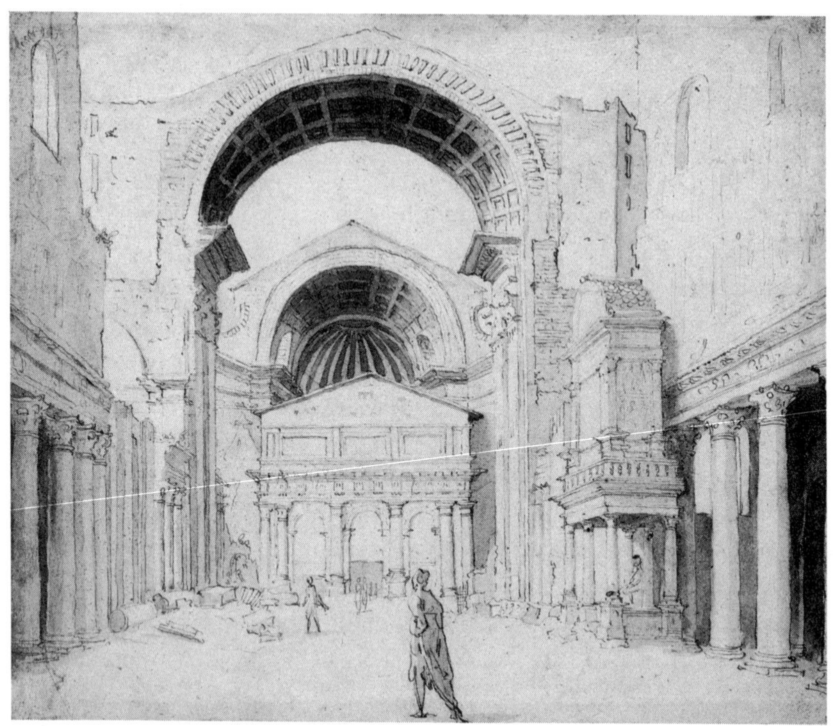

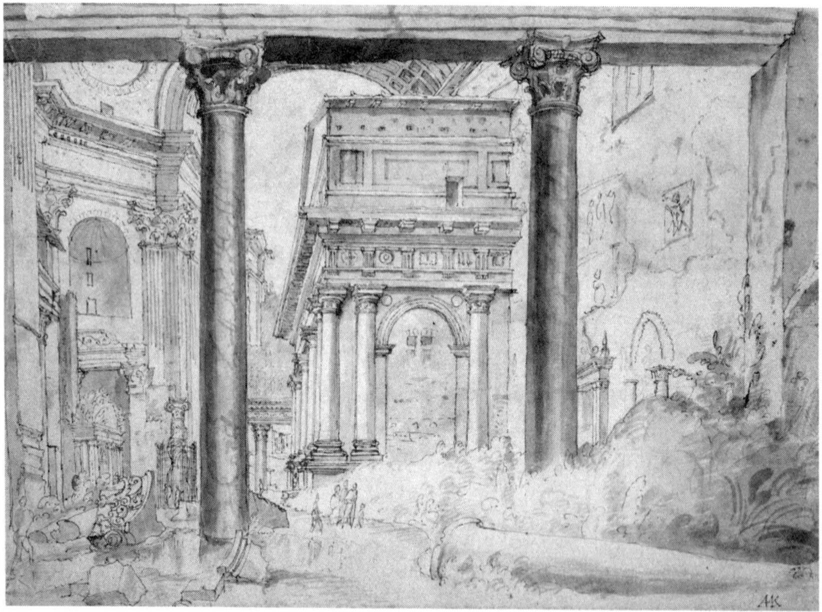

25.1–25.2 The continuity of the identity of St. Peter's between destruction and reconstruction.
Maarten van Heemskerck, *Tegurio Seen from the East*, pen and ink, 22.2 x 27.3 cm (1530s), Berlin,
Kupferstichkabinett; *Tegurio Seen from the North*, pen and ink, 20 x 27.7 cm (1530s), Stockholm,
National Museum. Bramante's temporary structure, or *tegurio*, as recorded in two drawings by the
Dutch artist Heemskerck, an assiduous and reliable topographer. The view of the *tegurio* from the side
shows its one-bay depth.

and the shed/hut—is a fairly exact rendition of Bramante's *tegurio*, three bays across and one deep, with one triglyph over every column and two over each bay. Or rather, it is an exact rendition of the *tegurio* as it would look if the structure were translated back into wood. The drawing's reverse engineering back from the *tegurio* illustrates Vitruvius's account of the wooden origins of Doric: the archways are gone and only the post and beam construction remains; the triglyphs here are not yet triglyphs but the front faces of beams cut flush with the structure's external face, just as Vitruvius says (4.2.2). Even before Bramante's structure acquired a roof in real life (as we just saw, it did not receive one until 1526), Raphael gives it a pitched roof here, like those of the prototypical wooden structures Vitruvius describes. Like so many artists before him, Raphael has turned the scene of the Nativity into a visualization of the history of architecture. Unusually, however, he folds his visualization into the drama then playing out at the site of St. Peter's, whose superintendency he had taken over after Bramante's death.

Rather than retelling the fable of proud architecture reduced to ruin, Raphael meditates on process. There is no rupture here, only graduation, hence the introduction of the third element, an anomaly in Nativity iconography, the Doric structure in wood that mediates between the advanced stone architecture and the hut. It softens the abrupt juxtaposition of grand architecture and humble shed, and the apocalyptic chronology that contrast implies, promising instead a reassuring and reversible movement up and down, backwards and forwards.

This improbable visualization was prompted, remarkably, by real architecture—by Bramante's modular intervention at the core of the "ruins" of St. Peter's. The Penni drawing after Raphael reveals that the spectacle at St. Peter's was a translated visualization, a three-dimensional staging of a drama of architectural destruction and succession, now projected into the world at a colossal scale. Bramante's own ambivalent vision in the Prevedari engraving (see figure 24.6) came true at St. Peter's and then here, in the drawing by Penni, was reconverted into a picture. Finally an engraver, a hand close to Raphael's sometime collaborator Marcantonio Raimondi, published the Penni drawing (figure 25.4).[12] When the epochal renovations at St. Peter's entered the pictorial register, they received a quasi-allegorical gloss—obviously in Penni's *Nativity*, more discreetly in Heemskerck's visual reports—and then these ideas about architectural history, about typology, about supersession could be reintroduced into architectural practice and back into images, without end. The feedback loop between buildings and representations of buildings accelerated the transmission of architectural ideas. But now, in addition, architecture itself

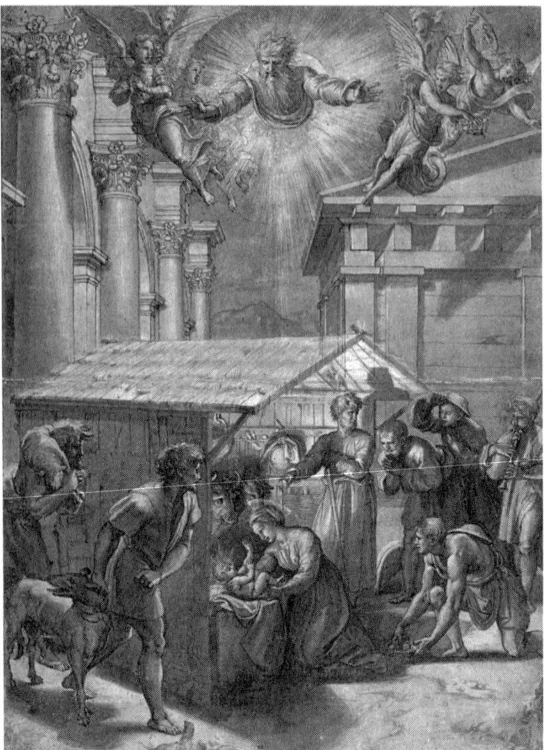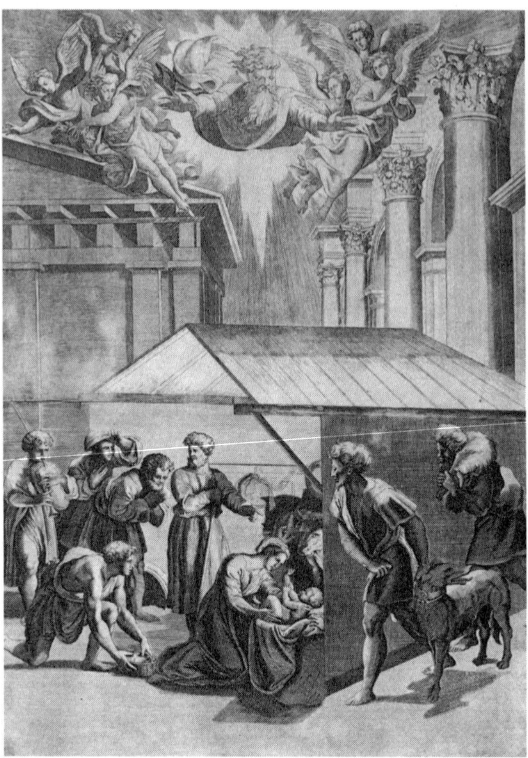

25.3 Bramante's *tegurio* staged as a phase in a Vitruvian history of architecture. Gian Francesco Penni, after Raphael, *Nativity*, drawing, 54 x 40.4 cm (ca. 1518–1520). Paris, Musée du Louvre. Real architecture here re-enters the more fluid realm of the architectural imagination. Bramante's *tegurio* appears here as a middle stage in the history of architecture, between the primitive hut and the grand stone architecture at the left. Or rather, not Bramante's *tegurio* but its own imagined wooden proto-type: for instead of Bramante's stone structure with its capitals, frieze, and triglyphs, we are shown a more primitive wooden structure not with triglyphs but only the ends of beams, just as described by Vitruvius.

25.4 Raphael's compressed history of architecture in published form. Raimondi school, *Nativity*, engraving, 61 x 43 cm (ca. 1520). New York, Metropolitan Museum. In the translation from drawing to print we lose the sensitive rendition of the wooden uprights of the shed and the thatch of its roof, a clear reference to Vitruvius's description of the "spars and thatch" of the most primitive architecture. Also, in the drawing Joseph is shown to be exactly the height of the shed's walls, possibly an indication of a basic modular logic in primitive architecture, a correspondence that is lost in the print. Nonethe-less, the engraving puts the drawing's basic program into circulation in the public realm. Print thus accelerates the loop between real and figurative architecture.

began to adapt to its own mirrorings in painting and print. Architecture in the Renaissance was no longer simply a process governed by a substi-tutional principle: it was now putting into practice the strategies of cita-tion, embedding, reframing, and staging that had been developed in the pictorial realm, especially in the depiction of architecture. Architecture took on a layer of reflexivity that had been unavailable to Brunelleschi, the last great architect before the age of mechanical reproducibility. Architecture had been figured, and before long it was itself engaged in the work of figuration.

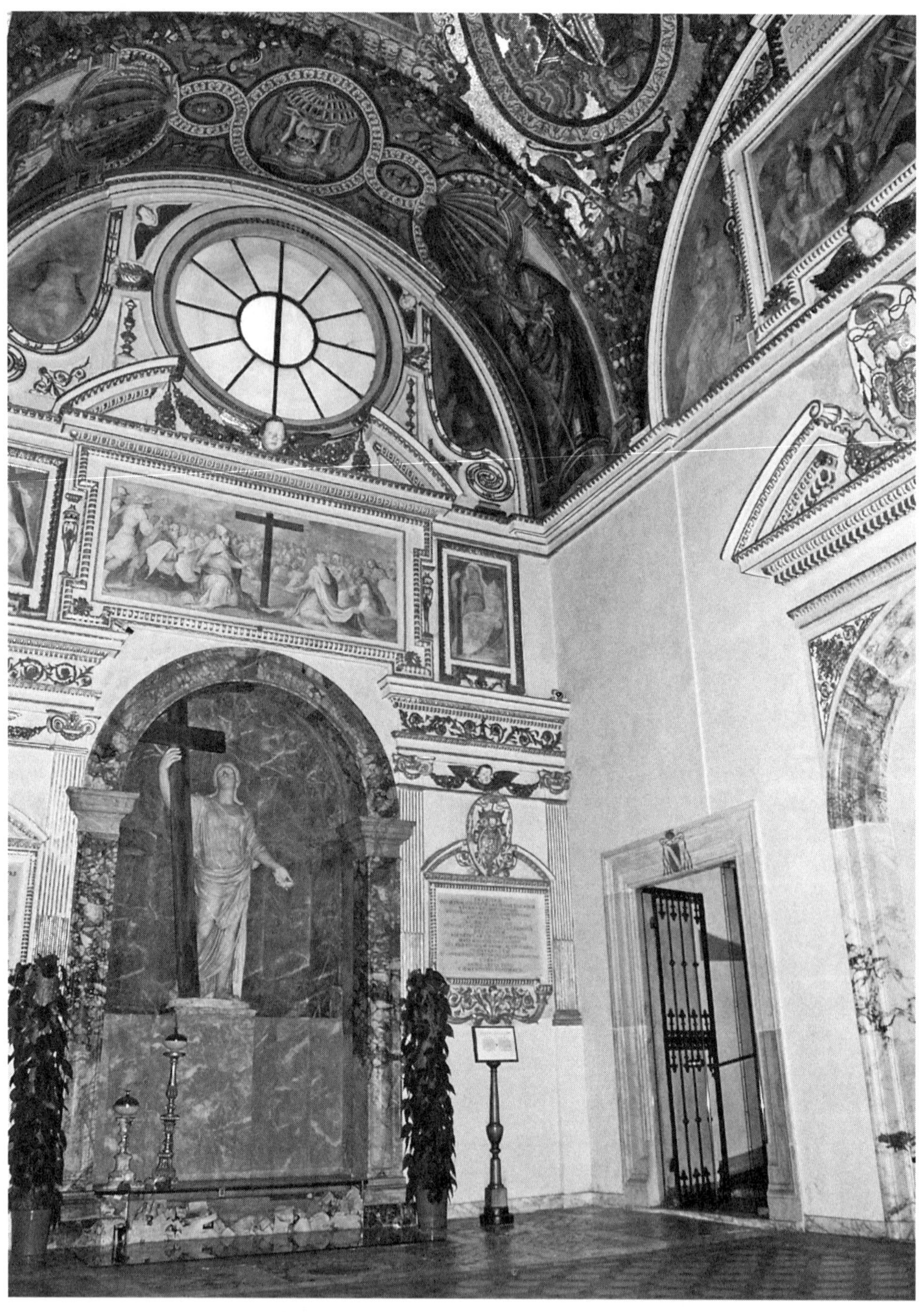

26.1 A substitution chamber. Jerusalem or Helena Chapel. Rome, Santa Croce in Gerusalemme. This chapel, supposedly once a room in the palace of St. Helena, the mother of the first Christian emperor Constantine and excavator of the Holy Sepulchre (324–325), sheltered the relics she brought back from Jerusalem. The statue on the altar is an ancient goddess reconditioned as a portrait of Helena and installed here in the eighteenth century.

TWENTY-SIX

Mosaic/Paint 1:

Limits of Substitution

The Jerusalem Chapel, a capsule of the Holy Land in Rome, is a chamber behind and below the apse of the basilica of Santa Croce in Gerusalemme (figure 26.1). For many centuries the chapel housed the relics of the Crucifixion, including large pieces of the cross itself, the Titulus or inscribed tablet once affixed to its top, and a shipload of earth from Golgotha, that St. Helena, according to some accounts, brought to Rome from Jerusalem. That chapel, today called the Helena Chapel, was itself a relic. When the heirs of Constantine in the middle of the fourth century converted an aula of an old imperial residence, the Sessorian Palace not far from Porta Maggiore, into a basilica, they left intact a single rectangular room of the palace.[1] Later this space was identified as Helena's own bedchamber, and indeed it may have been that room.[2] The chapel was outfitted with mosaics in the fifth century, some of which were still in place at the end of the fifteenth century. The church, reconstructed in the twelfth century and again in the eighteenth century, grew around and over the sanctuary. The authenticity of the chapel, like that of the Holy House at Loreto, was signaled by displacement. It sits two meters below the floor of the basilica. The steep, irregularly shaped ramp down to the chapel assured pilgrims that these walls had never been moved and the floor never raised; in other words, that the room had never been submitted to the ordinary, practical processes of displacement and accommodation.

The relationship between the reliquary chapel and the semicircular apse of the basilica repeated, by topological transformation, the relationship of the original Golgotha chapel, a two-storied space englobing the site of the Crucifixion, inside the Church of the Holy Sepulchre in Jerusalem, to Constantine's rotunda a few yards away. The basilica of Santa Croce, one of the principal destinations for all Rome pilgrims, became Jerusalem's map in Rome. In the Middle Ages the basilica and chapel together were simply known as "Jerusalem." In the mid-fifteenth century Niklas Muffel reported that a visit to the Jerusalem Chapel was equivalent, in the pilgrim's currency of indulgence or time off from purgatory, to a visit to the Holy Sepulchre itself (*do ist grosse gnad als zu dem heyligen grab*).[3]

Topomimesis of this sort was rare in Rome. The Romans of the Middle Ages, as if satisfied with their inherited Pantheon, built no imitation of the Rotunda of the Holy Sepulchre. Rome, self-absorbed and metropolitanist even during the centuries of political eclipse and severe population loss, took itself to be a total substitute for Jerusalem. The Holy City, lost to Christians except for a few decades in the twelfth century, and hard of access in the best of times, was an abstraction. Not until the late fifteenth century, under the control of a pair of Spanish cardinals, who together with the Spanish pope Alexander VI Borgia were involved in revivals of the Crusading project and the struggle against the Muslims in the Iberian peninsula, was the full symbolic potential of Santa Croce in Gerusalemme reactivated. Their projects parallel the interest taken by the Castilian monarchs Ferdinand and Isabella in the site of St. Peter's crucifixion. In 1502 Ferdinand and Isabella dedicated a crypt-like chapel on the Gianicolo, one of the two sites that competed for the honor.[4] Here Isabella displayed more interest in authenticity than when she commissioned the copy of the Miraflores altar by Rogier van der Weyden (see section 22). St. Peter's crucifixion in Rome repeated the execution of Christ himself; the Gianicolo was the doppelgänger of Golgotha. The doubling pointed to Rome's replacement of Jerusalem. Buried under the Tempietto (and discovered in 1627) was a marble stone believed to be a relic of the site of Peter's martyrdom; it was carved in 1502 with an inscription commemorating the foundation and used as a foundation stone.[5] Bramante's small round temple was built over the site.

The discovery of the Titulus relic at Santa Croce in 1492 and its reinstallation in the Jerusalem Chapel were implicated in a complex two-part renovation campaign. Cardinal Mendoza had a fresco painted on the main apse of the basilica, replacing, presumably, a mosaic which has left no traces. Several years later, probably in the second half of the first decade of the sixteenth century, his successor Cardinal Bernardino Carvajal, Mendoza's secretary and agent in Rome, and titleholder of Santa Croce from 1495–1511 and again from 1513–1523, outfitted the Jerusalem Chapel with a new mosaic ceiling.

The renovations of the main apse and the Jerusalem Chapel at Santa Croce in the 1490s and 1510s hardly number among the principal achievements of Italian Renaissance art. And yet the Santa Croce projects, engaged as they were in symbolic dialogue with the relics housed in the basilica, addressed basic and unresolved questions about the evidentiary authority of the image, the interference between the referential and fictional capacities of the image, the interchangeability of ancient and modern artifacts, the possible relic-status of some images, the sacrality of place, the virtues and meanings of the media of mosaic and paint, and the license of the individual artist to invent. The circuitry at Santa Croce was overcharged, as if the presence of the relics from Jerusalem were exerting pressure. The solutions at Santa Croce were only one degree removed from the paradigmatic and most influential projects of the Roman Renaissance: the Tempietto, the Stanza della Segnatura, the Sistine Chapel, the Chigi Chapel. By the middle of the second decade of the century, completely new concepts of the artwork and of the artist will have been spelled out so clearly that they have survived to the present day more or less intact, heavily protected by layers of conventions and institutions. The projects at Santa Croce in Gerusalemme were, in this sense, the hidden matrix of sixteenth-century art.

The new painted apse, undocumented but probably dating from about 1492 to 1495, represents, in a frieze-like narrative unscrolling before a landscape, Helena's Discovery and Proof of the True Cross and the Recovery of the Cross Relic by Emperor Heraclius (figure 26.2).[6] At the center, the cross is supported by Helena and the kneeling Cardinal Mendoza (figure 26.3). The subject was not common. Among prior treatments in fresco were the cycles by Agnolo Gaddi in the Cappella Maggiore of Santa Croce in Florence (ca. 1380) and the cycle by Piero della Francesca at Arezzo (no later than the mid-1460s), the most proximate model for the Roman fresco. From this point on, the subject wore a new layer of meaning, for Helena's discovery, narrated by the Church Father Eusebius and by Jacobus de Voragine in the *Golden Legend*, is a fable about historical research and identification. In the fifteenth century, European scholars developed disciplines—archeology and epigraphy—to settle disputes and slake curiosity about origins. The story of the discovery of the True Cross allegorizes the basic challenges of archeological scholarship: anxiety about the true site and the authenticity of the find, the necessity of relying on local knowledge, the application of empirical tests (the raising of the dead man by contact with the True Cross). Behind the apse fresco at Santa Croce loomed the contemporary problem of the identity of the Titulus fragment, legitimated as an authentic relic, finally, by papal fiat in 1496. The confusion about how to absorb the evidence of the Titulus stood in for a much larger concern about the legitimacy of the cult image. The problem of the True Cross was a comparatively manageable version of the problem of the religious sign, which when doubled—that is, when substitution failed or was revealed as incomplete—becomes a false sign.

The apse at Santa Croce is a late product of the workshop of Antoniazzo Romano, a leading Roman painter since the 1460s who made a speciality of repainting or interpreting older images, or generating new cult images with an archaic flavor.[7] It was he who painted the walls of the bedchamber of St. Catherine of Siena, a century after her death, paintings apparently taken by later observers to be the original decoration of the room (section 18). The apse paintings at Santa Croce were unmentioned by any writer before Onofrio Panvinio in 1570, and only ascribed to Antoniazzo by August Schmarsow in 1886. An inscription, "Maestro Delantoniazzo," recently discovered on the verso of a drawing, a study for the fresco, seems finally to secure the attribution.[8] In the upper part of the apse at Santa Croce, in a separate field marked off from the narrative below by a band of cherubim, Antoniazzo designed a Majestas Domini, an enthroned, gesturing Christ holding a book on his knee, inside a mandorla (figure 26.4). In the lower part of the apse Antoniazzo looked to relatively recent Tuscan painting for new ideas about narrative painting. Tuscany and Umbria were the great nurseries of painterly talent. Even before Raphael, the popes had hired central Italian artists to paint their apartments and chapels: Fra Angelico, Benozzo Gozzoli, Melozzo da Forlì, Botticelli, Perugino, Pinturicchio. But in the upper part of the apse, with its utopic, star-studded ground and supernatural diagram of Christ's overlordship, Antoniazzo invoked the decorative schemes of the early medieval Roman churches.

What was in the apse of Santa Croce before 1492? There are no records or remains that would help us decide. All the important early medieval churches in Rome had mosaic decoration in their apses, and all were restored and repaired over the years. The apse mosaics of the major basilicas, St. Peter's, San Paolo fuori le Mura, San Giovanni in Laterano, and Santa Maria Maggiore, were essentially redone in the twelfth and thirteenth centuries. No apses were left undecorated. The old basilica of Santa Croce must have had a mosaic apse, perhaps dating from the fifth century when Valentinian III and his mother Galla Placidia commissioned the mosaics on the ceiling vault of the Jerusalem Chapel. In the 1140s Cardinal Gerardo Caccianemici dal Orso, the future Pope Lucius II, upgraded the church into a standard three-aisled basilica with transept and added a portico and campanile. This was the moment that the Titulus relic was fabricated and deposited in a niche over the triumphal arch. The interior of the basilica was decorated with frescoes: Christ with Evangelist symbols on the triumphal arch, medallions with prophets and patriarchs on the upper part of the side walls of the nave. The original, fifth-century apse mosaic may have been restored during the twelfth-century rebuilding of the basilica, although there is no record of this. By the 1490s, at any rate, the apse mosaic had probably fallen badly into disrepair or else it would not have been stripped and replaced by a mere painting.[9]

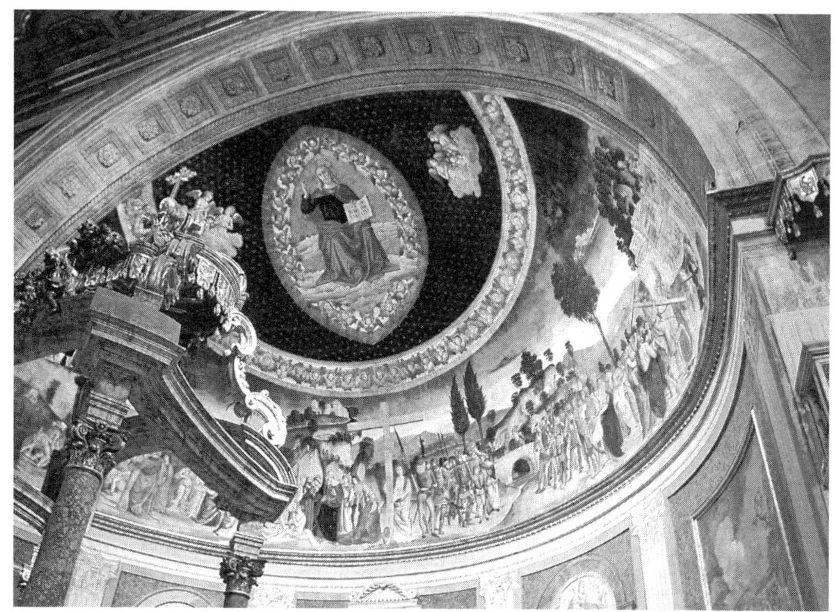

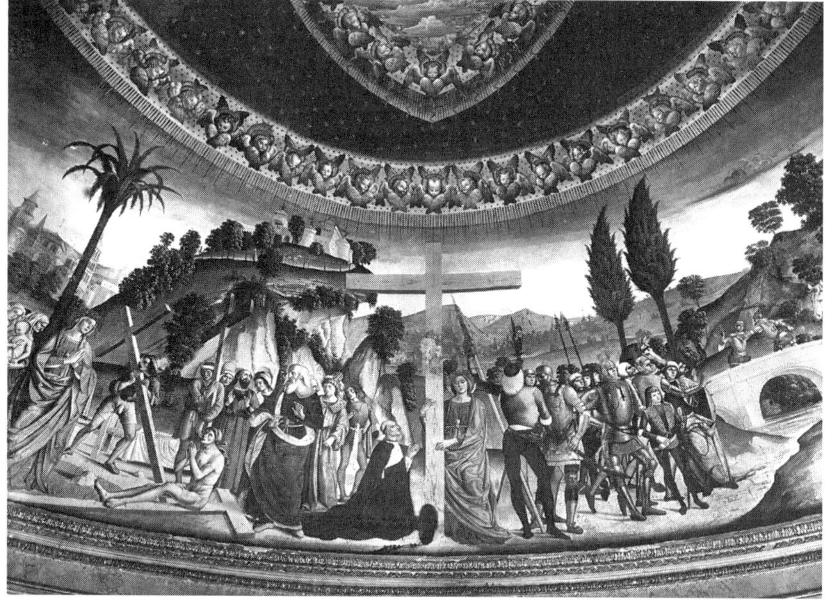

26.2 A painted apse substituting notionally for mosaic. Rome, Santa Croce in Gerusalemme, nave with view of apse painted by Antoniazzo Romano (ca. 1492–1495). The narrative frieze wrapping around the drum of the apse is partially obscured in this photograph by the baldachin (an eighteenth-century crown on twelth-century columns). It is not known what adorned the apse before this fresco—possibly an ancient mosaic.

26.3 The story of the discovery of the True Cross as a reflection on archeological scholarship. Antoniazzo Romano, *Story of the True Cross*, fresco, apse (ca. 1492–1495). Rome, Santa Croce in Gerusalemme. On the left, the True Cross revealed its identity by raising a dead man. At the center, Helena holds the cross while the patron Cardinal Mendoza kneels in reverence. On the right, Emperor Heraclius battles the Persian King Chosroes, in the year 628, for possession of a portion of the relic.

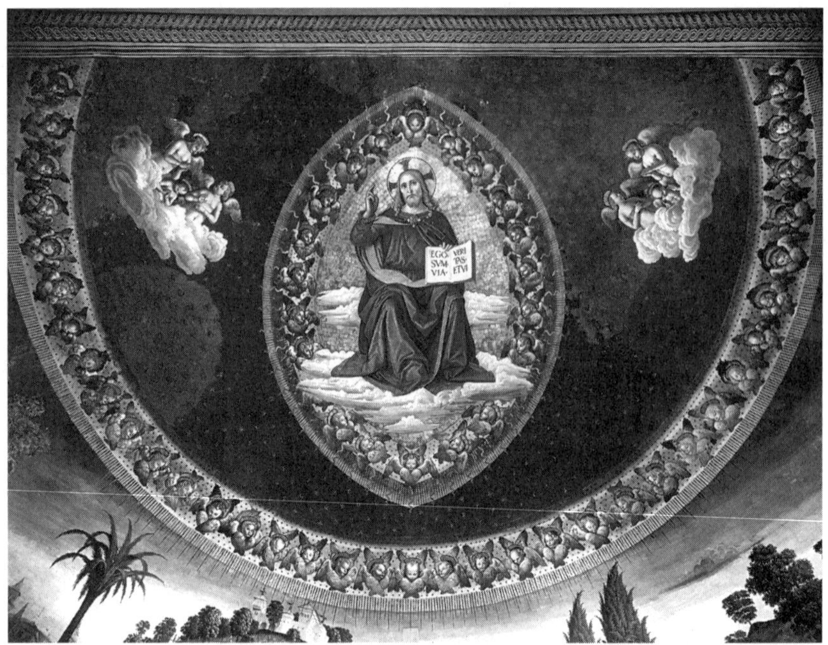

26.4 Christ in a mandorla, a motif with no ancient Roman pedigree. Antoniazzo Romano, *Majestas Domini*, fresco, apse (ca. 1492–1495). Rome, Santa Croce in Gerusalemme. The hieratic image recalls without duplicating an early medieval Roman apse in mosaic.

On the verge of their own decisions, Mendoza and Carvajal must have peered back upon the thinly documented, poorly understood life flow of the building, hoping to participate in the process. But creation entailed destruction. When Mendoza built a new ceiling, he left the twelfth-century frescoes on the triumphal arch visible but ended up covering those along the nave.[10] The ideal image of building history as an organic, unpunctuated flow of exchanges is a fiction that comes into view only from the vantage point of deliberate intervention in the present tense. Mendoza and Carvajal plotted self-advertising innovations that at the same time were meant to settle back into the historical fabric of the building. That is what it meant to work "anachronically": in and out of time, all at the same time. The artwork, by nature double-thinking, would find a way to shuttle between the interlopers' dream of seamless participation and their knowledge of their own destructive willfulness.

Mendoza and Antoniazzo's scheme for the apse involved an anachronism, for the enthroned Christ in a mandorla is not found in any early Roman apses. The early fifth-century mosaic apse of Santa Pudenziana, contemporary with the original apse of Santa Croce, shows Christ enthroned, gesturing, and holding a book, but not enclosed in a mandorla. Christ in a mandorla is an eastern form.[11] Antoniazzo chose a motif that, as far as we can tell, had no ancient Roman pedigree. The mandorla entered Roman iconography only in the fourteenth century. On the façade of Santa Maria Maggiore, in a mosaic by Filippo Rusuti dated to around 1300, Christ sits enthroned in a mandorla, holding a book, flanked by angels. To later fifteenth-century eyes, such an image, in the ancient medium of mosaic, was precedent enough. There was every reason for Antoniazzo and his contemporaries to believe in the antiquity of the motif. The figure of Christ in a mandorla matched an *idea* of ancient painting. Antoniazzo himself had placed Christ in a mandorla in his fresco for the chapel of Cardinal Bessarion at Santi Apostoli in the 1460s.[12] The Madonna in Pinturicchio's fresco in the chapel of Girolamo Basso della Rovere in Santa Maria del Popolo, where the artist was at pains to reconcile ancient forms with cultic function (see section 15), floats above her tomb in a mandorla. The form was also used by Perugino, with whom Antoniazzo collaborated at one point, in several paintings, and by Pinturicchio at the Bufalini Chapel in Santa Maria in Aracoeli, above the neo-cosmatesque floor (see figure 17.1). The family of fifteenth-century painted mandorlas, like the family of pseudo-antique architectural balustrades—and Pinturicchio, we recall, placed one of these in the Basso della Rovere chapel—was a self-authenticating network: each example corroborated the antiquity of the others, without any single example standing in secure relation to an ancient prototype. It was assumed that there was such a prototype, somewhere.

The restorations by Mendoza and Carvajal of the apse and the Jerusalem Chapel moved inside a force field established by one of the smallest yet most powerful artifacts in the building: the icon of Christ held to be the original image of the Man of Sorrows, a miraculous memorandum of Pope Gregory the Great's sixth-century vision which had occurred (some believed) at the basilica of Santa Croce (see figure 10.2).[13] Gregory, according to the legend, had prayed for a sign that would persuade a skeptic that the sacrament of the Eucharist really did recreate Christ's original sacrifice. He was answered by an apparition of Christ, on the altar before him, among the instruments of the Passion. Gregory had an image made recording this epiphany. The icon at Santa Croce was in fact made around 1300, probably in Constantinople, and was brought from the monastery of St. Catherine at Mount Sinai to Rome in the 1380s. This image was not a panel painting but a so-called micromosaic composed of tesserae so small that they resolve from a distance of even a few inches into a homogeneous surface. The icon thus defines two medial alternatives, painting and mosaic, but allows them to converge. Mosaic was the ancient medium

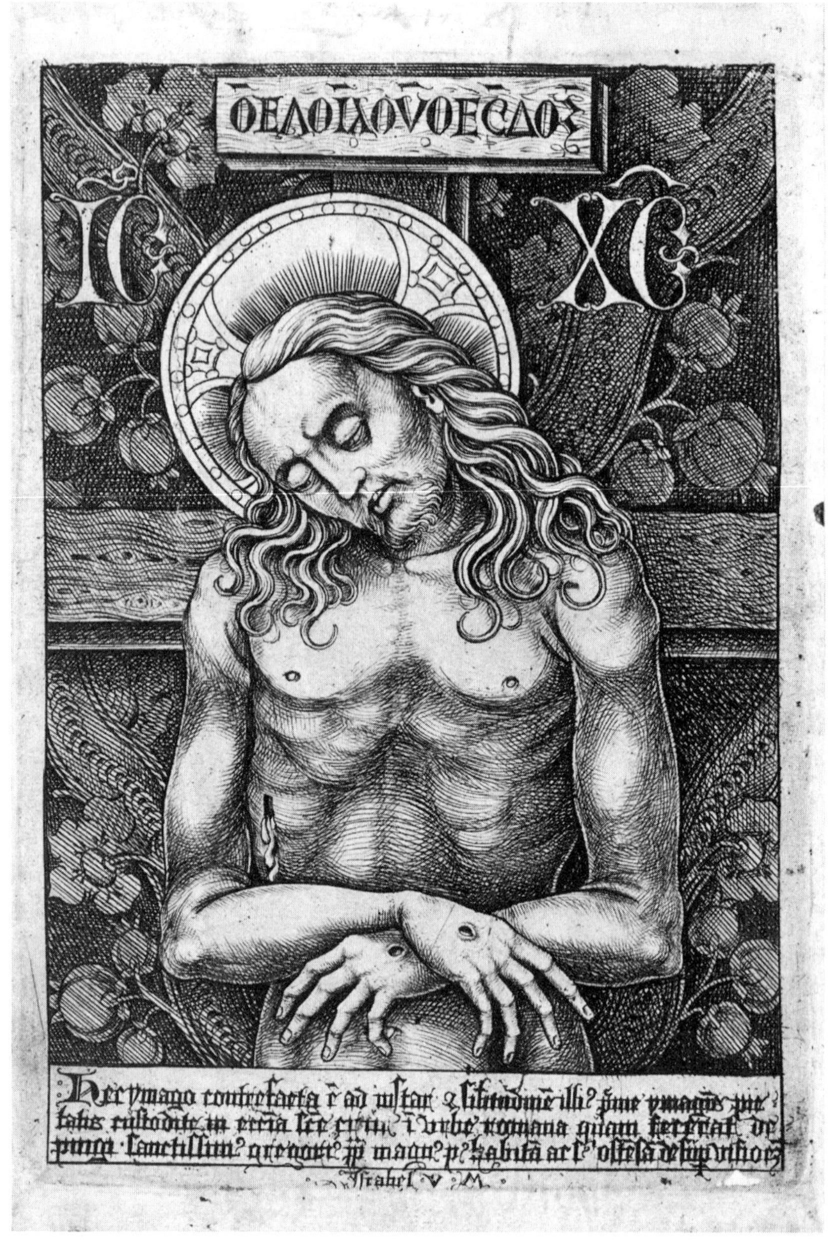

26.5 The mosaic icon of Santa Croce broadcast across Europe, and here identified as a painting.
Israhel van Meckenem, *Christ as Man of Sorrows*, engraving, 16.8 x 11.2 cm (ca. 1500). Berlin, Staatliche Museen, Kupferstichkabinett. This engraving reproduces the micromosaic icon associated with Pope Gregory and preserved at Santa Croce (see figure 10.2).

par excellence, the technique that the West lost, recovered, lost again; the technique preserved for centuries by Byzantine workshops. Few examples of micromosaic were known in late medieval Europe.[14] The intriguing technique gave the object a unique cachet.

Mosaic was a digital medium, and so eminently substitutable. The atomization of the representation into tesserae facilitated copying. The medium of mosaic therefore vitiated the performative quality of the St. Gregory image—its punctual, momentary quality—and thus its all-important status as a relic. To venerate the Santa Croce icon as a relic was to put strain on the substitutional assumption that automatically accompanied the medium of mosaic. The relic-cult insisted that this was the very picture created for Gregory, and not a copy. The object should have been a painting. Those unable to inspect the icon at close range could easily mistake the medium for paint. Israhel van Meckenem in his engraving of the icon described it as the image that Gregory "caused to be painted" (*fecerat depingi*) (figure 26.5).[15] A painting is patently handmade and so offers itself as a rhetorically effective trace of an event. St. Luke painted the Virgin in real time. Mosaic is not a real-time medium. All the prestigious Roman cult icons were painted; the medium of paint symbolized their rude and straightforward character and their status as direct traces of the eye's witness.

What was the significance of Mendoza's decision to replace the mosaic apse at Santa Croce, for many centuries the most expensive and prestigious of pictorial media, with a painting? In one sense it meant nothing, for there was no choice. There were no active mosaic workshops in fifteenth-century Rome. The last major program was the mosaic façade of San Paolo fuori le Mura from the first decades of the fourteenth century. Already in those years some smaller churches were forced to replace their crumbling mosaics with painting, for example San Giorgio al Velabro, where an apse fresco attributed to Pietro Cavallini replaced an older mosaic. The medial transition around 1300 is complicated by the historical fact of the emergence at that moment of a new paradigm of painting grounded in the authority of the painter. The significance of Giotto's and Cavallini's achievements as painters was hardly overlooked in fifteenth-century Italy. Still, the epochal shift in the significance of the medium of painting that Giotto represented is clearer in Albertian, and certainly Vasarian, retrospect than it was at the time. Giotto himself abandoned fresco and adopted mosaic when he designed a monumental allegory for the counter-façade of St. Peter's, the Navicella; as if here, in proximity to the burial site of the apostle, he felt compelled—or was compelled by his patrons—to revert to the traditionally more prestigious medium. Giotto's collapse back into mosaic, his renunciation of all the finer effects of the analogue medium in favor of the rough splendor of the tesserae, was remembered by the monument of ca. 1490 in the Duomo of Florence (see figure 12.1). Antoniazzo Romano himself, as if acknowledging the significance of Giotto's acknowledgement of the medium of mosaic, and moreover probably understanding Giotto's mosaic as a substitute for a pre-existing ancient work, painted a copy of the Navicella on panel.[16]

At any rate, Mendoza and Antoniazzo in the 1490s replaced the old mosaic with a fresco. They figured the choice between media — a choice that in practical terms they did not have — by dividing the apse into two fields, upper and lower. The narrative below describes a precisely dated and located series of events in a modern mode of painting. That lower narrative points beyond Rome to central Italy and, through Piero della Francesca, to the possibility of modernity in art, a modernity increasingly dominated by the medium of paint. The narrative frieze with its day-lit landscape and portrait-like physiognomies, brilliant effects of painting's analogue continuousness, would be all but unrepresentable in the digital medium of mosaic (see figure 26.3). The upper part or calotte of the apse, meanwhile, described a nonevent occurring in a nonplace. The mandorla and the abstract, homogeneous ground of the upper part of the fresco created the fiction of an artifact chain stretching all the way back to the fifth century, perhaps longer, a chain unbroken by the switch from mosaic to paint, here presented as trivial (see figure 26.4). The conceit of the painted mandorla pretended that the apse was a palimpsest, like the building itself. The contrast between the archaic-looking upper part of the fresco and the modern-looking lower register contributed to the fiction that the overall structure of the upper part had an ancient pedigree. The apse staged a contrast between, on the one hand, a custom-bound representational mode (pictures made much as they always had been) and, on the other hand, an ideally transparent modern mode (pictures unafraid to break with ancient tradition in order to show the true appearance of things).

The supposedly natural narrative mode of the lower register of the apse fresco at Santa Croce was in fact anything but natural. It had to be learned, and produced. Piero della Francesca, Perugino, Melozzo, and Pinturicchio developed a mode of painting whose criterion was the break with the very concept of "mode," or fashion. Piero's True Cross frescoes at Arezzo, and in its less inspired way the apse narrative at Santa Croce in Gerusalemme, were precisely *styleless*. In search of perfect narrative lucidity they started all over, breaking free from the conventional ways of painting; grounding themselves in the customs neither of antiquity nor of the recent masters, but in the look of life itself. But the styleless style was a time-bound style, as commentators of the late sixteenth and early seventeenth centuries recognized. Those later observers could not identify the author of the apse fresco at Santa Croce—Antoniazzo did not cultivate a personal style as distinctive as, say, Piero della Francesca's—but they recognized it as a work of its time, in the manner of Perugino but inferior in quality, perhaps therefore by Pinturicchio.[17]

Even the lower register of the apse, for all its rhetoric of descriptive straightforwardness, feigns an archaic virtue. For this is a simultaneous narrative: the protagonist Helena appears three times in the same field, without sectional dividers as was customary in fresco cycles.[18] Further to the right, events that took place three hundred years later, the winning back of the cross from the Persians by Heraclius and its restoration to Jerusalem, share the same landscape space. Heraclius, too, is tripled, once on the bridge battling Chosroes (visible at the right of our illustration), once on horseback, and once on foot entering Jerusalem. The continuous landscape stands in logical conflict with the figural narrative. Simultaneous narration looked archaic, but it was no such thing. Earlier painting had always partitioned the narrative in fields. The illogical folding over of the spatial continuum was in fact an invention of the Renaissance; it presupposes geometric and atmospheric perspective, the pictorial technology for representing spatial continuums.[19] The pseudo-archaism of the Santa Croce apse fresco was its true modernity.

Another ambiguous gesture to the tradition of medieval Roman apses is the giant cross supported by Helena in the center of the narrative frieze. The cross echoes the symbolic crosses depicted in the apses of Santa Pudenziana (fifth century), the chapel of Santi Primo e Feliciano at Santo Stefano Rotondo (seventh century), Santi Achilleo e Nereo (ninth century), San Clemente (twelfth century), and the Lateran (ca. 1290, by Jacopo Torriti). The anchor stabilizing all of these, their constant reference point, was the *crux gemmata* installed by Constantine in the Golgotha chapel of the Holy Sepulchre church in Jerusalem itself. The cross in the apse of Santa Croce in Gerusalemme, Jerusalem in Rome, is so distinct as to stand out in relief from the painted narrative around it, as if it were the true subject of the picture and all the surrounding figures and scenes merely a frame for it. If the apse as a whole stages a conflict between the upper and lower fields, then the lower part of the apse stages a conflict between the narrative and the iconic cross. The cross pushes Antoniazzo's frieze back into a substitutional relationship with the earlier apses.[20] Perhaps it was once easier to look through the styleless style of Antoniazzo's landscape and see, not Piero or Pinturicchio, but the palm-framed Jordan River friezes at the bases of the apses of Santi Cosma e Damiano (sixth century) and Santa Prassede (ninth century); Torriti's Lateran apse with its Nilotic flora and fauna; or the fourteenth-century painted frieze—a restoration of an older work?—in the lower part of the apse at San Clemente. Here, too, figures stand in an earthly landscape, unaware of the celestial diagram above their heads. It may make most sense, in other words, to see even the lower part of Antoniazzo's apse, the frieze, as a permissible updating of a standard type of Roman apse.

Antoniazzo's modern performance reveals the historical Roman mosaic apses as citable. They make everyone aware that the workshop tradition of mosaic-making had been broken; they make it necessary for the first time to *remember* mosaic. Both parts of the apse are equally intertextual. The calotte refers to early medieval models but so, too, does the narrative frieze below, in its way. Substitution, or participation in the tradition, is the mythic foil against which aesthetic performance emerged in the fifteenth century. But performance, the self-knowledge of presentness and will, was in turn always held back by the deeper knowledge of intertextuality, the knowledge that one is working with signs and possibilities that were never really one's own. The agency of the patron was diffracted by the artist's will; but then the agency of the artist was itself dispersed by form, medium, convention. Performance was therefore equally the conceptual foil for substitution. The substitutional ideal of picture production was recovered only after being routed through performance.

The subject of the frieze is a simple advertisement of the myth behind this church, a myth that until then was legible in the building fabric and in the relic treasures but not (as far as we know) pictorialized in this church. But the narrative of the Discovery of the True Cross was not a venerable subject for pictures. The introduction of any new subject onto the apse of an ancient Roman basilica was momentous. Such an innovation was a low-key rehearsal for the destruction of St. Peter's, on the horizon. The subject of the Discovery of the True Cross had a hidden relevance in the 1490s, however, for the story of Helena's successful expedition to the Holy Land in 324–325 was also a fable about the Crusades, a not yet dormant project even after four centuries of false starts and (mostly) failure, particularly in a world of Spanish patrons inspired by the reconquest of Granada. The painting at Santa Croce, and the entire renewed fascination with the Helena legend of the later fifteenth century, might well be interpreted as a surrogate Crusade. The atmosphere was one of European pessimism about Muslim power and increasing European self-absorption; a retreat from a full engagement with the Mediterranean sphere back into a smaller, tighter model of Europe. The Spanish patron celebrated in this painting the recent expulsion of Muslims and Jews from Iberia, a "successful" crusade. At the same time, by bringing Helena's expedition back into focus, the painting marked a disengagement from the futile modern project of the reconquest of the Holy Land and instead pointed, implicitly, to the new westward ambitions of the Spanish crown, an entirely new frontier for conquest and conversion. And indeed Cardinal Mendoza was instrumental in convincing Ferdinand and Isabella to support Christopher Columbus.[21]

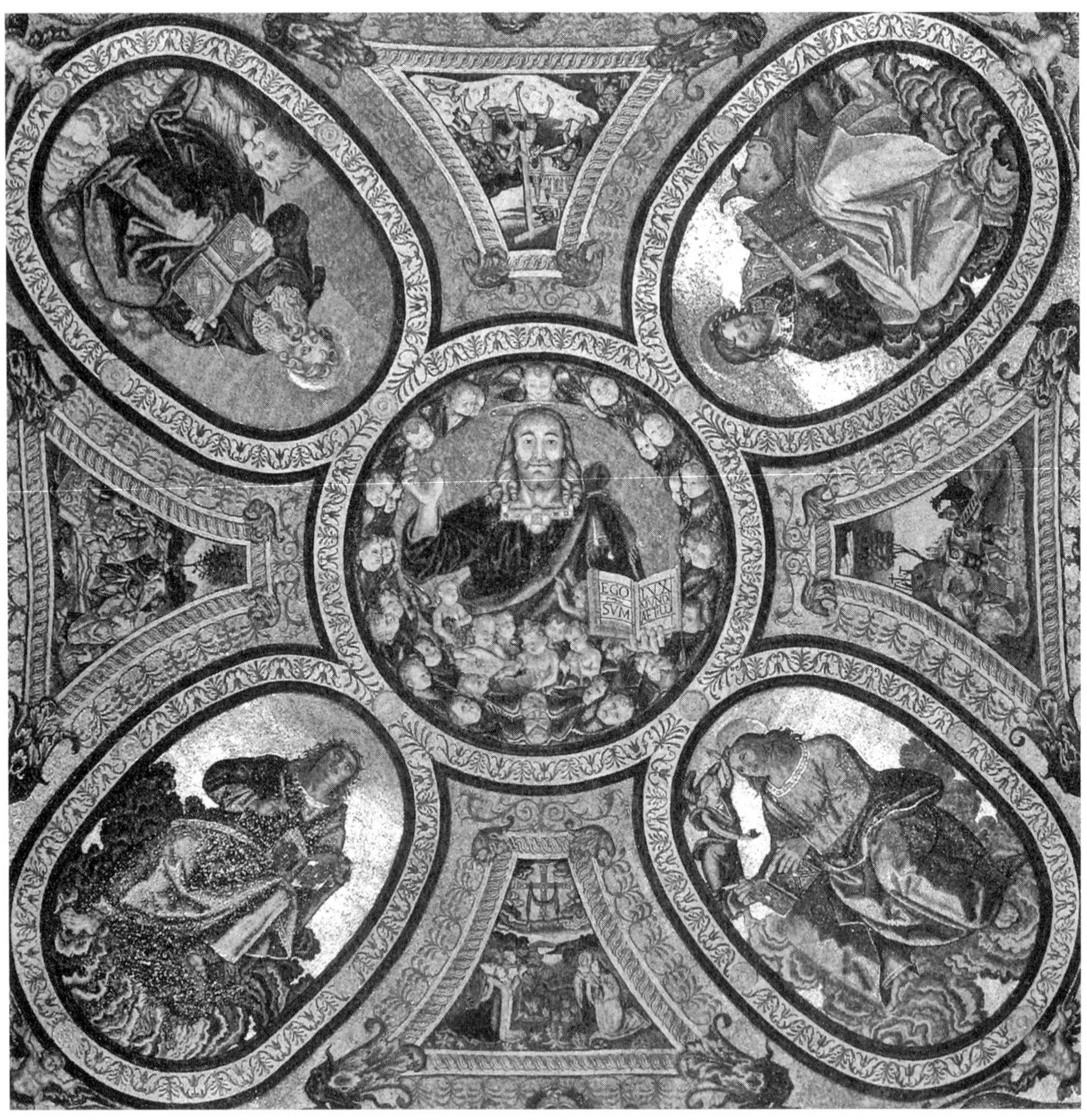

27.1 Archaism with medium specificity. Baldassare Peruzzi, mosaic ceiling (before 1509). Rome, Santa Croce in Gerusalemme, Jerusalem or Helena Chapel. An imitation of mosaic in the medium of mosaic, Peruzzi's ceiling probably reproduces features of a fifth-century mosaic that once existed on this same ceiling. The ceiling extends the mosaic revival initiated in Florence (see figure 12.4).

TWENTY-SEVEN

Mosaic/Paint 2:

Intermedial Comparison

The restoration, in fact replacement, of the mosaic ceiling of the Jerusalem Chapel at Santa Croce in Gerusalemme is undocumented but is reliably credited to the Sienese architect and painter Baldassare Peruzzi, who was paid for work at Santa Croce in the first decade of the sixteenth century (figure 27.1).[1] Giulio Mancini, a fellow Sienese, who as we learned earlier (section 23) took a special interest in attribution, named Peruzzi as the author of the mosaics in the early seventeenth century.[2] Peruzzi arrived in Rome in 1503 and the chapel was complete by 1509. At the center of the central vault is a circular medallion with the Christ Pantocrator holding an open book and with raised right hand, framed by a ring of cherubim. Arrayed around the central field, and like it enclosed in palmette borders, are four oval-shaped fields containing the four evangelists. These fields are fictive panels "nailed" to the ceiling with gold rivets and supported from below by half-figure putti. Between these fields are four trapezoidal scenes of the Legend of the True Cross.[3] The vault is contained by fruit-laden garlands; there are peacocks in the pendentives.

Cardinal Bernardino Carvajal, titular cardinal of the church and the patron, described the restoration project in a long inscription on majolica tiles, in blue roman capitals on a white ground, mounted on either side of the passageway that slopes down from the right transept of the basilica to the subterranean chapel.[4] According to this inscription, "the vault of the Jerusalem chapel and the mosaic figures, the work of Valentinian, were threatened with ruin, either by the age of the place or the negligence of its inhabitants." (The inscription makes no mention of the restoration of the church's main apse, incidentally.) Carvajal therefore had the mosaic in the Jerusalem chapel "entirely destroyed" and had "the vault and the mosaic images done anew on the model [*ad instar*] of the earlier one."[5] Some elements of Peruzzi's ceiling may reproduce features of the vanished fifth-century mosaic.[6] The peacocks in the corners and the vegetal garlands are common features in early Christian mosaics, for example in the Chapel of Santa Rufina in the Lateran Baptistery (fifth century). The

peacocks and the garlands and some other features of the ceiling may simply be one-to-one substitutes for motifs Peruzzi found in the predecessor
mosaic—survivals rather than revivals. Some elements of Peruzzi's mosaic,
however, were probably not carried over from the fifth-century ceiling,
for example the division of a vaulted ceiling into distinct pictorial fields.
The vaulted ceiling with scenes in the partitions was a favored format in
Rome around 1500: Pinturicchio used it for the chancel of Santa Maria
del Popolo and for the Borgia Apartments, as did the painter of the apse
mosaics at San Onofrio on the Gianicolo, possibly Jacopo Ripanda, possibly
Peruzzi. The initial designs Michelangelo projected for the Sistine Chapel
ceiling in 1508 also envisioned a compartmented vault of this kind.[7] The
compartmented, painted vault, like the Majestas Domini in the mandorla-
shaped frame in the apse of Santa Croce, was a device cultivated in the
late Middle Ages but easily assigned an ancient pedigree. The roundels in
the four groin vaults at the Upper Church of Assisi, for example, frescoes
by Jacopo Torriti, derived from Byzantine mosaic vaults such as those at
Hosios Loukas.[8] These ceilings were corroborated by the Golden Vault
of the Domus Aurea, recently discovered, or the vaults at Hadrian's Villa,
with circular, oval, octagonal, square, and rectangular fields articulated in
stucco.[9] Carvajal and Peruzzi likely could not distinguish—had no incentive to distinguish—between ancient models and more recent models
taken for trustworthy transmitters of ancient motifs and conventions.

The Christ Pantocrator in the medallion at the center of the ceiling is
another motif that may have been on the predecessor ceiling, or may have
been introduced by Peruzzi, a more than competent antiquarian. Peruzzi
could see such a mosaic Pantocrator medallion, carried by four angels,
on the ceiling of the Sancta Sanctorum. If he had copied that thirteenth-
century medallion, imagining that it transmitted older works, he would
not have been wrong. For the Pantocrator in a medallion at the crown of a
ceiling vault could also be found in the San Zeno chapel at Santa Prassede
(ninth century) and at Ravenna (sixth century).

The modern fascination with mosaic can be tracked in panel paintings,
which, although historically a less prestigious medium, had the power—and
over the course of the fifteenth century ever greater power—to describe all
the other media, including mosaic. Gentile da Fabriano, in the right hand
panel of the predella of his altarpiece for the Quaratesi of Florence in 1425,
described a scene of healing at the tomb of St. Nicholas (figure 27.2).[10] In
the apse above the tomb Gentile represented an enthroned Christ in Majesty enframed by a mandorla, apparently a gold-ground mosaic. Several
panel paintings and painted murals are visible to the right and left of the
tomb. More remarkably, the five scenes below the Majestas Domini in

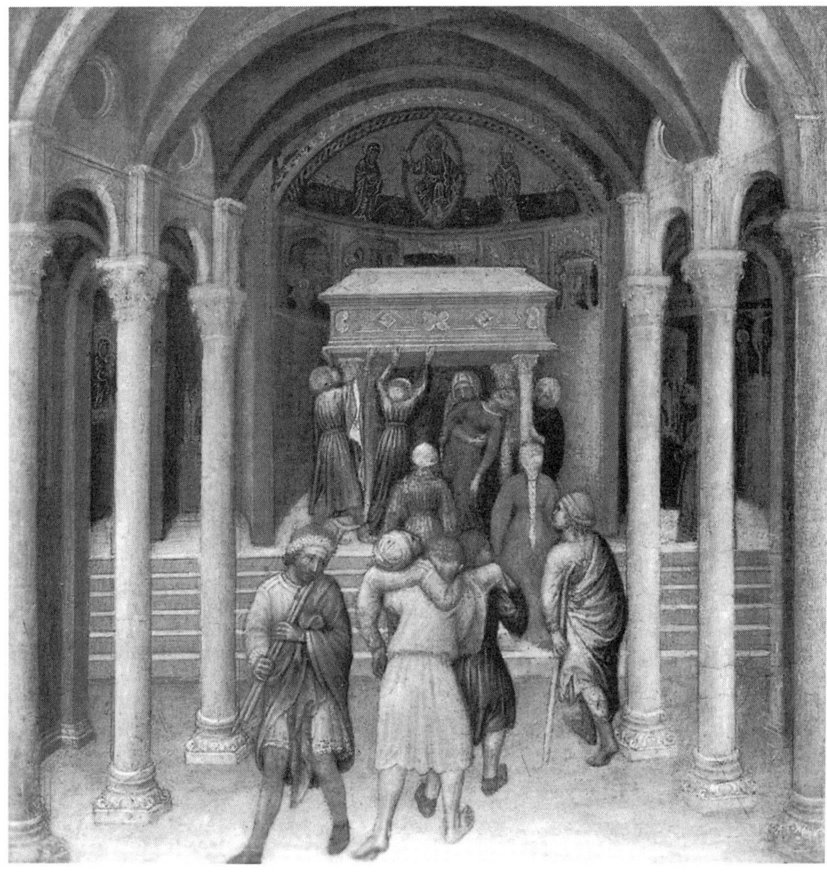

27.2 A painting imagines its own mosaic prototype. Gentile da Fabriano, *Tomb of Saint Nicholas*, from Quaratesi altarpiece, oil on panel, 36.4 x 35. 9 cm (1425). Washington, National Gallery of Art. This painting, one panel of the predella of an altarpiece, represents a mosaic apse with the same five scenes represented in the predella to which it belongs.

the apse reproduce the five scenes of Gentile's own altarpiece, including the very panel with the tomb and pilgrim and mosaic apse. Through this *mise-en-abyme* Gentile offers his own polyptych as the modern historical successor to the decorated apse.[11] This medial paragone finds its equivalent in Jan van Eyck's nearly contemporary *Annunciation* in the National Gallery of Art, where architecture, intaglio floor, stained glass, and sculpture are all corralled into the picture field and given a second optical life by paint (see figure 14.4). Such pictures made the case for the superiority of painting over the other media. We have already seen that Vittore Carpaccio, around 1503, depicted a small mosaic apse in the background of St. Augustine's study, reproducing a seraph from a thirteenth-century mosaic in the

337

basilica of San Marco in Venice (see figure 4.2). Cima da Conegliano, in his Montini altarpiece for the cathedral of Parma of 1507, depicted a mosaic apse behind the Virgin that copies with great care a scene from another mosaic in San Marco.[12] The conspicuous Venetian precedent for both Carpaccio and Cima da Conegliano was Gentile Bellini's altarpiece for the church of San Giobbe, commissioned in 1478, which represented a Sacra Conversazione beneath an apse decorated with a gold-ground mosaic with an inscription and a row of eight-winged seraphim (figure 27.3).[13] Bellini's and Carpaccio's citations, like those at Santa Croce, were at once distant and proximate. Apse mosaics were among the oldest and the newest works in Venice. The apse in the San Giobbe altarpiece refers to the ceiling of the chapter hall of the Scuola Grande della Carità, a work initiated in 1461.

Where did Carvajal find a mosaicist? When Raphael needed a mosaicist for the cupola of the chapel he designed for Agostino Chigi at Santa Maria del Popolo, about a decade later, he hired a Venetian, Luigi de Pace.[14] The Santa Croce ceiling, a larger surface than the cupola of the Chigi Chapel, had to have been done by an imported Venetian craftsman. It is not surprising that fifteenth-century Rome developed a strong tradition of feigned mosaics. On the ceiling vaults of the Basso della Rovere chapel at Santa Maria del Popolo, for example, Pinturicchio painted a gold ground with a grid pattern of veins. From floor level it closely resembles mosaic. There is uncertainty in such a work about whether the fictive mosaic was an ersatz for a real mosaic too expensive or unavailable (that is, the artist was hoping that his deception would not be uncovered), or simply another advertisement of painting's medial superiority (that is, the artist was hoping that his deception would be uncovered). That uncertainty is dispelled in the Jerusalem Chapel, where Peruzzi and his patron decided that nothing other than mosaic would do. A painted ceiling in the modern style would not strike the decorous imperial note. Nor was Peruzzi interested in making a virtue out of a necessity, as Pinturicchio seems to have done, by imitating mosaic in another medium. Instead he and Carvajal chose to archaize with medium specificity: to imitate ancient mosaic *in the medium of mosaic*; a perfect imitation.

The mosaic ceiling of the chapel, the micromosaic icon of the Man of Sorrows that was kept there, and the long inscription spread across several hundred majolica tiles amounted to a counterstatement to the modern reliance on painting. The digital mode now offered a clear alternative to the analogue mode of representation. Mosaic voluntarily renounced painting's capacities to register the direct trace of the artist's hand and to embrace the whole perceptible world, including all the other representational media, through optical illusions and perspective. Both the performative

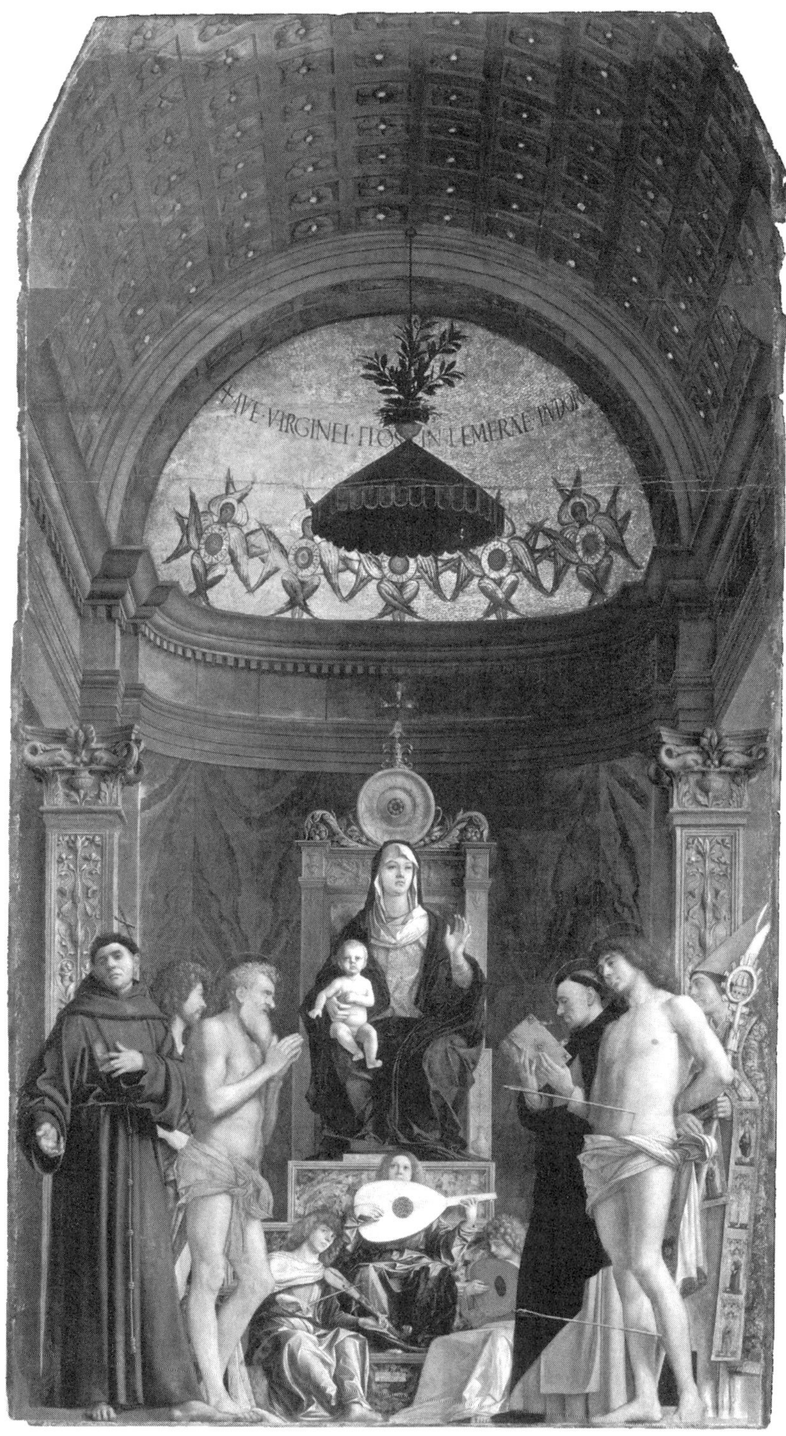

27.3 A comparison between media. Giovanni Bellini, *San Giobbe Altarpiece*, oil on panel, 471 x 258 cm (1478). Venice, Galleria dell' Accademia. Painting represents its authoritative precursor, mosaic, modestly effacing itself from the fictional world it creates. And yet painting is present, and prevails, as the medium capable of stage-managing such a fiction.

aspect of painting—its ability to register the circumstances of its own fabrication—and its illusionism were contingent on the continuity and homogeneity of its surface. Digital media, by contrast, which broke representational conventions down into replaceable modules, were media designed for substitution.

Peruzzi's mosaic ceiling in the Jerusalem Chapel at Santa Croce was not simply a substitute for the predecessor ceiling. It was an attempt to reinstate a substitutional mode of production in an age that felt it could no longer take for granted the smooth unpunctuated flow of content from one artifact to the next. Peruzzi's ceiling and the larger environment in which it worked offered a model of how a substitutional transmission process might ideally work.

By any measure Peruzzi's ceiling would seem to be one of the most successful antiquarian experiments made in Rome at the time. And yet the Jerusalem Chapel has never captured the imagination of historians of the period. The oblivion set in early; Vasari does not mention it at all. The Peruzzi mosaic looks like a blind pantomime of an early Christian work. The work, it would seem, does not sufficiently display its distance from its predecessor to qualify as an artistic performance. In fact, Peruzzi's chapel is a highly self-aware performance—a performance as sophisticated as Bellini's San Giobbe altarpiece—of an older mode of thinking about the historicity of artifacts. The ceiling performs a substitution, but commits the artistic infelicity of failing to signal its own performance, except in relatively minor ways, such as in the dramatic lighting from below on St. John's face.

The apse at Santa Croce by Antoniazzo Romano was an experiment in the modern idiom of illusionistic painting. A few steps away, and a decade later, Peruzzi reinstated the ancient medium of mosaic. The San Giobbe altar by Bellini and the *Saint Augustine in His Study* by Carpaccio also stage comparisons between media. Painting does not appear inside the fictive spaces created by Bellini's and Carpaccio's brushes, however, as it did for example in the Washington predella panel of Gentile da Fabriano's Quaratesi altarpiece, where the depicted church shows murals and altarpieces as well as a mosaic apse. In the ideal worlds invented by the Venetians—the nonspace of the Sacra Conversazione, the perfection of Augustine's study—the timeless and prestigious medium, mosaic, prevails. Painting modestly effaces itself from the fictional worlds it creates. Painting represents its own antithesis, a medium that submits to the disciplines of custom and craft and renounces the rhetoric of illusionism as much as authorial self-display. But painting is nevertheless present in the comparison as the framing medium. The picture proposes a comparison between,

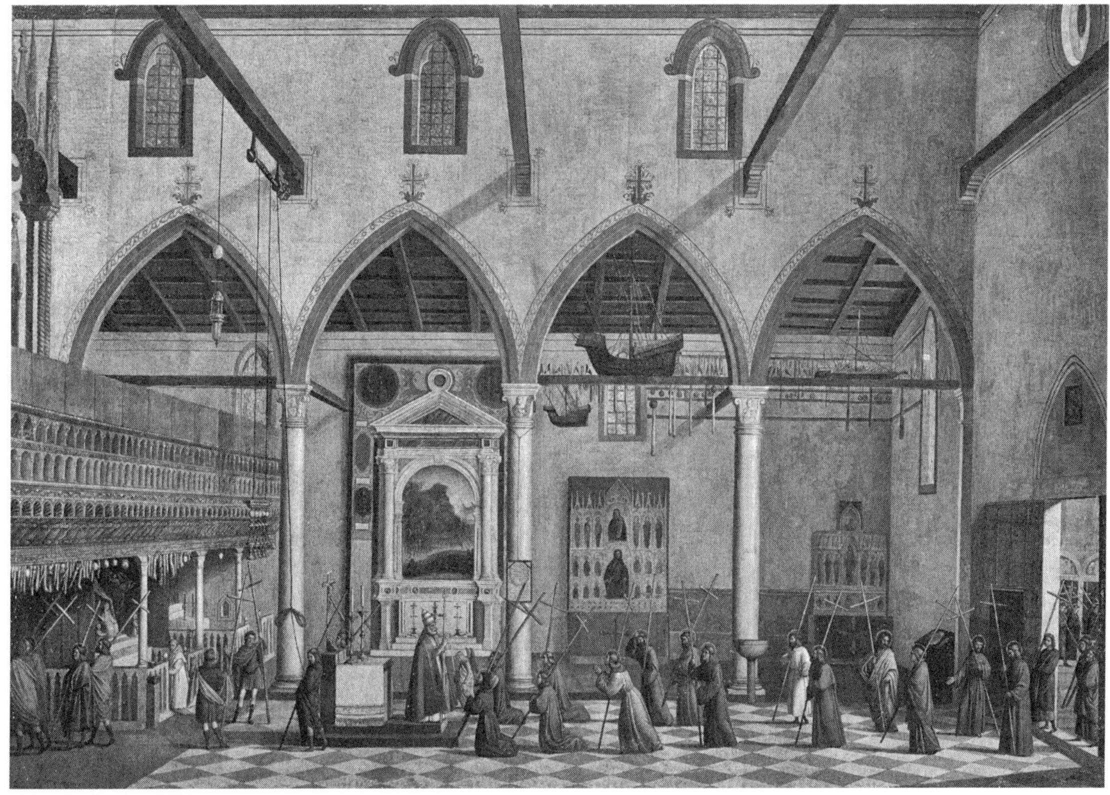

27.4 A catalogue of possible cult images. Vittore Carpaccio, *Vision of Prior Ottobon*, oil on canvas, 121 x 174 cm (ca. 1515). Venice, Galleria dell' Accademia. Under the rood screen, a cult statue surrounded by ex-votos; along the wall, two gold-ground polyptychs and an altarpiece in Carpaccio's own style offering a window onto an atmospheric landscape.

on the one hand, a fictive, depicted mosaic and, on the other hand, the real painting itself, Bellini's panel. To grasp the comparison, the beholder must submit to the fiction created by painting, and at the same time see the entire painting as a fiction-creating machine, thus breaking the fiction. A fictive thing is implicitly compared to a real thing. This is a special kind of comparison that happens across an ontological frontier. Only a painting capable of highly effective simulations of optical impressions can manage such a comparison. Carpaccio's *Vision of Prior Ottobon* of ca. 1515 in the Accademia in Venice is a catalogue of possible cult images (figure 27.4).[15] The prior, a small figure in white, is at prayer before a sculpted Virgin and Child of an archaic type, a so-called Throne of Wisdom. From the rafters of the church and from the rood screen hang votive offerings: batons of wax, wax body parts, ship models offered in gratitude for prayers

341

answered. In the aisle, two old-fashioned, multi-paneled, gold-ground altarpieces alongside a painting of Carpaccio's time, a mirror of his own art, a transparent window onto an atmospheric landscape. All these objects are trumped by Ottobon's vision—this happened in 1511—of the procession of the Ten Thousand Martyrs through this very church and towards St. Peter himself, stationed at an (imageless) altar.

By engulfing all the other media, painting prevails in the paragone with mosaic, a medium that for all its virtues would have great difficulty representing an oil painting inside itself. In this way painting emerges as the dominant medium of pictorial art. Art in the modern era, according to Niklas Luhmann, is characterized by the ability to demystify in a single operation the very fictions it creates. For Luhmann, all art "is constituted by an internal medium that shapes materials—paint, language, bodily movement, spatial arrangements—within an external medium that isolates the forms in their striking particularity and guarantees that they are perceived as art rather than as wood, a coat of paint, a simple communication, or human behavior."[16] Such a double framing creates and dismantles fictions in the same moment. Over the course of the fifteenth century, paint developed the power to function as both the internal and the external medium in Luhmann's sense. Paint created the illusion and at the same time signaled to the beholder the madeness, and the speciousness, of the illusion. It embraced illusion and disillusion within itself. Other media can do this, too, even architecture. The building physically enveloped by another building—the many imitations of the edicule of the Holy Sepulchre, the Holy House of Loreto, Bramante's Tempietto—were both buildings to be used, and models of buildings (of a sacred original or an ideal ancient temple). The architectural framing devices, including miniaturization, labeling by inscription, literal framing as well as literal enframing by a larger structure, signaled the fictional status of the edicule. Painting, however, is a peculiarly effective double frame. Paint is both an inferior substitute for mosaic and the privileged matrix for aesthetic performance. A painting such as Bellini's pretends to defer to the archaic medium of mosaic, but in reality does no such thing.

The comparison staged by Bellini's San Giobbe altarpiece is equally present at Santa Croce, except that in the Roman basilica the comparison is physically pried apart. The luxurious overlaying of possibilities in the Venetian panel, and the fine paradox of an intermedial comparison carried out inside a single medium which is itself one of the terms of comparison, is in the Roman church broken up and literalized as a plodding two-step sequence of hesitations: an apse painting that remembers an ancient iconographic tradition that in fact never existed (the mandorla), and a vaulted ceiling that attempts to bury its own performance in a medium not conducive to performances. Apse and ceiling at Santa Croce are a double framing dragged out in space and time.

Peruzzi's mosaic oscillates between two identities. It ornaments a reliquary chapel that is itself a structural relic of an imperial palace. But at the same time, insofar as it successfully restores the original fifth-century mosaic, the new ceiling is a relic in its own right. The mosaic is both container and contents, both frame and work. In the very next years Raphael, working in the papal apartments in the Vatican Palace, and well aware of Peruzzi's project at Santa Croce, would clarify the location of painting. Painting as an art in Rome would come to occupy a physically narrow but conceptually ample layer falling between the solid, load-bearing wall and the interior of the room occupied by bodies and things. The wall is a container, the contained are the movable objects in the room. The artwork can choose between two identities: it can ornament the container (a fresco or mosaic does this), or it can live inside the container, a precious movable thing. The painted panel or canvas of the Renaissance, neither wholly of the wall nor quite free of the wall, is caught between these two identities.

The decision to revert to mosaic in the Jerusalem Chapel had the effect of liberating painting from the substitutional project. Peruzzi imported his antiquarianism back into the old substitutional mode, and in the process masked his own artistry. Peruzzi was a painter of some virtue. The mosaics based on his designs are exceptionally painterly, rendering in nuanced cascades of tesserae the fine shading on Christ's face and the modeling of the upturned head of St. John, for example, a motif Peruzzi might have seen in Melozzo da Forlì's frescoes in the apse at Santi Apostoli, painted in the early 1480s.[17] But Peruzzi also created a new context for understanding the work of Antoniazzo Romano. Antoniazzo's apse at Santa Croce chronologically preceded Peruzzi's ceiling. But the moment that Peruzzi reverted to the older medium, mosaic, Antoniazzo became in effect his successor. For it was Antoniazzo's apse fresco, which dared to test the limits of the substitutional paradigm by replacing a mosaic with a mural painting, coating a wall with a garment of paint rather than of stones, that pointed forward to Raphael's and Michelangelo's Roman frescoes.

In 1509 the new Jerusalem Chapel at Santa Croce was complete, by which time Julius II, whose relations with Carvajal were poor, had hired Raphael of Urbino to decorate a nearly square room in the Vatican Palace: his library, it seems, although from at least 1513 the room was known as the Stanza della Segnatura (see figure 17.3). This was Raphael's first important commission in Rome. Nothing he had painted until then promised the amplitude and grace of the frescoes he would produce for this room:

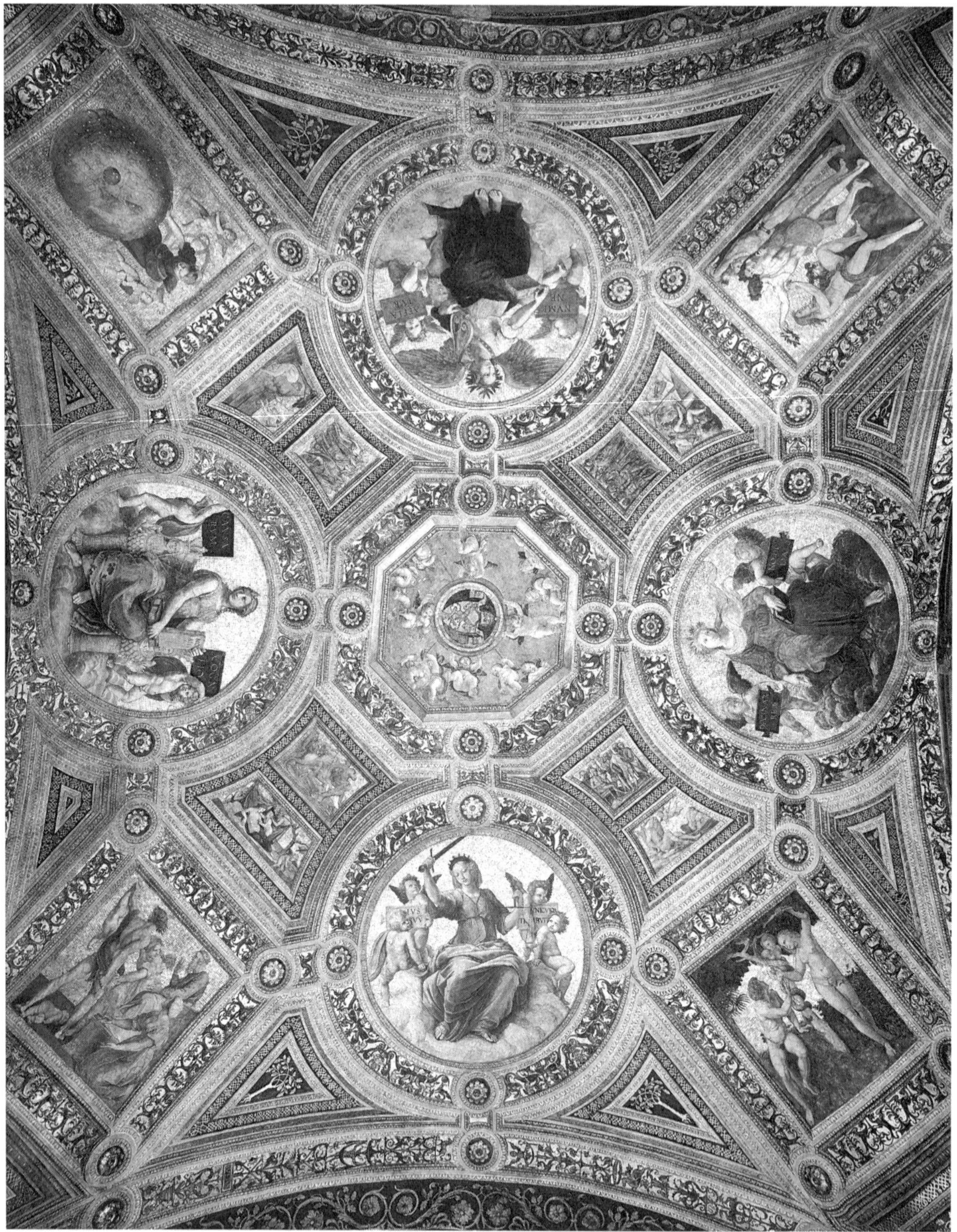

27.5 A rendering of a mosaic ceiling in paint. Raphael and associates, the ceiling of the Pope's library (ca. 1508). Vatican City, Vatican Palace, Stanza della Segnatura. Raphael was attending closely to the ceiling of the Jerusalem Chapel at Santa Croce. The tessellation is not real but fictive, and confined to the background. The false mosaic is interrupted by the continuous painted surfaces of the figures, signaling the painter's new sovereignty over the media.

the so-called *School of Athens*, the *Disputa*, the *Parnassus*, the *Allegory of Jurisprudence*. Together with Michelangelo's painted vault in the Sistine Chapel, which was begun in 1508 and completed in 1512, the murals of the Stanza della Segnatura made an instant, revolutionary sensation. But just above those unexpected wall paintings, Raphael designed a ceiling that was still tightly stitched into a substitutional web. The vaulted ceiling has four medallions surrounding a central oculus, divided by fictional partitions and supplemented by scenes in trapezoidal fields (figure 27.5). It is exactly the schema of Peruzzi's Jerusalem Chapel, except that in the Stanza della Segnatura the mosaic is not real but fictive: a tremulous, irregular grid incised into a gold ground. [18] Fictive mosaic was a staple of antiquarian-flavored wall painting in the last decades of the fifteenth and beginning of the sixteenth centuries. It was used by Andrea Mantegna in his *Camera picta* at Mantua (1465–1474); Pinturicchio, as noted, at the Basso della Rovere chapel, in Santa Maria del Popolo (ca. 1485); Peruzzi or Jacopo Ripanda at San Onofrio in Rome, another apse that "revived" the system of historiated partitions. Peruzzi used fictive mosaic backgrounds at the Villa Farnesina (c. 1511) and in his Ponzetti Chapel at Santa Maria della Pace (1516). In Florence, Ridolfo Ghirlandaio simulated mosaic in the vaults of the Cappella dei Priori in the Palazzo Vecchio (complete by 1515). In such simulated mosiacs it is the gold background alone, not the figures, to which the scored or drawn grid is applied, which is illogical, for in a real mosaic the entire surface would be composed of small tiles. The limiting of the fictive tesselation to the gold ground was the painters' way of indicating that in simulating mosaic they were in no way conceding the inferiority of paint to mosaic.

The floor of the Stanza della Segnatura, meanwhile, as noted in section 17, was neo-cosmatesque, in effect a completion of the incomplete floor of the Jerusalem Chapel as well as an imitation of the floor of the Sistine Chapel. It is as if the substitutional floor and ceiling were compensating for Raphael's radically unanticipated wall paintings between them, artistic performances that broke completely with any possible referential chain linking the present with the origins of painting. The parallel with the apse at Santa Croce is exact: again the archaizing work is found above and the modern scenic painting below.

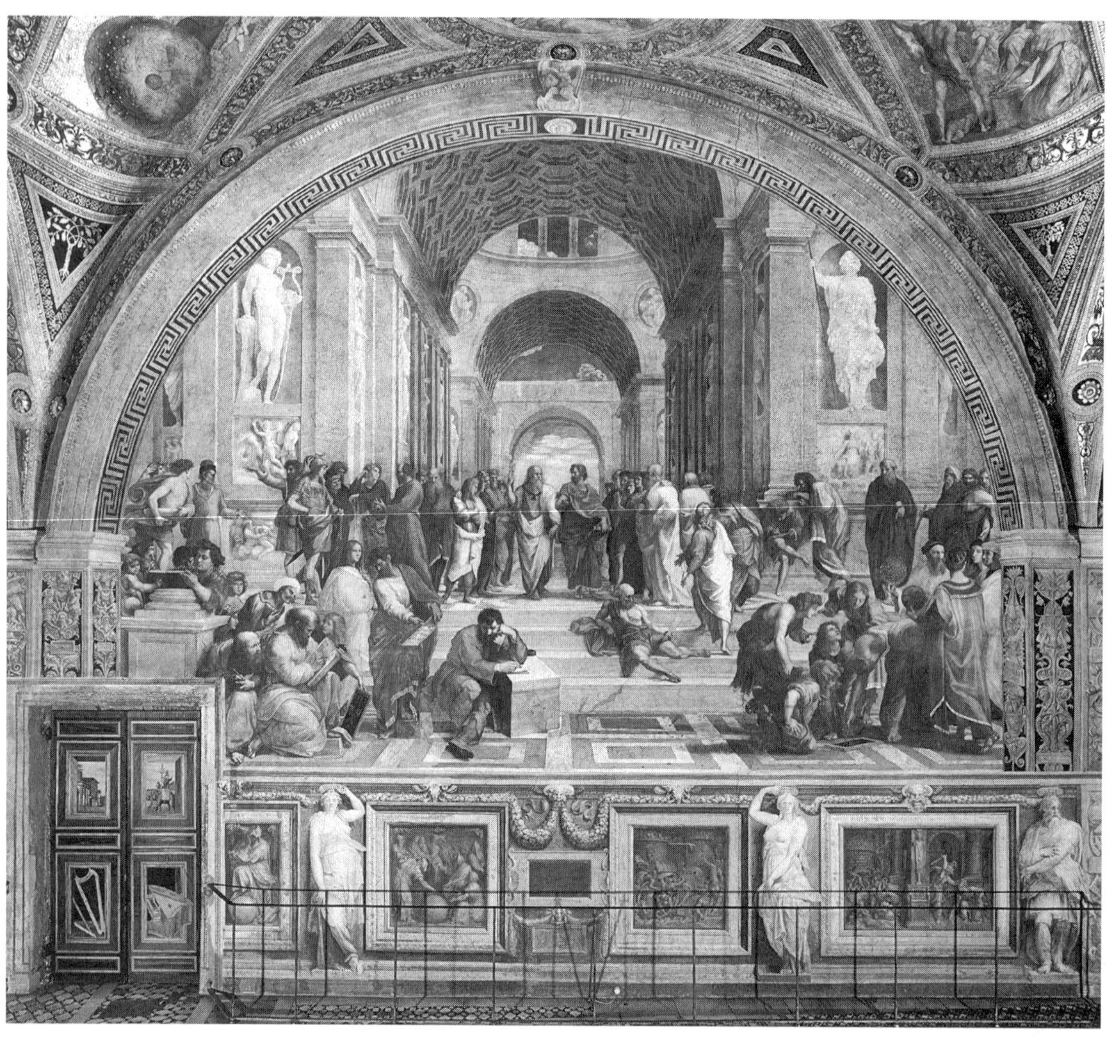

28.1 A sacra conversazione without a center. Raphael, *School of Athens*, fresco (ca. 1510). Vatican City, Vatican Palace, Stanza della Segnatura. The mural depicts a conversation that can never have taken place, among philosophers separated by vast expanses of space and time. The painting does not make it clear that they will ever resolve their differences.

TWENTY-EIGHT

Space for Fiction

The *School of Athens* by Raphael looks self-evident and deeply equilibrated (figure 28.1). In fact, this mural is the densest of cryptograms, a bundle of unresolved conceptual tensions masked by the animation and poised fluency of the represented bodies and the monumental harmony of the architecture. The conflicts absorbed by this painting are doubts about authority and transmission, about singular relic and numinous place, about the risks of creativity; the questions that had occupied late fifteenth-century buildings, sculptures, prints, paintings.

The *School of Athens* represents a population of ancient Greek philosophers and their pupils standing, strolling, sitting, above all talking, in pairs and small groups, on the steps and forecourt of a deep, barrel-vaulted, basilica-like structure. This is a picture of sociable interaction so harmonious and so inviting that one easily forgets the basic impossibility, the anachronism, of the scene. For this is a philosophical conversation carried out across time, gathering lives of the sixth century BCE (Zoroaster, Pythagoras) together with lives of the second century CE (Ptolemy), or even of the twelfth century, if the turbanned, moustachioed figure at lower left is indeed Averroës, the Cordoban commentator on Aristotle.[1] This conversation, which happened across the pages of books, is here thematized as live debate.

The interactive yet essentially outward-oriented company set off against an architectural foil was one of the basic templates of European painting. It was the schema of the oldest surviving decorated apse in Rome, the mosaic at Santa Pudenziana (early fifth century), and one of the most recent, Antoniazzo Romano's *True Cross* narrative at Santa Croce in Gerusalemme (see figure 26.3). To be sure, in the Santa Croce apse the figures are set off against a landscape, not a building, but then Raphael's building is so vast within the picture field that it comes to function as a landscape. In a sense Raphael has flattened an apse against a wall. The *Parnassus* on the adjacent wall (see figure 28.4) is a similar transformation of the fifth-century apse mosaic at Santa Sabina. The *School of Athens* secularizes an apse painting, just as the room's neo-cosmatesque pavement secularizes a church floor

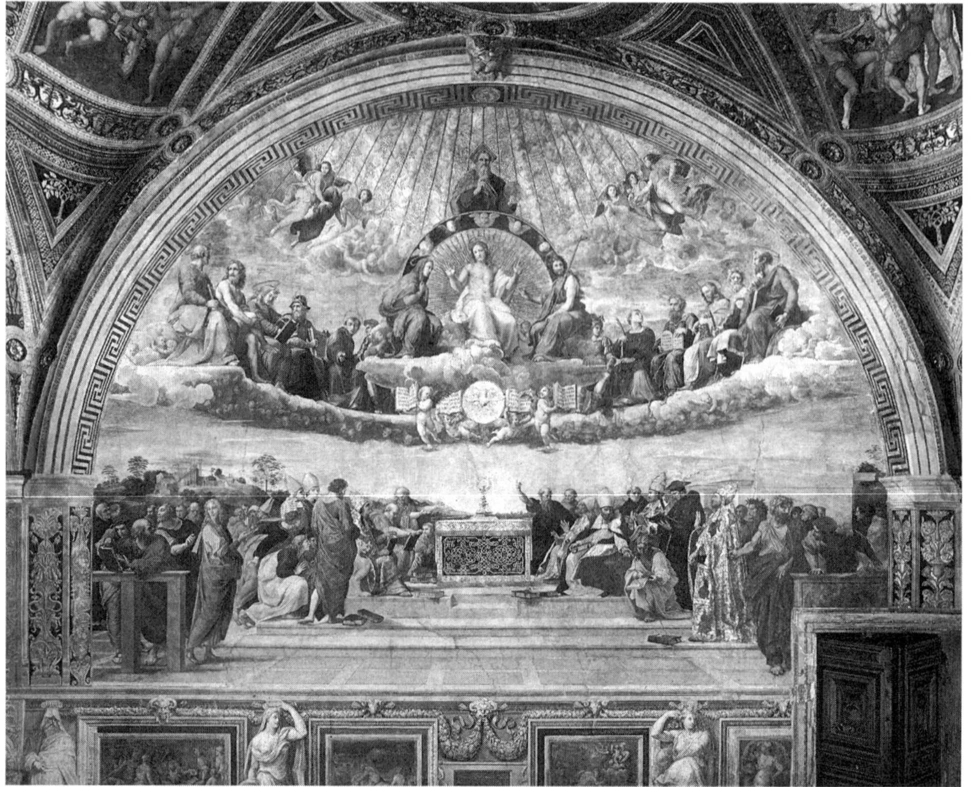

28.2 A fictive apse constructed of anthropomorphic building blocks. Raphael, *Disputa*, fresco (ca. 1510). Vatican City, Vatican Palace, Stanza della Segnatura. The truth of the Eucharist, an infinitely dense point at the center of the composition, is disseminated outwards, made comprehensible to human beings. Raphael's lunettes are flat but refer in their scale and iconographical ambitions to early medieval apse mosaics.

(see figure 17.3). It is a room masquerading as a church, each wall its own apse. The *Disputa* on the opposite wall of the Stanza della Segnatura makes this move clear (figure 28.2). Here Raphael constructed a fictive apse out of anthropomorphic building blocks: below, at ground level, a drum of standing and seated figures, above, a concave calotte of bodies supported by a cloud bank.

Even this idea was not new. The Florentine painter Francesco Botticini in his *Assumption of the Virgin* on panel (ca. 1475), now in the National Gallery, had flattened a celestial dome onto a plane surface and suspended it above an open tomb and a company of apostles in a landscape. Botticini was trying somewhat awkwardly to represent, on a picture plane, the meeting of spherical heaven and the plane of the earth, that "middling region" or "spherical shoreline where matter and spirit met."[2] Closer to Raphael, Fra Bartolommeo offered a similar adaptation in his *Vision of Saint Catherine* of 1508–1509, a painting Raphael knew (figure 28.3). The curving configuration of the upper, visionary portion of the painting, which shows God the Father with angels, is emphatically nonperspectival and can be compared (in form and motif: a figure of God surrounded by four whirling angels) to the Dome of the Ascension in San Marco in Venice, which Fra Bartolommeo had seen during his stay there in spring of 1508, while the *Vision of*

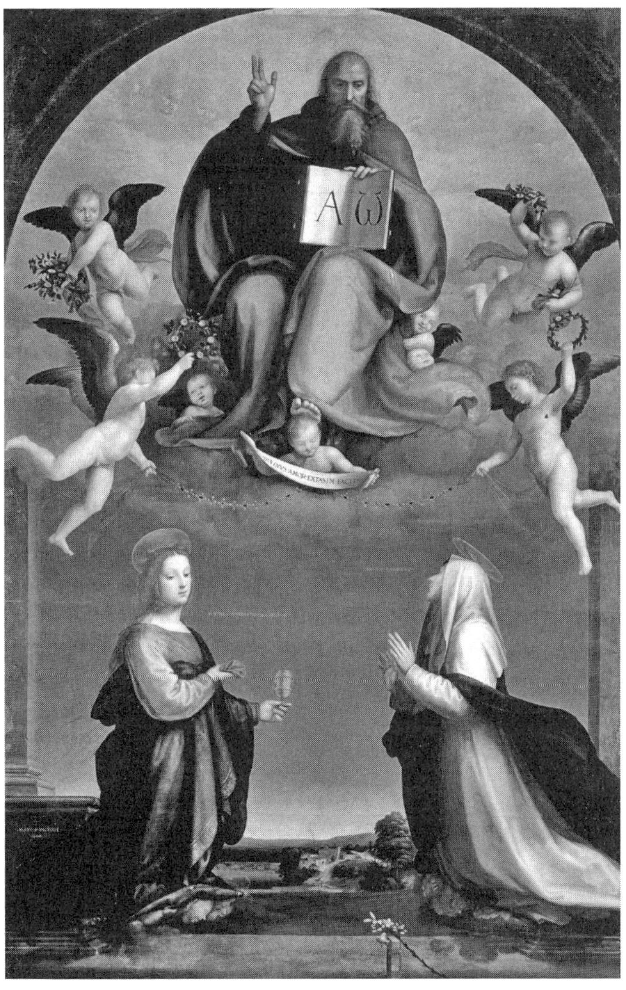

28.3 A Byzantine dome translated into two dimensions. Fra Bartolommeo, *Vision of Saint Catherine*, oil on canvas transferred from panel, 360 x 234 cm (1508–1509). Lucca, Pinacoteca Civica. This painting was well known to Raphael, who copied a portion of its landscape in the background of his *Disputa* (figure 28.2). Both paintings, in contrast to Antoniazzo's apse at Santa Croce, picture the meeting of heaven and earth.

Saint Catherine was in its gestation phase. At San Marco, the convexity suggested by the lightening of the blue field behind Christ contradicts the overarching concavity of the mosaic dome. Fra Bartolommeo adapted to the two-dimensional surface of his painting not the illusion of perspectival space but rather this kind of visual warping. Seeing it in 1508, Raphael took the impression of Fra Bartolommeo's painting with him when he went to Rome later that year. The *Disputa* fresco is throughout an homage to Fra Bartolommeo: the figures seated in a cloudy apse recall Fra Bartolommeo's *Last Judgment*, and in the background Raphael portrays rustic houses that are an exact quotation of the houses in the landscape of Fra Bartolommeo's *Vision of Saint Catherine* altarpiece.[3]

The *School of Athens* nests its figures in groups and subgroups and gathers chronologically separate moments into a unified space, just as Antoniazzo's apse at Santa Croce had done. Antoniazzo's "simultaneous narrative," which as we saw was not a traditional mode but a pseudo-archaism, prefigures the "softer" anachronism of Raphael. Freedom from temporal unity is not a distinctive feature of Raphael's mural, for it shared this feature with any fifteenth-century *sacra conversazione*, or assembly of saints. A typical example is Bellini's San Giobbe altarpiece (see figure 27.3), where historical individuals born in the fourteenth century BCE (?) (Job), first century BCE (John the Baptist and Mary), third century (St. Sebastian), twelfth century (St. Francis and St. Dominic), and thirteenth century (St. Louis of Toulouse) all gather under a barrel vault. The *School of Athens* is distinctive because, unlike a *sacra conversazione*, there is no center. Here the central figure that controlled every Christian cult image, Christ or Virgin or saint, or in the apse at Santa Croce the cross itself, is split into two figures, Plato and Aristotle.

Building and picturing in the fifteenth century were still much concerned to keep everything centered. Signs were meant to stay settled on their meanings, antitypes on their types, copies on their originals. Without that stability art could hardly expect to serve as a guide for belief or knowledge. Paintings themselves, panel and decorated wall, played their part in the stabilizing project. The portable icon, the painted altarpiece, the apse fresco were exerting pressure on space and on bodies, attempting to organize experience in time and of time. Doubling of origin points, hesitation about place, drift of meaning were all clues to the difficulty of the task.

The *School of Athens* withdraws from the stabilizing, centering project and instead finds a new, protected space and time. The picture practices a rhetoric of ideal classicism projecting an illusion of perfect alignment and the elimination of redundancy and excess. That rhetoric disguises the real subject matter of the picture. For this is a picture that withdraws from the effort to stabilize time through the production of antitypes, repetitions, and copies and instead takes the failure of that effort—marked by displacement and difference—as its content. The differences between original and copy and between then and now, temporal differences, are spatialized. Difference is laid out laterally on the surface of the wall. The difference between original and copy is the difference between Plato and Aristotle, teacher and disciple: a transmission problem presented by Raphael as a conversation, not a problem at all. Above the fresco, flanking the allegory of Philosophy, we read the words *Causarum Cognitio*, the inquiry into causes, reasons, explanations. The fresco affirms the plural *causarum*: the investigations are many and ongoing.[4]

The Stanza della Segnatura was the setting for a completely new conception of painting as an art. The break with the past is hard to recognize given the historical continuity of the papal chamber with the complex of medial experiments at Santa Croce in Gerusalemme. The Stanza della Segnatura combines elements of those slightly prior experiments and bundles them into a single room.

The wall paintings in the Stanza tear the substitutional web and create instant fictions, vast semicircular lunettes opening onto alternative worlds at once credible and incredible. On the wall across from the *School of Athens* is the *Disputation of the Sacrament*, or *Disputa*, a company of earthly and heavenly personages grouped around an altar and contemplating the mystery of the Eucharist. Between the two we find the *Parnassus*, Apollo together with the Muses and a gathering of poets ancient and modern (figure 28.4). On the fourth wall, there are two scenes of lawmaking: *Justinian Handing the Pandects to Trebonianus* and *Pope Gregory IX Handing the Decretals to Saint Raimund*. The overall model for the first three wall-sized scenes was Leonardo da Vinci's *Last Supper* mural in Milan, painted in the mid-1490s, known at the very least through copies to every Florentine and Roman artist, where one finds the same combination of a plausible constructed space and an overload of content. For in the *Last Supper*, as Leo Steinberg has shown, just as in the *School of Athens*, there is "too much time" packed into the space and a dense polyvalence folded into the many gestures.[5] Raphael also incorporates in these frescoes the idea of a multiplicity radiating from a packed center. The central gestures, of Christ in Leonardo's *Last Supper*, of Apollo in the *Parnassus*, and of Plato and Aristotle in the *School of Athens*, and the infinite density of the Eucharist in the *Disputa*, are all authoritative centers and yet replete with "multiplex" meaning. The density of the original message, powerful and yet cryptically encoded, is then distributed into looser, more individuated expression in the flanking figures—the Apostles, the Church fathers and theologians, the

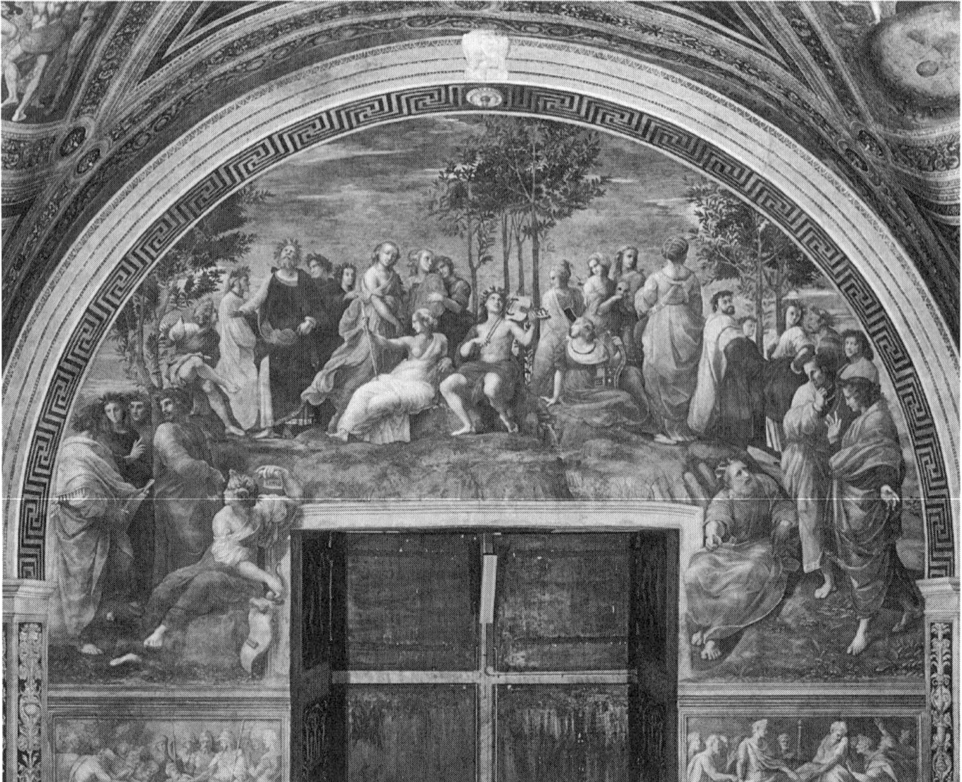

28.4 Orality to literacy. Raphael, *Parnassus*, fresco (ca. 1510). Vatican City, Vatican Palace, Stanza della Segnatura. Apollo sings and plays while the blind Homer intones. Writing comes later, in the tradition initiated by the scribe to the left and continued by the poets below him. The inscription of the spoken word, first in handwriting and eventually in printed books, will erode trust in the reliable transmission of truth and instead initiate the endless conversation figured in the *School of Athens* (figure 28.1).

poets in the various genres, and the various philosophers. Dissemination is essential to the original message, an outworking of the truth, and yet with distance and relays comes diversity. Leonardo predicts, in the Last Supper, the contentiousness that would mark the future of the church; Raphael then makes that diversity his theme.

The *School of Athens* had many other proximate models. Piero della Francesca's Brera Madonna, which used to be at San Bernardino near Urbino and was therefore well-known to Raphael, provided an example of a white, cassetted barrel vault. The overall architectural fantasy of the *School of Athens*, the proportions of the figures to the grandiose architecture, the roughly two-tiered disposition of the figures, and the two central figures framed by the arch are all modeled on the bronze relief by Lorenzo

Ghiberti depicting *The Meeting of Solomon and Sheba* on the doors of the Baptistery in Florence, the "Gate of Paradise," ca. 1430. Raphael submitted these paragons to hypertrophy, multiplying Leonardo's disciples until they could no longer fit within a single row and aggrandizing Ghiberti's architecture so that it no longer fits within the frame at all. But at the same time he defused the narrative charges in his models, exchanging the tight, urgent, emotional wavelengths of the *Last Supper*, and the world-historical clash figured by the confrontation of the powerful Jewish king and the skeptical Arabian queen, for the ceaseless circuitry, benign and almost anecdotal, of intellectual intercourse.

The content of Raphael's murals in the Stanza della Segnatura is reconciliation and harmony between the upper and the lower spheres. The knowledge that deciphers the mystery of the Eucharist flows from God far above to the humans below in a smooth passage, as oral teaching, *logos*, filters into scripture and eventually into the books of the theologians. Figures of the Old and New Testaments seated in the cloudbank above, prophets and evangelists, already write on tablets and books, preparing for their mediating missions. Four putti flanking the Holy Spirit hold open books. The jump across the gap between divine cloud bank and the massive, human-built pavilion below poses no difficulty. The inscription of abstract ideas is pictured just to the right of the altar, as a smooth relay: Peter, pointing skyward, explains a point to St. Ambrose. The next figure to the right is St. Augustine, holding a book in his lap and swiveling to dictate to a graceful scribe, parchment pressed against one knee, ink bottle squeezed between thumb and forefinger of the left hand. The potentially troubling split between the Eucharist, to all appearances a mere symbol, and its referent above is resolved by the magic of understanding. The vertical repetition, the downward cascade of divine substance, from God to Christ to Holy Spirit to Host, across a sequence of gold discs diminishing in size, is not allowed to become a displacement. In preparatory drawings, St. Peter and St. Paul intervened as mediators between Christ and altar; in the final work they are shifted to the sides.[6] The *Parnassus*, too, has a single center: Apollo, the singer, the oracle, surrounded by his muses. Here there are only two books in evidence, one in the hands of the figure in yellow at the lower left, sometimes identified as Horace, and one in the hands of the muse Clio.

The Stanza della Segnatura, the room as a whole, diagrams two competing modes of making.[7] Floor and ceiling, *opus sectile* and fictive mosaic, together model the substitutional system, the replica chain stretching back link by link to an invisible origin. The new floor is in the twelfth-century manner, which stood in for a lost ancient manner. The building itself, however, the Vatican Palace, was new, and no one could imagine for a moment—as they might at the Sancta Sanctorum, the Tempietto, or even in the Sistine Chapel—that the floor stood in any kind of substitutional relationship to an ancient floor. The floor and ceiling are not forgeries, they are forgeries of forgeries.

The wall paintings, meanwhile, imagine what it would be like to break out of the cycle of forgeries. The spacious wall paintings model authorial performance, the punctuation of history by the creative will. Moreover, they thematize individual invention. Each prophet, each theologian, each poet and philosopher had an individual voice and must be shown behaving in an individual fashion. Raphael even includes, to the right of the *Disputa*, the figure of the fiery preacher Girolamo Savonarola, who had been burned only a little over ten years earlier, in 1498, and whose legacy was the subject of real controversy at this time. The *School of Athens*, the *Disputa*, and the *Parnassus* are near absolute inventions, only weakly linked to their predecessors. In this room, performance takes the special form of the construction of experientially plausible fictional worlds that nevertheless carry such normative authority that they seem to escape time altogether. Figures by Raphael are designed to look as if they had never been designed; their freedom of movement and expression—so their rhetoric—is a function of their absolute necessity. The frescoes appear to be guided by nature, by the ideal examples of ancient art and architecture, by the artist's imagination, and not by mere blind tradition. The past does not force itself on this present. Apollo plays not an ancient lyre but a contemporary fiddle.[8]

The orchestration of modes, substitutional (floor and ceiling) and performative (painted walls), is itself a performance. The next step will be the construction of a painting that absorbs *this* performance; that is, a painterly performance whose content is a staged comparison between painting (standing for authorial performance) and architecture (standing for the transmission of content by a substitutional chain). And so on; every performance now potentially serving as the content of a future performance.

The *School of Athens* is a token in the total signifying system of the Stanza della Segnatura, whereby the room forces the picture to represent an idea about the origins of art within a collation of different ideas about origins. Yet the picture does not need the room any more. The picture depicts the dialectic of civilization, a critical, questioning conversation that takes place among rock-solid architectural accretions. In this way the painting absorbs into itself all the tensions between place and space, between custom and creativity, between building and painting, and puts them on display. This capacity to comment on architecture creates an asymmetry, since architecture has only a limited capacity to comment on painting. This asymmetry is the key to painting's conceptual, though not necessarily physical, break with architecture in the sixteenth century. The break that marks the advent of a "modern" art—and by that we mean an art whose premises and aims, whose institutional and theoretical justifications, are still more or less continuous with those of the art of our own time—will be the extraction of painting from the total context of the built space. In the sixteenth century, the art of painting liberated itself notionally from architecture, even if great quantities of painting through the eighteenth century and even beyond remained physically attached to walls. That is not to say that Raphael's paintings simply drifted off on their own. Rather, they took the room with them. The comparisons and stagings performed by the room were internalized by the paintings, complicating them almost unimaginably.

The substitution chain was a myth about the life of artifacts that justified the place of artifacts in life. The sequence of effective substitutes delivered intact an imagined primordial message. That message was materialized in an authoritative image or form. The original type together with all its subsequent tokens had the character of *inscriptions*, that is, they were held to be true in any conceivable context of reception. The whole point of the substitutional myth was to preserve the inscriptional character of the tokens. Undesirable were tokens suspected of being mere *utterances*, that is, local and occasional statements whose meanings derive from the circumstances of their enunciation. The hypothesis of substitution pretended that all the tokens were really maintaining the character of the original inscription instead of being utterances in their own right and therefore untrustworthy.

Raphael was *also* trying to make pictures that would be true in any context. In this sense they are "mobile" even though they are fixed to a wall. But Raphael's paintings do not deliver a message embodied in a primordial inscription. Raphael does entertain this idea. In the *Expulsion of Heliodorus* in the neighboring Stanza d'Eliodoro (ca. 1514) he may have incorporated an allusion to the Vera icon, the authentic portrait of Christ on cloth preserved in the Vatican.[9] And yet such references are not the real basis for the inscriptional character of Raphael's painting. Instead, the works create an effect of transcending their own local circumstances—of stepping out of the flow of custom—by adopting a timeless formal norm. The normative form automatically transforms every new work that complies with it into an authoritative work. Classic or normative works can be exchanged for other such works. In this way the character of the substitution chain is preserved, but not its structure of a descent through time. For the normative image disguises its own historical origins. Do the normative bodies and spaces of Raphael's fictive worlds derive from history or from nature? Are the forms authoritative because they are ancient, or because they are rational? Such doubts about the basis for the authority of the classical shunt attention away from the artistic performance that lies behind it. The artist who invents a timeless form hides behind the fiction of his own dispensability. This is not simply a performance that breaks with custom, it is a performance that masks its own existence. Precisely because it *is* a performance, normativity or classicism can never be a long-term or stable state in the modern West. The performance of the classical is always quickly fed back into the recursive mill to become raw material for the next performance.

Once liberated from their time-mending substitutional tasks, paintings can be understood for the first time as *texts*, that is, as self-sufficient, integrated wholes mysteriously more significant than the sum of their components. Once the picture is a text, it can be cited and no longer just copied, in the same way that later authors cite or allude to Dante's *Commedia* and do not just copy it. This accession to textual status was marked by the advent of printed reproductions. Among the first works to be reproduced as prints were the Madonna in the Robe of Wheat Ears (see figures 2.1 and 2.2) and Leonardo's *Last Supper*.[10] Raphael's frescoes were immediately reproduced in print.[11] Prints brought pictorial texts into contact with far-flung audiences and introduced the texts into an intertextual afterlife. Moreover, they flattened different kinds of imagery onto a consistent, often monochrome plane, a process of abstraction that enabled comparisons among disparate works and paved the way for the emergence of the idea of the artist's "corpus" and the idea of stylistic "schools." These ideas then fed back into art making. Textual pictures enter into a completely new temporal framework, the time of art: a virtual psychological process governed by the rhythms of recognition, connection, and interpretation.

Because pictorial representation is conventional, even if less so than language, every picture, even a picture by the new model of the self-ruled (that is, autonomous) artist, is linked to prior pictures. Painters learn to figure reality in paint by mimicking and revising other painters. Under a substitutional theory of the sacred image, that picture-to-picture chain is the guarantee of legitimacy. But when picture making begins to experiment with an alternative origin, less remote in time and place, for example the phenomenal world of bodies and spaces as routed through the sensory experience and the talent of the individual painter, then the picture-to-picture chain can come to seem like a confining bond. Against a new backdrop of multiple possible origins of the artwork—nature, geometry, the ideal manner of Greco-Roman statuary, the artist's own imagination— the link to an earlier work of art, whether ancient or recent, in, say, a painting by Raphael, carried a meaning in 1510 completely different from the meaning that retrospective links in a painting by Piero della Francesca had carried two generations earlier. Piero's *Resurrection* at the Palazzo Communale of Sansepolcro (1460s) closely resembles the former high altar of the abbey church (the modern cathedral), a painting of the same subject by Niccolò di Segna of around 1340.[12] Piero's relation to the earlier Resurrection in Sansepolcro could still be justified within the framework of a substitutional model, whereas such an explicit borrowing by Raphael, once he was in Rome, would have come across as mere dependence on another painter — unless it read as a citation. Citation secures the presence of the past in the present by an authorial decision, rather than by direct work-to-work survival. Citation symbolizes the capacity of the author to make decisions.

Aby Warburg was well aware of the risks of excessive citation. The modernist art of his own time was trying to break free of the layers and layers of neoclassicisms that had accumulated since Raphael painted his Stanze, and find its way back to archaic modes of image making. The so-called pathos formula (*Pathosformel*) was Warburg's own contribution to the problem. The pathos formula for Warburg was an image that crystallized archaic gestures and postures generated by fear and other passions.[13] His art history tracked the survival of those images across time and space. Warburg's model reverses a conventional history of art. Instead of the present selecting the past, the past selects its own future by fashioning bodily formulas so powerful that they compel their own future recognition. It is possible that Warburg was right about this; it is also possible that he was sometimes misrecognizing substitutional systems. For the constant effort to link back to the past is easily mistaken for a forward-moving "storing" of the past. Certainly it would seem that from this point on, after Raphael, European painting became so overwhelmingly citational that even Warburg felt compelled to abandon the search for pathos formulas. Warburg had little to say about European art after 1500. The threshold would seem to be marked by Michelangelo's cartoon for the mural of the Battle of Cascina (1504–1505).[14] Everyone at the time knew that the work's function was split: it was a design for a civic mural but it was also an entry in an artistic contest. And it was a work arrested at the stage of the design, the drawing stage, in which condition it could be "pulled apart." Michelangelo's drawing was metaphorically pulled apart as a source of motifs for the next generation of artists, until at last it was literally pulled apart and destroyed. Michelangelo's presentation of figures in varying states of readiness was taken by innumerable artists as an invitation to extract the figures from their context and to reuse them in new combinations. The process of decontextualization was ratified by Marcantonio Raimondi, who made individual figures from Michelangelo's cartoon, such as the "climber," the subject of self-sufficient prints. The generation of artists who studied this cartoon—and the list includes almost every artist of any note in Florence in the period—learned not only lessons in drawing the human nude, but also more basic lessons about making artworks through the recombination and redistribution of images.[15] The episode of the Cascina cartoon was a protracted demonstration of the new archeology of the work of art.

Are we to interpret the generative force of Michelangelo's figural abecedario as the continued transmission of *Pathosformeln*, or simply as a sterile exercise in artistic citation, on the road to academicism? The welter of cross-references became so dense in the sixteenth and seventeenth centuries that one despairs to distinguish survival from neoclassicism. When Warburg did approach sixteenth-century art, he avoided painting and dealt instead with theatrical *intermezzi* and stage design.[16]

The most powerful discursive compulsion of all in modern art history is the compulsion to end the account with Raphael. For a long time this strong sense of Raphael's career as a threshold between two incommensurable art-historical paradigms was linked to the decision of the German painters in Rome, in the early decades of the nineteenth century, to shuck off academicism and start all over again with the style of the young, pre-Roman Raphael. Warburg did not cross this threshold, nor did Panofsky in his *Renaissance and Renascences*, which winds up with an analysis of Raphael's introduction of the modern stringed instrument, the *lira da braccio*, in the *Parnassus*; the deliberate anachronism, according to Panofsky, that establishes the timelessness of the concept of "Parnassus," and the index of Raphael's new freedom.[17] And nor will we cross that threshold in this book. Perhaps in a deep sense our reasons are not so different from those of Warburg and Panofsky. But we also believe that any account that takes seriously print technology as a historical caesura will have to recognize that the rules of the game change suddenly in the first decades of the sixteenth century, at the moment when Raphael enters into alliance with the engraver Marcantonio.

Raphael's works, stretched across several media, from the many preparatory drawings, now collectors' items, to the paintings themselves, finally to the reproductive engravings, brought about an anamnesis. For substitutional transmission had been a kind of systematic oblivion, repetition without difference and without traces. The new conception of art proposed by Raphael's career involved both an integrated text—the painting—and the opening up of that text, the remembering of all the performances that fed into it, across a relay of medial transformations. The closed work and the open work were functions of one another.

The difference between direct (substitutional) and indirect (citational) transmission of form is the real content of Raphael's *School of Athens*. But the painter figures the problem of artistic transmission as the more familiar problem of oral transmission of knowledge giving way to a chain of written texts. The *School of Athens*, on the surface, is about the handing down of ancient wisdom from teacher to pupil. The picture transposes the problem of the histories of making, which is the basic existential concern of an artist — what is my debt to the past? — into the problem of the passage from a system of oral transmission to a system of written transmission, a problem of more universal concern and certainly appropriate subject matter for the wall of a library, if it was a library.[18] By 1510 mechanical printing of books had been established in Italy for half a century and the replacement of manuscripts by printed editions, volume by volume, was well underway. The transition from a textual culture reliant on handwritten books to one reliant on mechanically printed books forced a massive readjustment of traditional conceptions of the originality and evidentiary value of texts.[19] A comparably massive transition had occurred in the eleventh and twelfth centuries, when a society that conducted its business largely through face-to-face contact gave way to one that relied on written documents, involving revision of inveterate notions of trust and the legitimacy of suprapersonal institutions.[20] The print revolution was a recapitulation, three or four centuries later, of the transition from oral culture to written culture.

The introduction of movable type in the fifteenth century was accompanied by the introduction of mechanical procedures for reproducing images. Woodcut and engraving, like movable type, altered thinking about authorship and the truth value of images. The print was a collaboration between artist and machine, splitting the creative process into a multiple agency spread across the human and mechanical fields. Mechanization forced a reevaluation, indeed a new appreciation, of the merely handmade, clarifying the roles of mind and hand and in the end generating a more stable myth of artistic authorship. The conflict between oral and written transmission of knowledge in the *School of Athens* is thus an allegory of the problems of transmission and authority faced by builders and painters around 1500.

The protagonists at the center of the scene gesticulate with their right hands and hold their respective books, the *Timaeus* and the *Ethics*, in their left hands. The spoken words and gestures gloss the written words on the hidden pages. Such gestures are indecipherable because they draw their meaning from circumstances. This ambiguity, which is exactly what writing seeks to avoid—the inscription, again, is true (or false) in all circumstances—was the subject of Leonardo's *Last Supper.* As noted earlier, the *School of Athens*, unlike the *Disputa* and the *Parnassus*, was not organized around a stable center, nor does it offer any clear picture of a transmission process that carries knowledge reliably from one sphere to another. Here there is no source of understanding located in a celestial realm; and indeed since we are dealing with pagan not Christian wisdom, perhaps that is as it should be. Plato and Aristotle understand each other perfectly, but where is the source of their wisdom, and where is its outlet? Words ricochet endlessly from mouth to ear, carrying thought by an unwieldy person-to-person process.

Plato and Aristotle wrote books. Plato's teacher, however, standing at the head of the chain of European thought, was an oral teacher who, like Christ, left no books. Socrates's words were mediated by the books of others. It was the decision of Plato and other disciples to transpose Socrates's words onto pages that converted the teaching process into a philosophical tradition. Socrates as the source of this tradition might well have occupied the geometrical center of this mural, in parallel to Christ in the *Disputa* and Apollo in the *Parnassus.* But that would have placed Socrates in a theologically awkward rhyme with Christ and would have raised the difficult question of the source of Socrates's wisdom. Instead, Socrates appears just off to the side, shunted out of his rightful position in the center by his bookish followers Plato and Aristotle.[21] While Plato and Aristotle brandish their free arms with brusque authority, Socrates numbers arguments one by one, on his fingers, just as the twelve-year-old Christ did when debating the rabbis in the Temple (see, for example, the painting by Albrecht Dürer, which according to its inscription was executed in Rome in 1506[22]). Like Christ, Socrates has no need for books, for he knows by heart all the texts he needs to know. A bare-chested youth carrying scrolls and books, rushing in from the left to test or corroborate Socrates's points, is apparently rebuffed by one of the listeners. This enigmatic scene figures the troubled passage from orality to script. For to be modern is to learn to live in a world of endless writing and making of books, abandoning any dreams of straightforward, unmediated communication.

Plato, a writer, had Socrates offer a devastating critique of writing in the *Phaedrus.* The living word of knowledge, "of which the written word is properly no more than an image," has a soul and offers unvarying truth. But when speeches are written down things are not made more certain and fixed; instead, a confusing multiplicity of voices emerges, a multidirectional conversation that is the counterimage to what Raphael portrays in his celebratory fresco: speeches, once they are written down, "are tumbled about anywhere among those who may or may not understand them, and know not to whom they should reply, to whom not."[23] In this ironic light, the light cast by philosophy on its own degraded mediations, the confusion in Raphael's fresco, present but glossed by the painter's fluency, becomes starkly visible. The fresco is an effort to *reverse* the descent from orality to literacy, to the tumbling and chatter of proliferating texts, by putting the philosophers back into a virtual arena of orality, one register above the room's lowest zone, where the actual bookshelves of this library would have stood. And yet at the same time the philosophers' conversation is continually being woven back into texts, as they turn their backs on their colleagues to commit knowledge to writing and thus make it available to all those who would consult the Vatican's library.

The fall from unmediated wisdom to lesser forms of mediated knowledge was one of the primary themes of the sermon on the Golden Age delivered in the basilica of St. Peter's on December 21, 1507, in the presence of Julius II by Egidio da Viterbo, the pope's favored preacher. In the second golden age, Adam's mind was not "like ours, clouded by ignorance and unable to discern the meaning of things, but clear, endowed with the innate brightness of wisdom." And in the third golden age, that of the Etruscans, "[p]ractitioners of divination gathered their omens from human speech, and their auspices from the song, flight, or species of birds." But "it is in the nature of things to deteriorate," and their pure wisdom descended into superstition. The great philosophers of Greece understood that their knowledge was secondary, at a significant remove from the source; thus Pythagoras "preferred his doctrine to be called not wisdom, but philosophy; that is, love of wisdom. Apart from the Peripatetics, all philosophers disclaimed the odious and conceited name of wisdom, agreeing with Plato that wisdom and gold must be sought from God alone."[24]

The mural makes a veiled allusion to the dreadful possibility that Christ's winged words, like those of Socrates, might have suffered distortion at the hands of his posthumous deputies, so dedicated to the project of broadcasting the news over long distances and therefore to writing. This allusion is made explicit by Giorgio Ghisi's engraving after the painting published by Hieronymus Cock in Antwerp in 1550, which associates the scene with—indeed seems to *identify* the scene as—St. Paul preaching in Athens, by means of an inscription in the lower left citing Acts 17.[25] In the context of Vasari's account of the picture, published in that very year, Ghisi's identification is somewhat less enigmatic. Vasari described the subject of the painting not as the "School of Athens" (not before the seventeenth century is the work so described[26]) but as "how theologians harmonize Philosophy and Astrology with Theology." Admittedly this is not exactly what Paul did on the Areopagus, for Paul did not so much seek to absorb the doctrines of the pagans as refute them. Vasari even identified the figure of Pythagoras in the left foreground as St Matthew.[27] Ghisi and Cock's identification of the scene as Paul at Athens does not account for the figure at Paul's (that is, Plato's) side. It cannot have been Peter, since he was not in Athens with Paul. Yet the coupling of Peter and Paul, a doubling of Christ's authority that made space for a certain doctrinal flexibility, is an extrascriptural tradition reflected, for example, in the transfer of the patronage of the city of Rome from the twins Castor and Pollux, the Dioscuri, to Peter and Paul, or the ninth-century rededication of the Temple of Castor and Pollux in Naples to Peter and Paul. The coupling of the two apostles is registered in innumerable Roman images, such as the Peter and Paul portrait panel or panels preserved in the papal treasury in the Sancta Sanctorum (see section 20), the apse mosaic of Old St. Peter's, the bronze doors of St. Peter's by Filarete depicting the lives and martyrdoms of Peter and Paul in Rome, the two colossal statues of the saints flanking the entry to the church of St. Peter's by Paolo Romano and Mino da Fiesole,[28] or for that matter the scene of the *Repulse of Attila by Leo I* in the Stanza d' Eliodoro, painted by Raphael in 1513–1514, where the pope's modest army is backed up by an airborne duo of sword-brandishing apostles.[29]

The theme of the Stanza della Segnatura is thus the paradox of inscription, described by Plato in the *Phaedrus*, whereby writing compensates for an imperfect, distorting human memory but only at the price of a vertiginous loss of confidence in the referential authority of the verbal text. Print only extended the closing down of memory initiated by writing. In the face of print, the old-fashioned, handwritten transmission took over the place that memory had occupied in Plato's formula. Handwriting in contrast to speaking had once seemed secure; in contrast to print, it came to seem insecure. But that very insecurity, the margin of imprecision, error, and misprision that accompanied manuscript transmission, left room for creativity, change.

On the ceiling of the Stanza della Segnatura, in four roundels surrounding the central octagon (a fictive aperture over which putti hold a round shield with Julius's arms), appear the four disciplines that correspond to the four scenes on the walls below: Theology, Poetry, Philosophy, and Jurisprudence (see figure 27.5). Enthroned female figures supported by cloud banks and accompanied by putti bearing tablets with inscribed mottos personify these writerly and earthly disciplines, mere mediating devices designed for humans. Below, the results of the transcriptions embodying civil and canon law, the Pandects and the Decretals, are being promulgated; these are the authoritative sources to which all subsequent canon and civil lawyers will need to refer. Writing is a prosthesis that supplements the feeble powers of human memory. Divinities have no use for books or scholarship. And yet the disciplines are perched in the sky as if they had their true homes in the celestial realm. Whereas the real state of things, surely, is that although the truths that Theology, Poetry, Philosophy, and Jurisprudence mediate are grounded in timeless principles exceeding human experience, the disciplines themselves, like the technology of writing, are manmade. Three of the four personifications—Jurisprudence is the exception, hands full with sword and scales—hold books. Philosophy holds *two* books, labeled "Moralis" and "Naturalis," but also hinting at the possibility of conflict in this realm—after all, Philosophy's throne is adorned with a pair of alarmingly pagan sculptures of the multi-breasted Diana of Ephesus—and doubling the debate between Plato and Aristotle going on just below.

The Legend of the True Cross was about the search for something real to worship, a contact relic of Christ himself. Raphael's *Disputa* is the account of the debate that would, in principle, put an end to this search. The Eucharist, an ordinary wafer magically transformed into a relic, obviates the need for a literal relic. The disputants are gathered about an altar without an altarpiece, for the Eucharist, which has no material value and is easily replaced, if lost, with another exactly equivalent object, requires no container or frame. The *School of Athens*, which also pictures a "dispute,"[30] has no need of an altar at all. It says the same thing as the *Disputa*, but more radically: books break with mere utterance (a context-bound mode of communication) just as the Eucharist (a relic of Christ generated by ritual) breaks with the mere cult of bodily relics (common to many religions and vulnerable to fraud and mislabelling). Over the course of the sixteenth century some intellectuals took note, in effect, of the absence of any altar-like focal point in the *School of Athens* and dared to prefer the altarless, noncentered, nonritualized discourses of philosophy or, for that matter, the equally centrifugal force field of the creative arts pictured in the *Parnassus*, to the structures of dogma and liturgy. Books, the reference points for the philosophers, are not at all like relics. The circumstances of their material production do not bear on their informational value. It was still possible with handwritten books to preserve some fiction of a talismanic or magical efficacy. But print dispelled that idea. The printed book was perfectly interchangeable with all the other copies and in fact all other editions that delivered the same text. Of course printed books are also material artifacts; one copy differs from the next; each copy meets its own reception and bears the traces of that reception. The edition is not infinite but finite. The printed book is not at all like the Eucharistic wafer. But print proposed an ideal of the book as a transparent and infinitely reproducible vehicle for verbal texts. The mechanical procedure of printing cut the text off from its origin. Manuscripts had been produced in a chain of iterations made by bodies. The substitutional system, which governed manuscript production as much as it did artifacts, was a mechanism that allowed an original utterance to survive through a chain of iterations, *without difference*. That is, loss or distortion of meaning was not reckoned against the value of the iteration. Drift was just ignored. The printed book amounted to a cultural decision to stop ignoring the problem of drift. The printed book created an ideal model of frictionless transmission. Just as the philosophers of the *School of Athens* bear, in some cases, the features of modern people, contemporaries of Raphael, so too are they carrying in their hands, in effect, modern books, printed books.

Raphael provided a key to the thematics of transmission in the scenes in the rectangular fields in the spandrels of the vault: Adam and Eve about to surrender to temptation, Apollo punishing Marsyas, the judgment of Solomon. These three scenes are *decisions taken without the guidance of books*. Thus they are in tension with the two scenes of lawmaking on the fourth wall of the room, *Justinian Handing the Pandects to Trebonianus* and *Pope Gregory IX Handing the Decretals to Saint Raimund*, where bound volumes literally pass from hand to hand. Adam and Eve, with nowhere to turn but inward, to their own consciences, commit an error of judgment. Apollo, too, in cruelly condemning his rival artist, is guided by pride and spite. King Solomon, meanwhile, has internalized the God-given Word and needs to consult no manmade book when he hands down a correct judgment. (The fourth scene, Urania, Muse of Astronomy, blessing or calling into being a celestial sphere, cannot be interpreted as a decision.)

In the *Disputa*, one figure reminds us of a better mode of writing: Moses, whose inscribed tablets, an acheiropoietic book, were received and not made. In the *Parnassus*, blind Homer sings while a youthful scribe, colleague of Augustine's kneeling scribe in the *Disputa*, waits with pen poised.[31] Together these figures, Moses and Homer, represent the foil against which writing and printing unfold. (Socrates's story is more troubled, for his scribe, Plato, has engulfed him in his own writerly project as a mere character: the very marginalization pictured in the *School of Athens*.) In the same way, the icon and the acheiropoietic image, authoritative images, emerged in high relief in the fifteenth century, a resurfacing of the lost ground of artifact making that the work of art now chose to define itself against. Raphael's Roman work, through reproductive prints and through Rome's new status as the cynosure of European art, exerted a massive influence on all artists for more than three centuries. The great characteristic of Raphael's paintings is that they manage to mask so successfully any possible doubts about their own authority. Such doubts had been conspicuous in fifteenth-century art, in displacements, hesitations, and doublings. From this point on, once we step out of the Stanza della Segnatura, doubts about the authority and value of art are ever better disguised. Those doubts are everywhere *outside* the artwork, in society, in writing about art. But they are ever more difficult to perceive *in* art.

Acknowledgments

Many colleagues and friends, over a number of years, have stoked this project with ideas, support, assistance, and advice. We are profoundly grateful. These conversations have been a constant inspiration. Many colleagues have generously offered information and responded to requests, as registered in the endnotes to the book.

We would like to acknowledge the formal occasions and bodies that helped us realize the project as a book.

The Clark Art Institute offered us the opportunity to invite a team of scholars to a colloquium on "The Historical Imagination of Renaissance Art" in June 2002. We wish to thank Michael Ann Holly and Mariët Westermann for organizing the event, as well as the participants: Nicola Courtright, Patricia Emison, Hubertus Günther, Geraldine Johnson, Matt Kavaler, Alina Payne, Anne-Marie Sankovitch, Marvin Trachtenberg, and Gerhard Wolf.

We thank Jonathan Crewe and Adrian Randolph for the opportunity to present this project to an interdisciplinary audience at the Renaissance Seminar at the Leslie Humanities Center, Dartmouth College, in April 2004.

We are grateful to Marc Gotlieb, editor of the *Art Bulletin*, who asked us to contribute a pilot version of the argument of this book as the first in his series of "Interventions": "Toward a New Model of Renaissance Anachronism," *Art Bulletin* 87 (2005), pp. 403–32. We thank the three scholars who responded thoughtfully to the article in the same issue of the magazine: Michael Cole, Charles Dempsey, and Claire Farago. Informal debates in various venues followed the publication of this article. We wish to acknowledge in particular the ones held in October 2005 at the Center for Advanced Study in the Visual Arts, National Gallery, Washington, and at the Department of the History of Art at Yale University.

A portion of this project was presented at a conference on "Renaissance Medievalisms" held at the Center for Reformation and Renaissance Studies at the University of Toronto in October 2006. This paper has since been published as "What Counted as an Antiquity in the Renaissance?"

in *Renaissance Medievalisms*, ed. Konrad Eisenbichler (Toronto: Centre for Reformation and Renaissance Studies, 2009), pp. 53–74.

Two articles by Alexander Nagel presented material that pointed forward to this book: "Fashion and the Now-Time of Renaissance Art," *Res: Anthropology and Aesthetics* 46 (2004), pp. 33–52; and "Authorship and Image-making in the Monument to Giotto in Florence Cathedral," *Res: Anthropology and Aesthetics* 53–54 (2008), pp. 143–51. We are grateful to Francesco Pellizzi for his support.

The Center for Advanced Study in the Visual Arts at the National Gallery in Washington, the Wissenschaftskolleg zu Berlin, and the American Academies in Rome and Berlin provided havens for research to one or both of us during the production of this book. We wish to thank the directors of those institutions for their generosity and hospitality: Elizabeth Cropper, Luca Giuliani, Lester K. Little, and Gary Smith.

We wish to thank several research assistants: Sophie Collyer, Melissa L. Greenberg, Sarah K. Kozlowski, and Michael J. Waters.

Finally, we are grateful to Zone Books, especially to Jonathan Crary for supporting our project; to Meighan Gale for guiding the manuscript through its various stages; and to Julie Fry for so deftly and sympathetically coordinating word and image.

Notes

ONE — PLURAL TEMPORALITY
OF THE WORK OF ART

1. Simone de Beauvoir, *The Long March: A Book on
China*, trans. Austryn Wainhouse (Cleveland: World,
1958), pp. 64–65.

2. Suetonius, *Lives of the Twelve Caesars*, ed. and
trans. J. C. Rolfe (London: Heinemann; New York:
Putnam, 1930), vol. 2, pp. 140–41 (Life of Nero, §32).
The episode is attested nowhere else; see K. R. Bradley,
Suetonius' Life of Nero: An Historical Commentary
(Brussels: Latomus, 1978), and Annie Dubourdieu,
*Les origines et le développement du culte des Pénates à
Rome* (Rome: École Française de Rome, 1989). Further
examples of counterfeit heirlooms are the Japanese
imperial regalia, immemorial but apparently dating
no further back than the fifteenth century; see Joseph
Alsop, *The Rare Art Traditions: The History of Art Collect-
ing* (New York: Harper and Rowe, 1982), p. 156.

3. Plutarch, *Parallel Lives*, *The Lives of the Noble Grecians and Romans*, trans. John Dryden, vol. 1 (New York:
Modern Library, 1992), pp. 13–14. For other ancient
ship relics, see Friedrich Pfister, *Der Reliquienkult im
Altertum* (Giessen: Töpelmann, 1909–1912), p. 335. The
Ship of Theseus still poses a central problem of philosophy, continuity of identity; see Tamar Szabó Gendler,
*Thought Experiment: On the Powers and Limits of Imagi-
nary Cases* (New York: Routledge, 2000), pp. 65–109.

4. Rosalind Krauss, *The Originality of the Avant-
Garde and other Modernist Myths* (Cambridge, MA: The
MIT Press, 1985), p. 2, referring to a parallel myth
about the Argo.

5. Plato *Phaedon* 58B.

6. Denis Feeney, *Caesar's Calendar: Ancient Time
and the Beginnings of History* (Berkeley: University of
California Press, 2007), pp. 12–16.

7. See Ernst Gombrich, *Aby Warburg: An Intellectual
Biography* (Chicago: University of Chicago Press, 1986),
p. 248. See also Georges Didi-Huberman, *L'image
survivante: Histoire de l'art et temps des fantômes selon
Aby Warburg* (Paris: Les Éditions de Minuit, 2002),
p. 176. Didi-Huberman's book is one of the few of the
many recent studies of Warburg to take his Romantic
conception of the power of the symbol at face value.
Warburg's major texts on Renaissance art are translated in *The Renewal of Pagan Antiquity* (Los Angeles,
CA: Getty Research Institute, 1999).

8. On the development of the modern European
conception of historical time, see Anthony Grafton,
*Joseph Scaliger: A Study in the History of Classical Scholar-
ship*, vol. 2, *Historical Chronology* (Oxford: Oxford
University Press, 1993).

9. "*Geopolitics* has its ideological foundations in
chronopolitics," Johannes Fabian, *Time and the Other:
How Anthropology Makes its Object* (New York: Colum-
bia University Press, 2002), p. 144.

10. Cf. Walter Seitter who writes: "The inner
simultaneities have determined my reading of the
Nibelungenlied, and thus in a certain sense my reading
became a political one, insofar as politics consists in
the simultaneity (*Gleichzeitigkeit*) of numerous people,
places, actions, and differences." *Distante Siegfried-
Paraphrasen* (Berlin: Merve, 1993), p. 9.

11. Erich Auerbach, "Figura," in *Scenes from the Drama of European Literature* (New York: Meridian Books, 1956), pp. 11–76.

12. "[O]n substitue un ordre à un autre qui est initial," Paul Valéry, *Introduction à la méthode de Léonard de Vinci* (Paris: Gallimard, 1957), p. 41. See also pp. 17–18 and 31–32.

13. The picture of art history as a collection of "form-classes" made up of innovative "prime objects" and long sequences of replicas was introduced by George Kubler. See *The Shape of Time: Remarks on the History of Things* (New Haven, CT: Yale University Press, 1962).

14. The inability of the scholarly discipline of art history to acknowledge the unstable temporality of the image is a persistent and deeply developed theme in the writings of Georges Didi-Huberman. See, for example, *Devant l'image: Question posée aux fins d'une histoire de l'art* (Paris: Les Éditions de Minuit, 1990); *Confronting Images: Questioning the Ends of a Certain History of Art*, trans. John Goodman (University Park, PA: Penn State University Press, 2004); *Devant le temps: histoire de l'art et anachronisme des images* (Paris: Les Éditions de Minuit, 2000); and *L'image survivante*.

15. Letter of May 9, 1512 (Epistle 262), to Andrea Ammonio; presumably he made the trip soon afterwards. See also *Collected Works of Erasmus*, vol. 40 (Toronto: University of Toronto Press, 1998), p. 651 n.7.

16. J. C. Dickinson, *The Shrine of Our Lady of Walsingham* (Cambridge: Cambridge University Press, 1956).

17. Erasmus, *Collected Works*, vol. 40, pp. 631–32.

18. Jacques Rancière makes a similar distinction when he speaks of events and meanings as *anachronies*, attempting in this way to liberate historical thinking from linear temporality: "There is no anachronism. But there are modes of connection that we can in a positive sense call *anachronies*: events, notions, significations that are contrary to time, that make meaning circulate in a way that escapes any contemporaneity, any identity of time with 'itself.' An *anachronie* is a word, an event, a signifying sequence that has been cast out of its time, and in this way given the capacity to define completely original temporal switchings, to carry out leaps from one temporal line to another." "Il n'y a pas d'anachronisme. Mais il y a des modes de connexion que nous pouvons appeler positivement des anachronies: des événements, des notions, des significations qui prennent le temps à rebours, qui font circuler le sens d'une manière qui échappe à toute contemporanéité, à toute identité du temps avec 'lui-même.' Une anachronie, c'est un mot, un événement, un séquence signifiante sortis de leur temps, doués du même coup de la capacité de définir des aiguillages temporels inédits, d'assurer le saut d'une ligne de temporalité à une autre." Jacques Rancière, "Le concept d'anachronisme et la vérité de l'historien," *L'inactuel: Psychanalyse & Culture* 6 (1996), pp. 53–68, here 63–64.

19. An illuminating account of "chronology's hold on historical thought," especially since the seventeenth century, is Margreta de Grazia, "Anachronism," in Brian Cummings and James Simpson (eds.), *Cultural Reformations: Medieval and Renaissance in Literary History* (Oxford: Oxford University Press, 2010), pp. 13–32.

20. This is based on the translation of Claire J. Farago, *Leonardo da Vinci's "Paragone": A Critical Interpretation with a New Edition of the Text in the Codex Urbinas* (Leiden: Brill, 1992), pp. 186–90. Here is the original Italian text: "[Q]uesta non si coppia, come si fa le lettere, che tanto vale la coppia quanto l'origgine; questa non s'inpronta, come si fa scultura della quale tal'è la impressa qual'è la origgine in quanto alla virtude l'opera. Questa no' fa infiniti figlioli, come fa li libri stampati. Questa sola si resta nobbile, questa sola onora il suo Autore e resta pretiosa e unica e non partorisse mai figlioli eguali a sé. E tal singularita la fa più eccellente che quelle che per tutto sonno publicate."

21. See the analysis in Renate Lachmann, *Memory and Literature: Intertextuality in Russian Modernism* (Minneapolis: University of Minnesota Press, 1997), pp. 1–24.

22. "Onde andando un giorno Cimabue per sue bisogne da Fiorenza a Vespignano, trovò Giotto che, mentre le sue pecore pascevano, sopra una lastra piana e pulita con un sasso un poco apuntato ritraeva una pecora di naturale, senza aver imparato modo nessuno di ciò fare da altri che dalla natura." Giorgio Vasari, *Le vite de' più eccellenti pittori scultori e architettori*, vol. 2, ed. Rosanna Bettarini (Florence: Sansoni, 1966–1969), p. 96.

23. Xavier Barral i Altet (ed.), *Artistes, artisans et production artistique au Moyen Âge*, Colloque international, Centre national de la recherche scientifique, Université de Rennes II–Haute Bretagne, 2–6 mai 1983, 3 vols. (Paris: Picard, 1986–1990); Peter Cornelius Claussen, "Früher Künstlerstolz : Mittelalterliche Signaturen als Quelle der Kunstsoziologie," in Karl Clausberg (ed.), *Bauwerk und Bildwerk im Hochmittelalter: anschauliche Beiträge zur Kultur- und Sozialgeschichte* (Giessen: Anabas, 1981), pp. 7–34 and "Künstlerinschriften," in Anton Legner (ed.), *Ornamenta Ecclesiae: Kunst und Künstler der Romanik*, vol. 1 (Cologne: Stadt Köln, 1985), pp. 263–76; Maria Monica Donato (ed.), *Le opere e i nomi: Prospettive sulla "firma" medievale* (Pisa: Scuola Normale Superiore, 2000).

24. Richard A. Goldthwaite, *Wealth and the Demand for Art in Italy, 1300–1600* (Baltimore, MD: Johns Hopkins University Press, 1993); John Michael Montias, *Le marché de l'art aux Pays-Bas, XVe–XVIIe siècles* (Paris: Flammarion, 1996); Lisa Jardine, *Worldly Goods* (London: Macmillan, 1996); Evelyn Welch, *Art and Society in Italy, 1350–1500* (Oxford: Oxford University Press, 1997); Marina Belozerskaya, *Rethinking the Renaissance: Burgundian Arts across Europe* (Cambridge: Cambridge University Press, 2002); Evelyn Welch, *Shopping in the Renaissance: Consumer Cultures in Italy, 1400–1600* (New Haven, CT: Yale University Press, 2005); Neil De Marchi and Hans J. van Miegroet (eds.), *Mapping Markets for Paintings in Europe, 1450–1750* (Turnhout: Brepols, 2006); Michelle O'Malley and Evelyn Welch (eds.), *Material Renaissance* (Manchester: Manchester University Press, 2007).

25. Michael Cole, *Cellini and the Principles of Sculpture* (Cambridge: Cambridge University Press, 2002).

26. On the artwork as a recursive system and as second-order observation, see Niklas Luhmann, *Art as a Social System* (Palo Alto, CA: Stanford University Press, 2000), esp. chs. 1 and 2. For a theorization of hesitation as one of the political and aesthetic "fields" of modernity, see Joseph Vogl, *Über das Zaudern* (Zürich: Diaphanes, 2007), esp. pp. 22–24 where the "hesitation-system" is defined as a suspension of countervailing forces that simultaneously obstruct and motivate. Vogl ascribes a "meta-stability" to hesitation that distinguishes it from mere indecision, laziness, or lack of will. Hesitation provides for re-initiation of activity on new terms.

27. Hans Belting, *Likeness and Presence: A History of the Image before the Era of Art* (Chicago: University of Chicago Press, 1994); Gerhard Wolf, *Salus Populi Romani: Die Geschichte römischer Kultbilder im Mittelalter* (Weinheim: VCH, 1990); Giovanni Morello and Gerhard Wolf (eds.), *Il volto di Cristo* (Milan: Electa, 2000); Gerhard Wolf, *Schleier und Spiegel: Traditionen des Christusbildes und die Bildkonzepte der Renaissance* (Munich: Fink, 2002); Maryan Ainsworth, "'A la façon grèce': The Encounter of Northern Renaissance Artists with Byzantine Icons," in *Byzantium: Faith and Power (1261–1557)*, ed. Helen C. Evans (New York: Metropolitan Museum, 2004), pp. 545–55.

28. Francis Haskell, *History and its Images: Art and the Interpretation of the Past* (New Haven, CT: Yale University Press, 1993); Margaret Daly Davis (ed.), *Archäologie der Antike 1500–1700*, exhibition catalogue, Herzog August Bibliothek Wolfenbüttel (Wiesbaden: Harrassowitz, 1994); Patricia Fortini Brown, *Venice and Antiquity* (New Haven, CT: Yale University Press, 1996); Ingrid D. Rowland, *Culture of the High Renaissance: Ancients and Moderns in Sixteenth-Century Rome* (Cambridge: Cambridge University Press, 1998); Madeleine Viljoen, "Prints and False Antiquities in the Age of Raphael," *Print Quarterly* 21 (2004), pp. 235–47.

29. André Grabar, *Martyrium: Recherches sur le culte des reliques et l'art chrétien antique*, 2 vols. (Paris: Collège de France, 1946); Richard Krautheimer, "Introduction to an 'Iconography of Medieval Architecture'," *Journal of the Warburg and Courtauld Institutes* 5 (1942), pp. 1–33; Günter Bandmann, *Mittelalterliche Architektur als Bedeutungsträger* (Berlin: Mann, 1951); Wolfgang Götz, *Zentralbau und Zentralbautendenz in der gotischen Architektur* (Berlin: Mann, 1968); Paul Crossley, "Medieval Architecture and Meaning: The Limits of Iconography," *Burlington Magazine* 130 (1988), pp. 116–21; Matthias Untermann, *Der Zentralbau im Mittelalter: Form, Funktion, Verbreitung* (Darmstadt: Wissenschaftliche Buchgesellschaft, 1989).

30. Salvatore Settis, "Continuità, distanza, conoscenza. Tre usi dell'antico," in Salvatore Settis (ed.), *Memoria dell'antico nell'arte italiana*, vol. 3, *Dalla tradizione all'archeologia* (Turin, Einaudi, 1986), pp. 373–486; Michael Greenhalgh, *The Survival of Roman Antiquities in the Middle Ages* (London: Duckworth, 1989); Lucilla de Lachenal, *Spolia: Uso e reimpiego dell'antico dal III al XIV secolo* (Milan: Longanesi, 1995); Joachim Poeschke (ed.), *Antike Spolien in der Architektur des Mittelalters und der Renaissance* (Munich: Hirmer, 1996); *Ideologie e pratiche del riempiego nell'alto medioevo. 16–21 aprile 1998*, 2 vols. (Spoleto: Centro italiano di studi sull'alto Medioevo, 1999); Maria Fabricius Hansen, *The Eloquence of Appropriation: Prolegomena to an Understanding of Spolia in Early Christian Rome* (Rome: L'Erma di Bretschneider, 2003); Lukas Clemens, *Tempore Romanorum constructa: Zur Nutzung und Wahrnehmung antiker Überreste nördlich der Alpen während des Mittelalters* (Stuttgart: Hiersemann, 2003); Dale Kinney, "The Concept of Spolia," in Conrad Rudolph (ed.), *Companion to Medieval Art: Romanesque and Gothic in Northern Europe* (Malden, MA: Blackwell, 2006), pp. 233–52; and Michael Greenhalgh, *Marble Past, Monumental Present: Building with Antiquities in the Mediaeval Mediterranean* (Leiden: Brill, 2009).

TWO — "THE IMAGE OF THE IMAGE OF OUR LADY"

1. Kurt Rathe, "Ein unbeschriebener Einblattdruck und das Thema der Ährenmadonna," *Mitteilungen der Gesellschaft für vervielfältigende Kunst* 45 (1922), pp. 1–33.

2. Ulla Haastrup, "Det store bloktryk fra Dråby kirke," *Nationalmuseets Arbejdsmark* (1974), pp. 59–70. Thanks to Søren Kaspersen for pointing us to this article and to Gustav Percivall for helping us read it.

3. Friedrich Winkler, "Vorbilder primitiver Holzschnitte," *Zeitschrift für Kunstwissenschaft* 12 (1958), pp. 37–50.

4. W. L. Schreiber, *Handbuch der Holz- und Metallschnitte des XV. Jahrhunderts*, 8 vols. (Leipzig: Hiersemann, 1926–1930), no. 1000.

5. Zurich, Eidgenössische Technische Hochschule, Graphische Sammlung, inventory no. 656. Schreiber, *Handbuch*, vol. 8, no. 999y.

6. Rudolf Berliner, "Zur Sinnesdeutung der Ährenmadonna," *Die Christliche Kunst* 26 (1929/1930), pp. 97–112; Albert Walzer, "Noch einmal zur Darstellung der Maria im Ährenkleid," in *Beiträge zur schwäbischen Kunstgeschichte, Festschrift Werner Fleischhauer* (Konstanz and Stuttgart: Thorbecke, 1964), pp. 63–100.

7. Marshall McLuhan, *Understanding Media* (New York: McGraw-Hill, 1964), pp. 23–25.

8. See the exhibition catalogues *Die Frühzeit des Holzschnitts* (Munich: Staatliche Graphische Sammlung, 1970) and *Origins of European Printmaking: Fifteenth-Century Woodcuts and Their Public*, Washington, National Gallery of Art, and Nuremberg, Germanisches Nationalmuseum (New Haven, CT: Yale University Press, 2005).

9. On the relation of the earliest woodcuts to other media, see Hans Körner, *Der früheste deutsche Einblattholzschnitt* (Mittenwald: Mäander, 1979), pp. 32–37, and Peter Schmidt, "Die Anfänge des vervielfältigten Bildes im 15. Jahrhundert oder: Was eigentlich reproduziert das Reproduktionsmedium Druckgraphik?" in Britta Bussmann et al. (eds.), *Übertragungen: Formen*

und Konzepte von Reproduktion in Mittelalter und früher Neuzeit (Berlin and New York: de Gruyter, 2005), pp. 129–56.

10. Ulrich Firabet was active as a carver of woodblocks in Rapperswil (Switzerland) from the 1460s; see *Allgemeines Künstlerlexikon* (Leipzig: Seeman, 1983–), vol. 40, p. 248.

11. Suzanne Boorsch et al. (eds.), *Andrea Mantegna* (New York: Metropolitan Museum of Art, 1992), pp. 350–92; Helen C. Evans (ed.), *Byzantium: Faith and Power (1261–1557)* (New York: Metropolitan Museum of Art, 2004), no. 329.

THREE — WHAT IS SUBSTITUTION?

1. Tacitus *Histories* 4.53.

2. Richard Krautheimer, "Introduction to an 'Iconography of Medieval Architecture'," pp. 1–33.

3. Hans Belting, "In Search of Christ's Body: Image or Imprint?" in *The Holy Face and the Paradox of Representation*, eds. Herbert L. Kessler and Gerhard Wolf (Bologna: Nuova Alfa, 1998), pp. 1–11.

4. Cyril Mango, *The Art of the Byzantine Empire, 312–1453: Sources and Documents* (Englewood Cliffs, NJ: Prentice-Hall, 1972), p. 174. See also Gary Vikan, "Ruminations on Edible Icons: Originals and Copies in the Art of Byzantium," in *Retaining the Original: Multiple Originals, Copies, and Reproductions* (Washington: National Gallery of Art, 1989), pp. 47–59. See also the discussion of related problems in Charles Barber, *Figure and Likeness: On the Limits of Representation in Byzantine Iconoclasm* (Princeton, NJ: Princeton University Press, 2002), pp. 116–19.

5. For positions close to this within the well-developed debate about medieval forgery, see Giles Constable, "Forgery and Plagiarism in the Middle Ages," *Archiv für Diplomatik* 29 (1983), pp. 1–41; Horst Fuhrmann, "Die Fälschungen im Mittelalter," *Historische Zeitschrift* 197 (1963), pp. 529–601, and "'Mundus vult decepi': Über den Wunsch des Menschen, betrogen zu werden," *Historische Zeitschrift* 241 (1985), pp. 529–42.

See also the symposium proceedings *Fälschungen im Mittelalter: Internationaler Kongress der Monumenta Germaniae Historica, 1986*, 6 vols. (Hannover: Hahnsche Buchhandlung, 1988–1990).

6. Auerbach, "Figura," pp. 11–76; Henri de Lubac, *Exégèse médiévale: Les quatre sens de l'écriture*, 2 vols. (Paris: Aubier, 1959–1964).

7. Mary Carruthers, *The Book of Memory: A Study of Memory in Medieval Culture* (Cambridge: Cambridge University Press, 1992), p. 216.

8. *Ibid.*, p. 217.

9. Michael Baxandall, *Giotto and the Orators* (Oxford: Clarendon, 1971), pp. 81 and 148–49. We modified Baxandall's translation of Manuel Chrysolaras with the help of that of Salvatore Settis; see "Continuità, distanza, conoscenza. Tre usi dell'antico," in *Memoria dell'Antico nell'Arte Italiana*, vol. 3 (Turin: Einaudi, 1986), p. 456.

10. See Susan Buck-Morss, *The Dialectics of Seeing: Walter Benjamin and the Arcades Project* (Cambridge, MA: Harvard University Press, 1989), pp. 71–74 and 217–27.

11. See Hal Foster, *Compulsive Beauty* (Cambridge, MA: The MIT Press, 1993), pp. 172–74. See also the discussion of Ernst Bloch, Wilhelm Pinder, and the concept of nonsimultaneity in Frederic J. Schwartz, *Blind Spots: Critical Theory and the History of Art in Twentieth-Century Germany* (New Haven: Yale University Press, 2005), pp. 103–36.

12. "...strates, blocs hybrides, rhizomes, complexités specifiques, retours souvent inattendus et buts toujours déjoués"; Didi-Huberman, *L'image survivante*, p. 27.

FOUR — AN ANTIQUE STATUE OF CHRIST

1. Venice, Scuola di San Giorgio degli Schiavoni.

2. The subject was identified by Helen I. Roberts, "St. Augustine in 'St. Jerome's Study': Carpaccio's Painting and its Legendary Source," *Art Bulletin* 41 (1959), pp. 283–97.

3. See Christian Blinkenberg, *The Thunderweapon in Religion and Folklore* (Cambridge: Cambridge University Press, 1911); Alain Schnapp, *La conquête du passé* (Paris: Carré, 1993), pp. 318–19 and 346–47.

4. The identification of the figure as Bessarion was first suggested by Guido Perocco, "La scuola di San Giorgio degli Schiavoni," in *Venezia e l'Europa, Atti del XVIII Congresso Internazionale di Storia dell'Arte, Venice,* September 12–18, 1955 (Venice: Arte Veneta, 1956), p. 23. Vittore Branca proposed that the seal in the foreground could be that of the cardinal. See "Ermolao Barbaro e l'Umanesimo Veneziano," in Vittore Branca (ed.), *Umanesimo europeo e umanesimo veneziano* (Florence: Sansoni, 1964), pp. 163–212. Augusto Gentili argued compellingly against basing the identification on either the seal or the likeness. See "Carpaccio e Bessarione," in *Bessarione e l'umanesimo* (Naples: Vivarium, 1994), pp. 297–302. However, Patricia Fortini Brown strongly reaffirmed the identification with Bessarion on the basis of a close examination of the patronage context and the divergences between the preparatory drawing in Vienna and the final painting. See "Sant'Agostino nello Studio di Carpaccio: un ritratto nel ritratto?" in *Bessarione e l'umanesimo*, pp. 303–19.

5. Erwin Panofsky, *Early Netherlandish Painting* (Cambridge, MA: Harvard University Press, 1953), pp. 131–48.

6. Alfred Acres, "The Columba Altarpiece and the Time of the World," *Art Bulletin* 80 (1998), pp. 422–51, esp. 424–25 and 432–34.

7. Charles Dempsey, *The Portrayal of Love: Botticelli's* Primavera *and Humanist Culture at the Time of Lorenzo the Magnificent* (Princeton, NJ: Princeton University Press, 1992), pp. 65–78.

8. Acres, "The Columba Altarpiece and the Time of the World," p. 432.

9. Filarete, *Treatise on Architecture*, vol. 1, ed. and trans. John R. Spencer (New Haven, CT: Yale University Press, 1965), p. 12. The original Italian reads: "[C]osì colui che dipigne la sua maniera delle figure si cognosce, e così d'ogni facultà si cognosce lo stile di ciascheduno…." Filarete, *Trattato di Architettura*, ed. Anna Maria Finoli and Liliana Grassi (Milan: Il Polifilo, 1972), p. 28.

10. "[S]i conosce ciascun nel suo stil essere perfettissimo." Baldassare Castiglione, *Il libro del Cortegiano*, ed. Vittorio Cian (Florence: Sansoni, 1947), p. 93.

11. On the Venus and other items in the picture, see Zygmunt Wazbinski, "Portrait d'un amateur de l'art de la Renaissance," *Arte Veneta* 22 (1968), pp. 21–29.

12. See Karel Svoboda, *L'esthétique de Saint Augustin et ses sources* (Brno: Vydává Filosofická Fakulta, 1933), pp. 144 and 156.

13. On the tension between the sacred and secular characters of Augustine's study as depicted by Carpaccio, see Stephen J. Campbell, *The Cabinet of Eros: The Studiolo of Isabella d'Este and the Rise of Renaissance Mythological Painting* (New Haven, CT: Yale University Press, 2006), pp. 33–35.

14. Marcantonio Michiel noted a "statua de 'l Cristo, de bronzo, sopra l'altar" in the "capella del Salvatore" in the church of the Carità in Venice, and it is virtually certain that this is the one now in Milan. See *Notizia d'opere di disegno*, ed. Gustavo Frizzoni (Bologna, 1884), p. 231; *Der Anonimo Morelliano (Marcanton Michiel's Notizia d'opere del disegno)*, ed. Theodor Frimmel, *Quellenschriften für Kunstgeschichte*, N.F. 1 (1888), p. 114.

15. The chapel was gutted, together with the rest of the church, in 1807. Francesco Sansovino declared the chapel "notabilissima fra tutte della città, edificata da Domenico di Pietro gioielliero ricchissimo, & antiquario, con marmi, con porfidi, & con serpentini molto alla grande." See *Venetia città nobilissima et singolare, descritta in XIIII libri* (Venice: Sansovino, 1581), fol. 94v. Tommaso Temanza described it as "ricca di marmi porfidi e serpentini come di quei tempi era l'uso." See *Vite dei più celebri architetti e scultori veneziani* (Venice: Palese, 1778), p. 96. Some sense of Domenico di Piero's tastes can be gained from the façade of the Scuola di San Marco, commissioned from the Lombardos at his behest and under his direction during his tenure as

guardian grande of the Scuola; see Philip Sohm, *The Scuola Grande di San Marco 1437–1550: The Architecture of a Venetian Lay Confraternity* (New York: Garland, 1982), pp. 118–22. A 1548 document states that the chapel was finished in 1489; see Pietro Paoletti, *L'architettura e la scultura del rinascimento in Venezia; ricerche storico-artistiche*, vol. 1 (Venice: Ongania-Naya, 1893), p. 184. A recently discovered document shows that in April 1494 the chapel was still "almost finished"; see Rosella Lauber, "'Ornamento lodevole' e 'ornatissima di pietre': Marcantonio Michiel nella chiesa veneziana di Santa Maria della Carità," *Arte Veneta 55* (1999), p. 147. Nonetheless, it was sufficiently finished in 1493 to be noted by the diarist Marin Sanudo; see Wendy Stedman Sheard, "Sanudo's List of Notable Things in Venetian Churches and the Date of the Vendramin Tomb," *Yale Italian Studies* 1.3 (1977), p. 256.

16. The statue has not been clearly connected to an author. The Poldi Pezzoli catalogue offers an unconvincing attribution to Severo da Ravenna, *Museo Poldi Pezzoli: Tessuti-sculture-metalli islamici* (Milan: Electa, 1987), cat. 24. See also Lanfranco Franzoni, "Antiquari e collezionisti nel Cinquecento," in *Storia della cultura veneta*, vol. 3 (Vicenza: Nero Pozza, 1981), p. 237.

17. See Molly Teasdale Smith, "The Lateran Fastigium: A Gift of Constantine the Great," *Rivista di archeologia cristiana* 46 (1970), pp. 149–75; Sible de Blaauw, "Das Fastigium der Lateransbasilika: Schöpferische Innovation, Unikat oder Paradigma?" in Beat Brenk (ed.), *Innovation in der Spätantike* (Wiesbaden: Reichert, 1996), pp. 53–64.

18. "[P]rimum, si facultas esset, id est si non cum uxore cubuisset, matutinis horis in larario suo, in quo et divos principes sed optimos electos et animas sanctiores, in quis Apollonium, et, quantum scriptor suorum temporum dicit, Christum, Abraham, et Orpheum et huiuscemodi ceteros habebat ac maiorum effigies, rem divinam faciebat." *Scriptores Historiae Augustae*, Life of Alexander Severus, 29. Thanks to Björn Ewald for pointing out this passage. For an interpretation of the multifaith program of this *lararium*,

see Salvatore Settis, "Severo Alessandro e i suoi Lari," *Atheneum 50* (1972), pp. 237–51.

19. Gabriella Zarri, "Living Saints: A Typology of Female Sanctity in the Early Sixteenth Century," in Daniel Bornstein and Roberto Rusconi (eds.), *Women and Religion in Medieval and Renaissance Italy* (Chicago: University of Chicago Press, 1992), p. 223.

20. "Since I have mentioned this city (Paneas) I do not think it proper to omit an account which is worthy of record for posterity. For they say that the woman with an issue of blood, who, as we learn from the sacred Gospel, received from our Saviour deliverance from her affliction, came from this place, and that her house is shown in the city, and that remarkable memorials of the kindness of the Saviour to her remain there. For there stands upon an elevated stone, by the gates of her house, a bronze image of a woman kneeling, with her hands stretched out, as if she were praying. Opposite this is another upright image of a man, made of the same material, clothed decently in a double cloak, and extending his hand toward the woman. At his feet, beside the statue itself, is a certain strange plant, which climbs up to the hem of the bronze cloak, and is a remedy for all kinds of diseases. [...] They say that this statue is an image of Jesus. It has remained to our day, so that we ourselves also saw it when we were staying in the city. Nor is it strange that those of the Gentiles who, of old, were benefited by our Saviour, should have done such things, since we have learned also that the likenesses of his apostles Paul and Peter, and of Christ himself, are preserved in paintings, the ancients being accustomed, as it is likely, according to a habit of the Gentiles, to pay this kind of honor indiscriminately to those regarded by them as deliverers." Eusebius, *Historia Ecclesiastica*, ed. Philip Schaff, trans. Arthur Cushman McGiffert (New York: Christian Literature, 1890), bk. 7, ch. 18, p. 304. Eusebius was cautious, simply recording the local tradition that this was an image of Christ healing the hemorrhaging woman, as recounted in the Gospels (Mark 5:28). He also reported the popular belief that this group had in fact been erected

by that same woman, who had settled there after her healing. That association would have dated the statue group to the time of Christ, a hypothesis too tempting to let languish, as the later life of the legend shows.

21. Beate Fricke, *Ecce Fides: Die Statue von Conques, Götzendienst und Bildkultur im Westen* (Munich: Fink, 2007), p. 215.

22. The association of the work with the hemorrhaging woman persisted, however, and she came to be identified with St. Martha. Jacobus de Voragine writes: "Eusebius, in the fifth book [*sic*] of the *Ecclesiastical History*, relates the following story of the woman who was cured of an issue of blood. After she was healed, she erected a statue of Christ, dressed as she had seen him, in the court or garden of her house. And when the herbs which grew at the foot of the statue, and which had no power, were touched to the hem of the garment of Christ, they received such virtue therefrom that they cured the ills of many. And St. Ambrose says that Martha was the woman who was cured." "Life of St. Martha," in *Golden Legend*, trans. Granger Ryan and Helmut Ripperger, vol. 2 (New York: Arno, 1969), p. 393.

23. In a polemic against the Dutch humanist Erasmus, Alberto Pio da Carpi referred to the miracle-working statue of Christ in the city of Caesarea, invoking the authority of Eusebius. See Alberto Pio da Carpi, *Tres &uiginti libri in locos lucubrationum uariarum D [Erasmi Rhoteroda]mi, quos censet ab eo recognoscendos &retractandos*, with dedicatory letter to Altobello Averoldi (Florence: Giunta, 1531), fol. 100r–100v. For further sixteenth-century references to the legend see Giuseppe Scavizzi, *The Controversy on Images from Calvin to Baronius* (New York: Peter Lang, 1992), p. 170.

24. As noted by Wazbinski, "Portrait d'un amateur d'art," pp. 25–26. On Augustine's "collection," see Irene Favaretto, *Arte antica e cultura antiquaria nelle collezioni venete al tempo della Serenissima* (Rome: 'L'Erma' di Bretschneider, 1990), 68.

25. Brown, *Venice and Antiquity*, pp. 22–23.

26. Richard Brilliant, "I piedistalli del Giardino di Boboli: spolia in se, spolia in re," *Prospettiva* 31 (1982), pp. 2–17. Salvatore Settis develops the concept in "Continuità, distanza, conoscenza," pp. 375–486 and esp. 399–410. For more on "virtual spolia" see Dale Kinney, "Spolia: Damnatio and renovatio memoriae," *Memoirs of the American Academy in Rome* 42 (1997), pp. 117–48.

27. With some adjustments, however. The *Golden Legend* explicitly says that the statue showed Christ as the hemorrhaging woman had seen him when she was healed. And yet the statue now in Milan shows him in the form of the Resurrected Christ, not as the living, miracle-performing Christ. In his left hand is a perfectly cylindrical hole that would originally have held the banner of the Resurrection, much as we see it in Carpaccio's painting. It seems clear that here a fairly obscure theme has come under the typological demands of a dominant form. The free-standing statue, as a category, carried almost inherent associations with apotheosis and triumph; a bronze statue of Christ, even if rooted in the legendary tradition of the hemorrhaging woman, is naturally pulled towards the form of the triumphant, standing, resurrected Christ.

28. See the accounts by Eusebius and Jacobus de Voragine quoted above. This legend of the herbs touching Christ's robe recalls the Gospel account in which the hemorrhaging woman was healed by touching Christ's clothing: "If I may touch but his clothes, I shall be whole" (Mark 5:28).

29. Wendy Stedman Sheard noted that "lo stomaco, i cui muscoli, i *recti abdomini*, e i loro confini, o *inscripti tendinea*, sono resi con forme quasi astratte." See "Il torso antico nell'arte veneziana tra Quattro e Cinquecento. Una nuova lettura del torso," in Marcello Fagiolo (ed.), *Roma e l'antico nell'arte e nella cultura del Cinquecento* (Milan: Treccani, 1985), p. 436. Observing that there are no antique precedents for this treatment, she proposed to associate it with anatomy illustrations showing the structure of muscles beneath the layer of skin.

30. On the possible relations of the Bregno statue to Carpaccio's painting and to the Milan statue,

see Anne Markham Schulz, *Giambattista and Lorenzo Bregno: Venetian Sculpture in the High Renaissance* (Cambridge: Cambridge University Press, 1991), pp. 38–39 and n.14.

31. He missed, however, the telling detail of the dropping hem. The statue evidently carried authority for him without such "philological" support.

32. See Otto Demus, *The Mosaics of San Marco in Venice*, vol. 2, pt. 2 (Chicago: University of Chicago Press, 1984), color plate 35. The mosaic angels in the pendentives of the Creation cupola are blue, and are clearly identified by the inscription as cherubim. Carpaccio isolated the figure in the center of his little apse and made it red, thus promoting it to the level of Seraph.

33. Kurt Weitzmann, "The Genesis Mosaics of San Marco and the Cotton Genesis Miniatures," in Demus, *Mosaics of San Marco*, pp. 105–42.

34. In this sense Carpaccio and his contemporaries were continuing a well-known Byzantine tendency to regard images of later centuries as ancient. Robert Grigg explains the "puzzling" chronological confusions that abound in Byzantine writings as the result of Byzantine "credulity." The writers were "deceived into thinking there was no difference between ancient and Byzantine art." See "Byzantine Credulity as an Impediment to Antiquarianism," *Gesta* 25–26 (1987), pp. 3–9. The substitution model explains these phenomena without the need to speak of deception or error: the Byzantines knew that their images were postantique, and at the same time granted them antique status on the basis of their reference to ancient prototypes.

FIVE — THE PLEBEIAN PLEASURE
OF ANACHRONISM

1. Jorge Luis Borges, "Pierre Menard, Author of the *Quixote*," in *Labyrinths*, eds. Donald A. Yates and James E. Irby (New York: New Directions, 1964), p. 39.

2. Erwin Panofsky, *Renaissance and Renascences in Western Art* (Stockholm: Almqvist & Wiksels, Gebers Forlag, 1960), p. 38. Panofsky offered the clearest and most economical account of this argument in an article published in the *Kenyon Review* in 1940 as a response to a symposium, published in the *American Historical Review* the previous year, on the validity of the Renaissance as a period concept. He expounded and developed it in a number of essays and books, including "The First Page of Vasari's 'Libro': A Study on the Gothic Style in the Judgment of the Italian Renaissance," in *Meaning in the Visual Arts* (Garden City, NY: Doubleday Press, 1955), pp. 169–235, and "Iconography and Iconology: An Introduction to the Study of Italian Renaissance Art" also in *Meaning in the Visual Arts*, pp. 26–54. A sophisticated recent extension of Panofsky's thesis is Salvatore Settis, "Continuità, distanza, conoscenza," pp. 375–486, and "Von auctoritas zu vetustas: die antike Kunst in mittelalterlicher Sicht," *Zeitschrift für Kunstgeschichte* 51 (1988), pp. 157–79.

3. Ulrich Pfisterer has provided a dense discursive context for the early emergence of the concepts of historical, local, and personal style in the proximity of Donatello. See *Donatello und die Entdeckung der Stile 1430–1445* (Munich: Hirmer, 2002).

4. See also Jack M. Greenstein's close reading of the marks of time in the view of Jerusalem, or what he calls a "diachronic urban fabric" in the background of the *Agony in the Garden* from the San Zeno altarpiece. *Mantegna and Painting as Historical Narrative* (Chicago: University of Chicago Press, 1992), pp. 64–70, and generally ch. 3.

5. Elizabeth Eisenstein, *The Printing Press as an Agent of Change* (Cambridge: Cambridge University Press, 1979), p. 187. For general remarks on Panofsky's thesis, see pp. 181–225. Lucien Febvre, *The Problem of Unbelief in the Sixteenth Century: The Religion of Rabelais* (Cambridge, MA: Harvard University Press, 1982), pp. 393–400.

6. Frank L. Borchardt, *German Antiquity in Renaissance Myth* (Baltimore: Johns Hopkins Press, 1971); Walter Stephens, "Berosus Chaldeus: Counterfeit and Fictive Editors of the Early Sixteenth Century," PhD

diss., Cornell University, 1979, and *Giants in Those Days: Folklore, Ancient History, and Nationalism* (Lincoln: University of Nebraska Press, 1989); Anthony Grafton, *Forgers and Critics: Creativity and Duplicity in Western Scholarship* (Princeton, NJ: Princeton University Press, 1990), and *Defenders of the Text: The Traditions of Scholarship in an Age of Science, 1450–1800* (Cambridge, MA: Harvard University Press, 1991), pp. 76–103.

7. William J. Bouwsma sees this as a regrettable falling off from the clarity of the early sixteenth century. See *The Waning of the Renaissance 1550–1640* (New Haven, CT: Yale University Press, 2000), pp. 198–214.

8. Krautheimer, postscript to "Introduction to an 'Iconography of Medieval Architecture'," in *Studies in Early Christian, Medieval, and Renaissance Art* (New York: New York University Press, 1969), p. 149.

9. Marvin Trachtenberg, "Foreword" (1995), in Richard Krautheimer, *Rome: Profile of a City, 312–1308* (Princeton, NJ: Princeton University Press, 2000), pp. xix–xx.

10. See Panofsky, *Studies in Iconology*; and Ekkehard Kaemmerling (ed.), *Ikonographie und Ikonologie: Theorien, Entwicklung, Probleme* (Cologne: DuMont, 1979). See as well Georges Didi-Huberman, *Devant l'image*. This schema is dramatized at the historical juncture of the early Renaissance in Didi-Huberman, *Fra Angelico: Dissemblance et Figuration* (Paris: Flammarion, 1990); *Fra Angelico: Dissemblance and Figuration*, trans. Jane Marie Todd (Chicago: University of Chicago Press, 1995). On Panofsky's inability to grasp the "instability of history," see Schwartz, *Blind Spots*, p. 118.

11. Erwin Panofsky, *Perspective as Symbolic Form* (New York: Zone Books, 1991), p. 67.

12. Panofsky, *Studies in Iconology*, pp. 70–71.

13. Even the 1982 supplement to the *Oxford English Dictionary* lists only mineralogical usages of the term. *Webster's Third International* (1963), however, quotes Lewis Mumford on "the concept of the cultural pseudomorph." *Webster's Third New International Dictionary of the English Language*, s.v. "pseudomorphosis." Hans Jonas employed the concept, crediting Spengler,

in *Gnosis und spätantiker Geist* (Göttingen, Vandenhoeck & Ruprecht, 1934), p. 74.

14. Spengler, *Decline of the West*, vol. 1 (New York: Knopf, 1957), p. 209 and *Decline of the West*, vol. 2, pp. 189–90.

15. Thomas M. Greene picked up on it, though, in his study of Renaissance intertextuality. See *The Light in Troy: Imitation and Discovery in Renaissance Poetry* (New Haven: Yale University Press, 1982), p. 42. In effect, Greene was using Panofsky against the Spenglerian "tragic" view, whereas Panofsky's view may have been closer to Spengler's than to Greene's.

16. Silvia Ferretti, *Cassirer, Panofsky, and Warburg: Symbol, Art, and History* (New Haven, CT: Yale University Press, 1989), pp. 207–20.

SIX — ARCHITECTURAL MODELS

1. On the relation between the model, which "compensates for the renunciation of sensible dimensions by the acquisition of intelligible dimensions," and the work of art, see Claude Lévi-Strauss, *The Savage Mind* (Chicago: University of Chicago Press, 1966), pp. 23–24.

2. Varro *De lingua latina* 5.54, although here called *aedes Romuli*, which means both house and sanctuary. Dionysius of Halicarnassus states that the hut "is conserved as a sacred object by those in charge of it." *Roman Antiquities* 1.79.11. See Vitruvius *De Architectura* 2.1.5, which also mentions a hut "daubed with mud" that survives on the Areopagus in Athens, and Ovid *Fasti* 3.183–4. See André Balland, "La *Casa Romuli* au Palatin et au Capitole," *Revue des Études Latines* 62 (1984), pp. 57–80.

3. Andrea Carandini believes that they are the foundations of a symbolic royal residence already constructed in the late eighth or early seventh century, when the historical origin of the city was still alive in memory. That structure was destroyed within a century or so, Carandini hypothesizes, but the memory of it survived in oral tradition and governed the placement of the temples just above the site. See "Variazioni sul tema

di Romolo: Riflessioni dopo *La Nascità di Roma* (1998–1999)," in Andrea Carandini and Rosana Cappelli (eds.), *Roma: Romolo, Remo e la fondazione della città*, exhibition catalogue (Rome: Museo Nazionale Romano, 2000), pp. 130–31. See also Paolo Brocato, "Dalle capanne del *Cermalo* alla *Roma quadrata*," in *Roma: Romolo, Remo e la fondazione della città*, pp. 284–87.

4. Balland speculates that the Capitoline hut, meanwhile, was built in Augustus's time, reactivating an earlier, perhaps fourth-century, cult of the primordial *regia* or royal residence. See "La *Casa Romuli* au Palatin et au Capitole," p. 74.

5. T. P. Wiseman, "Reading Carandini," *Journal of Roman Studies* 91 (2001), pp. 188–91. Alexandre Grandazzi seems to accept the possibility of oral memory of at least the site. See *The Foundation of Rome: Myth and History* (Ithaca and London: Cornell University Press, 1997), p. 209.

6. Dionysius of Halicarnassus *Roman Antiquities* 1.79.11. The mythographer Conon suggested in the first century CE that the Capitoline hut was maintained in much the same way. Dion Cassius mentioned fires that destroyed the hut (probably the Palatine version) in the years 38 and 12. See Balland, "La *Casa Romuli* au Palatin et au Capitole," pp. 60 and 63. The Palatine hut was maintained until the end of the empire; St. Jerome visited it in the late fourth century.

7. On the tendency of "collective memory" to split into parallel, competitive sacred sites, see Maurice Halbwachs, *La topographie légendaire des évangiles en Terre Sainte* (Paris: Presses Universitaires de France, 1941), pp. 131 and 187–88; and Andrea Carandini, *Archeologia del mito: emozione e ragione fra primitivi e moderni* (Torino: Einaudi, 2002), pp. 152–53. Cf. the competing shrines in Genesis, at Jerusalem and Beth El (see the account of Jacob's Pillow in Genesis 28 and its destruction by King Josiah in 2 Kings 23). For other cases of the doubling of tomb sites and other topographical myths, see Friedrich Pfister, *Der Reliquienkult im Altertum* (Giessen: Töpelmann, 1909–1912), pp. 218–23 and 230–38; and Filippo Coarelli, "La doppia tradizione sulla morte di Romolo e gli Auguracula dell' Arx e del Quirinale," in *Gli Etruschi e Roma*, *Festschrift Massimo Pallottino* (Rome: Bretschneider, 1981), pp. 173–88.

8. It is also argued that the Palatine structure was the hut where the twins were raised by the shepherd Faustulus, and the Capitoline hut the later residence. Patrizio Pensabene, "Le reliquie dell' età romulea e della prima età regia," in *Roma: Romolo, Remo e la fondazione della città*, p. 78.

9. The original cabin was dismantled in 1868. Many replicas were built over the years, some claiming to incorporate original building materials. The cabin was not replicated on its original site until 1985. See W. Barksdale Maynard, *Walden Pond: A History* (Oxford: Oxford University Press, 2004), pp. 164–65, 202, 268, 279, 293–94, 319, 322–23.

10. On maintained and "reconditioned" wooden structures and imitations of primitive buildings in stone in the Near Eastern and East Asian, as well as Greek and Roman, traditions, see Joseph Rykwert, *On Adam's House in Paradise: The Idea of the Primitive Hut in Architectural History* (New York: Museum of Modern Art, 1972), ch. 6. Michael Meister, writing about Hindu temples of North India, describes "a process of 'symbolic substitution' [that] preserves a morphology of symbolic significance…but replaces practical elements of that morphology"; "Morphology for a Symbolic Architecture: India," *Res: Anthropology and Aesthetics* 12 (1986), p. 43.

11. Wada Atsumu, "The Origins of Ise Shrine," *Acta Asiatica* 69 (1995), pp. 63–83.

12. "We know that during a thousand years or more there have been some changes in the form of the Naiku and Geku sanctuaries and in the spatial order created by the placement of the various buildings. Yet during all this time some essential element has persisted unaltered behind all changes." Kenzo Tange and Noboru Kawazoe, *Ise: Prototype of Japanese Architecture* (Cambridge, MA: The MIT Press, 1965), p. 16.

13. The account by Martin Biddle is exceptionally careful. See *The Tomb of Christ* (Phoenix Mill, UK: Sutton, 1999), pp. 54–73.

14. Eusebius, *Life of Constantine*, ed. Averil Cameron and Stuart G. Hall (Oxford and New York: Oxford University Press, 1999), pp. 132–33.

15. Cornelis de Bruyn, *Reizen door de vermandste deelen van Klein-Asie…en Palastina* (Delft: Henrik van Krooneveld, 1698), fig. 144.

16. Biddle contests the traditional view that the structures were rebuilt by Emperor Constantine IX Monomachos in the 1040s. See *Tomb of Christ*, pp. 74–81. See also Robert Ousterhout, "Architecture as Relic and the Construction of Sanctity: The Stones of the Holy Sepulchre," *Journal of the Society of Architectural Historians* 62 (2003), p. 7. The Crusaders added an abbreviated basilica on the site of Constantine's courtyard.

17. Biddle, *Tomb of Christ*, pp. 100–103.

18. *Ibid.*, p. 36.

19. An example is the late tenth-century Byzantine reliquary now in Aachen. See Helen C. Evans and William D. Wixom (eds.), *Glory of Byzantium: Art and Culture of the Middle Byzantine Era, AD 843–1261*, exhibition catalogue (New York: Metropolitan Museum of Art, 1997), no. 300. See the small, lead models reproduced by I. Q. Regteren Altena, "Hidden Records of the Holy Sepulchre," in *Essays in the History of Architecture*, Festschrift Rudolf Wittkower (London: Phaidon, 1967), pp. 17–21. Such artifacts initiated feedback loops, for now the large-scale representations of the Holy Sepulchre themselves could imitate the reliquaries or ciboria. On this point, see Paul Naredi-Rainer, *Salomos Tempel und das Abendland: Monumentale Folgen historischer Irrtümer* (Cologne: DuMont, 1994), pp. 90–102.

20. Haarlem, Frans Hals Museum. See Alois Riegl, *The Group Portraiture of Holland* (Los Angeles: Getty Research Center for the History of Art and the Humanities, 1999), fig. 1, pp. 85–87; and Christopher P. Heuer, "*Bildraum* as Aporia," in Alexander Nagel and Lorenzo Pericolo (eds.), *Subject as Aporia in Early Modern Art* (Aldershot, UK: Ashgate, forthcoming 2010). See also Biddle, *Tomb of Christ*, p. 37.

21. Another background figure to the polygonal or round building was the (usually phantom) pagan temple on the same site, for example at the Baptistery in Florence.

22. Richard Krautheimer, "Introduction to an 'Iconography of Medieval Architecture'," pp. 3–4 and Robert Ousterhout, "Loca Sancta and the Architectural Response to Pilgrimage," in Robert Ousterhout (ed.), *The Blessings of Pilgrimage* (Urbana and Chicago: University of Illinois Press, 1990), p. 110. The chapel was rebuilt in the eleventh century and only traces of the original structure survive.

23. The structure is marble and measures 3.80 m in diameter; the wooden conical roof rests on dwarf columns. The replica was constructed before 1077. Karl Lanckoroński (ed.), *Der Dom von Aquileia* (Vienna: Gerlach and Wiedling, 1906), pp. 8–10, 105, 124–26. The structure at Aquileia is the only surviving example of a corpus of eleventh-century Holy Sepulchre replicas otherwise known only through textual sources; see Matthias Untermann, *Der Zentralbau im Mittelalter: Form, Funktion, Verbreitung* (Darmstadt: Wissenschaftliche Buchgesellschaft, 1989), pp. 70, 76.

24. The term was employed by Franco Cardini, "La devozione al Santo Sepolcro, le sue riproduzioni occidentali e il complesso stefaniano: Alcuni casi italici," in *Sette Colonne e Sette Chiese: La vicenda ultramillenaria del complesso di Santo Stefano in Bologna*, exhibition catalogue, Museo Civico Archeologico, Bologna (Bologna: Grafis, 1987), p. 47; see also p. 40 for the replica at Aquileia. Excellent surveys of the Europe-wide imitations of the Holy Sepulchre are André Grabar, *Martyrium: Recherches sur le culte des reliques et l'art chrétien antique*, 2 vols. (Paris: Collège de France, 1946), pp. 95–104; Wolfgang Götz, *Zentralbau und Zentralbautendenz in der gotischen Architektur* (Berlin: Mann, 1968), pp. 219–36; Geneviève Bresc-Bautier, "Les imitations du Saint-Sépulcre de Jérusalem (IXe–Xe siècles): Archéologie d'une dévotion," *Revue d'histoire de la spiritualité* 50 (1974), pp. 319–42; and Untermann, *Der Zentralbau im Mittelalter*, pp. 53–77.

25. The local, twelfth-century sources attributed

the whole complex to the city patron and bishop St. Petronius (fifth century). See Krautheimer, "Introduction to an 'Iconography of Medieval Architecture,'" pp. 5 and 17–19; *Sette Colonne e Sette Chiese*; and Luigi Vignali, *Santo Stefano* (Bologna: Edizioni Luigi Parma, 1991).

26. Damiano Neri, *Il Santo Sepolcro riprodotto in Occidente* (Jerusalem: Franciscan Printing Press, 1971), p. 68; Annabel Jane Wharton, *Selling Jerusalem: Relics, Replicas, Theme Parks* (Chicago: University of Chicago Press, 2006), pp. 49–96.

27. Gustav Dalman, *Das Grab Christi in Deutschland* (Leipzig: Dietrich, 1922), pp. 44–56; Untermann, *Zentralbau im Mittelalter*, p. 72. The plan of the Augsburg chapel survives in a drawing made at the time of its destruction in 1611. There are also images of it on sixteenth-century maps and views.

28. At the abbey church at Bebenhausen a line on the wall two meters long is labeled, apparently on the basis of direct measurement in Jerusalem, the "true dimension" of the Lord's sarcophagus. The depth and breadth are also rendered by inscribed lines though less accurately. See Dalman, *Das Grab Christi in Deutschland*, p. 90; Krautheimer, "Introduction to an 'Iconography of Medieval Architecture'," p. 12.

29. See Carlo Ginzburg, *The Enigma of Piero* (London: Verso, 2000), pp. 68–70. On measurement relics generally, see Ernst Kitzinger, "Cult of Images," *Dumbarton Oaks Papers* 8 (1954), p. 105 and Lenz Kriss-Rettenbeck, *Bilder und Zeichen religiösen Volksglaubens* (Munich: Callwey, 1963), p. 138 n.70.

30. W. L. Schreiber, *Handbuch*, no. 1795. Richard S. Field, *Fifteenth Century Woodcuts and Metalcuts* (Washington, D.C.: National Gallery of Art, 1965), no. 260; Peter Parshall and Rainer Schoch (eds.), *Origins of European Printmaking: Fifteenth-Century Woodcuts and Their Public*, exhibition catalogue, National Gallery of Art and Germanisches Nationalmuseum (New Haven, CT: Yale University Press, 2005), no. 78. See also David S. Areford, "The Passion Measured: A Late-Medieval Diagram of the Body of Christ," in Alasdair

A. MacDonald et al. (eds.), *The Broken Body: Passion Devotion in Late-Medieval Culture* (Groningen: Egbert Forsten, 1998), pp. 211–38.

31. Schreiber, *Handbuch*, no.1942; Albert Bühler, "Die Heilige Lanze: Ein ikonographischer Beitrag zur Geschichte der deutschen Reichskleinodien," *Das Münster* 16 (1963), pp. 100–101; Mark P. McDonald, *The Print Collection of Ferdinand Columbus (1488–1539)*, vol. 1 (London: British Museum, 2004), fig. 12; and *The Print Collection of Ferdinand Columbus (1488–1539)*, vol. 2, no. 2959; *Origins of European Printmaking*, no. 59.

32. Wolfgang Seibrich, "Die Hl.-Rock-Ausstellungen und Hl.-Rock-Wallfahrten von 1512 bis 1765," in Erich Aretz (ed.), *Der heilige Rock zu Trier: Studien zur Geschichte und Verehrung der Tunika Christi* (Trier: Paulinus, 1995), p. 178 n.15.

33. Throughout the Middle Ages, the centrally planned structure functioned as a diacritical marker acknowledging a break with custom, namely the basilical cross plan. See Marvin Trachtenberg, "On Brunelleschi's Choice: Speculations on Medieval Rome and the Origins of Renaissance Architecture," in Cecil L. Striker (ed.), *Architectural Studies in Memory of Richard Krautheimer* (Mainz: Philipp von Zabern, 1996), p. 170.

34. Biddle, *Tomb of Christ*, p. 81.

35. Jocelyn Toynbee and John Ward Perkins, *The Shrine of St. Peter and the Vatican Excavations* (London: Longmans, 1956), pp. 141, 161, 201–203. Matthew 27:60 describes Christ's tomb as the "new tomb" of Joseph of Arimathea, a "rich man." Thus one might well have imagined Christ's tomb as a small mausoleum, not a rude cave.

36. "[I]n questo caso la mente delli homini pò sattisfare standossi nel letto, e non andare nè lochi fatticosi e pericolosi nè pellegrinaggi come al continuo far si vede. Ma se pure tai pellegrinaggi al continuo sono in essere, che li move sanza necessità? Certo tu confessarai essere tal simulacro." Claire J. Farago, *Leonardo da Vinci's Paragone: A Critical Interpretation with a New Edition of the Text in the Codex Urbinas* (Leiden: Brill, 1992), p. 188.

37. Renate Stegmaier-Breinlinger, "'Die hailigen Stett Rom und Jerusalem': Reste einer Ablaßsammlung im Bickenkloster in Villingen," *Freiburger Diözesan-Archiv* 91 (1971), pp. 176–201.

38. William Hood, "The Sacro Monte of Varallo: Renaissance Art and Popular Religion," in Timothy Verdon (ed.), *Monasticism and the Arts* (Syracuse: Syracuse University Press, 1984), pp. 291–311; Alessandro Nova, "'Popular' Art in Renaissance Italy: Early Response to the Holy Mountain at Varallo," in Claire Farago (ed.), *Reframing the Renaissance: Visual Culture in Europe and Latin America, 1450–1650* (New Haven, CT: Yale University Press, 1995), pp. 112–26 and 319–21; and Wharton, *Selling Jerusalem*, pp. 97–144. A parallel phenomenon was the family of models of the Nativity crib, for example, in Santa Maria Maggiore, Santa Maria in Trastevere, and St. Peter's in Rome. See Neri, *Il Santo Sepolcro riprodotto in Occidente*, pp. 47–49.

39. See n.19 above, as well as the many artifacts assembled ingeniously under the rubric *temples-objets* in the exhibition catalogue *Le temple: Représentations de l'architecture sacrée*, exhibition catalogue, Musée National Message Biblique Marc Chagall, Nice (Paris: Éditions de la réunion des musées nationaux, 1982). See also Justin E. A. Kroeser, *The Sepulchrum Domini Through the Ages* (Leuven: Peeters, 2000).

40. Niklas Luhmann, *Art as a Social System* (Palo Alto, CA: Stanford University Press, 2000), p. 227, following Jan Assmann. Luhmann points out that "the evolution of an imaginary space of art can begin with a sense for ornamentation, because ornamentation does not presuppose a distinct artistic realm."

41. Hans Caspary, *Das Sakramentstabernakel in Italien bis zum Konzil von Trent* (Munich: Uni-Druck, 1964), pp. 97–99.

SEVEN — DOUBLE ORIGINS
OF THE CHRISTIAN TEMPLE

1. Rotterdam, Museum Boijmans van Beuningen, inventory no. 2449. The attribution to Jan van Eyck has been accepted by many but not all authorities. For the bibliography, see *Van Eyck to Bruegel, 1400–1550: Dutch and Flemish Painting* (Rotterdam: Museum Boijmans van Beuningen, 1994), pp. 35–36.

2. An example is the ivory relief in the Bargello. See Franco Cardini, "La devozione al Santo Sepolcro, le sue riproduzioni occidentali e il complesso stefaniano: Alcuni casi italici," in *Sette Colonne e Sette Chiese*, p. 31.

3. Robert Ousterhout, "Architecture as Relic and the Construction of Sanctity: The Stones of the Holy Sepulchre," *Journal of the Society of Architectural Historians* 62 (2003), p. 4. Good examples are the ivory relief in the Bayerisches Nationalmuseum, Munich, ca. 400; see *Le temple: Représentations de l'architecture sacrée*, document no. 18, or Cardini, "La devozione al Santo Sepolcro," p. 32; and the Bargello relief cited in the previous note. See also the scene painted on the inside cover of the relic case of the Sancta Sanctorum in Rome in Gary Vikan, *Byzantine Pilgrimage Art* (Washington, D.C.: Dumbarton Oaks Center for Byzantine Studies, 1982), pp. 18–20, figs. 13a–b.

4. Jacobus de Voragine, *Legenda Aurea*, trans. Richard Benz (Heidelberg: Schneider, 1984), pp. 269–70.

5. On portraits of Jerusalem in fifteenth-century northern painting, see Carol Herselle Krinsky, "Representations of the Temple of Jerusalem before 1500," *Journal of the Warburg and Courtauld Institutes* 33 (1970), pp. 1–19; Eva Frodl-Kraft, "Der Tempel von Jerusalem in der 'Vermählung Mariae' des Meisters von Flémalle," in *Études d'art médiéval offertes à Louis Grodecki* (Paris: Ophrys, 1981), pp. 293–309; and Reiner Haussherr, "Spätgotische Ansichten der Stadt Jerusalem (oder: war der Hausbuchmeister in Jerusalem?)," *Jahrbuch der Berliner Museen* 29/30 (1987/1988), pp. 47–70.

6. On the Dome of the Rock, see Oleg Grabar, *The Shape of the Holy: Early Islamic Jerusalem* (Princeton, NJ: Princeton University Press, 1996), and most recently on the mysteries surrounding its construction, Gülru Necipoğlu, "The Dome of the Rock as Palimpsest: 'Abd al-Malik's Grand Narrative and Sultan Süleyman's Glosses," *Muqarnas* 25 (2008), pp. 17–105. We are

grateful to Kathryn Moore for guidance on this topic. The rock was held by Muslims—not necessarily in the earliest period but eventually—to be the site of Mohammed's ascension, a repetition and displacement of Christ's Ascension from the Mount of Olives a few hundred yards to the east, site of a centrally planned Christian sanctuary since the late fourth century (the Imbomon, which survives today only in outline).

7. The strong case for the observance of the scriptural proportions in church architecture, running from the earliest times deep into the Middle Ages, and based on computer surveys, is made by John Wilkinson, *From Synagogue to Church: The Traditional Design* (London: Routledge, 2002). The derivation of the Christian basilica is controversial, to say the least; for basic orientation, see Richard Krautheimer, *Early Christian and Byzantine Architecture* (Harmondsworth and New York: Pelican, 1986), p. 41 n.6.

8. Walter Cahn, "Solomonic Elements in Romanesque Art," in Joseph Gutmann (ed.), *The Temple of Solomon: Archaeological Fact and Medieval Tradition in Christian, Islamic, and Jewish Art* (Missoula, MT: Scholars Press for American Academy of Religion, 1976), pp. 45–72 and "Architecture and Exegesis: Richard of St.-Victor's Ezekiel Commentary and Its Illustrations," *Art Bulletin* 96 (1994), pp. 53–68.

9. John Wilkinson, *Jerusalem Pilgrims before the Crusades* (Warminster, UK: Aris & Phillips, 2002), p. 266. See pp. 357–59 for other early accounts of the temple area. On the misidentifications of the Dome of the Rock and the confusion of Temple, Dome, and Holy Sepulchre, see Naredi-Rainer, *Salomos Tempel und das Abendland*, pp. 13–90.

10. On the identity of temple and palace in royal building systems, see Jonathan Z. Smith, *To Take Place: Toward Theory in Ritual* (Chicago: University of Chicago Press, 1987), pp. 22, 47–73.

11. Some modern archeologists doubt that the Temple stood on the Rock.

12. M. C. Seymour (ed.), *Mandeville's Travels* (Oxford: Clarendon Press, 1967), p. 61.

13. For a fifteenth-century pictorial example, see Helen Rosenau, *Vision of the Temple: The Image of the Temple of Jerusalem in Judaism and Christianity* (London: Oresko, 1979), p. 66.

14. Michael Greenhalgh suggests that the Dome of the Rock was a "worthy successor to what early Islamic legends of Solomon's Temple describe as 'sheathed inside and out with white, yellow, and green marble'"; *Marble Past, Monumental Present*, p. 284.

15. John Wilkinson with Joyce Hill and W. F. Ryan, *Jerusalem Pilgrimage 1099–1185* (London: Hakluyt Society, 1988), p. 132.

16. "Est enim in ea [Jerusalem] primum sacratissimum templum Domini a Salomone antiquitus [sic] constructum, quo penitus totum quasi ruptum est. An aliquid tamen de priori templum remanserit ambiguum est. Sufficiat nobis eundem locum esse in quo templum prius edificatum erat." See *Itinéraire d'Anselme Adorno en Terre Sainte (1470–71)*, ed. and trans. Jacques Heers and Georgette de Groer (Paris: Editions du Centre National de la Recherche Scientifique, 1978), p. 258.

17. Wilkinson, *Jerusalem Pilgrimage*, p. 293.

18. "Salomons tempel...mitt rondem werck und kriechescher arbeyt erbuwen mit behauwen und polyrten oder geebnetten steynen, welcher Tempel serre hoch und wyt ist, mit bly bedeckt. Darauff haben die heiden eyn halben mon als ob er were eclipseret das ist verdunckelt." Bernhard von Breydenbach, *Peregrinatio in terram sanctam* (Mainz, 1486), fol. 32v–33r. Breydenbach concedes that the Saracens "hold Solomon's Temple in great honor."

19. Lotte Brand Philip, *The Ghent Altarpiece and the Art of Jan van Eyck* (Princeton, NJ: Princeton University Press, 1971), pp. 180–92; Heribert Müller, *Kreuzigungspläne und Kreuzzugspolitik des Herzogs Philipp des Guten von Burgund* (Göttingen: Vandenhoek & Ruprecht, 1993).

20. The most recent archeological evidence suggests that the Imbomon (Church of the Ascension) was originally circular in plan and that the Crusaders later made it octagonal in imitation of the Dome of the

Rock. See Adrian J. Boas, *Jerusalem in the Time of the Crusades: Society, Landscape, and Art in the Holy City under Frankish Rule* (London: Routledge, 2001), p. 113.

21. Hans Caspary, *Das Sakramentstabernakel in Italien bis zum Konzil von Trent* (Munich: Uni-Druck, 1964), p. 96. Of course liturgical references were also made to the Holy Sepulchre. Joseph Braun discusses a number of textual sources that describe the eucharistic receptacle as "corporis Christi novum sepulcrum," see *Das christliche Altargerät in seinem Sein und in seiner Entwicklung* (Munich: Hueber, 1932), p. 669. Braun's suggestion is taken up and developed by Doris Carl, *Benedetto da Maiano: A Florentine Sculptor at the Threshold of the High Renaissance* (Turnhout: Brepols, 2007), p. 202 and subsequent pages.

22. Round interiors were generally not represented on paper before the late fifteenth century; see for example the drawing by Cronaca of Santo Stefano Rotondo, Uffizi 161s, in *Le temple*, no. 61.

23. Robert Ousterhout, "Architecture as Relic and the Construction of Sanctity," p. 13.

EIGHT — ICON MAINTENANCE

1. The legend of Luke as portraitist dates no earlier than the sixth century, and it did not achieve widespread dissemination in the West until the twelfth century. See Regine Dölling, "Byzantinische Elemente in der Kunst des 16. Jahrhunderts," in Johannes Irmscher (ed.), *Aus der byzantinistischen Arbeit der DDR*, vol. 2, Berliner Byzantinistische Arbeiten 6 (Berlin: Akademie, 1957), p. 160 and Michele Bacci, *Il pennello dell'evangelista: Storia delle immagini sacre attribuite a San Luca* (Pisa: GISEM, 1998), esp. pp. 250–80.

2. On the Veronica and its relation to the traditions of the Mandylion, the basic reference works are: Ernst von Dobschütz, *Christusbilder: Untersuchungen zur christlichen Legende* (Leipzig: J. C. Hinrichs, 1899); Giovanni Morello and Gerhard Wolf (eds.), *Il volto di Cristo*, and Herbert L. Kessler and Gerhard Wolf (eds.), *The Holy Face and the Paradox of Representation* (Bologna: Nuova Alfa, 1998).

3. "[C]ome vedemo in ne' pittori dopo i Romani, i quali senpre imitarono l'uno dall'altro e di età in età senpre andava detta arte in dechinazione." Jean Paul Richter (ed.), *Literary Works of Leonardo da Vinci*, vol. 1 (Oxford: Oxford University Press, 1939), pp. 331–32, no. 660 (= Codex Atlanticus, fol. 139r).

4. Carlo Bertelli, *La Madonna di Santa Maria in Trastevere: Storia, iconografia, stile di un dipinto romano del ottavo secolo* (Rome: n.s., 1961). The icon at Santa Maria in Trastevere includes a portrait of the pope who commissioned it, and at the same time claims in an inscription that the image of the Virgin was "made by itself." This is proof for Charles Barber that the "icon could be a copy of a miraculous original and still claim the same status as the original." See Barber, *Figure and Likeness*, p. 29. On the five oldest Roman Marian icons, see Gerhard Wolf, "Icons and Sites: Cult Images of the Virgin in Medieval Rome," in Maria Vassilaki (ed.), *Images of the Mother of God: Perceptions of the Theotokos in Byzantium* (Aldershot, UK: Ashgate, 2005), pp. 23–49.

5. See Wolf, *Salus Populi Romani: Die Geschichte römischer Kultbilder im Mittelalter* (Weinheim: VCH, 1990).

6. Most scholars agree that the latest interventions on the St. Luke icon in Santa Maria Maggiore and the early eighth-century Madonna della Clemenza in Santa Maria in Trastevere date to the thirteenth century. Gerhard Wolf convincingly disproved Joseph Wilpert's dating of the panel to ca. 1250, arguing that the original painting was done in the sixth century, shortly after the founding of the church. See *Salus Populi Romani*, pp. 24–28 and Bertelli, *La Madonna di Santa Maria in Trastevere*. The Madonna of San Sisto in Santa Maria del Rosario was apparently also last retouched in the thirteenth century, to judge from the prerestoration photos. Unfortunately, the main study on the work does not consider this question. See Carlo Bertelli, "L'immagine del 'Monasterium Tempuli' dopo il Restauro," *Archivum Fratrum Praedicatorum* 31 (1961),

pp. 82–111. Besides some overpainting of the nineteenth century removed in 1950, the latest layer of repainting on the seventh-century icon from Santa Maria Antiqua, now in Santa Francesca Romana, was a layer of tempera paint dating to the thirteenth century; see Ernst Kitzinger, "On Some Icons of the Seventh Century," in Kurt Weitzmann (ed.), *Late Classical and Medieval Studies in Honor of Albert Mathias Friend, Jr.* (Princeton, NJ: Princeton University Press, 1955), pp. 132–50. In this case, the thirteenth-century restoration also involved the preservation and insertion of the faces of the Virgin and Child in their original state, as relics, thus signaling a move towards a more modern approach to restoration already at that stage; see Pico Cellini, "Una Madonna molto antica," *Proporzioni* 3 (1950), pp. 1–6. The Madonna of the Pantheon is the exception as it was repainted several times up to the eighteenth century; see Carlo Bertelli, "La Madonna del Pantheon," *Bollettino d'Arte* 46 (1961), pp. 24–32 and 30 n.3.

7. Carmen Gómez-Moreno, Elizabeth H. Jones, Arthur K. Wheelock, and Millard Meiss, "A Sienese *St. Dominic* Modernized Twice in the Thirteenth Century," *Art Bulletin* 51 (1969), pp. 363–66. See also Cathleen Hoeniger, *The Renovation of Paintings in Tuscany, 1250–1500* (Cambridge: Cambridge University Press, 1995), pp. 88–99.

8. Enzo Carli and Cesare Brandi, "Relazione sul Restauro della Madonna di Guido da Siena del 1221," *Bollettino d'Arte* 36 (1951), pp. 248–60 and esp. 252 and 254.

9. Cesare Brandi, *Duccio* (Florence: Vallecchi, 1951), pp. 94–120.

10. James Stubblebine, *Guido da Siena* (Princeton, NJ: Princeton University Press, 1964), p. 40 and Julian Gardner, "Guido da Siena, 1221, and Tommaso da Modena," *Burlington Magazine* 121 (1979), pp. 107–108. The basic evidence for the association with St. Dominic is the inscription placed in the chapel by Domenico Venturini, patron of the chapel, in 1706: "GUIDO DE SENIS HANC TABULAM PINXIT ET/ DIVUS DOMI-NICUS OCCUMBIT ANNO MCCXXI/ FELIX PICTOR CUIUS PITTURA FORTASSE CELIS OSTENDIT QUI EA COMPLETA CELIS ASCENDIT." However, Venturini's connection of the date to the death of St. Dominic has no particular authority. Moreover, the second part of the inscription makes it clear that Venturini understood the inscription on the painting to mean that Guido actually painted it in 1221 (thus making it possible that St. Dominic "displayed it to heaven upon ascending there"). Indeed, in the document that records the installation of Guido's panel in the Venturini chapel, it is said that the installation greatly pleased Domenico Venturini "per havervi divozione speciale e perché pittura di Guido da Siena, in tempo che per l'Italia era perduta l'arte di dipingere. E detta immagine è quella istessa tanto nominata da' sanesi nelle loro historie, per abbattere l'oppinione falsa di quelli che dicono che Giovanni Cimabue fosse il ritrovatore della pittura nella Toscana, essendo questa immagine dipinta 59 anni avanti che egli nascesse, come si vede dall'inscrizzione che è sotto il medesimo quadro." See Peter Anselm Riedl and Max Seidel (eds.), *Die Kirchen von Siena*, vol. 2 (Munich: Bruckmann, 1992), p. 936. In other words, Domenico Venturini had adopted an art-historical view of artifacts, one which saw paintings as indices of their time. His desire to establish a precise historical chronology led him to think nonsubstitutionally about production.

11. This was proposed by Enzo Carli, *Dipinti senesi del contado e della maremma* (Milan: Electa, 1955), p. 177.

12. Cesare Brandi, *Duccio*, pp. 102–103.

13. A few years later, in 1226, the Dominicans were granted the current site on Campo Regio, where Tizio places the parish church of San Gregorio. The Dominicans began building a new church on the site in 1227, see *Die Kirchen von Siena*, vol. 2, pp. 452–53.

14. The case of the chapterhouse in the Dominican church at Treviso was adduced by Gardner, "Guido da Siena, 1221, and Tommaso da Modena," who reports the inscription: ANNO DOMINI MILLMO CCXXI FRATRES PRAEDICATORES PRIMO TARVISIUM VENERUNT ET EODEM ANNO COMMUNITAS TARCISINA EISDEM

AEDIFICAVIT CONVENTUM S. NICOLAI IN QUO
NUNC AD LAUDEM DEI ET SUAE MATRIS VIRGINIS
GLORIOSAE B. NICOLAI AC UTILITATEM POPULI
TARVISINI COMMEMORANTUR. The inscription
commemorates the date 1221 because it was the date
of the first building of the church of the Dominicans
in Treviso. Gardner takes this as evidence that the
date 1221, death date of St. Dominic, carried universal
importance for the order. However the inscription
does not refer to the death of Dominic; it only refers to
the first Trevisan foundation. If this first building had
been built in, say, 1223 then presumably that is the date
that would have appeared in the inscription.

15. On the Madonnas for the high altar of Siena
Cathedral, see chs. 2 and 3 in Henk van Os, *Sienese
Altarpieces*, vol. 1 (Groningen: Bousma, 1984). On
Daddi and Orsanmichele, see Walter and Elizabeth
Paatz, *Die Kirchen von Florenz*, vol. 4 (Frankfurt am
Main: Klostermann, 1952), p. 499 and Nancy Fabbri
and Nina Rutenberg, "The Tabernacle of Orsanmichele
in Context," *Art Bulletin* 63 (1981), pp. 385–405.

16. Bruce Cole, "Old and New in the Early
Trecento," *Mitteilungen des Kunsthistorischen Institutes
in Florenz* 17 (1973), pp. 229–40.

17. Suzana Skalova, "The Seventeenth-Century
Icon 'Mother of God of Smolensk,' Rediscovered,"
ICOM Committee for Conservation, Preprints (Los
Angeles, CA: Getty Conservation Institute, 1987),
pp. 1127–31. Cathleen Hoeniger refers to this article
in *Renovation of Paintings in Tuscany*, p. 32.

18. Alessandro Conti discusses in these terms the
documented restorations of paintings and sculptures
carried out by Martino di Bartolomeo in 1404 in the
Cathedral of Siena. According to Conti, "The work
completed by Martino came as a modernization of
the altarpiece in relation to new cultic requirements,
changing and adding figures of saints and restoring colors that had ceased to operate with their former optical
efficacy, as we might say in the modern language of
conservation. The intervention occurs only (and also
necessarily) in the service of the functionality of the
panel as a cult object and as a piece of furnishing that
gives prestige to the cathedral. [*Il lavoro compiuto da
Martino si individuava come un aggiornamento della pala
a nuove esigenze di culto, cambiando ed aggiungendo figure
di santi e come un recupero dei colori che non rispondevano
più alla loro funzionalità ottica, diremmo con un linguag-
gio da restauro moderno. L'intervento avviene unicamente
(ma anche necessariamente) in nome della funzionalità
della tavola come oggetto di culto e parte dell'arredo
che dà prestigio alla cattedrale.*]" See *Storia del restauro
e della conservazione delle opere d'arte* (Milan: Electa,
1988), p. 12.

19. This is essentially the argument of Hoeniger,
as she lays it out in ch. 2 of *Renovation of Paintings in
Tuscany*. Less convincing is her contention that the
restorations were intended to link up the old images
with the modern style of Duccio, which since the
installation of the *Maestà* in 1311 had become associated
with "religious efficacy." See *Renovation of Paintings in
Tuscany*, p. 26.

20. See Hoeniger, *Renovation of Paintings in Tuscany*,
ch. 2. Michael Viktor Schwarz argues that the *Madonna
del Bordone* was left half-restored in order to call attention to the panel's great age. See "Übermalungen und
Remakes: Stil als Medium," in Bruno Klein and Bruno
Boerner (eds.), *Stilfragen zur Kunst des Mittelalters* (Berlin: Reimer, 2006), p. 197.

21. Michele Cordaro, noting the presence of oil
paint in the overpainting, argued that it was done much
later, in the eighteenth century. See "Il problema dei
rifacimenti e delle aggiunte nei restauri con due esempi
relativi a dipinti medievali," *Arte Medievale* 1 (1983),
pp. 263–76. In this he was followed by Joseph Polzer,
"The Virgin and Child Enthroned from the Church of
the Servites in Orvieto Generally Given to Coppo di
Marcovaldo: Recent Laboratory Evidence and a Review
of Coppo's Oeuvre," *Antichità Viva* 23.3 (1984), pp.
5–18. Hoeniger also concurs with this view, see *Renovation of Paintings in Tuscany*, p. 160 n.1. Conti, however,
argued that the oil medium was used in binding agents
in the early period, as indicated by Theophilus writing

in the twelfth century and Cennino Cennini writing
ca. 1400. According to Conti the repainting was
done by a painter influenced by Cimabue ca. 1280.
See *Storia del restauro*, p. 9 and p. 329 n.4. According
to Miklos Boskovits the repainting was done early,
by the late thirteenth-century Master of the Madonna
of San Brizio. See "Intorno a Coppo di Marcovaldo,"
in Maria Grazia Ciardi Dupré Dal Poggetto and
Paolo Dal Poggetto (eds.), *Scritti di storia dell'arte in
onore di Ugo Procacci*, vol. 1 (Milan: Electa, 1977),
pp. 94–105.

22. Hoeniger dates the original painting to ca. 1260
and the repainting to ca. 1270–1275, believing the
repainting to be by Margarito's shop. See *Renovation
of Paintings in Tuscany*, pp. 77–82. Anna Maria Maetzke
believes the repainting to have been done in the
Florentine ambient of the Magdalen Master. See
"Nuove Ricerche su Margaritone d'Arezzo," *Bollettino
d'Arte* 58 (1973), p. 108.

23. "The principal heads were completely repainted
as a result of probable damage from fire. [*Le teste
principali erano state completamente ridipinte in seguito ai
probabili danni di bruciature.*]" Conti, *Storia del Restauro*,
p. 9. "The second version...conforms closely to the
underlying figure (which perhaps had been ruined). [*La
seconda stesura...ricalca fedelmente la figura sottostante
(che si era forse rovinata).*]" Maetzke, "Nuove Ricerche
su Margaritone d'Arezzo," p. 108. On Margarito,
Hoeniger sees "no reason to believe that the image was
repainted to repair a damaged original," arguing that
it was done instead to emphasize different aspects of
the saint's personality; see *Renovation of Paintings in
Tuscany*, p. 82. Interestingly, no restoration-as-repair
hypothesis has been proposed for the Ducciesque
repainting of Coppo's *Madonna del Bordone*, probably
because in this case the fifty-year interval does not
so urgently demand it.

24. Klaus Krüger, "Medium and Imagination:
Aesthetic Aspects of Trecento Panel Painting," in
Victor M. Schmidt (ed.), *Italian Panel Painting of the
Duecento and Trecento*, Studies in the History of Art 37
(Washington, D.C.: National Gallery of Art, 2002),
pp. 57–81.

25. The later art-historical consequences of this
problematic are analyzed in Klaus Krüger, *Das Bild als
Schleier des Unsichtbaren: Ästhetische Illusion in der Kunst
der frühen Neuzeit in Italien* (Munich: Fink, 2001).

26. See Carl Brandon Strehlke, "Carpentry and
Connoisseurship: The Disassembly of Altarpieces
and the Rise in Interest in Early Italian Art," in Clay
Dean, Laurence B. Kanter, and Carl Brandon Strehlke,
Rediscovering Fra Angelico: A Fragmentary History (New
Haven, CT: Yale University Art Gallery, 2001), p. 44.
For the identification of the panel now in San Diego,
see Federico Zeri, "Due appunti su Giotto," *Paragone*
8 (1957), pp. 75–87. The fifteenth-century Florentine master Neri di Bicci also recuperated several
thirteenth-century gabled panels by fitting them into
frameworks. See chs. 3 and 5 of Hoeniger, *Renovation
of Paintings in Tuscany*. On the problem more generally,
see Martin Warnke, "Italienische Bildtabernakel bis
zum Frühbarock," *Münchner Jahrbuch der bildenden
Kunst* 19 (1968), pp. 61–102, and Klaus Krüger,
"Medium and Imagination: Aesthetic Aspects of
Trecento Panel Painting," pp. 57–58.

27. "In the year 1706 lord Domenico Venturini
decorated said chapel with stuccoes on the walls, had
the entire vault painted, commissioned the walnut
panelling, and on the altar the Pietà was removed and
is now in storage, and [in its place] was installed the
image of the Madonna that had earlier been placed
above the principal door on the interior of the church,
a most ancient painting. [*L'anno 1706 il signore Domenico
Venturini adornò la detta cappella con stucchi alle par[e]ti
laterali, pitturò tutta la volta, vi fece le spalliere di noce,
e nell'altare fu levata la Pietà, che di presente è posta in
crino, e vi fu collocata l'immagine della Madonna in atto
di sedere, che prima era situata sopra la porta maggiore,
nella parte interiore della chiesa, pittura antichissima.*]"
Riedl and Siedel (eds.), *Die Kirchen von Siena*, vol. 2,
p. 933. On Venturini's appreciation of the painting as a
historical relic, see the document quoted in n.10 above.

NINE — FASHION IN PAINTING

1. Donato Salvi (ed.), *Regola del governo di cura familiare* (Florence: Garinei, 1860), p. 113.

2. This form is an adverb, but English would rather have an adverbial prepositional phrase here.

3. Literally something like "as in other letters" or "as with other letters."

4. See note 2.

5. Symeon of Thessalonica, *Dialogus Contra Haereses*, in J.-P. Migne (ed.), *Patrologiae cursus completus*, Series Graeca (Paris, 1857–1866), vol. 155, col. 112. An excerpt of this passage is offered in Cyril Mango, *The Art of the Byzantine Empire, 312–1453* (Englewood Cliffs, NJ: Prentice Hall, 1972), pp. 253–54. Here we provide a larger excerpt of the text, newly translated by Kyle Mahoney.

6. See the excellent recent study of Charles Barber, *Figure and Likeness: On the Limits of Representation in Byzantine Iconoclasm* (Princeton, NJ: Princeton University Press, 2002).

7. Henry Maguire, *The Icons of their Bodies: Saints and their Images in Byzantium* (Princeton, NJ: Princeton University Press, 1996), p. 11.

8. "[N]on autem praeterire quicquam in aeterno, sed totum esse praesens; nullum vero tempus totum esse praesens." Augustine *Confessiones* 11.11.

9. *Ibid.*, 11.15.

10. "[E]t paululum rapiat splendorem semper stantis aeternitatis." *Ibid.*, 11.11.

11. Maguire, *Icons of their Bodies*, p. 11.

12. "For if the prophets saw in graphic terms that God had hair, then surely that hair existed for the purpose of honoring both nature and God's own intention for us. Those who cut the remaining hair are doing this against God's own intention and for the purpose of dishonoring His nature. And even priests and monks do these things—people who especially ought to give up serving the flesh." Symeon, *Dialogus Contra Haereses*, vol. 155, col. 112 (trans. Kyle Mahoney).

13. Max von Boehn correlated it to the rise of the burgher class in the cities of fourteenth-century Europe: "[F]ashion, in the sense of incessant fluctuation, perpetual striving after improvement, now came on the scene." *Modes and Manners*, trans. Joan Joshua, vol. 1 (Philadelphia: Lippincott, 1952), p. 215. On p. 216 he also claims: "[C]ostume of the fourteenth and fifteenth centuries…no longer follows any definite style, the whole tendency is toward violation of style." See also Anne Hollander, who states: "Fashion as we know it thus began roughly with the rise of towns and the middle class, along with the consolidation of monarchical power." Until the twelfth century, in Hollander's view, clothes show "a fairly static simplicity of shape…. Once pronounced formal elements began to distinguish elegant dress, fashion could become truly competitive, as it has been ever since, in a battle fought chiefly on aesthetic grounds between members of the same class, generation after generation." *Seeing Through Clothes* (New York: Viking, 1978), pp. 362–63. According to Carole Frick, "The first mention in Florentine records of a phenomenon called 'fashion,' of the need to constantly change and update one's (still-wearable) clothing, is probably to be found in Villani's early fourteenth-century Cronica." *Dressing Renaissance Florence: Families, Fortunes, and Fine Clothing* (Baltimore, MD: Johns Hopkins University Press, 2002), p. 180.

14. Diane Owen Hughes, "Sumptuary Laws and Social Relations in Renaissance Italy," in John Bossy (ed.), *Disputes and Settlements: Law and Human Relations in the West* (Cambridge: Cambridge University Press, 1983), pp. 69–99.

15. Georg Simmel, "Fashion," in Simmel, *On Individuality and Social Forms: Selected Writings*, ed. Donald Levine (Chicago: University of Chicago, 1971), p. 297.

16. Boehn, *Modes and Manners*, vol. 2, pp. 102–11.

17. George Kubler, *The Shape of Time*, pp. 38–39.

18. Heinrich Wölfflin, "Prolegomena to a Psychology of Architecture," in *Empathy, Form, and Space: Problems in German Aesthetics 1873–1893*, ed. and trans. Eleftherios Ikonomou and Henry Francis Mallgrave (Santa Monica, CA: Getty Center for the History of Art and the Humanities, 1994), p. 183.

19. "How people like to move and carry themselves is expressed above all in costume, and it is not difficult to show that architecture corresponds to the costume of its period." Wölfflin, "Prolegomena to a Psychology of Architecture," p. 182.

20. Frederic J. Schwartz, "Cathedrals and Shoes: Concepts of Style in Wölfflin and Adorno," *New German Critique* 76 (1999), pp. 3–48.

21. Schwartz, "Cathedrals and Shoes," p. 27.

22. *Ibid.*, p. 35, citing Wölfflin's own source, Hermann Weiss's *Kostümkunde*.

23. See Walter Benjamin's fourteenth thesis, "Über den Begriff der Geschichte": "So war für Robespierre das antike Rom eine mit Jetztzeit geladene Vergangenheit, die er aus dem Kontinuum der Geschichte heraussprengte. Die französische Revolution verstand sich als ein wiedergekehrtes Rom. Sie zitierte das alte Rom genau so wie die Mode eine vergangene Tracht zitiert. Die Mode hat die Witterung für das Aktuelle, wo immer es sich im Dickicht des Einst bewegt. Sie ist der Tigersprung ins Vergangene." *Gesammelte Schriften*, vol. 2.2 (Frankfurt: Suhrkamp, 1974), p. 701. Benjamin's idea is a positive construction on the famously wry opening paragraphs of Karl Marx: "And just when [the living] seem engaged in revolutionizing themselves and things, in creating something that has never yet existed, precisely in such periods of revolutionary crisis they anxiously conjure up the spirits of the past to their service and borrow from their names, battle cries and costumes in order to present the new scene of world history in this time-honoured disguise and this borrowed language." *The Eighteenth Brumaire of Louis Bonaparte* (New York: International Publishers, 1962), p. 15. Many thanks to Ian Balfour for helpful discussions on the Benjamin passage.

24. Charles Baudelaire, *Le peintre de la vie moderne*, in *Oeuvres complètes*, vol. 2 (Paris: Gallimard, 1976), p. 684.

25. Erasmus, *Ciceronianus*, in *Collected Works of Erasmus*, vol. 28, ed. A. H. T. Levi (Toronto: University of Toronto Press, 1988), p. 381. It is simple enough to find examples of each of these fashions in works of art made during the previous century. Many of them could, in fact, have been described by Erasmus as "pictures that aren't all that old, painted, say, sixty years ago." For "horns and pyramids and cones sticking out from the top of the head" see Jan van Eyck, *Portrait of Margaret van Eyck*, Vienna, Kunsthistorisches Museum (horns); Hans Memling, *Portrait of Maria Baroncelli*, New York, Metropolitan Museum (cone); Master of Mary of Burgundy, "Mary of Burgundy at Prayer," *Hours of Mary of Burgundy*, Berlin, Kupferstichkabinett of the Staatliche Museen. "[B]row and temples plucked so that nearly half her head is bald": *Profile Portrait of a Lady* sometimes attributed to the Limbourgs, Washington, D.C., National Gallery; Master of the Virgo inter Virgines, *Annunciation*, Rotterdam, Museum Boijmans van Beuningen. "[M]en wearing those hats stuffed like a cushion with a great tail hanging down": Pisanello, *Costume Study*, Bayonne, Musée Bonnat; Eyck School, *Portrait of Marco Barbarigo*, London, National Gallery. "[C]oats with scalloped borders and enormous padded shoulders": Domenico Veneziano, *Adoration of the Magi*, Berlin, Staatliche Museen. "[H]air shaved off an inch above their ears": Robert Campin, *Portrait of a Man (Robert de Masmines?)*, Madrid, Thyssen Collection; Jan van Eyck, *Virgin of the Chancellor Rolin*, Paris, Louvre. "[T]unics far too short to reach the knees, hardly covering their private parts": Master of René of Anjou, "Amour takes the Heart of the King," *Livre du Cuer d'Amour Espris*, Vienna, Nationalbibliothek. "[S]lippers with a long pointed beak sticking out in front": Rogier van der Weyden, *Bladelin Triptych*, Berlin, Staatliche Museen.

26. Wölfflin, "Prolegomena to a Psychology of Architecture," p. 185; Riegl, "Der moderne Denkmalkultus, sein Wesen und seine Entstehung," in *Gesammelte Aufsätze* (Augsburg: Filser, 1928), pp. 145–46.

27. Jocelyn Penny Small, "The Tarquins and Servius Tullius at Banquet," *Mélanges de l'École Française de Rome* 103 (1991), pp. 247–64.

28. Filarete, *Treatise on Architecture; being the treatise*

by Antonio di Piero Averlino, known as Filarete, trans. John R. Spencer (New Haven, CT: Yale University Press, 1965), vol. 1, p. 306; vol. 2, fol. 179v. On the representation of historical costume in paintings, see Reiner Haussherr, *Convenevolezza: historische Angemessenheit in der Darstellung von Kostüm und Schauplatz seit der Spätantike bis ins 16. Jahrhundert* (Mainz: Akademie der Wissenschaften und der Literatur, 1984), who contends that the issue was discussed in Florence already in the 1430s, but not thought through until the mid-sixteenth century. On northern Europe, especially in the sixteenth century, see Leonie von Wilckens, "Das 'historische' Kostüm im 16. Jahrhundert," *Waffen-und Kostümkunde* 3 (1961), pp. 28–46.

29. "Li abiti delle figure siano accomodati all'età e al decoro, cioè che 'l vecchio sia togato, il giovane ornato d'abito che manco occupi il collo da li omeri della spalle in su, eccetto quegli che fanno professione in religione, e fugire il più che si può gli abiti della sua età, eccetto quando si scontrassino essere delli sopradetti, e non si debbono usare se non nelle figure ch'anno a somigliare a quelli che son sepolti per le chiese, acciò che si riservi riso nelli nostri successori delle pazze invenzioni degli uomini, ovvero che gli lascino admirazione della loro dignità e bellezza." Leonardo da Vinci, *Treatise on Painting: Codex urbinas latinus 1270*, trans. A. Philip McMahon (Princeton, NJ: Princeton University Press, 1956), vol. 1, fol. 107r.

30. "Questa pittura, ancora che non sia molto bella, considerandosi il disegno di Bonamico e la invenzione ell'è degna di esser in parte lodata, e massimamente per la varietà de' vestiti, barbute et altre armature di que' tempi; et io me ne sono servito in alcune storie che ho fatto per il signor duca Cosimo, dove era bisogno rappresentare uomini armati all'antica e altre somiglianti cose di quell'età.... E da questo si può conoscere quanto sia da far capitale dell'invenzioni et opere fatte da questi antichi, comeché così perfette non siano, et in che modo utile e commodo si possa trarre dalle cose loro." (On paintings by Bruno di Giovanni and Buffalmacco in Santa Maria Novella, Florence.)

Giorgio Vasari, *Le vite de' più eccellenti pittori, scultori e architettori nelle redazioni del 1550 e 1568*, vol. 2, ed. Rosanna Bettarini, with commentary by Paola Barocchi (Florence: Studio per Edizioni Scelte, 1967), p. 173. It is likely that Vasari used them for details in *The Expansion of Florence* in the Salone dei Cinquecento. He says similar things about the frescoes depicting the Longobard queen Theodelinda in the Cathedral of Monza, "dove si vedeva che eglino dalla parte di dietro erano rasi e dinanzi avevano le zazzere e si tignevano fino al mento; le vestimenta erano di tela larga, come usarono gl'Angli et i Sassoni, e sotto un manto di diversi colori, e le scarpe fino alle dita de' piedi aperte e sopra legate con certi correggiuoli." *Le vite de' più eccellenti pittori, scultori e architettori*, vol. 1, p. 23. A very legible inscription on the wall dates the paintings at Monza to 1444. Nevertheless Vasari apparently took them to be context-sensitive records of sixth-century dress. On the fresco cycle, see Janice Schell, "La cappella di Teodolinda: gli affreschi degli Zavattari," in *Il Duomo di Monza*, vol. 1, *La storia e l'arte* (Milan: Electa, 1990), pp. 189–214.

TEN — ANCIENT PAINTING

1. Some basic literature on the reception of the Byzantine icons in the West: Ernst Kitzinger, "The Byzantine Contribution to Western Art of the Twelfth and Thirteenth Centuries," *Dumbarton Oaks Papers* 20 (1966), pp. 25–47; James H. Stubblebine, "Byzantine Influence in Thirteenth-Century Italian Panel Painting," *Dumbarton Oaks Papers* 20 (1966), pp. 85–101; Hans Belting, *The Image and its Public in the Middle Ages: Form and Function of Early Paintings of the Passion* (New Rochelle, NY: Caratzas, 1990), pp. 31–85; Hans Belting, "The 'Byzantine' Madonnas: New Facts about their Italian Origin and Some Observations on Duccio," *Studies in the History of Art* 12 (1982), pp. 7–22; Hans Belting, *Likeness and Presence: A History of the Image before the Era of Art* (Chicago: University of Chicago Press, 1994), pp. 330–47; Anne Derbes, *Picturing the Passion in Late Medieval Italy: Narrative*

Painting, Franciscan Ideologies, and the Levant (Cambridge: Cambridge University Press, 1996); Anne Derbes, "Siena and the Levant in the later Dugento," *Gesta* 28 (1989), pp. 190–204; Annemarie Weyl Carr, "East, West, and Icons in Twelfth-Century Outremer," in V. Goss and C. Bornstein (eds.), *The Meeting of Two Worlds: Cultural Exchange between East and West during the Period of the Crusades*, *Studies in Medieval Culture*, vol. 21 (Kalamazoo, MI: Medieval Institute Publications, Western Michigan University, 1986), pp. 347–59; Rebecca W. Corrie, "The Political Meaning of Coppo di Marcovaldo's Madonna and Child in Siena," *Gesta* 29 (1990), pp. 61–76; Annemarie Weyl Carr, "Byzantines and Italians on Cyprus: Images from Art," *Dumbarton Oaks Papers* 49 (1995), pp. 339–57; Anthony Cutler, "From Loot to Scholarship: Changing Modes in the Italian Response to Byzantine Artifacts, ca. 1200–1750," *Dumbarton Oaks Papers* 49 (1995), pp. 237–68; Rebecca W. Corrie, "Coppo di Marcovaldo's Madonna del Bordone and the Meaning of the Bare-Legged Christ Child in Siena and the East," *Gesta* 35 (1996), pp. 43–65.

2. C. Wolters, "Beobachtungen am Freisinger Lukasbild," *Kunstchronik* 17 (1964), p. 85ff.

3. See Helen C. Evans (ed.), *Byzantium: Faith and Power (1261–1557)* (New York: Metropolitan Museum, 2004), cat. 132.

4. Carlo Bertelli, "The Image of Pity in Santa Croce in Gerusalemme," in Douglas Fraser, Howard Hibbard, and Milton J. Lewine (eds.), *Essays in the History of Art Presented to Rudolf Wittkower* (London: Phaidon, 1967), pp. 40–55.

5. Evans (ed.), *Byzantium: Faith and Power*, cat. 128.

6. The chronology of the object resists clarification even under the microscope of modern art-historical analysis. Cutler believes the mosaic itself was commissioned by Perotti in the 1450s. See "From Loot to Scholarship," p. 253. Fabrizio Lollini dates the mosaic to 1320–1350 but believes that the revetment and frame date to ca. 1600. See "Bessarione e Perotti diffusori della cultura figurativa bizantina," *Res publica litterarum* 14 (1991), pp. 127–42 and esp. 128–29. Jannic Durand argues that the mosaic dates to the early fourteenth century, apart from the interpolation of Perotti's coat of arms on the saint's shield, and that the revetment was commissioned by Perotti in the mid-fifteenth century. See Evans (ed.), *Byzantium: Faith and Power*, cat. 139. It is unlikely that the inscription was invented by Perotti, and the eagles are distinctly Palaiologan. It is more likely that the revetment is a Palaiologan antiquarian venture, and that Perotti believed in it. Thanks to John Monfasani and Alice-Mary Talbot for sharing their views on the work with us.

7. See Adolph Goldschmidt and Kurt Weitzmann, *Die Byzantinischen Elfenbeinskulpturen des X.–XIII. Jahrhunderten* (Berlin: Cassirer, 1930–1934), no. 54. See also Anthony Cutler, *The Hand of the Master: Craftsmanship, Ivory, and Society in Byzantium (9th–11th Centuries)* (Princeton, NJ: Princeton University Press, 1994), pp. 45–48, 65, 84, 207 and 217. Since the Goldschmidt and Weitzmann publication, the revetment and nielli have been separated from the ivory and are now in the Oberlin Museum of Art.

8. "[I]magines sanctorum operis antiqui ex Graecia allatas, quas illi iconas vocant." Eugène Müntz, *Les arts à la cour des papes pendant le XVe et le XVIe siècle*, vol. 2 (Paris, 1878–1882), p. 132.

9. "Non passerò che io non dica qui una singulare loda de' Greci. E' Greci in anni mille cinquecento o più, non hanno mai mutato abito, quello medesimo abito avevano eglino in quello tempo, ch'eglino avevano avuto nel tempo detto, come si vede ancora in Grecia nel luogo si chiama I campi Filippi, dove sono molte storie di marmo, drentovi uomini vestiti a la greca, nel modo erano alora." Vespasiano, *Le vite*, 2 vols., ed. Aulo Greco (Florence: Istituto Palazzo Strozzi, 1970), p. 19.

10. See Paul Durrieu, *Les Très Riches Heures de Jean de France, Duc de Berry* (Paris: Plon-Nourrit, 1904), p. 98. The costumes are analyzed in detail by Stella Mary Newton, *Renaissance Theatre Costume and the Sense of the Historic Past* (London: Rapp & Whiting, 1975), pp. 64–66.

11. See Evans (ed.), *Byzantium: Faith and Power*, cat. 318 AB; Michael Vickers, "Some Preparatory Drawings for Pisanello's Medallion of John VIII Palaeologus," *Art Bulletin* 60 (1978), pp. 417–24.

12. Charles D. Cuttler, "Exotics in Fifteenth-Century Netherlandish Art: Comments on Oriental and Gypsy Costume," in *Liber Amicorum Herman Liebaers* (Brussels: Amis de la Bibliothèque Royale Albert Ier, 1984), pp. 419–34.

13. James Joyce, *Ulysses: The Corrected Text*, ed. Hans Walter Gabler (New York: Random House, 1986), p. 302.

14. The bust was attributed to Filarete by its discoverers Michele Lazzaroni and Antonio Muñoz, who believed it was made in Florence in the first half of 1439 during the Florence portion of the Ferrara-Florence Council. See *Filarete, scultore e architetto del secolo XV* (Rome: Modes, 1908), pp. 125–30. It was attributed, with powerful arguments, to Donatello by Jane Schuyler. See *Florentine Busts: Sculpted Portaiture in the Fifteenth Century* (New York, NY, and London: Garland, 1976), pp. 103–13.

15. See Stephen K. Scher, *The Currency of Fame: Portrait Medals of the Renaissance* (New York: Abrams, 1994), pp. 44–46.

16. Some examples of Byzantine costumes in European art after the Ferrara-Florence Council of 1438–1439 include: paintings by Apollonio di Giovanni; a manuscript of Boccaccio's *Filocolo* in Kassel—see Leo Olschki, "Asian Exoticism in Italian Painting of the Early Renaissance," *Art Bulletin* 26 (1944), pp. 95–108; an engraving by the Master of Mount Calvary—see Fischer, *Geschichte der deutschen Zeichnung und Graphik* (Munich, 1951), p. 130, fig. 97. See also Julian Raby, *Venice, Dürer and the Oriental Mode* (London: Islamic Art Publications, 1982), p. 18. Roberto Weiss gives several examples of adaptations of the figure represented in Pisanello's medal, especially for figures from antiquity. See *Pisanello's Medallion of the Emperor John VIII Palaeologus* (Oxford: Oxford University Press, 1966), pp. 21–28. A manuscript from the 1470s shows on the title page a portrait of the author, Aristotle, wearing an adaptation of John VIII's hat. See Jonathan J. G. Alexander (ed.), *The Painted Page: Italian Renaissance Book Illumination, 1450–1550* (Munich: Prestel, 1994) cat. 35, p. 97.

17. Ernst von Dobschütz, *Christusbilder: Untersuchungen zur christlichen Legende* (Leipzig: J. C. Hinrichs, 1899), p. 292.

18. "Graeci etiam utuntur pingentes illas, ut dicitur, solum ab umbilico supra, et non inferius, ut omnis stultae cogitationis occasio tollatur." Durandus *Rationale Divinorum Officiorum* 2.3.2. See also Sixten Ringbom, *Icon to Narrative: The Rise of the Dramatic Close-up in Fifteenth-Century Devotional Painting* (Doornspijk, Netherlands: Davaco, 1984), pp. 39–40.

19. Otto Pächt, "The 'Avignon Diptych' and its Eastern Ancestry," in M. Meiss (ed.), *De Artibus Opuscula XL, Essays in Honor of Erwin Panofsky* (Princeton, NJ: Princeton University Press, 1961), pp. 402–21.

20. Otto Pächt, "The Limbourgs and Pisanello," *Gazette des Beaux-Arts* 62 (1963), pp. 109–22.

21. Basic studies are Deno J. Geanakoplos, *Byzantine East and Latin West: Two Worlds of Christendom in Middle Ages and Renaissance* (New York: Harper & Row, 1966) and the collection by John Monfasani (ed.), *Byzantine Scholars in Renaissance Italy: Cardinal Bessarion and Other Emigrés: Selected Essays* (Aldershot, UK: Variorum, 1995).

22. Hans Belting made the simple point that Giovanni Bellini's interest in icons was continuous with the antiquarian studies pursued in the Paduan workshop of Francesco Squarcione, the master of Mantegna. See *Giovanni Bellini, Pietà: Ikone und Bilderzählung in der venezianischen Malerei* (Frankfurt: Fischer, 1985), p. 19.

23. "It is reasonable to suppose that princes of the Roman church preferred overtly Christian artifacts, but it is also necessary to recall that these same works were prized because, in the fifteenth century, they were already regarded as antiquities." Cutler, "From Loot to Scholarship," p. 251.

24. Tilmann Buddensieg, "Gregory the Great, the Destroyer of Pagan Idols," *Journal of the Warburg and Courtauld Institutes* 28 (1965), pp. 44–65.

25. Leonard Barkan, *Unearthing the Past: Archeology and Aesthetics in the Making of Renaissance Culture* (New Haven, CT: Yale University Press, 1999).

26. In the rhetoric of reform one favorite metaphor for this process of correction and reversal was the restoration of a work of art. In describing the reform of humanity and its restoration to the image and likeness of God, the Church fathers repeatedly compared it to the process of cleaning a painting that has been marred but not completely ruined by the addition of unsuitable colors and by the accumulation of dirt. See Gerhard B. Ladner, "The Concept of the Image in the Greek Fathers and the Byzantine Iconoclastic Controversy," *Dumbarton Oaks Papers* 7 (1953), pp. 1–34 and esp. p. 12; and *The Idea of Reform: Its Impact on Christian Thought and Action in the Age of the Fathers* (Cambridge, MA: Harvard University Press, 1969), pp. 91–94, 128, and 194–95.

27. In "From Loot to Scholarship," Cutler insists on the absence of attention paid to Byzantine artifacts before the later fifteenth century. In *Picturing the Passion in Late Medieval Italy*, Anne Derbes contests his views and demonstrates that Italian painting of the thirteenth century shows informed and sustained attention paid to Byzantine models — pictorial evidence that, she argues, counterbalances the dearth of textual documentation of Byzantine artifacts known to be in Italy at that time. It does appear that the initial interest in Byzantine artifacts in the wake of the Sack of Constantinople in 1204 waned in the fourteenth century only to wax in the fifteenth.

28. Müntz, *Les arts à la cour des papes*, vol. 2, pp. 202–205.

29. *Ibid.*, pp. 298–304.

30. Eugène Müntz and A. L. Frothingham, *Il Tesoro della Basilica di San Pietro in Vaticano* (Rome: Società Romana di Storia Patria, 1883), pp. 111–12. Bessarion presented his spectacular reliquary of the True Cross to the Scuola Grande di San Giovanni Evangelista in Venice on his initiation into the order in August 1463, a ceremony attended by Niccolò Perotti, the owner of the St. Demetrios icon in Sassoferrato discussed above. The reliquary did not reach the Scuola until July 1472, the year Bessarion died; in the meantime it stood beneath the Pala d'Oro in the church of San Marco. These bequests went hand in hand with Bessarion's famous donation of 482 Greek and 264 Latin manuscripts to the Republic of Venice, May 1, 1468.

31. Laurie Fusco and Gino Corti, *Lorenzo de' Medici: Collector and Antiquarian* (Cambridge: Cambridge University Press, 2006), p. 74.

32. D. S. Chambers, *A Renaissance Cardinal and his Worldly Goods* (London, 1992), cat. 598, p. 164. In the copies of Greek manuscripts commissioned by Cardinal Francesco Gonzaga (1444–1483) the illustrations mingle elements copied from Roman antiquities, such as Trajan's column and imperial coins, with elements copied from Greek manuscripts from the eleventh century clearly thought to be ancient.

33. See Mario Cattapan, "Nuovi elenchi e documenti dei pittori in Creta dal 1300 al 1500," *Thesaurismata* 9 (1972), pp. 202–35.

34. See Maria Constantoudaki-Kitromilides, "Taste and the Market in Cretan Icons in the Fifteenth and Sixteenth Centuries," in Myrtale Acheimastou-Potamianou (ed.), *From Byzantium to El Greco: Greek Frescoes and Icons* (Athens: Byzantine Museum, 1987), pp. 51–53, and "La pittura di icone a Creta Veneziana (secoli XV e XVI): Questioni di mecenatismo, iconografia, e preferenze estetiche," in Gherardo Ortalli (ed.), *Venezia e Creta: atti del convegno internazionale di studi Iraklion-Chaniaà, 30 settembre–5 ottobre 1997* (Venice: Istituto Veneto di Scienze, Lettere ed Arti, 1998), pp. 463–66.

ELEVEN — SUBSTITUTION SYMBOLIZED

1. See Hans Belting, *Likeness and Presence: A History of the Image before the Era of Art* (Chicago: University of Chicago Press, 1994), pp. 342–48.

2. Not everyone wanted to impose miraculous or acheiropoietic origins on local images. Robert Maniura shows that some parties in the debate about the origins of the Madonna dell'Impruneta in the 1450s preferred to attribute the image to a local painter. See "The Icon is Dead, Long Live the Icon: The Holy Image in the Renaissance," in Anthony Eastmond and Liz James (eds.), *Icon and Word: The Power of Images in Byzantium* (Aldershot, UK: Ashgate, 2003), pp. 93–94.

3. The manuscript is in the Vatican Library, Vat. Lat. 3921. See Gerhard Wolf's edition and analysis in *Salus Populi Romani: Die Geschichte römischer Kultbilder im Mittelalter* (Weinheim: VCH, 1990), pp. 213–20 and 330–38. See also Anna Cavallaro, "Il rinnovato culto delle icone nella Roma del Quattrocento," in Antonio Iacobini and Mauro della Valle (eds.), *L'arte di Bisanzio e l'Italia al tempo dei Paleologi, 1261–1453* (Rome: Argos, 1999), p. 285.

4. Anna Cavallaro, *Antoniazzo Romano e gli Antoniazzeschi: Una generazione di pittori nella Roma del Quattrocento* (Udine: Campanotto, 1992), pp. 58–59. It is also likely that Bessarion commissioned Antoniazzo to restore the original in Santa Maria in Cosmedin, which is heavily overpainted in Antoniazzo's manner.

5. See Corrado Ricci, "La Madonna del Popolo di Montefalco," *Bollettino d'Arte* 4 (1924–1925), pp. 97–102; Bonita Cleri, "Dalla committenza di Alessandro Sforza, Signore di Pesaro, Opere di Melozzo da Forlì e Antoniazzo Romano," in Sergio Rossi and Stefano Valeri (eds.), *Le due Rome del Quattrocento: Melozzo, Antoniazzo e la cultura artistica del '400 romano* (Rome: Lithos, 1997), pp. 94–104.

6. Belting, *Likeness and Presence*, p. 342.

7. On the copy by Hans Holbein the Elder, dated 1493 and now in Oberstorf (Bavaria), and on other German renderings of ancient Madonnas, see Regine Dölling, "Byzantinische Elemente in der Kunst des 16. Jahrhunderts," in Johannes Irmscher (ed.), *Aus der byzantinistischen Arbeit der DDR*, vol. 2, Berliner Byzantinistische Arbeiten 6 (Berlin: Akademie, 1957), pp. 148–86.

8. Maryan Ainsworth, "'A la façon grèce': The Encounter of Northern Renaissance Artists with Byzantine Icons," in Evans (ed.), *Byzantium: Faith and Power*, pp. 545–55, esp. 553–54, and cat. no. 349.

9. Three copies were commissioned from Petrus Christus in 1454. See Paul Rolland, "La Madone Italo-Byzantine de Frasnes-le-Buissenal," *Revue Belge d'archéologie et d'histoire de l'art* 17 (1947–1948), p. 102 n.14. Twelve copies were commissioned from Hayne de Bruxelles in 1454–1455; see Jacques Dupont, "Documents: Hayne de Bruxelles et la copie de Notre-Dame de Grâces de Cambrai," *L'amour de l'art* 6 (1935), pp. 363–66 and Paul Rolland, "La Madone Italo-Byzantine," p. 102 n.15. See also *Byzantium: Faith and Power*, cat. 349–50.

10. Otto Pächt, "The 'Avignon Diptych' and its Eastern Ancestry," pp. 416–17. As Pächt notes on p. 417, the "wart on which there stood a tuft of hair" was in fact a distinguishing feature of King René himself, as can be seen in the alabaster medallion portrait of him in the Museum at Aix-en-Provence and in the medals based on it by Pietro da Milano, as well as in Nicolas Froment's altarpiece in the Cathedral of Aix. This is another conspicuous instance of the entwined relationship between contemporary portraiture and the Greek icons.

11. Evans (ed.), *Byzantium: Faith and Power*, fig. 17b and cat. 338.

12. Klaus Krüger suggests that Giotto had already adopted archaic formats and picture types "in order to form within this framework his modern artistic language." See "Medium and Imagination: Aesthetic Aspects of Trecento Panel Painting," in Victor M. Schmidt (ed.), *Italian Panel Painting of the Duecento and Trecento*, Studies in the History of Art 37 (Washington, D.C.: National Gallery of Art, 2002), pp. 63–64.

13. Sixten Ringbom, *Icon to Narrative: The Rise of the Dramatic Close-Up in Fifteenth-Century Devotional Painting* (Doornspijk: Åbo Akademi, 1965); Hans Belting, *The Image and its Public in the Middle Ages: Form and Function of Early Paintings of the Passion*, trans.

Mark Bartusis and Raymond Meyer (New Rochelle, NY: Aristide D. Caratzas, 1990).

14. Rona Goffen, "Icon and Vision: Giovanni Bellini's Half-Length Madonnas," *Art Bulletin 57* (1975), pp. 487–519, here 492 and 503.

15. Amy Powell, "'A Point Ceaselessly Pushed Back': The Origin of Early Netherlandish Painting," *Art Bulletin 88* (2006), pp. 540–62.

16. The lack of resemblance between Rogier's Marian icons and the Cambrai panel does not prove Rogier's indifference to the icon. Powell seems to say just this, however, when she points out that "very few of the extant early Netherlandish Virgin and Child panels in half-length are painted in an archaizing manner" and asserts that the emphasis in Rogier's diptychs is not on "adequation of the Virgin to an ancient and faraway model," "'A Point Ceaselessly Pushed Back,'" p. 713. A substitutional model of replication provides for identity across stylistic difference. The painter who enters into a substitutional system does not need to take recourse to an "archaizing manner." We are not suggesting that Rogier van der Weyden was innocently hoping that his own panels would be taken for antiquities, nor that he was blind to the morphological gap between the Cambrai icon and his own panels. Rather, we are proposing that the possibility that a modern-looking copy of the Cambrai icon could nevertheless extend the chain of reference carried by the icon was part of the content of Rogier's work.

17. Ricci, "La Madonna del Popolo di Montefalco."

18. The epigrams, from the Biblioteca Angelica in Rome, MSS Fondo Antico 603 miscellaneo, were published by Constantino Corvisieri in *Antoniazzo Aquilio Romano* (Rome, 1869), pp. 133–34. See also Rezio Buscaroli, *Melozzo da Forlì nei documenti* (Rome: Reale Accademia d'Italia, 1938), pp. 15–18. Our thanks to Hérica Valladares for help with translating the epigrams that follow.

Ad Mariam de Populo.
Hanc divus Lucas vivo de virginis ore

pinxerat; haec propria est Virginis effigies. Sfortia Alexander iussit, Melotius ipsam effinxit, Lucas diceret esse suam.

[At Santa Maria del Popolo. This was painted by Saint Luke after the Virgin from life; this is the authentic portrait of the Virgin. Alexander Sforza commissioned it, Melozzo painted it, Luke would say it was his own work.]

Ad Mariam Maiorem.
Virginis est Romae quam Lucas pinxit imago tam sancta: errorem quis putet esse suam hanc? Antoniatus pictor romanus ab illa duxit. Alexander Sfortia solvit opus.

[At Santa Maria Maggiore. In Rome there is the very holy image of the Virgin which St. Luke painted: who could imagine his [image] to be an error? The Roman painter Antoniazzo took it as his model. Alexander Sforza paid for the work.]

19. The picture has been dated from ca. 1485 to the 1490s and is currently on loan to the National Gallery of Art, Washington, D.C.

20. Strong arguments in favor of the originality of the present arrangement were put forward by Richard Stapleford, "Botticelli's Portrait of a Young Man Holding a Trecento Medallion," *Burlington Magazine* 129 (July 1987), pp. 428–36. Damian Dombrowski finds Stapleford's case convincing, and associates the roundel more generally with Siena, pointing to the panel with three saints by Simone Martini in the Fitzwilliam Museum, Cambridge; "'Terrae prasens non abest ab aethere': Botticellis 'Mann mit Medaille' als Beitrag zum Menschenbild des späteren Quattrocento," *Wallraf-Richartz-Jahrbuch* 65 (2004), pp. 35–70, here p. 54.

21. Keith Christiansen, letter in *Burlington Magazine* 129 (November 1987), p. 744. Cf. Roberto Longhi, "Uno sguardo alle fotografie della Mostra 'Italian Art and Britain' alla Royal Academy di Londra," *Paragone* 11, 125 (1960), p. 60, proposing that the icon was

inserted at a later date to replace an original, more fitting object, like a pastiglia medal, such as we see in Botticelli's famous portrait in the Uffizi. David Alan Brown suggested that that original object might have been a mirror; *Virtue and Beauty: Leonardo's Ginevra de' Benci and Italian Renaissance Portraits of Women* (Washington, D.C.: National Gallery, 2001), cat. 26, p. 177.

22. Ulrich Pfisterer, *Lysippus und seine Freunde: Liebesgaben und Gedächtnis im Rom der Renaissance, oder: Das erste Jahrhundert der Medaille* (Berlin: Akademie, 2008), pp. 34–35. Even if Pfisterer is right that the original occupant of the recess in Botticelli's panel was a portrait of a contemporary—a betrothed portrayed by another artist, a gift to the sitter—then it would stand to reason that that portrait was removed sooner rather than later. One can imagine various scenarios in which the portrait of the youthful lover, after a few years or a decade, no longer seemed appropriate and needed to be replaced. It is harder to imagine that a nineteenth-century dealer or restorer would extract a fifteenth-century portrait of a woman from Botticelli's panel and replace it with a fragment of an old religious picture.

23. The conservation documentation at the National Gallery of Art shows no damage to the edge of the cavity, arguing against a complicated history of removals and replacements. The delicate painting of highlights on the frame immediately surrounding the roundel is all intact, save for one area of damage, lower left, which extends across both the surface of the Botticelli-painted frame and the icon, and thus occurred after the icon was inserted. Our thanks to David Bull, Miguel Falomir, and Nicholas Penny for sharing their views on the matter.

24. We thank Carl Strehlke for this suggestion. Bulgarini is known to have worked in Florence. Stapleford, "Botticelli's Portrait," p. 432, associates the fragment in the Botticelli portrait with the altarpiece Bulgarini made for the Florentine church of Santa Croce, dated 1350, pieces of which still belong to the Museo dell'Opera di Santa Croce.

25. Pfisterer also remarks that Botticelli, if he had himself inserted a gold-ground icon into the panel, would have furnished it with a proper gilded frame and not a plain brown frame; *Lysippus und seine Freunde*, pp. 34–35. But it is not clear that the frame of the roundel is, or was, plain brown. The frame today has a metallic, silver-brown tone. The matter is discussed by Stapleford and Christiansen as well as by Petra Kathke, *Porträt und Accessoire: Eine Bildnisform im 16. Jahrhundert* (Berlin: Reimer, 1997), p. 186. True icons came with engaged gilded frames. Once the image of the saint was excised from its original setting, however, it became a collector's item and was no longer expected to sit in a conventional gilded frame. A comparable example is the twelfth-century micromosaic icon in the collection of Lorenzo de' Medici, held in an ebony frame (see figure 12.5). A note of 1605 added to the Medici inventory of the Tribuna of 1589 describes the object as "un Christo di musaico, in adornamento d'ebano, alto braccia 1 in circa." In earlier inventories, admittedly, no mention is made of the frame. See Luisa Marcucci, *I dipinti toscani del secolo XIII. Scuole bizantine e russe dal secolo XI al secolo XVIII* (Florence: Galleria Nazionale di Firenze, 1958), p. 179; Italo Furlan, *Le icone bizantine a mosaico* (Milano: Stendhal, 1979), p. 19 and pp. 53–55; Michele Bacci's entry in *Eredità del Magnifico*, ed. Giovanni Gaetà Bertelà, Beatrice Paolozzi Strozzi and Marco Spallanzani (Florence: Studio per edizioni scelte, 1992), no. 117, pp. 132–34; and Laurie Fusco and Gino Corti, *Lorenzo de' Medici, Collector and Antiquarian* (Cambridge: Cambridge University Press, 2006), pp. 74 and 388.

26. Note also that Piero de' Medici is known to have sought out a painting he considered a Cimabue, the double-sided panel depicting *Christ Leaving the Virgin in the Care of St. John* and the *Lamentation* now in the Fogg Museum and attributed to Lippo di Benivieni; see Luciano Bellosi, "Un Cimabue per Piero de' Medici e il 'Maestro della Pietà di Pistoia'," *Prospettiva* 65 (1992), pp. 49–52.

27. Belting, *Likeness and Presence*.

28. Nathaniel Jones in a seminar paper (Yale

University, 2007) connected Botticelli's device of a youth holding a round image to Byzantine images, including two in Tuscany: a steatite icon of Gabriel (twelfth century, now in Fiesole) and a painted icon of St. Michael (fourteenth century, now in Pisa), both holding round icons of Christ. For the latter, see also David Talbot Rice, *The Art of Byzantium* (New York: Abrams, 1959), figs. 162 and 189. Petra Kathke connects Botticelli's arrangement to a Byzantine tradition of portraits of iconodules holding round icons of Christ, for example, the portrait of Niketas of Medikon in a tenth-century manuscript; *Porträt und Accessoire*, p. 189 and fig. 137.

29. "Tiene in sé la pittura forza divina non solo quanto si dice dell'amicizia, quale fa gli uomini assenti essere presenti, ma più i morti dopo molti secoli essere quasi vivi, tale che con molta ammirazione dell'artefice e con molta voluttà si riconoscono. Dice Plutarco, Cassandro uno de' capitani di Allessandro, perché vide l'immagine d'Allessandro re tremò con tutto il corpo; Agesilao Lacedemonio mai permise alcuno il dipignesse o isculpisse: non li piacea la propia sua forma, che fuggiva essere conosciuto da chi dopo lui venisse. E così certo il viso di chi già sia morto, per la pittura vive lunga vita. E che la pittura tenga espressi gli iddii quali siano adorati dalle genti, questo certo fu sempre grandissimo dono ai mortali, però che la pittura molto così giova a quella pietà per quale siamo congiunti agli iddii, insieme e a tenere gli animi nostri pieni di religione." Alberti, *Della pittura*, in *Opere Volgari*, 3 vols., ed. Cecil Grayson (Bari: Laterza, 1973), vol. 3, pp. 44–45 (bk. 2, section 25).

30. Ringbom, *Icon to Narrative*, p. 40.

31. *Ibid.*, pp. 39–52. The connection between icons and portraits was drawn forcefully by Rona Goffen, addressing the case of Giovanni Bellini: "Icon and Vision: Giovanni Bellini's Half-Length Madonnas."

32. The diptych is now separated. The *Madonna and Child* is at the Henry E. Huntington Library, San Marino, while the *Portrait of Philippe de Croÿ* is at the Koninklijk Museum voor Schone Kunsten, Antwerp.

33. John Oliver Hand, Catherine A. Metzger, and Ron Spronk (eds.), *Prayers and Portraits: Unfolding the Netherlandish Diptych* (New Haven, CT: Yale University Press, 2006), cat. 38, pp. 252–57.

34. See François Souchal, "Les bustes reliquaires et la sculpture," *Gazette des Beaux-Arts* 67 (1966), pp. 205–216; Jane Schuyler, *Florentine Busts: Sculpted Portraiture in the Fifteenth Century* (New York: Garland, 1976), pp. 33–76.

35. Irving Lavin, "On the Origins and Meaning of the Renaissance Portrait Bust," *Art Quarterly* 33 (1970), pp. 207–26.

36. Lavin, "On the Origins and Meaning of the Renaissance Portrait Bust," p. 212.

37. Dombrowski makes a similar but slightly different point: the embedded icon, the product of *Kult* and *Kunst*, offers a more substantial kind of truth than Botticelli's portrait, which with its thin paint layer and bloodless complexion makes life seem precarious and fugitive; "'Terrae prasens non abest ab aethere,'" p. 54.

TWELVE — AUTHOR AND *ACHEIROPOIETON*

1. ILLE EGO SVM PER QVEM PICTVRA EXTINCTA REVIXIT

CVI QVAM RECTA MANVS TAM FVIT ET FACILIS

NATVRAE DEERAT NOSTRAE QVOD DEFVIT ARTI

PLVS LICVIT NVLLI PINGERE NEC MELIVS

MIRARIS TVRRIM EGREGIAM SACRO AERE SONANTEM

HAEC QVOQVE DEMODVLO CREVIT ADASTRA MEO

DENIQVE SVM IOTTVS QVID OPVS FVIT ILLA REFERRE

HOC NOMEN LONGI CARMINIS INSTAR ERAT

OB AN MCCCXXXVI CIVES POS B M MCCCCLXXXX.

Many thanks to Hérica Valladares and Caroline Elam for consulting on the translation. Originally the date of death read MCCCXX. It is still possible to see even in reproduction that when the date was corrected

CONCIVES was reduced to CIVES to make room for the extra numerals. Although the inscription says it was "erected by the citizens," this monument, together with several others to illustrious Florentine citizens erected in the Cathedral at this time, was conceived by Lorenzo de' Medici. See Doris Carl, "Il ritratto commemorativo di Giotto di Benedetto da Maiano nel Duomo di Firenze," in *Santa Maria del Fiore: The Cathedral and its Sculpture*, ed. Margaret Haines (Fiesole: Cadmo, 2001), pp. 129–47.

2. Ille ego sum Scorpus, clamosi Gloria Circi,/ plausus, Roma, tui deliciaeque breves,/ invida quem Lachesis raptum trieteride nona,/ dum numerat palmas, credidit esse senem.

3. Several examples, all beginning with *ille ego* or *ille ego sum*, have been collected by Edward Brandt. See "Zum Aeneis-Prooemium," *Philologus* 83 (1928), pp. 331–35. See also Antonio La Penna, "Ille ego qui quondam e i raccordi editoriali nell'antichità," *Studi Italiani di Filologia Classica* 78 (1985), pp. 76–91.

4. Louise Pratt, "The Seal of Theognis, Writing, and Oral Poetry," *The American Journal of Philology* 116 (1995), pp. 171–84.

5. "Ille ego qui fuerim, tenerorum lusor amorum,/ quem legis, ut noris, accipe posteritas./ Sulmo mihi patria est, gelidis uberrimus undis,/ milia, qui novies distat ab Urbe decem." Gerhard Wolf proposes another Ovidian reference, the "Iste ego sum" uttered by Narcissus on recognizing himself in his reflection (*Met.* 3.463), a reference Wolf associates with Alberti's famous identification of Narcissus as the founder of the art of painting, which is here "linked to a Christo-logical myth of origins." See *Schleier und Spiegel: Traditionen des Christusbildes und die Bildkonzepte der Renaissance* (Munich: Fink, 2002), p. ix. While not excluding this reading, the widespread presence of the "ille ego sum" formula in other contexts suggests a broader literary framework, one in which questions of authorship are consistently brought to bear on the arena of image production.

6. "[A]rma dedi uobis: dederat Vulcanus Achilli;/

uincite muneribus, uicit ut ille, datis./ sed quicumque meo superarit Amazona ferro,/ inscribat spoliis 'Naso magister erat'./ ecce, rogant tenerae, sibi dem prae-cepta, puellae: uos eritis chartae proxima cura meae!" Other examples can be found in Horace's *Epistulae* 1.20.20, in Propertius's *Elegiae* 1.1, 1.22, and 3.4, and in Ovid's *Amores* 3.15.

7. Virgil, *Works*, vol. 2, trans. H. Rushton Fairclough (Cambridge, MA: Harvard University Press, 1916), p. 241. The original reads: "Ille ego, qui quondam gracili modulatus avena/ carmen, et egressus silvis vicina coegi/ ut quamvis avido parerent arva colono,/ gratum opus agricolis, at nunc horrentia Martis."

8. The verses were resoundingly rejected by R. G. Austin in "Ille Ego Qui Quondam...," *The Classical Quarterly* 18 (1968), pp. 107–15, only to be defended by P. A. Hansen in "Ille Ego Qui Quondam.... Once Again," *The Classical Quarterly* 22 (1972), pp. 139–49.

9. There is some shifting, however. The Bologna 1485 edition of the *Opera* gives the "ille ego" incipit as part of Servius's preface, but starts the poem proper with "Arma virumque cano." The Nuremberg edition of 1492 of the *Opera* with Cristoforo Landino's com-mentary gives the "Ille ego" incipit as part of Ser-vius's commentary, but then gives the verses again at the bottom of fol. LXXVIIIv, followed by the "Arma virumque cano" incipit with a large initial at the head of fol. LXXIXr. This way the "Ille ego" verses stand at the beginning at the poem and yet the "Arma virumque cano" verses still stand at the head of the page—a reasonable compromise obtained through formatting. In the Venetian 1493 edition of the *Opera* the "Ille ego" incipit is given a proper position at the beginning of the poem *and* at the top of the page.

10. Michael Viktor Schwarz and Pia Theis, *Giottus pictor* (Vienna: Böhlau, 2004).

11. One of Poliziano's drafts for this epigram, indeed, invokes the *Navicella* "variis compacta lapillis"; see Angelo Ambrogini Poliziano, *Prose volgari inedite e poesie latine e greche edite e inedite*, ed. I. Del Lungo and G. Barbera (Florence, 1867), p. 159. Strangely, Alberti

calls it the "nave dipinta a Roma" by "nostro toscano dipintore Giotto," forgetting that it was a mosaic — or perhaps he considered the mosaic a modality of painting. See Leon Battista Alberti, *Della pittura*, in *Opere Volgari*, ed. Grayson, 3:74–75 (bk. 2, section 42). Nonetheless, others very clearly saw the work as an instance of Giotto's expertise in the mosaic art, as in Filarete's account which is discussed below. In 1606, Pierleone Casella set Giotto's work in mosaic higher than his work in painting: "[o]n canvas and on panels he excelled others in constructing a scene. But with coloured tesserae Giotto adorns the twin brides and conducts them to his dwelling." See Ernst Gombrich, "An Early Seventeenth-Century Canon of Artistic Excellence: Pierleone Casella's *Elogia Illustrium Artificum* of 1606," *Journal of the Warburg and Courtauld Institutes* 50 (1987), p. 229. Many thanks to Carolina Mangone for this reference.

12. Doris Carl also notes the discrepancy between Poliziano's text and the portrayal of Giotto as a mosaicist; see *Benedetto da Maiano: A Florentine Sculptor at the Threshold of the High Renaissance* (Turnhout: Brepols, 2007), p. 149.

13. On the authorless image, or *acheiropoieton*, see pp. 16 and 97. John White, *Art and Architecture in Italy 1250–1400* (New Haven, CT: Yale University Press, 1993), p. 152, notes that the bust of Christ is a remnant of the fourth- or fifth-century mosaic, preserved by Jacopo Torriti in his restoration of the apse mosaic in the thirteenth century.

14. Eugène Müntz, "Les mosaïques byzantines portatives," *Bulletin Monumental* 52 (1886), pp. 223–40; Furlan, *Le icone bizantine*; and Arne Effenburger, "Images of Personal Devotion: Miniature Mosaic and Steatite Icons," in Evans (ed.), *Byzantium: Faith and Power*, pp. 209–14.

15. Marco Spallanzani and Gaeta Bertelà (eds.), *Libro d'inventario dei beni di Lorenzo il Magnifico* (Florence: Associazione Amici del Bargello, 1992), pp. 27, 80 and 47–48. See also Fusco and Corti, *Lorenzo de' Medici: Collector and Antiquarian*, p. 74.

16. Hetty Joyce, "Grasping at Shadows: Ancient Paintings in Renaissance and Baroque Rome," *Art Bulletin* 74 (1992), pp. 219–46.

17. "Zotum Florentinum, qui primus ex antiquis et musaicis figuris modernas mirum in modum configuravit." Michele Savonarola, *Commentariolus de laudibus Patavii*, ed. L. A. Muratori, *Rerum Italicarum Scriptores*, vol. 24 (Milan, 1738), col. 1169.

18. "E certo è che il musaico è la più durabile pittura che sia, imperò che l'altra col tempo si spegne e questa nello stare fatta di continuo s'accende, et inoltre la pittura manca e si consuma per se medesima, ove il musaico per la sua lunghissima vita si può quasi chiamare eterno." "Introduction," Giorgio Vasari, *Le vite de' più eccellenti pittori scultori e architettori nelle redazioni del 1550 e 1568*, ed. Rosanna Bettarini, with comments by Paola Barocchi, 8 vols. (Florence: SPES, 1966–1984), vol. 1, ch. 29, p. 148. In the life of Ghirlandaio, he writes: "Usava dire Domenico la pittura essere il disegno, e la vera pittura per la eternità essere il musaico." *Le vite*, vol. 3, p. 494.

19. Carlo Bertelli, "Rinascimento del mosaico," in *Il mosaico*, ed. Carlo Bertelli (Milan: Mondadori, 1997), pp. 225–32. See esp. p. 232, where he quotes a document from the Florence Baptistery records stating that Baldovinetti was rehired successively, in 1487, 1489, 1490, and 1491, as conservator of mosaics, "non si trovando chi sappia altri."

20. On the Lorenzo-driven mosaic revival, see Ruth Wedgewood Kennedy, *Alesso Baldovinetti* (New Haven, CT: Yale University Press, 1938), p. 191; Werner Haftmann, "Ein Mosaik der Ghirlandaio Werkstatt aus dem Besitz des Lorenzo Magnifico," *Mitteilungen des Kunsthistorischen Institutes in Florenz* 7 (1940), pp. 97–107; André Chastel, "Une mosaïque Florentine du XVe siècle au Musée de Cluny" (1958), in *Fables Formes Figures*, vol. 1 (Paris: Flammarion, 1978), pp. 349–56; and Bertelli, "Rinascimento del mosaico." See also Angela Dressen, *Pavimenti decorati del Quattrocento in Italia* (Venezia: Marsilio, 2008), p. 272.

21. See "Life of Baldovinetti," in Vasari, *Le vite*,

vol. 3, pp. 317–18. Vasari reports that when Lorenzo told Graffione, a pupil of Baldovinetti, that he wanted to cover the interior of Brunelleschi's cupola in the Cathedral with mosaic decoration, Graffione reminded him of the difficulty of finding masters of the technique: "Il Graffione rispose 'Voi non ci avete maestri'; a che replicò Lorenzo: 'Noi abbiam tanti danari che ne faremo'; il Graffione subitamente soggiunse: 'Eh, Lorenzo, i danari non fanno maestri, ma i maestri fanno i danari.'"

22. Only the ribs in the vaults were completed. See Margaret Haines, "Il principio di 'mirabilissime cose': i mosaici per la volta della cappella di San Zanobi," in Marco Dezzi Bardeschi (ed.), *La difficile eredità: Architettura a Firenze dalla repubblica all'assedio* (Florence: Alinea, 1994), pp. 38–55.

23. Discussed by Haines, "Il principio di 'mirabilissime cose'," p. 43.

24. "Questa arte, come è detto, è perduta, ché da Giotto in qua poco s'è usata. Lui ne fe': solo a Roma se ne vede di sua mano la nave di Santo Pietro. E uno Piero Cavallino romano ancora lui ne lavorò ne' suoi tempi, il quale era bonissimo maestro. Honne veduto ancora in tavola piccola in Vinegia, fatta molto solennemente, e molto minuti, i quali dicono essere fatti di guscia d'uova." Filarete, *Trattato di Architettura*, vol. 2, ed. Anna Maria Finoli and Liliana Grassi (Milan: Il Polifilo, 1972), pp. 671–72. The misidentification of the materials appears to have been common at the time; according to Vasari, in the early fourteenth century Gaddo Gaddi made small mosaic panels with tesserae made of egg shells: "[P]er che datosi a fare piccole tavolette di musaico, ne condusse alcune di guscia d'uova con diligenza e pacienza incredibile, come si può fra l'altre vedere in alcune che ancor oggi sono nel tempio di S. Giovanni di Firenze." See Vasari, *Le vite*, vol. 2, p. 83.

25. Marco Collareta has pointed out that in this portrait of the artist as author of a sacred image was modeled according to a formula for images of St. Luke. See "Le luci della Fiorentina Gloria," *Artista* 3 (1991),

p. 139. In basic disposition and in detail, Collareta points out, it resembles in particular the painting of *St. Luke Painting the Virgin* by Neri di Bicci, now in Pescia, a painting Benedetto da Maiano had already used as a model in his relief of *St. Luke* for the Holy House of Loreto.

26. Furlan, *Le icone bizantine*, p. 19. For further bibliography, see section 11 above, n.25.

27. Thus raising the question: Who made it? The mosaic in the tondo is quite crude, and thus cannot be ascribed to Monte and Gherardo, whose St. Zenobius panel in the Museo dell'Opera del Duomo shows greater smoothness and compactness. Nor can it be attributed to the Ghirlandaio brothers, whose *St. Peter* in the Louvre reveals a sophisticated capacity for quasi-pictorial effects. On the other hand, the crudeness may itself be a rhetorical feature, a mark of archaic authenticity. It may also be coarse for purposes of legibility, given how high the monument is on the façade wall. (Thanks to Jeffrey Hamburger for suggesting this point.) In any case, it is possible that it was done by Benedetto da Maiano himself, for this monument.

THIRTEEN — ANTIQUITY OF BUILDINGS OVERRATED

1. See Kathleen Olive, "Creation, Imitation, and Fabrication: Renaissance Self-Fashioning in the Codex Rustici," PhD diss., University of Sydney, 2004.

2. In the preface to book 1 of *Le vite*, Vasari says that the eleventh-century architects of San Miniato were able to emulate "l'ordine buono antico" that they recognized in the "antichissimo tempio di San Giovanni nella città loro." See *Le vite*, vol. 2, p. 25. In the "Life of Andrea Tafi" he refers again to the Baptistery as "quel tempio antico...la quale è dagli architetti moderni come cosa singolare lodata, e meritamente: perciocchè ella ha mostrato il buono che già aveva in sè quell'arte," and confirms that Brunelleschi, Donatello, and other masters used both the Baptistery and Santi Apostoli as models for their own work. See *Le vite*, vol. 2, p. 74.

3. For this concept, see Ingrid D. Rowland, "Antiquarianism as Battle Cry," in Allen J. Grieco et al. (eds.), *The Italian Renaissance in the Twentieth Century*, Acts of an International Conference, Florence, Villa I Tatti, 1999 (Florence: Olschki, 2002), p. 407. See also E. H. Gombrich, "From the Revival of Letters to the Reform of the Arts: Niccolò Niccoli and Filippo Brunelleschi," *The Heritage of Apelles: Studies in the Art of the Renaissance* (Oxford: Phaidon, 1976), pp. 93–110.

4. Franklin Toker, "A Baptistery below the Baptistery," *Art Bulletin* 58 (1976), pp. 157–67. Karl M. Swoboda, "Zur Analyse des Florentiner Baptisteriums," *Kunstwissenschaftliche Forschungen* 2 (1933), pp. 63–74, and Walter Horn, "Das Florentiner Baptisterium," *Mitteilungen des Kunsthistorischen Insitutes in Florenz* 5 (1938), pp. 99–151, established the eleventh-century date of the present building. See most recently Piero Degli Innocenti, *Le origini del bel San Giovanni* (Florence: CUSL, 1994), pp. 21–34 on the possibility of a late antique origin, and pp. 75–109 on the late medieval tradition of the building's antiquity; and Larry Shenfield, *How Much of the Florence Baptistery Is a Surviving Roman Building? A Re-evaluation of the Archaeological, Architectural and Artistic Evidence* (Oxford: John and Erica Hedges Ltd., 2008).

5. Adolph Goldschmidt, "Die Bedeutung der Formenspaltung in der Kunstentwicklung," in *Independence, Convergence, and Borrowing in Institutions, Thought, and Art*, Harvard Tercentenary Publications (Cambridge, MA: Harvard University Press, 1937), pp. 167–77. According to Goldschmidt, when later artists copied earlier art, they tended to barbarously pull the forms apart and reassemble them in strange ways.

6. As stressed, for instance, by Uta Schedler in *Filippo Brunelleschi: Synthese von Antike und Mittelalter in der Renaissance* (Petersberg: Michael Imhof, 2004), pp. 101 and 109–10.

7. William Heckscher, "Relics of Pagan Antiquity in Medieval Settings," *Journal of the Warburg and Courtauld Institutes* 1 (1937–1938), p. 204; Norberto Gramaccini, *Mirabilia: Das Nachleben antiker Statuen vor der Renaissance* (Mainz: Philipp von Zabern, 1996).

8. See Francis Morgan Nichols (ed.), *The Marvels of Rome: Mirabilia urbis Romae* (New York: Italica, 1986), pp. 18–19. Dale Kinney argues that the *Mirabilia* was no empty rhetorical exercise but was based on research and aimed at accuracy. See "Fact and Fiction in the *Mirabilia urbis Romae*," in Éamonn ó Carragáin and Carol Neuman de Vegvar (eds.), *Roma Felix—Formation and Reflections of Medieval Rome* (Aldershot, UK: Ashgate, 2007), pp. 235–52.

9. Phyllis Pray Bober and Ruth Rubinstein, *Renaissance Artists and Antique Sculpture: A Handbook of Sources* (London: Harvey Miller, 1986), no. 125.

10. *Ibid.*, no. 176.

11. "L'imitatione delle cose antiche è piv laudabile che quella delle moderne." *Literary Works of Leonardo da Vinci*, ed. Jean Paul Richter (Oxford: Oxford University Press, 1939), vol. 2, no. 1445. For the dating of the entry, see Carlo Pedretti, *Commentary on the Literary Works of Leonardo da Vinci compiled and edited by Jean Paul Richter*, vol. 2 (London: Phaidon, 1977), p. 343.

12. Orietta Rossi Pinelli, "Chirurgia della memoria: scultura antica e restauri storici," in Settis (ed.), *Memoria dell'antico*, vol. 3, pp. 191–92.

13. Michael Greenhalgh, *The Survival of Roman Antiquities in the Middle Ages*, pp. 91–97. For an impressive recent study of the engagement with ancient remains in northern Europe, see Lukas Clemens, *Tempore Romanorum constructa: Zur Nutzung und Wahrnehmung antiker Überreste nördlich der Alpen während des Mittelalters* (Stuttgart: Hiersemann, 2003).

14. The last three examples are discussed in Hubertus Günther, "Die Vorstellung vom griechischen Tempel und der Beginn der Renaissance in der venezianischen Architektur," in Paul Naredi-Rainer (ed.), *Imitatio: von der Produktivität künstlerischer Anspielungen und Missverständnisse* (Berlin: Reimer, 2001), p. 127 n.109. Günther lists fifteen authorities between the fourteenth and the seventeenth centuries who identify San Lorenzo with a temple of Hercules.

15. Amato Pietro Frutaz, *Il complesso monumentale*

di Sant'Agnese (1960) (Rome: Nova officina poligrafica Laziale, 2001), pp. 111–12 and esp. n.10 which contains a bibliography of Renaissance commentators. On the fascination Santa Costanza held for Renaissance scholars and artists, see Maria Fabricius Hansen, "Representing the Past: The Concept and Study of Antique Architecture in 15th-Century Italy," *Analecta Romana Instituti Danici*, vol. 23 (1996), pp. 83–116.

16. Ingrid D. Rowland, "L'*Historia Porsennae* e la conoscenza degli Etruschi nel Rinascimento," *Res publica litterarum* 12 (1989), p. 186. For more on Egidio's Etruscanizing imagination, see Rowland, *Culture of the High Renaissance*, pp. 148–50.

17. Hartmann Schedel, *Weltchronik* (Nuremberg, 1493), fol. 23r.

18. Beatus Rhenanus, *Rerum germanicarum* 3. See Wolfgang Binsfeld, "Triers Altertümer und die Humanisten, " *Landeskundliche Vierteljahrsblätter* (*Trier*) 14 (1968), p. 68.

19. Lukas Clemens, *Tempore Romanorum constructa*, p. 424 n.611, with reference to Bruschius's *Monasteriorum Germaniae praecipuorum* (1551).

20. See Giovanni Villani, *Nuova Cronica*, ed. Giuseppe Porta, vol. 1 (Parma: Guanda, 1990), p. 90 and Charles Davis, "Topographical and Historical Propaganda in Early Florentine Chronicles and in Villani," *Medievo e Rinascimento* (1988), pp. 33–51.

21. Oscar Wilde, "The Decay of Lying," in *The Complete Works of Oscar Wilde* (New York: Barnes & Noble Books, 1994), p. 973. We would not want to interrupt Wilde in mid-sentence: "'He either falls into careless habits of accuracy, or takes to frequenting the society of the aged and the well-informed. Both things are equally fatal to his imagination, as indeed they would be fatal to the imagination of anybody, and in a short time he develops a morbid and unhealthy faculty of truth-telling, begins to verify all statements made in his presence, has no hesitation in contradicting people who are much younger than himself, and often ends by writing novels which are so life-like that no one can possibly believe in their probability.'"

22. "Templum non graeco non tusco more factum, sed plane romano." See Gombrich, "From the Revival of Letters to the Reform of the Arts," p. 104 n.54. Cf. the comment by Giovanni da Prato (ca. 1425) on the Baptistery, also analyzed by Gombrich: "in the most ancient form of building according to the custom and method of the Romans" (*in forma di fabrica antichissima al costume e al modo romano*).

23. Hubertus Günther, *Das Studium der antiken Architektur in den Zeichnungen der Hochrenaissance* (Tübingen: Wasmuth, 1988), pp. 42–43, 70–71, figs. 1–7; pp. 121–22, fig. 3.14. Maria Fabricius Hansen, *Ruinbilleder: Antikfascinationens baggrunde i 1400-tallets italienske maleri* (Copenhagen: Tiderne Skifter, 1999), p. 111, fig. 80; p. 141, fig. 94.

24. Richard Schofield and Grazioso Sironi, "New Information on San Satiro," in Christoph L. Frommel, Luisa Giordano, and Richard Schofield (eds.), *Bramante Milanese e l'architettura del Rinascimento Lombardo* (Venice: Marsilio, 2002), pp. 281–97 and esp. 282–83.

25. Hansen, "Representing the Past." Marvin Trachtenberg makes the same point in "On Brunelleschi's Choice: Speculations on Medieval Rome and the Origins of Renaissance Architecture," in *Architectural Studies in Memory of Richard Krautheimer*, pp. 169–73.

26. "Comparison of Old and New Rome," a letter to the Byzantine emperor clearly meant to be read by Romans as well. The translation is by Christine Smith, see *Architecture in the Culture of Early Humanism: Ethics, Aesthetics, and Eloquence, 1400–1470* (New York: Oxford University Press, 1992), p. 212.

27. The letter of the Fabbriceri to Cardinal Ascanio Sforza describing their efforts is published in Rodolfo Maiocchi, *Codice diplomatico-artistico di Pavia dall'anno 1330 all'anno 1550*, vol. 1 (Pavia: Bianci, 1937–1949), doc. 1330. See the discussion by Richard Schofield, "Bramante e un Rinascimento locale all'antica," in Francesco Paolo di Teodoro (ed.), *Donato Bramante: ricerche, proposte, riletture* (Urbino: Accademia Raffaello, 2001), pp. 62–63.

28. "Attento che per essere fatto quello edifizio

sul garbo antiquo non molto dissimile da quello viso fantastico de messer Baptista di Alberti, io per ancho non intendeva se l'haveva a reussire in chiesa o moschea o synagoga." Cornel von Fabriczy, "Die Baugeschichte von S. Sebastiano in Mantua," *Repertorium für Kunstwissenschaft* 27 (1904), p. 84.

29. For all these observations and hypotheses, see Gülru Necipoğlu, *The Age of Sinan: Architectural Culture in the Ottoman Empire* (London: Reaktion, 2005), pp. 77–92 and esp. 84–87 and 89–92. On the possible mutual awareness of Palladio and Sinan, see pp. 98–101.

30. Gombrich, "From the Revival of Letters to the Reform of the Arts," p. 106. See the general discussion in Erwin Panofsky, *Renaissance and Renascences in Western Art*, pp. 20–23. There is a vast literature on Brunelleschi's and Alberti's reception of ancient and medieval architecture; see the recent survey of Giuseppe Rocchi Coopmans de Yoldi, "Riflessioni sulla storiografia delle origini dell' architettura fiorentina e sullo svolgimento della fabbrica del Battistero" and "Il Brunelleschi e il Battistero," both in Coopmans de Yoldi (ed.), *Santa Maria del Fiore*, vol. 2, *Piazza, Battistero, Campanile* (Florence: Il Torchio, 1996), pp. 27–34 and 64–65.

31. John Onians, "The System of the Orders in Renaissance Architectural Thought," in *Les traités de l'architecture de la renaissance* (Paris: Picard, 1988), p. 169.

32. Howard Burns, "Quattrocento Architecture and the Antique: Some Problems," in R. R. Bolgar (ed.), *Classical Influences on European Culture, A.D. 500–1500* (Cambridge: Cambridge University Press, 1971), p. 277. Schedler goes so far as to say that everything in Brunelleschi can be accounted for by the Baptistery and the Duomo. See *Filippo Brunelleschi*, pp. 93–100.

33. Rudolf Wittkower described Santa Maria Novella as a "posthumous member of the twelfth-century family of Proto-Renaissance buildings." See *Architectural Principles in the Age of Humanism* (1949; New York: Norton, 1971), pp. 43–44.

34. See ch. 1 in Irving Lavin, *Past-Present: Essays on Historicism in Art from Donatello to Picasso* (Berkeley: University of California Press, 1993), pp. 1–26.

35. See H. W. Janson, *The Sculpture of Donatello* (Princeton: Princeton University Press, 1957), pp. 137–38 and Michael Greenhalgh, *Donatello and his Sources* (London: Duckworth, 1982), pp. 113–18. Greenhalgh's introduction to *Donatello and his Sources* (pp. 1–30) is exceptionally sensitive to the whole paradoxical problem of misdating and chronological confusion in the *rinascimento dell' antichità*.

36. Lavin, *Past-Present*, pp. 5–6.

37. John Onians argued that Brunelleschi knew perfectly well that the Baptistery was not an ancient building. He was attempting, according to Onians, to reanimate and perfect a medieval Tuscan tradition of building. See *Bearers of Meaning: The Classical Orders in Antiquity, the Middle Ages, and the Renaissance* (Princeton, NJ: Princeton University Press, 1988), pp. 130–36. Burns also believes that Renaissance architects knew that these buildings were of recent centuries, but were interested in them for the "antique deposit" that they contained. See "Quattrocento Architecture and the Antique."

38. Enzo Bentivoglio and Simonetta Valtieri, *Santa Maria del Popolo* (Rome: Bardi, 1976), pp. 15–22.

39. Deborah Howard, "Responses to Ancient Greek Architecture in Renaissance Venice," *Annali di Architettura* 6 (1994), pp. 23–38, here 28.

40. Richard Krautheimer, *Early Christian and Byzantine Architecture* (New Haven: Yale University Press, 1986), p. 341.

41. Franz Graf Wolff-Metternich, "Der Kupferstich Bernardos de Prevedari aus Mailand von 1481. Gedanken zu den Anfängen der Kunst Bramantes," *Römisches Jahrbuch für Kunstgeschichte* 11 (1967–1968), p. 63. He writes: "Der Sakralbau, den das grosse graphische Blatt darstellt, folgt in den Grundlagen trotz des antikischen Gewandes, das ihn umhüllt, nachweisbaren mittelalterlichen Vorbildern."

42. Günther, "Die Vorstellung vom griechischen Tempel und der Beginn der Renaissance in der venezianischen Architektur."

43. G. F. Hill, *A Corpus of Italian Medals of the*

Renaissance (London: British Museum, 1930), no. 361. These examples are discussed by Hubertus Günther, who notes that the quincunx form is also predominant in Filarete's projections of his Greek ideal city Plusiapolis. See "Geschichte einer Gründungsgeschichte: San Giacomo di Rialto, San Marco und die venezianische Renaissance," in *Per assiduum studium scientiae adipisci margaritam: Festgabe für Ursula Nilgen zum 65. Geburtstag* (St. Ottilien: EOS, 1997), pp. 231–60 and esp. 253–55.

44. For the Venetian revival of the form, see John McAndrew, "Sant'Andrea alla Certosa," *Art Bulletin* 51 (1969), pp. 15–28 and *Venetian Architecture of the Early Renaissance* (Cambridge, MA: The MIT Press, 1980), pp. 302–305. See also James Ackerman, "Observations on Renaissance Church Planning in Venice and Florence," in Sergio Bertelli, Nicolai Rubinstein, and Craig Hugh Smyth (eds.), *Florence and Venice, Comparisons and Relations*, vol. 2 (Florence: La Nuova Italia, 1980), pp. 287–308; Manfredo Tafuri, *Venezia e il Rinascimento* (Turin: Einaudi, 1985), esp. ch. 2. For the use of the type in the rest of Italy, see Bruno Adorni (ed.), *La chiesa a pianta centrale: tempio civico del rinascimento* (Milan: Electa, 2002).

45. Cesariano, *De architectura libri dece* (Como, 1521), fol. 52r and 52v.

46. On the interest in pre-Gothic forms in Renaissance Lombardy, see James S. Ackerman, "The Certosa of Pavia and the Renaissance in Lombardy," *Marsyas* 5 (1947–49), pp. 23–37.

47. Uffizi A20.

48. Robert S. Nelson, "Byzantium and the Rebirth of Art and Learning in Italy and France," in *Byzantium: Faith and Power*, pp. 521–23; D. S. Chambers, *A Renaissance Cardinal and his Worldly Goods: The Will and Inventory of Francesco Gonzaga (1444–1483)* (London: Warburg Institute, 1992), pp. 60–63.

49. B. L. Ullmann, *The Origin and Development of Humanistic Script* (Rome: Edizioni di Storia e Letteratura, 1960); James Wardrop, *The Script of Humanism: Some Aspects of Humanistic Script, 1460–1560* (Oxford:

Clarendon Press, 1963); Stanley Morison, *Politics and Script*, ed. Nicholas Barker (Oxford: Oxford University Press, 1972), ch. 6; Martin Steinmann, "Die humanistische Schrift und die Anfänge des Humanismus in Basel," *Archiv für Diplomatik* 22 (1976), pp. 376–437.

50. Otto Pächt, "Notes and Observations on the Origin of Humanistic Book Decoration," in D. J. Gordon (ed.), *Festschrift Fritz Saxl* (London and Edinburgh: Nelson, 1957), pp. 184–94 and *Italian Illuminated Manuscripts*, exhibition catalogue (Oxford: Bodleian Library, 1948). More recently Melania Ceccanti showed that the modern imitations of medieval white-vine ornament improved in accuracy between 1400 and 1425; see "Proposte per la storia dei primi codici umanistici a bianchi girari," *Miniatura* 5/6 (1993/1996), pp. 11–16. See also J. J. G. Alexander and A. C. de la Mare, *The Italian Manuscripts in the Library of Major J. R. Abbey* (London: Faber & Faber, 1969), pp. xxxiii–xxxiv; Albinia C. de la Mare, "Vespasiano da Bisticci as Producer of Classical Manuscripts in Fifteenth-Century Florence," in Claudine A. Chavannes-Mazel and Margaret M. Smith (eds.), *Medieval Manuscripts of Latin Classics: Production and Use*, Proceedings of the Seminar in the History of the Book to 1500, Leiden 1993 (Los Altos Hills, CA: Anderson-Lovelace; London: Red Gull Press, 1996), figs. 2–3, p. 169; and Fabrizio Crivello, "'Vetustioris litere maiestas': un manoscritto di Sant' Agostino del Petrarca, gli umanisti e qualche osservazione sulle iniziali a 'bianchi girari,'" *Italia medioevale e umanistica* 44 (2003), pp. 227–34.

51. Barbara A. Shailor, *Catalogue of the Medieval and Renaissance Manuscripts in the Beinecke Rare Book and Manuscript Library, Yale University*, vol. 3, Marston MSS (Binghamton: Medieval and Renaissance Texts and Studies, 1992), pp. 101–102.

52. Robert G. Babcock et al., *Catalogue of the Medieval and Renaissance Manuscripts in the Beinecke Rare Book and Manuscript Library, Yale University*, vol. 4, MSS 481–85 (Turnhout: Brepols, 2004), fig. 23, pp. 61–62.

53. Pächt, "Notes and Observations," p. 189.

54. Vat. Lat. 182, fol. 129r; Leopold D. Ettlinger,

The Sistine Chapel Before Michelangelo (Oxford: Clarendon Press, 1965), pp. 79–80.

55. Erika Doberer partially summarizes some of her earlier publications on this topic in "Abendländische Skulpturen des Mittelalters und ihre metamorphische Veränderungen," *Wiener Jahrbuch für Kunstgeschichte* 46–47 (1993–1994), pp. 161–63. See also Heinrich Magirius, *Geschichte der Denkmalpflege: Sachsen von den Anfängen bis zum Neubeginn 1945* (Berlin: VEB, 1989), pp. 10–11, and Volkmar Greiselmayer, "Anmerkungen zum Nordportal der Schottenkirche St. Jakob in Regensburg," *Das Münster* 48 (1995), pp. 143–50.

56. Christoph Luitpold Frommel, "'In pristinam formam': Die Erneuerung von S. Maria in Navicella durch Leo X," in Joachim Poeschke (ed.), *Antike Spolien*, pp. 309–20.

57. "[O]pera di tanto buona maniera che tira alla vera bontà antica, avendo, come si è detto di sopra, tutte le colonne di pezzi, misurate e commesse con tanta diligenza che si può molto imparare a considerarle in tutte le sue parti." Vasari, *Le vite*, vol. 1, p. 74. Cf. "In Fiorenza poi, migliorando alquanto l'architettura, la chiesa di S. Apostolo, che fu edificata da Carlo Magno, fu, ancorché piccola, di bellissima maniera; perché oltre che i fusi delle colonne, se bene sono di pezzi, hanno molta grazia e sono condotti con bella misura, i capitelli ancora e gli archi girati per le volticciuole delle due piccole navate mostrano che in Toscana era rimaso overo risorto qualche buono artefice. Insomma l'architettura di questa chiesa è tale che Pippo di ser Brunellesco non si sdegnò di servirsene per modello nel fare la chiesa di S. Spirito e quella di S. Lorenzo nella medesima città." Vasari, *Le vite*, vol. 1, p. 24.

FOURTEEN — NON-ACTUAL HISTORIES OF ARCHITECTURE

1. Paul Durrieu, *Les antiquités judaïques et le peintre Jean Fouquet* (Paris: Plon, 1908), fig. 8. Although usually considered the only work securely linked to Fouquet, by virtue of a late fifteenth-century inscription in volume one, the *Antiquités judaïques* have been reattributed by François Avril to the Master of the Munich Boccaccio; see *Jean Fouquet, Peintre et enlumineur du XVe siècle*, exhibition catalogue, Bibliothèque nationale de France (Paris: Hazan, 2003), cat. 34, pp. 310–14. Durrieu suggests that Fouquet gave his temple an unorthodox form in order to distinguish the First Temple from the Second Temple, and that as a guide he took Orsanmichele in Florence; see "Le temple de Jérusalem dans l'art français et flamand du XVe siècle," in *Mélanges offerts à Gustave Schlumberger* (Paris: Librairie Orientaliste Paul Geuthner, 1924), pp. 510–11.

2. Fol. 213v. See also fol. 248, where the temple is visible in the background, now with bell towers. Already in the scene of the Destruction of the Temple, an ambiguous element rises from behind the building, cut off at the edge of the picture; presumably this, too, is a bell tower.

3. There are some earlier but less significant examples in Friedrich B. Polleross, *Sakrale Identifikationsporträt: Ein höfischer Bildtypus vom 13. bis zum 20. Jahrhundert* (Worms: Werner, 1988).

4. Millard Meiss, *French Painting in the Time of Jean de Berry: The Limbourgs and Their Contemporaries* (New York: Braziller, 1974), pp. 202–206. Meiss points to some partial precedents in fourteenth-century Italian painting. Most striking are the elements of the Sienese cityscape in the scenes on the back of Duccio's *Maestà*.

5. Elisabeth Dhanens credits van Eyck himself, and not Jan van Scorel who restored the painting in the sixteenth century, with the portrait of the tower of the cathedral of Utrecht on the horizon of the Adoration of the Lamb. See *Hubert et Jan van Eyck* (Antwerp: Mercatorfonds, 1980), p. 96, 100, and 106.

6. See the analysis in Hans Belting and Christiane Kruse, *Die Erfindung des Gemäldes: das erste Jahrhundert der niederländischen Malerei* (Munich: Hirmer, 1994), pp. 115–16.

7. Paris, Musée du Louvre, Département des arts graphiques, R.F. 1679. François Avril and Nicole

Reynaud, *Les manuscrits à peinture en France 1440–1520* (Paris: Bibliothèque Nationale, 1993), no. 68B.

8. Nicole Verhaegen, "Le maître de la légende de Ste.-Lucie: Précisions sur son oeuvre," *Bulletin de l'Institut Royal du Patrimoine Artistique* 2 (1959), pp. 73–82.

9. Dirk de Vos, *Hans Memling: The Complete Works* (Ghent: Ludion Press, 1994), no. 83, pp. 296–303.

10. Lotte Brand Philip, *The Ghent Altarpiece*, p. 195 n.386; Didier Martens, "L'illusion du réel," in Brigitte de Patoul and Roger van Schoute (eds.), *Les primitifs flamands et leur temps* (Louvain-la-Neuve: La Renaissance du Livre, 1994), pp. 259–64. Bret Rothstein's discussion of the portrait of the Poortersloge in Bruges in the background of Gerard David's *Justice of Cambyses* (1498) makes explicit the contemporary political relevance of the story; see "Looking the Part: Ruminative Viewing and the Imagination of Community in the Early Modern Low Countries," *Art History* 31 (2008), p. 25.

11. Otto Benesch, *Collected Writings*, vol. 3, *German and Austrian Art of the Fifteenth and Sixteenth Centuries* (London: Phaidon, 1972), fig. 204.

12. Felicity Ratte, "Re-presenting the Common Place: Architectural Portraits in Trecento Painting," *Studies in Iconography* 22 (2001), pp. 87–110; Marvin Trachtenberg, *Dominion of the Eye: Urbanism, Art, and Power in Early Modern Florence* (Cambridge: Cambridge University Press, 1997), pp. 214–16; Alessandro Gambuti, *L'architettura dei pittori: nel Quattrocento italiano* (Florence: Alinea, 1994); Sylvia Ferino Pagden, "Painted Architecture," in *The Renaissance from Brunelleschi to Michelangelo: The Representation of Architecture* eds. Henry Millon and Vittorio Magnago Lampugnani (London: Thames and Hudson, 1994), pp. 446–52.

13. Brand Philip, *Ghent Altarpiece*, p. 195. On Florence as a New Jerusalem see Dale Kent, *Cosimo de' Medici and the Florentine Renaissance* (New Haven: Yale University Press, 2000), pp. 50 (on the city's divine mission to become an earthly Jerusalem), 78 (on various prophecies), 188 (on Holy Sepulchre replicas based on the vision of Florence as a New Jerusalem), and 305 (on pageants in which Florence became Jerusalem).

14. Marilyn Aronberg Lavin, *Piero della Francesca's Baptism of Christ* (New Haven, CT: Yale University Press, 1981), pp. 23–32.

15. Mircea Eliade, *Patterns in Comparative Religion* (New York: Meridian, World Publishing, 1971), p. 448.

16. See Kathleen Biddick's ingenious discussion of the woodcut view of Nuremberg in Schedel's *Weltchronik* (1493) in *The Typological Imaginary: Circumcision, Technology, History* (Philadelphia: University of Pennsylvania Press, 2003), pp. 48–52. Such city portraits, according to Biddick, represented not "secularization" but rather an "occupation" of Jerusalem that perpetuated the deception of typology, enabling modern viewers to sustain links across time and space to a "preconstituted" Christian self.

17. Erwin Panofsky, *Early Netherlandish Painting*, pp. 131–40.

18. Vienna, Österreichische Nationalbibliothek, Cod. Vind. 2554, fol. 50v. Rainer Haussherr, "Templum Salomonis und Ecclesia Christi: Zu einem Bildvergleich der Bible moralisée," *Zeitschrift für Kunstgeschichte* 31 (1968), pp. 101–102. Haussherr concedes that the example is exceptional but argues that it confirms Panofsky's argument about fifteenth-century painting; he discusses the paradox of Fouquet's Gothic temple on p. 116.

19. Julius von Schlosser compares the poetic descriptions of the temple of the Grail in the late medieval *Younger Titurel* to the depictions of fantastic architecture in fifteenth-century Netherlandish and Italian paintings. See *Quellenbuch zur Kunstgeschichte des abendländischen Mittelalters* (Vienna: Graeser, 1896), p. xv.

20. Madrid, Prado, inventory no. 1887. Eva Frodl-Kraft, "Der Tempel von Jerusalem in der 'Vermählung Mariae' des Meisters von Flémalle," pp. 293–309 and esp. 296–97.

21. Panofsky, *Early Netherlandish Painting*, p. 136. The portal is a portrait of Notre-Dame du Sablon

in Brussels; see Felix Thürlemann, *Robert Campin* (Munich and New York: Prestel, 2002), p. 55, fig. 35.

22. See Werner Körte, "Die Wiederaufnahme romanischer Bauformen in der niederländischen und deutschen Malerei des 15. und 16. Jahrhunderts," PhD diss., Leipzig, 1929 and Hans Tietze, "Romanische Kunst und Renaissance," *Vorträge der Bibliothek Warburg 1926–1927* (1930), pp. 43–57. On images of Romanesque architecture and sculpture in fifteenth-century painting, see Jurgis Baltrušaitis, *Reveils et prodiges: Le gothique fantastique* (Paris: Colin, 1960), pp. 186–94. Jan van Eyck's *Madonna of Canon van der Paele* (Bruges, 1436) is set in a round-arched temple modeled either on the Anastasis of the Holy Sepulchre itself or on a local imitation of it such as Saint-Bénigne in Dijon; see G. Joseph Kern, "Perspektive und Bildarchitektur bei Jan van Eyck," *Repertorium für Kunstwissenschaft* 25 (1912), pp. 34–50; Stephan Hoppe, "Die Antike des Jan van Eyck: Architektonische Fiktion und Empirie im Umkreis des burgundischen Hofs um 1435," in Dietrich Boschung and Susanne Wittekind (eds.), *Persistenz und Rezeption: Weiterverwendung, Wiederverwendung und Neuinterpretation antiker Werke im Mittelalter* (Wiesbaden: Reichert, 2008), pp. 351–94.

23. See Jacob Wamberg, "Ghiberti, Alberti, and the Modernity of Gothic," *Analecta Romana Instituti Danici* 21 (1993), pp. 173–211.

24. This point about the parallel modernities of mid-fifteenth-century Netherlandish painting and Italian architecture was made by Heinrich Klotz, following a clue of Dagobert Frey. See *Der Stil des Neuen: Die Europäische Renaissance* (Stuttgart: Klett-Cotta, 1997), pp. 42–51.

25. Stephan Hoppe, "Romanik als Antike und die baulichen Folgen," in Norbert Nussbaum, Claudia Euskirken, and Stephan Hoppe (eds.), *Wege zur Renaissance: Beobachtungen zu den Anfängen neuzeitlicher Kunstauffassung im Rheinland und den Nachbargebieten um 1500* (Cologne: SH-Verlag, 2003), pp. 89–131. Hoppe also gives examples of the integration of such motifs into real, built architecture.

26. Howard Burns, "Building against Time: Renaissance Strategies to secure Large Churches against Changes to their Design," in Jean Guillaume (ed.), *L'église dans l'architecture de la renaissance* (Paris: Picard, 1995), pp. 107–31. Marvin Trachtenberg argues that Alberti's antidote to an organic, evolutionary conception of building, and the essential character of his sense of authorship, was the attempt to build according to ideal principles invulnerable to time; see "Building Outside Time in Alberti's *De re architectura*," *RES: Anthropology and Aesthetics* 48 (2005), pp. 123–34, and *Building-in-Time: From Giotto to Alberti and Modern Oblivion* (New Haven: Yale University Press, 2010).

27. Washington, National Gallery of Art, inventory no. 1937 and *Building-in-Time from Giotto to Alberti and Modern Oblivion* (New Haven : Yale University Press, 2010).

28. Panofsky, *Early Netherlandish Painting*, p. 138 and Hoppe, "Die Antike des Jan van Eyck." See also van Eyck's *Virgin in the Church* in Berlin. Some real buildings did manage to jumble styles, casting some doubt on the meaning of van Eyck's painted church. See the examples from Tournai assembled by Thomas W. Lyman, "Architectural Portraiture and Jan van Eyck's Washington Annunciation," *Gesta* 20 (1981), pp. 263–71. The decagon of St. Gereon in Cologne, completed in 1227, involves late Romanesque tribunes and a dwarf gallery over Gothic windows; Willibald Sauerländer, "Romanesque Art 2000: A Worn Out Notion?" in Colum Hourihane (ed.), *Romanesque Art and Thought in the Twelfth Century: Essays in Honor of Walter Cahn* (Princeton: Index of Christian Art, and Dept. of Art and Archeology, Princeton University; University Park: Penn State University Press, 2008), pp. 40–56, here 47–49. Robert Suckale sees behind stylistic gradients and contrasts within Gothic buildings a deliberate will to stage formal contrasts, creating dynamic "architectural compositions"; see "Peter Parler und das Problem der Stillagen," in Suckale, *Stil und Funktion: ausgewählte Schriften zur Kunst des Mittelalters*, eds. Peter Schmidt and Gregor Wedekind (Munich: Deutscher Kunstverlag, 2003), pp. 257–86.

The unreal clarity of van Eyck's image does suggest, however, that he was seeking with his clash of styles to make a more distinctive point than anything attempted in real buildings.

29. This is the formulation of Hoppe, "Die Antike des Jan van Eyck," p. 384

30. Van Eyck anticipated the classical revival of architecture in Italy in his Rolin and van der Paele Madonnas, which describe the dwellings of the Virgin as Romanesque or early Christian structures—massive and round-arched. In these pictures, it is no longer Gothic that figures as the ideal style. Instead, Stephan Hoppe argues in "Die Antike des Jan van Eyck," pp. 373–81, van Eyck sought out authentic forms at the Holy Sepulchre itself, a structure he would have seen if the artist visited Jerusalem in 1426 (as others have proposed; see for example Brand Philip, *The Ghent Altarpiece*, pp. 180–84). If so, then van Eyck's antiquarianism was arguably more ambitious than that of Alberti and Brunelleschi.

31. Wolfgang Kemp, *Die Räume der Maler: Zur Bilderzählung seit Giotto* (Munich: Beck, 1996), pp. 16–64.

32. Howard Burns, "Quattrocento Architecture and the Antique," p. 281.

33. Marvin Trachtenberg, *The Dominion of the Eye: Urbanism, Art, and Power in Early Modern Florence*, pp. 214 and 241.

34. On the so-called Romanesque Renaissance in German architecture, see Vojtěch Birnbaum, *Románská Renesance koncem středověku* (Prague: Jan Štenc, 1924); Hans Tietze, "Romanische Kunst und Renaissance," pp. 43–57; Michael Schmidt, *Reverentia und Magnificentia: Historizität in der Architektur Süddeutschlands, Österreichs und Böhmens vom 14. bis 17. Jahrhundert* (Munich: Schnell und Steiner, 1999), pp. 130–45; Stephan Hoppe, "Romanik als Antike und die baulichen Folgen," pp. 89–131 and esp. 105–15.

35. Henry-Russell Hitchcock, *German Renaissance Architecture* (Princeton, NJ: Princeton University Press, 1981), pp. 3–21; Bruno Bushart, *Die Fuggerkapelle bei St. Anna in Augsburg* (Munich: Deutscher Kunstverlag, 1994).

36. See Michael Baxandall, *The Limewood Sculptors of Renaissance Germany* (New Haven, CT: Yale University Press, 1980), pp. 135–42; Andrew Morrall, "The 'Deutsch' and the 'Welsch': Jörg Breu the Elder's Sketch for the Story of Lucretia and the Uses of Classicism in Sixteenth-Century Germany," in Stuart Currie (ed.), *Drawing 1400–1600: Invention and Innovation* (Aldershot, UK: Ashgate, 1998), pp. 109–25.

37. Piero Tomei, *L'architettura a Roma nel Quattrocento* (Rome: Multigrafica, 1977), pp. 103–105.

38. Henri Zerner, *Art de la renaissance en France: L'invention du classicisme* (Paris: Flammarion, 1996), pp. 14–53. The question of a "Renaissance Gothic" has recently received renewed attention; see Ethan Matt Kavaler, *Renaissance Gothic : Architecture and the Arts in Northern Europe 1470–1540* (New Haven: Yale University Press, 2012).

FIFTEEN — TEMPLES PAINTED, PRINTED, AND REAL

1. *Grandes Chroniques de France enluminées par Jean Foucquet* (Paris: Berthaud, 1906), Coronation of Marie de Brabant, second wife of Philip III in the Sainte-Chapelle, fol. 292, fig. 31; and Burial of Philippe le Bel at St. Denis, fol. 323, fig. 33. For the latter image, see also François Avril and Nicole Reynaud, *Les manuscrits à peinture en France 1440–1520* (Paris: Bibliothèque Nationale, 1993), p. 139, no. 70. Generally on Fouquet's adjustments of real Parisian buildings in his historical scenes, see Camille Serchuk, "Images of Paris in the Middle Ages: Patronage and Politics," PhD diss., Yale University, 1997, pp. 218–24.

2. Christine Smith argues that the Florentine Duomo "meets [Alberti's] criteria for good architecture through its effect on the spectator and the principles of its design. There is no hint that its formal vocabulary is other than classical." *Architecture in the Culture of Early*

Humanism: Ethics, Aesthetics, and Eloquence, 1400–1470 (New York: Oxford University Press, 1992), p. 60. See page 61 for a discussion of Alberti and arches. Hubertus Günther makes a series of comparably surprising observations about the reception of Gothic in "Das architektonische Urteil in der Renaissance," *Der Architekt: Zeitschrift des Bundes Deutscher Architekten* 7 (1998), pp. 394–402; see also his essay "The Renaissance of Antiquity," in Millon and Lampugnani (eds.), *The Renaissance from Brunelleschi to Michelangelo*, pp. 259–305. Anne-Marie Sankovitch makes the paradoxical argument that Vasari, too, saw medieval architecture—with the exception of the bizarre *maniera tedesca*, which in her reading of the text does not simply map onto Gothic—as a set of variations on classical architecture, and not always unsuccessful. See "The Myth of the 'Myth of the Medieval': Gothic Architecture in Vasari's *Rinascita* and Panofsky's Renaissance," *Res* 40 (2001), pp. 28–50.

3. The Crusaders also introduced Western innovations into the Holy Land. But as Robert Ousterhout has pointed out, the technically new ribbed groin vaults introduced by the Latins go unrecorded in the early sources: "visitors to the church were more concerned with its antiquity than with its novelty." See "The French Connection? Construction of Vaults and Cultural Identity in Crusader Architecture," in Daniel H. Weiss, Lisa J. Mahoney, Lisa Cindrich (eds.), *France and the Holy Land: Frankish Culture at the End of the Crusades* (Baltimore: Johns Hopkins University Press, 2004), p. 80. Before the Latin introduction of the ribbed groin vaults, Holy Land architecture was marked by somewhat more massive vaults, but they were still groin vaults over pointed arches. The continuity would have been much more apparent than the innovation, which is recognized only by the eye of the architectural historian.

4. Enea Silvio Piccolomini, *Deutschland, der Brieftraktat an Martin Mayer und Jakob Wimpfelings Antworten und Einwendungen*, trans. and ed. Adolf Schmidt (Cologne: Böhlau, 1962); Paul Frankl, *The Gothic: Literary Sources and Interpretations through Eight Centuries* (Princeton: Princeton University Press,

1960), pp. 244–48; Gernot Michael Müller, *Die "Germania generalis" des Conrad Celtis: Studien mit Edition, Übersetzung und Kommentar* (Tübingen: Niemeyer, 2001), pp. 250–63; Smith, *Architecture in the Culture of Early Humanism*, pp. 63–66.

5. Hermann Hipp shows how rarely northern European writers disapproved of Gothic architecture before 1700. See "Studien zur 'Nachgotik' des 16. und 17. Jahrhunderts in Deutschland, Böhmen, Österreich und der Schweiz," PhD diss., Tübingen, 1979, p. 594.

6. Toledo Museum of Art, 1939.501. *Byzantium: Faith and Power*, cat. no. 347. Sandra Hindman and Nina Rowe (eds.), *Manuscript Illumination in the Modern Age*, exhibition catalogue (Evanston: Block Museum of Art, 2001), fig. 3, fig. 26, and p. 299. The Evanston exhibition catalogue argues that this collage and several others like it were made in the nineteenth century. But the evidence is ambiguous. It is not clear why the Madonna and Child and the frame, which fit together perfectly, could not have been united already in the early sixteenth century.

7. Anthony Geber, "Name Inscriptions: Solution or Problem?" *Italian Plaquettes: Studies in the History of Art* 22 (Washington: National Gallery of Art, 1989), pp. 247–50.

8. On this apparent paradox, see Anne Dunlop, "Pinturicchio and the Pilgrims: Devotion and the Past at S. Maria del Popolo," *Papers of the British School at Rome* 71 (2003), pp. 265–91.

9. Cesariano, *De architectura libri dece* (Como, 1521), fol. 14r–15v.

10. Carol H. Krinsky, "Cesare Cesariano and the Como Vitruvius Edition of 1521," PhD diss., New York University, 1965, p. 112.

11. Cesariano, *De architectura libri dece*, fol. 13r–14r. This point is well explained by Marco Rossi, "Cesariano in Duomo," in *Cesare Cesariano e il classicismo di primo Cinquecento: Atti del seminario di studi, Varenna 7–9 ottobre 1994*, ed. Maria Luisa Gatti Perer e Alessandro Rovetta (Milan: Vita e Pensiero, 1996), pp. 45–66, here p. 54.

12. Mario Carpo, *Architecture in the Age of Printing: Orality, Writing, Typography, and Printed Images in the History of Architectural Theory* (Cambridge, MA: The MIT Press, 2001).

13. Marco Rossi and Alessandro Rovetta, "Indagine sullo spazio ecclesiale immagine della Gerusalemme celeste," *La Gerusalemme celeste*, exhibition catalogue, Milan, Università Cattolica del S. Cuore (Milan: Vita e Pensiero, 1983), pp. 111–12. Brunelleschi's stupendous octagonal cupola for the cathedral of Florence, however, to this day the largest masonry dome in the world, was described by Alberti, in the dedication (addressed to Brunelleschi) of his own treatise in painting, as a "feat of engineering…that people did not believe possible these days and was probably equally unknown and imagined among the ancients." *Della Pittura*, in *Opere Volgari*, ed. Grayson, vol. 3, pp. 7–8. The cupola, with its ribs and pointed profile, was both the culmination of Gothic architecture, a Tuscan triumph over the French and German builders, and at the same time a complete novelty, an original without prototype; see Smith, *Architecture in the Culture of Early Humanism*, p. 26.

14. Willibald Sauerländer pursues a suggestion by Panofsky in "Abwegige Gedanken über frühgotische Architektur und 'The Renaissance of the Twelfth Century,'" in *Études d'art médiéval offertes à Louis Grodecki* (Paris: Ophrys, 1981), pp. 167–79; and see also Sauerländer, "'Première architecture gothique' or 'Renaissance of the Twelfth Century'? Changing Perspectives in the Evaluation of Architectural History," *Sewanee Mediaeval Colloquium Occasional Papers* 2 (Sewanee, TN: The University Press, 1985).

15. Bernhard von Breydenbach, *Peregrinatio in Terram Sanctam* (Mainz, 1486). For further examples of such emendations, including illustrations in Schedel's *Weltchronik*, see Werner Körte, *Die Wiederaufnahme romanischer Bauformen in der niederländischen und deutschen Malerei des 15. und 16. Jahrhunderts* (Wolfenbüttel: Heckner, 1930).

16. See *Le temple: Représentations de l'architecture sacrée*, exhibition catalogue, Musée National Message Biblique Marc Chagall, Nice (Paris: Éditions de la Réunion des musées nationaux, 1982) and Paul Naredi-Rainer, *Salomos Tempel und das Abendland*.

17. Eunice Howe, "A Temple Facade Reconsidered in Botticelli's *Temptation of Christ*," in *Rome in the Renaissance: The City and the Myth* (Binghamton, NY: Medieval and Renaissance Texts and Studies, Center for Medieval and Early Renaissance Studies, 1982), pp. 208–21, complicates the traditional identification of Botticelli's structure with the Roman Hospital of Santo Spirito, pointing out, among other things, that the church's present-day façade is a restoration of the 1920s and is no guide to the original appearance, since it is based in large part on Botticelli's fresco.

18. Turin, Museo Civico, fol. 48v. See also the panel in the Ca'd'Oro, Venice, possibly by the same artist, known as "Hand H," of the 1440s. In both pictures the Temple has the polygonal drum of the Rotterdam rendering (the drum of the Dome of the Rock is cylindrical), and is much too tall. Albert Châtelet, *Early Dutch Painting* (New York: Rizzoli, 1981), pp. 200–201, nos. 28 and 32; Hans Belting and Dagmar Eichberger, *Jan van Eyck als Erzähler: Frühe Tafelbilder im Umkreis der New Yorker Doppeltafel* (Worms: Werner'sche Verlagsgesellschaft, 1983), fig. 42.

19. British Museum, Egerton MS. 1070, fol. 5r. Otto Pächt, "René d'Anjou–Studien I," *Jahrbuch der Kunsthistorischen Sammlungen* 69 (1973), pp. 93–95, fig. 83.

20. F. W. Kent argues that this and other letters of Rucellai are eighteenth-century forgeries or creative adaptations. Even if true, the letters may yet transmit elements of lost originals. See "The Letters Genuine and Spurious of Giovanni Rucellai," *Journal of the Warburg and Courtauld Institutes* 37 (1974), pp. 343–48.

21. Ludwig Heydenreich, "Die Cappella Rucellai von San Pancrazio in Florenz," in Millard Meiss (ed.), *De artibus opuscula XL: Essays in Honor of Erwin Panofsky*, vol. 1 (New York: New York University Press, 1961), pp. 219–29; Riccardo Pacciani, "La cappella Rucellai

a San Pancrazio," in *Leon Battista Alberti e l'architettura*, exhibition catalogue (Mantua: Casa del Mantegna, 2006), pp. 368–73.

22. Martin Biddle, *The Tomb of Christ*, pp. 28–40. See also section 6 above. The edicule was completely rebuilt in 1555.

23. Millon and Lampugnani, *Renaissance from Brunelleschi to Michelangelo*, p. 456, no.44.

24. H. W. Davies, *Bernhard von Breydenbach and his Journey to the Holy Land 1483–4, A Bibliography* (London: Leighton, 1911), and Elizabeth Ross, "Picturing Knowledge and Experience in the Early Printed Book: Reuwich's Illustrations for Breydenbach's *Peregrinatio in terram sanctam* (1486)," PhD Diss., Harvard University, 2004.

25. Gustav Dalman, *Das Grab Christi in Deutschland* (Leipzig: Dietrich, 1922), pp. 96–102; Bruno Bushart, *Die Fuggerkapelle bei St. Anna in Augsburg* (Munich: Deutscher Kunstverlag, 1994), pp. 331–33, fig. 206.

26. Krautheimer said that architectural copies were drained of their content as they became more accurate, "Introduction to an 'Iconography of Medieval Architecture,'" p. 20.

27. Norberto Gramaccini, "Riccios Tiere und die Theorie des Naturabgusses seit Cennino Cennini," in Herbert Beck and Peter Bol (eds.), *Natur und Antike in der Renaissance* (Frankfurt: Liebieghaus, 1985), pp. 198–226, and Georges Didi-Huberman, *La ressemblance par contact: Archéologie, anachronisme et modernité de l'empreinte* (Paris: Minuit, 2008), pp. 92–111.

28. Note, however, that in his Vitruvius commentary *Unterrichtung zu rechtem Verstandt der lehr Vitruvii* (1547), the physician and minor humanist Walter Rivius or Ryff of Strasbourg was happy to follow Cesariano in offering the interior elevation of Milan Cathedral, a church built by Germans, as a modern exemplar of Vitruvian architecture.

29. For a sample of the considerable literature on centrally planned churches in the Renaissance, see Rudolf Wittkower, *Architectural Principles in the Age of Humanism*, pp. 1–32, and Bruno Adorni (ed.), *La chiesa*

a pianta centrale: Tempio civico del Rinascimento.

30. Erik Thunø, "The Miraculous Image and the Centralized Church: Santa Maria della Consolazione in Todi," in Thunø and Gerhard Wolf (eds.), *The Miraculous Image in the Late Middle Ages and Renaissance* (Rome: 'L'Erma' di Bretschneider, 2004), pp. 29–57.

31. Fra Mariano da Firenze, *Itinerarium urbis Romae*, ed. P. Enrico Bulletti (Rome: Pontificio istituto di archeologia cristiana, 1931), p. 98.

32. Ludwig H. Heydenreich, "Baluster und Balustrade: eine 'Invenzione' der toskanischen Frührenaissancearchitektur," in *Studien zur Architektur der Renaissance* (Munich: Fink, 1981), pp. 214–22. Paul Davies and David Hemsoll argue that a balustrade appeared in a painting—Filippo Lippi's *Annunciation* at Spoleto, 1460s—before it appeared in a real building; see "Renaissance Balustrades and the Antique," *Architectural History* 26 (1983), p. 5. See also the entry "Docke" in *Reallexikon zur deutschen Kunstgeschichte*, vol. 4 (Stuttgart: Metzler, 1937), col. 103.

33. Georg Satzinger, "Spolien in der römischen Architektur des Quattrocento," in Joachim Poeschke (ed.), *Antike Spolien*, p. 258.

34. Hans-Christoph Dittscheid, "Form versus Materie: Zum Spoliengebrauch in den römischen Bauten und Projekten Donato Bramantes," in Poeschke (ed.), *Antike Spolien*, p. 279 n.14. See also Perugino's *Betrothal* at Caen (1500–1504).

35. It is not known how the upper edge of the edicule was really decorated in the late fifteenth century. There is circumstantial evidence that there was some sort of parapet that Reuwich adapted into a balustrade. See Heydenreich, "Die Cappella Rucellai von San Pancrazio in Florenz," p. 224 n.24. See also the drawing in the Scorel painting, fig. 6.2. The tablets with urns on the façade of the Holy Sepulchre chapel constructed in Görlitz between 1491 and 1504 may be a misunderstanding of the balustrade in the Breydenbach woodcut; see *Le temple: Représentations de l'architecture sacrée*, doc. 19.

36. Hubertus Günther, "La ricezione dell' antico

nel Tempietto," in Francesco Paolo de Teodoro (ed.), *Donato Bramante*, p. 275, referring to Cod. Vat. Barb. lat. 4424. Heydenreich characterizes these drawings, like Alberti's Holy Sepuchre for Rucellai, as "ideal reconstructions;" see "Baluster und Balustrade," p. 219.

37. See also above, section 13, p. 139; and Günther, "La ricezione dell' antico nel Tempietto," pp. 268–69. The Kassel Codex, which can be dated between 1528 and 1541, describes the Tempietto and an entablature from the Baths of Diocletian on a single page; Günther, *Das Studium der antiken Architektur*, p. 373 and fig. 124. According to Heydenreich, no author prior to 1735 noted that the balustrade was actually an invention of the Renaissance; see "Baluster und Balustrade," p. 214.

38. See *Raffaello, L'architettura 'picta': percezione e realtà*, ed. Gianfrancesco Spagnesi, Mario Fondelli, and Emma Mandelli, exhibition catalogue, Palazzo Venezia, Rome (Rome: Multigrafica, 1984), p. 100. The balustrade in his *Sacrifice at Lystra* looks more permanent. Note that in the *School of Athens* (1509) Raphael referred to Bramante's plan for the cupola of St. Peter's.

SIXTEEN — CITATION AND SPOLIATION

1. Corrado Ricci, *Il Tempio Malatestiano* (Milan and Rome: Bestetti & Tumminelli, 1925); Wittkower, *Architectural Principles*, pp. 37–41; Robert Tavernor, *On Alberti and the Art of Building* (New Haven, CT: Yale University Press, 1998), pp. 49–77; Francesco Paolo Fiore, "Tempio Malatestiano—1453–1454 e seguenti," in *Leon Battista Alberti e l'architettura*, pp. 282–95; Maria Fabricius Hansen, *Eloquence of Appropriation*, p. 279.

2. Although there is evidence that the bricks of the inner structure may have once been faced with plaster, thus diminishing the contrast.

3. See the letter from Alberti to Matteo de' Pasti (1454) about the problem of the nonconcordance between the chapel windows and the shell; Ricci, *Il Tempio Malatestiano*, p. 587. It is not clear exactly when

Alberti joined the project; according to Wittkower, he "carefully watched over the execution of the exterior from Rome." *Architectural Principles in the Age of Humanism*, p. 37.

4. See Trachtenberg, "Building Outside Time in Alberti's *De re aedificatoria*."

5. Renate Lachmann, *Memory and Literature*, pp. 4–10.

6. "[I]n San Pietro di Roma, rovinandosi le mura vecchie di quella chiesa per rifar le nuove della fabrica, pervennero i muratori a una pariete dove era una Nostra Donna et altre pitture di man di Giotto; il che veduto Perino, che era in compagnia di messer Niccolò Acciaiuoli, dottor fiorentino e suo amicissimo, mosso l'uno e l'altro a pietà di quella pittura, non la lasciarono rovinare, anzi, fatto tagliare attorno il muro, la fecero allacciare con ferri e travi e collocarla sotto l'organo di San Piero in un luogo dove non era né altare né cosa ordinata; et innanzi che fusse rovinato il muro che era intorno alla Madonna, Perino ritrasse Orso dell'Anguillara senator romano, il quale coronò in Campidoglio messer Francesco Petrarca, che era a' piedi di detta Madonna; intorno alla quale, avendosi a far certi ornamenti di stucchi e di pitture, et insieme mettervi la memoria di un Niccolò Acciaiuoli, che già fu senator di Roma, fecene Perino i disegni e vi messe mano sùbito; et aiutato da' suoi giovani e da Marcello Mantovano suo creato, l'opera fu fatta con molta diligenza." Vasari, *Le vite*, vol. 5, pp. 152–53.

7. W. S. Heckscher, "Relics of Pagan Antiquity in Mediaeval Settings," pp. 204–20; Hans Peter l'Orange, *Der spätantike Bildschmuck des Konstantinsbogens* (Berlin: de Gruyter, 1939); Friedrich Wilhelm Deichmann, "Säule und Ordnung in der frühchristlichen Architektur," *Römische Mitteilungen* 55 (1940), pp. 114–30; Arnold Esch, "Spolien. Zur Wiederverwendung antiker Baustücke und Skulpturen im mittelalterlichen Italien," *Archiv für Kulturgeschichte* 51 (1969), pp. 1–64; Salvatore Settis, "Continuità, distanza, conoscenza," pp. 373–486; Michael Greenhalgh, *The Survival of Roman Antiquities*; Lucilla de Lachenal, *Spolia*; Joachim

Poeschke (ed.), *Antike Spolien; Ideologie e pratiche del reimpiego nell'alto medioevo. 16–21 aprile 1998*, 2 vols. (Spoleto: Centro Italiano di studi sull'alto Medioevo, 1999); Maria Fabricius Hansen, *Eloquence of Appropriation*; Lukas Clemens, *Tempore Romanorum constructa*; Dale Kinney, "The Concept of Spolia," pp. 233–52; and Greenhalgh, *Marble Past, Monumental Present*.

8. Thuri Lorenz, "Beobachtungen an der Reiterstatue des Marc Aurel auf dem Kapitolsplatz," in Kurt Gschwantler and Alfred Bernhard-Walcher (eds.), *Griechische und römische Statuetten und Grossbronzen, Akten der 9. Internationalen Tagung über antike Bronzen* (Vienna: Kunsthistorisches Museum, 1988), pp. 124–29.

9. Greenhalgh, however, warns that the assumption that there was no quarrying in the Middle Ages needs "re-evaluation." He points to evidence of medieval awareness of the great Egyptian quarries, and massive stockpiles of usable material lying about at the closed quarries; *Marble Past, Monumental Present*, pp. 90–124, 138.

10. See, for example, the analysis of the reuse of ancient sarcophagi at Pisa Cathedral by Salvatore Settis, "Continuità, distanza, conoscenza," pp. 395–98.

11. Hansen, *Eloquence of Appropriation*.

12. See the documents in Julius von Schlosser, *Schriftquellen zur Geschichte der karolingischen Kunst* (Vienna: Graeser, 1892), p. 26 n.101. See also the discussions by Richard Krautheimer, "The Carolingian Revival of early Christian Architecture," *Art Bulletin* 24 (1942), p. 35 and W. Eugene Kleinbauer, "Charlemagne's Palace Chapel at Aachen and its Copies," *Gesta* 4 (1965), p. 3. Charlemagne also found antique models and materials closer to home. Sven Schütte shows that the recently excavated fourth-century octagon in the praetorium in Cologne was the same size as that of Aachen and carried several features, including wings with apses, which also appear at Aachen. See "Überlegungen zu den architektonischen Vorbildern der Pfalzen Ingelheim und Aachen," in Mario Kramp (ed.), *Krönungen: Könige in Aachen—Geschichte und*

Mythos, vol. 1 (Mainz: Zabern, 2000), pp. 203–11. Moreover, the octagon in Cologne was damaged by an earthquake between 785 and 790, just a few years before the building of the Pfalzkapelle. Thanks to Carol Krinsky for pointing out this reference.

13. Wolfgang Götz, "Der Magdeburger Domchor: Zur Bedeutung seiner monumentalen Ausstattung," *Zeitschrift des deutschen Vereins für Kunstwissenschaft* 20 (1966), pp. 97–120. On Magdeburg, and generally on the use of ancient marbles by Charlemagne and his successors, see Greenhalgh, *Marble Past, Monumental Present*, pp. 333–44.

14. Beat Brenk, "Sugers Spolien," *Arte medievale* 1 (1983), p. 102.

15. Hansen, *Eloquence of Appropriation*, p. 14 n.10. Vitruvius 6.1 speaks of rubble reused as paving material as *redivivus*.

16. Brunelleschi was relatively uninterested in aggregation and heterogeneity, but rather strove for overall unity of form. In this respect, Hansen argues, he extends a "Gothic" aesthetic; see *Eloquence of Appropriation*, p. 278.

17. On Eugene IV's attempts to ban spoliation, see Rodolfo Lanciani, *Storia degli scavi di Roma e notizie intorno le collezioni romane di antichità*, vol. 1 (1902; reprinted Rome: Quasar, 1989), pp. 57–58. Cyriacus of Ancona, meanwhile, visiting the ruined temple of Hadrian at Cyzicus in Anatolia in 1444, tried to convince the local Ottoman authorities to prohibit further spoliation; see Greenhalgh, *Marble Past, Monumental Present*, p. 9.

18. On Nicholas V's excavations, see Lanciani, *Storia degli scavi di Roma*, p. 62, and Georg Satzinger, "Spolien in der römischen Architektur des Quattrocento," pp. 251–54. The buildings of Rome were eventually frozen. Around 1600, agents of Pope Clement VIII tried to requisition four splendid, colored columns from Sant' Agnese fuori le Mura but were prevented by an alert cardinal. See Amato Pietro Frutaz, *Il complesso monumentale di Sant'Agnese* (1960) (Rome: Nova officina poligrafica Laziale, 2001), p. 167 n.85.

19. See the transcription of the Munich manuscript by Ingrid Rowland, "Raphael, Angelo Colocci, and the Genesis of the Architectural Orders," *Art Bulletin* 76 (1994), pp. 100–103. See also John Shearman, *Raphael in Early Modern Sources, 1483–1602*, vol. 1 (New Haven, CT: Yale University Press, 2003), p. 521. For a concise account of ancient Greek and Roman spoliation practices, which heavily informed the understanding of spoliation in the Renaissance, see Dale Kinney, "*Spolia*: *Damnatio* and *renovatio memoriae*," pp. 117–48.

20. Lex Bosman, *The Power of Tradition: Spolia in the Architecture of St. Peter's in the Vatican* (Hilversum: Verloren, 2004), pp. 147–48; Dale Kinney, "Spolia," in William Tronzo (ed.), *St. Peter's in the Vatican* (Cambridge: Cambridge University Press, 2005), pp. 16–47.

21. Hans-Christoph Dittscheid, "Form versus Materie: Zum Spoliengebrauch in den römischen Bauten und Projekten Donato Bramantes," in Poeschke (ed.), *Antike Spolien*, p. 281.

22. Dittscheid, "Form versus Materie," p. 278. Derek A. R. Moore contends that fifteenth-century builders did not use spolia and that the practice was basically revived by Bramante. See "Notes on the Use of Spolia in Roman Architecture from Bramante to Bernini," in Cecil R. Striker (ed.), *Architectural Studies in Memory of Richard Krautheimer* (Mainz: Philipp von Zabern, 1996), pp. 119–22. Moore believes, as do others, that the columns of the Tempietto are spolia.

23. Satzinger, "Spolien in der römischen Architektur des Quattrocento," p. 257.

24. For this concept, see Richard Brilliant, "I piedistalli del Giardino di Boboli: Spolia in se, spolia in re," *Prospettiva* 31 (1982), pp. 2–17. See also section 4 above.

SEVENTEEN — NEO-COSMATESQUE

1. The orthodox scholarly opinion is that fifteenth-century "neo-cosmatesque" floors simply continued the medieval tradition. See, for example, Georg Satzinger, "Spolien in der römischen Architektur des Quattrocento," in Joachim Poeschke (ed.), *Antike Spolien in der Architektur des Mittelalters und der Renaissance* (Munich: Hirmer, 1996), p. 257. Angela Dressen argues instead—and, we believe, correctly—that the fifteenth-century floors must be understood as an aspect of the revival of antiquity. See *Pavimenti decorati del Quattrocento in Italia* (Venezia: Marsilio, 2008), p. 268.

2. Alessandra Guiglia Guidobaldi complicates the traditional picture of the westward transmission by revealing multiple entry points into the peninsula and stressing the local Italian contributions—perhaps in continuity with ancient Roman traditions—to pattern and color choice. See "Tradizioni locali e influenze bizantine nei pavimenti cosmateschi," *Bollettino d'arte* 69 (1984), pp. 57–72.

3. Edward Hutton, *The Cosmati: The Roman Marble Workers of the XIIth and XIIIth centuries* (London: Routledge and Paul, 1950); Dorothy F. Glass, *Studies on Cosmatesque Pavements* (Rome: British Academy, 1980); Herbert Bloch, "The New Fascination with Ancient Rome," and Ernst Kitzinger, "The Arts as Aspects of a Renaissance: Rome and Italy," in Robert L. Benson and Giles Constable (eds.), *Renaissance and Renewal in the Twelfth Century* (Cambridge, MA: Harvard University Press, 1982), pp. 616–21 and 639–41; Peter Cornelius Claussen, *Magistri doctissimi Romani: Die römischen Marmorkünstler des Mittelalters* (Stuttgart: Steiner, 1987), *Die Kirchen der Stadt Rom im Mittelalter, 1050–1300: A–F* (Stuttgart: Steiner, 2002), and *Die Kirchen der Stadt Rom im Mittelalter, 1050–1300: S. Giovanni in Laterano* (Stuttgart: Steiner, 2008); Paloma Pajares Ayuela, *Cosmatesque Ornament: Flat Polychrome Geometric Patterns in Architecture*, trans. Maria Fleming Alvarez (New York: Norton, 2001); and Dressen, *Pavimenti decorati*. Most of the surviving floors are in Rome and Latium; several are found in Tuscany and Campania. The outstanding far-flung example is the pavement of the sanctuary of Westminster Abbey, composed in the 1260s by workmen fetched, together with the colored stones, by the abbot; see Lindy Grant and Richard Mortimer

(eds.), *Westminster Abbey: The Cosmati Pavements* (Aldershot, UK: Ashgate, 2002).

4. Claussen puts the cosmatesque work in the overall context of reuse. See "Marmi antichi nel Medioevo romano: L'arte dei Cosmati," in Gabriele Borghini (ed.), *Marmi antichi*, exhibition catalogue (Rome: De Luca, 2001), pp. 65–79. Note that in some sections of later floors the simpler patterns of the Carolingian floors survive to this day, for example in the San Zeno chapel in Santa Prassede in Rome.

5. Greenhalgh describes the cosmatesque pavements as the end-phase of a long process of "miniaturization," involving successive fragmentations of floors into smaller and smaller bits. Although this process was determined by lack of materials, "style accommodated diminishing supplies"; *Marble Past, Monumental Present*, p. 373.

6. See the comparative illustrations assembled by Pajares Ayuela, where the only major difference seems to be that the Roman examples are opus tesselatum (where the smaller forms are composed of regularly-sized tesserae arrayed in even rows) and the cosmatesque examples are *opus sectile* (where each small form, corresponding to a piece of stone, is individually shaped and fitted). See *Cosmatesque Ornament*, pp. 136–38.

7. Rodolfo Lanciani, *Storia degli scavi di Roma*, vol. 1, p. 47; Dressen, *Pavimenti decorati*, pp. 67–70, 105–106, cat. A3.

8. Dressen, *Pavimenti decorati*, cat. nos. A36, A41, A42.

9. *Ibid.*, p. 272.

10. *Ibid.*, pp. 37–39, 42–43, cat. A27. Alberti, in the section on marble revetments and pavements in his treatise on architecture (1452), seems uninterested in cosmatesque design; see *De re aedificatoria; On the Art of Building in Ten Books*, bk. 6 (Cambridge, MA: The MIT Press, 1988), p. 178.

11. See Irving Lavin, *Past-Present: Essays on Historicism in Art from Donatello to Picasso* (Berkeley: University of California Press, 1993), pp. 1–26. The pulpits were assembled and installed only in 1515 in preparation for the visit of Leo X, leaving open the question of their form and even of whether the bronze panels were always meant for two pulpits. Cf. the balanced discussion of Nirit Ben-Aryeh Debby, who concludes that two pulpits were planned from the beginning. See ch. 8 of *The Renaissance Pulpit: Art and Preaching in Tuscany, 1400–1550* (Turnhout: Brepols, 2007).

12. Alexandra Herz, "Cardinal Cesare Baronio's Restoration of SS. Nereo ed Achilleo and S. Cesareo de' Appia," *Art Bulletin* 70 (1988), pp. 590–620.

13. "Pavimentum totum ex fragmentis marmorum. Alicubi cernebantur reliquiae primi pavimenti (et fortasse Constantiniani) vermiculato opera phrigiato ex albis, porphyretis serpentinisque lapillis. In hoc sacro vermiculato solo magnae rotae errant, meo tempore has notavi: Tres amplae nobilissimae et integrae, quarum una fracta nunc est in novo pavimento ante sepulcrum Clementis VIII, visebantur ante solium pontificis apsidae veteris; Jacobus a Porta architectus rogatus a multis, ut integras inde elevaret sub dicto Clemente, quia volebant apsidam diruere, verba dedit et tales lapides flocci pendit. Fabricatores murorum massas super ipsas rotas deiciendo in plures partes fregerunt, multae licet crassitudinis essent; huiusmodi lapidis materia cinericius erat, orientale granitum vocant. Illinc non longe alia rota similes minor erat, quam integram elevarunt. Mirabantur inspicientes et priscorum Romanorum potentiam inde arguebant." Giacomo Grimaldi, *Descrizione della Basilica Antica di S. Pietro in Vaticano, Codice Barberini Latino 2733*, ed. Reto Niggl (Vatican City: Biblioteca Apostolica Vaticana, 1972), p. 141.

14. Claussen, *Magistri doctissimi Romani*, pp. 10–11.

15. Pajares Ayuela, *Cosmatesque Ornament*, pp. 82–84.

16. On Solomon's Temple and the Sistine Chapel as "palace chapels," and on other ancient associations of Sixtus's structure, see Eugenio Battisti, "Il significato simbolico della Cappella Sistina," *Commentari: Rivista di critica e storia dell'arte* 7 (1957), pp. 96–104 and Silvia Danesi Squarzina, "La Sistina di Sisto IV e l'eredità del

pensiero religioso medievale," in Sergio Rossi and Stefano Valeri (eds.), *Le due Rome del Quattrocento: Melozzo, Antoniazzo e la cultura artistica del '400 romano* (Rome: Lithos, 1997), pp. 109–26.

17. Dressen, *Pavimenti decorati*, pp. 75, 104–106, cat. A37.

18. L. D. Ettlinger, *The Sistine Chapel before Michelangelo: Religious Imagery and Papal Primacy* (Oxford: Clarendon Press, 1965), pp. 12–13; Deoclecio Redig de Campos, *I Palazzi Vaticani* (Bologna: Cappelli Editori, 1967), pp. 66–67; Carol F. Lewine, *The Sistine Chapel Walls and the Roman Liturgy* (University Park, PA: Penn State University Press, 1993), p. 13. John Shearman correctly says that the antiquity of this type of floor was "overestimated" in the Renaissance, see *Raphael's Cartoons in the Collection of Her Majesty the Queen and the Tapestries for the Sistine Chapel* (London: Phaidon, 1972), p. 7 n.39; see also pp. 22–23.

19. Ernst Steinmann, *Die Sixtinische Kapelle*, vol. 1 (Munich: Bruckmann, 1901–1905), p. 181.

20. The association of the floor with Nicholas V is proposed by Arnold Nesselrath, for example in *Carlo Magno a Roma* (Rome: Retablo, 2001), p. 161. See also John Shearman, *The Vatican Stanze: Functions and Decoration* (Rome: British Academy, 1971), p. 15. Dressen concedes that the floor between the windows is attributable to Leo X rather than Julius II but does not believe that any elements of the floor predate the sixteenth century. See *Pavimenti*, p. 56, cat. A54

21. Sara Magister, *Arte e politica: La collezione di antichità del Cardinale Giuliano della Rovere nei palazzi ai Santi Apostoli* (Rome: Accademia nazionale dei Lincei, 2002), p. 39. Dressen, *Pavimenti decorati*, p. 56, cat. A38.

22. "At vero pro commoditate conventus mons crucifixionis in medio claustri remanens, adaequavit. Ibique magnum marmoreumque ciborium columnis ornatum ad magnitudinem ablate collis cum altare et cavernula Amadaei, ut visitor, exstruxit." Fra Mariano da Firenze, *Itinerarium urbis Romae*, ed. Enrico Bulletti (Rome: Pontificio Stato di Archeologia Cristiana, 1931), p. 98.

23. Dressen, *Pavimenti decorati*, pp. 108–109, cat. A50. The floor is rarely discussed. Arnaldo Bruschi, listing the Tempietto's floor among the other main neo-cosmatesque pavements of the Quattrocento, states that the origins of the form were imagined to be classical; see *Bramante Architetto* (Bari: Editori Laterza, 1969), p. 473 n.15.

24. Bruschi, *Bramante Architetto*, pp. 132–33.

25. Fra Mariano da Firenze, *Itinerarium urbis Romae*, p. 98.

26. J. M. Huskinson, "The Crucifixion of St. Peter: A Fifteenth-Century Topographical Problem," *Journal of the Warburg and Courtauld Institutes* 32 (1969), pp. 135–57.

27. A majolica inscription at Santa Croce dating from 1520 speaks of "terraque sancti montis Calvariae navi inde advecta supra quam Christi sanguis effusus fuit." See Ilaria Toesca, "A Majolica Inscription in Santa Croce in Gerusalemme," in Douglas Fraser, Howard Hibbard, and Milton J. Lewine (eds.), *Essays in the History of Art Presented to Rudolf Wittkower* (London: Phaidon, 1967), pp. 102–105, here p. 105. The Spanish traveller Pero Tafur, visiting Rome in 1436, heard a somewhat different story: "All this church, with the floor and the walls and everything else, was made from earth of Jerusalem brought as ballast in ships, when St. Helena sent the holy relics to Rome." Tafur, *Travels and Adventures, 1435–1439* (London: Routledge, 1926), p. 41.

28. Claussen, *Die Kirchen der Stadt Rom*, pp. 441–42.

29. The rest of the floor is plain red tile with several embedded inscriptions, crucially the tablet describing the renovation of Carvajal at the beginning of the sixteenth century. Further alterations to the chapel were undertaken from the 1590s through the first years of the seventeenth century. It is possible that the isolation and, in effect, framing of the cosmatesque patch in front of the altar was carried out at some point well after the intervention of Carvajal and Peruzzi that concerns us here.

30. For photos and diagrams see Maria Letizia

Accorsi, "S. Croce in Gerusalemme a Roma: recenti scoperti nella Cappella di S. Elena," *Palladio* 23 (1999), pp. 5–20. A similar case is the patch of opus sectile pavement, probably eleventh century, in the Cappella del Bagno at Santa Cecilia in Rome. This was a site associated with the murder of the saint. When Cardinal Sfrondrato, in 1599, restored the chapel in the modern style, he preserved a patch of the old floor, apparently believing that it belonged to the original (second-century) floor of Cecilia's home. See Caroline J. Goodson, "Material Memory: Rebuilding the Basilica of St. Cecilia in Trastevere, Rome," *Early Medieval Rome* 15 (2007), pp. 30–32.

EIGHTEEN — MOVABLE BUILDINGS

1. Ulysse Chevalier made the strong case against the authenticity of the house relic, see *Notre-Dame de Lorette: Étude historique sur l'authenticité de la Santa Casa* (Paris: Picard, 1906). Georg Hueffer made a similar argument, laying the entire fable of the flying house on the head of Pietro Giorgio Tolomei (Teramano), the author of the early pamphlet on the miracle (ca. 1470), accusing Teramano of crediting a mere vision of the event. See *Loreto: eine geschichtskritische Untersuchung der Frage des heiligen Hauses*, vol. 1 (Münster: Aschendorffsche Verlagsbuchhandlung, 1913–1921), pp. 35–36. Nanni Monelli, however, presents modern archeological evidence that some of the stones in the house really do come from the Holy Land. See *La Santa Casa a Loreto—La Santa Casa a Nazareth* (Loreto: Congregazione Universale della Santa Casa, 1997). Monelli is biased but the evidence is admittedly rather convincing. The twelfth-century Crusader church in Nazareth seems to have sheltered a house relic. Jaroslav Folda argues that the chapel at Walsingham and possibly some fourteenth- and fifteenth-century representations of the Annunciation, as well as the baldachin forms associated with Loreto iconography (see figure 18.2), registered some awareness of the form of the relic at Nazareth or the shrine-monument constructed around

it; *The Nazareth Capitals and the Crusader Shrine of the Annunciation* (University Park: Penn State University Press, 1986), pp. 20–26.

2. Luca da Monterado gives evidence of simple measures taken perhaps already in the late thirteenth century to encase the relic stones in a wall, followed by the construction probably in the early fourteenth century, of a containing wall, the *muro bono et grosso* mentioned by the treatise of Teramano; see *Storia del culto e del pellegrinaggio a Loreto* (Loreto: s.p., 1979), pp. 161–69. That wall was apparently at least partially removed at the time of the ensheathing in marble two centuries later.

3. On the early cult, including fairs, an obvious motive for local encouragement of this cult, see Monterado, *Storia del culto e del pellegrinaggio a Loreto*, pp. 111–42. In the 1360s Pope Urban V, as a consolation to the local inhabitants, sent an image of the Virgin to Tersatto, the village in Illyria, near Rijeka (Fiume), the port city in modern Croatia, where according to the legend the House had made a brief layover before continuing to Italy. Gregory XI issued an indulgence in 1375 acknowledging miracles accomplished through contact with the Virgin at Loreto.

4. Erwin Panofsky, *Early Netherlandish Painting*, p. 30 n.1.

5. According to Lucetta Scaraffia the angels were nothing more than a framing device with no reference to the myth of a flying house; see *Loreto* (Bologna: Il Mulino, 1998), p. 69. The oldest such image securely linked to Loreto is a fresco fragment datable to the 1370s at Valcora di Fiuminata, in the Marches; see Luca Bortolotti et al., "Iconografia, devozione e culto lauretano: analisi e riflessioni," and Floriano Grimaldi, "L'iconografia della Vergine Lauretana nell' arte: i prototipi iconografici," in Floriano Grimaldi and Katy Sordi (eds.), *L'iconografia della Vergine di Loreto nell' arte*, exhibition catalogue (Loreto: Cassa di risparmio di Loreto, 1995), pp. 31–45 and 15–30. See also Corrado Ricci, "Per l'iconografia Lauretana," *Rassegna d'arte antica e moderna* III (1916), vol. 1, pp. 265–74; and

Giuseppe Santarelli, *La Santa Casa di Loreto: Tradizione e ipotesi* (Loreto: Congregazioni Universali della Santa Casa, 1996), pp. 401-72.

6. Bortolotti et al., "Iconografia, devozione e culto lauretano," pp. 31-32.

7. Paris, Bibliothèque Nationale, Ms. Lat. 248, vol. 1, fol. 8v; see *Art au temps des Rois maudits: Philippe le Bel et ses fils, 1285-1328* (Paris: Réunion des musées nationaux, 1998), no. 191, pp. 286-87. See also Kathleen Morand, *Jean Pucelle* (Oxford: Clarendon Press, 1962), pp. 41-42.

8. James Hastings, "Loreto," *Encyclopedia of Religion and Ethics*, vol. 8 (New York: Scribner's, 1916), p. 140.

9. *Illustrated Bartsch*, vol. 24, *Commentary*, Part 1, *Early Italian Masters*, Mark J. Zucker (ed.) (New York: Abaris, 1993), no. 2402.023; Zucker, "*The Madonna of Loreto*: A Newly Discovered Work by the Master of the Vienna Passion," *Print Quarterly* 6 (1989), pp. 149-60. Our thanks to Mark Zucker for the photograph.

10. Dale Kinney, "Spolia from the Baths of Caracalla in Sta. Maria in Trastevere," *Art Bulletin* 68 (1986), pp. 379-97.

11. On the woodcuts of the Triumphal Arch, see *Albrecht Dürer, das druckgraphische Werk*, vol. 2 (Munich and New York: Prestel, 2002), no. 238, pp. 398-412.

12. *1495—Kaiser, Reich, Reformen—Der Reichstag zu Worms*, exhibition catalogue (Koblenz: Landeshauptarchiv, 1995), no.B6. See also Günther Franz (ed.), *Kostbare Bücher und Dokumente aus Mittelalter und Neuzeit*, exhibition catalogue (Trier: Stadtbibliothek and Stadtarchiv, 1984), nos. 66-67.

13. Mechthild Flury-Lemberg, "Das Reliquiar für die Reliquie vom Heiligen Rock Christi," in Erich Aretz (ed.), *Der heilige Rock zu Trier: Studien zur Geschichte und Verehrung der Tunika Christi* (Trier: Paulinus, 1995), pp. 699-702.

14. Mario Cempanari and Tito Amodei, *Scala Santa e Sancta Sanctorum* (Rome: Quasar, 1999), pp. 14-19.

15. Laura Donadono, *La Scala Santa a San Giovanni in Laterano* (Rome: Quasar, 2000), n.1.

16. The round map by Taddeo di Bartolo in the Palazzo Communale in Siena; see Cempanari and Amodei, *Scala Santa e Sancta Sanctorum*, p. 19, fig. 7.

17. On the range of Holy Land souvenirs or *pignora*—pebbles, earth, lamp-oil, water, palm-leaves—see Franco Cardini, "La devozione al Santo Sepolcro, le sue riproduzioni occidentali e il complesso stefaniano: Alcuni casi italici," in *Sette Colonne e Sette Chiese*, p. 32.

18. M. C. Seymour (ed.), *Mandeville's Travels*, p. 55. For the crystal cross reliquary in Tongres containing Holy Land pebbles set like jewels, see Henk van Os, *The Way to Heaven: Relic Veneration in the Middle Ages* (Baarn: de Prom, 2000), p. 57, fig. 54.

19. According to Marilyn Aronberg Lavin the mimetic link of the town to Jerusalem was secured by labeling alone. It is as if the relic stones had generated a virtual Holy Sepulchre whose reference to the original was so powerful that it did not even need to resemble, as so many others did, that original; see her *Piero della Francesca's Baptism of Christ*, pp. 29-31. The fragment of the tomb was housed in the village church, converting the entire town into a substitute for the destroyed Jerusalem; see section 14 above. Cf. the sixteenth-century reliquary in the church of Villers-Saint-Sépulchre (Oise) containing a stone tile pilfered from the tomb in the twelfth century; *Les trésors des églises de France*, exhibition catalogue (Paris: Musée des Arts Décoratifs, 1965), no. 96.

20. C.R. Morey, "The Painted Panel from the Sancta Sanctorum," in *Festschrift Paul Clemen* (Düsseldorf: Schwann, 1926), p. 151. The box is now in the Museo Sacro in the Vatican Palace.

21. Sible de Blaauw, *Cultus et decor: Liturgia e architettura nella Roma tardoantica e medioevale* (Vatican City: Biblioteca Apostolica Vaticana, 1994), pp. 400-401. Although the Nativity relics were not mentioned until an inventory of the eleventh century, the church was described as *ad praesepe* already in the seventh century and a chapel of the *presepio* was mentioned in the eighth century.

22. Diane Cole Ahl, "Camposanto, Terra santa:

Picturing the Holy Land in Pisa," *Artibus et Historiae* 24 (2003), pp. 95–112.

23. Beat Wyss, *Vom Bild zum Kunstsystem* (Cologne: König, 2006), pp. 212–15 and 219–26. He coins the phrase "Loreto principle" to describe the displacement, enveloping, and multiplication of sacred places. He also relates the Loreto myth to Julius II's ambitions at St. Peter's.

24. Robert Maniura, "The Icon is Dead, Long Live the Icon: The Holy Image in the Renaissance," in *Icon and Word*, pp. 87–104 and esp. 95.

25. The ecclesiastical context was the key for miraculous images; see Richard Trexler, "Being and Non-being: Parameters of the Miraculous in the Traditional Religious Image," in *The Miraculous Image*, pp. 15–27.

26. The nature of the original shelter for the House is unclear. There are records of altars and chapels around or near the Santa Casa from at least 1429. See Monterado, *Storia del culto e del pellegrinaggio a Loreto*, pp. 169–78; also Nanni Monelli et Giuseppe Santarelli, *La basilica di Loreto e la sua reliquia* (Loreto: Congregazione universale della Santa Casa, 1999), pp. 14–19.

27. Scaraffia, *Loreto*, p. 18.

28. The manuscript, preserved in Lucca, was published as Giacomo Ricci, *Virginis Mariae Loretae Historia*, ed. Giuseppe Santarelli (Loreto: Congregazioni Universali della Santa Casa, 1987). The text was probably composed in the 1470s.

29. Tolomei's text is datable to ca. 1465–1472. See Hueffer (ed.), *Loreto*, vol. 1, pp. 22–26.

30. Mario Fanti, "La leggenda della Madonna di San Luca di Bologna. Origine, fortuna, sviluppo e valore storico," in Mario Fanti and Giancarlo Roversi (eds.), *La Madonna di San Luca di Bologna* (Bologna: Le Arti, 2001), pp. 69–101, here 71–79.

31. See the essays by Cornelia Ringer, Holger Klein, Thomas Hensel, and others in *Die Alte Kapelle in Regensburg*, Arbeitshefte des Bayerischen Landesamtes für Denkmalpflege, vol. 114 (Munich: Bayerisches Landesamt für Denkmalpflege, 2001); and Achim Hubel, "Das Gnadenbild der Alten Kapelle,"

in Werner Scheidermair (ed.), *Die Alte Kapelle in Regensburg* (Regensburg: Schnell und Steiner, 2002), pp. 219–44.

32. See J. C. Dickinson, *The Shrine of Our Lady of Walsingham* (Cambridge: Cambridge University Press, 1956).

33. Gabriella Airaldi, "'Ad mortem festinamus…' Genova, il Mandylion e Leonardo Montaldo," in Gerhard Wolf et al. (eds.), *Mandylion: Intorno al "Sacro Volto," da Bisanzio a Genova*, exhibition catalogue (Milan: Skira, 2004), pp. 275–81.

34. Rebecca Müller, "Il 'sacro catino': percezione e memoria nella Genova medievale," in Anna Rosa Calderoni Masetti (ed.), *Intorno al Sacro Volto: Genova, Bisanzio e il Mediterraneo (secoli XI–XIV)* (Venezia: Marsilio, 2007), p. 95. Daniele Calcagno, "Il Sacro Catino specchio dell' identità genovese," *Xenia Antiqua* 10 (2001), pp. 49–54.

35. Calcagno, "Il Sacro Catino," p. 50.

36. Maria Montesano, "Da Genova a Parigi, da Parigi a Genova: Il furto e il ritorno del Mandylion nel primo Cinquecento," in *Mandylion*, pp. 285–91.

37. A bull of Sixtus IV in the same year mentions the Mandylion; see Colette Dufour Bozzo, *Il 'Sacro Volto' di Genova* (Rome: Istituto Nazionale d'Archeologia e Storia dell'Arte, 1974), p. 64. Dufour Bozzo also suggests that the silence proves that Montaldo did not receive the relic as a gift but stole it. She mentions a document of 1388 confirming receipt of the relic at San Bartolomeo but concedes that it cannot be found anymore. It has also been argued that the relic was held privately and enjoyed no official civic status in the fifteenth century; see Valeria Polonio, "A Genova tra XIV e XV secolo: Icone e reliquie d' oltremare," in *Mandylion*, p. 125.

38. Montesano, "Da Genova a Parigi, da Parigi a Genova," p. 290.

39. Alberto Rizzi, "La Madonna Nicopeia," *Quaderni della Soprintendenza ai Beni artistici e storici di Venezia* 8 (1979), p. 11–21; Rizzi, "Un'icona constantinopolitana del XII secolo a Venezia: la Madonna

Nicopeia," *Thesaurismata* 17 (1980), pp. 290–306; and Martin Schulz, "Die Nicopea in San Marco: Zur Geschichte und zum Typ einer Ikone," *Byzantinische Zeitschrift* 91 (1998), pp. 475–501.

40. Grażyna Jurkowlaniec, "Cult and Patronage: the *Madonna della Clemenza*, the Altemps and a Polish Canon in Rome," *Zeitschrift für Kunstgeschichte* 72 (2009), pp. 69–98, here 69–70. Jurkowlaniec dismisses a pair of ambiguous references from the seventh century and ca. 900; Gerhard Wolf is more open to the possibility that they refer to the Santa Maria in Trastevere icon; "Icons and Sites: Cult Images of the Virgin in Medieval Rome," in Maria Vassilaki (ed.), *Images of the Mother of God: Perceptions of the Theotokos in Byzantium* (Aldershot, UK: Ashgate, 2005), pp. 38–39.

41. Steven Ostrow, *Art and Spirituality in Counter-Reformation Rome: The Sistine and Pauline Chapels in S. Maria Maggiore* (Cambridge: Cambridge University Press, 1996), pp. 24–25.

42. Marilyn Aronberg Lavin, "Images of a Miracle: Federico Barocci and the Porziuncula Indulgence," *Artibus et historiae* 54 (2006), pp. 9–49.

43. Adolf Gottschewski, *Die Fresken des Antoniazzo Romano im Sterbezimmer der heiligen Catarina von Siena zu S. Maria sopra Minerva* (Strasbourg: Heitz, 1904), pp. 7–8. Gisela Noehles, "Antoniazzo Romano: Studien zur Quattrocentomalerei in Rom," PhD diss., University of Münster, 1973, pp. 239–41. See also Cavallaro, *Antoniazzo Romano e gli Antoniazzeschi*, no. 76.

44. Ricci, *Virginis Mariae Loretae Historia*, p. 56.

45. *Ibid.*, pp. 58 and 44–45. There is archeological evidence that the putative house of the Virgin in Nazareth had been transformed into a shrine in early Christian times.

46. Dickinson, *The Shrine of Our Lady of Walsingham*. The dimensions of the replica at Walsingham do not match the Holy House at Loreto.

47. Ricci, *Virginis Mariae Loretae Historia*, p. 63.

48. Nichols (ed.), *The Marvels of Rome*, pp. 29–30. On the Solomonic origins of the columns in St. Peter's, see Dale Kinney, "Spolia," pp. 29–30 and 35. The connection to the Jewish temple seems to emerge in the fifteenth century. On the spiral columns generally, see Toynbee and Perkins, *The Shrine of St. Peter and the Vatican Excavations*, pp. 247–50.

49. Ricci, *Virginis Mariae Loretae Historia*, pp. 65–66. In fact there had been a Marian cult site in that forest since at least 1194.

50. Dickinson, *The Shrine of Our Lady of Walsingham*, pp. 124–30. The unique copy of the imprint is preserved at Magdalene College, Cambridge. Later records name a patron, Richelde of Fervaques, and date the foundation to the twelfth century.

51. Francesco Suriano, for example, a Franciscan pilgrim to the Holy Land, doubted the Loretan legend because Joseph and Mary, he had learned, had lived in a rock-hewn cave, not a house; see Scaraffia, *Loreto*, pp. 45–46.

52. Ricci, *Virginis Mariae Loretae Historia*, pp. 116–17: "Sed quid loquor: transportaretur? Non enim immobile transportatur. Cur ergo incredibilia refero? Eloquor an sileam? Sed bonum est opera Dei revelare."

53. *Ibid.*, pp. 106–107.

54. *Ibid.*, p. 61; cf. Hueffer, *Loreto*, vol. 1, p. 28.

55. Ricci, *Virginis Mariae Loretae Historia*, p. 38.

56. *Ibid.*, p. 60.

57. Interestingly, Erasmus published in 1523 a mass to the Virgin of Loreto, not mentioning of course the flying house; *Collected Works of Erasmus*, vols. 85–86 (Toronto: University of Toronto Press, 1993), pp. 360–63. See also *Collected Works of Erasmus*, vol. 40, p. 659 n.75, on Erasmus's many compositions in praise of the Virgin, including several prayers embedded in the colloquy that mocks the shrine at Walsingham (see section 1 above).

58. Vienna, Albertina, inventory no. AZ Italien 118. The drawing must date from the period of the construction of the encasing marble structure, even if the script at the top is rather later. See Mario Luni, "Le fasi edilizie del Sacello della Santa Casa di Loreto alla luce dei recenti restauri," in Floriano Grimaldi (ed.), *Il Sacello della Santa Casa* (Loreto: Cassa di Risparmio di

Loreto, [1991]), pp. 74–76, fig. 2; Nereo Alfieri et al., "Gli scavi nella Santa Casa di Loreto e il problema delle origini," in Ferdinando Citterio and Luciano Vaccaro (eds.), *Loreto: Crocevia religiosa tra Italia, Europa ed Oriente* (Brescia: Morcelliana, 1997), pp. 427–40, fig. 83.

59. On the possibility that topography or other conditions dictated the alignment of the basilica, see Monelli and Santarelli, *La basilica di Loreto e la sua reliquia*, pp. 81–83. Monelli agrees, however, p. 83, that the misalignment of the house demonstrates that it was *intangibile, inamovibile*. He makes the same point in *La Santa Casa*, pp. 165–69.

60. On the Capitoline temple, see Dionysius of Halicarnassus, *Roman Antiquities* 3.69.5; Livy, *Ab urbe condita* 1.55.3–4; Ovid, *Fasti* 2.667–70; and Servius, *Commentary on the* Aeneid *of Virgil* 9.448. For bibliography and an account of the latest archeological findings, see Margherita Albertoni (ed.), *Il tempio di Giove e le origini del Colle capitolino* (Milan: Electa, 2008). Joseph Rykwert discusses these and other examples and concludes that "the Etruscans, as well as the Romans, seemed to cultivate such irregularities as tokens or even assertions of the primitive and rustic sanctity of their urban temples"; see *The Dancing Column: On Order in Architecture* (Cambridge, MA: The MIT Press, 1996), p. 359.

61. Hansen argues that misalignment, obliquity, and imprecision in such early medieval churches as Santa Costanza, the Lateran basilica, Santo Stefano Rotondo, and San Lorenzo fuori le Mura, even if not strictly deliberate, complied with the overall period sensibility and taste for obscurity and may have even been understood as registrations of the mystical referentiality of the churches; see *Eloquence of Appropriation*, pp. 220–21.

62. The project was initiated by Julius II although Weil-Garris found no evidence that construction was underway before 1513 and only "sparse" evidence of Bramante's involvement. Kathleen Weil-Garris, "The Santa Casa di Loreto: Problems in Cinquecento Sculpture," PhD diss., Harvard University, 1965, pp. 6–11.

63. Arnaldo Bruschi, "Loreto: Città santuario e cantiere artistico," in Ferdinando Citterio and Luciano Vaccaro (eds.), *Loreto: Crocevia religiosa tra Italia, Europa ed Oriente* (Brescia: Morcelliana, 1997), pp. 441–70. See also Nanni Monelli, *"Architettore" e architettura rinascimentale per la Santa Casa di Loreto* (Loreto: Congregazione universale della Santa Casa, 2001).

64. Werner Oechslin and Anja Buschow Oechslin, *Die Kunstdenkmäler des Kantons Schwyz*, vol. 3 (Bern: Gesellschaft für Schweizerische Kunstgeschichte, 2003).

65. *Meister E. S.: Ein oberrheinischer Kupferstecher der Spätgotik* (Munich: Staatliche Graphische Sammlung, 1987), nos. 31–33. Barbara Welzel, "Die Engelweihe in Einsiedeln und die Kupferstiche vom Meister E. S.," *Städel-Jahrbuch* N. F. 15 (1995), pp. 121–44.

66. Oechslin and Buschow Oechslin, *Die Kunstdenkmäler des Kantons Schwyz*, fig. 199.

67. Linus Birchler confirms that Meinrad's cell could not be moved, *Die Kunstdenkmäler des Kantons Schwyz*, vol. 1, *Einsiedeln, Höfe und March* (Basel: Birkhäuser, 1927), p. 29.

68. Oechslin and Buschow Oechslin, *Die Kunstdenkmäler des Kantons Schwyz*, p. 375.

NINETEEN — THE TITULUS CRUCIS

1. Stefano Infessura gives the date February 1, 1492; see Oreste Tommasini (ed.), *Diaro della Città di Roma di Stefano Infessura* (Rome, 1890), pp. 269–71. Other sources give the date as the last Sunday in January. Granada fell in early January but the news did not arrive until some weeks later; see Francesca Cappelletti, "L'affresco nel catino absidale di Santa Croce in Gerusalemme a Roma: La fonte iconografica, la committenza e la datazione," *Storia dell'arte* 66 (1989), p. 124 and Meredith J. Gill, "Antoniazzo Romano and the Recovery of Jerusalem in Late Fifteenth-Century Rome," *Storia dell'arte* 83 (1995), pp. 32–33.

2. "[O]b demselben altar [i.e., the high altar] in einem fenster...ist auch die überschrift des heiligen

creutz, daran stet: Jhesus Nazarenus rex Judaeorum."
Wilhelm Vogt (ed.), *Niklas Muffels Beschreibung der
Stadt Rom*, Bibliothek des litterarischen Vereins in
Stuttgart, 128 (Tübingen, 1876), p. 35. Pero Tafur noted
the presence of the Titulus at Santa Croce in 1436 but
did not claim to have seen it; see Tafur, *Travels and
Adventures*, p. 41.

3. Good photos of the object are published in
Maria Luisa Rigato, "'Titulus crucis': Reliquia custodita
nella Basilica Santa Croce in Gerusalemme a Roma,"
in L. Padovese (ed.), *Atti del VII Simposio di Efeso su
S. Giovanni Apostolo* (Rome: Istituto Francescano di
Spiritualità, Pontificio Ateneo Antoniano, 1999),
pp. 333–36.

4. Cf. Luke 23:38, which gives a different sequence
of languages, and Matthew 27:37 and Mark 15:26,
which give a version of the text in Greek only. All
four texts give the core phrase "King of the Jews"; as a
prefix to these words Luke adds "this is"; Matthew adds
"this is Jesus"; and John adds "Jesus the Nazorean."

5. Carsten Peter Thiede and Matthew d'Ancona,
The Quest for the True Cross (London: Weidenfeld and
Nicolson, 2000), pp. 58 and 91, arguing for the authen-
ticity of the relic, as does Michael Hesemann, *Die
Jesus-Tafel: Die Entdeckung der Kreuz-Inschrift* (Freiburg:
Herder, 1999).

6. Francesco Bella and Carlo Azzi, "^{14}c Dating
of the 'Titulus Crucis,'" *Radiocarbon* 44 (2002),
pp. 685–89.

7. Anna Pontani points out, however, that there
is no secure documentation of the presence of the
Titulus relic at Santa Croce before 1492. The box with
the seal of Caccianemici was not preserved. See "Note
sull' esegesi e l'iconografia del *Titulus crucis*," *Aevum:
Rassegni di scienze storiche linguistiche e filologiche* 77
(2003), p. 150.

8. Christopher S. Wood, *Forgery Replica Fiction:
Temporalities of German Renaissance Art* (Chicago:
University of Chicago Press, 2008), pp. 128–35.

9. On Renaissance epigraphy, see Roberto Weiss,
The Renaissance Discovery of Classical Antiquity, 2nd ed.

(Oxford: Blackwell, 1988), and Ida Calabi Limentani,
"Primi orientamenti per una storia dell'epigrafia latina
classica," *Acme* 19 (1966), pp. 155–219.

10. Johann Burchard, *Johannis Burchardi Diarium
sive Rerum Urbanarum Commentarii (1483–1506)*, ed. Louis
Thuasne, vol. 1 (Paris: Leroux, 1883), pp. 449–50;
Liber Notarum, ed. Enrico Celani, vol. 1 (S. Lapi, 1907),
p. 341.

11. See the discussion and transcription of Leonardo da Sarzana's letters of 1492 in n.36 below.

12. Bruce M. Metzger, *Textual Commentary on the
Greek New Testament*, 4th ed. (Stuttgart: Deutsche
Bibelgesellschaft, 1994), p. 217. See also Thiede and
d'Ancona, *Quest for the True Cross*, pp. 81–83. Erasmus's
Greek New Testament and, following this, the Autho-
rized Version give Hebrew, Greek, and Latin; one
might wonder whether Erasmus had been influenced
in his choice by extraphilological evidence, namely the
Titulus itself. Luke 23:38 reports a completely different
sequence of languages: Greek, Latin, and Hebrew.

13. On medieval reconstructions of the trilingual
Titulus, see Pontani, "Note sull' esegesi e l'iconografia
del *Titulus crucis*," pp. 159–67.

14. One cannot reject the possibility that the
twelfth-century forgers were copying a much older
artifact, perhaps a fourth-century forgery; perhaps
a fourth-century copy of the original Titulus; perhaps
even the Titulus itself.

15. The most damning is the omission of the Greek
ho, or "the," before "King of the Jews."

16. Regensburg, Diözesanmuseum, inv. no. L
1982/18 a, b, c. *Ratisbona Sacra: Das Bistum Regensburg
im Mittelalter*, exhibition catalogue, Diözesanmuseum
Obermünster (Munich: Schnell & Steiner, 1989), no.
66. See also Franz Fuchs, "Die Regensburger Diony-
siussteine vom Jahre 1049," in Renate Neumüllers-
Klauser (ed.), *Vom Quellenwert der Inschriften: Fachtagung Esslingen 1990* (Heidelberg: Winter, 1992), p. 150
n.24.

17. The text of the inscription on the lid of the
reliquary was preserved by Emmanuele Cicogna, *Delle

iscrizioni Veneziane vol. 1 (Venice: Orlandelli, 1824), p. 90.

18. Leo Planiscig, *Andrea Riccio* (Vienna: Schroll, 1927), pp. 211–34.

19. Munich, Bayerische Staatsbibliothek, Rar. 287 = Cim. 187, fol. 334r–334v. See the online catalogue: http://daten.digitale-sammlungen.de/~db/0010/ bsb00102722/images/. The sheet on fol. 334r shares a watermark with a map published in Nuremberg in 1492 by Erhard Etzlaub. The print is reproduced in Beatrice Hernad, *Die Graphiksammlung des Humanisten Hartmann Schedel* (Munich: Prestel, 1990), p. 55, fig. 25, and in Rainer Budde and Roland Krischel (eds.), *Genie ohne Namen: der Meister des Bartholomäus-Altars*, exhibition catalogue (Cologne: DuMont, 2001), p. 410. The print on fol. 334v is reproduced in *Genie ohne Namen*, p. 408.

20. "…ist dits die breyt lenng und grosse von der tafel und gleich alle buchstaben und form als dann in dem pret gegraben sint als ich dann mit meinen augen hab gesehen und es ist vast pöß zulesen wann die wurm haben es durchfressen…" (text from woodcut on Rar. 287, fol. 334v). The two woodcuts give different information about the lettering on the titulus relic, however, and thus seem to follow different models, perhaps drawings brought or sent from Rome. The text below the woodcut on fol. 334r is similar, describing the discovery of the relic and testifying to the accuracy of the representation, but omitting the comment about the worms. The print on fol. 334v, although claiming more insistently its eyewitness status, makes a greater effort to complete the Hebrew lettering at the top edge and extends the truncated letter at the end of the Greek line into a BA.

21. An Augsburg broadsheet dated 1493 gives the news of the discovery and a woodcut image of a trilingual tablet, but with no fidelity to the actual relic. *Genie ohne Namen*, no. 78, pp. 408–409. All the prints, even the most faithful, render the Latin line as "Nazarenus," following the Gospel, whereas the titulus relic itself reads "Nazarinus."

22. Gad Sarfatti, Anna Pontani, and Stefano Zamponi, "Titulus Crucis," in Marco Ciatti and Max Seidel (eds.), *Giotto: The Santa Maria Novella Crucifix* (Florence: Edifir, 2001), pp. 191–202.

23. Rüdiger Fuchs (ed.), *Die Inschriften der Stadt Worms*, Die Deutschen Inschriften, vol. 29 (Wiesbaden: Reichert, 1991), no. 331, fig. 92a.

24. Cologne, Wallraf-Richartz-Museum, inventory no. WRM 180. *Genie ohne Namen*, no. 62, pp. 376–77.

25. Philadelphia Museum of Art, John G. Johnson Collection, no. 744. *Genie ohne Namen*, no. 77, pp. 406–407. See also nos. 75 and 80, *Depositions from the Cross* by the same master in Paris and London that depict the titulus but not in compliance with the relic. Mauro Lucco compares the Paris picture to Giovanni Bellini's *Correr Crucifixion*, whose titulus derives its Greek text from a variant textual tradition; see "Greek Inscriptions in Two Venetian Renaissance Paintings," *Journal of the Warburg and Courtauld Institutes* 60 (1997), pp. 111–29. Renate Schumacher-Wolfgarten discusses the Cologne painting but seems unaware of the same master's other versions as well as of the prints; see "Eine römische Passionsreliquie, Präsentation und Indienstnahme. Zum Kreuz-Altar des Bartholomäus-meister in Köln," in Ulrike Lange and Reiner Sörries (eds.), *Vom Orient bis an den Rhein*, Festschrift Peter Poscharsky (Dettelbach: Röll, 1997), pp. 257–75.

26. Pisa, Museo Nazionale di San Matteo, no. 1723. The Greek inscription gives the Biblical *Nazoraios*, however, rather than the spelling of the relic. Gozzoli was active in Pisa until 1494. See Diane Cole Ahl, *Benozzo Gozzoli* (New Haven, CT: Yale University Press, 1996), pp. 268–69, fig. 322.

27. José Joaquin Yarza Luaces, "El Retablo Mayor de la Cartuja de Miraflores," in *Actas del Congreso Internacional sobre Gil Siloe y la escultura de su época* (Burgos: Centro Cultural "Casa del Cordon," 2001), pp. 207–38.

28. This picture of the 1510s is the name-piece of the Lower Bavarian Master of the Oberaltaicher Schmerzensmann. See Christian A. zu Salm and Gisela Goldberg, *Altdeutsche Malerei*, Alte Pinakothek München, Katalog II (Munich: Bruckmann, 1963),

pp. 141–42; Avraham Ronen, "Iscrizioni ebraiche nell'arte italiana del Quattrocento," in *Studi di storia dell'arte sul medioevo e il rinascimento*, vol. 2, Festschrift Mario Salmi (Florence: Polistampa, 1992), pp. 601–24, here p. 606, fig. 6.

29. New York, Pierpont Morgan Library, no. 1950.1. *100 Master Drawings from the Morgan Library and Museum* (Munich: Hirmer, 2008), no. 63. Fedja Anzelewsky, "Eine Gruppe von Malern und Zeichnern aus Dürers Jugendjahren," *Jahrbuch der Berliner Museen* 27 (1985), pp. 35–59.

30. Tilman Falk, *Katalog der Zeichnungen des 15. und 16. Jahrhunderts im Kupferstichkabinett Basel* (Basel: Schwabe, 1979), p. 54, no. 44, fig. 17. R. S. Field (ed.), *Illustrated Bartsch (Supplement), German Single Leaf Woodcuts before 1500*, vol. 162, *Anonymous Artists (.401–.735)* (New York: Abaris, 1989), nos. 661 and 669. *Die Karlsruher Passion*, exhibition catalogue, Staatliche Kunsthalle Karlsruhe (Ostfildern-Ruit bei Stuttgart: Hatje, 1996), p. 165 and fig. 11. These works are hard to date; it cannot be excluded that they all postdate the discovery of the titulus relic, even if none of them shows a scribe preparing an object resembling the panel found in Rome.

31. The backward majuscule N is frequently found in fifteenth-century German inscriptions in paintings and elsewhere, including representations of the Crucifixion; see for example the panel from Kempten, dated to the 1460s, in the Germanisches National-museum, Nuremberg, reproduced in Mitchell B. Merback, *The Thief, the Cross, and the Wheel: Pain and the Spectacle of Punishment in Medieval and Renaissance Europe* (London: Reaktion, 1999), p. 118, fig. 50. The strange form suggested ancient and exotic origins; see Renate Neumüllers-Klauser, "Epigraphische Schriften zwischen Mittelalter und Neuzeit," in *Epigraphik 1988, Fachtagung für mittelalterliche und neuzeitliche Epigraphik, Österreichische Akademie der Wissenschaften, Philosophisch-historische Klasse, Denkschriften*, vol. 213, Walter Koch (ed.) (Vienna: Österreichische Akademie der Wissenschaften, 1990), pp. 315–28.

32. Paul L. Meier, "The Inscription on the Cross of Jesus of Nazareth," *Hermes* 124 (1996), p. 65.

33. See Ernst Bammel, "The Titulus," in Ernst Bammel and C. F. D. Moule (eds.), *Jesus and the Politics of his Day* (Cambridge: Cambridge University Press, 1984), pp. 353–64, here 360.

34. *Etymologiae* 9.1.3.

35. Burchard, in his entry dated March 12, 1492, described the artifact as *semiconsumpta*; see *Johannis Burchardi Diarium*, pp. 449–50 and *Liber Notarum*, vol. 1, p. 341. Infessura's account of the missing letters is confusing: "[S]ed illud IUDEORUM non erat perfectum, quia illud RUM non erat nisi usque ad R inclusive. Illud UM ceciderat, ut dixi, quia erat ab ea parte corrosa et vetustate defecit"; see *Diario della Città di Roma di Stefano Infessura*, p. 270. This observation is strangely at variance with all the other accounts of the state of the inscription. Unless Mendoza gave a really significant portion of the relic to Girolamo Donato (see above), and the Titulus relic found in the wall niche in 1492 was therefore originally wider by several inches, Infessura carelessly mistook the R at the left edge of the lowest line as part of the word IUDEORUM rather than the beginning of REX.

36. A faulty transcription of these letters can be found in Gaetano Marini, *Degli Archiatri Pontificij*, vol. 2 (Rome: Pagliarini, 1784), pp. 238–44. We provide new transcriptions here. Letter of February 4 from Leonardo da Sarzana in Rome to Jacobus Volaterranus, otherwise known as Giacomo Gherardi, papal nuntio of Innocent VIII in Florence; Vatican Library, Vat. Lat. 3912, fol. 43v.: "Titulus Graecus, & Latinus haud facile, etiam a peritissimis earum linguarum, legi poterat. Sunt enim figurati eo ordine scribendi retrogrado, quo et litterae hebraicae conscribuntur. Ex quo et major fides et religio huic rei adhibenda videtur. Primo namque ordini litterarum Hebraicarum inscribendi modo contrarie noluerunt." And the letter of the February 14, fol. 44v.: "Titulus ipsum sanctae Crucis, in palincesto figuratum, eisdem characteribus, ea litterarum longitudine, et scriptionis retrogradae

ordine, ut Hebrei solent, & quantum in ipso veneran-
dissimo Ligno reperitur, paucis post diebus, quam ad
ipsam Paternitatem tuam scripseram, ad Magnificum
Laurentium Medices, certum peritorum Virorum
confugium, misi."

37. Leonardo da Sarzana to Giacomo Gherardi,
February 14, 1492, Vat. Lat. 3912, fol. 44v.: "Domini
Antistiti Aretino [Gentile Becchi], Pico, Acciajolo,
Politiano me deditissimum esse ostendes, quibus & me
diligenter commendabis." Gherardi often functioned
as a go-between for Poliziano in relation to humanist
scholars elsewhere. See *Dispacci e lettere di Giacomo
Gherardi nunzio pontificio a Firenze e Milano*, ed. Enrico
Carusi (Rome: Tipografia Poliglota Vaticana, 1909),
pp. xlvii, lvii, 369, and 391. Poliziano, moreover, was
a friend of Girolamo Donato, who received a piece of
the Titulus relic from Mendoza.

38. Kathleen Weil-Garris Brandt et al. (eds.),
Giovinezza di Michelangelo (Florence and Milan:
ArtificioSkira, 1999), no. 36, p. 288.

39. Alessandro Parronchi, "Titulus Crucis,"
Antichità Viva 4 (1966), pp. 41–42. Signorelli made
two paintings for Lorenzo de' Medici around 1490,
the now-lost *Pan* and the *Medici Madonna* in the Uffizi,
although it is possible that he came to know about
the relic independently.

40. The Greek on the Titulus relic would appear
to be a simple transliteration of the Latin. Thiede,
believing the relic to be real, argued for the plausibility
of the Greek spelling on the tablet; see Thiede, *Quest
for the True Cross*, pp. 96–97. His arguments were
severely criticized by Pontani; see "Note sull' esegesi
e l'iconografia del *Titulus crucis*," p. 148 n.36. Note
that Giotto's titulus at Santa Maria Novella gave the
nonscriptural ναζαρινος.

41. Many thanks to Peter Schäfer of Princeton
University and Elizabeth Eisenberg, M.A. Candidate
at the Institute of Fine Arts, New York University,
for their help with the Hebrew inscription.

42. Note the careful copy of the Titulus—with
the Hebrew line filled out at the top, however—by

Francisco de Holanda in his *Codex Escurialensis*; see
Rodolfo Lanciani, *Storia degli scavi di Roma*, vol. 1
(Rome: Quasar, 1989), p. 116, fig. 47.

43. Walther Dolch (ed.), *Bibliographie der Öster-
reichischen Drucke des XV. und XVI. Jahrhunderts*, vol. 1,
no. 1, *Trient—Wien—Schrattenthal* (Vienna: Gilhofer
and Ranschburg, 1913), p. 47, no. 29.

44. The other inscriptions on the sheet, composed
by a humanist scholar, perhaps Conrad Celtis or Johann
Cuspinian, who both worked with the printer Winterburger, read: "Behold the figures sent down from the
height of heaven, those which the mystical hand of God
had given to Moses. Following this language are the
Greek and Latin characters, which, joined to [the letter
of] Jerusalem, your cross, Christ, carried. Therefore let
us worship these little marks on account of the triple
power of the divine, lest the savage trident of Jupiter do
us harm." Thanks to Kyle Mahoney for assistance with
the translation.

45. Carl Wehmer (ed.), *Leonhard Wagners Proba
centum scripturarum*, 2 vols. (Leipzig: Insel, 1963).

TWENTY — THE FABRICATION
OF VISUAL EVIDENCE

1. G. F. Hill, *A Corpus of Italian Medals of the Renaissance* (London: British Museum, 1930), pp. 231–32,
nos. 898–901 and 903. See also Georg Habich, "Zum
Medaillen-Porträt Christi," *Archiv für Medaillen- und
Plaketten-Kunde* 2 (1920–21), pp. 69–78; G. F. Hill,
Medallic Portraits of Christ (Oxford: Clarendon Press,
1920); Philine Helas, "Lo 'smeraldo' smarrito, ossia
il 'vero profilo' di Cristo," in Giovanni Morello and
Gerhard Wolf (eds), *Il Volto di Cristo*, exhibition catalogue (Milan: Electa, 2000) pp. 215–26; Gerhard Wolf,
*Schleier und Spiegel: Traditionen des Christusbildes und
die Bildkonzepte der Renaissance* (Munich: Fink, 2002),
pp. 298–302. It is not certain which artist stands behind
the medal type. Luke Syson, National Gallery, London,
in oral communication, attributes the entire series to
Niccolò Fiorentino.

2. Hill, *Corpus of Italian Medals of the Renaissance*, no. 898.

3. Byzantine cameos and intaglio gems with images of Christ did exist; for example, see the green jasper cameo of Christ, full-length and holding a book, eleventh century; Alice Bank (ed.), *Byzantine Art in the Collections of Soviet Museums* (Leningrad: Aurora, 1985), fig. 165.

4. See the authoritative discussion by Helas, "Lo 'smeraldo' smarrito ossia il 'vero profilo' di Cristo," in Morello and Wolf (eds.), *Il Volto di Cristo*, pp. 216–17, and catalogue 5.6.

5. Maria Pia Billanovich, "Falsi epigrafici," *Italia medioevale e umanistica* 10 (1967), pp. 25–110.

6. See the five-volume symposium proceedings *Fälschungen im Mittelalter*, Monumenta Germanica Historica, Schriften, vol. 33 (Hannover: Hahn, 1988). Not a single contribution in these volumes addressed sculpture or painting.

7. "I'm flummoxed [*cedo per deos flumini*] as to how you have come to the conclusion that it is a bust of Socrates or who on earth said this to you. It should certainly have a 'snub nose and protruding eyes' [Plato *Theaetetus* 209c], and it should look like a satyr, for these, they say, were his distinguishing features. I'd really like to learn this from you. For a statue of one of the Roman emperors or indeed of certain Greeks, even if damaged, can be easily identified by means of the coins of them which survive." Translation by Andrew Gregory and Jonathan Woolfson, "Aspects of Collecting in Renaissance Padua: A Bust of Socrates for Niccolò Leonico Tomeo," *Journal of the Warburg and Courtauld Institutes* 58 (1995), pp. 264–65.

8. William Stenhouse, *Reading Inscriptions and Writing Ancient History: Historical Scholarship in the Late Renaissance* (London: Institute of Classical Studies, University of London School of Advanced Study, 2005), pp. 101–102.

9. For these passages, see Lorenzo Valla, *On the Donation of Constantine*, trans. G. W. Bowersock, I Tatti Renaissance Library (Cambridge, MA: Harvard University Press, 2007), pp. 59, 63, and 53, as well as the passage on inscriptions on "old stones, bronze tablets, or coins" as evidence of the authority of the Roman Senate and people, p. 69; or Lorenzo Valla, *Discourse on the Forgery of the Alleged Donation of Constantine*, trans. Christopher B. Coleman (New Haven, CT: Yale University Press, 1922), pp. 75, 81, 70–71 and 87.

10. "Yet for all my agonizing about this, I am not a difficult or ill-mannered person and firmly believe that it is none other than Socrates, the son of Sophronicus and the teacher of Plato, the man, if you like, who died in prison at Athens after drinking hemlock. Just make sure that I get the statue…" Gregory and Woolfson, "Bust of Socrates," p. 265.

11. For the correspondence, which was credited by Jerome and Augustine, see M. R. James, *The Apocryphal New Testament* (Oxford: Oxford University Press, 1924), pp. 480–84.

12. Anthony Grafton, *Forgers and Critics: Creativity and Duplicity in Western Scholarship* (Princeton, NJ: Princeton University Press, 1990).

13. Hill, *Corpus of Italian Medals of the Renasance*, no. 162.

14. There are portraits of Christ on coins from the seventh century, but these had no influence on the Renaissance tradition; see Hill, *Medallic Portraits of Christ*, p. 11.

15. Ernst von Dobschütz, "Zum Lentulus-Briefe," *Zeitschrift für wissenschaftliche Theologie* 42 (1899), pp. 457–66.

16. Munich, Staatliche Graphische Sammlung, inventory no. 118193. The sheet is a unicum and the woodcut is hand-colored. F. W. H. Hollstein, *German Engravings, Etchings, and Woodcuts, ca. 1400–1700*, 68 vols. (Amsterdam: Hertzberger, 1954–), vol. 5, no. 55. *Hans Burgkmair: Das Graphische Werk*, exhibition catalogue (Augsburg, Städtische Kunstsammlungen: 1973), no. 8.

17. "Hanc Epistolam scripsit pilatus a jherusalem in Romam Tyberio et toti senatui. Apparuit temporibus nostris et ad huc est homo magne virtutis: cui nomen

est cristus jesus: suscitans mortuos: et sanans languores: Qui dicitur propheta veritatis: quem discipuli eius vocant filium dei: homo quidem statura procerus et spectabilis: vultum habens venerabilem: quem intuentes possunt diligere et formidare: capillos habens coloris nucis avelane premature planos vere usque ad aures: ab auribus vero crispos aliquantum et ceruliores et fulgentiores ab humeris ventilantes: discrimen habens in medio capitis iuxta morem nazarenorum: faciem habens sine ruga aliqua et macula: quam rubor moderatus venustat: nasi et oris nulla prorsus est reprehensio: oculis varijs glancis et claris existentibus: Barbam habens copiosam et non longam: scilicet capillis concolorem et impuberem sed in medio bifurcatam[:] manus habens et brachia visu delectabilia[:] in increpatione terribilis. in ammonitione placidus et amabilis: hylaris servata gravitate[:] qui nunquam visus est ridere: flere autem: Sic in colloquio rarus et modestus. speciosus inter filios hominum." *Hans Burgkmair: Das Graphische Werk*, no. 8. Thanks to Ashley West for help with the Latin translation.

18. The text still appeared without a framing device in the earliest editions of the letter. See Dobschütz, *Christusbilder*, pp. 308–10**.

19. Valla, *On the Donation of Constantine*, pp. 120–21; Valla, *Discourse on the Forgery of the Alleged Donation of Constantine*, pp. 142–43: "Huic simile est, quamquam decem milia huiusmodi Rome sunt, quod inter religiosa demonstratur in tabella effigies Petri et Pauli, quam Silvester Constantino ab eisdem apostolis in somnis admonito in confirmationem visionis exhibuit. Non hoc dico, quia negem effigies illas esse apostolorum — utinamque tam vera esset epistola nomine Lentuli missa de effigie Christiquae non minus improbe ementita est quam privilegium quod confutavimus! — sed quia tabella illa a Sylvestro non fuerit exhibita Constantino; in quo non sustineo admirationem animi mei continere." On the Peter and Paul panels, which date from the eighth century, see Hans Belting, *Likeness and Presence: A History of the Image before the Era of Art* (Chicago: University of Chicago Press, 1994), p. 121, fig. 73.

The panels, bust portraits, measure 8.5 x 5.8 cm.

20. Christopher S. Wood, *Forgery Replica Fiction: Temporalities of German Renaissance Art* (Chicago: University of Chicago Press, 2008), pp. 1–7, 11–12, 111 and 241.

21. Annius, *De marmoreis Volturrhenis tabulis*. See Roberto Weiss, "An Unknown Epigraphic Tract by Annius of Viterbo," in C. P. Brand (ed.), *Italian Studies Presented to E. R. Vincent* (Cambridge: Heffer, 1962), pp. 101–20. For more on Annius, see Walter Stephens, "Berosus Chaldeus: Counterfeit and Fictive Editors of the Early Sixteenth Century," PhD diss., Cornell University, 1979, and Anthony Grafton, *Defenders of the Text: The Traditions of Scholarship in an Age of Science, 1450–1800* (Cambridge, MA: Harvard University Press, 1991), pp. 76–103.

22. *Corpus Inscriptionum Latinarum*, vol. 11 (Berlin, 1863), 1.347*. Italo Faldi, *Museo Civico di Viterbo* (Viterbo, 1955), no. 40; Brian Curran, "*De sacrarum litterarum aegyptiorum interpretatione*: Reticence and Hubris in Hieroglyphic Studies of the Renaissance: Pierio Valeriano and Annius of Viterbo," *Memoirs of the American Academy in Rome* 43–44 (1998–99), pp. 139–82, here 172–77, and *The Egyptian Renaissance: The Afterlife of Ancient Egypt in Early Modern Italy* (Chicago: University of Chicago Press, 2007), pp. 121–31.

23. *Corpus Inscriptionum Latinarum*, vol. 11, 1.339*.

24. Faldi, *Museo Civico di Viterbo*, no. 38; Weiss, "An Unknown Epigraphic Tract by Annius of Viterbo," p. 119 n.53; Brian Curran, "The *Hypnerotomachia Poliphili* and Renaissance Egyptology," *Word and Image* 14 (1998), pp. 165–69, fig. 17; Curran, "*De sacrarum litterarum aegyptiorum interpretatione*," pp. 172–76 and fig. 10; and Curran, *The Egyptian Renaissance*, pp. 125–28 and fig. 47.

25. Annius, *Antiquitatum variarum volumina XVII* (Paris, 1512), fol. 26r; see also his *Auctores vetustissimi* (Rome, 1498), fol. f I r–f III v.

26. Paola Mattiangeli, "Annio da Viterbo ispiratore di cicli pittorici," in *Annio da Viterbo: Documenti e ricerche*, vol. 1 (Rome: Consiglio Nazionale delle

Ricerche, 1981), pp. 257–339 and esp. 297–301. The oak itself was the letter of Osiris. The lizard or crocodile symbolized evil, that is, the Giants. The birds, finally, were the Italians who appealed to Osiris for help; and so forth. Annius also believed he saw an eye in the branches of the tree. A tablet with an explanatory inscription was appended to the object in 1587.

27. Curran rightly compares them to the profile heads on the pulpit at Ravello in Campania; see "The *Hypnerotomachia Poliphili* and Renaissance Egyptology," n.76. That pulpit dates from about 1270 and has been attributed to Niccolò di Bartolommeo da Foggia, an artist not far from Niccolò Pisano; John Pope-Hennessy, *Italian Gothic Sculpture* (London: Phaidon, 1996), p. 12; Lachenal, *Spolia*, p. 332 and plate 35.

28. Giorgio Vasari, *Vite de' più eccellenti pittori scultori e architettori*, vol. 1, ed. Rosanna Bettarini (Florence: Sansoni, 1966–1969), p. 220.

29. Riccardo Fubini compares Annius's forged Viterban inscriptions to the etymological "nuclei" that linked the distant traditions and confirmed his historical theories; see "Annio da Viterbo nella tradizione erudita toscana," in Riccardo Fubini (ed.), *Storiografia dell'Umanesimo in Italia da Leonardo Bruni ad Annio da Viterbo* (Rome: Edizioni di Storia e Letteratura, 2003), pp. 335–42 and esp. 337–38.

30. C.R. Ligota pointed out that Annius frequently noted problems in the texts he had forged; see "Annius of Viterbo and Historical Method," *Journal of the Warburg and Courtauld Institutes* 50 (1987), pp. 44–56. Either this was all part of the ruse or the texts had taken on some measure of authenticity in his eyes.

31. In addition to the literature cited in section 3, n.5, see the exhibition catalogue *Fälschungen und Fiktionen* (Munich: Bayerisches Hauptstaatsarchiv, 1986); P. Herde and A. Gawlik, "Fälschungen," in *Lexikon des Mittelalters*, vol. 4 (Munich and Zurich: Artemis, 1988), column 246ff.; and Alfred Hiatt, *The Making of Medieval Forgeries: False Documents in Fifteenth-Century England* (London: British Library; Toronto: University of Toronto Press, 2004), pp. 1–21.

32. Annius, *Antiquitatum variarum*, fol. 28v; Stephens, "Berosus Chaldeus: Counterfeit and Fictive Editors of the Early Sixteenth Century," p. 174.

TWENTY-ONE — RETROACTIVITY

1. C.R. Ligota, "Annius of Viterbo and Historical Method," *Journal of the Warburg and Courtauld Institutes* 50 (1987), p. 48.

2. Horst Bredekamp, "Der simulierte Benjamin: mittelalterliche Bemerkungen zu seiner Aktualität," in Andreas Berndt et al. (eds.), *Frankfurter Schule und Kunstgeschichte* (Berlin: Riemer, 1992), pp. 125–33.

3. Peter Parshall, "Imago contrafacta: Images and Facts in the Northern Renaissance," *Art History* 16 (1993), pp. 554–79.

4. Roberto Weiss, *The Renaissance Discovery of Classical Antiquity* (Oxford: Blackwell, 1969), pp. 178–79; Francis Haskell, *History and its Images: Art and the Interpretation of the Past* (New Haven, CT: Yale University Press, 1993), pp. 28–30; and most recently on the emergence of numismatic scholarship, Pfisterer, *Lysippus und seine Freunde*, pp. 129–203.

5. Tilman Falk, *Hans Burgkmair: Studien zu Leben und Werke des Augsburger Malers* (Munich: Bruckmann, 1968), pp. 46–47. See also ch. 2 in Ashley West, "Hans Burgkmair the Elder (1473–1531) and the Visualization of Knowledge," PhD diss., University of Pennsylvania, 2006.

6. Campbell Dodgson, "Drei neue Cäsarenköpfe Hans Burgkmairs," *Mittheilungen der Gesellschaft für vervielfältigende Kunst* 56 (1933), p. 227.

7. An idea already entertained by G. F. Hill; see *Medallic Portraits of Christ*, (Oxford: Clarendon Press, 1920), p. 36. See also Georg Habich, "Zum Medaillenporträt Christi," *Archiv für Medaillen- und Plakettenkunde* 2 (1920–1921), pp. 69–78. The proposal was recently taken up and developed by Gerhard Wolf; see "Profil Christi und Locken des Thomas: Überlegungen zum 'Nachleben' von Verrocchios Salvator und zur kunsttheoretischen Bedeutung der Gruppe,"

in Herbert Beck, Maraike Bückling, and Edgar Lein (eds.), *Die Christus-Thomas Gruppe von Andrea del Verrocchio* (Frankfurt: Henrich, 1996), pp. 197–205, and *Schleier und Spiegel: Traditionen des Christusbildes und die Bildkonzepte der Renaissance* (Munich: Fink, 2002), pp. 282–304. See also Andrew Butterfield, *The Sculptures of Andrea Verrocchio* (New Haven, CT: Yale University Press, 1997), pp. 57–80.

8. Luca Landucci, *A Florentine Diary from 1450 to 1516*, ed. Iodoco del Badia (London: Dent, 1927), p. 38. Wolf suggests that Verrocchio's Christ may itself have emerged out of a search for the true face of the Savior, in the icons; see *Schleier und Spiegel*, pp. 288–94.

9. "Nec non & fictores in effigiandis ex aere aliove metallo Deorum, aut heroum imaginibus, & numismatum inscriptionibus imprimendes utebantur. Ut cum Romae essem in felicioribus Iulij Secundi Pontificius maximi, & in Sequentibus Leonis Decimi temporibus memimi me vidissi in aeneis numismatis. Et anno praeterito in aere constatam servatoris nostri imaginem, cum litteris samaritanis, ostendit, mihi madrona illa sanctissime credita vita, cuius nomen (nec illam custitissimasque cuius aures offendam) silentio involvam cum Ferrariam per transiret [fol. 22r] navisque Venetias profectura per Padum veheret, in cuius altera numismatis, parte litterae conflatae seu percussae videbantur, qualum sensum talis erat: Messias rex venit in pace, Deus homo factus est, vel incarnatus est." Teseo Ambrogio, *Introductio in Chaldaicam linguam, Syriacam, atque Armeniam, et decem alias linguas* (Pavia: Simoneta, 1539), fol. 21v–22r. For a translation see Hill, *Medallic Portraits of Christ*, pp. 47–48. The last indications suggest that he was looking at a medal of the type represented by the medal reproduced in *Il Volto di Cristo*, cat. no. 5.11, which contains a similar inscription in Hebrew.

10. "Nuper a Con. Cel. inventum in plumbea lamina in Stiria in Colle: in quo est Ecclesia circa Sanctum Andream. Anno M.D." Petrus Apianus and Bartholomeus Amantius, *Inscriptiones sacrosanctae vetustatis* (Ingolstadt, 1534), p. 385.

11. G. F. Hill, *A Corpus of Italian Medals of the Renaissance* (London: British Museum, 1930), nos. 421–423.

12. Horst Appuhn and Christian von Heusinger, "Der Fund kleiner Andachtsbilder des 13. bis 17. Jahrhunderts in Kloster Wienhausen," *Niederdeutsche Beiträge zur Kunstgeschichte* 4 (1965), no. 88, fig. 212.

13. Max Lehrs, *Geschichte und kritischer Katalog des deutschen, niederländischen und französischen Kupferstichs im XV. Jahrhundert*, vol. 7 (Vienna: Gesellschaft für vervielfältigende Kunst, 1930), no. 3, 10.3 x 8.3 cm. See also G. F. Hill, "Renaissance Medals with the Head of Christ," *The Reliquary* 11 (1905), pp. 242–43. On the prints after the medal portrait, see Hill, *Medallic Portraits of Christ*, pp. 32–43.

14. Paul Kristeller, *Andrea Mantegna* (Berlin: Cosmos, 1902), pp. 422, document 152, and pp. 566–77.

15. "[A]dvertendo havere il suo Naturale; pocho io gli haveva dicto che Mro Baptista dela Fiera havea retrovata la sua similitudine." Kristeller, *Mantegna*, p. 566.

16. Paris, Musée du Louvre, R.F. 439. Ronald Lightbown, *Mantegna* (Berkeley: University of California Press, 1986), pp. 189 and 463–64, no. 85. *Mantegna: 1431–1506*, exhibition catalogue, Paris, Musée du Louvre (Paris: Hazan, 2008), p. 344, no. 144. Obviously Mantegna had a mind of his own, since in the drawing Virgil is holding a book and is not wearing sandals.

17. *Splendours of the Gonzaga*, eds. David Chambers and Jane Martineau (London: Victoria and Albert Museum, 1982), pp. 155–56.

18. Umberto Eco, "Tipologia della falsificazione," in *Fälschungen im Mittelalter*, Monumenta Germanica Historica, Schriften, vol. 33 (Hannover: Hahn, 1988), pp. 69–82; here 73.

19. The portrait group has been studied by Giulio Bodon in an informative series of articles, occasionally skewed by the untenable view that this group of Livy portraits originated in an authentic ancient bust; see "La tradizione dell'iconografia di Tito Livio: dal ritratto antico al ritratto rinascimentale," *Bollettino del Museo Civico di Padova* 81 (1992), pp. 135–46; "Studi

antiquari fra XV e XVII secolo: la famiglia Maggi da Bassano e la sua collezione," *Bollettino del Museo Civico di Padova* 80 (1991), pp. 23–172; "L'immagine di Tito Livio a Padova nella tradizione artistica rinascimentale," *Bollettino del Museo Civico di Padova* 78 (1989), pp. 69–92; "Nuovi elementi per lo studio del busto di Tito Livio al Palazzo della Ragione di Padova," *Bollettino del Museo Civico di Padova* 77 (1988), pp. 81–95. The best account of the various images of Livy produced in Padua between the fourteenth and fifteenth centuries is Joseph Trapp, "The Image of Livy in the Middle Ages and the Renaissance," in *Studies of Petrarch and His Influence* (London: Pindar, 2003), pp. 279–339. On the issues raised by the cinquecento Livy monument, see Dagobert Frey, "Apokryphe Liviusbildnisse der Renaissance," *Wallraf-Richartz-Jahrbuch* 17 (1955), pp. 132–64. More broadly on the question of invented author portraits, including the Livy and the Virgil terracotta discussed above, see Sarah Blake McHam, "Renaissance Monuments to Favourite Sons," *Renaissance Studies* 19 (2005), pp. 458–86.

20. Vienna, Kunsthistorisches Museum, inventory no. 7499.

21. For example Andrea Riccio's bust of the Abbot Antonio Trombetta in the Santo in Padua, as well as the two death masks he placed at the top of the della Torre tomb in San Fermo in Verona. See also the bronze bust of the doctor and humanist Girolamo Fracastoro, sometimes attributed to Danese Cattaneo, now in the Kunsthistorisches Museum in Vienna, as well as the unattributed Paduan bust of an old man in the Landesmuseum in Oldenburg.

22. "Il y a une salle, la plus grande, sans pilliers, que j'aie jamais veue où se tient leur justice; et à l'un bout est la teste de Titus Livius maigre, rapportant un home studieus et malancholicq, ancien ouvrage auquel il ne reste que la parole. Son epitaphe aussi y est, lequel ayant trouvé, ils l'ont ainsi élevé pour s'en faire honneur, et avecque raison." Michel de Montaigne, *Oeuvres complètes*, eds. Albert Thibaudet and Maurice Rat (Paris: Gallimard, 1962), p. 1182.

23. According to Charles Davis, "Although it is not wholly clear how Bassano and his contemporaries reconciled their conviction that the bust of Livy represented an accurate and antique likeness of their ancient compatriot with the knowledge the head had been formed in modern times with the aid of a death mask, such must have been the case." "Aspects of Imitation in Cavino's Medals," *Journal of the Warburg and Courtauld Institutes* 41 (1978), p. 333.

24. See Norberto Gramaccini, "Riccios Tiere und die Theorie des Naturabgusses seit Cennino Cennini," pp. 198–226.

25. Frey, "Apokryphe Liviusbildnisse," pp. 161–62.

26. See Carla Gottlieb, "The Mystical Window in Paintings of the Salvator Mundi," *Gazette des Beaux-Arts* 56 (December 1960), pp. 313–32.

27. See *The Illustrated Bartsch, German Book Illustration before 1500*, vol. 80, part 1, no. 1473/63.

28. Rostock, University Library, UBR Fa-1119(69).13. The Rostock impression is the only one that preserves the texts. Hollstein, *German Engravings, Etchings, and Woodcuts, ca. 1400–1700*, vol. 5, no. 53. Arthur Burkhard, *Hans Burgkmair der Ältere* (Berlin, Klinkhardt and Biermann 1932), no. 30, p. 38, fig. 25. *Hans Burgkmair: Das Graphische Werk*, no. 83.

29. The line must have measured 17.8 cm, one tenth of the traditional height of Christ. On such "measurement relics," see Carlo Ginzburg, *The Enigma of Piero* (London: Verso, 2000), pp. 68–70.

30. Munich, Graphische Sammlung, inventory no. 67 874D. Hollstein, *German Engravings, Etchings, and Woodcuts, ca. 1400–1700*, vol. 5, no. 52. *Hans Burgkmair: Das Graphische Werk*, no. 71.

31. *Die Bibliothek Konrad Peutingers: Edition der historischen Kataloge und Rekonstruktion der Bestände*, vol. 1, *Die autographen Kataloge Peutingers: der nicht-juristische Bibliotheksteil*, eds. Hans-Jörg Künast und Helmut Zäh (Tübingen: Niemeyer, 2003), p. 710, no. 767.

32. Peter Volz, "Conrad Peutinger und das Entstehen der deutschen Medaillensitte zu Augsburg 1518," PhD diss., University of Heidelberg, 1972.

33. Max Geisberg, *The German Single-Leaf Woodcut, 1500–1550* (New York: Hacker, 1974), vol. 1, p. 48, no. 56-1. Two other German prints based on the medal are Schreiber, *Handbuch der Holz- und Metallschnitte des XV. Jahrhunderts*, no. 757m, with a proof impression in Washington, see Richard S. Field, *Fifteenth Century Woodcuts in the National Gallery of Art* (Washington, D.C.: National Gallery of Art: [1965]), no. 110; and a unicum in Dresden, Max Lehrs, *Geschichte und kritischer Katalog des deutschen, niederländischen und französischen Kupferstichs im XV. Jahrhundert*, vol. 7 (Vienna: Gesellschaft für vervielfältigende Kunst, 1930), no. 3.

34. As noted by Hill, *Medallic Portraits of Christ*, p. 22, no. 901.

35. *Ibid.*, nos. 898–99.

36. "[P]ro indelibili immortalique memoria facienda fuerat rursus erea aureaque tabella mirabili sculptura excussa: pene ad modum numismatis huiusce proprie speciei ac quantitatis (ut hic oculis coram facile intueri poteris) multo ingenio arte et sagacitate (nullum denique a prothotypo discrimine preseferens [sic]) diligentissime fabrefacta."

37. Maurice Halbwachs, *La topographie légendaire des Évangiles en Terre Sainte* (Paris: Presses Universitaires de France, 1941), pp. 80–89, 187–88.

38. Kimbell Art Museum, AP 2005.04. The model for the relief is probably the medal reproduced as fig. 22 in Hill, *Medallic Portraits of Christ*, p. 45. This medal also served as the basis for the miniature roundel, formerly attributed to Leonardo da Vinci, in the Castello Sforzesco, Milan.

39. Thanks to Alison Luchs for her observations on this point.

40. Anne Markham Schulz, "Cristoforo Solari at Venice: Facts and Suppositions," *Prospettiva* 52–56 (1988–1989), pp. 309–16 and esp. 312. See also the bust by Lorenzo Bregno in the Scuola di San Rocco; see Schulz, "Lorenzo Bregno," *Jahrbuch der Berliner Museen* 26 (1984), pp. 143–79 and esp. 171.

41. The painting has been placed into the context of ca. 1500 portraits of Christ by Nicholas Penny, *National Gallery Catalogues: The Sixteenth-Century Italian Paintings*, vol. 1, *Paintings from Bergamo, Brescia, and Cremona* (London National Gallery, 2004), pp. 300–302.

42. Tancred Borenius, *The Picture Gallery of Andrea Vendramin* (London, 1923), fol. 12r and 12v, pp. 19–20, and fig. 1.

43. As observed by Nicholas Penny, *The Sixteenth Century Italian Paintings*, vol. 1 (London: National Gallery, 2004), p. 300.

44. Max Geisberg, *The German Single-Leaf Woodcut 1500–1550*, vol. 2 (New York: Hacker, 1974), pp. 616–17; Joseph Leo Koerner, *The Moment of Self-Portraiture in German Renaissance Art* (Chicago: University of Chicago Press, 1993), pp. 116–19.

45. Milan, Pinacoteca di Brera. The presence of the medal-type portrait in the architecture was noted by Hill, *Medallic Portraits of Christ*, p. 15.

46. Utrecht, Rijksmuseum het Catharijneconvent, inv. BMR s2. See also M. L. Caron, "Het beeld van Christus in de Vrouwen. Kloosters en bij de zusters van het Gemene Leven," *Ons Geestelijk Erf* 59 (1985), pp. 457–69, fig. 1; *Prayers and Portraits: Unfolding the Netherlandish Diptych*, exhibition catalogue, National Gallery of Art (New Haven, CT: Yale University Press, 2006), no. 29. The panel may date from around 1500 suggesting that the Netherlandish painter and the German printmaker independently conceived of connecting the medal-based profile to the Lentulus letter. See also the panel in Berlin attributed to the Bruges Master of 1499 and possibly also dating from around 1500. It is only 18 x 13 cm and the blessing hand—an awkward, narrativizing supplement to the medal profile, here as in the Utrecht picture—seems to have been cut off at the left. Berlin, Gemäldegalerie, inv. no. 528A. Wilhelm von Bode, "Ein neu erworbenes Profilbild des Heilands von Jan van Eyck in der Berliner Galerie," *Zeitschrift für christliche Kunst* 1 (1888), cols. 344–52; Max J. Friedländer, *Early Netherlandish Painting*, vol. 4 (Leiden: Sijthoff, 1967–1976), p. 89, fig. 118.

47. *Mandylion*, pp. 268–71; and Robert S. Nelson, "Byzantine Icons in Genoa before the 'Mandylion,'"

in Anna Rosa Calderoni Masetti (ed.), *Intorno al Sacro Volto: Genova, Bisanzio e il Mediterraneo (secoli XI–XIV)* (Venezia: Marsilio, 2007), pp. 79–92.

48. American Academy in Rome, inventory no. 9521. The relief, which has never been published, sits on the porch of the academy. Anne Markham Schulz, on the basis of a photograph, connected it to Roman work, perhaps near Isaia da Pisa, of the third quarter of the fifteenth century. Francesco Caglioti, also on the basis of a photograph, judges it a rather minor work and quite late, perhaps even late sixteenth century.

49. The modern relief may have been inserted into the ancient frame at a later point. There is reason to believe that the relief was cut down: the rays of the nimbus are short at the top. The possibility that the relief is a reworked ancient portrait cannot be ruled out.

50. In the phrase of the epigrapher Renate Neumüllers-Klauser, "Zur Problematik epigraphischer Fälschungen," in Klaus Herbers et al. (eds.), *Ex ipsis rerum documentis. Festschrift Harald Zimmermann* (Sigmaringen: Thorbecke, 1991), pp. 173–93.

51. Raphael and others, in the formulation of Gerhard Wolf, were caught between claims to truth and the desire to compete and exceed; see *Schleier und Spiegel*, pp. 295–96.

52. John Shearman, *Raphael's Cartoons in the Collection of Her Majesty the Queen, and the Tapestries for the Sistine Chapel* (London: Phaidon, 1972), pp. 50–51.

53. A tapestry of 1720 excerpted this portrait, returned it to the bust format, and added an inscription explaining that this image had been copied from the emerald given to Pope Innocent VIII by the Turkish Sultan. The inscription carries errors; for example, it says that the gift of the emerald was part of a ransom to free the sultan's brother, whereas the original legend on the medal had said that it was in thanks for keeping his brother safely in prison. It also adds the detail, never before mentioned, that the emerald was originally made for the Emperor Tiberius. The inclusion of an allusion to Tiberius may well be a garbled memory of the Lentulus letter, whose opening line,

in some versions, was an address to Tiberius. All of this suggests that the inscription of 1720 is not a fresh invention, but a somewhat confused mish-mash of older associations, perhaps going all the way back to the period of the creation of Raphael's tapestry, that is, the moment when documentary images of Christ were first making a sensation.

54. Philine Helas identified the standing figure on the back as a rendition of the Minerva Christ, see "Lo 'smeraldo' smarrito, ossia il 'vero' profilo," in *Il Volto di Cristo*, p. 238. Another example was published by Hill, see *Medallic Portraits of Christ*, p. 66, fig. 38. Paola Gallamini published an oval version of this medal designed to be worn as a pendant but apparently cast from a common mold; see "La medaglia devozionale cristiana: secoli XVII–XVIII–XIX (parte I)," *Medaglia* 17, 24 (1989), p. 49, no. 45.

55. Vasari, *Le vite*, vol. 4, p. 281. The artist must have remembered Plutarch, *Life of Publicola* (Poplicola), 19.6, who reported that a bronze statue of the Etruscan king used to stand near the senate-house, "of plain and antique workmanship" *The Lives of the Noble Grecians and Romans*, trans. John Dryden, vol. 1 (New York: Modern Library, 1992), p. 141.

56. The bust is in a private collection in Montepulciano. See Ciro Girolami, "Il Porsenna e il Galba di Andrea Sansovino," *Rivista d'Arte* 18 (1936), pp. 179–91, as well as the exhibition catalogues *Il Giardino di San Marco: Maestri e compagni del giovane Michelangelo* (Florence: Silvana, 1992), no. 26; and *L'Officina della maniera: varietà e fierezza nell'arte fiorentina del Cinquecento fra le due repubbliche (1494–1530)* (Venice: Marsilio, 1996), no. 46. The surface of the head is painted, perhaps to resemble bronze. Vasari also mentioned a pair of terracotta heads by Sansovino representing the emperors Nero and Galba and "ritratte da medaglie antiche," see Giorgio Vasari, *Le vite*, vol. 4, p. 510.

57. Franco Borsi (ed.), *Fortuna degli Etruschi* (Milan: Electa, 1985), pp. 37–39. The tomb—if it ever existed—had vanished by Pliny's time; he relied on Varro. *Natural History* 36.19.

58. Ingrid D. Rowland, "L'*Historia Porsennae* e la conoscenza degli Etruschi," pp. 185–93.

59. Giovanni Cipriani, *Il mito etrusco nel rinascimento fiorentino* (Florence: Olschki, 1980), p. 31.

60. On fifteenth-century interest in Etruscan antiquities, see C. C. van Essen, "Elementi etruschi nel Rinascimento toscana," *Studi etruschi* 13 (1939), pp. 497–99; André Chastel, *Art et humanisme à Florence au temps de Laurent le Magnifique: Études sur la Renaissance et l'humanisme platonicien* (Paris: Presses Universitaires de France, 1959), pp. 63–71; André Chastel, "L''etruscan revival' du XVe siècle," *Revue archéologique* 1 (1959), pp. 165–80; Marvin Trachtenberg, "An Antique Model for Donatello's Marble *David*," *Art Bulletin* 50 (1968), pp. 266–69; Cristina Frulli, "Caratteri etruschi nella scultura fiorentina al tempo di Lorenzo il Magnifico," and Franco Borsi, "Architettura" in Borsi (ed.), *Fortuna degli Etruschi*, pp. 102–108 and 36–43. On the Etruscanizing imagination of the Biblical scholar, theologian, and cardinal Egidio da Viterbo, see Rowland, *Culture of the High Renaissance: Ancients and Moderns in Sixteenth-Century Rome* (Cambridge: Cambridge University Press, 1998), pp. 148–50.

61. Spinello Benci, *Storia della cittá di Montepulciano* (Florence, 1641), frontispiece and p. 7.

TWENTY-TWO — FORGERY 1: COPY

1. Berlin, Gemäldegalerie, inventory no. 534A.

2. New York, Metropolitan Museum of Art, inventory no. 22.60.58.

3. According to Erwin Panofsky, the possibility that the Granada/New York panels are copies commissioned by Isabella after the Berlin triptych "has never been considered by the experts and is indeed the most improbable from a stylistic point of view." Panofsky did not pursue this hypothesis, asserting that when the Berlin and New York panels were recently compared side by side "no stylistic and technical differences indicative of an interval of circa fifty years could be discovered." See *Early Netherlandish Painting*, pp. 259

and 460–61 n.3. Rainald Grosshans determined on the basis of technical and stylistic analysis that the Berlin paintings were the originals; see "Rogier van der Weyden: Der Marienaltar aus der Kartause Miraflores," *Jahrbuch der Berliner Museen* 23 (1981), pp. 49–112.

4. Maryan Ainsworth, "Implications of Revised Attributions in Netherlandish Painting," *Metropolitan Museum of Art Journal* 27 (1992), pp. 59–68, and *From Van Eyck to Bruegel* (New York: Metropolitan Museum of Art, 1998), no. 46.

5. Umberto Eco, *A Theory of Semiotics* (Bloomington: Indiana University Press, 1976), pp. 178–79.

6. Marcantonio Michiel, *Notizia d'opere di disegno*, ed. Gustavo Frizzoni (Bologna, 1884), p. 219 and *Der Anonimo Morelliano (Marcanton Michiel's Notizia d'opere del disegno)*, ed. Theodor Frimmel, *Quellenschriften für Kunstgeschichte*, N.F. 1 (1888), pp. 107–108. Van Eyck's panel is in Berlin, Gossaert's in the Galleria Doria-Pamphilj in Rome.

7. E. H. Gombrich, *Art and Illusion: A Study in the Psychology of Pictorial Representation* (Princeton: Princeton University Press, 1960), pp. 140–41. Most recently on Roman copies of Greek works, and in fact arguing that they were not copies but interpretations, Miranda Marvin, *The Language of the Muses: The Dialogue between Roman and Greek Sculpture* (Los Angeles: J. Paul Getty Museum, 2008).

8. See Elizabeth Bartman, *Ancient Sculptural Copies in Miniature* (Leiden: Brill, 1992), p. 13.

9. Lucian *Philopseudes* 18. See the discussion in Michael Koortbojian, "Forms of Attention: Four Notes on Replication and Variation," in Elaine K. Gazda (ed.), *The Ancient Art of Emulation: Studies in Artistic Originality and Tradition from the Present to Classical Antiquity* (Ann Arbor: University of Michigan Press, 2002), pp. 173–204.

10. According to Longinus: "Was Herodotus the only devoted imitator of Homer? No, Stesichorus even before his time, and Archilochus, and above all Plato, who from the great Homeric source drew to himself

innumerable streams. And we might have found it necessary to prove this by examples, had not Ammonius and his followers selected and noted the particulars. This proceeding is not plagiarism [lit.: stealing]; it is instead like taking an impression (as it is acceptable to do) from beautiful statues or other works of art (Solusne Herodotus fuit magnus Homeri imitator? Stesichorus etiam ante eum idem fuit, et Archilochus: Plus autem, quam hi omnes, Plato fuit, qui ab Homerico illo fonte innumeros rivulos ad se deduxit. Et forsitan nobis opus fuisset exemplis, nisi ea sigillatim etiam Ammonius eligens in suis scriptis notasset. Haec vero res non est furtum ullum, sed (ut a bonis moribus fieri potest) sive simulacrorum sive operum expressa effigies)." See *De Sublimitate* 13. Our thanks go to Michael Koortbojian for pointing out this passage.

11. The often equivocal phrasing of Domenico Mustilli—"falsi o per lo meno imitazioni," "falsificazioni o, almeno, copie"—reveals the flexibility of the ancient categories; see "Falsificazione," *Enciclopedia dell'Arte Antica Classica e Orientale* (Rome: Istituto della Enciclopedia Italiana, 1995), pp. 576–89. Pliny discusses disputed attributions of works, but even here it is not clear whether he is talking about invention or execution; see *Natural History* 36.27–29.

12. Pliny *Natural History* 35.92; Katherine Jex-Blake, *The Elder Pliny's Chapters on the History of Art* (Chicago: Ares, 1977), pp. 128–29.

13. Wolfgang Speyer, *Die literarische Fälschung im heidnischen und christlichen Altertum* (Munich: Beck, 1971).

14. Francis Haskell and Nicholas Penny, *Taste and the Antique: The Lure of Classical Sculpture, 1500–1900* (New Haven, CT: Yale University Press, 1981).

15. The distinction, which creates a sharp price differential on the open market, only began to matter to scholars and curators in the last two or three decades. A similar distinction was drawn in the field of classical sculpture in the nineteenth century, when museums sent their modern copies to the basement and displayed only "originals." Of course, many of those originals were themselves Roman copies of Greek works, or Greek copies of older Greek works.

16. Kurt Gschwantler, "Der Jüngling von Magdalensberg: Ein Forschungsprojekt der Antikensammlung des Kunsthistorischen Museums Wien," in *Griechische und römische Statuetten und Grossbronzen*, pp. 17–27.

17. Wolfgang Wohlmayer, "Der Jüngling vom Magdalensberg—Versuch einer stilistischen Neubestimmung," *Mitteilungen der Gesellschaft für Salzburger Landeskunde* 131 (1991), p. 14 n.26.

18. Pliny *Natural History* 35.91.

19. The modern commentator on Pliny, Katharine Jex-Blake, misunderstood this point when she contradicted Pliny's report that the picture had been replaced; see *The Elder Pliny's Chapters on the History of Art*, p. 128 n.3. She pointed out that the picture of Apelles seems still to have been in existence under Vespasian, when Suetonius speaks of its being again restored: "Coae Veneris…refectorem insigni congiario magnaque mercede donavit;" see *Vesp.* 18. In fact, Suetonius's comment only confirms that Dorotheos produced a true substitute rather than a new picture of his own invention. Note that although Suetonius refers to the Aphrodite of Kos, another work altogether, he was almost certainly talking about the work in the Temple of Divus Julius; see Jerome J. Pollitt, "The Impact of Greek Art on Rome," *Transactions of the American Philological Association* 108 (1978), p. 168 n.15.

20. *Byzantium: Faith and Power*, cat. no. 353. See also Larry Silver, "Fountain and Source: A Rediscovered Eyckian Icon," *Pantheon* 41 (1983), pp. 95–104.

21. *Byzantium: Faith and Power*, cat. no. 353.

22. Klaus Schreiner, "'Discrimen veri ac falsi': Ansätze und Formen der Kritik in der Heiligen- und Reliquienverehrung des Mittelalters," *Archiv für Kulturgeschichte* 48 (1966), pp. 1–53; František Graus, "Fälschungen im Gewand der Frömmigkeit," in *Fälschungen im Mittelalter*, vol. 5, *Fingierte Briefe; Frömmigkeit und Fälschung; Realienfälschung* (Hannover: Hahn, 1988), pp. 261–82.

23. Michiel, *Notizia d'opere di disegno*, pp. 188 and

37; *Der Anonimo Morelliano*, pp. 98–99 and 16. The *St. Jerome* in the home of Antonio Pasqualino, according to Michiel, was attributed by some to Antonello da Messina (correctly, as it happens), but might actually be by Memling or by Jacometto. The relief, representing a pair of centaurs and a female centaur (not found at all in ancient art) was still judged an antiquity into the nineteenth century. Michiel saw it in the home of Niccolò Leonico Tomeo. See also L. Planiscig, "Del Giorgionismo nella scultura veneziana all' inizio del Cinquecento," *Bollettino d'arte* 28 (1934), pp. 148–49.

24. Having learned of the "desiderio che tiene lo Illustrissimo signor Marchese d'haver il mio quadro di Santa Maria Maddalena per farne dono a la signora marchesa di Pescara, et perchè non ho cosa al mondo ch'io non vogli che sia parimente di Sua Excellentia, mi fu di grandissima satisfattione veder ch'ella havesse tal desiderio et subito le havrei mandato il quadro, ma perché ne ho voluto far prima far un simile, è stato necessario ritenerlo fin tanto che'il pittore se ne sia servito in prenderne l'essempio, hora ch'egli l'ha finito, lo mando pel medesimo portatore di questa mia, et lo indrizzo a voi…." See Diane H. Bodart, *Tiziano e Federico II Gonzaga: Storia di un rapporto di commitenza* (Rome: Bulzoni, 1998), p. 264.

25. Ermanno Ferrero and Giuseppe Müller (eds.), *Vittoria Colonna, Marchesa di Pescara. Carteggio* (Turin: Loescher, 1892), p. 104.

26. Karl Frey, *Michelangelo: Quellen und Forschungen* (Berlin: K. Curtis, 1907), p. 139.

27. See Alexander Perrig, *Michelangelo-Studien I: Michelangelo und die Zeichnungswissenschaft—Ein methodologischer Versuch* (Bern and Frankfurt: H. Lang, 1976) and *Michelangelo's Drawings: The Science of Attribution*, trans. Michael Joyce (New Haven and London: Yale University Press, 1991). On the painted copies of the presentation drawings, see William Wallace, "Michelangelo and Marcello Venusti: A Case of Multiple Authorship," in Francis Ames-Lewis and Paul Joannides (eds.), *Reactions to the Master: Michelangelo's Effect on Art and Artists in the Sixteenth Century* (Aldershot, UK:

Ashgate, 2003), pp. 137–56. On the copied afterlife of the presentation drawings, see Maria Ruvoldt, "Copies after Michelangelo's 'Dream' for Ottavio Farnese," *Source: Notes in the History of Art* 30.4 (2011), pp. 18–25.

28. "La qual cosa dispiacendo molto al magnifico Ottaviano, che non arebbe voluto privar Fiorenza d'una sì fatta pittura, si maravigliò che il Papa l'avesse corsa così a un tratto; pure rispose che non mancherebbe di servire il duca, ma che essendo l'ornamento cattivo, ne faceva fare un nuovo, il quale come fusse messo d'oro, manderebbe sicurissimamente il quadro a Mantoa. E ciò fatto messer Ottaviano per salvare, come si dice, la capra et i cavoli, mandò segretamente per Andrea e gli disse come il fatto stava, e che a ciò non era altro rimedio che contrafare quello con ogni diligenza, e mandandone un simile al Duca, ritenere, ma nascosamente, quello di mano di Raffaello. Avendo dunque promesso Andrea di fare quanto sapeva e poteva, fatto fare un quadro simile di grandezza et in tutte le parti, lo lavorò in casa di messer Ottaviano segretamente: e vi si affaticò di maniera che esso messer Ottaviano, intendentissimo delle cose dell'arti, quando fu finito non conosceva l'uno dall'altro, né il proprio e vero dal simile, avendo massimamente Andrea contrafatto insino alle macchie del sucido, come era il vero apunto." Vasari, *Le vite*, vol. 4, pp. 378–79. See also Roger Jones and Nicholas Penny, *Raphael* (New Haven, CT: Yale University Press, 1983), p. 159.

29. Vasari, *Le vite*, vol. 4, pp. 379–80.

30. An example is the portrait of a man by Robert Campin (or the Master of Flémalle) in the Thyssen collection and in Berlin; see the exhibition catalogue *Der Meister von Flémalle and Rogier van der Weyden* Berlin, Gemäldegalerie, Staatliche Museen zu Berlin (Ostfildern: Hatje Cantz, 2008), nos. 16–17, pp. 265–71. On multiples of sixteenth-century portraits, see Lorne Campbell, *Renaissance Portraits* (New Haven, CT: Yale University Press, 1990), pp. 182–85.

31. J. C. Dickinson, *The Shrine of Our Lady of Walsingham*, p. 126.

32. For the case against the referential capacities

of images, see Kendall Walton, *Mimesis as Make-Believe: On the Foundations of the Visual Arts* (Cambridge: Cambridge University Press, 1990).

33. Joseph Leo Koerner, *The Moment of Self-Portraiture*, pp. 249–51.

34. The episode is recounted by Vasari, but, interestingly, otherwise unattested; see *Le vite*, vol. 5, p. 7. A thoughtful recent account is Lisa Pon, *Raphael, Dürer, and Marcantonio Raimondi: Copying and the Italian Renaissance Print* (New Haven, CT: Yale University Press, 2004).

35. Bartman, *Ancient Sculptural Copies in Miniature*, p. 13.

36. Andrew Burnett, "Coin Faking in the Renaissance," in Mark Jones (ed.), *Why Fakes Matter: Essays on Problems of Authenticity* (London: British Museum Press, 1993), pp. 15–22 and esp. 18.

37. Jonathan Woolfson and Andrew Gregory, "Aspects of Collecting in Renaissance Padua," pp. 252–65 and esp. 264–65.

38. "Las mejores de todas [modern productions] son las de un Paduano q contrahaze las mejores medallas de las antiguas que agora tenemos, y estas estan tan bien hechas, que es gran plazer mirallas: y fino fuesse por algunos errores que hai o en las letras, o en las cosas debuxadas, no havria q dessear mejores." Burnett, "Coin Faking," pp. 16–17. According to Lanfranco Franzoni, even Cavino cannot clearly be indicted of fraudulent intentions: for was he not simply "reframing" the old images? See "Antiquari e collezionisti nel Cinquecento," in *Storia della Cultura Veneta*, vol. 3 (Vicenza: Nero Pozza, 1981), pp. 239–41.

TWENTY-THREE — FORGERY 2:
PASTICHE

1. Wolfgang Karrer, *Parodie, Travestie, Pastiche* (Munich: Fink, 1977), p. 74. See pp. 47–49 on pastiche and forgery and pp. 118–19 on the pastiche signalling its own status by framing devices.

2. *Fabulae* 5.11.4–9. On the extensive and ruthless

art market in Augustan Rome, see Pollitt, "The Impact of Greek Art on Rome," p. 162.

3. Julius von Schlosser, "Die ältesten Medaillen und die Antike," *Jahrbuch der Kunsthistorischen Sammlungen* 18 (1897), pp. 64–108; Mark Jones, *A Catalogue of the French Medals in the British Museum* (London: British Museum, 1982), pp. 17–28; Scher (ed.), *Currency of Fame*, pp. 32–37. Ulrich Pfisterer agrees that the medals belong to a category beyond truth and falsehood: they are invented evidence; *Lysippus und seine Freunde*, pp. 93–96.

4. See Luigi Beschi, "Le sculture antiche di Lorenzo il Magnifico," in *Lorenzo il Magnifico e il suo mondo. Atti del convegno internazionale di studi* (Florence: Olschki, 1994), pp. 291–317.

5. A. de Rinaldis cites a letter from Summonte to Michiel of 1524: "In this city in the house of Sig. Conte Matalona, by the hand of Donatello is the most beautiful cast colossal horse;" see "Di un'antica testa di cavallo in bronzo attribuita a Donatello," *Bollettino d'Arte* 5 (1911), p. 245 n.3.

6. Vasari, *Le vite*, vol. 3, p. 213 (Life of Donatello): "Et in casa del conte di Matalone, nella città medesima [Naples], è una testa di cavallo di mano di Donato tanto bella che molti la credono antica." See also vol. 3, p. 227: "Attribuiscongli alcuni che e' facesse la testa del cavallo che è a Napoli in casa del conte di Matalone; ma non è verisimile che così sia, essendo quella maniera antica e non essendo egli mai stato a Napoli."

7. Hans Semper, *Donatello: seine Zeit und seine Schule* (Vienna: Graeser, 1875), p. 307.

8. Ulrich Pfisterer, *Donatello und die Entdeckung der Stile*, pp. 13–22.

9. "Dilettossi anco di contraffare i conii delle medaglie antiche...." Vasari, *Le vite*, vol. 3, p. 78.

10. On Bellano's discipleship to Donatello, whom he admired so much and whose manner he adopted so fully that some of his works were confused with the master's, see Vasari, *Le vite*, vol. 3, p. 321; on the life of Bandinelli and his early training in copying ancient heads, see *Le vite*, vol. 4, p. 240; on the life of Andrea

del Sarto and his copy of Raphael's portrait of Leo X, already discussed above, see *Le vite*, vol. 4, p. 379; on the life of Michelangelo and his early training copying an antique head of a faun in the Medici garden and his efforts to imitate Donatello in the early *Madonna of the Stairs*, see *Le vite*, vol. 6, p. 10 and 11; on Valerio Belli's imitations of antique medals, "delle quali ne cavò grandissima utilità," see *Le vite*, vol. 4, p. 627; and on Leone Leoni's "prontezza infinita" in imitating "medaglie antiche," see *Le vite*, vol. 4, p. 628; and on Titian's early assimilation of the style of Giorgione—"E così datosi a lavorare et a contrafare dell'opere di colui, si fece tale che venne in bonissimo credito"—see *Le vite*, vol. 6, p. 170. The only case when Vasari uses the word to describe a forgery is in the account of the Raimondi–Dürer; see *Le vite*, vol. 5, p. 7.

11. For a good summary of the history and reception of the Turin Shroud, see Robin Cormack, *Painting the Soul: Icons, Death Masks, and Shrouds* (London: Reaktion, 1997), pp. 114–26.

12. On forged documents, see p. 31 above. On forged inscriptions, see Billanovich, "Falsi epigrafici," pp. 25–110; Franzoni, "Antiquari e collezionisti," pp. 243–44; and Speyer, *Die literarische Fälschung*, p. 315 n.2.

13. Grafton, *Forgers and Critics*, pp. 49–50.

14. Several fifteenth-century German examples include: Bernhard Bischoff, "Ein Reichenbacher Codex des XV. Jahrhunderts in imitierter romanischer Minuskel," in *Mittelalterliche Studien: Ausgewählte Aufsätze zur Schriftkunde und Literaturgeschichte* vol. 1 (Stuttgart: Hiersemann, 1966), pp. 63–67; Martin Steinmann, "Von der Übernahme fremder Schriften im 15. Jahrhundert" and J. P. Gumbert, "Italienische Schrift—humanistische Schrift—Humanistenschrift," in Johanne Autenrieth (ed.), *Renaissance- und Humanistenhandschriften* (Munich: Oldenbourg, 1988), pp. 51–62 and 63–70.

15. Laurie Fusco and Gino Corti, "Giovanni Ciampolini, a Renaissance Dealer in Rome and his Collection of Antiquities," *Xenia* 21 (1991), p. 10.

16. For a still relevant discussion, see Ernst Kris, *Meister und Meisterwerke der Steinschneidekunst in der italienischen Renaissance*, vol. 1 (Vienna: Schroll, 1929), pp. 26–27.

17. Fusco and Corti, "Giovanni Ciampolini," p. 8.

18. Marcantonio Michiel, *Notizia d'opere di disegno*, p. 181. He also writes: "In casa de M. Francesco Zio, 1512…. La tazza de porfido cun li 3 maneghi et el bocchino fu de mano de Pietro Maria intagliatore de corneole, Fiorentino la qual ascose in Roma sotta terra, alla intrata de re Carlo cun molte altre sue cosse, oue si schiappo alquanto, sicchè fu bisogno cingerla d'uno cerchio de rame, la qual è stata uenduta più fiate per opera antica a gran precio." See *Der Anonimo Morelliano (Marcantonio Michiel's Notizia d' Opere del Disegno)*, p. 96. For a sensitive discussion of this and other instances, see Luke Syson and Dora Thornton, *Objects of Virtue: Art in Renaissance Italy* (Los Angeles: The J. Paul Getty Museum, 2001), pp. 102–34.

19. Vasari, *Le vite*, vol. 6, pp. 8–9. For a more sustained examination of the accounts of these drawings in relation to Michelangelo's early drawing practice, see Alexander Nagel, *Michelangelo and the Reform of Art* (Cambridge: Cambridge University Press, 2000), pp. 2–8.

20. Michael Hirst elucidates this episode most clearly; see "The Artist in Rome 1496–1501," in Michael Hirst and Jill Dunkerton, *The Young Michelangelo* (London: National Gallery, 1994), pp. 20–28. See also, Paul Eberhard, "Falsificazioni di antichità dal rinascimento al XVIII secolo," in Settis (ed.), *Memoria dell'antico nell'arte italiana*, vol. 2, pp. 413–39; Kathleen Weil-Garris Brandt, "Sogni di un Cupido Dormiente smarrito," in *Giovinezza di Michelangelo*, pp. 315–17 and the entries on 318–22.

21. Stephen J. Campbell, *The Cabinet of Eros: Renaissance Mythological Painting and the Studiolo of Isabella d'Este* (New Haven, CT: Yale University Press, 2004), pp. 91–102.

22. Franzoni, "Antiquari e collezionisti," pp. 236–39.

23. For this phrase, see Madeleine Viljoen, "Prints

and False Antiquities in the Age of Raphael," p. 244 n.26.

24. Munich, Bayerisches Nationalmuseum, inventory no. 35.386. See Hans Weihrauch, *Kataloge des Bayerischen Nationalmuseum*, vol. 13, pt. 5, *Die Bildwerke in Bronze und in anderen Metallen* (Munich: Bruckmann, 1956), no. 50; see also Christopher S. Wood, "Maximilian I as Archeologist," *Renaissance Quarterly* 58 (2005), p. 1156, fig. 8.

25. Ann Hersey Allison, "The Bronzes of Pier Jacopo Alari-Bonacolsi, called Antico," *Jahrbuch der Kunsthistorischen Sammlungen in Wien*, 89–90 (1993–1994), p. 92, docs. 74–75.

26. Giovanni Gaye, *Carteggio inedito d'artisti dei secoli XIV, XV, XVI*, vol. 2 (Florence, 1839–40), pp. 192–93.

27. Madeleine Viljoen, "Paper Value: Marcantonio Raimondi's *Medaglie Contraffatte*," *Memoirs of the American Academy in Rome* 48 (2003), pp. 203–26. On p. 223, Viljoen points out that the "counterfeit [was] closely linked to notions of the substitute."

28. On Desiderio's relief, see John Pope-Hennessy, *Italian Renaissance Sculpture* (Oxford: Phaidon, 1985), p. 258, and Leo Planiscig, *Desiderio da Settignano* (Vienna: Schroll, 1942), pp. 16–17 and 42. For Mino da Fiesole's Marcus Aurelius, see Gianni Carlo Sciolla, *La scultura di Mino da Fiesole* (Turin: G. Giappichelli, 1970), p. 112, no. 70, and Shelley Zuraw, "The Sculpture of Mino da Fiesole (1429–1484)," PhD diss., New York University, 1993, pp. 91–93, no. 9, fig. 25.

29. Debra Pincus, "Tullio Lombardo as Restorer of Antiquities: an aspect of fifteenth century Venetian antiquarianism," *Arte Veneta* 33 (1979), pp. 29–42.

30. Franzoni, "Antiquari e collezionisti," p. 241. See also Panofsky, *Renaissance and Renascences in Western Art*, p. 41; Panofsky made this work the frontispiece to the book.

31. Joseph Alsop, *The Rare Art Traditions*, pp. 95–96 and 157–58.

32. Vico, *Discorsi sopra le medaglie degli antichi*. Burnett notes that Antonio Agustín (*Dialogos de medallas*, pp. 451 and 464) criticised Fulvio on just this point, see "Coin Faking," pp. 18–19.

33. Jacopo Strada, *Epitome Thesauri Antiquitatum* (Lyon: Jean de Tournes, 1553). Hubert Goltz takes the same approach, see *Vivae omnium fere imperatorum imagines* (Antwerp: Gillis Coppens van Diest, 1557). Milan Pelc also discusses the issue, see *Illustrium Imagines: Das Porträtbuch in der Renaissance* (Leiden: Brill, 2002), pp. 75–77.

34. Hans Huth, *Künstler und Werkstatt der Spätgotik* (Augsburg: Filser, 1923).

35. Vasari, *Le vite*, vol. 7, pp. 148–49.

36. Speyer, *Die literarische Fälschung*, pp. 318–20. Alberti's play *Philodoxeos Fabula* was attributed to "Lepidus," whom many early readers took to be a newly discovered Latin author; see Gary R. Grund (ed.), *Humanist Comedies*, I Tatti Renaissance Library (Cambridge, MA: Harvard University Press, 2005). Leonardo Bruni's translations of Demosthenes's speeches were understood by many to be Cicero's lost translations. On the pastiche of the classical author as a staple of Renaissance pedagogy, see Robert Black, *Humanism and Education in Medieval and Renaissance Italy* (Cambridge: Cambridge University Press, 2001), pp. 331–65. For guidance on this topic we are grateful to Stefano Cracolici.

37. Greene, *The Light in Troy*, p. 46.

38. Barkan, *Unearthing the Past*.

39. In an important recent essay Jonathan Hay describes the forgery as a non-authored production scorned by an art system oriented to authorship, and misunderstood by the modern discourse of art history. He goes on to provide a macrohistorical context for forgery, arguing that because "the forgery is the artifact that can escape its historical moment by not having an author," it is "always narratologically (as against evolutionally) modern, wherever in history it is produced." "The Value of Forgery," *Res: Anthropology and Aesthetics* 53/54 (Spring/Autumn 2008), pp. 5–19, here p. 15.

TWENTY-FOUR — ANTI-ARCHITECTURE

1. See Ralph Toledano, *Francesco di Giorgio Martini: Pittore e scultore* (Milan: Electa, 1987), pp. 102–105.

2. See the comments on ruins by Georg Simmel, cited in Sabine Forero-Mendoza, *Le temps des ruines: L'éveil de la conscience historique à la Renaissance* (Seysel: Champ Vallon, 2002), p. 9 n.1. At the moment when the collapse of the building destroys the form, the opposing parts of the building break down into their originary and universal "hostility," revealing the inability of form to overcome matter.

3. Toledano, *Francesco di Giorgio Martini*, p. 102.

4. Jacobus de Voragine, *Legenda aurea: Vulgo historia lombardica dicta*, ed. Johann Georg Theodor Graesse (Dresden: Arnold, 1846), p. 42.

5. The ruined building as a theme emerged already in Tuscan painting of the fourteenth century; for examples, as well as analyses of several fifteenth-century Nativity scenes, see Hansen, *Ruinbilleder*.

6. On the anti-architectural theme in the Judeo-Christian tradition, see John Onians, "The Last Judgment of Renaissance Architecture," *The Royal Society for the Encouragement of Arts, Manufactures and Commerce Journal* 128 (1980), pp. 701–18.

7. See the entry by François Viatte in Leonardo da Vinci, *Master Draftsman*, ed. Carmen C. Bambach (New York: Metropolitan Museum of Art, 2003), cat. no. 27, pp. 316–20.

8. *Italian Paintings of the Fifteenth Century*, ed. Miklós Boskovits (Washington: National Gallery of Art, 2003), pp. 161–66.

9. *Die Kirchen von Siena*, ed. Peter Anselm Riedl and Max Seidel, I, 1 (Munich: Bruckmann, 1985), pp. 117–19. See also the entry by Roberto Bartalini, Giovanni Agosti, and Cecilia Alessi, *Domenico Beccafumi e il suo tempo* (Milan: Electa, 1990), pp. 250–52.

10. See *Domenico Beccafumi e il suo tempo*, p. 146.

11. A similar motif occurs in the *Nativity* by Pinturicchio in the Baglione chapel in Santa Maria Maggiore in Spello, where real vines grow over and occlude the stylized vegetal motif of the pilaster of the ruined Roman building.

12. Joseph Rykwert, *On Adam's House in Paradise: The Idea of the Primitive Hut in Architectural History*, 2nd ed. (Cambridge, MA: The MIT Press, 1981), p. 183.

13. "[I]tem in Capitolio commonefacere potest et significare mores vetustatis Romuli casa et in arce sacrorum stramentis tecta." Vitruvius *De architectura* 2.1.5. The English text is from *Vitruvius: Ten Books on Architecture*, trans. Ingrid Rowland (Cambridge, MA: Harvard University Press, 1999), p. 35.

14. Massimo Mussini, *Francesco di Giorgio e Vitruvio: Le Traduzioni del "De Architectura" nei Codici Zichy, Spencer 129 e Magliabecchiano II.I.141* (Florence: Olschki, 2003), p. 339. This is a short work made between the first and second renditions of his *Trattati d'Architettura*. A corresponding passage, with interesting variations, can be found in the *Trattati*; see Francesco di Giorgio Martini, *Trattati di Architettura, Ingegneria ed Arte Militare*, vol. 2, ed. Corrado Maltese (Milano: Il Polifilo, 1967), pp. 29–98.

15. See Christof Thoenes and Hubertus Günther, "Gli ordini architettonici: Rinascita o invenzione?" in Marcello Fagiolo (ed.), *Rome e l'antico nell'arte e nella cultura del Cinquecento* (Rome: Istituto della Enciclopedia Italiana, 1985), pp. 261–310.

16. Francesco di Giorgio used features of his painted triumphal arch in his own architecture—the dolphin-volute capitals on his triumphal arch, for example, can be found in the portal of the church of San Bernardino in Urbino. For a reproduction, see Francesco Paolo Fiore and Manfredo Tafuri (eds.), *Francesco di Giorgio Architetto* (Milan: Electa, 1993), p. 236. On p. 243, Tafuri discusses an ancient example of such a dolphin capital, and on pp. 343–45 Howard Burns discusses a drawing showing such a capital on the monument to Epaphroditus near the mausoleum of Cecilia Metella.

17. Besides the bibliography discussed below, see David Landau and Peter Parshall, *The Renaissance Print* (New Haven, CT: Yale University Press, 1994), pp. 104–108.

18. The building has been interpreted as an inscribed quincunx; see Arnaldo Bruschi, *Bramante Architetto* (Bari: Laterza, 1969), pp. 745–50, and Mario Dal Mas, "Donato Bramante—L'incisione Prevedari—studio di restituzione prospettica," *Bollettino del Centro di Studi per la Storia dell'Architettura* 25 (1979), pp. 15–22. Franz Graf Wolff-Metternich reconstructed it as a basilical plan, although he adduces cross-in-square plan Romanesque churches as possible sources for the conception; see "Der Kupferstich Bernardos de Prevedari aus Mailand von 1481," pp. 7–108.

19. Franco Borsi, with critical catalogue by Stefano Borsi, *Bramante* (Milan: Electa, 1989), p. 161.

20. See Lorenzo Pericolo, "Heterotopia in the Renaissance: Modern Hybrids as Antiquities in Bramante, Cima da Conegliano and the *Hypnerotomachia Poliphili*," *Getty Research Journal* 1 (2009), pp. 1–16. Pericolo's point about the "Prevedari" engraving, Cima da Conegliano's *Madonna and Child with Sts. Michael and Andrew* in Parma, and the woodcuts of the *Hypnerotomachia Poliphili* is that they create hybrid architectures that involve both ancient and modern motifs. But it could not have been clear to the artists which building elements were ancient and which were modern. The rose window with balusters in the Prevedari print is a good example: it seems unlikely that a quattrocento observer would have read this as a specifically medieval form.

21. Werner Haftmann, *Das italienische Säulenmonument* (Hildesheim: Gerstenberg, 1972), pp. 42–45, 112–14 and passim.

22. The simile is Stefano Borsi's in Borsi, *Bramante*.

23. Constantine prudently built new basilicas rather than directly confronting the pagan aristocracy. There are no examples in Rome of direct occupation of pagan structures by Christians earlier than the Pantheon in 609. But the Pantheon is so exceptional that some have thought it evidence that the Pantheon wasn't really a temple, or at least wasn't understood as such by the Christians. San Lorenzo in Miranda, which occupies the temple of Antoninus and Faustina in the Roman Forum, was consecrated probably no earlier than the eleventh century. For good discussions of this whole issue, including the possible relationship between typological thinking and early medieval spoliation, see Maria Fabricius Hansen, *The Eloquence of Appropriation,* pp. 144–50, 225–35, 247–60, and 265–75.

TWENTY-FIVE — THE PRIMITIVE HUT AMIDST THE RUINS OF ST. PETER'S

1. Paolo Cortesi, *Pauli Cortesii Protonotarii Apostolici in libros de Cardinalatu ad Iulium Secundum Pont[ifex] Max[imus]* (Castro Cortesio: Nardi, 1510), fol. 21v, cited by Hubertus Günther, "I progetti di ricostruzione della Basilica di S. Pietro negli scritti contemporanei: giustificazioni e scrupoli," in Gianfranco Spagnesi (ed.), *L'Architettura della Basilica di San Pietro: Storia e costruzione* (Rome: Bonsignori, 1997), p. 143. See also Hubertus Günther, "'Als wäre die Peterskirche mutwillig in Flammen gestetzt': zeitgenössische Kommentare zum Neubau der Peterskirche und ihre Massstäbe," *Münchner Jahrbuch der bildenden Kunst* 48 (1997), p. 82.

2. Horst Bredekamp, *Sankt Peter in Rom und das Prinzip der Produktiven Zerstörung: Bau und Abbau von Bramante bis Bernini* (Berlin: Wagenbach, 2000), p. 49. See also James Ackerman, "Notes on Bramante's Bad Reputation," in *Studi Bramanteschi: Atti del convegno internazionale* (Rome: De Luca, 1974), pp. 339–50 and esp. 347–48.

3. Andrea Guarna da Salerno, *Scimmia*, trans. Eugenio Battisti (Rome: De Luca, 1970), discussed by Günther, "I progetti di ricostruzione della Basilica di S. Pietro," pp. 144–45.

4. Lex Bosman has made the most forceful argument to this effect, see *The Power of Tradition: Spolia in the Architecture of St. Peter's in the Vatican* (Hilversum: Uitgeverij Verloren, 2004). See also his review of William Tronzo (ed.), *St. Peter's in the Vatican* (Cambridge: Cambridge University Press, 2005) in *Art Bulletin* 89 (2007), pp. 162–64.

5. John Shearman, "Il 'Tiburio' di Bramante," in *Studi*

Bramanteschi: Atti del Congresso Internazionale. Milano, Urbino, Roma (Rome: De Luca, 1974), pp. 567–73.

6. William Tronzo, "Il Tegurium di Bramante," in Spagnesi (ed.), *L'Architettura della Basilica di San Pietro*, p. 163.

7. "[N]onnulli ex ulva palustri componunt tuguria tecta." Vitruvius 2.1.5. For the use of the word to describe the hut of Romulus throughout ancient literature, see the references in Joseph Rykwert, *On Adam's House in Paradise: The Idea of the Primitive Hut in Architectural History*, 2nd ed. (Cambridge, MA: The MIT Press, 1981), ch. 6 n.128.

8. Berlin, Kupferstichkabinett, inventory no. 79 D2a, fol. 52a.

9. Stockholm, Nationalmuseum, Coll. Ankersvärd 637. For Heemskerck's drawings of St. Peter's, see Christoph Thoenes, "St. Peter als Ruine: zu einigen Veduten Heemskercks," *Zeitschrift für Kunstgeschichte* 49 (1986), pp. 481–501. The attributions of the drawings are disputed; we feel that they are either by Heemskerck or closely copied from him.

10. Paul Joannides, *The Drawings of Raphael* (Oxford: Phaidon, 1983), p. 31.

11. John Onians, *Bearers of Meaning: The Classical Orders in Antiquity, the Middle Ages, and the Renaissance* (Princeton, NJ: Princeton University Press, 1988), pp. 260–61.

12. Madeline Cirillo Archer, *The Illustrated Bartsch*, vol. 28 (New York: Abaris, 1995), p. 14. It is also briefly discussed, together with some later printed copies, by Stefania Massari, in *Raphael Invenit* (Rome: Istituto Nazionale per la Grafica, 1985), pp. 139–40 and 588–89.

TWENTY-SIX — MOSAIC/PAINT 1: LIMITS OF SUBSTITUTION

1. The residence can be traced back to the late second century. Later it was incorporated into the villa of Heliogabalus (218–222). In the late third century it was still in imperial hands and therefore possibly a residence of Constantinus Chlorus and Helena. The *Liber Pontificalis* says

that Constantine founded the church, but this is unreliable. See Walther Buchowiecki, *Handbuch der Kirchen Roms*, vol. 1 (Vienna: Hollinek, 1967), pp. 604–606, and Richard Krautheimer, *Corpus basilicarum christianarum Romae*, vol. 1 (Città del Vaticano: Pontificio Istituto di archeologia cristiana, 1937–1977), pp. 165–94.

2. The link between Helena and the Sessorian palace is plausible, for it was mentioned already in the *Gesta Xysti* (500–550). Helena's role in the founding of the church is dubious, however. The oldest source to report that Helena brought the True Cross relic to Rome is the *Descriptio Lateranensis Ecclesiae* (1073–1118). Not before Flavio Biondo's *Roma instaurata* (1444–1446) does any source connect her to Santa Croce. For these and other demystifications, see Sible de Blauuw, "Jerusalem in Rome and the Cult of the Cross," in Renate L. Colella et al. (eds.), *Pratum Romanum: Richard Krautheimer zum 100. Geburtstag* (Wiesbaden: Reichert, 1997), pp. 55–73. De Blauuw considers the story of Helena's discovery of the cross relic a fiction created in Jerusalem in the 350s.

3. Vogt (ed.), *Niklas Muffels Beschreibung der Stadt Rom*, p. 35.

4. Huskinson, "The Crucifixion of St. Peter," pp. 135–57 (see p. 416 n.26 above). Deborah Howard proposes that Ferdinand and Isabella's involvement did not reach beyond the initial reliquary chapel; see "Bramante's Tempietto: Spanish Royal Patronage in Rome," *Apollo* 136 (1992), pp. 211–17.

5. Jack Freiberg argues that the Tempietto was commissioned with the subterranean chapel in 1502; see "Bramante's Tempietto and the Spanish Crown," *Memoirs of the American Academy in Rome* 50 (2005), pp. 151–205.

6. On the commission of the apse frescoes, see Francesca Cappelletti, "L'affresco nel catino absidale di Santa Croce in Gerusalemme a Roma," pp. 119–26, esp. p. 124 for arguments against a dating of the frescoes prior to 1492; and Meredith J. Gill, "Antoniazzo Romano and the Recovery of Jerusalem in Late Fifteenth-Century Rome," pp. 28–47. Cappelletti's and Gill's findings are not in conflict. See also Vitaliano Tiberia, *L'affresco restaurato con Storie della Croce nella*

Basilica di Santa Croce in Gerusalemme a Roma (Todi: Ediart, 2001).

7. See Noehles, "Antoniazzo Romano: Studien zur Quattrocentomalerei in Rom"; Cavallaro, *Antoniazzo Romano e gli Antoniazzeschi*, pp. 263–64, no. 140; Sergio Rossi, "Roma anno 1500: immagini per un giubileo," in Bonita Cleri (ed.), *Homo viator: nella fede, nella cultura, nella storia* (Urbino: Quattroventi, 1997), pp. 245–56; and Rossi, "Tradizione e innovazione nella pittura romana del Quattrocento: i maestri e loro botteghe," in Rossi and Valeri (eds.), *Le due Rome del Quattrocento*, pp. 19–39. See esp. p. 34 where he attributes the overall design of the fresco and some important figures to Antoniazzo, but the rest to the workshop under the direction of his son Marcantonio Aquili.

8. Christa Gardner von Teuffel, "Light on the Cross: Cardinal Pedro Gonzalez de Mendoza and Antoniazzo Romano in Sta. Croce in Gerusalemme, Rome," in Lars R. Jones and Louisa C. Matthew (eds.), *Coming About—A Festschrift for John Shearman* (Cambridge, MA: Harvard University Art Museums, 2001), pp. 49–55.

9. Examples of early medieval apses completely redone in the fifteenth century are the Duomo at Spoleto (Filippo Lippi) and Santi Apostoli in Rome (Melozzo da Forlì). Gardner von Teuffel believes that the documents suggest that the old mosaic did survive to the fifteenth century; see "Light on the Cross," pp. 51–52. See also Gill, "Antoniazzo Romano and the Recovery of Jerusalem in Late Fifteenth-Century Rome," pp. 35–36.

10. All the twelfth-century paintings were completely covered by the eighteenth-century rebuilding and only rediscovered at the beginning of the twentieth century. See Gill, "Antoniazzo Romano and the Recovery of Jerusalem in Late Fifteenth-Century Rome," p. 37.

11. Christa Belting-Ihm has examples from Thessalonica and Sinai, see *Programme der christlichen Apsismalerei vom vierten Jahrhundert bis zur Mitte des achten Jahrhunderts* (Wiesbaden: Steiner, 1960), figs. 13.1, 20.1, 23.1, 25.1; see also "Theophanic Images of Divine Majesty in Early Medieval Italian Church Decoration," in William Tronzo (ed.), *Italian Church Decoration of the Middle Ages and Early Renaissance* (Bologna: Nuova Alfa, 1989), pp. 43–58.

12. The frescoes, already whitewashed in the sixteenth century and partially destroyed by the eighteenth century, were only rediscovered in 1959. The Christ figure seems to have occupied a mandorla-shaped aperture in a solid field of cherubim. See Noehles, *Antoniazzo Romano*, no. 85; and Vitaliano Tiberia, *Antoniazzo Romano per il Cardinale Bessarione a Roma* (Rome: Ediart, 1992), p. 17, fig. 2 and p. 61, fig. 23.

13. Carlo Bertelli, "The Image of Pity in Santa Croce in Gerusalemme," pp. 40–55; Hans Belting, *Das Bild und sein Publikum im Mittelalter: Form und Funktion früher Bildtafeln der Passion* (Berlin: Mann, 1981), pp. 66–67; Gerhard Wolf, *Schleier und Spiegel*, pp. 163–66; *Byzantium: Faith and Power*, no. 131. Bertelli points to confusion among the sources about whether the Santa Croce icon was the original image.

14. Anthony Cutler states that apart from the Santa Croce icon and the Twelve Feasts diptych now in the Museo dell'Opera del Duomo in Florence, micro-mosaic icons were "all but unknown" in Italy before the fall of Constantinople; see "From Loot to Scholarship," p. 251.

15. *Byzantium: Faith and Power*, no. 329. On the engraving, see Peter Parshall, "Imago Contrafacta," pp. 554–79, and Wolf, *Schleier und Spiegel*, pp. 164–65.

16. Avignon, Musée du Petit Palais. Noehles, *Antoniazzo Romano*, no. 84; Antonio Paolucci, *Antoniazzo Romano: Catalogo completo dei dipinti* (Florence: Cantini, 1992), no. 30.

17. On the early reception, see Cappelletti, "L'affresco nel catino absidale di Santa Croce in Gerusalemme a Roma," pp. 122–23.

18. On simultaneous representation, see E. Kluckert, "Die Simultanbilder Memlings, ihre Würzeln und Wirkungen," *Das Münster* 27 (1974), pp. 284–95; Lew Andrews, *Story and Space in Renaissance Art: The Rebirth of Continuous Narrative* (Cambridge: Cambridge

University Press, 1995), pp. 14–17, 70–71, 98–102; Wolfgang Kemp, *Die Räume der Maler*, p. 48; and Silvia Tomasi Velli, *Le immagini e il tempo: Narrazione visiva, storia e allegoria tra Cinquecento e Seicento* (Pisa: Edizioni della Normale, 2007), pp. 64–88.

19. As argued by Andrews, *Story and Space*.

20. Gardner von Teuffel wonders whether the symbolic cross may not have been the subject of the predecessor mosaic. "Light on the Cross," p. 51.

21. Cappelletti, "L'affresco nel catino absidale di Santa Croce in Gerusalemme a Roma," p. 125.

TWENTY-SEVEN — MOSAIC/PAINT 2: INTERMEDIAL COMPARISON

1. Christoph Luitpold Frommel, "Baldassare Peruzzi als Maler und Zeichner," *Römisches Jahrbuch für Kunstgeschichte* 11 (1967/68), pp. 56–59. See also Simona Antellini, "Cappella di Sant' Elena: Restauro del mosaico e degli affreschi della volta," in Anna Maria Affani (ed.), *La Basilica di S. Croce in Gerusalemme a Roma* (Viterbo: Beta Gamma Editrice, 1997), p. 129.

2. Another early source linking Peruzzi to Santa Croce was an inscription on the project drawing for the apse fresco discovered by Christa Gardner von Teuffel, naming "Baldassari." That name was subsequently crossed out and changed—as we saw in the previous section—to "Maestro Delantoniazzo"; see "Light on the Cross," pp. 49–50.

3. The best illustrations can be found in Cynthia A. Payne, "Lux mundi: The Vault Mosaic in the Cappella S. Elena, S. Croce in Gerusalemme, Rome," *Athanor* 17 (1999), pp. 35–43.

4. Ilaria Toesca, "A Majolica Inscription in Santa Croce in Gerusalemme," pp. 102–105. Some of the tile inscription was destroyed in the eighteenth century. The entire text was published in 1592.

5. "Inde vero vetustate murorum aut inhabitantum incuria fornice sacelli istius Hierusalem ruinam minante et musivis figuris operis Valentiniani…: omnino deletis R.mus D. Bernardinus Lupi Carvaial Epus Ostien. S.R.E. cardinalis/s.+ in Hierusalem patriarcha hyerosolymitan. et fornicem ipsum ac figuras musivas denuo ad instar prior. refecit."

6. Frommel published a drawing of the chapel (Uffizi A 4000) that appears to show remains of the paleochristian mosaic on the upper register of the southwest wall; see "Progetto e archeologia in due disegni di Antonio da Sangallo il Giovane per Santa Croce in Gerusalemme," in Silvia Danesi Squarzina (ed.), *Roma, centro ideale della cultura dell'Antico nei secoli XV e XVI* (Milan: Electa, 1989), pp. 382–89.

7. Michelangelo said that he was expected to provide the "usual ornamentation" on the ceiling of Sistine Chapel: "un certo partimento ripieno d'adornamento, come si usa." Charles de Tolnay, *The Sistine Ceiling (Michelangelo*, vol. 3) (Princeton, NJ: Princeton University Press, 1945), pp. 14–15.

8. Hans Belting, *Die Oberkirche von San Francesco in Assisi* (Berlin: Mann, 1977), p. 74.

9. See Jones and Penny, *Raphael*, p. 56, figs. 65–66.

10. Washington, National Gallery of Art, inventory no. 379. Miklós Boskovits and David Alan Brown, *Italian Paintings of the Fifteenth Century* (Washington: National Gallery of Art, 2003), pp. 293–95; Andrea de Marchi, *Gentile da Fabriano* (Milan: Federico Motta, 2006), pp. 215–16, fig. 65. The relics of the saint, who died in Myra in Asia Minor in 343, were stolen and transferred to Bari in Puglia in 1087. Gentile has imagined the tombsite at the basilica of St. Nicholas at Bari, a structure built to house the relics.

11. See also Gentile's *Stigmatization of St. Francis*, which shows an image of an Annunciation in thirteenth-century style on the wall of the chapel; de Marchi, *Gentile da Fabriano*, p. 225 n.133, fig. 32. For other examples of fifteenth- and even fourteenth-century retrospectives on older styles of painting, see Krüger, "Medium and Imagination: Aesthetic Aspects of Trecento Panel Painting," pp. 60–63.

12. Peter Humfrey, "Cima da Conegliano a Parma," *Saggi e Memorie di Storia dell'arte* 13 (1982), pp. 33–46.

13. See Deborah Howard, "Bellini and Architecture," in Peter Humfrey (ed.), *Cambridge Companion to Giovanni Bellini* (Cambridge: Cambridge University Press, 2004), pp. 152–54. See also Bellini's San Zaccaria altarpiece (1505), depicting a mosaic apse with vine scrolls.

14. John Shearman, "The Chigi Chapel in S. Maria del Popolo," *Journal of the Warburg and Courtauld Institutes* 24 (1961), pp. 129–60; Derek A. R. Moore describes the Chigi Chapel as a "*summa* of the period's command of spolia and other materials"; see "Notes on the Use of Spolia in Roman Architecture from Bramante to Bernini," in Striker (ed.), *Architectural Studies in Memory of Richard Krautheimer*, p. 120.

15. Patricia Fortini Brown, *Venetian Narrative Painting in the Age of Carpaccio* (New Haven, CT: Yale University Press, 1988), pp. 186–89. Augusto Gentili, *Le storie di Carpaccio* (Venice: Marsilio, 1996), pp. 100–102.

16. Luhmann, *Art as a Social System*, p. 110.

17. On the mosaic technique in the chapel, see Antellini, "Cappella di Sant' Elena," p. 128. In the older scholarly literature, before the involvement of Peruzzi had been established, the mosaics at Santa Croce were sometimes attributed to Melozzo.

18. When Raphael took over, the ceiling was already planned and underway, in the hands of the painter Sodoma. The parts usually attributed to Sodoma have gold grounds but no incised lines simulating mosaic. Roberto Bartalini confirms that the techniques used, on the one hand, in the architectural divisions, the grotesque friezes, and the small narrative scenes (attributed to Sodoma) and, on the other, in the roundels with the allegories and the rectangular scenes in the corners (by Raphael) are clearly different: buon fresco used by Raphael in contrast to a mixed technique used by Sodoma; "Sodoma, the Chigi and the Vatican Stanze," *Burlington Magazine* 143 (2001), pp. 544–53. There are also clear irregularities in the plaster joins at the frontiers between these two zones. Thus the different treatment of the gold grounds corresponds to the different approaches of the two artists.

TWENTY-EIGHT — SPACE FOR FICTION

1. On the identifications of the philosophers, see Ingrid D. Rowland, "The Intellectual Background of the *School of Athens*: Tracking Divine Wisdom in the Rome of Julius II," in Marcia Hall (ed.), *Raphael's "School of Athens"* (Cambridge: Cambridge University Press, 1997), pp. 131–70.

2. See Robin Evans, *The Projective Cast: Architecture and its Three Geometries* (Cambridge, MA: The MIT Press, 1995), pp. 22–23, fig. 11.

3. On the connections between Fra Bartolommeo and Raphael, see Ludovico Borgo, "Fra Bartolommeo e Raffaello: L'Incontro Romano del 1513," in Micaela Sambucco Hamoud and Maria Letizia Strocchi (eds.), *Studi su Raffaello* vol. 1 (Urbino: Quattro Venti, 1987), pp. 499–507, and Patricia Emison, "Raphael's Dresden Cherubs," *Zeitschrift für Kunstgeschichte* 65 (2002), pp. 242–50.

4. According to Ernst Gombrich, the true title of the work, which like the others in the room has to be read from the ceiling downward, is indeed "The Search for the Knowledge of Causes" or *causarum cognitio*: difference along the vertical axis, in other words; see "Raphael's *Stanza della Segnatura* and the Nature of its Symbolism," in Gombrich, *Symbolic Images: Studies in the Art of the Renaissance* (London: Phaidon, 1972), pp. 88–89.

5. Leo Steinberg, *Leonardo's Incessant Last Supper* (New York: Zone Books, 2001).

6. See the analysis in Jones and Penny, *Raphael*, p. 60.

7. Gombrich pointed out that we need to look at nineteenth-century engravings to grasp the floors, walls, and vaults of the room all at once; he reproduced two of them. See "Raphael's *Stanza della Segnatura*," p. 86.

8. Panofsky, *Renaissance and Renascences in Western Art*, pp. 204–205.

9. Matthias Winner sees the theme of relics and typological correspondences echoed throughout the room; see "Allusio auf die Reliquie der Veronika in

Raffaels Eliodor," in Kessler and Wolf (eds.), *The Holy Face and the Paradox of Representation*, pp. 310–17.

10. An engraving by G. P. da Birago, ca 1500, was the first printed reproduction of a painting. See Steinberg, *Leonardo's Incessant Last Supper*, p. 19 and fig. 4; on painted copies of the picture, see also his Appendix E, p. 227ff.; see also the engraved reproduction of the *Last Supper* by Marcantonio Raimondi, after a drawing by Raphael, on p. 23, fig. 7.

11. Grazia Bernini Pezzini et al. (eds.), *Raphael Invenit* (Rome: Instituto Naztionale per la Grafica, 1985).

12. Christa Gardner von Teuffel, "Niccolò di Segna, Sassetta, Piero della Francesca and Perugino: Cult and Continuity at Sansepolcro," *Städel-Jahrbuch* N.F. 17 (1999), pp. 163–208.

13. On Warburg's concept of the *Pathosformel*, see E. H. Gombrich, *Aby Warburg: An Intellectual Biography* (London, The Warburg Institute, 1970), p. 263 and passim; Silvia Ferretti, *Cassirer, Panofsky, and Warburg: Symbol, Art, and History* (New Haven, CT: Yale University Press, 1989), p. 2 and passim; Kurt W. Forster, "Introduction" to Warburg, *The Renewal of Pagan Antiquity* (Los Angeles, CA: Getty Research Institute, 1999), pp. 36–38; and Georges Didi-Huberman, *L'image survivante: Histoire de l'art et temps des fantômes selon Aby Warburg* (Paris: Minuit, 2002), pp. 191–202.

14. Luwig Goldscheider, *Michelangelo* (New York: Phaidon, 1953), p. 259.

15. Vasari gives the extraordinary list of artists who studied the cartoon: Aristotile da Sangallo, Ridolfo Ghirlandaio, Raphael, Francesco Granacci, Baccio Bandinelli, Alonso Berruguete, Andrea del Sarto, Franciabigio, Jacopo Sansovino, Rosso Fiorentino, Maturino, Lorenzetto, Niccolò Tribolo, Jacopo da Pontormo, Perin del Vaga. See *Le vite*, vol. 6, pp. 24–25.

16. Warburg, "The Theatrical Costumes for the Intermedi of 1589," in *The Renewal of Pagan Antiquity*.

17. Panofsky said that Raphael "must have known" that the *lira da braccio* was not an ancient instrument, *Renaissance and Renascences in Western Art*, p. 205. Lisa Pon, however, points out that Marcantonio Raimondi depicted mythological figures playing the *lira da braccio* four times before he ever met Raphael; *Raphael, Dürer, and Marcantonio Raimondi*, p. 89. Raphael had reason to believe, in other words, that the modern instrument was substitutionally linked to an ancient instrument—that is *was* the ancient instrument.

18. For two different views on this, see Gombrich, "Raphael's *Stanza della Segnatura*," p. 86, and John Shearman, *The Vatican Stanze*.

19. Elizabeth Eisenstein, *The Printing Press as an Agent of Change* (Cambridge: Cambridge University Press, 1979).

20. Brian Stock, *The Implications of Literacy: Written Language and Models of Interpretation in the Eleventh and Twelfth Centuries* (Princeton, NJ: Princeton University Press, 1983).

21. On Marsilio Ficino's rehabilitation of Socrates as a type of Christ, see James Hankins, *Plato in the Italian Renaissance* (Leiden: Brill, 1990), pp. 321–29.

22. Madrid, Museo Thyssen-Bornemisza. Fedja Anzelewsky, *Albrecht Dürer: Das malerische Werk* (Berlin: Deutscher Verlag für Kunstwissenschaft, 1991), pp. 206–10, no. 98. The word "Roma" is illegible in the painting but is attested by old drawn copies.

23. Plato *Phaedrus* 276a and 275e, in the translation of Benjamin Jowett.

24. Francis X. Martin, "Fulfillment of the Christian Golden Age under Julius II," in *Friar, Reformer, and Renaissance Scholar: Life and Work of Giles of Viterbo 1469–1532* (Villanova, Augustinian Press, 1992), pp. 228, 238, and 241.

25. Bartsch 24. Suzanne Boorsch and Michal and R. E. Lewis, *The Engravings of Giorgio Ghisi* (New York: Metropolitan Museum of Art, 1985), pp. 61–63, no. 11.

26. Jeremy Wood points out that Karel van Mander described it as "de Schole" already in 1604; see "Cannibalized Prints and Early Art History: Vasari, Bellori and Fréart de Chambray on Raphael," *Journal of the Warburg and Courtauld Institutes* 51 (1988), pp. 213–14.

27. Vasari, *Le vite*, vol. 4, pp. 329 and 332. Also see Rowland, "The Intellectual Background of the

School of Athens," p. 154 n.56. Most commentators simply dismiss Vasari's identification as a blunder. For the different explanations for Vasari's comment, see Wood, "Cannibalized Prints and Early Art History," pp. 212–17. The basis for Vasari's confusion seems to have been the engraving by Agostino Veneziano of the "Pythagoras" figure and the group around him (1523; Bartsch 492) which inscribes a Gospel text onto the book. For a modern reading that pursues Agostino's and Vasari's syncretism, see Harry B. Gutman, "The Medieval Content of Raphael's 'School of Athens,'" *Journal of the History of Ideas* 2 (1941), pp. 420–29.

28. The statues were carved in 1461–1463 for Pius II. They were removed in 1847 and are now in the Vatican Palace. Hannes Roser, *St. Peter in Rom im 15. Jahrhundert* (Munich: Hirmer, 2005), pp. 89–93.

29. See Birte Poulsen, "The Dioscuri and the Saints," *Analecta Romana Instituti Danici* 21 (1993), pp. 141–52.

30. "[D]ove sono ritratti tutti i savi del mondo che disputano in varij modi." Vasari, *Le vite,* vol. 4, p. 330.

31. Jones and Penny doubt that the unwreathed scribe of the *Parnassus* could be the early Roman poet Ennius, who imagined himself the successor to Homer; see *Raphael,* p. 72.

Index

AACHEN, PALACE CHAPEL, 69, 181.
Abd-al-Malik, Caliph, 64.
Accaiauoli, Niccolò, 179.
Accarisi, Graziolo, 204–205.
Acheiropoieton; acheiropoieta, 16, 64, 72, 97, 128, 205–207, 270. *See also* Vera icon; Mandylion; Portraits of Christ, indexical.
Acre, 195, 208.
Adorno, Anselm, 67, 207.
Agustín, Antonio, 287.
Albergati, Niccolò, 204.
Alberti, Leandro, 40.
Alberti, Leon Battista, 119, 128, 140–42, 157, 161, 165, 168, 175–79, 214, 274, 297, 329, 398 nn.5, 11, 410 n.13, 415 n.10, figs. 15.5, 16.1.
Alexander VI, Pope, 182, 239, 322.
Altdorfer, Albrecht, 182; *Crucifixion* (Budapest), 14.
Altemps, Marco Sittico, Cardinal, 207.
Amantius, Bartholomeus, 253.
Ambrogio, Teseo, 253.
Ambrose, Saint, 220, 353.
Ammanati, Jacopo, Cardinal, 101.
Ammonio, Andrea, 370 n.15.
Anachronic artifacts, 18, 75, 86, 326; compared to anachronistic artifacts, 13–14, 45.
Anachronism, 10, 141, 298; in painting, 35–41, 43–44, 151, 155, 347, 350, 358; and fashion, 92–93.
Anastasis, *see* Jerusalem, Holy Sepulchre.
Angelico, Fra, 324.
Angelita, Girolamo, 212.
Annius of Viterbo (Giovanni Nanni), 247, 249–51, 294, fig. 20.3.
Anselm, Thomas, 263.
Antico (Pier Jacopo Alari Bonacolsi), 41, 295, fig. 4.1.
Antiquarianism, 94; and ancient inscriptions, 221; archeological, 18, 27, 136–46, 154, 188, 323; and architecture, 138, 142–43, 145–146, 157; and coins and medals, 286, 290; and conception of the antique, 138, 161–63, 257; and icons, 105–107, 116, 128; and manuscripts, 144; and mosaic, 128–33, 336–45; and likeness, 286; and substitution, 144–46, 256, 343. *See also* Misdating.
Antonello da Messina, 112, 119, 282.
Antoniazzo Romano, 109–10, 114–15, 208, 323–24, 326–27,

330–32, 340, 343, 347, 350, figs. 26.2, 26.3, 26.4, 28.3.
Apelles, 279–80.
Apianus, Petrus, 253.
Apollo, 209, 302, 351, 353–54, 360, 364, fig. 28.4.
Apollonio de Giovanni, 392 n.16.
Aquileia, Cathedral, Holy Sepulchre, 56–57, fig. 6.3.
Aragon, Louis, 33.
Archaism, 50, 81, 111–12, 114, 324, 338, 345. *See also* Pseudo-archaism.
Architecture: ancient and limited knowledge of, 138–40, 142–43; ancient and reconstruction of, 308–309; and authorship, 157, 175–77, 309, 319; citation of historical styles of, 153–154; diagrams its own history, 157, 177–78, 317–19; misdating of, 135–42, 146; and print technology, 163, 168; Renaissance, postantique sources for, 140–46, 161, 172–74; represented, 63–66, 70, 147–61, 165–67, 170–72, 177–78, 307, 317–19; and substitution, 30, 51–61, 64–70, 135–36, 138, 140–46, 157, 165–66, 174; treatises on, 163; typology, 155, 159, 168–70, 311, 321. *See also* Models.
Arezzo, 150, 323, 330; Cathedral, 137.
Aristotle, 347, 350–51, 360, 363.
Art, modern conception of, 38, 217, 296, 355, 358, 364.
Art collecting, culture of, 275, 278–83, 285, 295, 296.
Assisi, 336.
Aste, Niccolò delle, 203.
Athens, 8, 136, 143.
Atri, Jacopo d', 255.
Attavanti, Attavante, 161.
Auerbach, Erich, 33.
Augsburg, 158, 222, 239, 245, 251, 257; St. Anna, 168; Sts. Ulrich and Afra, 220–21
Augustine, Saint, 35–39, 44, 87, 93, 267, 353, fig. 4.1.
Augustus, Emperor (Octavian), 180, 280, 290, fig. 13.1.
Authorship, artistic, 27, 38, 123–24, 126–28, 133, 323, 359; and art market, 275, 296; as performance, 14–16, 18, 49–50, 177; and style, 37–38.
Authorlessness, 43, 117. *See also Acheiropoieton*; Stylelessness; Vera icon.
Aurispa, Giovanni, 105.

BALDUNG, HANS, 285.
Balzac, Honoré de, 289.
Barbari, Jacopo de', 269.

Barbo, Pietro, *see* Paul II.

Baronio, Cesare, Cardinal, 188.

Barthes, Roland, 8.

Bartolommeo, Fra, 43; *Vision of Saint Catherine*, Lucca, 349–50, fig. 28.3.

Basil the Great, Saint, 87.

Bassano, Alessandro, 256.

Baudelaire, Charles, 90–91.

Bayezid II, Sultan, 140, 241.

Beatus Rhenanus, 137.

Beauvoir, Simone de, 7, 12, 18.

Bebenhausen, 381 n.28.

Beccafumi, Domenico, 305, fig. 24.5.

Bellini, Giovanni, 112, 114, 119, 182, 268, 392 n22, 423 n.25, fig. 11.5; *San Giobbe Altarpiece*, 338, 340–42, 350, fig. 27.3.

Bellini, Jacopo, 112, 119.

Benci, Spinello, 274.

Benedetto da Maiano, 123, 127–28, 133, fig. 12.1.

Benedict VIII, Pope, 205.

Benjamin, Walter, 33–34, 90.

Bentivoglio, Sante, 205.

Bessarion, Basilius, Cardinal, 37, 98, 105, 107, 205, 327.

Bethlehem, 35, 69, 149, 154, 201.

Bible moralisée, 151, 157.

Biondo, Flavio, 441 n.2.

Bladelin, Pieter, 149.

Bloch, Ernst, 373 n.11.

Boccaccio, 392 n.16.

Boldù, Giovanni, 253.

Bologna, 205; Madonna del Monte, 204; Santo Stefano, 57.

Borges, Jorge Luis, 45.

Borgo San Sepolcro, 150, 201, 357.

Boschini, Marco, 296.

Botticelli, Sandro, 10, 324; *Adoration of the Magi*, Washington, 305, fig. 24.3; *Portrait of Youth Holding an Icon*, private collection, 115–19, 122, 123, 128, 155, 178–79, 184, fig. 11.7; *Primavera*, Florence, Uffizi, 37; *Temptations of Christ*, Sistine Chapel, 166, 170, fig. 15.4.

Botticini, Francesco, 348.

Bramante, Donato, 143–44, 213–14, 309, 313–14, figs. 10.5, 18.6, 24.6; *Tegurio*, 183, 314–19, figs. 25.1, 25.2, 25.3, 25.4; *Tempietto*, 139–40, 172, 174, 184, 188, 190, 193–94, 299, 314, 322–23, 342, 354, figs. 15.8, 17.5.

Brandi, Cesare, 75.

Bregno, Andrea, 139.

Bregno, Giambattista, 43.

Breydenbach, Bernhard von, 67, 165, 168.

Bronze, as anachronic medium, 103, 265.

Bruges, 149, 207; Church of the Holy Sepulchre, 67.

Brunelleschi, Filippo, 131, 135–36, 138, 141–42, 150, 157–58, 187, 319, 410 n.13.

Bruni, Leonardo, 438 n.36.

Bruschius, Caspar, 138.

Bruyn, Cornelis de, fig. 6.1.

Bulgarini, Bartolommeo, 116.

Burchard, Johann, 223, 234.

Burgkmair, Hans, 245, 251–53, 257, 259, 263, 265–67, 269, 286, figs. 21.5, 21.6, 21.7, 21.8.

Byzantium: as conduit to antiquity, 101–103, 241, 270, 329; images imported to West from, 97–107, 128, 130, 207, 230, 243.

CACCIANEMICI, GERARDO, *see* Lucius II.

Caesar (Juius Caesar), Emperor, 93, 252, 296.

Caimi, Bernardino, 61.

Callixtus III, Pope, 188.

Cambrai, Cambrai Madonna, 110–13, 116, 299, figs. 11.3, 11.4.

Campagnola, Domenico, 256.

Campin, Robert, 105, 119, 158, 389 n.26, 435 n.30; *Betrothal of the Virgin*, 152–53, 157, 177–79, fig. 14.3.

Carafa, Diomedes, Count, 290–91, fig. 23.2.

Carpaccio, Vittore: *Saint Augustine in His Study*, Scuola di San Giorgio degli Schiavoni, 35–44, 50, 52, 65, 93, 116, 133, 174, 184, 252, 267, 299, 337–38, 340, figs. 4.1, 4.2, 4.3; *Vision of Prior Ottobon*, 341–42, fig. 27.4.

Carpi, Alberto Pio da, 376 n.23.

Carvajal, Bernardino, Cardinal, 322, 326–27, 336, 338, 343.

Castiglione, Baldassare, *The Courtier*, 38.

Catherine of Alexandria, Saint, 97, 222.

Catherine of Siena, Saint, 208, 324.

Cavallini, Pietro, 132, 329.

Cavino, Giovanni, 256, 287.

Celtis, Conrad, 247, 249, 253, 425 n.44.

Cennini, Cennino, 387 n.21.

Centrally planned buildings, 56, 59–61, 67, 136–37, 139–40, 172. *See also* Holy Sepulchre, replicas; Jerusalem, Dome of the Rock; Jerusalem, Imbomon; Rome, Tempietto.

Cesariano, Cesare, 143, 163, 170, fig. 15.3.

Charlemagne, Emperor, 69, 146, 181, 312.

Chiusi, 274.

Christian temple: as successor to Temple of Jerusalem, 64–65, 151; basilical plan of, 69; origins of, 63–69, 151; and quincunx plans , 140, 143.

Christus, Petrus, 111.

Chrysoloras, Manuel, 33, 105, 140.

Ciampolini, Giovanni, 294.

Cicero, 91, 177.

Cima da Conegliano, 43, 182, 338.

Cimabue, Giovanni, 75, 82, 105, 197, 396 n.26.

Ciriaco d' Ancona, 143, 413 n.17.

Citation, 35–41, 43–44, 115–18, 122, 357–59; of historical style, 81, 151–58, 184. *See also* Archaism.

Clement VI, Pope, 103.

Clement VII, Pope, 283.

Clement VIII, Pope, 413 n.18.

Cock, Hieronymus, 361–62.

Cologne, 149, 161, 225, fig. 14.2.

Colonna, Vittoria, 283.

Commodus, Emperor, 136.

Como, San Fedele, 137.

Constantine I, Emperor, 40, 54–55, 60, 64, 67, 69, 101, 136–37, 146, 167–68, 180, 188, 193, 209, 214, 219, 224, 242, 246, 290, 294–95, 311–12, 321, figs. 6.1, 10.8, 23.1, 26.1.

Constantine X Momomachos, Emperor, 380 n.16.

Constantinople, 72–73, 101, 105, 107, 119, 121, 128, 205, 207, 241, 252, 265, 269, 327, figs. 11.2, 20.1; *Hagia Sophia*, 140.

Copies: architectural, 56–61, 69–70; activating prototypes, 30, 42, 44, 52, 113, 202, 243, 281, 253–54, 256–59, 263, 266–67, 271–74, 327; of drawings, 282–83, 295; of icons, 109–15, 280; of medals, 241–47, 257–73; of paintings, 275–85; of prints, 21–26; print technology eliminates drift of, 251, 254, 256, 263, 265–66, 280–81, 362–63; and prototype theory, 86–87; relationship of original to, 60–61; of sculpture, 43, 254–57, 259–73; and substitution, 281; and Titulus Crucis, 225–30, 236–39; typological vs. documentary, 280–81.

Coppo di Marcovaldo, 79.

Cortesi, Paolo, 313.

Cosmatesque pavements: of twelfth and thirteenth centuries, 185–88, 190, 194, fig. 17.6: of fifteenth century (neo-cosmatesque), 185–90, 299, 327, 345, 348, figs. 17.1, 17.2, 17.3, 17.4, 17.5.

Cosmati, 185–86, 188.

Costume, *see* Fashion.

Cotton Genesis, 44.

Council of Ferrara and Florence, 101, 103, 110, 119, fig. 10.6.

Cranach, Lucas, the Elder, 269.

Cranach, Lucas, the Younger, 269.

Cronaca, il (Simone del Pollaiuolo), 139, 384 n.22.

Croÿ, Philippe de, 97, 119–20, figs. 10.1, 11.8, 11.9.

Crusades, Crusaders, 56–57, 59–60, 66, 68–69, 72, 161, 165, 208, 214, 332.

Cult image, as class of objects, 115–18, 122, 128, 204.

Cuspinian, Johann, 290, 425 n.44.

Cyriacus, Pope, 154.

DADDI, BERNARDO, 78.

Dante, 356.

Dati, Lorenzo, 274.

David, Gerard, 281, 406 n.10.

Decembrio, Pier Candido, 297.

Demetrios, Saint, 98, fig. 10.4.

Denis, Saint, 224.

Desiderio Settignano, 296.

Desiderius, Abbott, 185.

Desiderius, King, 247.

Diana, Benedetto, 267, fig. 21.10.

Diogenes, 42.

Dion Cassius, 379 n.6.

Dionysius of Halicarnassus, 51–52.

Dominic, Saint, 74–75.

Dominici, Giovanni, 85.

Donatello, 45, 103, 122, 141–42, 170, 187, 291–94, figs. 10.7, 23.2.

Donato, Girolamo, 224.

Donatus, 124.

Dorotheos, 280.

Double-think, 31, 46, 53, 135, 326.

Dråby, 21.

Duccio di Buoninsegna, 78–79, 166, 386 n.19, 405 n.4.

Durandus, William, 68, 103, 112.

Dürer, Albrecht, 199, 285, 360, fig. 18.3.

ECO, UMBERTO, 256, 275.

Edessa, 205.

Edicule, *see* Jerusalem, Holy Sepulchre.

Egeria, 220, 223.

Egidio da Viterbo, 137, 361.

Einsiedeln, 215–17, fig. 18.7.

Einstein, Carl, 34.

Eliade, Mircea, 150–51.

Ennius, 446 n.31.

Erasmus, Desiderius, 12–13, 91–93, 212, 299, 376 n.23, 422 n.12.

Este, Francesco d', Cardinal, 107.

Este, Isabella d', Marchioness, 255, 283, 295–96, 333.

Eucharist, 351, 353, 363–64.

Eugene IV, Pope, 182, 275, fig. 22.1.

Eusebius, 40, 42, 54, 220, 243, 323, 376 n.23, fig. 4.4.

Evans, Walker, 279.

Evidence: artifacts and images as, 18, 112, 224, 231, 235, 241–43, 246, 249, 251, 273, 293, 296, 322, fig. 21.15; of Christ's appearance, 245–46, 252, 257, 268–69, 271, figs. 20.1, 21.6, 21.7, 21.8; fabrication of, 243, 246, 249, 273–74, 296, 299; medals and coins as, 242, 246, 251–52, 257, 286, 296, figs. 21.7, 21.8, 21.10, 21.11; relics as, 31; Titulus Crucis as, 221, 224, 229, 233, 236, 239, 323. *See also* Icons, documentary function of; Referential images, artifacts, and artworks.

Eyck, Jan van, 49, 105, 111–12, 119, 141, 147–48, 153, 157, 167, 278, 280–82, 389 n.25, 407 n.22; *Annunciation*, Washington, 155, 158, 337, fig. 14.4; *Three Marys at the Tomb of Christ*, Rotterdam, 63–68, 70–71, 88, 167, fig. 7.1.

FABRI, FELIX, 67.

Fashion, 85–95, 159–60, 243.

Febvre, Lucien, 46.

Ferdinand the Catholic of Aragon, King, 219, 228, 322, 333.

Ferdinand of Habsburg, Archduke, 280.

Fiera, Battista, 255, figs. 21.1, 21.2.

Filarete (Antonio di Pietro Averlino), 38, 93–94, 103, 132, 141, 143, 274, 362, fig. 10.7.

Firabet, Ulrich, 27, fig. 2.2.

Florence, 33, 126, 139, 150, fig. 12.1; Baptistery (San Giovanni), 130, 135, 138–41, 146, 165, 168, 172, 187, 312, 353, fig. 13.1; Cathedral, 123, 130–31, 133, 135, 150, 165; Old Sacristy, 142; Orsanmichele, 78, 141, 252, 272–73; Palazzo Vecchio, 345; San Lorenzo, 141–42, 187–88; San Miniato al Monte, 141, 187; San Pancrazio, 168, fig. 15.5; Santa Croce, 323; Santa Maria Novella, 141, 166, 175; Santi Apostoli, 141, 146, 187; Santo Spirito, 141.

Forgery, 31, 50, 115, 223–24, 236, 239, 241, 247, 249, 256, 271, 274, 279–87, 289, 293–99, 303, 354. *See also* Pastiche.

Fouquet, Jean, 147, 150–51, 159–60, figs. 14.1, 15.1.

Francesca, della, Piero, 150, 323, 330–33, 352, 357.

Francesco di Giorgio Martini, 137, 301, 303, 308, fig. 24.1.

Freud, Sigmund, 33, 47.

Fulda, Chapel of St. Michael, 56.

Fulvio, Andrea, 251–52, 286, 296.

Fursy de Bruille, 110.

GADDI, AGNOLO, 323.
Gaddi, Taddeo, 141, 166.
Galba, Emperor, 8, 12.
Galla Placidia, 324.
Genoa, 205–207, 270; San Bartolommeo degli Armeni, 205, 207, fig. 18.4.
Gentile da Fabriano, 336, 340, fig. 27.2.
George of Trebizond, 105.
Germigny-des-Prés, 69, 143.
Gervasius of Tilbury, 103, 112.
Gherardi, Giacomo, 234–35.
Ghiberti, Lorenzo, 165, 293, 352–53.
Ghirlandaio, Davide, 130.
Ghirlandaio, Domenico, 82, 130, 150, 166, 301.
Ghirlandaio, Ridolfo, 345.
Ghisi, Giorgio, 361–62.
Giambono, Michele, 112.
Gil de Siloe, 228.
Giorgione, 38, 268.
Giotto, 16, 75, 79, 88, 105, 131, 150, 179, 394 n.12; *Coronation of the Virgin*, Baroncelli Chapel, 82, fig. 8.4; *Crucifix*, Santa Maria Novella, 225; Monument to Giotto, Florence, Cathedral (by Benedetto da Maiano), 123–28, 131–38, 178, 303–304, 330, figs. 12.1, 12.2, 12.3; *Navicella*, St. Peter's, 329–30.
Giovanni, Gherardo, 130.
Giovanni, Monte di, 130–31, fig. 12.4.
Giovanni Baptista, 109, 204.
Giuliano da Maiano, 214.
Giustiniani, Agostino, 205–207.
Golden Legend (*Legenda Aurea*), 40, 42, 64, 243, 302, 323, 376 nn.22, 27, fig. 24.1.
Goldschmidt, Adolph, 136.
Goltzius, Hubert, 290.
Gombrich, Ernst, 278, 402 n.22.
Gonzaga, Federico, Marquis and Duke, 283–84.
Gonzaga, Francesco, Cardinal, 140, 144, 393 n.32.
Gonzaga, Francesco, Marquis and Duke, 255–56.
Gossaert, Jan, 278, 282.
Gothic architecture, 159–61, 163–65, 178, 181.
Gozzoli, Benozzo, 225, 324.
Granada, 219, 275, 332.
Grassis, Paris de, 313.
Greenberg, Clement, 48.
Gregory the Great, Emperor and Saint, 40, 97, 109, 222–23, 314, 327, 329, figs. 10.2, 26.5.
Gregory XI, Pope, 417 n.3.
Greiffenklau, Richard von, Archbishop, 198.
Grimaldi, Giacomo, 188.
Guarino da Verona, 105.
Guarna, Andrea, 314.
Guido da Siena: *Maestà*, 75–80, 83, figs. 8.2, 8.3, 8.5; *Madonna del Voto*, 78.
Gutenberg, Johannes, 222.
Gypsies (Roma), 103.

HAARLEM BROTHERHOOD OF JERUSALEM PILGRIMS, 56, fig. 6.2.
Haider, Ursula, 61.
Hadrian, Emperor, 54, 66, 139, 336.
Hakim, Caliph, 56, 69.
Halbwachs, Maurice, 379 n.7.
Hannibal, 93.
Hayne de Bruxelles, 111, fig. 11.4.
Heemskerck, Maarten van, 315, figs. 25.1, 25.2.
Helena, Empress and Saint, 67, 193–94, 197–98, 201, 219–20, 223, 321, 323, 331–32, figs. 17.6, 19.1, 26.1, 26.3.
Henry II, Emperor, 161, 205.
Heraclius, Emperor, 290, 294–95, 323, 331, figs. 10.8, 26.3.
Herodotus, 33.
Hesse, Eobanus, 297.
Holbein, Hans, the Elder, 394 n.7.
Holy Face, *see* Vera icon.
Holy Lance, 229, 241.
Holy Robe of Trier (Tunica Domini), 198–200, 229, fig. 18.3.
Holy Sepulchre, replicas (Aquileia, Augsburg, Bologna, Fulda, London, Metz, Pisa, Segovia), 56–60, fig. 6.3.
Homer, 278, 364, fig. 28.4; *Iliad*, 144.
Hory, Elmyr de, 289.
Hosios Loukas, 336.

ICONS: and antiquarianism, 105, 106–107, 128; bust format of, 103–105, 112, 119, 121, 298; Byzantine, 97–101, 103–107, 109–11, 121, 207; fifteenth-century copies of, 109–15, 208; documentary function of, 72, 86, 119, 229–31, 284; Italian altarpieces and, 72–83; origin myths of, 109–11, 327; as relics, 72–73, 80–83, 121–22, 204–207, 222, 231, 298, 327–29; repainting of, 73, 79–80, 231; and secular portraiture, 115–22; stylelessness of, 105–106, 112; attributed to St. Luke 72, 97, 109–11, 115, 204–207, 231–32, figs. 11.1, 11.2, 11.3, 11.6. *See also Acheiropoieton*; Mandylion; Micromosaic; Misdating; Vera icon.
Imperial Palace, Beijing, 7, 12, 15, 18.
India, temple architecture of, 379 n.10.
Indulgences, 61, 110, 202–204, 321.
Infessura, Stefano, 234.
Innocent VIII, Pope, 61, 182, fig. 20.1.
Inscriptions, 220–25, 232–33, 355, 360, 362; in painting, 75, 77–78, 114; and icons, 97–98; and costume, 102; on Monument to Giotto, 123–27.
Intermedial comparisons, 329–30, 337–45, 354.
Isabella of Castile, Queen, 219, 228, 275, 280, 284, 322, fig. 22.1.
Ise Shrine (Japan), 54.
Isidore of Seville, 233.

JEAN, DUKE OF BERRY, 102, 147, 290, fig. 23.1.
Jerome, Saint, 35, 379 n.6.
Jerusalem, 57, 72–73, 150–51, 168, 194, 201, 220, 223, 331; Aqsa mosque, 66; Dome of the Rock, 56, 64–70, 161, 165–68, 170, 172, 174, 207, figs. 7.1, 7.2, 15.6, 15.7; Holy Sepulchre, 54–61, 63–65, 68–70, 139, 150, 159, 161, 167–68, 174, 214, 265, 321–22, 331, 342, 408 n.30, figs. 6.1,

6.2, 26.1; Imbomon (Church of the Ascension), 56, 67, 383 n.6, 383 n.20; Rome as substitute for, 193–94, 321–22, 331, 364; Temple of Solomon, 21–27, 64–66, 70, 147, 150–51, 154, 159, 161, 165–67, 174, 188, 266, figs. 2.1, 2.2, 7.2, 14.1, 15.6, 15.7.
Johann von Baden, Archbishop of Trier, 59.
John VIII Palaiologos, Emperor, 102–103, 121–22, 244, figs. 10.6, 10.7, 10.8, 20.2.
Josephus, Flavius, 147, 150.
Joyce, James, 103.
Juan II, King, 275, fig. 22.1.
Juan de Flandes, 275, 278, fig. 22.2.
Julian (the Apostate), Emperor, 66.
Julius II, Pope, 98–99, 141, 190, 194, 213, 270, 313–14, 322, 343, 361–62, figs. 10.5, 17.3, 17.4.
Julius III, Pope, 56.
Justinian, Emperor, 98, 140, fig. 10.4.

KRAUTHEIMER, RICHARD, 30, 46–47, 56, 146.
Kubler, George, 89, 370 n.13.

LABELS, 70, 71, 81, 201, 232–33, 242, 282, 311–12.
Landucci, Luca, 252.
Lanfranchi, Ubaldo, 201.
Lanzi, Luigi, 274.
Lars Porsenna, 273–74, fig. 21.15.
"Lentulus" letter (also attributed to Pilate), 245–46, 263, 267, 269, figs. 21.7, 21.8.
Leo X, Pope, 146, 182, 283, 314.
Leonardo da Vinci, 11, 14–15, 38, 60, 72–73, 93, 95, 137, 139, 305, 351–52, 356, 360, fig. 24.2.
Liber Pontificalis, 40, 188, 441 n.1.
Limbourg brothers, 105, 119, 147, 389 n.26.
Lippi, Filippino, 190, 193.
Lippi, Filippo, 442 n.9.
Livy, 256–57, figs. 21.3, 21.4.
Longhi, Roberto, 116.
Longinus (author of *On the Sublime*), 278.
Lorenzetti brothers, 111, fig. 11.3.
Loreto: Holy House (Casa Santa) of Loreto, 13, 195–98, 201–204, 208–15, 217, 253, 313–14, 321, 342, figs. 18.1, 18.2, 18.5, 18.6; copies of Holy House of Loreto, 202.
Louis IX, King, 159.
Lucian, 278.
Lucius II, Pope, 220, 324.
Lucius Verus, Emperor, 136.
Luhmann, Niklas, 342, 371 n.26.
Luke, Saint, *see* Icons, attributed to.

MCLUHAN, MARSHALL, 25.
Magdeburg, 181.
Mainardi, Bastiano, 82.
Madonna Nicopeia, 207.
Madonna degli Occhi Grossi (Siena), 78.
Madonna in the Robe of Wheat Ears (Madonna del Coazzone), 21–29, 38, 50, 203, 356, figs. 2.1, 2.2, 11.6.
Makarios, Bishop, 54.

Malouel, Jean, 105.
Mancini, Giulio, 296, 335.
Mandeville, John (*Mandeville's Travels*), 66, 201.
Mandylion, 205–207, 229, 266, 270, 293, figs. 12.2, 18.4.
Manetti, Antonio, 138.
Mantegna, Andrea, 38, 45, 94, 112, 255–56, 345, 392 n.22, fig. 21.1; *Triumphs of Caesar*, 27.
Mantua, 140, 255, 257, 283, 345.
Manuel II Palaiologos, Emperor, 101, 147.
Marcus Aurelius, Emperor, 135, 137, 296.
Margarito d'Arezzo, 79.
Mariano da Firenze, Fra, 190, 193.
Marmion, Simon, 162.
Martial, 123.
Martin V, Pope, 186.
Martini, Simone, 58, 395 n.20.
Marvels of Rome (*Mirabilia urbis Romae*), 136, 209.
Marx, Karl, 389 n.23.
Marziale, Marco, 166.
Master E.S., 215–17, fig. 18.7.
Master of the Herpin Manuscript, 229, figs. 19.5, 19.6.
Master of René of Anjou, 103, 112, 389 n.26.
Master of the St. Bartholomew Altarpiece, 225, 236, fig. 19.4.
Master of the St. Lucy Legend, 149.
Master Thomas, 225.
Master of the Vienna Passion, 197.
Matteo de' Pasti, 244, 253, 259, 267, fig. 20.2.
Maupassant, Guy de, 289.
Maximianus, Emperor, 137.
Maximilian I of Habsburg, Emperor, 198, 200, 280, fig. 18.3.
Mazzocchi, Jacopo, 251.
Meckenem, Israhel van, *Christ as Man of Sorrows*, 27, 329, fig. 26.5.
Medals and coins, 103, 241–45, 251–54, 256–73, 286, 290.
Medici, Cosimo de', 141–42, 187–88.
Medici, Giovanni de', *see* Leo X.
Medici, Lorenzo de', 107, 128, 130–31, 133, 135, 234–36, 274, 290–91, 293–94, 396 n.25, 398 n.1, figs. 12.1, 12.4, 12.5.
Medici, Lorenzo di Pierfrancesco de', 295.
Medici, Ottaviano de', 283.
Medici, Piero de', 396 n.26.
Meegeren, Han van, 289.
Mehmet II, Sultan, 140.
Meinrad, Saint, 215, 217.
Melozzo da Forlì, 114–15, 324, 330, 343, 442 n.9, fig. 11.6.
Memling, Hans, 149, 153–54, 157, 282, 389 n.26, fig. 14.2.
Mendoza, Pedro González de, Cardinal, 219, 224, 243, 322–23, 326–27, 329–30, 333, fig. 26.3.
Michelangelo Buonarotti, 38, 188, 235–36, 272–73, 275, 283, 294, 297, 336, 343, 345, 357–58, figs. 10.5, 19.7, 21.14; *David*, Florence, Accademia, 196; *Risen Christ*, Santa Maria sopra Minerva, 272, 296, fig. 21.14.
Michiel, Marcantonio, 278, 282, 294.
Micromosaics, 97–98, 107, 128, 133, 327–29, 338.
Milan, 141, 143, 180, 182, 309; Cathedral, 21–27, 144, 163, figs. 2.1, 2.2, 15.3; San Lorenzo, 137, 144; San Satiro, 139, 143; Sant'Ambrogio, 309.

Mino da Fiesole, 296, 362.
Mirabilia urbis Romae, see Marvels of Rome.
Miraflores, 225, 275, 322.
Misdating, 50, 135–42, 146, 249; of Byzantine artifacts, 142–44, 185, 207; of icons and micromosaics, 97–101, 103–106, 327; of medals, 253, 290; of mosaics, 327; of neo-cosmatesque pavements, 185–88, 194, 353; of Romanesque buildings, 139–40. *See also* Florence, Baptistery; Spolia.
Models: artwork as, 70, 217, 353–54; of buildings, 12, 51–52, 54, 56, 60–61, 69, 70, 155, 165, 342, fig. 6.3; buildings as, 27, 51, 54, 59, 69, 139, 141, 157, 197–98, 202, 209, 309, 314, 340, fig. 15.8; of origins or temporality of artwork, 11, 16–18, 21, 25, 29, 49, 71, 117, 127, 166, 195, 231, 299, 311–12.
Montagna, Bartolommeo, 269.
Montaigne, Michel de, 257, fig. 21.3.
Montaldo, Leonardo, Doge, 205, 207.
Monte Cassino, 185.
Montepulciano, 273–74, fig. 21.15.
More, Thomas, 286.
Mosaic: as antique medium, 128–33, 135, 327–30, 338; Medicean revival of, 130–31, 133; as nonauthorial medium, 128, 129–31, 133, 330, 338, 343; renovation of, 335–36; represented, 43–44, 338, 345. *See also* Antiquarianism; Intermedial comparison; Misdating.
Moses, 27, 29, 145–46, 364, fig. 2.1.
Motis, Cristoforo de, 24.
Mount Sinai, Monastery of St. Catherine, 97.
Muffel, Niklas, 219, 321.
Multscher, Hans, 163.
Muscat, Jörg, 295.
Myron, 278.
Mys, 289–90.

NAPLES, 255, 283, 290, 362.
Nazareth, 12, 195, 197, 204, 209, 212, 214.
Neri di Bicci, 387 n.26.
Nero, Emperor, 8, 12, 280.
Niccolò Fiorentino, 252, 272.
Niccolò di Segna, 357.
Nicholas II, Pope, 135.
Nicholas III, Pope, 189.
Nicholas V, Pope, 158, 182, 189–90.
Nikephoros, 86.
Nonsubstitutability: and painting, 60, 385 n.10; and pilgrimage, 60, 195; of relics, 31, 83, 203, 214, 231–32.
Notker, 69.
Nuremberg, 168.

ORALITY AND LITERACY, 359–64.
Orley, Bernd van, 281.
Orsini, Fulvio, 242.
Orsini del Balzo, Raimondello, fig. 10.2.
Orso dell'Anguillara, 179.
Otto I, Emperor, 181, 312.
Ovid, 124, 307.

PACE, LUIGI DE, 338.
Pacher, Michael, 150.
Pächt, Otto, 103, 111–12.
Padua, 141, 222, 256–57, fig. 21.3.
Painting: changing status of, 338, 342–45, 351, 354–55; as performative medium, 44, 71, 73, 129, 178, 329, 338, 340, 342, 345; and paragone, 337, 342.
Palladio, Andrea, 174, 403 n.29, fig. 15.8.
Paneas (Banyas), 40.
Panofsky, Erwin, 45–49, 136, 197, 358.
Panvinio, Onofrio, 207, 324.
Paolo Romano, 362.
Paragone, 337, 342.
Paris, 147, 149–50, 159, 205–206.
Paschal I, Pope, 146.
Pastiche, 289–299. *See also* Forgery.
Paul II, Pope, 101, 107, 110, 202–203, 212.
Penates, 8, 12.
Penni, Gian Francesco, 316–17, figs. 25.3, 25.4.
Performance: authorial, 15–16, 30, 37, 44, 49–50, 71, 94, 157, 176, 239, 246, 293, 295, 297, 299, 312, 329, 332, 340, 343, 345, 356, 358, fig. 15.5; contrasted to substitution, 16, 30, 44, 49–50, 71, 123, 128, 146, 155, 157, 177, 296, 299, 312, 332, 354, 358; painting as, 73, 94, 340, 342, 354.
Perino del Vaga, 179.
Perotti, Niccolò, 98.
Perspective, 47–48, 331.
Perugino, Pietro, 324, 327, 330–31; *Christ Handing the Keys to Saint Peter*, Sistine Chapel, 170, 174, fig. 15.6.
Peruzzi, Baldassare, 274, 335–36, 338, 340, 343, 345, fig. 27.1.
Petrarch, 179.
Peutinger, Conrad, 251–52, 263.
Phaedrus, 289–90.
Philip the Good, Duke of Burgundy, 68, 70.
Philippe III the Bold, King, 159.
Philippe IV le Bel, King, 160, 197.
Piccolomini, Aeneas Silvius, *see* Pius II.
Pico della Mirandola, Giovanni, 235.
Pienza, 161, fig. 15.2.
Piero, Domenico di, 40, 42.
Pilate, Pontius, 59, 64, 154, 201, 219, 229, 232–34, 245, 253, 257, 259, 263.
Pilgrimage: outside Holy Land, 73, 198, 202–3, 208, 210, 217, 321; to Holy Land, 56, 59; and nonsubstitutability, 60, 195; and skepticism, 12; virtual, 56, 61, 73.
Pinder, Wilhelm, 373 n.11.
Pinturicchio, Bernardo, 163, 173–74, 324, 327, 330–31, 336, 338, 345; *Christ Among the Doctors*, Spello, 170, fig. 15.7.
Pisa, 142, 201–202, 225.
Pisanello (Antonio di Puccio Pisano), 102–103, 111, 119, 244, 389 n.26, figs. 10.6, 10.8.
Pius II, Pope, 161, 202, fig. 15.2.
Pius IV, Pope, 188.
Pius V, Pope, 208.
Plato, 15, 350–51, 360–64.
Pliny, 92, 136, 274, 279–80.
Plutarch, 8, 432 n.55.

Poggio a Caiano, Villa Medici, 172.

Pole, Reginald, 283.

Poliziano, Angelo, 123–24, 126, 235–36, 247, fig. 12.1.

Polo, Agnolo di, 252.

Polycleitus, 278, 298.

Pontano, Giovanni, 255.

Pontelli, Baccio, 214.

Portiuncula, Chapel of St. Francis, 208.

Portraits: anachronistic, 37, 147–50; and authenticity, 251–59, 263–73, 286; secular, 118–22. *See also* Medals and coins.

Portraits of Christ, 27, 30–31, 39, 86, 111, 267–73, 281, figs. 2.1, 21.10, 21.13, 21.14; iconic, 73, 97–99, 103, 119, 128, 133, 229–30, 303, 327, figs. 10.1, 10.2, 10.5, 12.2, 12.5, 18.4, 26.5; in antiquity, 40–42, 274, fig. 4.3; indexical, 59, 293; medallic, 241–46, 252–54, 256–67, 299, figs. 20.1, 20.2, 21.5, 21.6, 21.7, 21.8; relief, 267, 271, figs. 21.19, 21.12; statuary, 39–44, 50, 52, 116, 184, 252, 272–74, 299, figs. 4.2, 4.3, 4.4, 21.11, 21.14. *See also Acheiropoeiton*; Mandylion; Rome, Santa Croce in Gerusalemme, mosaic icon of Christ as Man of Sorrows; Vera icon.

Praxiteles, 278, 280, 289–90, 292, 295.

Prevedari, Bernardo, 309, 311, 317, fig. 24.6.

Primitive hut, myth of, 305–308, 313–17.

Print technology: authority of, 168; eliminates drift in replica chain, 251, 254, 256, 263, 265–66, 280–81, 362–63; and status of painting, 356, 358, 364; and texts, 359, 363–64.

Probus, Emperor, 295.

Proust, Marcel, 289.

Pseudo-antique, 297, 327. *See also* Virtual antiquity.

Pseudo-archaism, 331, 350.

Pseudo-relic, fig. 17.6. *See also* Virtual relics; Virtual spolia.

Pseudomorphosis, pseudomorphic, 48, 50, 136.

Pucelle, Jean, 197.

Pynson, Richard, 210.

Pythagoras, 347, 361–62.

QUINTILIAN, 177.

RAIMONDI, MARCANTONIO, 285, 295–96, 317, 358, fig. 25.4.

Ramusio, Giovan Battista, 207.

Rancière, Jacques, 370 n.18.

Raphael (Raffaello Sanzio), 38, 166, 172, 174, 182, 190, 251, 285, 315, 317, 324, 338, figs. 25.3, 25.4; *Miraculous Draught of Fishes*, Sistine Chapel, cartoon, 271, fig. 21.13; *Portrait of Leo X with Two Cardinals*, Florence, 283–84; *Sermon of Saint Paul at Athens*, Sistine Chapel, cartoon, 174; Stanza d'Eliodoro, *Expulsion of Heliodorus*, 355, 362; Stanza della Segnatura, 42, 343–65, figs. 27.5, 28.1, 28.2, 28.4.

Ratdolt, Erhard, 245, 259, fig. 21.5.

Ravenna, 181, 336; Mausoleum of Theodoric, 56, 139, 175; San Vitale, 56, 139.

Recanati, 195, 203.

Referential images, artifacts, and artworks, 9, 11, 13, 16, 18, 24, 29, 33, 37, 42, 61, 71–73, 75, 80–81, 94, 99, 106, 113, 126, 129, 141–42, 178, 183–84, 187–88, 202, 232, 239, 249, 252, 281, 284, 298, 322, 345. *See also* Evidence.

Reform of images, 85–88, 94, 106, 235–39, 284.

Regensburg, 224; Alte Kapelle, 205.

Reims, 165, 181.

Relics, 13, 17, 18, 54; architectural, 175–77, 183, 195–98, 212–14, 313–14, 321; artworks as, 279, 285, 294–95; cult of, 220; definition of, 8, 231, 233; forged or fabricated, 52, 223–224, 293; as formless, 197, 201–202, 233; and reliquaries, 198–201, 208; rediscoveries of, 219–21, 224, 229; skepticism about, 224, 229–31, 233. *See also* Mandylion; Pseudo-relic; Titulus Crucis; Vera icon; Virtual relics.

René of Anjou, King, 112.

Replicas, *see* Copies.

Reuwich, Erhard, 165, 168, 174.

Riario, Raffaelle, 295, 297.

Ricci, Giacomo, 203–204, 208–12.

Riccio, Andrea, 224, 256, 295.

Riegl, Alois, 92, 181.

Rieter, Sebastian, 168.

Ripanda, Jacopo, 336, 345.

Romano, Giulio, 283.

Rome, 10, 135, 180–82, 185, 205, 222, 280, 301, 311, 322, 362; Ara Pacis, 190; Arch of Constantine, 182, 308; Arch of Septimius Severus, 308; Arcus Argentariorum, 190; Basilica of Maxentius ("Temple of Peace"), 170, 302, 315, fig. 24.1; Baths of Agrippa, 182; Baths of Caracalla, 129, 137, 198; Baths of Diocletian, 182; Capitoline Hill, 30, 51, 53, 179, 209, 212–13, 306; Casa Romuli, 51–53, 165, 209, 266, 303, 306, 313; Colosseum, 182; *Dioscuri* (Horse Tamers), 136; Domus Aurea, 336; Mausoleum of Hadrian, 56; Palatine Hill, 51–53, 209; Pantheon, 56, 69, 73, 136, 138–39, 168, 182, 322, 385 n.6, 440 n.23; St. Peter's (New), 60, 69, 103, 107, 128, 132, 140, 143, 145–46, 179, 183, 189, 209, 213, 241, 313–19, 324, 362, 382 n.38; St. Peter's (New), *Tegurio*, 183, 313–19, figs. 25.1, 25.2, 25.3, 25.4; St. Peter's (Old), 141, 146, 153–55, 166, 182–83, 188, 198, 313–19, 332, 362, fig. 14.2; San Cesareo, 188; San Clemente, 188–89, 331–32; San Giorgio al Velabro, 190, 329; San Giovanni in Laterano, 40, 59, 69, 73, 128, 136, 182, 186, 188, 201, 209, 324, 331; San Giovanni in Laterano, Baptistery, 56, 129, 139, 335; San Lorenzo fuori le Mura, 142, 421 n.61; San Onofrio, 336, 345; San Paolo fuori le Mura, 324, 329; San Sisto, 73; San Teodoro, 158; Sancta Sanctorum, 186, 201, 207, 336, 354, 362, 382 n.3; Sancta Sanctorum and Holy Stair (Scala Santa), 201, 205, 207; Sant' Agnese fuori le Mura, 413 n.18; Sant' Agostino, 109; Santa Cecilia, 417 n.30; Santa Costanza, 137, 139–40, 412 n.61; Santa Croce in Gerusalemme, 219–24, 321–27, 329–31, 340, 351, figs. 19.1, 26.5; Santa Croce in Gerusalemme, apse fresco (Antoniazzo Romano), 347, 350, figs. 26.2, 26.3, 26.4; Santa Croce in Gerusalemme, Helena Chapel (Jerusalem Chapel), 193–94, 321–24, 335–36, 338, 340, 342–45, figs. 17.6, 26.1, 27.1; Santa Croce in Gerusalemme, mosaic icon of Christ as Man of Sorrows, 27, 97, 222, 327, 338, figs. 10.2, 26.5; Santa Francesca Romana, 205; Santa Maria Antiqua, 73, 385 n.6; Santa Maria Aracoeli, 109, 187, 327, fig. 17.1; Santa Maria in Cosmedin, 110; Santa Maria in Domnica, 146; Santa Maria Maggiore, 129, 201, 208, 324,

327, 382 n.38; Santa Maria Maggiore, *Salus Populi Romani*, 73, 109–10, 114–15, 204; Santa Maria sopra Minerva, 182, 187, 190, 208, 272, fig. 21.14; Santa Maria della Pace, 345; Santa Maria del Popolo, 163, 173, 327, 336, 338, 345; Santa Maria del Popolo, Chigi Chapel, 323, 338; Santa Maria del Popolo, *Madonna del Popolo*, 109–11, 114, 116, 142, figs. 11.1, 11.6; Santa Maria in Trastevere, 73, 198, 207, 382 n.38, fig. 8.1; Santa Prassede, 331, 336, 415 n.4; Santa Pudenziana, 326, 331, 347; Santa Sabina, 190, 347; Santi Achilleo e Nereo, 188, 331; Santi Apostoli, 110, 190, 327, 343, 442 n.9, fig. 17.3; Santi Cosma e Damiano, 331; Santi Quattro Coronati, 188; Santo Stefano Rotondo, 139, 158, 331, 384 n.22, 421 n.61; Septizodium, 139; Tempietto (San Pietro in Montorio), 139–40, 172, 174, 184, 188–190, 193–94, 299, 314, 322–23, 342, 354, figs. 15.8, 17.5; Trajan's Column, 144; Villa Farnesina, 345.

Rome, Vatican Palace: Borgia Apartments, 336; Casino of Pius IV, 188; Sistine Chapel, 166, 170, 174, 188–90, 194, 271, 299, 323, 335, 345, 354, figs. 15.4, 15.6, 17.2, 21.13; Stanza d'Eliodoro, 355; Stanza della Segnatura, 42, 188, 190, 194, 323, 343, 345–48, 350–64, figs. 17.3, 17.4, 28.1, 28.2, 28.4.

Romulus, 51–53, 73, 165, 209, 266, 303, 306.

Rossellino, Bernardo, 158, 161, fig. 15.2.

Rovere, Giuliano della, *see* Julius II, Pope.

Rucellai, Giovanni, 167, fig. 15.5.

Rusuti, Filippo, 327.

SAINT-DENIS (ABBEY), 160, 165, fig. 15.1.

Salutati, Coluccio, 138.

Sangallo, Antonio da, 274, fig. 18.6.

Sangallo, Giuliano da, 139, 143, 172–74, 214, 274.

San Germano (Cassino), 143.

San Vittore delle Chiuse (Marches), 143.

Sansovino, Andrea, 214, 272, 274, 313, figs. 18.6, 21.15.

Santa Croce (Sassoferrato), 143.

Santa Maria delle Carceri (Prato), 173.

Santa Maria delle Moie (Jesi), 143.

Sanudo, Marin, 375 n.15.

Sarto, Andrea del, 283.

Sarzana, Leonardo da, 234–35.

Savonarola, Girolamo, 354.

Savonarola, Michele, 129.

Schedel, Hartmann, 137, 168, 224–25, 229, 236, 238, figs. 19.2, 19.3, 19.8.

Schlosser, Julius von, 406 n.19.

Schmarsow, August, 324.

Schongauer, Martin, 229.

Scorel, Jan van, 56, 405 n.5.

Scripts, 97, 98, 144.

Septimius Severus, Emperor, 136, 139.

Serbaldi, Pier Maria, 293–95.

Servius, 124.

Severo da Ravenna, 375 n.16.

Sforza, Alessandro, 110, 114–15, fig. 11.6.

Sforza, Francesco, 143.

Sforza, Ginevra, 205.

Shakespeare, William, 13, 89, 91.

Shroud of Turin, 207, 293.

Siena, 274, 301; Cathedral, 78, 139, 174, 386 n.18; Church of the Carmine, 110–11; Church of the Servi, 79; San Domenico, 75–80, figs. 8.2, 8.3, 8.5, 24.1; San Gregorio, 76–77; Santa Maria Maddalena, 75.

Signatures, artists', 27, 75, 78, 285.

Signorelli, Luca, 236.

Simpertus, Saint, 220–21.

Simultaneous narrative, 331, 350.

Sinan, 140.

Sixtus IV, Pope, 97–98, 110, 119, 142, 145, 188, 190, 194, 203, 293, 419 n.37, figs. 10.1, 11.1, 17.3.

Skepticism about relics, 12, 210, 212, 293.

Socrates, 242, 286, 360–61, 364.

Sodoma, il (Giovanni Antonio Bazzi), 305, 444 n.18, fig. 24.4.

Solari, Cristoforo, 267.

Solari, Pietro Antonio, 24.

Solomon, King, 65–67, 69, 147, 150–51, 159–60, 166, 353, 364, fig. 14.1.

Spagnuoli, Baptista (il Mantovano or Mantuanus), 211, 255.

Spengler, Oswald, 48.

Spinario, 298.

Spolia, spoliation, 179–84, 185–86, 214, 312. *See also* Virtual spolia.

Stella, Giorgio, 207.

Strada, Jacopo, 290, 296.

Style, 35, 37–38, 80–81, 83, 106, 130, 151, 153–54, 157, 179, 289, 291, 317.

Stylelessness, 50, 106, 112, 330–32, 350, 354–56.

Substitution: and chain structure, 16, 29–30, 51, 94, 232, 242; contrasted to performance, 16, 30, 44, 49–50, 71, 123, 128, 146, 155, 157, 177, 296, 299, 312, 332, 354, 358; as cultural program, 144–46; definitions of, 29–33, 94, 177, 284, 355; and formal drift, 56–59, 68–69, 78, 111, 159, 168–70, 292; of icons, 71–73, 75, 78, 106, 110–18, 229, 231; outside of Europe, 54, 379 n.10; and print technology, 168–70, 251, 254, 265–66, 356; in the Renaissance, 49–50, 51; staging of, 250, 337, 340; as time-bending mechanism, 32–33, 45, 131, 133, 141, 150–51; typological, 11, 29–33, 71, 86–87, 151, 155, 159, 168–70, 321, 336.

Sudarium, *see* Vera icon.

Suetonius, 8, 144.

Suger, Abbot, 160.

Surrealism, 33.

Sylvester I, Pope, 246.

Symeon of Thessalonica, 85–88, 116.

TACITUS, 30.

Tafur, Pero, 416 n.27, 422 n.2.

Tarquin the Proud, King, 212.

Tempio Malatestiano (Rimini), 175–78, 183, 214, fig. 16.1.

Terence, 102.

Tertullian, 233.

Theodore the Studite, Saint, 30–31, 87.

Theoderic (monk), 67.

Theoderic the Great, 136–37, 175.

Theodosius, Emperor, 101.

Theophilus, 386 n.21.

Theseus, Ship of, 8, 12, 80.

Thoreau, Henry David, 53.

Tiberius, Emperor, 64, 245, 290.

Tifernas, Lilius, 145.

Titulus Crucis, 219–39, 247, 267, 321, 323–24, figs. 19.1, 19.2, 19.3, 19.4, 19.5, 19.6, 19.7, 19.8, 19.9, 21.9.

Titus, Emperor, 66, 201.

Tizio, Sigismondo, 75.

Toesca, Pietro, 249.

Tolomei, Pietro Giorgio, 203–204, 211–12.

Tomeo, Niccolò Leonico, 241–42, 435 n.23.

Tommaso di Modena, 78.

Torrigiani, Pietro, 252, 272.

Torriti, Jacopo, 331, 336.

Tours, 147, 150.

Traversari, Ambrogio, 105.

Trier, 59, 137–38, 198, 201.

Trubert, Georges, 112.

Tucher, Hans, 168.

Tullio Lombardo, 267, 296, 299, fig. 21.9.

Typology: architectural, 19, 29, 71, 138, 151, 154–55, 159, 161, 168–69, 184, 282; theological, 10, 32–33, 61, 86, 181, 251, 311–12, 317.

URBAN II, POPE, 68.

Urban V, Pope, 417 n.3.

VALENTINIAN III, EMPEROR, 324, 335.

Valéry, Paul, 11.

Valla, Lorenzo, 242, 246–47, 263, 265.

Varallo, Sacro Monte, 61.

Varro, 51.

Vasari, Giorgio, 16, 49, 75, 92–93, 95, 105, 130, 135–37, 146, 161, 170, 179, 239, 249, 273–74, 283, 285, 291, 293–95, 297, 329, 340, 361–62, fig. 21.15.

Velletri, 109.

Vendramin collection (Venice), 268, 278.

Veneziano, Agostino, 446 n.27.

Veneziano, Domenico, 389 n.26.

Venice, 143, 158, 165, 224, 267, 285; Basilica of San Marco, 41, 43–44, 140, 143, 166, 207, 338, 393 n.30, fig. 4.2; Santa Maria della Carità (Scuola Grande della Carità), 40, 42–43, 243, 252, 267, 273, 338, fig. 21.11; Scuola di San Giorgio degli Schiavoni, 35.

Venturini, Domenico, 80, 83, fig. 8.5.

Vera icon (Sudarium, Holy Face), 26, 29, 64, 72, 103, 128, 205–207, 266, 270–71, 293, 303, 355, fig. 18.4.

Vermeer, Johannes, 289.

Verrocchio, Andrea del, 187, 252, 259, 263, 272–73.

Vespasian, Emperor, 30, 201.

Vespasiano da Bisticci, 101.

Vico, Enea, 286–87, 296.

Vienna, 150, 161.

Vignola, Jacopo Barozzi da, 208.

Villani, Giovanni, 138.

Villingen (Swabia), 61.

Vincent Ferrer, Saint, 207.

Virgil, 51, 124, 254–56, figs. 21.1, 21.2.

Virtual antiquity, 116, 184, 295. See also Pseudo-antique.

Virtual relics, 178, 214. See also Pseudo-relic.

Virtual spolia, 184, 376 n.24.

Viterbo, 247, 249.

Vitruvius, 143, 163, 170, 303, 305–6, 315, 317, figs. 15.3, 24.2, 24.3, 25.4.

Vittorino da Feltre, 105.

Vivarini, Alvise, 43.

Voragine, Jacobus de, see Golden Legend.

WAGNER, LEONHARD, 239, fig. 19.9.

Walsingham, 12–13, 73, 205, 209–10, 212, 299.

Warburg, Aby, 9–10, 33–34, 357–58.

Wey, William, 197.

Weyden, Rogier van der, 27, 37, 112–14, 119–20, 148–49, 154, 275, 278, 284, 322, 389 n.25, figs. 11.8, 11.9, 22.1, 22.2.

Wilde, Oscar, 402 n.21.

Winterburger, Johann, 238, fig. 19.8.

Wölfflin, Heinrich, 80, 92.

Woodcuts, 21–28.

World Chronicle (Nuremberg, 1493), 168, 224, 238.

YOUTH OF MAGDALENSBERG, 279.

ZAINER, GÜNTHER, 257, fig. 21.6.

Zenobius, Saint, 130–31, 135, 150, fig. 12.4.

Zeuxis, 278–79, 289–90.

Zio, Francesco, 294.

Zoppo, Agostino, 256, fig. 21.4.

PHOTO CREDITS

akg-images: 21.15
Albertina Museum (Vienna): 18.5
Archiv des Bistums Augsburg: 19.9
Art Resource (New York): 4.1, 4.2, 8.5, 12.1, 15.2, 16.1, 18.3, 26.4
Art Resource/Alinari: 7.2, 8.4, 15.7, 15.8, 18.1, 18.6, 24.4, 27.3
Art Resource/Bildarchiv Preussischer Kulturbesitz: 22.1, 25.1, 26.5
Art Resource/Erich Lessing: 6.3, 10.8, 11.5, 14.2, 23.1
Art Resource/Nicolò Orsi Battaglini: 12.5
Art Resource/Réunion des Musées Nationaux: 10.6, 21.1, 24.2, 25.3
Art Resource/Scala: 8.1, 8.2, 11.9, 12.4, 14.3, 15.4, 15.6, 17.2, 17.3,
    17.4, 19.7, 24.1, 24.5, 27.4, 27.5, 28.1, 28.2, 28.3, 28.4
Art Resource/Victoria and Albert Museum: 21.13
Bayerische Staatsbibliothek (Munich): 19.2, 19.3, 19.8, 21.6
Beinecke Rare Book Library, Yale University (New Haven):
    6.1, 13.2, 13.3, 15.3
Bibliothèque nationale de France: 14.1, 15.1
British Museum (London): 18.7, 20.1, 24.6
Eidgenössische Technische Hochschule, Graphische Sammlung
    (Zurich): 2.2
Foto Böhm (Venice): 21.3
Fototeca Nazionale (Rome): 20.3
Frans Hals Museum (Haarlem): 6.2
Julie Fry: 17.5
Huntington Library, Art Collections and Botanical Gardens
    (San Marino, California): 11.8
Kimbell Art Museum (Fort Worth): 21.9
Kunsthistorisches Institut, Fotothek (Florence): 15.5
Kunsthistorisches Museum (Vienna): 21.4
Ralph Lieberman: 21.14
Metropolitan Museum of Art (New York): 10.3, 22.2, 25.4
Museo della Città (Mantua): 21.2
Museo Poldi Pezzoli (Milan): 4.3, 21.11
Museum Boijmans van Beuningen (Rotterdam): 7.1
Alexander Nagel: 4.4, 17.6, 23.2
National Gallery (London): 21.10
National Gallery of Art (Washington): 14.4, 20.2, 24.3, 27.2
National Museum (Stockholm): 25.2
Nelson Atkins Museum of Art (Kansas City): 11.4
Robert S. Nelson: 8.3
Philadelphia Museum of Art: 19.4
Pierpont Morgan Library (New York): 19.5, 19.6
Staatliche Graphische Sammlung (Munich): 21.5, 21.8
University Library (Rostock): 21.7
Michael J. Waters: 12.2, 12.3
Christopher S. Wood: 2.1, 17.1, 21.12, 26.1
Mark Zucker: 18.2

Typesetting by Meighan Gale
Layout and production by Julie Fry
Printed and bound by Maple Press